I0213080

ZIONISTS IN INTERWAR CZECHOSLOVAKIA

THE MODERN JEWISH EXPERIENCE

Deborah Dash Moore and Marsha L. Rozenblit, editors
Paula Hyman, founding coeditor

A Helen B. Schwartz Book

Published with the support of the Helen B. Schwartz Fund for New Scholarship in Jewish Studies of the Robert A. and Sandra B. Borns Jewish Studies Program, Indiana University

ZIONISTS IN INTERWAR CZECHOSLOVAKIA

Minority Nationalism and the Politics of Belonging

TATJANA LICHTENSTEIN

INDIANA UNIVERSITY PRESS

Bloomington & Indianapolis

This book is a publication of

INDIANA UNIVERSITY PRESS
Office of Scholarly Publishing
Herman B Wells Library 350
1320 East 10th Street
Bloomington, Indiana 47405 USA

iupress.indiana.edu

The paper used in this publication meets the minimum requirements of the American National Standard for Information Sciences–Permanence of Paper for Printed Library Materials, ANSI Z39.48–1992.

Manufactured in the United States of America

Library of Congress Cataloging-in-Publication Data

Lichtenstein, Tatjana, author.
Zionists in interwar Czechoslovakia : minority nationalism and the politics of belonging / Tatjana Lichtenstein.
pages cm – (The modern Jewish experience)
Includes bibliographical references and index.
ISBN 978-0-253-01867-0 (cloth : alk. paper) – ISBN 978-0-253-01872-4 (ebook) 1. Zionism – Czechoslovakia – History. 2. Jews – Czechoslovakia – History – 20th century. 3. Czechoslovakia – Ethnic relations. I. Title.
DS149.5.C94L53 2016
320.54095694094370'9041 – dc23
2015033435

1 2 3 4 5 21 20 19 18 17 16

FOR MY PARENTS

Contents

Acknowledgments

AT THE END OF THIS JOURNEY, IT IS A PLEASURE TO BE ABLE TO thank the many institutions and people that I am indebted to.

My research has been funded by several different organizations. At the University of Toronto, I had the honor of receiving a Connaught Scholarship, the Israel and Golda Koschitzky Fellowship in Jewish Studies, the Naim S. Mahlab Graduate Scholarship, the Liebe Sharon Wilensky Lesk Graduate Scholarship in Jewish Studies, the Arthur Vaile Memorial Graduate Prize in Jewish Studies, and a grant from the Canadian Friends of the Hebrew University. In the early stages of my research, the Simon Dubnow Institute for Jewish History and Culture hosted me in Leipzig. The Memorial Foundation for Jewish Culture also supported my research. At the University of Texas at Austin, I am especially grateful for the financial support of the Department of History, the Schusterman Center for Jewish Studies, the Center for Russian, East European, and Eurasian Studies, the Center for European Studies, and the College of Liberal Arts. In 2012–2013, I was fortunate to be a fellow at the University of Michigan's Frankel Institute for Advanced Judaic Studies. This book is published with the generous support of a University of Texas at Austin Subvention Grant awarded by the Office of the President.

I would also like to thank the archivists and librarians who helped me navigate their collections. In Prague, I am grateful to Alena Jelínková and Vlastimila Hamáčková of the Jewish Museum in Prague; Vlasta Měšt'ánková, Vladimír Waage, and Jiří Křest'an of the National Archives; Jindřiška Baušteinová of the National Library; and Vojtech Scheinost of the Tyrš Museum for Physical Education and Sport. The staff at the periodical section at the University Library in Olomouc provided an excellent working environment. In Israel, Roni Dror of the Joseph Yekutieli Maccabi Sports Archive provided me with exceptional working conditions. I am also grateful to Rochelle Rubinstein at the Central Zionist Archives for her advice. Martin J. Wein shared generously his knowledge of the collections at the Central Zionist Archives. In New York, I would like to thank the staff at the Leo Baeck Institute.

I was fortunate to have wonderful mentors in the early stages of my career as a historian. Derek J. Penslar's patience, encouragement, and intellectual rigor provided solid ground for me from the outset of this project. Doris L. Bergen never failed to provide advice, support, and outstanding mentorship in all aspects of this profession. I am grateful for their continued generosity and friendship.

Colleagues and friends have offered invaluable advice and assistance along the way. I am grateful to Veronika Ambros, Kate Bell, Petr Brod, Karl Brown, Kateřina Čapková, Anna Cichopek-Gajraj, Paula Daccarett, Barbara Di Lella, Lois Dobin, the Frankel fellows 2012–2013, Michal Frankl, Ben Frommer, Libuše Heczková, Dana Jandová, Steve Jobbitt, Hillel J. Kieval, Petrine Kjær Wolfsberg, Rebekah Klein-Pejšová, Jan Láníček, Paul R. Magocsi, Pamela S. Nadell, Isabelle Sirois, Jindřich Toman, Veronika Tuckerová, Ruti Ungar, and Lynne Viola. Wendy and David Ernst provided vital intellectual and human support. I also want to thank the scholars who gave me the opportunity to present and publish my work: Pieter M. Judson, Morgane Labbé, and Tara Zahra. In Austin, I have benefited from the friendship and support of my colleagues. I am grateful for the unwavering encouragement I have received from Robert H. Abzug, Ruramisai Charumbira, David Crew, Heather Hindman, Anne Martinez, Joan Neuberger, Mary Neuburger, James M. Vaughn, and Charters Wynn. Charters and David along with Judith G. Coffin and Michael B. Stoff have welcomed me into the community that is the Frank Denius Normandy Scholar Program on World War II. For that I am especially thankful.

Deborah Dash Moore and Marsha L. Rozenblit accepted this book as part of the Modern Jewish Experience series, and I appreciate their advice and support throughout this process. At Indiana University Press,

I am grateful to Dee Mortensen and her team, especially Darja Malcolm-Clarke, Jennifer Witzke, Debra Hirsch Corman, and Sarah Jacobi.

I am grateful to the publishers of *East European Jewish Affairs* and the *Austrian History Yearbook* for allowing me to reproduce some material for this book and to Centropa for permission to use the cover image.

I could never have completed this book without the support of my parents, Olga and Jiří Lichtenstein. As far back as I can remember, they have encouraged me to pursue my interest in history, even when it took me far away from them. While their immigrant experience might have equipped them to understand better the choices I have made, I know that, at times, that same experience makes our separation even more painful. Nevertheless, they have taken a great interest in my work. For over a decade, my father has worked tirelessly in libraries and archives in Prague retrieving and cataloguing materials, assisting with translations, and numerous other tasks. I am grateful to them for their support and to my brother, Jan D. Lichtenstein, for his friendship and encouragement.

Finally, I want to thank my partner, Chris Ernst. If it weren't for his intellectual curiosity, willingness to spend countless hours discussing ideas, and enthusiasm and love for our dogs, Huxley and River, I would not have been able to complete this book. Over the past years, our companionship has sustained me, and I am grateful to him for his love and patience.

Place Names

BOHEMIAN LANDS: CZECH/GERMAN

Boskovice/Boskowitz
Brno/Brünn
České Budejovice/Budweis
Hodonín/Göding
Holešov/Holleschau
Hradec Králové/Königgrätz
Jihlava/Iglau
Karlovy vary/Karlsbad
Liberec/Reichenberg
Litoměřice/Leitmeritz
Mikulov/Nikolsburg
Moravská Ostrava/Mährisch Ostrau
Moravská Třebová/Mährisch-Trübau
Plzeň/Pilsen
Poděbrady/Podiebrad
Praha/Prag
Praskolesy/Praskoles
Prostějov/Prossnitz
Sedlčany/Seltschan
Semily/Semil
Teplice-Šanov/Teplitz-Schönau
Terezín/Theresienstadt
Ústí nad labem/Aussig

SLOVAKIA: SLOVAK/GERMAN/HUNGARIAN

Banska Bystrica/Neusohl/Besztercebánya
Bardejov/Bartfeld/Bártfa
Bratislava (Prešporok)/Pressburg/Pozsony
Košice/Kaschau/Kassa
Michalovce/Grossmichel/Nagymihály
Nitra/Neutra/Nyitra
Prešov/Eperies/Eperjes
Trenčin/Trentschin/Trencsén
Trnava/Tyrnau/Nagyszombat
Žilina/Sillein/Zsolna

SUBCARPATHIAN RUS': CZECHOSLOVAK/ HUNGARIAN/YIDDISH/RUSYN

Mukačevo/Munkács/Munkatsch/Mukacheve
Užhorod/Ungvár/Uzhhorod

ZIONISTS
IN INTERWAR
CZECHOSLOVAKIA

Map 1. Successor states

GERMANY
Litoměřice/Leitmeritz
x Terezín/Theresienstadt
Prague
Plzeň/
Pilsen
BOHEMIA
České Budejovice/Budweis
POLAND
Moravská Ostrava/
Mährisch Ostrau
MORAVIA-SILESIA
Brno/Brünn
Žilina/
Sillein/Zsolna
SLOVAKIA
Banska Bystrica/
Neusohl/Besztercebánya
Bratislava/Pressburg/Pozsony
Prešov/Eperies/
Eperjes
Košice/Kaschau/Kassa
Užhorod/Ungvár / Uzhhorod
SUB-CARPATHIAN RUS'
Mukačevo/Munkács/
Munkatsch/Mukacheve
AUSTRIA
HUNGARY
ROMANIA

Map 2. Czechoslovakia

Introduction

MINORITY NATIONALISM AND ZIONISTS' POLITICS OF BELONGING

IN TODAY'S PRAGUE, TOURISTS AND LOCALS EAGER TO EXPLORE the city's Jewish past trek through the streets of the old Jewish quarter, Josefov, in the inner city. Here a handful of synagogues, a sixteenth-century town hall, and a mysterious old cemetery wedged in between towering fin-de-siècle apartment buildings and glossy luxury stores embody what most visitors experience as Jewish Prague. Some also venture further afield to the Strašnice neighborhood to visit Franz Kafka's grave in the New Jewish Cemetery. Across from the cemetery is an area known as Hagibor. It houses several tennis courts, the sports club TJ Bohemians, and the headquarters of Radio Free Europe. Besides a Jewish seniors' home, little remains to suggest to the visitor that this was once a Jewish space.

The name Hagibor has insinuated itself into the city's topography, all but divested of its Jewish origins. The fact that Hagibor is Hebrew for "the hero" escapes most, as does the Jewish history of the area. Toward the end of the Second World War, the sporting ground served as an internment camp and forced labor site for people of mixed ancestry, for Jews married to so-called "Aryans," and for some non-Jews who resisted the pressures to divorce their Jewish spouses. Earlier in the war, it was used as a playground for Jewish children and youths excluded from the city's public spaces by German racial laws. Yet, its origin as a Jewish space dates back before the war to the mid-1920s, when Hagibor was synonymous with the well-known Jewish sports club Hagibor Praha/Prag. The club was part of a network of Zionist institutions that emerged across Czechoslovakia, a testament to the significance of Zionism as a cultural and political force in Jewish life in the two decades between the World Wars.

This book explores the appeal and impact of Zionism in interwar Czechoslovakia. It shows that Zionists envisioned nation building as the basis for achieving civic equality and social integration. Zionist activists' aspiration was to make Jews insiders by insisting that their respectability as citizens, and hence their belonging, depended on maintaining a distinctive Jewish national identity.[1] This study examines the projects that Zionists undertook to nationalize Jews' identities and claim belonging in this new multinational state. National communities – much like belonging – had to be constructed. Zionists, like other nation makers, worked hard to create and maintain institutions, such as schools and sports clubs – a stateless nation's territory – through which the Jewish nation was to come to life. Unlike many histories of Zionism, this book moves beyond questions of how Zionists theorized the nation and the intricacies of high-level political and intellectual debates, to look at the nitty-gritty of nation building, the everyday work that went into creating a nation. It shows that Zionist activism, its narratives, priorities, and strategies, was profoundly shaped by the legislative, political, and discursive framework for national mobilization that had emerged in late Habsburg Austria and was sustained in interwar Czechoslovakia. By shifting the focus away from the traditional modes of inquiry into Zionism – the international congresses, party politics, factionalist showdowns, and the Zionist project in Palestine – this book shows that for Zionists in interwar Czechoslovakia, the most significant and in many ways constitutive framework for their activism was the state. Here, the process of state building engendered avenues for minority nation building.

In interwar Czechoslovakia, Zionists adopted a model for citizenship that combined an ethno-national Jewish identity with patriotism. Indeed, to Zionists, the nationalization of Jewish society was a necessary precondition for good citizenship.[2] While the country's constitution guaranteed Jews equal rights, actual social and civic equality depended on a broader public identification of Jews as belonging in the state as well as Jews' own feeling of being at home. Zionists' political project of belonging aimed to define the boundaries and loyalties of the Jewish nation as well as to contest narratives that marked Jews as outsiders and excluded them from the community of equal citizens.

The question of Jews' suitability for citizenship, for equal rights and admittance into society at large, has been at the center of modern Jewish history. In some states, Jews were admitted to full citizenship without formal preconditions, while in others, such as the Habsburg Monarchy, Jews were expected to transform themselves into loyal, acculturated, and moral subjects in return for equal rights. Jews' status was contested and the willingness to accept Jews in their difference fluctuated on a spectrum between inclusion and exclusion. At the same time, Jews considered the conditions for their admittance and equality. Some assimilated, others retreated into tradition. Many developed new forms of Jewish culture, identity, and community that allowed them to retain aspects of their difference that they found meaningful. In the wake of the First World War, Zionists in Czechoslovakia created a model for citizenship that cast Jews' ethno-national difference, and Jews' loyalty to their ancestral community, as a precondition for Jews' readiness to assume citizenship.

In interwar Czechoslovakia, Zionism was not an exit strategy for Jews, but a ticket of admission to the societies in which they already lived. In this new multinational state, Zionists saw nationalism as a way for Jews to stake their claim as a collective, as one of the country's national minorities, that belonged as much as any other. Nationalism thus allowed Zionists to normalize and legitimize Jews' difference. It was a position shaped, on the one hand, by Zionists' political ambitions and personal loyalties. On the other, it reflected their belief that Zionism – as an assertion of Jews' respectability and expression of Jews' Czechoslovak patriotism – would not only appeal to the country's Jewish population, but also gain them acceptance as model citizens. Rather than looking to Palestine, Zionists focused on sustaining Jewish life in the Diaspora. Their goal was to transform Jews from outsiders to insiders in Europe.

Hagibor as a Jewish space was destroyed by the wartime dispossession, deportation, and murder of the city's Jews. The memory of it was suppressed by postwar antisemitism and the marginalization of the Jewish experience by the Communist regime. The traumatic events of the

Second World War and its aftermath have shaped not only the lives of people and their communities, but also the ways in which Jewish life there has been remembered. Although the Zionist project in Czechoslovakia ultimately failed, exploring its history reveals the challenges and opportunities facing minority nationalists in interwar Eastern Europe. This study gives voice to Zionists' diverse aspirations and thereby uncovers a bold and creative form of Jewish politics long overshadowed by post-Holocaust memories.

JEWS AND THE STATE

In Eastern Europe, the First World War created unprecedented dislocations. Millions of people were uprooted from their communities by war and forced deportations. The relatively stable empires, which had enveloped the region's diverse religious, linguistic, and ethnic societies for centuries, collapsed. The successor states that followed in their wake aspired to national homogeneity. Across the region, minorities were called upon to justify their presence and to demonstrate that they belonged within the new political boundaries. With the international community watching, minority questions assumed center stage in Eastern Europe's restructured political landscape.[3] Yet, the new state elites aspired not only to national homogeneity, but also to political, social, and economic stability. To international audiences, eager to contain revolutionary Russia and an expansionist Germany, stability was a key indicator whether the East European peoples deserved their sovereignty. In Czechoslovakia – a new state created out of former Austrian and Hungarian territories with large linguistic and religious minorities – the interconnected needs for stability and legitimacy created new possibilities for minority nationalist activists.[4]

Looking beyond the legacies of the years of genocide and ethnic cleansing that destroyed Eastern Europe's multinational states during and after the Second World War, this book shows that the interwar period was a time of experimentation and innovation in state and nation building. As new political elites sought to establish their dominance, minority activists faced fresh challenges and opportunities. Drawing on local models for nationalist activism cobbled together with a strategic allegiance to central authority, Zionists pursued a role as partners in the Czechoslovak state-building project.[5] Zionists capitalized on the Czech political elite's uncertainty regarding the loyalty of the diverse communities within the newly amalgamated territories. They did so by casting Zionism as a cultural and political force that would transform Jews into loyal citizens and a model national minority.

In their efforts to create an alliance with the state, Zionists tapped into a long-standing Jewish political custom of fostering partnerships with central governments or powerful elites. Like previous generations of Jewish reformers and modernizers, Zionists in Czechoslovakia looked to the state for assistance in transforming Jewish society.[6] As a new force on the Jewish political stage and unsure of their influence among Jews, Zionists sought to harness the authority and resources of the state to their own cultural programs. To them, the new political circumstances offered a chance to improve their community's sociocultural, political, and economic position. Zionists developed their projects within the context of an emerging welfare state, where authorities were expected to care for citizens' educational, cultural, and social welfare needs. This included support for those institutions created by and for national minorities. The book shows that state authorities and Zionist activists engaged in a complex process of negotiation to balance the interests of the state with those of the country's Jewish minority. It was a process that allowed Zionists to contest the ethnic and linguistic boundaries that marked Jews as outsiders by insisting on the integrative potential of their nation-building project.

The cooperation between state authorities – ministerial bureaucrats, members of state agencies, elected officials – and minority activists was central to a local tradition for nationalist mobilization that dated back to the late Habsburg era. Since the 1880s, German and Czech nationalists had succeeded in shaping legislation and securing public resources that enabled them to expand and strengthen their capacity for national mobilization. After 1918, in the new Czechoslovakia, Zionists looked with admiration and envy at some of the country's other, larger nationalities' expansive state-funded network of social welfare, educational, and cultural institutions. And because the Czechoslovak authorities had recognized Jews as one of the country's nationalities, Zionists expected to be included among the recipients of state support. Since funding depended on activists' political clout and their nation's size, the population censuses, which counted Jews as not only a religious but also a national minority, assumed central importance.[7]

This book reveals that while the state authorities recognized Jews as a nationality, contrary to Zionists' expectations they did not extend full national rights to Jews. In Czechoslovakia, as in Habsburg Austria, the belief that Jews lacked a shared national language turned out to be a significant obstacle for Zionists' ability to obtain equal national rights for Jews. In a context in which nationality was marked primarily by language, Jews' multilingualism and the absence of a shared Jewish mother tongue posed a serious problem for Zionists. Jews' contested nationality status barred Zionist activists from access to urgently needed public funds, limited their authority vis-à-vis the country's Jews, and posed a challenge to the legitimacy of the Zionist project as a whole. Nevertheless, by looking closely at the ways in which state authorities and Jewish minority advocates negotiated policies toward the country's Jews, this study demonstrates that initiatives from above were at times shaped and even engineered by Zionists. This was an important mode of governance through which activists assumed and exercised power vis-à-vis their own communities and the state elites. Yet, when the interests of the state and Zionists were perceived to be at odds, in the absence of outside support the latter had little recourse. The unequal power relationship should not, however, overshadow that, as this book shows, the relationship between the successor states and their minorities in the interwar years was complex. At times it was cooperative, at others adversarial, but always dynamic.

LOCAL TRADITIONS FOR MINORITY NATIONALIST ACTIVISM

This book focuses on Zionist activists in the Bohemian Lands, the former Austrian provinces of Bohemia and Moravia and part of Austrian Silesia that made up Czechoslovakia's western half. Although the Zionist project must be considered within the context of Czechoslovakia as a whole, the Zionist elite consisted of people who had been part of grassroots Zionist circles in Bohemia and Moravia during the last decades of the Habsburg Monarchy.[8] In the 1920s and '30s, they retained their leadership position within the country's Zionist institutions. The study's main protagonists, such as the statistician František Friedmann, the parliamentarians Ludvík Singer and Angelo Goldstein, and the community administrator Gustav Fleischmann, were all from the Bohemian Lands, and their nation-building efforts were shaped by local traditions for minority nationalist activism. In Czechoslovakia, Zionists created a movement for Jews' social, cultural, and political empowerment by adapting legible and legitimate narrative forms, political strategies, and institutional models developed by German and Czech nationalists.

The Bohemian Lands had been one of the centers for nationalist activism in the late Habsburg era. During those years, Jewish society was not only transformed by urbanization and sociocultural changes, but also affected by the power struggle between Czech and German nationalists.[9] The outlook of the interwar Zionist leaders reflected their experience of nationalist mobilization and the antisemitism that accompanied it.[10] In the Bohemian Lands, the nationalist battle was so intense in part because nationalists competed over the same population. In this region, where there were few cultural differences that separated the overwhelmingly Catholic population from each other, linguistic differences became the main marker of Czech or German national belonging in the course of the late nineteenth century. This was by its very nature an unstable and fluid national marker in an area where many people were multilingual.

Recently, scholars have overturned the long-standing assumptions that in Eastern Europe people's national belonging were firmly rooted in age-old ethnic loyalties by showing that people's national identities remained malleable and contested well into the twentieth century.[11] By studying how national categories were constructed and to what extent they transformed societies, historians argue that it was precisely the persistence of fluid identities and behaviors, of national indifference, that radicalized nationalists' tactics.[12] As a result, by the early 1900s, assisted by the Austrian courts and legislators, nationalists were increasingly empowered to ascribe national belonging to individuals and communities. By then, state elites acted on the assumption that citizens belonged to ethno-national groups and worked hand in hand with nationalists to impose fixed identities and ideal behaviors.

Thus historians argue that ethnic boundaries were created and hardened only in the late nineteenth century for the region's Catholic German- and Czech-speakers and even so remained porous. In contrast, before the emergence of nationalism in the region in the early 1800s, Jews did constitute a distinct ethnic community. Jews were bounded as a group by religious, legislative, institutional, social, and economic markers that distinguished them from the Catholic majority population.[13] Over the course of the nineteenth century, however, urbanization, acculturation, and social integration softened the boundaries between Jews and non-Jews. Czech and German nationalists recognized Jews' distinctiveness but considered Jews "nationally indeterminate." For some time, Czech and German nationalists alike appealed to Jews to join their nations – and some Jews did.[14]

Yet, by the 1880s, Czech and German activists began pointing to Jews as particularly chauvinist "Czechs" or "Germans" or as indifferent side switchers. These accusations reflected, on the one hand, the broader anxieties that nationalists harbored about assimilation, opportunism, and national indifference and, on the other, the increasing influence of racialism on Czech and German nationalism.[15] When Zionist circles emerged in the Bohemian Lands in the 1890s, their members agreed that it was Jews' transgression of the boundaries of "other" nations that fueled antisemitism. They called on Jews to "return" to their ancestral Jewish nation by becoming Zionists. In the wake of the First World War, when anti-Jewish sentiment and violence reached new heights, activists promoted Zionism as the remedy. By assuming a Jewish national identity, they argued, Jews would no longer be suspected of interloping, treason, or indifference, a behavior that harmed Jews and non-Jews alike. As Zionist activists and their Czech and German colleagues saw it, good fences made good neighbors.[16]

Zionism was not an awakening of preexisting, slumbering national feelings, but an ideology that served to give meaning to Jews' difference. It was individual activists' response to a specific cultural and political context and its challenges. In the Bohemian Lands before and after the

First World War, most Zionist activists shared a similar social, cultural, and educational background. Many were lawyers, doctors, writers, or businessmen; most had attended university in Vienna or Prague. These middle-class men's activism was shaped by their class- and gender-based identities as well as by the affront to these identities that the nationalist conflict and growing antisemitism posed. Zionists were driven by a search for respect and recognition by their social peers, for political influence and civic equality, and for integration, a process in which individual worthiness was inseparable from collective respectability.[17] To them, Jews' indeterminate nationality, what they saw as national indifference, was a mark of shame, a denial of oneself and one's community. Zionism was in its most basic sense a movement for ethnic pride, an assertion of Jews' dignity and equality.

In interwar Czechoslovakia, Zionists joined the efforts of other nationalists to eradicate indifference to questions of national belonging and instill correct national behavior. Jews' decisions about where to send their children to school, where and with whom to enjoy gymnastics, what sports team to support, how to vote in elections, and what nationality to choose on the census now became subjects of intense scrutiny. By nationalizing people's private and public worlds, Zionists alongside other activists worked to create parallel national universes.[18] For Zionists, nationalism was a legitimate and legible mode of political action that aspired to place Jews on par with the country's other nationalities, a message intended for Jewish and non-Jewish audiences alike. For Zionists, nationalization was a process of physical and moral regeneration that promised to restore Jews' honor, bestow dignity on Jews and the Jewish nation, and thereby end Jews' marginalization. Nationalism was thus a way to stake out Jews' claim to belonging and insider status.

Zionists succeeded in creating visibility for Jewish nationhood in political life, in urban neighborhoods, and in social scientific discourse, a visibility that allowed Jews and non-Jews alike to imagine a Jewish nation. They succeeded in creating new Jewish spaces, such as youth groups, sports clubs, and cultural and educational associations, which allowed Jews to build community on the basis of a Jewish ethnic rather than religious identity. Yet, only a minority of the country's Jews signed up in Zionist organizations. Even the ones that did continued to seek out community elsewhere, such as in internationalist socialist youth groups and on non-Jewish sports teams. To be sure, Zionist leaders were themselves blurring national boundaries. Some were active in multiple political parties and organizations; others married non-Jews. Indeed, in the interwar years, despite Zionists' efforts, Jews' identities and communities remained fluid and diverse, with considerable regional and generational differences. Yet, rather than dismissing Jews' indifference altogether, Zionists adapted their message. Instead of demanding that Jews commit unequivocally to Jewish nationhood, they promoted Zionism as a form of national neutrality, an expression of ethnic Jewish pride and Czechoslovak patriotism. Along with other recent works on nationalism in Eastern Europe, this study of Zionist activists thus shows that nationalization was a contested process shaped by the reciprocal roles of state elites, nationalists, and ordinary people.

Zionists' politics of belonging – the projects they undertook to nationalize Jewish society and transform others' perception of Jews – have to be understood as framed by the particular historical experience that they shared with their Czech and German peers among bureaucrats, politicians, journalists, and social scientists. This similarity facilitated Zionists' ability to position themselves as junior partners in a broader civilizing mission undertaken by Czech elites. Although the Czechoslovak Zionist Organization was formally headquartered in the Moravian industrial city Moravská Ostrava/Mährisch Ostrau, in the middle of the elongated country, Prague Zionists were the most influential on the domestic stage thanks to their proximity to political power and the outlook they shared with the political and administrative elites in the capital. Indeed, as respectable political agents, Zionists stood at the ready to assist the state authorities in the moral, social, and cultural improvement of the country's eastern regions and populations, areas where the majority of Czechoslovakia's Jews lived. By acting as a junior partner of the state, employing statistics, social science, and top-down reforms to transform Jews into model citizens, Zionists were empowered by their participation in the consolidation of Czechoslovak hegemony, a position that aligned them with the state's Czech elite.

JEWS AS CZECHOSLOVAKS

In recent years, historians have dismantled the myth of Czechoslovakia.[19] Constructed by the interwar Czech political elite, it depicts Czechoslovakia as a liberal and democratic island whose progressive, western Czech leaders held out against the anti-democratic and chauvinist nationalist forces that engulfed the rest of Central and Eastern Europe in the interwar years. Scholars point to the ways in which the state and its political elite subsumed individual rights to those of national collectives, restricted democratic rights, and favored Czech hegemony at the expense of the country's other nationalities. One of the key components of the myth has been the claim that the authorities' recognition of Jews as one of the country's nationalities reflected the Czech leadership's tolerance and forthcoming attitude toward the country's Jews and, by extension, other minorities. This book shows that the Czechoslovak state authorities' cooperation with Zionists was less a sign of their acceptance of the latter's demand for national rights as a legitimate one than a desire to consolidate Czechoslovak hegemony in the country. The Czech elite's support for Zionists' projects was therefore determined by the former's priorities rather than Zionists' needs.

Paradoxically, the myth of Czechoslovakia as an exceptional state in Eastern Europe also sustained another misconception, namely that in the interwar years, "Jews were the only real Czechoslovaks," a vague saying used by scholars to suggest that Jews alone remained faithful to the state's alleged multinational, democratic, and liberal ideals while everyone else descended into exclusionary ethno-racial nationalism.[20] The saying thus ascribes to Jews the moral high ground as well as denies Jews political agency. It does so by implying not only that Jews' nationalist aspiration was indeed a neutral position, as Zionists claimed, but also that Jews alone remained separate from the nationalist struggle, preferring to stand on the sidelines of the broader political battle.[21] In reality, I argue, Zionists positioned themselves as loyal supporters of the state's Czech elite and dominant national group. In fact, the myth of Jews as the only "real" Czechoslovaks was constructed by Zionist activists. Seeking to cast Zionists as partners in Czechoslovak state building, and by extension the Jewish minority as an integrative force, Zionists produced and disseminated an image of the country's diverse and dispersed Jewish societies as united by an underlying sociological and cultural sameness, by their Jewish nationhood. Jews, they argued, perhaps belonged more than any of the country's other nationalities. Zionists thus accommodated rather than resisted the dominant nationalizing paradigm that ascribed national identity to people based on ethnic origin. Zionism was a vehicle for Jews' participation in rather than withdrawal from the process of nationalization in Czechoslovakia, a process that increasingly undermined individuals' rights and enforced ethnic boundaries.

The persistence of these intertwined myths does reflect that the Jewish experience in Czechoslovakia was different from that of Jews in neighboring countries in the interwar years. Czechoslovakia did stand out, with its absence of overt, state-sponsored antisemitism and a general commitment among public officials to honor the state's legal commitments to its Jewish citizens and communities. If the reasons for this exceptionalism are not as idealistic as historians imagined, it did shape Jews' experience. As conditions deteriorated for Jews in neighboring countries, Czechoslovakia – with its relative political stability and socioeconomic prosperity – did appear, and was perhaps experienced, as a uniquely welcoming place for Jews in Eastern Europe.

The work of scholars studying Jewish and East European history has been shaped by the breakdown of the region's diverse societies during and after the Second World War. The interethnic violence that swept the region was interpreted as evidence of the societies' prewar dysfunctionality rather than as a result of wartime mobilization and a deliberate deepening of social, ethnic, religious, and regional differences.[22] In contrast, this book shows that as the supranational Habsburg Monarchy was replaced by successor states with new criteria for belonging, ones that centered on ethnicity and loyalty to the state, Jews were in search of new models for citizenship. In Czechoslovakia, Zionists believed that nationalism enabled Jews to embrace and cultivate their ethnic difference meanwhile becoming loyal, equal, and respected citizens of the state that they shared with their non-Jewish neighbors. As a study of Jewish politics, this book shifts the focus away from what emerged as the dominant form of Zionism after 1945, namely the Palestine-focused and state-seeking kind whose aspiration came to fruition by the creation of the State of Israel. It thereby seeks to recover the diversity of Zionist voices that existed before the Holocaust, including ones that remained committed to Jewish national life in Europe.

"WHERE IS MY HOME?" ZIONISTS AND THE DIASPORA

The title of the Czech national anthem "Where Is My Home?" embodies an important tension within Zionism. Some Zionists dismissed the Jewish Diaspora as a historical aberration and looked to the ancestral homeland in Palestine as the only place that offered a future for the Jewish people. Yet, the majority of Zionist activists, supporters, and sympathizers continued to live in the Diaspora, and many did not plan to emigrate to Palestine until the onset of the Second World War. In fact, even though Zionist ideology maintained that the Jewish Question – the problem of antisemitism, poverty, spiritual emptiness, and political powerlessness – could only be resolved by returning Jews to the Land of Israel, this project depended on Zionists' ability to mobilize the financial resources, political influence, and national aspirations of Jews living in the Diaspora. Thus, paradoxically, the Zionist project depended on the well-being of Diaspora Jewry.

By the time the Budapest-born and Vienna-based Theodor Herzl (1860–1904) founded the Zionist Organization in Basel in 1897, proto-Zionist groups had been active in the Russian Empire for well over a decade, organizing small-scale agricultural communities in Ottoman Palestine. From the outset, the Zionist Organization's program to create a homeland for the Jewish people appealed to Jews from across Europe but was met with particular enthusiasm from Jewish activists in Russia and Austria-Hungary. Zionism attracted people with diverse social, political, and cultural backgrounds, a diversity that was reflected in the different visions for the organization.[23] Some activists were focused on encouraging immediate Jewish emigration to Palestine, others on the foundation of some form of Jewish sovereign entity, a state or a homeland, and still others on the creation of a modern Jewish national culture in the Diaspora.

Regardless of their differences, these Zionists were all driven by a sense of urgency in finding a solution to the perceived ills of Jewish societies. For some Zionists, antisemitism in all parts of Europe signaled that the promise of emancipation had fallen short. Despite Jews' acculturation and integration, non-Jews rejected them with a new, more forceful hostility. Estranged from traditional Jewish culture, some were looking to infuse Jews' socioeconomic, cultural, and linguistic difference with new meaning. For many Zionists in France, Germany, and parts of the Habsburg Monarchy, securing Jews' ethnic and cultural continuity and mobilizing a defense against antisemitism were the central concerns. For many East European Zionists, it was the deepening socioeconomic crisis among the Jewish masses that required new action. What united them was an "ethos of activism."[24]

Zionism shared with other minority nationalisms in Eastern Europe a strong remedial impulse. They saw their nation's present as a state of decline and deficiency for which a national awakening, a process of internal reform, was the only remedy. This internal transformation would in turn pave the way for the renegotiation of the nation's position vis-à-vis the state or the dominant elite. In Eastern Europe at the turn of the twentieth century, minority nationalists imagined national liberation as a simultaneous internal and external process of empowerment.[25]

In Zionist ideology, this state of deficiency was embodied in the notion of the "negation of the Exile (*Galut*)."[26] According to this view, Jews' existence as a minority in the Diaspora, the dispersal of the Jewish people and its separation from the Land of Israel, had produced a state of being that was uniformly negative. To them, the Diaspora embodied Jews' humiliation, powerlessness, a parasitic socioeconomic and cultural relationship to non-Jews, linguistic and cultural hybridity, rootlessness, and passivity. In the Diaspora, as one author put it, "we did not make our history, but the gentiles made it for us . . . it [our history] has no deeds or plots, no heroes or world conquerors, no rulers or men of deeds, only a community of pained, dragged along, groaning and crying people seeking mercy."[27] While the negative view of the Diaspora centered on powerlessness and passivity, these views were also nurtured by a more entrenched religious tradition that viewed exile as divine punishment, as an ugly, shameful state of being.[28] To many

Zionist ideologues, the remedy for the exilic condition was the return of the Jewish people to the Land of Israel. Only here could Jews develop an authentic and pure national culture, engage in productive economic and cultural pursuits, restore their sense of honor, and make their own history. Yet, at the same time as Herzl articulated his vision for a Jewish state, in Austria-Hungary, most prominently in Galicia, Jewish activists adopted nationalism as a vehicle for Jews' collective political empowerment in Austria in sync with local modes of minority nationalist mobilization and politics.[29]

By the early 1900s, as Ottoman authorities proved opposed to Zionist goals in Palestine, Zionist leaders accepted the need to prioritize equally the Palestine project and the efforts to secure Jews' civil and minority rights in the Diaspora. Indeed, the Jewish national awakening had to begin in Eastern Europe, where most Jews lived. Before long, Zionism developed into an all-inclusive ideology engaged in every aspect of Diaspora Jewish life. The more Zionist activists became integrated into and invested in the existing Jewish societies, the more they became committed to and dependent on the continuity of life in the Diaspora. As one historian notes, "Zionism was transformed into an effective instrumentality for the *preservation* of Jewish life and culture in the diaspora."[30]

The Zionist Organization's embrace of the Diaspora was in part a response to the competition Zionists' faced from other Jewish nationalist movements. In Eastern Europe, there were important non-Zionist Jewish nationalist organizations. These Jewish nationalists believed, much like Zionists did, that Jews were a nation connected by history, religion, and language. But they rejected the notion that national autonomy involved statehood or another form of territorial claim. In the Russian Empire and in Austria-Hungary, Jewish Diaspora nationalists, some inspired by the work of the historian Simon Dubnow (1860–1941) and the writer Nathan Birnbaum (1864–1937), worked to secure Jews legal equality and national minority rights (especially rights regarding education and language) within the framework of the continent's multinational states. They did not share Zionists' negative view of the Diaspora. Yet, these activists were critical of what they perceived as Jews' passivity, political ignorance, and unsustainable socioeconomic structure, in particular Jews' propensity for commerce.

The most significant Diaspora nationalist institution was the General Union of Jewish Workers in Lithuania, Poland, and Russia, known as the Bund (Der Algemeyner Yidisher Arbeter Bund in Lite, Poyln, un Rusland), which would become the largest Jewish socialist trade union and party in Eastern Europe.[31] Although an important member of the broader socialist revolutionary movement in Russia, the Bund insisted on the inclusion of Jewish workers' national rights as part of the struggle for civic equality and social justice. They were particularly invested in the recognition of Yiddish as Jews' national language. In the decade before the First World War, a multitude of Jewish nationalist organizations emerged; some were Zionists, other were anti-Zionists, some were religious, others secular, and some were socialists, others anti-socialist. The main distinction between them remained whether the Jewish nation belonged *here* (in Europe) or *there* (in Palestine).

From the outset, the differences between Zionism and Diaspora nationalism, although they remained sharp in theory, were quite blurred in practice. By 1905, democratic reforms in Russia and Austria-Hungary opened up new possibilities for Zionist political activism. The prospect of elections emboldened activists who were critical of some Zionists' disregard for the immediate and pressing socioeconomic, political, and cultural problems of the Jewish minority in Europe. By 1906, "work in the present" became an important part of the Zionist agenda. Although Zionists in some parts of Austria-Hungary formed political parties and ran in general elections, in the Bohemian Lands Zionists focused on cultural renewal. Some, most famously the Prague circle of Jewish writers, imagined Zionism as a movement of spiritual regeneration. Inspired by the work of German and Czech nationalists and eager to participate in new forms of Jewish community, Zionists here also created gymnastics and sports clubs, student organizations, and cultural associations and supported an emerging Zionist press.[32] Thus, before the First World War, Zionists and Diaspora nationalists alike, and often working together, were at the forefront of a broad movement of Jewish cultural renewal and political mobilization and found themselves increasingly at the center of the battle for recognition of Jews' civic and national rights. After the war, they took the fight to the Paris Peace Conference, now seeking to create an alliance with western Jewish leaders to ensure the protection of Jews and their rights in Eastern Europe's successor states.[33]

The First World War transformed the prospects for the Zionist movement in a number of ways. In the wake of the war, Palestine became a British Mandate. By 1922, the British government's wartime support for the creation of a national home for the Jewish people in Palestine became an internationally recognized commitment. In Eastern Europe, Jews became citizens or subjects of nationalist successor states or fell under Bolshevik rule, a regime that was hostile to Zionism but not always to Jewish nationalism. Indeed, the Soviet Union would prove to be the most significant ideological and practical challenge to Zionists in the interwar years.[34]

In Palestine, the British authorities initially favored the Zionist Organization as a partner on the ground. They welcomed Zionist leaders' plans for investment in and modernization of the area's agriculture and industry. Zionists in turn expected the British authorities to open up Palestine to Jewish arrivals and to commit public resources to facilitate the immigration and settlement of Jews. Before long, they had to adjust those expectations. Not only did the British quickly become aware of local Palestinian Arab opposition to Jewish immigration, but they also believed that the economic realities of Palestine made it unsuitable for a mass influx of European immigrants. Thus, from the outset, the British authorities, who were supportive of the Zionist project, regulated Jews' entry into Palestine.[35] They did so by issuing visas in the form of work certificates for specific sectors of the economy, by requiring financial guarantees for most immigrants, and by restricting any use of public resources for immigration purposes. The financial and logistic burden of immigration, land purchase, and settlement fell to the Zionist Organization. Zionists in turn appealed to world Jewry, including non-Zionist Jews, to support the creation of a national home.

Between 1919 and 1932, a little more than 125,000 Jews immigrated to Palestine. The majority of these immigrants arrived before 1926. In some years, substantial numbers of immigrants left Palestine, either returning to their old homes or headed to new destinations. As conditions deteriorated for Jews in Germany after 1933, the number of immigrants increased substantially. Between 1933 and 1939, almost 230,000 Jewish immigrants entered Palestine.[36] As a result, the Jewish population in Palestine grew from 83,790 (11% of the total population) in 1922 to 174,606 (17%) in 1931. As immigration from Poland and Germany increased in the 1930s, the number of Jews in Palestine increased to 474,102 (30%) by 1941.[37]

Despite Zionist leaders' success in mobilizing the support of non-Zionist Jews for the Palestine project, in the late 1920s and early 1930s the internal ideological, political, and social differences between Zionists became more divisive. By the mid-1930s tensions over the ideological and political direction of the Palestine project divided Zionists in Palestine and in Europe. In 1935 the Zionist radical right, the Revisionists, created an alternative New Zionist Organization. The Revisionists were especially popular in Poland, home to the largest Zionist movement and the source of most immigrants to Palestine. Thus, on the one hand, the project to create a Jewish homeland in Palestine brought together Zionist and non-Zionist Jews in an effort to raise funds for land purchase, immigration, and settlement. On the other, the political realities of building a national Jewish society as well as the broader European political landscape had a polarizing effect, creating deep divisions among Zionists in Europe and in Palestine.

Nevertheless, the establishment of a British mandate in Palestine energized Zionists in Europe. With the national home seemingly at hand, activists redoubled their efforts to shore up financial support for the Zionist cause among Jews in the Diaspora. As mentioned earlier, most Zionists in Europe and the Americas did not intend to immigrate to Palestine, yet they devoted themselves wholeheartedly to making sure that others could. For some, fundraising for Zionist agencies became an end in itself. Others viewed their activism as a substitute for emigration. While western Jewish donors supplied the funds, the majority of immigrants to Palestine in the 1920s came from Eastern Europe, primarily Poland. Across Europe, Zionist activism expanded considerably in the 1920s and '30s alongside other forms of Jewish political activism, most prominently the Jewish socialist movement.[38]

In interwar Eastern Europe, activists oversaw the expansion of Zionist networks of political parties, schools, youth and sports organizations, agricultural and industrial training facilities, and other institutions that simultaneously were symbols of and vehicles for Jews' national mobilization. In Poland, Zionists also supported a Hebrew-language school system. Despite the Zionist movement's growth and visibility, nowhere in Europe did Zionists dominate Jewish political life, nor did they command most Jews' political loyalties.[39]

This was also the case in Czechoslovakia, where Zionists never overcame the opposition from powerful, traditional Jewish leaderships in Slovakia and Subcarpathian Rus' and only managed to organize a minority of Jews within Zionist organizations. Yet, in the Bohemian Lands, despite their modest following, Zionists gained influence in communal Jewish politics and eventually on the national stage. They did so by toning down Zionist doctrine in favor of a more moderate position of Jewish pride and solidarity as well as loyalty to the state.[40] This pragmatism was perhaps in part due to the departure of some of the prominent prewar Zionist ideologues for Palestine in the early 1920s.[41] Most Zionists stayed in Czechoslovakia and over the next two decades negotiated the tensions embedded in Zionist theory and practice. Zionists here supported the Jewish homeland in Palestine financially and ideologically, but they were ambivalent about the prospects of young Jews' emigration to Palestine. Not only did emigration drain the Jewish nation in Czechoslovakia of its future elite, but it also diminished the political weight of Jews in the country. Indeed, in Czechoslovakia, with its political stability, nationalist traditions, and relative social and economic prosperity, Zionists believed they had been presented with a unique opportunity to create Jewish national life in Europe.

The traditional paradigm for the study of Zionism in interwar Europe has tended to understand the movement as developing within an almost purely "Jewish framework" shaped by the interplay between Zionist leaderships in Palestine, activists in the Diaspora, and the broader Jewish societies whose resources and support Zionists were working to mobilize. These narratives, even when they adopt a comparative perspective, play out almost entirely within a Jewish context upon which the broader European environment, its people, institutions, and traditions, intrudes mostly as antisemitism and to underline Jews' powerlessness as a minority.[42] As this book shows, this old framework is inadequate if one seeks to understand how Zionism functioned in European societies in the interwar period.[43] In Czechoslovakia, Zionists identified with the broader Zionist movement's ideals and supported the project in Palestine with funds and "human material," but they also developed their own political agendas and partnership and pursued their goals using dynamic and multifaceted strategies. In interwar Europe, Zionism was a way for Jews to participate as equal citizens in the societies in which they lived and articulate their belonging in the places they already called home.

CHAPTER OVERVIEW

The Zionist project in Czechoslovakia was shaped in important ways by the diversity of Jewish societies and cultures in the new state. In the Bohemian Lands, Jews were mostly middle class, acculturated, and German- and Czech-speaking. In Slovakia, German, Hungarian, and Yiddish were widely used languages among the region's lower middle class and Orthodox Jews. Further east, in Subcarpathian Rus', most Jews lived in traditional Yiddish-speaking Jewish societies. As chapter 1, "The Jews of Czechoslovakia: A Mosaic of Cultures," demonstrates, despite their differences, the Jews of Czechoslovakia shared a historical experience as subjects of the Habsburg state. Significantly, in the decades before the First World War, many observers considered the monarchy's Jews staunch allies of the dominant German and Hungarian elites and among the monarchy's most loyal supporters. When the Habsburg state collapsed in 1918, Jews' patterns of identification, a complex of ethnic, political, and cultural loyalties, had to be reconfigured.[44] Yet, the Habsburg legacy continued to shape debates about Jews' political loyalties and national belonging, and hence Zionist priorities and strategies, in the decades that followed.

It was in the immediate aftermath of the First World War, amid a volatile atmosphere of intense antisemitism and anti-Jewish violence, that Zionists first appeared on the political stage in Czechoslovakia. Zionists presented their position as one of neutrality, as an attempt to withdraw Jews from the national conflict and thereby diminish attacks on Jews. Historians have generally accepted this assertion. From the outset, however, it was clear that in the Bohemian Lands, the nationality conflict left no room for neutrality. From most German and Czech nationalists' perspective, this was a zero-sum game. And in practice, Zionists' neutrality effectively meant loyalty to the new Czech elites. Chapter 2, "Jewish Power and Powerlessness: Zionists, Czechs, and the Paris Peace Conference," explores how in the fall of 1918, Prague-based Zionists set out to protect Jews by creating an alliance with the dominant Czech leaders in Prague and at the Paris Peace Conference. Zionists' mission was to convince Czech and Slovak elites that attacks on Jews were detrimental to the internal stability of the new state and to Czechoslovak interests abroad. Historians often focus on how the Czech leadership bestowed rights on Jews. In contrast, my analysis centers on the role played by Jewish activists in creating the coalition with the new authorities. It shows that Jewish activists, spurred on by the calamitous events around them and their own political ambitions, skillfully manipulated widely held perceptions about international Jewish power to convince Czech leaders to discourage antisemitism and curb anti-Jewish violence. Zionists were thus instrumental for the success of Czech leaders in creating Czechoslovakia's image as a particularly welcoming and tolerant place for Jews, a central component of the myth of Czechoslovakia as an island of democracy in Eastern Europe.

Scholars who view Czechoslovakia as exceptionally welcoming to Jews hold up as evidence of their claim the fact that the state authorities allowed Jews to opt for Jewish national belonging in the population censuses of 1921 and 1930, an interpretation disseminated by Zionists in the interwar years. The census was among the most significant political institutions in interwar Czechoslovakia. Yet, few have considered what the recognition of Jews as a nationality actually meant. The interwar alliance between Zionist and Czech elites rested on the belief that Jewish nationalism would neutralize Jews' effect on the balance of power between the country's nationalities. More specifically, Czechs and Zionists alike hoped that Jews, if given the opportunity to choose Jewish national belonging, would no longer identify as Germans and Hungarians, as they had during the Habsburg era. The Czechoslovak population census was an important test of the promise made by Zionists to the Czechs. Chapter 3, "Mapping Jews: Social Science and the Making of Czechoslovak Jewry," focuses on the importance that Zionist activists invested in the inclusion of the category "Jewish nationality" in the country's censuses. It examines how statistics and social science became a vehicle for mapping a Jewish nation that appeared as a natural and integral part of Czechoslovakia's ethnographical landscape. In the interwar years, Zionists hailed the statistical recognition of Jewish nationhood as a reflection of Czech tolerance and commitment to scientific truths over politics. As the chapter demonstrates, however, the census makers envisioned the census as a blueprint for state- and nation-building in Czechoslovakia more than an imprint of social reality. The chapter examines the work of Jewish statistician and activist František Friedmann and shows that Zionists produced narratives that depicted the country's Jews as a unified ethnic community whose historical boundaries conformed with and even predated those of Czechoslovakia. Exploring the debates surrounding the census design and its political uses, I argue that in response to what they perceived as Jews' national indifference and opportunism, Jewish activists contributed to the increasingly racialized understandings of Jewishness in the 1920s and '30s.

While Zionists used social science to make Jews visible as an integral part of Czechoslovakia, they also looked to existing Jewish institutions as vehicles for Jews' integration. In Europe, the most prominent Jewish institution was, and remains, the formal Jewish community. Historically, Jewish community leaders had extensive social, religious, legal, and political responsibilities. As the public face of local Jewry, the community was an institution invested with significant authority and important symbolic meaning. It was the seat of power in Jewish life. The quest to assume control of the Jewish communities was therefore a priority formulated by Theodor Herzl himself in his call for Zionists "to conquer the communities." In contrast to the imagery of popular revolt and sweeping victories bandied about by the Zionist press, in the Bohemian Lands Zionists' conquest took subtle, cooperative forms.

Historians have shown that among European Jews, there was "a search for community" in the interwar years.[45] This desire for a collective framework within which Jewish ethnicity could be expressed and nurtured was reflected in the creation of new Jewish social and cultural spaces as well as in the ethnification of Jews' identities. In Czechoslovakia, this process was mediated in important ways by the cooperation between Jewish elites from the Bohemian Lands and the state authorities. Both parties were eager to facilitate Jews' successful adaption to the momentous political and cultural changes brought about by the war. Chapter 4, "Conquering Communities: Zionists, Cultural Renewal, and the State," examines the efforts of Prague's various Jewish leaders – Zionists and non-Zionists, Czech- and German-speakers, religious and secular activists – to reconcile the needs of the Jewish communities with the priorities of the Czechoslovak authorities. Embarking on the creation of state-supported Czechoslovak Jewish institutions, the reformers articulated a position of simultaneous cultural distinctiveness *and* adaptation as the basis for a model Jewish citizenry. They envisioned the modernized community – with its well-maintained, century-old synagogues and cemeteries, a new cohort of modern rabbis, Jewish museums and libraries – as the locus of Jewish life, as evidence of Jews' belonging and deep-rooted local presence. Zionist activists were front and center in these reform efforts. They worked behind the scenes as experts in the Prague Jewish community, lobbied for their cause with state bureaucrats, and shepherded reform legislation through the parliament in the late 1930s. Significantly, chapter 4 shows that Jewish leaders more broadly, and thus not Zionists alone, believed that the sustainability and vitality of Jewish life depended on the community becoming a site for Jews' ethnic and cultural identification. This was a program of cultural renewal that depended on a strengthening of ties between Jews and the state. This chapter demonstrates that when historians turn their gaze away from traditional arenas for politics – election campaigns, debates about party platforms, and national parliaments – and toward the bureaucracies that work behind the scenes, one discovers the more subtle yet ultimately more influential ways in which minority activists were able to assert power. Working within the legal and administrative framework of the state, these Jewish activists negotiated reforms with the state bureaucrats that not only created a new centralized Jewish leadership, but also empowered this new institution vis-à-vis the state as well as individual Jewish communities in the Bohemian Lands.

The collaboration between Jewish activists and the state authorities on projects of Jewish cultural renewal was a continuation of a tradition established by earlier generations of Jewish reformers. Past collaborations focused on how to meet the state's demands for Jews' cultural and linguistic adaptation as a path to emancipation. Seeking to assure the state of Jews' potential as loyal citizens, Zionists now insisted on the right and need to cultivate Jews' national distinctiveness. For Zionists, the state's support for Jewish national institutions was the hallmark of equality. Chapter 5, "A Stateless Nation's Territory: Zionists and the Jewish Schools," shows that while in public the government in Prague paid lip service to the Zionist cause, the state authorities rejected Zionists' repeated requests for support for a Jewish national school system, an institution widely perceived as a nation's cradle.

Recently, historians of nationalism have pointed to the crucial role children and the schools they attended played in activists' effort to nationalize individuals' identities and their communities in the Bohemian Lands.[46] Children, whom nationalists invested with the responsibility for the future of the nation, were seen as particularly vulnerable to "denationalization" and assimilation. Thus, over time in the Bohemian Lands, people's formal and informal practices for bilingual education were undermined by discourses on the harmful effects of bilingualism and by activists' increasing ability to use the power of the state to enforce compliance with the demand for monolingual education. Parents, children, and the schools they attended became the major focal point for Czech, German, and, as we shall see, Jewish nationalist activists.

The Habsburg authorities had awarded its subjects the right to an education in their own language in an effort to deescalate the conflict between German and Czech nationalists. Yet, nationalists molded this legislation into a system of denunciation and surveillance that marginalized individuals' linguistic choices in favor of external, expert assessments of people's real nationality. Language remained the most significant yet most contested marker of nationality. At the time, in the Bohemian Lands, Jews were considered by many social scientists to be a distinct ethnic and religious group, but one without a linguistic marker to set them apart from non-Jews. This chapter shows how Zionist goals, strategies, and narratives were simultaneously enabled and constricted by the local tradition for nationalist activism. Indeed, "the lack of a Jewish national language" would prove to be a significant obstacle in Zionists' nation-building efforts. As a result, Zionists did not have the same authority and ability to influence, even coerce, parents' choices that were available to their Czech and German peers. While Zionists labored to mobilize parents for the new Jewish schools, in the 1920s and '30s, most Jewish children funneled into the newly established and well-funded Czech- and Slovak-language schools, a development both welcomed and encouraged by the state. Zionists, having failed to secure a public Jewish national alternative, watched with dismay. Chapter 5 reveals the tension between the state authorities' formal commitment to minority rights and the assimilationist pressures the state exerted on its diverse populations. It was a contest in which minority representatives were no match for the executive powers and resources of the state.

As efforts to establish Jewish national schools failed, the Jewish sports and gymnastics movement Maccabi Czechoslovakia took on greater importance for the Zionist project. In the minds of Zionist activists, Maccabi became a substitute for the school and hence the most significant educational institution within the country's Jewish societies. Many young Jews encountered Zionist symbols, ideology, or community for the first time because of their love for sports and gymnastics. Eager to tap into state resources for physical education, activists promoted Maccabi as an institution through which young Jews were transformed into dedicated, loyal, and able citizens of Czechoslovakia. Playing on widespread stereotypes, in particular Jewish men's unmanliness, their assumed physical ineptness and cowardice, Maccabi activists championed physical education and Zionism as a remedy for Jews' civic deficiencies. Chapter 6, "Making New Jews: Maccabi in Czechoslovakia," highlights how Jewish activists drew upon familiar, local models of nationalist mobilization to make a Jewish nation come alive. This chapter notes the significance of mundane, everyday spaces – the gymnasiums, soccer fields, pools, and clubhouses – for the imagining, constructing, and performing of Jewish nationhood and belonging in towns and cities across Czechoslovakia.

Although the Zionist movement celebrated a cult of youth – strong, young, healthy bodies that symbolized the movement's vigor and promise – Zionist leaders were ambivalent about what they considered to be the radicalism of young people. Zionist elites sought to foster Zionism's mass appeal among Jews in Czechoslovakia by cultivating an image of political neutrality and moderation and by appeals to ethnic Jewish unity and solidarity. Yet, they were alarmed as members of Zionist youth groups – the nation's elite – abandoned Zionism for more radical political alternatives. Young Jews appeared to do so *not* for another nationalist cause, but for an internationalist one, for Communism. Indeed, as chapter 7, "Promised Lands: Zionism and Communism in Interwar Czechoslovakia," shows, in the interwar years, Zionist leaders viewed the country's dynamic Communist movement as the main threat to the Jewish nation-building project not only in Czechoslovakia, but also in Palestine. By the late 1920s, Prague Zionists founded the Zionist Propaganda Bureau, an institution imagined as a command center for a counteroffensive against Communists' anti-Zionist campaign. As they faced off with the Communist rival and its threat of "red assimilation," Zionist activists adopted what they considered their enemy's successful methods. In the 1930s, Zionists embraced a political culture that emphasized ideological discipline, education, and surveillance in an effort to halt the defection of Jewish youths to the red banner.

The epilogue, "The Storm of Barbarism," brings together the strands created by each of the preceding chapters in a reflection on the wartime fate of a generation of activists and the institutions they helped form. Although some Zionists emigrated to Palestine, Britain, and other places of refuge when the German occupation began, many stayed behind. They soon faced the onslaught of genocidal destruction. Some activists reacted to the crisis by assuming roles that were familiar to them: statisticians turned to their craft to develop rational communal policies in light of German demands, Jewish politicians acted as national leaders in London, and others turned their classrooms or athletic practices into spaces where young Jews could regain a sense of normalcy and dignity. The epilogue is a tale of what happened to the people whose worlds were destroyed in ways no one could have imagined.

A NOTE ON TERMINOLOGY AND SOURCES

In interwar Czechoslovakia, Zionists consciously and consistently employed a political-legal terminology derived from the country's minority protection laws. Terms like *Židovská národní rada* (Jewish National

Council), *Židovská národnost* (Jewish nationality), and *národnostní menšina* (national minority) cast Jews as belonging as one of the country's national minorities with legitimate collective rights. In the Czechoslovak political context, Zionists made reference to the international Zionist movement when it empowered or added prestige to their cause. In a lecture to a Czechoslovak student society, the Jewish social scientist František Friedmann noted that while all Zionists were Jewish nationalists, not all Jewish nationalists were Zionists.[47] However, in Czechoslovakia, there was considerable, if not complete, overlap between Jewish nationalists and Zionists, a fact that underlines the rhetorical importance of the use of the local terminology. In this book, I will thus be using the terms "Jewish nationalist" and "Zionist" interchangeably.

In Czechoslovakia, Zionists often referred to their opponents as "assimilationists," a strategy they employed to taint their rivals with the negative moral connotations of assimilation that were especially prominent in Czech nationalist discourse.[48] However, as this study shows, non-Zionist Jewish activists such as the Czech-Jewish nationalists, who promoted Czech language and culture among Jews, were committed to Jewish continuity but not to Jewish nationalism in the interwar years.

This book is based on a wide range of published and archival sources held at institutions in the Czech Republic, Israel, and the United States. Since one of the main themes of this study is the interplay between Zionist activists and state authorities, I have utilized materials from various archival collections in the Czech National Archives and Prague's City Archive. From the Central Zionist Archives, I have drawn on correspondence between the leadership of the WZO, the Jewish National Fund, and Zionist activists in Czechoslovakia. Some Zionist organizations' own archives – for example, that of the sports organization Maccabi – were destroyed or disappeared during the Second World War, leaving only traces in Israel (such as the materials brought by individual activists to the Maccabi Archives in Ramat Gan) and the Czech Republic (in the archives of the Jewish Museum in Prague). I have also made use of Bohemia and Moravia's Zionist press (including weeklies, yearbooks, and pamphlets). In the 1920s and 1930s, there were two main German-language Zionist papers. One was the Prague-based *Selbstwehr* (established 1907). The other was *Jüdische Volksstimme,* which was published in Brno/Brünn between 1904 and 1934. While the latter remained independent from the Zionist Organization, *Selbstwehr* and its Czech-language equivalent *Židovské zprávy* (established in 1918) served as the official organs of the Zionist Organization in Czechoslovakia. They shared contributors and at times offices. Yet *Selbstwehr* had a distinctly international Zionist focus while *Židovské zprávy* was more preoccupied with domestic affairs.[49]

Finally, maps and place names are powerful tools for depicting towns, regions, or countries as of a particular national character. When deciding on the use of place names, interwar Czechoslovakia – which consisted of multilingual regions that had formerly been under Austrian and Hungarian administration – poses particular difficulties if one wishes to avoid reproducing the claims that nationalists made on specific territories. Scholars writing on the Bohemian Lands often use both the Czech and German place names, a practice I have adopted here (aside from well-known places that have English names), since it does not impede the reader and since this region is the book's main focus. For Slovakia and Subcarpathian Rus', the situation is far more complicated, reflecting the linguistic and cultural diversity of these regions. In order not to make reading about these places too cumbersome, I have chosen as a general rule to use the official Czechoslovak name but to include the name in its other forms on first mention – for example, Bratislava/Pressburg/Pozsony. A list of place names in the various languages spoken in Czechoslovakia's regions is included with the maps. I thereby hope to do justice to the complex historical context in which this study plays out.[50]

ONE

The Jews of Czechoslovakia

A MOSAIC OF CULTURES

ONE WINTER, SOMETIME IN THE 1930S, HANA SHAFAR, A YOUNG Jewish woman, traveled with her fiancé, Ivo Karajich, from Moravská Ostrava/Mährisch Ostrau, a bustling industrial center, eastward to Hana's home village Polana, deep in the valleys of Subcarpathian Rus'. Hana had been in the city for only a short time. She had moved there to join a newly established Zionist commune and prepare for emigration to Palestine. She, like so many others in Polana, had been mesmerized by the visiting young Zionist activists' fiery speeches about Palestine, work, prosperity, and freedom. But Hana also joined the commune to escape the bleak future awaiting a village girl with no dowry.[1] Before long, the beautiful Hana attracted the attention of a salesman and atheist publicist, Ivo Karajich. Formerly known as Isaac Cohen, Karajich had renounced his Jewishness and changed his name, though he could neither escape his own physiognomy ("What a nose!") nor his attraction to the exotic yet familiar Jewish girl from Polana ("it is his blood calling him").[2] Within weeks, Ivo "liberated" Hana from factory work as well as from the Zionist commune by securing her a position at his journal *The Free Thinker*. It was as if a whirlwind carried Hana away from her village, from all the truths that she had hitherto known, from all that had been self-evident. She wondered, "Aren't there any Jews here in Ostrava? Are there only Jews in Polana and then a few in Košice and no more anywhere else? What is the truth, then? What sort of Jews do you call them if they haven't their own tongue and talk *goy* even to each other and dress like *goyim* and do not keep the Sabbath, if they eat *treyfe* food and don't pray and don't do any of the things that make a Jew a Jew?"[3] Hana's confusion grew deeper when Ivo, in proposing to her, revealed, "I am not a Jew."[4] Despite her reservations, Hana loved Ivo and agreed to marry him. Soon, the couple found themselves on the road through Slovakia to Subcarpathian Rus' and Polana to introduce him to her family.

As they traveled eastward, it was as if the changing landscape, the picturesque townships and villages, the vast forests, mountains, and valleys, signaled that this was a journey not only in space but also in time. While Ivo was excited by the exotic, dramatic landscape, as they neared her village, Hana's trepidation intensified. At first Hana's parents welcomed the couple. They had not recognized Karajich as a Jewish name and were relieved when they set eyes on Ivo's "great big nose, the like of which has never been seen in Ruthenia!"[5] But their happiness soon turned to horror when they learned that Ivo, arrogantly confident in his cultural and intellectual superiority vis-à-vis the devout villagers, was an atheist. Not simply a converted Jew, which they would have understood, but a Jew who had "forsaken God."[6] A drama unfolded, as the Shafars kidnapped their daughter, the village dignitaries attempted to convince Ivo to "return to Israel," and a village mob gathered to settle the affront. Both Ivo and the villagers alike demanded respect for their principle of faith. It was only with help of Czechoslovak gendarmes that Ivo managed to wrest Hana from her family and the village. By then, Hana was cast out of the community, dead both to her family and her people. As she left, walking through the village, Hana passed "one Jewish cottage after another, and in front of everyone the families were gathered and the men were wailing in a loud chorus, each mingling with the next: "You shall be pure and free of all defilement . . . so the Lord purifies Israel." Hana, "the outcast[,] walked down the empty street with her impure lover by her side and two Czechoslovak policemen ten paces in front of her. She was as white as the path she trod, calling desperately to her aid the blood of her forebears, accustomed to shame and humiliation and suffering, she moved on through the terrible funeral prayers of her grandfather, her face set forward and her eyes fixed in a strange gleam on some far-off point."[7] Although in mourning, the village was cleansed, the old order restored. Ivo got his bride, but Hana had changed; a grain of hardness had entered her wonderful, sorrowful eyes.[8]

Yet, it was not only Hana who had sinned. It was all the Jews of Polana who had grown tired of waiting for the Messiah, lost faith in divine redemption, and allowed their youngsters to dabble in Zionism. Ever since the *ḥalutsim* (pioneers, socialist Zionist youth) and the youngsters from Mizraḥi (the most prominent religious Zionist movement) appeared in Polana, seducing the villagers with tales of the Promised Land, the righteous Pinches Yakubovich had pleaded with God to have mercy on the sinful, ungrateful villagers. Just prior to Hana and Ivo's arrival, an angel appeared before him demanding a sacrifice:

> Thus speaketh the Lord unto you, in my words, *lamet vav* Pinches, son of Yankel! Your cries have reached Me and not passed unheard. I thought to break the Jewish congregation of Polana with an iron rod for their sins, like a potter's vessel, and scatter it like the sands of the desert. My wrath and anger have been turned aside by thy prayers, and I have taken pity upon them. Behold, there are no *halutz* and no *mizrakhi* wrongdoers anymore; I have swept them from the face of the earth as a thing unclean, and Polana will be one again as of old. But I demand a peace offering on behalf of the whole congregation. Only one, yet more terrible than any other. Death! Death! Death! Such a death as Polana has never seen, more terrible than the armed man, than fire or the grave, the death of all deaths. Tomorrow. Make this sacrifice without reluctance![9]

Thus, as Hana walked through the village, the Jews scorned and shamed her, unaware that she was the scapegoat for their sins. Only Pinches Yakubovich knew and,

> as he gazed at the young girl going towards a death worse than the armed man, worse than fire and the grave, towards the death of all deaths, spiritual death, did not see what the rest of Polana saw. Behold the scapegoat of the Lord, that hath taken away the sins of Israel! She alone in the name of all! Behold the greatest sacrifice of all, laid upon the altar of the Lord as a solemn peace offering. Great, eternal, holy and unfathomable is God the Lord of Hosts. Praise be to his name![10]

As Hana is cast out, as she dies "the death of all deaths," the village is purified. The heresy of Zionism, its promise of revolution and redemption, is expunged. Yet, anyone looking on could see that a stain remained.

The tragedy of Hana Shafar was the fictional creation of Ivan Olbracht (1882–1952), a towering figure in interwar Czechoslovakia's literary circles and one of the most important Czech writers of the twentieth century. Born in Semily/Semil, a town in northern Bohemia, to the German-speaking Jewish Kamila Schönfeld and the Czech Catholic writer and lawyer Antal Stašek (1843–1931, whose real name was Antonín Zeman), Ivan Olbracht (Kamil Zeman) embarked on his literary and political career well before the First World War.[11] Olbracht was not a Zionist. Rather, by the 1920s, he was a major figure in Prague's Communist milieu as the editor of the party organ *Rudé Právo*. Having split from the Communist Party in 1929, after which he lost his position as an editor, Olbracht began exploring Czechoslovakia's east. He spent much of the 1930s living in Subcarpathian Rus', the country's easternmost province, a region dominated by the Carpathian Mountains and known for its beauty, harshness, and the poverty of its people. Indeed, it was Olbracht's documentary essays, novels, and short stories about Subcarpathian Rus' that brought him much literary fame and popularity.[12] More than nine hundred kilometers from Prague, for most of Olbracht's readers, Subcarpathian Rus' was a mysterious, unfamiliar, and exotic place, a different civilization, one that could be (safely) discovered through the writings of, among others, Ivan Olbracht.

Published in 1937 as part of the collection *Golet v údolí* (Exile in the Valley), "The Sorrowful Eyes of Hana Karajich" was one of three short stories set among Hasidic villagers in Subcarpathian Rus'. The story of Hana and Ivo is, on the one hand, a universal story about rebellion and loss of faith and family. On the other, Olbracht's tale is one particular to Jewish life in Czechoslovakia in the interwar years. This was a time of rapid social and cultural change, of momentous political and economic challenges. Olbracht's work brilliantly captured the restlessness of youth as well as the efforts of political activists to harness this impatience to their utopian visions. Because it symbolized the most radical and rapid ways Jewish life was changing in Czechoslovakia, it was no coincidence that Olbracht placed Zionism at the center of his Subcarpathian tale. Subcarpathian Rus', with its large, poor, and fiercely traditional Jewish society, was an important arena for Zionist activism in the 1920s and '30s. At that time, Zionists from the Bohemian Lands and Palestine, together with representatives from the American Jewish Joint Distribution Committee, descended on the region seeking to lift its Jews out of poverty and "backwardness" by providing social welfare programs and education.[13]

Unlike that of their American colleagues, the Zionists' intervention in the region was driven by political rather than humanitarian concerns. Indeed, the mobilization of Subcarpathian Jewry for the Zionist cause was a key step in their program for Jews' integration and equality in Czechoslovakia. On the one hand, Zionists from the Bohemian Lands imagined Subcarpathian Jews as constituting an authentic Jewish *Volk* that had remained untouched by decades of assimilation and denationalization policies that had eroded Jewish national life in Bohemia and Moravia. On the other, Zionists were taken aback by the poverty, religious traditionalism, and cultural foreignness of the Jews in the country's east. Zionist activists depended ideologically, politically, and demographically on the eastern Jews. Yet, the latter threatened to undermine Jews' broader social and cultural respectability that underpinned the Zionist project in Czechoslovakia. Zionists' vision for Jewish nationhood as a vehicle for Jews' social, economic, political, and cultural prosperity and participation in Czechoslovak society was, in some ways, a radical challenge to the assimilationist paradigm, which for more than a century had promised Jews emancipation in return for their social and cultural assimilation. But Zionists did not seek "to push Jews back into the ghetto," as some critics claimed. Rather, they pursued a program of simultaneous acculturation and nationalization that aimed to transform Jews into model citizen in the new multinational state.

In 1918, the Austrian provinces of Bohemia, Moravia, and part of Austrian Silesia (referred to here as the Bohemian Lands) and territories in the northern part of the Kingdom of Hungary (later known as Slovakia and Subcarpathian Rus') became provinces in Czechoslovakia. A complex country with great regional diversity, including at least six major languages and many more religious denominations, the landscape ranged from the highly industrialized towns and cities of Bohemia and Moravia to the fields worked by subsistence farmers below the Carpathian Mountains.[14] Czechoslovakia's Jewish societies reflected the diversity of the country as a whole. In the Bohemian Lands, Jews constituted an acculturated German- and Czech-speaking middle-class community. In Slovakia, German, Hungarian, and Yiddish were the dominant languages among less prosperous middle-class Jews, many of whom considered their Orthodoxy a point of pride. In Subcarpathian Rus', most Jews lived in traditional Yiddish-speaking Hasidic village communities.

The Zionist project in Czechoslovakia was shaped in important ways by this diversity. Czechoslovakia's Jews spoke a multiplicity of languages but shared no one language. Jews' religious practice varied greatly, as did their class and national identifications. Yet, even though there were important differences among the country's Jewish societies, there were cultural and historical commonalities. In these newly amalgamated regions, Jews' shared a historical experience. It was an experience shaped, on the one hand, by their place within the larger Central and East European Ashkenazi Jewish world – a cultural network sustained by economic, kinship, and scholarly ties; and, on the other, by their belonging within the realm of the Habsburg Monarchy, a state that since the late eighteenth century offered Jews some degree of equality and protection in return for political loyalty and assimilation. Although Jews were treated by the state and by many non-Jewish observers as one, undifferentiated group, when Zionists set out to unite Jews under a Jewish nationalist banner, they were faced with what appeared as insurmountable cultural, social, and political divisions. It was a paradox shaped by the Habsburg legacy.

BEFORE THE HABSBURGS

Before they became Habsburg possessions, Bohemia and Moravia, the so-called Crown Lands, had been part of the Central European realm ruled by the medieval Přemysl dynasty. The regions that would become Slovakia and Subcarpathian Rus' were part of the Kingdom of Hungary. As in other parts of medieval Europe, Jews were considered "serfs of the royal chamber" (*servi camerae regis*).[15] In return for their taxes and other financial services, the king granted Jews a charter stipulating their right of residence, communal autonomy, and royal protection. Jews were thus subjects of the royal court, not of the local authorities. Although it is impossible to say how many Jews lived in the Bohemian Lands in the Middle Ages, Jewish communities did exist in important trade centers such as Prague, Brno/Brünn, and Jihlava/Iglau.[16] Further south, in the territories that would later become Slovakia, from the middle of the eleventh century on, Pressburg/Pozsony (later Bratislava), Nitra/Neutra/Nyitra, and Trnava/Tyrnau/Nagyszombat had substantial communities with charters similar to the ones granted Jews in the Bohemian Lands. As elsewhere in medieval Europe, moneylending, trades, and commerce formed the economic backbone of Jewish life.

By the fifteenth century, the weakening of royal authority vis-à-vis burghers and the nobility led to the expulsion of Jews from the royal towns and a dispersion of the bulk of the Jewish population into privately owned noble town and villages.[17] Over time, in Bohemia and Moravia, Jews' settlement patterns shaped distinctive communal and cultural traditions that defined Jewish life in these regions well into the twentieth century. In Moravia, Jews lived in midsized, urban communities excluded from the region's cities. Living under the protection of noble magnates, they were part of the agricultural economy as moneylenders, merchants, peddlers, tradesmen, and leaseholders, as mediators between peasants and the nobility and between rural and urban areas. The Moravian communities, similar in size and political, economic, and religious stature, were able to develop a supra-communal authority, much like the one that emerged among Jews in the Polish-Lithuanian Commonwealth.[18] This institution acted as a representative of the communities to the authorities, collaborated on fulfilling Jews' tax obligations, and sought to resolve intercommunal disputes and issues.

In Bohemia, things looked different. Here, the majority of Jews lived dispersed in small settlements ranging from a few families to a few hundred Jews.[19] The important exception was the community in Prague, one of Central Europe's major Jewish religious, economic, and cultural centers. This imbalance in influence and prestige, which more often than not pitched rural and small-town Jews against Prague Jewry, frustrated the development of supra-communal institutions such as the ones that emerged in Moravia. The different settlement patterns helped shape traditions for unity and cooperation in Moravia and disunity and intercommunal competition in Bohemia. It was only in the interwar years that Jewish reformers, Zionists among them, succeeded in creating an institution that united the Jewish communities in Bohemia with the ones in Moravia.

UNDER THE HABSBURGS

The Bohemian Lands became part of the Habsburg Monarchy in 1526. The early modern Habsburg rulers' attitude toward the Jews in their realm moved on a spectrum marked at one end by acceptance and co-operation and at the other by hostility and exclusion. Thus, at times, individual Jews, mostly financiers and scholars, achieved unprecedented access to the royal court. In some years, however, the court would placate burghers, nobles, and church leaders and – with an eye to its own debt obligations to local Jews – expel entire Jewish communities from their hometowns.[20]

As the Habsburg state grew stronger, state authorities developed a gradually more interventionist approach toward their Jewish communities. In the mid-1720s, they created laws intended to limit the growth of the Jewish population in Bohemia and Moravia by allowing only one son in every Jewish household to marry.[21] The so-called Familiant Laws had significant impact on Jewish life. As Jews' settlement and migration patterns changed in response to the legislation, important social and cultural connections were established between Jews in the Bohemian Lands and the Kingdom of Hungary. In response to the Familiant Laws, in Bohemia, Jews dispersed even more. They settled in villages and small towns in part as a way to evade the state's watchful eye.[22] Moravian Jews, who were restricted to live in fifty-two communities in the region, meanwhile began migrating to other parts of the Habsburg Monarchy where the Familiant Laws were not in effect.[23] Many settled in the neighboring Kingdom of Hungary, especially in its northern provinces (known as Oberland) that bordered Moravia. The migrants established new communities, such as the one in Trenčin/Trentschin/Trencsén, just across the border, and contributed significantly to the growth of existing ones in Pressburg and Nitra.[24] These were areas that along with adjacent Hungarian territory to the east bordering Galicia would become known as Slovakia and Subcarpathian Rus' after World War I. Since the emigrants often settled in close proximity to the border, they were able to maintain familial, economic, and cultural ties to their old communities. In contrast to the Moravian tradition for compact, urban Jewish communities, in Oberland the majority of Jews lived in villages with only one or two Jewish families, much as in Bohemia.

If Oberland Jews had strong ties to Moravian Jewry, then in the northeastern part of Hungary (known as Unterland), the Jewish population was connected to communities in the Polish-Lithuanian Commonwealth's borderlands (what would later become the Austrian territory of Galicia and Bukovina).[25] Indeed, by the second half of the nineteenth century, Jews in these Hungarian counties constituted a western outpost of the expanding cultural network of Hasidic dynasties centered to the east, across the Carpathian Mountains, in Galicia and the adjacent borderlands of the Russian Empire. A revivalist, populist movement, Hasidism, alongside the strong Orthodox communities in Oberland, ensured that religious traditionalism thrived among Jews in this area until the Second World War. Although there were some exchange and migration between the Jewish societies in Oberland and Unterland, they would remain somewhat distinct sociocultural communities until 1918, when these northern Hungarian counties became part of Czechoslovakia.[26] In the interwar years, Zionists invoked the memory of the social and cultural networks that linked Jews in Moravia to communities in Slovakia as a source of legitimacy for Jews' belonging in Czechoslovakia.

ACCULTURATION, INTEGRATION, AND EMANCIPATION

By the late 1700s, the Habsburg state began a process of centralization of the state apparatus and Germanization of its population. Among the monarchy's Jews, the reforms and Jews' adaptation to them brought about new Jewish cultures and changed the relations between Jews and non-Jews. A century later, the legacy of these reforms would shape how Jews responded to the emergence of nationalism as well as to a new virulent antisemitism.

The single most important ruling that affected Habsburg Jews in the late eighteenth century was Joseph II's 1781 Edict of Toleration, which introduced reforms intended to create a direct relationship between the state and its Jewish subjects. Until the late 1700s, Habsburg Jews, like many other Jews across much of Europe, lived in autonomous communities ruled by religious and economic elites. Jewish societies were governed by the law of the land as well as by Jewish law (*halakhah*), a traditional body of legislation that touched upon every aspect of individual and communal Jewish life. Although Christian authorities would on occasion intervene in Jewish internal affairs, they only began doing so systematically by the 1780s. By then the emperor hoped to transform Jews into "useful subjects" through a process of carefully managed economic and cultural change.[27] Between 1781 and 1790, as the authorities expanded the edict's geographic and legislative reach, new laws encouraged Jews to enter "productive" occupations such as farming and crafts, restricted Jewish authorities' jurisdiction to religious matters alone, and conscripted Jews into the army. Perhaps most significantly, the state mandated elementary, secular education for its Jews.[28]

Beginning in the 1780s, and continuing well into the twentieth century, state authorities and Jewish reformers would turn to education again and again as a vehicle for broader cultural change among Jews. Having instituted universal compulsory education in 1774, Habsburg authorities directed Jewish community boards to establish state-supervised, community-funded, secular schools (*Normalschulen*). These German-Jewish schools would provide Jewish boys, and later girls, with an elementary education in German language, reading, and writing, as well as arithmetic and ethics.[29] At the same time, the authorities granted Jews access to general public elementary and secondary schools, thereby creating a path to institutions of higher learning.

In Bohemia, the Jewish community in Prague established the region's flagship German-Jewish school, and soon rural and small-town communities followed suit with their own schools.[30] In Moravia, where the Jewish communities were larger, almost every community had a Jewish *Normalschule* by 1784. With the reforms of the 1780s, the Habsburg authorities promised emancipation and integration in return for Jews' economic and cultural transformation. The schools, as Hillel J. Kieval notes, became "both the symbol of a promised integration into state and society and one of the main vehicles of its implementation."[31] Over time, Jewish families in the Bohemian Lands came to see German high culture as a means for integration and upward social mobility.

The Josephinian reforms were extended to the Kingdom of Hungary in 1783, but with different results. Although the state authorities initiated reforms, their implementation was not a priority for local Jewish and non-Jewish authorities.[32] Thus, unlike in Bohemia and Moravia, in Hungary a secular Jewish school system parallel to the religious one did not emerge. It was not until 1850 that the Habsburg authorities renewed their push for secular Jewish education in Hungary. By then the decree was followed by an allocation of state resources for German-Jewish schools and a teachers' seminary. Between 1850 and 1860, the number of school increased from thirty to three hundred, and German began replacing Yiddish in many communities in Oberland.[33] By 1868, German was replaced by Hungarian as a language of instruction in the public Jewish schools.[34] Despite the rapid linguistic Magyarization, German remained an important language among Jews in Oberland.[35]

By the mid-nineteenth century, German language and culture had become a sign of Jews' commitment to the emancipation program and loyalty to the Habsburg Monarchy. By then, most Jews in the Bohemian Lands had exchanged western Yiddish for German as their everyday language. Many also knew Czech, which they had learned in elementary school or by living in Czech-speaking environments. From then on and well into the twentieth century, Marsha L. Rozenblit argues, "for many Jews, German became and remained a Jewish language."[36] Among Jews in the Kingdom of Hungary, Hungarian language, and for some the adoption of Hungarian national identity, embodied their alliance with Hungarian elites. In return for Jews' political allegiance, the Budapest government promised Jews upward social mobility and protection from antisemitism.[37] In 1848 and in the years that followed, the authorities lifted residence and occupational restrictions on Jews, setting in motion years of intense Jewish urbanization in many parts of the monarchy. Thousands of Jews from Oberland emigrated to nearby Vienna (a mere sixty-three kilometers from Pressburg).[38] In 1867, Jews across the monarchy received full emancipation. By then, Jewish middle classes, educated and acculturated, were emerging in Hungary's towns and cities.[39] Before long, the growing urban communities were divided by tensions over acculturation and religious change. In 1868, the Hungarian government, in an effort to create a supra-communal Jewish authority, inadvertently sparked a hardening of the religious divisions. In Hungary, Jewish communities split into denominations, Neolog and Orthodox, while some remained unaffiliated (Status Quo). As a result, in Oberland, the communities were somewhat evenly divided between Neolog and Orthodox; meanwhile in Unterland, traditionalism, whether Orthodox or Hasidic, dominated Jewish societies.[40]

In the Bohemian lands, Jews gradually achieved full emancipation in the years from 1840 to 1867. Restrictions on residency, occupations, economic activity, and travel were lifted. In 1848, the Familiant Laws were abolished. In Bohemia, the authorities ended Jewish communities' last vestiges of autonomy. They were now purely religious institutions. In contrast to the situation among Hungary's Jews, in the Bohemian Lands Jewish communities did not break into denominations. In Moravia, twenty-seven of the region's fifty-two Jewish communities retained their status as Jewish townships, providing municipal services such as policing and schools.[41] In 1867, after almost a century, the state authorities removed the last formal barriers to Jews' equality. Alongside broader social and economic developments in the 1860s, urbanization and upward social mobility changed the character of Jewish life in Bohemia and Moravia.

In Bohemia, Jews moving from the Czech-speaking countryside to the region's cities challenged the hegemony of the German-speaking Jewish elites. This "cultural revolution" was particularly dramatic in the provincial capital Prague. Between 1869 and 1910, the city's Jewish population doubled, and it became home to a third of Bohemia's Jews.[42] By 1921, 60 percent of all Prague Jews had been born outside the city; eight out of ten came from Czech-speaking areas of Bohemia, the remaining from German-speaking ones.[43] In a process that Hillel J. Kieval defines as "secondary acculturation," Bohemia's Jewish society underwent a cultural reorientation. The move of rural and small-town Jews to the cities, along with the newfound political power of the Czech-speaking majority population in the region, challenged the social and cultural hierarchy in the existing urban Jewish communities.

Unlike the German-speaking old-timers, many newcomers were Czech-speakers and identified with the linguistic, cultural, and political aspirations of the region's Czech majority.[44] In 1876, Jewish academics, businessmen, professionals, and students organized the first Czech-Jewish association (Spolek českých akademiků židů). Czech-Jews set out to promote the use of the Czech language and familiarity with Czech culture among Jews as well as to challenge the assumptions among Christians that all Jews identified as Germans. In 1893, they founded an activist political group, the National Union of Czech-Jews (Národní jednota českožidovská) and began publishing the first Jewish newspaper in Czech, *Českožidovské listy,* in 1894. In 1904, the most significant Czech-Jewish periodical, *Rozvoj,* began appearing and did so until 1938. As educated, middle-class Jews, these activists were bilingual but identified as members of the Czech nation and sought to voice their cultural and political aspirations as Czech nationalists.[45] Despite the widespread bilingualism among Jews in the Bohemian Lands, the elevation of Czech to a language of education and high culture, as well as the emergence of the Czech-Jewish movement, Jews in the Bohemian Lands continued to use German in communal affairs, in religious life, in private, and in education. As Hillel J. Kieval notes, "Nowhere – with the possible exception of the Jewish elementary schools – was the institutional identification of Bohemian Jewry with German culture more pronounced than in its synagogue. Public ritual throughout the Czech lands, whether in the cities or in the smallest villages, shared one key feature: the language of discourse for everything but the ancient Hebrew texts was German."[46]

In Moravia, Jews also flocked to the growing industrial centers in large numbers. The new Jewish communities in the provincial capital Brno/Brünn as well as the region's industrial center, its Manchester, Moravská Ostrava/Mährisch Ostrau, attracted thousands of Jews. Many Moravian Jews also left for nearby Vienna (connected by railway and only 130 kilometers away).[47] In Moravia, Jews retained an allegiance to German language, culture, and politics. This was, according to the historian Michael L. Miller, in part because urbanization did not challenge the German-language Jewish culture of the small-town communities, as the Moravian Jewish communities did not experience an influx of Czech-speaking Jews and thus no internal "culture war."[48] Some Moravian towns were inhabited mostly by German-speakers but surrounded by Czech-speaking rural populations. In these towns, Jews could comfortably retain German as their everyday public and private language. Many knew enough Czech to manage social and economic interactions, since Moravia's German-Jewish schools continued to teach Czech as part the curriculum even after other German-language schools abandoned it.[49]

By 1900, rural Jewish communities in Bohemia and Slovakia had given way to growing urban ones, while in Moravia old Jewish centers were being replaced by new ones. After World War I, the largest communities in the Bohemian Lands were Prague, Brno/Brünn, and Moravská Ostrava/Mährisch Ostrau, home to 38 percent of the regions' Jews.[50] In Slovakia, Pressburg and Košice were the largest Jewish centers (about 15% of the province's Jews). The majority of Slovakia's Jews lived in mid-sized towns with Jewish populations of a few thousand.[51] In Subcarpathian Rus', Mukačevo/Munkács/Munkatsch/Mukacheve had the largest Jewish community. In this province, more than 70 percent of the province's Jews lived in rural areas, in villages and small towns.[52] Thus, after the First World War, Jewish communities in Czechoslovakia encompassed very different kinds of institutions and societies, from large urban communities to village ones. They were multilingual societies with different cultural and religious traditions, a diversity that fascinated writers such as Ivan Olbracht.

In the course of the late eighteenth and through the nineteenth century, the state authorities limited Jews' communal autonomy while expanding their opportunities for participation in the economic, social, political, and cultural spheres. As a result, Jewish societies were increasingly divided along denominational and national lines. Zionists soon discovered that these were cultural divides that were difficult to bridge.

ONE RELIGION, MANY FAITHS

In the interwar years, it was the religious differences among Jews in Czechoslovakia that proved particularly challenging to Zionists' unification efforts. Zionists had an ambiguous relationship to Judaism. In the Bohemian Lands, they viewed Jews' indifference to religion as an obstacle to the cultural and communal renewal they envisioned. Meanwhile, in Slovakia and Subcarpathian Rus', it was Jews' traditionalism that hindered Zionists' work.

The Austrian, Hungarian, and Czechoslovak population censuses counted Jews as a religious community and thus grouped all Jews into the same category, "Israelite." This was a simplification that obscured the very important religious and cultural differences between Jews. By 1900, the most significant distinctions were between traditionalists, such as the Orthodox and Hasidic communities in Hungary and Galicia, and modernizing forms of Judaism such as the Neolog in Hungary and many communities in the Bohemian Lands. Although there were pockets of religious traditionalism in Bohemia and Moravia, by the turn of the twentieth century, many Jews had abandoned much of Jewish ritual observance, received little religious instruction beyond what was required in public schools, and rarely attended synagogue.

Nevertheless, many did retain a connection to Judaism through family and family rituals. The differences were often generational. Memoirists recall the vestiges of Judaism that grandparents and parents retained, practices that the younger generation looked upon as curious, and to some intriguing, remnants of the past. In his memoir, the Czech writer František Langer (1888–1965), who spent summers in his grandparents' village, noted that his grandfather and father prayed daily, attended synagogue, and kept kosher. Yet, in every generation the commitment and knowledge of Judaism declined. For Langer himself, his observance ended (as it had begun it seems) with his bar mitzvah. Yet, even within the Langer family there were great variations. Langer's younger brother Jiří Langer (1894–1943) became very observant and lived for a time among Hasidim in Belz/Bełz in Galicia. After the First World War, when he returned to Prague, the young Langer remained an observant Jew.[53] By and large, Jews in the Bohemian Lands had transformed their Judaism in ways that allowed them to blend into non-Jewish society, with few religious customs to distinguish them from their Christian neighbors.

In contrast, for much of the nineteenth century, northern Hungary was one of the most significant Orthodox centers in Central Europe, a status these communities retained until the Second World War. Although there were substantial Neolog communities in the region's towns and cities, the well-organized and centralized Orthodox communities had strong and charismatic leaders, many of whom were trained at the prestigious Sofer yeshiva in Pressburg and invested in the creation of new Orthodox institutions in the growing urban centers.[54] Similarly, in Subcarpathian Rus', the authority of the Hasidic *rebbes* remained strong and was not significantly diminished in the first decades of the twentieth century. In these communities, strict boundaries were maintained between Jews and Christians through language, customs, and dress. Here, Zionists were, as Olbracht's stories reflect, often met with virulent hostility from rabbis and their faithful communities.[55]

JEWS AND MULTILINGUALISM

One of the major challenges that Zionists faced in their quest to create a Jewish nation in Czechoslovakia was the fact that Jews lacked the most significant marker of nationality, a shared national language. In the 1920s and '30s, Hebrew remained for the most part, as it had been for centuries, a language of Jewish religious high culture. While Zionists promoted Hebrew as a symbol of Jewish nationhood, they tentatively cast Jews' multilingualism as a marker of Jewish nationality in the Diaspora. They argued that while Jews adopted the languages of other nations, their language use did not reflect their national belonging, as it did among non-Jews. This was a tenuous political and cultural position to inhabit, as many nationalists viewed multilingualism as the very embodiment of someone's national indifference or opportunism. The languages shared by most Jews in Czechoslovakia were German and Yiddish. While the former was linked, in the minds of Czech nationalists, to Jews' sympathy for the old Austrian order, the latter was shunned by many Jews from the Bohemian Lands as an embarrassing reminder of the ghetto, of Jews' denigration, isolation, and poverty in Christian Europe. Thus, both languages were politically and culturally suspect. Zionists had little choice but to embrace multilingualism. They did so, however, while promoting a linguistic reorientation among Jews toward Czech and Slovak. Although critical voices continued to lambast Jews for clinging to German and Hungarian, in the interwar years, Jews' language use was complex and in flux, with significant intergenerational, rural and urban, and regional differences. Jews' multilingualism was the only constant.

As we shall see, Habsburg language policies and their legacies shaped the Zionist project in Czechoslovakia in profound ways. In the course of the second half of the nineteenth century, the non-national Habsburg Monarchy became a multinational state. For the Viennese authorities seeking to satisfy yet control the monarchy's dominant German, Hungarian, and Polish elites, language rights and other concessions to minority nationalities became an important political tool to keep the monarchy intact.[56] In 1867, the Kingdom of Hungary was granted autonomy, and the following year, Polish-dominated Galicia was given home rule within the Habsburg Monarchy. At the same time, the Viennese authorities also expanded the rights and in effect gave equality to the monarchy's other ethnic peoples, or nationalities (*Volksstämme*). The state did not recognize the monarchy's Jews as one of these nationalities. One of the areas in which the nationalities now were to experience greater equality was in language use, the right to use their vernaculars in public life.[57] Soon, language rights, particularly the right to minority language education, became a rallying point for minority nationalists. By this time, in many communities, people's language use went from being situational to a behavior that nationalists invested with explosive political significance as they sought to stake their claim for public space and resources.[58]

By 1880, when the Habsburg authorities began registering individuals' everyday language in the census, the political battle over language rights intensified as individuals' and groups' language use became the focus of attention for politicians, journalists, and neighbors.[59] Significantly, respondents could declare only one language from a list of approved ones. The census's simplification of people's linguistic behavior and especially its erasure of individual and social multilingualism did much to cement stereotypes in the political battles over the meaning of the census data. Eager to count as large a nation as possible, dominant and non-dominant nationalists alike equated individuals' everyday language with national identity, thereby politicizing people's public and private language use.[60] Multilingual communities, such as many villages and towns in provincial border regions and the monarchy's Jewish populations, were considered nationally indeterminate. They now came under intense scrutiny by nationalists of all stripes. Even though multilingualism was widespread among Jews and non-Jews alike, in the late nineteenth century, nationalists increasingly constructed Jews' multilingualism as uniquely opportunist and morally suspicious, thereby seeking to marginalize multilingual practices more broadly.

In Slovakia, Rebekah Klein-Pejšová notes, the Jewish geographic-linguistic map reflected historical migration patterns and divided along German-, Yiddish-, and Hungarian-speaking lines.[61] While across the entire territory Jews spoke German and Hungarian in public, in western and central Slovakia, they would use German or Judeo-German at home. In south Slovakia, it was Hungarian, and in the eastern parts, Yiddish. In parts of Subcarpathian Rus' especially, Yiddish was the dominant everyday language in public and in private. As in the Bohemian Lands, Jews also used local vernaculars such as Slovak and Rusyn.

In the Habsburg Monarchy, outside observers often viewed Jews' language use with suspicion. In the late 1700s, Jewish and non-Jewish Enlightenment reformers alike had seen Jews' Hebrew and Yiddish language as a source of distrust between Christians and Jews. By the late nineteenth century, Czech and Slovak minority nationalists perceived Jews' use of German and Hungarian as an affront and impediment to their national aspirations. What had been a vehicle for Jews' integration into state and society was in the course of the nineteenth century transformed into a symbol of Jews' allegiance to the monarchy's dominant German and later, in the Kingdom of Hungary, Magyar elites. In the Hungarian regions that had substantial non-Magyar minorities, such as in the north and east with their large Slovak, Rusyn, and Romanian populations, critics viewed Jews as Magyarizing outposts serving as tools for the Budapest authorities in their efforts to marginalize non-Hungarian nationalities. Similarly, in mixed German- and Czech-speaking communities in the Bohemian Lands, activists accused Jews of serving as "Germanizers."[62] By 1900, Czech nationalists were especially incensed by the presence of the German-Jewish schools, what they considered to be "German bastions," in otherwise Czech-speaking communities.[63] As a result of this legacy, for Zionist activists in interwar Czechoslovakia, Jews' adoption of Czech and Slovak languages was a symbol of Jews' political loyalty to the new state and its dominant nationalities.

In Czechoslovakia, the national revolution that ushered in the new state was forcefully expressed in the elevation of Czech and Slovak to privileged languages in the territories that now made up Czechoslovakia. This shift was particularly stark in Slovakia and Subcarpathian Rus', where Slovak and Rusyn had not hitherto had a status as languages of education and high culture, a position Czech had enjoyed in the Bohemian Lands since the late 1860s. In the course of the 1920s and '30s, Czech and Slovak languages became more widely used among Jews alongside German and Hungarian.[64] Already by the mid-1920s, a majority of Jewish children attended Czech- and Slovak-language elementary schools. In the Bohemian Lands, many Jewish students went on to attend secondary schools that used German as the language of instruction.[65] In the Bohemian Lands as well as Slovakia and Subcarpathian Rus', multilingualism remained an important characteristic of Jewish life.

Despite the linguistic reorientation in elementary schooling, German remained the most significant intergenerational and cross-regional language among Jews in Czechoslovakia. After all, German had been the vehicle for secular education and social mobility among Jews for generations. Over time, it had come to be an integral part of Jewish communal and religious life, connecting Jews in the Bohemian Lands and Slovakia to broader Jewish religious-cultural networks in Austria, Germany, and Hungary.[66] For many Jews, German was not a "foreign" language, but a Jewish one, intimately tied to Jews' sense of self and community.[67] In the interwar years, in the Bohemian Lands, Czech increasingly opened up avenues for education and social mobility. Among Jews, especially in the Bohemian Lands and Slovakia, it did so alongside German.

Before the First World War, Zionist activists in the Bohemian Lands were part of an Austrian-wide organization, and German was the language in which activists debated, published, and lectured. In Prague and Brno/Brünn, Zionists founded periodicals, *Selbstwehr* (1907) and *Jüdische Volksstimme* (1904), which reached audiences beyond the Bohemian Lands. In early 1918, Bohemian Zionists began a systematic campaign to create "Zionism in Czech," that is, to give the movement here a bilingual, more homegrown profile. They did so by publishing a Czech-language Zionist paper, *Židovské zprávy,* as well as other materials in Czech, and they arranged meetings and public lectures about Zionism in

Czech. At the time, Zionists aimed to inform Czech-speaking audiences, Jewish and non-Jewish ones alike, about their goals and thereby create a political alternative to the Czech-Jewish movement. Zionists were well aware that Jews' adoption of Czech and Slovak languages was a particularly important signal about Jews' loyalty to the emerging political order, and they wasted no time in adapting to the new reality.

As we shall see, in the 1920s and '30s, Zionists pointed to Jews' multilingualism – Jews' knowledge and situational use of the multiple local languages used in the country without attaching national meaning to any of them – as a national trait unique to Jews. Since Jews were a nation considered to "have lost their national language," Zionists declared Jews' linguistic behavior "nationally neutral." This was an assertion that dovetailed with their broader claim that Jewish national belonging was a position of "neutrality" in the national conflict between Czechs and Germans, Slovaks and Hungarians, a way for Jews to "withdraw" themselves from the competition. Significantly, it allowed Zionists in practice to continue to use German as a tool of communication, a lingua franca, in the interwar years. In this way, Zionists could reach across regional and generational divides within Czechoslovakia, for example, by dispatching activists with German-language educational materials from the center to budding Zionist groups across the country. For a political movement with limited financial resources, whose success depended on activists' ability to mobilize Jews across the country, the practical value of German as well as its emotional and symbolic power as a Jewish language, outweighed any embarrassment caused by Czech-Jews' and others' accusations that Zionism was merely a way for Jews unwilling to accept the new political reality "to cling to German."

ANTISEMITISM

By 1900, German- and Czech-Jewish nationalists – and before long Zionist activists – accepted the trope that it was Jews' indeterminate national position, Jews' alleged indifference to and opportunism in questions of national belonging, that was the root cause of an ever more virulent antisemitism. As in other parts of Europe, religious, socioeconomic, and cultural tensions between Jews and Christians were part and parcel of life in the Habsburg Monarchy. In the Bohemian Lands as well as in Slovakia, the Catholic Church, its clergy and press, played an important role in transforming long-lived stereotypes and suspicions about Jews into a powerful critique of economic, political, and social changes in the late nineteenth century.[68] Anti-Jewish violence occasionally erupted especially in political and economic uncertain times, such as during the 1848–1849 revolutions. In the 1880s and 1890s, first in Hungary and then in the Bohemian Lands, ritual murder trials preoccupied wide readerships, prominent politicians, journalists, and judges.[69] In the last decades of Habsburg rule, attacks on Jews and their property did become more frequent, yet the main arenas for antisemitic excesses were newspapers, pamphlets, and books.

By the late nineteenth century, along with the gradual extension of male suffrage, political activists of all stripes adopted antisemitism as part of their political ideology and mobilizing repertoire. Long-standing stereotypes and the particularities of Jewish societies in the Habsburg Monarchy allowed every political party their own "Jewish adversary." Socialists rallied against the "Jewish capitalist," conservatives against "Jewish liberalism" and "Jewish socialism," nationalists of all stripes against the "assimilating Jew" and the "Jewish usurer."[70] By the 1890s, Jews were increasingly drawn into the nationality conflict that dominated political life in the Habsburg Monarchy. In Hungary, Slovak nationalists painted Jews as "oppressors" of Slovaks in economic and national terms, a powerful image that conjured up old and new grievances against Jews. Similarly, in Bohemia in the 1890s, narratives of economic exploitation and national oppression sustained a Czech economic boycott movement against Germans and by extension Jews, known as "To Each His Own" (*Svůj k svému*).[71]

In the Bohemian Lands, the national struggle was particularly intense because Czech and German activists competed for the same population.[72] As mentioned earlier, in this part of the Habsburg Monarchy, nationalists worked to create nationally segregated public and private spheres. Since nationalists' access to public resources and political influence depended on the size of their nation, whether counted in the census or at the ballot box, they sought to ensure that individuals remained loyal to their nation by creating obstacles to assimilation and so-called side switching. Hence, in both urban and rural communities, there were parallel Czech- and German-language schools, gymnastic clubs, cooperatives, pubs, and musical societies. These parallel German and Czech public spheres left contemporary and subsequent observers with the impression that nationalists had indeed succeeded in segregating Czechs from Germans. Yet, recently historians have shown that it was precisely people's continued "crossing" of national boundaries, for example by attending theater performances and concerts wherever they pleased, that drove nationalist activists to insist on the need to create nationally separate spheres and to police people's behavior. Jews, who were "neither obviously German nor obviously Czech," became part of the conflict on a practical as well as on a symbolic level.[73] Frustrated by people's lack of commitment to the nation, German and Czech nationalists projected their own anxieties about assimilation, opportunism, and national indifference on to "the Jews" as especially chauvinist Czechs or Germans or as indifferent and opportunist side switchers. By the last decade of the nineteenth century, Jews' multilingualism and alleged national side switching were used by various nationalists as a negative type against which they defined ideal national behavior.[74]

AFTER THE HABSBURG

The First World War and the collapse of the Habsburg Monarchy destabilized the identities of the more than two million Jews who lived within its borders.[75] As Marsha L. Rozenblit argues, for more than half a century, the supranational Habsburg state had facilitated the development of a tripartite identity among its Jews. This was an identity that allowed them to combine different loyalties: political loyalty to Austria-Hungary, cultural loyalty to German or other linguistic communities such as Czech, Polish, and Hungarian, and ethnic loyalty to the Jewish people. In the diverse Jewish societies within the monarchy, the meaning and significance of each of these loyalties varied. The state authorities did demand political loyalty, and Jews responded by becoming fervent Austrian patriots. Jews' divergent cultural and ethnic identities were not an obstacle to their inclusion in the community of loyal subjects.[76]

In 1918, following the collapse of Austria-Hungary, the Jews of the Bohemian Lands, Slovakia, and Subcarpathian Rus' became residents of Czechoslovakia. Interwar Czechoslovakia was a multinational state dominated by the Czechs and Slovaks (65.5% of the country's 13.6 million residents, the vast majority of them Czechs), but inhabited by significant minority populations. Most minorities were concentrated in specific parts of the country, most significantly Germans in the Bohemian Lands (23.4% of the total population), Hungarians in Slovakia (5.6%), Rusyns in Subcarpathian Rus' (3.5%), and Poles in Silesia (0.6%).[77] Jews, who were counted as a religious and a national minority, made up 3.6% of the country's population. Most Jews lived in Slovakia (135,918 in 1921), constituting about 4.4% of the population in that region. In Subcarpathian Rus', there were 93,341 Jews, who made up about 15.3% of the population. In the Bohemian Lands, there were 125,083 Jews (1.2% of the population in Bohemia and Moravia).[78] Unlike the other minorities, the majority of Jews were not concentrated in one specific region, but lived in communities across Czechoslovakia.

In contrast to the Habsburg Monarchy, the successor states were "conceived as of and for one nation."[79] As Rogers Brubaker argues, the new dominant national elites imagined their nations as ethnic ones, as cultural communities of descent. They rejected the idea of a supranational state and idealized unified political, cultural, and ethnic identities (e.g., Czech citizens, of Czech culture and Czech ethnicity). At the same time, the core nations' elites had to come to terms with the fact that their states were what they considered to be "insufficiently national," their ideal homogeneity marred by the presence of significant linguistic, religious, and ethnic minority populations. These state elites did not accept the presence of minorities as an unfortunate and immutable fact. Rather, they employed nationalizing processes and policies to make up for the lack in national homogeneity.[80] Many of these policies focused on displacing minorities from the economy through land reforms, on excluding minority members from the civil service and certain sectors of the economy, and on privileging the new state language in all areas of public life including the school system.

Yet, despite the dominant ethno-national paradigm that populated the imagination of the new state elites, boundaries between national groups were not always as rigid as the discourse would suggest. Through educational policies and preferential treatment for members of the core nation, states encouraged cultural and linguistic assimilation of minority populations. Thus, as the dust settled – and in East Central Europe violence and war continued for at least two years after the armistice in November 1918 – in the new nation-states (such as Czechoslovakia and Poland) and in the reconfigured ones (such as Hungary and Romania), minorities had to realign their identification and public loyalties, find ways in which to justify their belonging, and begin to negotiate the possibilities and terms for inclusion and equality.

* * *

In interwar Czechoslovakia, Zionist leaders faced a Jewish community that they believed, to adapt Brubaker's observation, to be "insufficiently national." The Jewish nation had to be created. This was a process that required, on the one hand, an internal process of homogenization, creating cultural, social, national, and linguistic uniformity among Jews. On the other, it involved a hardening of the nation's external boundaries by defining the Jewish nation as a community of descent. Although Zionists rejected the assimilationist paradigm, they did advocate acculturation, especially Jews' adoption of Czech language as a sign of political loyalty and a vehicle for social mobility, a strategy that resembled that of previous generations of Jewish reformers. Indeed, even though the new political order in East Central Europe was hailed as a revolution and as a fundamental break with past nationality policies, the relationship between the state and its Jews – and by extension Zionists' priorities and strategies – continued, as we shall see, to be shaped by the Habsburg legacy.

TWO

Jewish Power and Powerlessness

ZIONISTS, CZECHS, AND THE PARIS PEACE CONFERENCE

IN OCTOBER 1940, THE LONDON-BASED NATIONAL COUNCIL OF Jews from Czechoslovakia published an illustrated, English-language pamphlet entitled *Jews of Czechoslovakia.*[1] Its woodcuts depicting iconic Jewish sites in Czechoslovakia were accompanied by a text written by Viktor Fischl (1912–2006), a prominent young Zionist from Prague now in exile in London. Fischl's narrative recalled the exceptional character of the Jewish experience in his native land since 1918. "In the Czechoslovak Republic" he wrote, "the Jews enjoyed all civic rights." Touting the equality and minority protection extended to Jews "and other national entities" as a model for other states in Eastern Europe, Fischl's text mourned the demise of Czechoslovakia as a uniquely tolerant and welcoming place for Jews. Reminding his readers of Jews' "value to the state" and their exceptional loyalty to Czechoslovakia in times of crisis, he continued, "The country of Masaryk and those who followed in his political footsteps never deprived the Jews of Czechoslovakia of any of their rights which they retained in their entirety even when, in the neighboring countries the storm of barbarism broke over the reign of justice." Pointing to the ways in which Czech leaders had distanced themselves from antisemitism in the past, Fischl observed, "So far [to] Czechoslovak statesmen, good relationship with the Jewish population was a matter of self-evidence." But now, the "firm bonds" between Jews and Czechs were coming undone.[2]

Fischl published his pamphlet during an anxious time for Czechoslovak Jewish activists in London. In the course of the first year of the war, it had become increasingly clear that the partnership between

Czech leaders and Zionists, to which Fischl attributed "the twenty happy years" in Czechoslovakia, was floundering.[3] The unraveling of the interwar alliance went hand in hand with the gradual dissolution of Czechoslovakia that began in the fall of 1938. The exiled Czech political elite blamed the country's national minorities for the downfall of the republic. Soon, Edvard Beneš (1884–1948), the former president and leader of the provisional Czechoslovak government-in-exile, and others began developing plans for a postwar Czechoslovakia as a country without minorities. In September 1940, a month before Fischl's publication appeared, Beneš had told Zionist representatives that in a restored Czechoslovakia, Jews, like other national minorities, would have to assimilate or leave.[4] When Zionists objected to statements that depicted all national minorities as disloyal, thereby equating the behavior of the country's Jews with that of separatist Sudeten Germans and Slovaks, Beneš dismissed their objections. The confrontation between Beneš and the Zionist representatives came on the heels of a spring and summer when disagreement had intensified between Zionist and Czech leaders over Czechoslovak Jewish refugees' military obligations. The tension was further exacerbated by reports of rampant antisemitism in the British-based Czechoslovak army. Then, Beneš rejected requests to include a representative of the Jewish national minority in the exile government. By October 1940, the activists on the National Council of Jews in London grew increasingly alarmed.

It was in this crisis atmosphere that Viktor Fischl penned his pamphlet. Addressed to Western audiences and to the exiled Czech leaders, Fischl attempted to garner support for the budding Czechoslovak government-in-exile among what he and others believed to be powerful Jewish circles in the United States and Britain. This demonstration of Zionist activists' ability to call on powerful American and British Jewish representatives alerted Czech leaders to the risks involved in jeopardizing the alliance between Jews and Czechs. In short, the pamphlet *Jews of Czechoslovakia* reminded Czech politicians that their attitude toward the country's Jews was important to their wartime allies. In what might seem like a paradoxical move – just as he and his colleagues experienced a new, undisguised antisemitism among their fellow Czechoslovaks in London – Fischl chose to celebrate the myth of Czechoslovakia and its Czech leadership as uniquely tolerant, democratic, and Western, indeed as friends of Jews. In doing so, he continued a tradition established in the wake of the First World War by a generation of Zionists before him.

Since the end of the First World War, the image of Czechoslovakia as an unusually favorable environment for Jews has been a trope in narratives about the country's Jews.[5] At the same time, it is one of the key ingredients in the myth of Czechoslovakia as an exceptional democratic and Western state in interwar Eastern Europe.[6] Czech leaders, such as the first president Tomáš G. Masaryk (1850–1937) and his then foreign minister Edvard Beneš, are often depicted as tolerant, progressive, and politically sophisticated strategists bestowing rights on their Jews. Even historians more critical of Masaryk's and Beneš's mythmaking tell only part of the story.[7] They do not take into account that in the aftermath of Austria-Hungary's collapse, local Zionist activists worked hard to convince Czech leaders that the fate of Jews was important. In fact, a closer look at Zionists' strategies and Czech leaders' perceptions of Jews tells a somewhat different story, one marked by distrust and manipulation.

In the tumultuous months after the end of the First World War, Zionist leaders from the Bohemian Lands were unsure of the Czech authorities' attitude toward Jews. On the one hand, Czech leaders expressed support for Zionism and a commitment to equal rights for minorities in the new state. On the other, they did little to quell the anti-Jewish hostility, violence, and looting that swept Bohemia and Moravia as well as Slovakia in the immediate postwar months and continued through the summer of 1919. Concerned about what the future might hold, Zionists from Czechoslovakia joined the broader international Jewish efforts to secure protection and rights for Eastern Europe's Jews at the Paris Peace Conference.

At the time, Czech leaders were somewhat uncertain about the strength of their case for state sovereignty at the Paris Peace Conference. Although the Allied powers had signed declarations in support of a Czechoslovak state, the exact contours of its borders were still up in the air. Having already established a reputation as more Western, more mature, and more capable statesmen than other East European leaders, Czech politicians strove to uphold an image of Czechoslovakia as the exception to the rule among the new states. Seeking international legitimacy and support, Czech leaders courted, among others, American Jewish leaders.

The Jewish minority in Czechoslovakia was not a concern to Czech leaders, the way Jews were to the Polish and other East European delegations in Paris. Jewish power, however, was top of mind for the Czechs. Both Paris and Prague leaders believed that Jews, through their alleged control of the press and their international financial and political networks, held considerable influence with Western statesmen and public opinion. Although they were determined not to give in to calls for extensive minority rights, Czech leaders were unsure of the extent of Jews' power on the international stage and of their ability to influence Czech fortunes abroad. In this, they were encouraged by Zionists. Keenly aware of the importance the Czech leaders placed on their international image, these Jewish activists played along, confirming Czechoslovak exceptionalism, meanwhile spelling out the damage the country's reputation might suffer should anti-Jewish violence go unchecked. Thus, Czech leaders' attention to Jews and their somewhat forthcoming pose toward them was not a reflection of trust between the two parties, as Zionists subsequently claimed. Rather, it was a sign of Czech leaders' respect for Jewish power.

Focusing on how Zionists made attacks on Jews in small-town Bohemia and Moravia relevant to the participants at the Paris Peace Conference, this chapter examines the interplay between Jews' power and powerlessness in the postwar international and domestic political arena. It is a story of risky and daring actions by people with little experience in high politics but who were energized and emboldened by the events of the war. At a time of crisis, when their communities were vulnerable and isolated, Zionists had little other choice than to rely on Czech leaders' respect for Jewish power and their belief in Jews' ability to influence Czechoslovakia's fortunes on the international stage. When, in 1940, Viktor Fischl invoked the memory of this alliance between Jews and Czechs – reminding the exiled Czech leaders why Jews mattered – he did so in ways established by his predecessors in a previous world war.

THE FIRST WORLD WAR: JEWISH POWER AND POWERLESSNESS

For Jews and Jewish activists, the First World War created a paradoxical situation. As the historian Jonathan Frankel observed, during and after the war, the victimization of Jews, evidence of Jews' powerlessness and vulnerability, coexisted with a widespread belief in Jewish power and in the growing influence of a financial and political network connecting Jews across the world.[8] This perception was nurtured not only by traditional beliefs about Jews' influence and solidarity, but also by the work and claims by Jewish activists lobbying for their cause. At the end of the war, there was a growing sense among state authorities on all sides of the conflict that Jews had the will *and* ability to influence world affairs.

Although often overshadowed by the cataclysmic events of the Second World War, the First World War caused enormous destruction and dislocation in Eastern Europe. In contrast to the famously static yet devastating trench warfare in the west, when the eastern front moved, it did so across vast swaths of territory. With front lines stretching hundreds of kilometers, advancing and retreating armies alike wrought havoc on communities and the natural environment. During the first two years of the war, the eastern front lines swept through the borderlands between Austria-Hungary and the German and Russian Empires. These were regions of extraordinary linguistic, ethnic, and religious diversity, a complexity that made civilian populations in these areas vulnerable to the anxieties and desires of the competing imperial armies. Significantly, these border regions constituted the heartland of East European Jewry. Since the late 1700s, Russian authorities had restricted Jewish populations to the vast former Polish lands absorbed into Russia and known as the Pale of Settlement. Adjacent to the Pale, the Austrian provinces of Galicia and Bukovina were also home to a large number of Jews. No one expected the war that broke out in August 1914 to last more than a few months. Few anticipated the enormous dislocation, violence, and material destruction about to befall the Jewish communities in the war zones of Eastern Europe.

In the course of the first two years of the war, about 750,000 of the four million Jews in the war zone were expelled or fled their home communities.[9] Terrifying rumors and evidence of the invading Russian soldiers' mistreatment of Jews created panic among Jews in Galicia and Bukovina in the war's early months. Historians believe that between 200,000 and 450,000, or half of Galicia's Jews, fled the area.[10] In parts of Austria-Hungary well away from the front lines, such as the Bohemian Lands, the impact of war on civilians in the east was felt early on. In the fall and early winter of 1914, 16,000 Jewish refugees reached Prague.[11] In those first months of the war, Austrian authorities estimated that more than 75,000 refugees from Galicia and Bukovina arrived in the Bohemian Lands.[12] Even more fled to Vienna at that time, and thousands were displaced to other parts of Austria-Hungary and beyond. The following spring, the Russian authorities began expelling Jews from the front, eventually displacing more than half a million people from the front lines to the Russian interior.[13] Thousands more fled the fighting on their own accord. The Austro-Hungarian authorities managed to repatriate tens of thousands of Galician Jewish refugees in the summer and fall of 1915. The refugees returned home, some only to be uprooted again in the years that followed.[14] Thus, from the very beginning of the war, Jewish refugees were a familiar sight along roads, in train stations, and on city streets in Russia and Austria-Hungary.

With the Bolshevik Revolution in Russia and the Civil War that followed, the victimization of Jews in Eastern Europe reached new heights. In the chaos that erupted with the crumbling of German authority in Russian Poland and Ukraine in the fall of 1918, the warring parties targeted Jews, whom they suspected of harboring Bolshevik and German loyalties.[15] Thousands of Jews were attacked and killed, entire communities destroyed, its members left destitute and homeless. Thousands more died of the hunger and epidemics that ravaged the war-torn region. In all, historians estimate that between 1917 and 1921, more than one hundred thousand Jews were killed and tens of thousands more died as a result of the war.[16] When the First World War came to an end in November 1918, it was already clear to many observers that the continued violence and chaos in the former Russian borderlands threatened to create a Jewish refugee crisis of yet unseen proportions. Furthermore, since Bolshevik forces were widely regarded as the only *anti*-antisemitic force among the various belligerents, some worried that sympathy for the Bolshevik regime was strengthening among Jews in Eastern Europe and beyond.

During the war, Jews on the home fronts in Germany, Austria-Hungary, and Britain and in neutral countries such as the United States were confronted with news of the destruction of Jewish societies in Eastern Europe in different ways. Some witnessed the arrival of destitute refugees in their communities, others read press reports and letters from the front, and some listened to stories from returning soldiers. Many read the articles and reports filed by Jewish activists who documented the devastation to mobilize humanitarian aid.[17] Stories of wanton murder, mass rapes, torture, and destruction and dislocation of entire Jewish communities shocked readers. Jewish relief organizations sprang into action in Vienna, Berlin, Paris, Petrograd, New York, and London, collecting funds and disseminating information about the hardship of the refugees and the mounting pressures on the communities sheltering them.

The help other Jews extended to Eastern Europe was unmatched by any previous crisis, in part because total war mobilized the home fronts in unprecedented ways. The main German-Jewish aid organization (Hilfsverein der deutschen Juden) raised 15.5 million marks for Jews in German-occupied territories in the east.[18] In the Habsburg Monarchy, Jewish private individuals, communities, and organizations stepped up to shelter, feed, and assist the Jewish refugees from Galicia and Bukovina. Most prominent was the refugee aid organization Israelitische Allianz zu Wien. With a network of volunteers and employees organized in regional committees, the Allianz spent more than 4 million crowns between 1915 and 1918 assisting refugees in the Austrian Lands.[19] Its work was funded by state aid, private and communal Jewish donations, and resources provided by American Jews. Indeed, until April 1917, when the United States entered the war, the Allianz's work was paid for in large part by the American Jewish Joint Distribution Committee (JDC), the premier American relief organization established in 1914.[20] Working with different local Jewish relief organizations, the JDC distributed more than $38 million from 1914 to 1920 and facilitated the distribution of an additional $10.5 million in private funds sent from American Jews to their families in Eastern Europe.[21] Aid to Jewish soldiers and refugees marshaled the resources of Jewish societies to an unmatched extent and added a unity of purpose in communities often divided by social, cultural, political, and religious differences.

Alongside the aid efforts, Jewish activists also pursued political goals. Indeed, Jewish leaders inside and outside the region saw the war as an opportunity to shape the future for the Jews of Eastern Europe. On both sides of the front lines, Jewish leaders looked to make headway on the improvement of Jews' status in East European society. In Germany, Jewish leaders promoted Eastern Europe's Jews as a force for Germanization.[22] Meanwhile American Jewish leaders made the case that if only given equal opportunity, Russia's Jews would prove themselves as loyal and patriotic citizens.[23] As Marsha L. Rozenblit has shown, in Austria-Hungary, Jews rallied behind the monarchy, which they saw as the guarantor of their own rights and as the liberator of Jews from Russian oppression.[24] When antisemitism intensified at home and as it became increasingly clear that the war would engineer constitutional reforms in the Austrian Lands, Jewish political activists sought to create an institution that could act as the voice of Austria's Jews.[25]

Despite multiple attempts, the efforts to create an Austrian Jewish Congress or other representative institution failed. Jewish leaders were unable to find common ground, divided as they were by regional, religious, sociocultural, and political differences. What they did agree on, however, until the very end of the war was that for Jews, the monarchy's continuity held out the most promise.[26] Once it became clear that the war had brought down the old order, these Jewish elites worked to convince the Allies to make the question of equality for Jews and guarantees of their rights part of the postwar agenda. Among these Jewish lobbyists was a group of relative newcomers: representatives of the World Zionist Organization (WZO).

In the course of the First World War, the Zionist movement emerged as a significant political presence in Jewish life. Zionist wartime politics were many-sided and dynamic, shifting with developments in the war itself. When the war broke out in August 1914, the World Zionist Organization was headquartered in Berlin. At the time, German Zionists formed the most influential faction within this international and diverse institution. In the war's early days, influential German Zionists, such as Max Bodenheimer (1865–1940), the director of the Jewish National Fund, an institution that collected money for land purchase and colonization in Palestine, sought to align the movement as a whole with the German war effort. Meeting with German authorities in August, Bodenheimer proposed that in the east, an estimated six million Jews would act as a loyal political group in a future German-dominated multinational state located in the territory between Germany and what would remain of the Russian Empire.[27] At the same time, he argued, support for Jewish settlement in Palestine, then under Turkish control, would help solidify German influence in the territories of its Turkish ally and in the Middle East more broadly.[28] By aligning Zionist goals with German imperial interests, Bodenheimer and his wartime allies hoped to secure national rights and civic equality for Jews in Eastern Europe as well as the establishment of a Jewish homeland in Palestine.

Although Zionists in Germany and Eastern Europe continued to work with the German authorities through the war, from the very beginning there was resistance to Bodenheimer's initiative from other Zionist leaders. They deemed the WZO's involvement with German imperialism too risky. By December 1914, the organization's main office was relocated to Copenhagen, thereby signaling the WZO's official position of neutrality in the war. Regardless, Zionist leaders in Germany, Britain, and later the United States continued to approach their governments and military authorities casting Jews and Zionists in particular as useful partners in the pursuit of the Great Powers' wartime and postwar goals.[29] Although it created great excitement and hope among Zionists, and among Jews more broadly, the Balfour Declaration, the letter expressing British support for a Jewish homeland in Palestine issued in early November 1917, reflected only one of several different political alliances and visions pursued by Zionist activists. As the war came to an end, the Zionist movement had gained prominence on the Jewish political stage in Eastern Europe and in Allied countries, most significantly among American Jews.[30]

With a looming Jewish refugee crisis sparked by wartime displacement and postwar violence, Jewish representatives were invited by the Allies to participate in the Paris Peace Conference. In their efforts to secure equality and minority rights for Jews, western Jewish leaders were joined by Jews from Eastern Europe acting as spokesmen for the region's Jewish populations. As fear of Bolshevism intensified in the west, along with a growing unease about the prominent role played by Jews in the Russian, Bavarian, and Hungarian Communist revolutions, Zionists garnered support for their plan for a Jewish homeland in Palestine as a solution to the Jewish Question, a compelling alternative to "Judeo-Bolshevism."[31] In the wake of the war, the paradox of Jewish power and powerlessness ensured Jewish representatives a highly contested seat at the table in Paris.

FROM PRAGUE TO PARIS AND BACK

For Zionists as well as for many of Eastern Europe's nationalist movements, the war served as a catalyst for international activism in the capitals of the Great Powers. Polish nationalists, for example, were active in Berlin, London, Petrograd, and Washington. There they mingled with other nationalist activists, among them the Czech and Slovak leaders Edvard Beneš, Tomáš G. Masaryk, and Milan R. Štefánik (1880–1919) as well as prominent Zionists such as Chaim Weizmann (1874–1952) and Nahum Sokolow (1859–1936), who were all on similar missions to get international support for their national projects.[32] Claiming to represent the political will of their people, these activists struck alliances, outlined plans, and taught audiences about their land and people. Their task was often complicated by competing leaderships on opposite sides in the war and by the shifting attention of Great Power leaders, whose interest in these activists waxed and waned. However, in the wake of the Bolshevik Revolution in November 1917 and Russia's subsequent withdrawal from the war, the calls for a new order in Eastern Europe, one that would contain Bolshevism, gained traction among both the Allies and the Central Powers. In Eastern Europe, political activism thus had domestic as well as international dimensions. As the war came to a close, hectic activity ensued among these self-appointed representatives of Eastern Europe's peoples. In the capitals of the victors and at home in the territories of the defeated Central Powers, new leaderships emerged as the old order crumbled.

In mid-October 1918, Zionists in the Bohemian Lands severed their ties definitively to the Austrian Zionist leaders in Vienna. Since it was now clear that the Habsburg Monarchy would dissolve, Zionists in Prague needed a free hand to chart their own course.[33] In Prague and Brno/Brünn, Zionists established Jewish National Councils, as did Jews in many parts of Eastern Europe at this time.[34] These political bodies consisted primarily of Jewish nationalists, including Zionists, claiming to represent local Jews. The Moravian and Bohemian councils merged soon thereafter to form the Prague-based Jewish National Council for the Czechoslovak State.[35] With the establishment of the Jewish National Council, Zionists sought to usurp the traditional leaders at the helm of the region's Jewish communities, then the only Jewish institutions authorized by the state to represent the Jewish population.

Indeed, on October 28, 1918, the day Czech leaders declared Czechoslovakia's independence, Bohemian Zionist leaders Ludvík Singer (1876–1931), Karel Fischel, and Max Brod (1884–1968), representing the Jewish National Council, approached the new authorities. On behalf of the country's Jews, they pledged loyalty to the provisional Czechoslovak government. During the meeting, the Zionist representatives delivered a memorandum to the Czechs outlining concrete demands on behalf of the country's "nationally conscious Jews."[36] Modeled on the manifesto "The Demands of the Jewish People" issued a few days earlier by the Zionist Office in Copenhagen, the Prague activists called for "recognition of the Jewish nationality and freedom of individuals to profess that nationality, full civil and legal equality for the Jewish people, national minority rights for the Jewish people, including cultural autonomy, and democratization and unification of the Jewish communities."[37] Although the memorandum used an existing template, the Prague Jewish National Council had a more moderate agenda than the ones pursued by their colleagues in Vienna and other places.[38] The Prague Zionists were asking for civic equality for Jews, the state's recognition of Jews as a national *and* a religious minority (including the right for Jews to declare Jewish nationality on the census), the right to publicly funded Jewish national schools, and state-mandated democratization of the country's Jewish communal institutions.[39] The Jewish National Council's swift approach of the Czech leaders, almost a week before other Jewish representatives pledged their communities' loyalty to the Czechs, was symptomatic of the Zionists' efficient organization, political acumen, and self-confidence.

Although making more cautious demands, the Prague Jewish National Council's efforts were part of a coordinated attempt by Zionists and Jewish nationalists in Eastern Europe and beyond to present a united front on the domestic as well as on the international stage. Across Eastern Europe, Jewish National Councils presented similar manifestos aimed at securing national rights for Jews and solidifying their own authority as national leaders.[40] Indeed, Jews' war experience and the international Zionist movement's recent successes encouraged activists seeking recognition for Jews as a nation. By claiming to speak for a national minority rather than a religious one, Jewish activists sought legitimacy for their demands, ranging from the right to public Jewish national schools and support for Jewish cultural institutions to language rights and guarantees of political representation in the form of Jewish national cadasters or Jewish government representatives. In short, as representatives of one nation among others, Jewish nationalists sought to tap into the triumphant discourse on national self-determination and thereby frame national rights for Jews as part of the new democratic order in Eastern Europe. It was a political strategy shaped by these activists' wartime experiences.

The catastrophes that befell Eastern Europe's Jews during the war served to rally Jews from a wide variety of political, cultural, and social backgrounds in areas outside of the immediate war zones. The Bohemian Lands were no exception. When thousands of Jewish refugees arrived in the region in the fall of 1914, Jews in Prague and Brno/Brünn rushed to their aid.[41] The Austro-Hungarian authorities repatriated many of the more than 75,000 refugees that arrived in the fall and winter 1914–1915 the following summer. Thousands were uprooted again in the summer of 1916 by renewed fighting. By the end of that year, about 90,000 Jewish refugees languished in camps near Uherské Hradiště/Ungarisch Hradisch in Moravia.[42] A year later, Austrian authorities estimated that there were more than 108,000 Jewish refugees in the Bohemian Lands. As the number of destitute refugees continued to grow, so did the financial burden on the local Jewish communities in the Bohemian Lands and Hungary. Although the Austrian authorities did provide aid for the refugees, their resources were limited, and before long Jewish individuals, communities, and organizations as well as international Jewish relief organizations stepped in to meet the needs of the ever-growing number of refugees.[43] Initially, the various competing factions within Jewish society in Bohemia and Moravia, religious traditionalists and secularists, conservatives and socialists, Zionists and assimilationists, joined forces to assist the Jewish refugees through the Committee for the Assistance of Jewish War Refugees from Galicia and Bukovina (Hilfskomite für die jüdische Flüchtlinge aus Galizien und Bukowina).[44] Even though they were brought together by the plight of the refugees, these activists were nevertheless deeply divided on how to respond to the growing antisemitism and to the increasing political uncertainty.

The Czech-Jewish movement, which promoted Jews' assimilation to Czech culture and coveted an alliance with Czech nationalists, had experienced several setbacks during the war.[45] Czech nationalists' enthusiasm for Russia's symbolic pan-Slavic leadership made Czech-Jewish activists uncomfortable as Jewish victims of pogroms perpetrated by the tsar's forces appeared in the Bohemian Lands.[46] Furthermore, accusations of Jews' parasitical character, exploitation of non-Jews, and loyalty to Austria caused a surge in Czech antisemitism. This made Czech-Jews increasingly uneasy among their Russophile peers as the war dragged on.[47]

At the same time as Czech-Jews were met with suspicion by other Czechs and by the Austrian authorities, who were distrustful of any form of Czech nationalism, Zionist groups continued unhindered in their political activities promoting Jewish nationalism. Heartened by Jews' expression of solidarity with other Jews, embodied in the broad Jewish support for the refugees, they were nevertheless frustrated by their lack of influence in the established Jewish communities.[48] As mentioned earlier, during the war there were several attempts to create a leadership organization for Austria's Jews, but every one of them had failed.[49] One Prague Zionist, the editor of *Selbstwehr,* Siegmund Kaznelson (1893–1959), had worked tirelessly to build support among Jewish leaders for a so-called Austrian Jewish Congress. Kaznelson envisioned a leadership institution that would enable the monarchy's Jews to speak with a degree of unity and thereby add political weight to their voice, something that had become especially urgent as antisemitism mounted on the home front in 1915. Although Kaznelson was eager to see Zionists win more influence among Austria's Jews, he set aside divisive questions over Jews' national rights. Instead, he pursued a moderate, "all-Jewish" platform, intended to create common ground among Jews, a strategy that angered his Viennese Zionist colleagues. By the spring of 1918, it was clear that Kaznelson had failed. As he fell ill, no one picked up the mantle.[50] By October 1918, however, as Zionists in the Bohemian Lands broke with the Zionist leadership in Vienna, they adopted a strategy similar to Kaznelson's, one that prioritized Jewish unity and representation – an "all-Jewish" agenda – over ideological commitments.

While Kaznelson had hoped that the fight against antisemitism was something that could unite Jews, it soon became clear that the onslaught of anti-Jewish agitation was divisive. As antisemitism intensified, so too did Zionists' frustration with the communal elites. To them, the existing leadership's inability to respond effectively to the mounting hostility of non-Jews to their Jewish neighbors only confirmed that German or Czech assimilation as a strategy for coexistence was a dead end. Zionists saw the popular vilification of Jews as proof that the assimilationists' claim that Jews would achieve acceptance and equality if they became Czech or German in language, culture, and national feeling was false. To Zionists, it was time for a revolution on the Jewish street. If the various political factions within Jewish society had buried the hatchet during the war, then once it became clear that the tables had turned – that Austria-Hungary's so-called small and oppressed nationalities, among them Czechs and Slovaks, had become partners of the Allied powers – Zionists began their quest for recognition as leaders of the Jews in the areas slated to become part of the new Czechoslovak state.

On October 28, 1918, Czech leaders in Prague declared Czechoslovak independence. The next day, German nationalist leaders in the Bohemian Lands seceded by declaring their intention to join German Austria. Indeed, as Austria-Hungary disintegrated in the fall of 1918, it was by no means clear what the outcome of the monarchy's dissolution would be. In the months that followed, the scholar Joseph Rothschild observed, "the territorial consolidation of Czechoslovakia and the delimitation of its frontiers, which included provinces and regions of disparate historical, cultural, and economic development, were the products of extremely intricate diplomatic maneuvers."[51]

Early on in the war, Czech politicians, at home and abroad, had floated different ideas for a new arrangement for the Czechs after the war. In the course of the next four years, it was the plan for an independent state uniting Czechs and Slovaks advocated by a group of Czech and Slovak activists abroad led by Tomáš G. Masaryk and Edvard Beneš that came to fruition.[52] While Beneš mainly cultivated his connections with power brokers in Paris, Masaryk spent the war in Britain, France, and Russia before going to the United States in May 1918. Here, he drummed up support for Czech and Slovak independence in émigré circles and among other groups he deemed influential, such as American Jewish leaders. Eventually, in September 1918, the Wilson administration endorsed the project of uniting Czechs and Slovaks in an independent state.[53] Yet, up until the last year of the war, few of his colleagues in the Bohemian Lands imagined that there would be a postwar solution for the Czechs separate from Austria-Hungary. What appeared much more likely, and for which there was support among other minority nationalist leaders, was the transformation of the Habsburg Monarchy into a federation of nationalities.

In Pittsburgh in late May 1918, Czech and Slovak leaders committed to a shared vision for statehood that called for the unification of the Bohemian Lands and part of northern Hungary inhabited largely, but not only, by Slovak-speaking populations. The Czech and Slovak nations were to be equal partners in the new country.[54] At the same time, Masaryk and Beneš worked to convince French and American leaders that an independent Czechoslovak state would serve alongside other successor states to curb German expansionism to the east and to halt the spread of Bolshevism westward. However, as soon as the Prague leaders declared Czechoslovak independence on October 28, German leaders in Bohemia, Moravia, and Silesia organized in four regional groupings and declared their intent to join what remained of Austria. This was a sign of dissent and conflict that challenged Beneš and Masaryk's claim that national self-determination for Czechs and Slovaks would be a source of stability in the region. In December 1918, Czech forces moved in and suppressed German opposition in the borderlands.[55] The Czech and Slovak leaders could now set out for Paris formally, if not firmly in control of the territory that they were claiming for the new Czechoslovakia. At the Paris Peace Conference, which opened on January 20, 1919, Rusyn activists joined the Czechoslovak delegation, legitimizing Beneš's request to include Subcarpathian Rus', territory populated by Slavic Rusyn-speakers in Hungary's northeast, as the "tail," the easternmost part of Czechoslovakia.

In Paris, the Czechoslovak delegation had to joggle two different principles for statehood in order to legitimize their territorial demands. On the one hand, Beneš and Karel Kramář (1860–1937), as foreign and prime ministers of Czechoslovakia, demanded that the historical boundaries and territorial integrity of the Bohemian Lands remain intact. Although Czech-speakers formed a majority in these areas, the regions were also inhabited by a large German minority, a fact that caused some, but not decisive, concern among some Allied leaders.[56] On the other hand, the delegation asked for Hungarian territory to be included as part of Czechoslovakia in accordance with the right to national self-determination for the Slovaks and Rusyns in these regions.[57] The Czechoslovak delegates thus legitimized their territorial demands through the right to national self-determination as well as "historic frontiers," a move that, of course, disregarded the rights of German- and Magyar-speakers as well the integrity of Hungary's borders. In the course of the spring and summer 1919, the Czechoslovak delegation secured Allied approval of its territorial demands. Whatever misgivings remained were swept aside as Hungarian Bolshevik forces invaded Slovakia, yet again alerting hesitant decision makers to the importance of Czechoslovakia "as part of the cordon sanitaire against Bolshevism."[58]

By satisfying their territorial appetite, including wresting a significant part of the strategically important, but miniscule Těšín/Teschen/Cieszyn region from Poland in the summer of 1920, Czechoslovakia's leaders ended up in a position of fundamental insecurity. There was bad blood between Czechoslovakia and most of its neighbors. Many Czech and Slovak leaders distrusted their German- and Hungarian-speaking fellow citizens, substantial populations living in what came to be seen by the Prague government and by Czech and Slovak nationalists as volatile borderlands. Furthermore, Czech leaders had assured Slovak and Rusyn delegates that they would enjoy significant autonomy within the new state in order to assuage the latters' fears of being dominated by the more numerous and powerful Czechs. By the time Czechoslovakia was consolidated, however, the Czechs backtracked. Instead, they sought to shore up the legitimacy and stability of the country through a program of centralization and cultural and linguistic homogenization. It was this desire on the part of the Czech leadership to integrate these newly amalgamated territories – regions marked by extraordinary socioeconomic, linguistic, religious, and cultural diversity – that presented Zionists with an opportunity to declare that they, and by extension the country's Jews, were partners in Czechoslovak state building.

As an emerging Jewish leadership, the Jewish National Council considered its contact with Czech leaders to be of great importance for its bid for influence. From the outset, the council, chaired by Bohemian Zionists Ludvík Singer and Max Brod, represented itself as enjoying the support of the new authorities. It cultivated this image by publicizing statements about the virtues of the Zionist movement and its goals made by the Czechs' most prominent leader, Tomáš G. Masaryk, and reiterated by other Czech politicians.[59] When, in mid-November 1918, Masaryk, then still on his propaganda tour in the United States, expressed "sympathy" for Zionism in a message to the Zionist Organization of America, the Jewish National Council in Prague immediately spun it as an "act of state" in support of their program.[60] They invoked the authority of Masaryk's statement repeatedly both when addressing Jewish audiences and when intervening on behalf of Jews with local authorities. Zionists were unsure about Jews' political loyalties, divided as they were by language, cultural traditions, religious practices, and class. In addition, Jews lived dispersed in large and small communities across the territory of the new state where authority was still changing hands. Zionists were, however, fairly certain that as a vulnerable minority, Jews would be looking to the central government for protection. By presenting themselves as close to political power in Prague, Zionists sought to appear as effective leaders among Jews as well as loyal partners to the new Czech leadership and their allies.

As mentioned earlier, Prague Zionists had been at the forefront of wartime efforts to unite Austria's Jews. In November 1917, Ludvík Singer reported that there was broad support among prominent Prague Jews, Zionists and non-Zionists alike, for an institution that would allow Jews to speak with one voice and help secure rights, although not necessarily national ones, for Austria's Jews.[61] By early January 1919, Zionists in the Bohemian Lands, now freed from the squabbles with Viennese and Galician colleagues, convened a Jewish National Congress for Czechoslovakia. Over 340 delegates attended this first congress, along with dignitaries from Czech political and cultural life.[62] When the congress opened on January 4, 1919, the hosts greeted delegates and guests with a message from Masaryk, whose portrait was displayed alongside the other members of the Zionists' trinity, Theodor Herzl, the founder of the World Zionist Organization, and President Woodrow Wilson.[63]

The January congress selected a number of local activists to speak on behalf of Czechoslovak Jewry at the Paris Peace Conference.[64] Having been symbolically vested with representing the Jews of Czechoslovakia, these activists joined other Jewish nationalists from Eastern Europe and Jewish leaders from the Allied countries in Paris. As in Prague, across Europe and North America, Zionists, Diaspora nationalists, and other Jewish activists had organized congresses, passed resolutions, and dispatched delegates. They now met up in the French capital to make a bid for Jews' civic equality and national minority rights in the new Europe.

Despite Jewish leaders' great expectations, the first months of the negotiations brought little progress on minority issues. Internal fighting between the various Jewish groups was exacerbated by the Allied Powers' unwillingness to commit to the protection of minorities.[65] By late March 1919, Jews renewed their efforts to overcome their differences over what kinds of rights and protection should be pursued for Jews in Eastern Europe.[66] While they all sought civic equality for Jews, East European delegates wanted Jews recognized as a national minority. Influential French and British Jewish leaders would agree only to work for equality for Jews as a religious minority. Under American Jewish leadership, Jewish nationalists established a committee meant to unite the efforts to ensure protection for Jews in Eastern Europe, known as the Committee of Jewish Delegations to the Paris Peace Conference

(Comité des Délégations juives auprès de la Conférence de la paix). Delegations representing Jewish National Councils across Eastern Europe, including the Czechoslovak one, joined the committee.[67] In a resolution of May 10, 1919, the committee demanded recognition of equal civic and national rights for Jews, cultural autonomy, state support for Jewish schools, minority language rights, and protection of Sabbath observance.[68]

As the negotiations between the Allied Powers and the new East European state leaderships entered its final stages in the summer of 1919, Jewish delegates met with representatives of the successor states. Edvard Beneš, who led the Czechoslovak delegation in Paris, was firmly opposed to the kind of minority protection assurances pursued by the Committee of Jewish Delegations to the Paris Peace Conference and others, including representatives of the region's German minorities. He viewed such conditions as a breach of sovereignty.[69] Indeed, Beneš worried that rights for specific minorities would unduly empower Czechoslovakia's largest minority, the over three million German-speakers (about a quarter of the country's population) living within the territory claimed by the new state. As we have seen, the Czechoslovak leaders had already had to overcome strong internal German opposition to their authority, including serious riots in the borderlands in March 1919. The Allies' final decision to award Czechoslovakia all of the historical territory of Bohemia and Moravia was made only in April that year. Indeed, throughout the course of the Paris Peace Conference, from January through August 1919, Czechoslovakia's borders were contested by local populations as well as by neighboring Poland and Hungary.

Beneš's misgivings about a connection between German goals and Jewish activists were not accidental. On a regional level, the efforts to secure minority rights for Jews coincided with Germany's campaign to limit its territorial losses and secure national rights for millions of Germans about to be absorbed into the new East European states. Furthermore, seeking to limit Poland's demands for German secession of territory, the German Foreign Office assisted in the dissemination of news about ethnic conflict in areas under Polish control. Evidence of Polish authorities' discrimination and violence against Jewish populations, for example, became fodder for the German authorities' efforts to raise suspicion about the ability of Polish leaders to assume the responsibility of statehood. Assisting Jewish minority rights activists was one way for the German Foreign Office to bolster the case for Germany retaining its territory and populations.[70] Thus, the question of rights for Jews, and minority rights more broadly, was for Beneš, as it was for his Polish colleagues, a matter of upholding state sovereignty as well as securing his territorial and strategic goals at the Paris Peace Conference. Although the Jewish minority was not a concern to Beneš, he believed that awarding special rights to particular minorities would set a dangerous precedent.

In late August 1919, weeks after the Poles had signed a treaty that incorporated some of the demands of the Committee of Jewish Delegations to the Paris Peace Conference, Jewish delegates from Czechoslovakia made a last attempt to move Beneš to adopt what they viewed as a more cooperative attitude on the question of Jews' rights.[71] In Paris, the leader of the Czechoslovak Jewish delegation, Ludvík Singer, was accompanied by two Zionists from Prague: Hugo Bergmann (1883–1975), a writer and philosopher, who had already made a name for himself in the international Zionist movement, and Norbert Adler (1897–?), a lawyer and community activist. These Bohemian Jews were joined by a delegate from Slovakia, Marcus Ungar. As the Jewish National Council's envoy in Slovakia, Ungar acted as a self-appointed spokesman for Slovak communities and an expert on conditions in that region.[72] The negotiations between the Jewish delegates and Beneš were less than smooth. When Singer and his colleagues impressed on Beneš the need for special protection for Jews, he rebuffed them. As he had in the past, Beneš dismissed their concerns with reference to Czechoslovakia's general assurances of equal rights and freedoms for all its citizens.[73] In no uncertain terms, Beneš told the delegation that he considered their campaign a form of defamation. It was a level of distrust he found inappropriate considering Czechoslovakia's democratic, Western, and civilized character.

A few days later, Ludvík Singer made another attempt to make inroads with Beneš. When he arrived in the latter's Paris office for a scheduled meeting, Singer was handed a letter. In it, Beneš warned that it was in the interest of Jews as well as Czechs that the question of special rights for Jews be abandoned. Hinting at the swell of hostility against Jews in the Bohemian Lands and Slovakia in the spring and summer of 1919, Beneš warned that "a number of complaints and criticisms concerning certain Jewish elements have come to our attention." Beneš hinted that further Jewish pressure might "provoke renewed recriminations from one side or the other."[74] The Jewish delegates found themselves in an awkward position. Over the past months, in an effort to hold Czech leaders to their assurances of protection for Jews, the Jewish National Council had supported the image of Czechoslovakia and its leaders as uniquely tolerant, democratic, and Western, an image carefully produced by Masaryk and Beneš.[75] Now, Beneš claimed that precisely because Czechoslovakia was an exception to the rule among the new states, Jews should satisfy themselves with the commitment to equality for minorities already made by the Czech leaders.

The Jewish delegates were infuriated by Singer's humiliation. Chillingly, it alerted them to the risk of alienating Czech leaders.[76] Torn between their dual loyalties – their simultaneous commitments to the international Jewish cause and their own communities – and fearful of repercussions at home, they disagreed about how to proceed. In the end, the Zionists from Czechoslovakia handed the case over to the international Jewish leadership and left Paris. A few days later, the leader of the international Zionist delegation in Paris, Nahum Sokolow, made a last attempt to reason with Beneš. His efforts were in vain. The Allied Powers had already accepted the Czechs' position.[77]

Beneš's challenge to the Jewish delegates was just one instance that revealed broader rifts among members of the Committee of Jewish Delegations to the Paris Peace Conference – disagreements that undermined their efforts on behalf of Jews in Eastern Europe and Palestine.[78] While some Jewish National Councils demanded more extensive autonomy and guarantees of political representation, the Zionists from the Bohemian Lands were more cautious. Their main concern was the state authorities' recognition of Jews as a nationality and with that status the right to public Jewish national schools, to state support for Jewish cultural institutions, and to organize a countrywide Jewish representative body.[79] The lack of progress in securing rights for Jews in all the new states made some delegates uneasy about the wisdom of a united, international Jewish front and more open to pursuing local solutions to their communities' future. Hugo Bergmann commented in his diary that Ludvík Singer's fear of a possible backlash at home hampered his ability to remain true to the committee's demands and the shared interest of East European Jewry.[80] He noted with disdain how Singer "would have been completely content with *that* letter [Beneš's letter]."[81] Bergmann was unrelenting in his criticism of Singer.[82] Since he was climbing the ladder in the Zionist movement and preparing for immigration to Palestine, Bergmann had little sympathy for the Jewish activists who were anxious to secure alliances with their local governments. Furthermore, having spent the spring and summer abroad in Bern, Paris, and London, Bergmann was perhaps less aware of the volatile situation back home than his colleagues who had arrived in Paris from Czechoslovakia.[83] The conflict between Singer and Bergmann was symptomatic of the differing interests within the committee. In this case, the disagreement between the Palestine-bound Bergmann and Singer, who was concerned about Jews' future in Czechoslovakia, also reflected a fundamental divide within the Zionist movement. For some Zionists, the prospect of securing national rights for Jews in Eastern Europe made the need to open Palestine for Jewish immigration less urgent. For others, the uncertain future for Jews in the successor states created an opportunity to push hard for an Allied commitment to a Jewish homeland in Palestine. It was a chance that could not be missed.[84] Having to make a choice, Singer determined that he had too much to lose by alienating the Czech leaders. The Czechoslovak Jewish delegation was, after all, not after as extensive rights as those sought by, for example, Polish Jews. As Bergmann's comments imply, Singer's concern reflected an awareness that in the end the future of Czechoslovakia's Jews depended on the Prague government's will to protect them and to ensure their rights. For Singer, the larger Jewish cause had to be sacrificed in the interest of Jews at home.

Despite the tension between Edvard Beneš and the Jewish delegates, upon his return to Prague in early September 1919, Ludvík Singer showed no sign of defeat. Addressing an assembly of the Jewish National Council two weeks later, Singer pointed out that since the Czechs had already adopted general minority protection clauses and considering the "exceptional character of the conditions for Jews in this country," the delegation had not found it necessary to insist on special protections for Jews such as the ones included in the Allied treaty with Poland.[85] Making no mention of a disagreement between the delegates and Beneš, Singer presented the lack of protection for Jews as a sign of the smooth cooperation between the Jewish National Council and the Czech leaders. It was an alliance, according to Singer, built on mutual trust between Jews and Czechs. Singer's claim was meant to reassure his colleagues in the assembly. No doubt, he was well aware that it hardly reflected Jewish activists' experience in the preceding months when they had watched antisemitism and violence against Jews reach new, unchecked heights in the Bohemian Lands and Slovakia.

POSTWAR VIOLENCE AND INTERNATIONAL AUDIENCES

On November 22, 1918, the Polish army entered Lwów/Lemberg/Lviv, a city in the former Austrian Galicia. In a rampage that lasted for more than two days, Polish soldiers and civilians attacked the city's Jews, killing 72 and wounding more than 440. Soon, panicked messages made their way to the west spreading the news. International publicity campaigns brought the continuing atrocities to the attention of Western audiences. Their indignation with the violence against Jews soon became an important tool for activists concerned with the fate of Jews in the region.[86] To Jewish and non-Jewish observes alike the pogrom highlighted the urgent need for protection for civilians, minorities in particular, in Eastern Europe. Having followed the news of pogroms closely, Jewish leaders in the Bohemian Lands breathed a collective sigh of relief that the collapse of the monarchy had not resulted in the chaos experienced elsewhere. Just as they did so, anti-Jewish sentiments and occasional attacks spilled over into widespread violence and looting. As soon as the "pogrom atmosphere" emerged in the newly established Czechoslovakia, the Prague-based Jewish National Council rose to the challenge, feverishly intervening with local authorities and dispatching reports abroad in an effort to ensure government action to stop attacks on Jews.

A few days after the pogrom in Lwów, anti-Jewish violence erupted in parts of Bohemia and Moravia.[87] By early December, it had spread to the capital. In a communiqué to Jewish news organizations abroad about the violence, the Jewish National Council reported that Jewish officers as well as civilians had been beaten up and robbed in the streets of Prague.[88] Even though the council highlighted the antisemitism stirred up by the Czech nationalist press, they also reported that German nationalist groups had been stoking the fire at the city's German university in the days preceding the larger outbreak of violence.[89] While the unrest in Prague was subdued, attacks continued in other areas of Bohemia and Moravia in the days following. Most riots took the form of looting and beatings, some of which resulted in deaths. The Jewish National Council had anticipated violence and was ready to dispatch messages abroad.

Already on October 18, 1918, Max Brod, the vice chair of the Jewish National Council, had written to Leo Hermann (1888–1951), a Prague colleague and a high-ranking member of the WZO, now based in London.[90] Brod reported that in small towns where Czech nationalist tensions ran high, rioters were already pillaging Jewish homes. He anticipated that a Czechoslovak declaration of independence would be accompanied by violence, perhaps even full-blown pogroms, against Jews. In his letter, Brod included a set of codes with which he would telegraph the extent of any violence to Hermann. "Congratulations on the wedding" would indicate that there was a risk of a pogrom in Prague, while a telegram reading "The best wishes for the wedding" signified that a pogrom was already under way in the city. Other codes communicated the location, extent, and identity of the perpetrators to Hermann. Brod assured his colleague that he would use these codes only if the situation was serious and the reports confirmed. At that point, Hermann should not hesitate informing the Zionist headquarters in Copenhagen, Anglo-Jewish organizations, the British and American governments, as well as President Wilson and Tomáš G. Masaryk. Brod's hope was that by dispatching the news abroad, these international players would be moved to send "warning" letters and telegrams to Karel Kramář and Václav Klofáč (1868–1942), the most prominent Czech politicians in Prague, who had strong ties to the Czech nationalist press and political parties.

When two Jews were murdered and scores of Jewish businesses and homes robbed and burned in the town of Holešov/Holleschau in Moravia on December 3–4, 1918, the Jewish National Council intervened with the new provisional Czechoslovak government in Prague.[91] In their open letter, the Jewish leaders condemned the local town authorities' passivity in the face of widespread looting and violence and warned of the spread of anti-Jewish unrest.[92] They urged the central authorities to suppress further pogroms by prosecuting the perpetrators and stopping the press's anti-Jewish goading.[93] The vicious campaign, however, continued unabated and was followed by a call for a boycott of Jewish businesses in early 1919. Using the slogan "Each to His Own" (*Svůj k svému*), Czech nationalists invoked the memory of previous boycotts of German- and Jewish-owned businesses. They did so to cast this postwar campaign against Jews as a continuation of the struggle by Czechs against "German domination."[94]

To the Jewish press, the thin veil of a national struggle was a poor disguise for blatant antisemitism.[95] As attacks became "the order of the day" Jews grew increasingly anxious.[96] By March 1919, the "topics of daily discussions and worries among Jews [were] the boycott against everything Jewish, the untruthful press campaign, the unjust and inhumane treatment of the [Jewish] refugees, attacks on Jewish citizens, [and] the recent assaults in the streets which has created a state of panic among Jews."[97] By then reports of renewed attacks on Jews in Slovakia were also adding to the increasing uncertainty as to the authorities' ability and willingness to protect Jews and their livelihoods.[98] In Slovakia, Jews had been victims of widespread looting and violence in the immediate aftermath of the war, when they were accused of harboring Hungarian sympathies. As in the Bohemian Lands, the Slovak-language press and the new authorities cast the violence as punishment for Jews' wartime betrayal and exploitation of their Slovak neighbors. The authorities let the perpetrators go unpunished. When Hungarian Bolshevik forces, in an effort to restore the territory to Hungary, entered Slovakia in March 1919, accusations of Jews' Magyar, Bolshevik, and anti-Slovak sentiments fueled the press's calls for punishment of the region's Jews through economic boycotts and expulsions.

In the Bohemian Lands, the Zionist papers blamed the Czech nationalist and Agrarian press for stirring up the violence against Jews by encouraging an anti-Jewish mood.[99] In January, during their first meeting with President Masaryk, members of the Jewish National Council pointed to the "hostile and injurious tendencies of the Czechoslovak press" when discussing the recent "pogrom-like incidents."[100] Nevertheless, to

Jewish reporters the government remained passive in the face of continued incitement against Jews. As tensions ran high through the spring of 1919, with riots in the Sudetenland and the Hungarian invasion of Slovakia, and as new incidents of violence against Jews occurred in Prague, the Czech-language Zionist paper *Židovské zprávy* accused the Czech press of "systematic incitement of the people against their Jewish fellow citizens."[101] When a mob attacked a Jewish couple for their alleged wartime spying for the Austrians, one writer noted that Jews had become objects of "street justice." "In Prague under the eyes of the authorities, the crowd severely maltreated Jewish citizens," an incident that proved, according to the author, that the authorities' assurances of equality and protection for Jews were little more than empty words.[102]

The postwar months were far more chaotic and violent in Poland than in the Bohemian Lands and Slovakia. Nevertheless, events there shaped the way Jewish writers experienced and presented the outbreak of antisemitism in Czechoslovakia.[103] Despite the pervasiveness of anti-Jewish violence during and in the wake of the war, the pogroms in Poland still attracted considerable attention in the Jewish press in Prague and Brno/Brünn. The "mass murder in Lemberg" was described as the "most horrible pogrom in world history." Inflated estimates of Jewish casualties and reports of atrocities both reflected and sustained a sense of apocalyptic destruction descending on East European Jewry.[104] The "violent attacks, lootings, mutilations, and arsons" were described as a "war of extermination [*Vernichtungskrieg*]" and "the systematic destruction of eastern Jewry [*die systematische Ausrottung der Ostjuden*]."[105] Once the familiar Polish routine of civilians and soldiers joining forces to attack Jews and their property appeared in the Bohemian Lands, Jews were alarmed.[106] Unable to separate fully the pogrom images disseminated by reports about Poland from the slander, looting, and violence in their own communities, Jews were increasingly uncertain as to what the future would bring.

PERCEPTIONS OF JEWISH POWER

As anti-Jewish unrest intensified, exposing Jews' vulnerability and isolation, the Jewish National Council stepped up its efforts to convince the new authorities to intervene. They did it by highlighting the damaging effects to Czechoslovakia's image abroad should the authorities fail to protect Jews at home. In doing so, Zionist activists relied on the widespread belief in Jewish power, especially the influence of international Jewish financial and political networks based in Britain and the United States. On the one hand, this strategy reflected local Jews' admiration for their American and British allies and what they believed to be the latter's political thrust. On the other, it also betrayed that Jews had few other tools at their disposal. In the face of immediate danger to their communities, Zionist activists had little other choice than to play on non-Jews' inflated perceptions of Jewish power.

The war and its aftermath nurtured beliefs about Jews' global power. The presence of vocal and active Jewish rights and relief organizations in France, Britain, the United States, and Germany and their ability to mobilize significant resources in support of Jewish war victims gave the impression that Jews wielded considerable financial power. Jewish activists themselves encouraged the notion that Jews, particularly American Jewish leaders, were able and willing to act on behalf of other Jews.[107] Although Jews might have used these shared notions strategically, they did so because to some extent they believed them. As the United States emerged as a major political and economic power, so did American Jewry in the eyes of European Jews. Thus, at the same time as these perceptions informed and fueled antisemitism, they were also internalized and reshaped to serve Jews' interests.[108] In Paris, Jewish activists pleaded with, cajoled, and threatened representatives of the new states with the power of international Jewry. This was a tactic that heightened the sense among politicians and their publics that Jews could be an asset as well as an obstruction in the delicate negotiations under way.[109]

From the outset, the notion of Jews' power influenced Czech leaders' attitude toward antisemitism and anti-Jewish unrest as well as their perceptions of the consequences that these events might have for Czechoslovakia. In contrast to the Polish leaders, the Czechs were not worried about the presence of Jews in the new state (Jews made up less than 4% of the population). The Czechs were concerned about the much larger number of Germans (24%) and Hungarians (6%) living within Czechoslovakia's proposed borders. Nonetheless, Czech leaders were preoccupied with Jews' influence in the international political arena. In their wartime correspondence, Masaryk and Beneš discussed the significance of American Jews' support for the Czechoslovak cause. Both believed that Jews were influential with President Wilson and with Western public opinion more broadly. This belief did not, however, endear Jews to either of these men. Beneš had what one historian has called "a confused fear of Jews." Suspicious of their role on the international political stage, he warned Masaryk to watch out for Jews.[110]

Masaryk shared with Beneš this perception of Jewish power, and like his colleague, he never divested himself of an emotional suspicion and fear of Jews and their foreignness.[111] In his political life, Masaryk was able to overcome his negative emotional predisposition toward Jews, his prejudice and distrust, and support Jews even when it was unpopular to do so, such as during the 1899 Hilsner ritual murder trial.[112] Masaryk placed great significance on the support of American "Zionists and other Jews who have publicly endorsed our program" during and after the First World War.[113] By facilitating personal contacts to Wilson and by otherwise supporting the Czechs, they had, Masaryk believed, rewarded him for his opposition to antisemitism. Looking back on his accomplishments years later, Masaryk evaluated the role of Jewish power as follows: "In the United States, as in Europe, Jewish influence is strong in the press; it was very beneficial for us that this great power was not against us."[114] Uneasy about Jews and unsure of the extent of the power they wielded, Masaryk and Beneš were convinced that if they were seen as harboring or tolerating antisemitism, it would be detrimental to the Czech cause.

The perception of Jews' ability to control the Western press – and by extension influence Western public opinion – caused concern among Czech leaders as violence against Jews erupted throughout newly independent Czechoslovakia. In December 1918, having only recently returned to Prague, Masaryk wrote to Beneš of the need to frame the recent attacks on Jews as food riots, noting, "There is great dislike of Jews here. . . . I will endeavor to get it under control."[115] With an eye to the international outcry against the pogroms in Poland, Masaryk warned the provisional government against giving in to local public pressure to deport the Galician Jewish war refugees who remained in the Bohemian

Lands. He argued that "it is half the victory, if we can keep things tidy up to the peace conference."[116] At the same time, Karel Pergler (1882–1954), a Czech-American activist and Czechoslovakia's newly appointed ambassador to the United States, warned Masaryk of a "campaign of falsehood against us, charging for instance that an order was issued to deport all Jews from the Czechoslovak Lands. As you see, they do not differentiate between the Galician refugees and our own Jews." "It is essential," claimed Pergler, "that our people at home are quite careful in the handling of the Jewish situation."[117]

Both international Jewish leaders and activists from the Bohemian Lands were aware of Masaryk and Beneš's strategy to create an image of Czechoslovakia as a respectable, Western state in order to ensure that Czechoslovak demands were satisfied in the negotiations with the Allies. The Czechoslovak delegation's demands were after all contested.[118] As Zionists abroad intervened with Czech and Slovak leaders on behalf of Jews, they invoked the importance of Czechoslovakia's reputation on the international stage. The Zionist leader Chaim Weizmann wrote in a letter protesting Slovak authorities' antisemitic policies and arrest of local Zionists in July 1919, "No one would regret more than ourselves if as a result of these occurrences in Slovakia, the Jewish and non-Jewish circles of England, America and other Entente countries, which have always inclined to the Republic, should call public attention in their respective countries to the dangerous position of the Jews in Slovakia."[119] Similarly, in the wake of Beneš's humiliation of Singer and the Czechoslovak Jewish delegation in late August 1919, Nahum Sokolow explained to Beneš that "disappointing" news of his lack of cooperation on the question of Jewish rights was making its way to American Jewish leaders.[120] When Beneš did not budge, Sokolow cautioned that should the Czechs fail to accept his demands for special protection for Jews, "the Jews who until now have been friends of the Republic will be thunderstruck, and a press campaign might very well begin which we will not be in a position to avert."[121] Even though he was unsure of the extent of Jews' influence, Beneš did not give in to Sokolow's demands.[122]

At home in the Bohemian Lands, Zionists countered allegations of Jews' wartime treason with grandiose depictions of Jews' intervention on behalf of Czechoslovakia. The Zionist press never missed an opportunity to point out that prominent Zionist leaders, such as Supreme Court Justice Louis Brandeis (1856–1941), were influential in the circle of advisors surrounding President Wilson.[123] *Selbstwehr* reported that Brandeis and Henri Bergson (1859–1941), a French-Jewish scholar and member of the French Mission in Washington, had worked with Masaryk to deploy Czechoslovak volunteer soldiers in Siberia, the so-called Czechoslovak Legions, thereby securing the recognition of the Czechoslovak National Council as an Allied partner. Thus, the writer concluded, "Jews had played a decisive role in fulfilling the Czech aspirations through the Entente."[124] Eager to depict Jews as influential supporters of the Czechoslovak cause, the writer noted that "it is clear that the Czech people should be very grateful to these Jews, representatives of the world's most powerful states, for the freedom and independence that it enjoys today." Sparing no effort in highlighting the future importance of this partnership between Jews and Czechs, the writer continued:

> It is obvious that the policy of the Czechoslovak state has to take this circumstance into account along with the more important consideration that the Jewish people, which is already a very important international power, once organized on a national basis will gain a still unforeseeable influence on world politics as well as financial and economic affairs.[125]

Although the authors of these reports worked to convince Czechs of the importance of international Jewish leaders' support for Czechoslovakia, they also warned that Jews' influence could be used against the Czechs should the latter fail to protect Jews.[126] Wary of the censors, direct criticism of the Prague government was subdued in the Zionist press.[127] Instead, Jewish writers highlighted how the Polish government's antisemitic policies had damaged that country's prestige on the international stage.[128] In an article describing attacks on Jews and looting of Jewish property, one author warned, "It would be a shame if the Czech nation, who enjoys so much sympathy abroad, would attract the attention of the Allies in the same manner that the Poles have done."[129] Another cautioned against more Polish-style Jew bashing, as "the Czechs now see for themselves the detrimental effects that the Polish pogroms against the Jews have had on that country's prestige."[130] With an eye to the negotiations in Paris, Zionist leaders reminded the Czech authorities that the negative effects of antisemitism on the country's reputation could be limited if action was taken to restrict incitement and violence, a step the Polish government had failed to take.

If Beneš and Masaryk were certain that Jews, whether as pogrom victims or as political players, were able to influence the fate of the Czechoslovak cause, so were the Czechs from the home guard. At a public meeting on October 25, 1918, only days before the establishment of Czechoslovakia, Václav Klofáč, whom Max Brod had identified early on as a key political actor in Prague, cautioned that "we should not consider all Jews equally guilty [of profiteering and other crimes during the war] and should not forget that the Jews are very influential advisors of Entente leaders like Wilson. Proceeding thoughtlessly in this matter could result in a setback."[131] Similarly in the aftermath of the pogroms in December 1918, Karel Kramář, now as newly appointed prime minister of Czechoslovakia, warned in a speech to the provisional National Assembly, "Allow me to say as someone who oversees foreign affairs and receives reports from abroad that any violence [against Jews] would cause real damage to our freedom."[132]

Even though Czech politicians at home and abroad called for an end to anti-Jewish violence, they displayed a certain amount of unease about suppressing popular calls for punishment of Jews for their alleged profiteering and treason. In order not to run the risk of appearing as if in the pocket of Jews or protecting the nation's enemies, Czech politicians played on the widely held, exaggerated belief in Jewish power to present antisemitism as detrimental to Czech interests. They claimed to act in the interest of the Czech nation and the future of Czechoslovakia when calling for protection of Jewish refugees and restraint in public displays of antisemitism. During the December 1918 parliamentary session, the social democrat Josef Stivín (1879–1941) warned that "this fashion [of antisemitism] might harm us at the peace conference and in the eyes of the civilized world."[133] In explaining how antisemitism would damage the "exceptional respect" that the Czech nation enjoyed abroad, Karel Kramář argued "that it would be a monstrous crime if we were to damage the good name of our legionaries because of disorder, pogroms, looting, and pillaging. Every [Jewish] window pane that is destroyed in a store, and every scrap that is stolen, the Czechoslovak Republic will have to pay for with her future."[134] Even if humanitarian concerns motivated these politicians to condemn attacks on Jews, they thought it prudent not to phrase their disapproval in those terms. In short, they condemned antisemitism not out of sympathy for Jews, but out of respect for Jewish power.

Distancing the Prague government from "certain Jewish elements" became particularly important to Czech leaders in the spring of 1919 when Bolshevik Hungarian forces entered territory claimed by the Prague government. As the armies clashed, more violence descended on the Jews in Slovakia and Subcarpathian Rus'.[135] One of the voices on the right who demanded the government take action against Jews was the prominent historian and later chancellor of Prague's Charles University Josef Pekař (1870–1937). In the Czech nationalist paper *Národní listy,* he thundered against "Jewish Bolshevism" and suggested that the increasing popular support for socialism "proved the power of world Jewry's solidarity [with each other] and that internationalism is a special and particularly interesting form of Jewish nationalism."[136] Following a script popularized by *The Protocols of the Elders of Zion,* the Russian-produced and widely distributed antisemitic hoax, Pekař cast Jewish capitalists and revolutionaries as pursuing shared ends. Jews' goal, he maintained, was to create more "Jewish states" in Europe alongside Hungary and the Soviet Union. Similar sentiments warning against the Jews' contamination of Slav culture were also voiced in the Czech Catholic weekly *Mír.*[137] Still unsure of their political authority, their ability to maintain order and hold on to the territory they had claimed for Czechoslovakia, Czech leaders found themselves in a bind. On the one hand, they sought to appear forthcoming to local and western Jewish leaders in order to maintain a favorable international reputation. On the other, they were hesitant to suppress popular calls for punishment of Jews, incitement that occasionally spilled over into violence. Thus, even if Slovak authorities arrested perpetrators of violence and looting, they promptly released them without trial. They thereby sent a message that disorder was impermissible, but antisemitism was not.

The conflicting notions of Jews' simultaneous power and powerlessness were reflected in the Czech leadership's understanding of Zionist activists' position. Edvard Beneš, for example, although careful not to appear uncooperative toward Jews, cautioned them against not supporting the government. Hinting at possible retribution, he capitalized on the Jewish delegates' anxiety, knowing full well the precarious position of Jews back home. In other words, although sensitive to the possibility of damaging publicity about antisemitism in Czechoslovakia, Beneš also used the recurring anti-Jewish violence as a way of repelling Jews' demands. Similarly, while the authorities were careful to censor reports in the Zionist press about the anti-Jewish violence in Slovakia, worried as they were that the news about the extent of the violence would reach audiences abroad, Czech leaders did little in response to Jews' complaints about the antisemitic campaign in the Czech press. Thus, even if Czech leaders believed that international Jewish financial and political networks held considerable influence with Allied governments and Western public opinion, they also acted on the assumption that local Jews, as pariahs, and increasingly vulnerable ones, would be reluctant to damage their relations with the central government, dependent as they were on its protection. This was a fact that Zionist activists were acutely aware of.

If the strategy of invoking Jewish power reflected local Jews' admiration and trust in their American allies, it also betrayed the fact that Jews had few other options. In the face of waning support for minority protection among the Great Powers, Jews had little choice but to play on non-Jews' inflated perceptions of Jewish power. While this strategy might have worked to hold the attention of Czechs to Jews' concerns, the encouragement of this discourse became a threat once Jews' goals were no longer in sync with those of the Czech leaders. Furthermore, while Zionists worked to create an image of shared interest between themselves and the Czechoslovak leadership, their voices were hard to hear amid the clamor of a much broader and more ingrained discourse of the threat of Jewish power to the Czech and Slovak nations. Indeed, one wonders to what extent Zionists' deployment of these discourses – their exaggerated depictions of Jews' influence with American leaders and world politics and their threats of international press campaigns and sanctions – nurtured anti-Jewish perceptions. Trapped in the midst of an avalanche of antisemitism, Jews were damned if they didn't utilize these beliefs – and damned if they did.

* * *

From the outset, Zionists participated in the construction of the myth of Czechoslovakia as unique among the states in Eastern Europe. This was not a reflection of trust between Jews and Czechs. Rather, Zionists played along because the only way to get the attention of the Czech leaders – to move them to protect the Jewish communities under their jurisdiction and to hold them to their assurances of equality for Jews in the new state – was to rely on the latter's respect for Jewish power. In short, Zionists convinced the Czechs that the fate of Jews at home was important to the fortunes of Czechoslovakia abroad. After the formal establishment of Czechoslovakia with the Treaty of Saint-Germain on September 10, 1919, Tomáš G. Masaryk and Edvard Beneš continued to view the country's international image as a significant strategic tool in the new European order.

This had an immediate impact on the authorities' relationship to Jews. Rebekah Klein-Pejšová has shown that the Czechoslovak authorities cooperated with local Jewish communities and the American Jewish Joint Distribution Committee to shelter, feed, and find permanent homes abroad for Galician and other Jewish war refugees in the years after the war. Sensitive to the damage the anti-Jewish violence in the Bohemian Lands and Slovakia in 1918–1919 might have done to Czechoslovakia's image abroad, the authorities extended Jews a refuge in Czechoslovakia that in turn facilitated local and international Jewish actors' ability to provide aid for the refugees until they were able to emigrate.[138] Klein-Pejšová argues that at least domestically this forthcoming attitude toward the Jewish refugees nourished Jews' loyalty to the new state. Indeed, as Marsha L. Rozenblit suggests, Czechoslovakia offered Jews in the Bohemian Lands an opportunity to continue to cultivate a "tripartite" identity: ethnically Jewish, culturally Czech and German, but now politically loyal to Czechoslovakia instead of the Habsburg Monarchy. It was a transfer of political allegiance that became embodied by Jews' reverence for Tomáš G. Masaryk, who now replaced the emperor as the object of Jews' affection and trust.[139]

The Czech leadership's enormous investment in cultural diplomacy – in the publication and dissemination of propaganda materials in multiple language, the public lecture tours and other cultural events abroad, and the cultivation of alliances with domestic constituents in Great Power states – reflects that they placed significant emphasis on creating and maintaining an image of Czechoslovakia that would garner favor with international, and especially British, French, and American, audiences.[140] Masaryk, Beneš, and other leading Czech politicians' concern about image and uncertainty about Jews' ability to influence it created an opening for local Zionists. They managed to convince the Czechs that the fate of vulnerable Jews at home mattered because powerful Jews abroad cared. Thus, thanks to "Jewish power," local Zionists gained access to the corridors of high politics from which they would otherwise have been excluded. This was the case as much in 1919 as it was in 1940.

The experience of the First World War, the unprecedented victimization of Jews and the upsurge in antisemitism, coexisted with a bold and public Jewish activism. If Zionists did not in the end have the ability to convince Czech leaders to give in to international Jewish demands for special protection, it was not because they did not try. In the Bohemian Lands, Jews brought together by their Zionism and wartime activism worked hard, relentlessly, to secure the authorities' protection of the country's Jews. They alerted the Czech leaders to the risks involved in remaining tolerant of antisemitism and unresponsive to Jews' pleas for help. Zionists succeeded in convincing Czech leaders to stand up to popular calls for the immediate expulsion of Jewish refugees and to suppress violence against Jews, even if this happened only in the name of public order. They persuaded the Czechs that they could make international political gains by appearing forthcoming to Jews' concerns. In the years that followed, Zionists continued to uphold the image of Czechoslovakia as an exceptional place for Jews in Eastern Europe. Although in the early postwar years this was more aspiration than experience, Zionists made a decision to play along and to hold the Czechs to their promises of protection and equal rights for Jews. It was a strategy that remained central to Zionist politics in Czechoslovakia in the interwar years.

The Czechoslovak Constitution of February 29, 1920, did grant equality to the country's minorities, as had been agreed in Paris. It did not award rights to specific minorities. Jews' rights were included under the general provision securing equality before the law for the country's religious, racial, and linguistic minorities. But aside from equality for Jews, the Czechoslovak National Assembly did include another one of the Zionist leadership's requests. The constitutional articles that accompanied the main text specified that Jewish citizens were free to identify nationally as Jews regardless of their language abilities and use. As they would in the years to come, Czech leaders gave in to Zionist demands when they believed it was in their interest to do so. On the question of the census, as the next chapter shows, Czech priorities and Zionist goals coincided, and both parties could celebrate a political victory. The Jewish National Council welcomed this implicit recognition of Jews as a national minority as a sign of Czech leaders' commitment to full equality for Jews by ensuring them individual civil and collective national rights.[141] Ludvík Singer and his colleagues believed that despite the breakdown of talks in Paris, the ongoing attacks and hostility against Jews, and the lack of an explicit recognition of Jews' national rights, this was nevertheless a moment of victory for the Jewish National Council, a turning point for Zionists in Czechoslovakia. Yet, for these Jewish activists, part of a nationalist movement that had only recently entered the political stage in the Bohemian Lands and whose popular support among Jews in Czechoslovakia as a whole remained untested, the battle for the legitimacy of their leadership and of Jews' national rights had just begun.

THREE

Mapping Jews

SOCIAL SCIENCE AND THE MAKING OF CZECHOSLOVAK JEWRY

IN THE SUMMER OF 1941, THE WELL-KNOWN CZECH DEMOGRAPHER Antonín Boháč (1882–1950) was asked by the leadership of the Czech resistance to compose a memorandum on the nationality question in postwar Czechoslovakia. Not surprisingly, his book-length treatise focused on the historical relationship between Germans and Czechs. At one point, when discussing the social scientific definition of nationhood, he noted about Jews:

> Jews are an interesting example of a defective nation, one that used to be a nation in the full meaning of the term. Jews had their own state and territory, language and distinct culture. When they lost their political freedom and were dispersed across the world, [Jews] lost not only their homeland, but, in these foreign environments, also their national language. Yet even then, they preserved a sense of national difference, a strong emotional connection to the land of their ancestors and do therefore constitute a distinct nation. It is, however, an impaired one that does not live a full national life. Nevertheless, Jews do not stop being a nation, much like a person who goes blind or deaf is still a human being.[1]

Although Boháč did not otherwise concern himself with Jews in this piece of writing, he had done so in the interwar years as one of Czechoslovakia's leading experts on nationalities. In 1919, he had overseen the design of Czechoslovakia's first census that included Jews as a national minority. Unlike the country's other nationalities, Jews did not have to provide ethno-linguistic evidence for their national identification. By making an exception for Jews, the Czechoslovak census makers accommodated Jews' particularity purportedly caused by centuries of dispersion. Yet, regardless of this exemption, in interwar Czechoslovakia, the normative ideal for nationhood was that of an ancestral community defined by a shared language, a mother tongue passed on from generation to generation that distinguished one nation from another.

If Jews' distinctiveness as a nation – one that lacked the most significant of national features, a shared language – had been granted legitimacy by the census makers, other observers and institutions were less willing to accommodate Jews' "impairment." Through the 1920s and '30s, Jews' status as a national minority was contested by the courts, by political elites, and by a diverse array of critics. In response, Zionist activists, who had been instrumental in convincing the state authorities to grant Jews' national – and not merely religious – minority status, marshaled wide-ranging statistical, ethnographical, and historical evidence to counter the voices that questioned Jews' nationhood. Zionist experts worked to transform perceptions of Jews' inadequacies, their imperfection and want as a nation, from a topic of shame and inferiority into a point of pride and distinction; indeed, into evidence of the Jewish nation's authenticity and historical uniqueness. In doing so, they aimed at changing Jews' self-perception as well as non-Jews' attitudes toward Jews. To Zionists, the state authorities and other observers' willingness to accommodate Jews' particularity tested their commitment to equal rights for Jews as individuals and as a national collective. For Zionists, the inclusion of the category "Jewish nationality" in the census was a significant step on the path to equality for Jews in interwar Czechoslovakia.

This chapter examines how the interwar population census, the statistical representation of the country's population, became a vehicle for Zionists' construction of a legitimate place for Jews in Czechoslovakia. Faced with demands of Jews' unconditional commitment to the new state in the postwar years, Zionists were eager to produce evidence that demonstrated that Jews were a loyal and integrative force in Czechoslovakia. The census (and the statistical data it produced) was an important mode of nation building for Zionist activists. For them, nationalism created order out of the perceived chaos of Jews' fluid and diverse linguistic and cultural identities. They wanted to transform Jews into a unified national community, a nation with firm boundaries and stable political loyalties. The census's summarizing and homogenizing categories in general, and its creation and enumeration of ethnic collectives in particular, facilitated the construction of a Jewish nation in Czechoslovakia.[2] In turning to statistics as an instrument for political assertion, Zionists adopted an important mode of governance and legitimization developed by the modern state.

Since the mid-nineteenth century, social sciences and statistics have played an important role in the modern state's management of its population and resources. Statistical practices made territories and their inhabitants legible to the administrative centers often far from their objects in geography and culture.[3] This process of mapping, however, rather than depicting an objective reality, as its practitioners trusted, reflected the way in which technocrats imagined the landscapes, economic and social networks, and communities they were studying. Even though these statistical practices were first developed by states eager to control and extract resources from within their borders, the authority of numbers to convey "facts" became useful to other groups competing for power. For the disenfranchised, statistics was also a language of social contestation. As Jacqueline Urla suggests, statistics and social sciences was a way in which marginalized groups made themselves visible, enabling them to articulate their differences and make claims upon the state and its resources.[4]

This chapter examines how Zionist social scientists and activists successfully lobbied the census designers and politicians to include "Jewish" among the census's choices of national identification. Although the visibility afforded by statistics was important, the data needed interpreters to become useful political narratives. Jewish experts took the lead in explaining the meaning of the results produced by the census. They did so in ways that weaved Jews into Czechoslovakia's ethnographical fabric on a local and a countrywide level, threads that held the whole together, past and present.

Zionists turned to statistics as a means for establishing themselves as a political force in Czechoslovakia. In the 1920 parliamentary elections, Zionist candidates did not receive enough votes to gain representation in the National Assembly. Furthermore, at this time Zionists were unsure of their appeal among Jews. They therefore tapped into a familiar tradition for measuring the size and political weight of a nation: the census. In the late Habsburg period, Czech and German minority activists, regardless of their formal political influence, had successfully used the census results to make claims on public resources.[5] Zionists now turned to the census for political legitimacy as they cast themselves as a natural Jewish leadership even though they lacked both parliamentary representation and a well-established position at the helm of the country's Jewish communities. At the same time, Zionists were well aware that their success depended on their ability to ally themselves with the country's new elite by aligning Jewish with Czechoslovak interests. Eager to portray the country's Jews as a loyal and useful minority, activists put the census data to use countering voices that questioned Jews' belonging in and commitment to the new state.

By doing so, Zionists in the Bohemian Lands adopted a well-established practice among Jewish activists in Central Europe of using statistics and social science as a form of resistance to dominant discourses about Jews. Historians have shown how Jewish scholars employed statistics and social science to diagnose and prescribe solutions to the so-called Jewish Question. Whether they perceived the crisis in Jewish life to be of a socioeconomic, cultural, medical, political, or national nature, the discourses they created were often simultaneously self-critical and apologetic.[6] In other words, they sought to remedy the Jewish condition and challenge misconceptions about Jews, meanwhile insisting on their amenability and equality. By drawing on the power of numbers and science, Jewish experts sought to shape the ways in which Jews and non-Jews alike perceived Jews' difference. By the late nineteenth century, Zionists were at the forefront in the collection and publication of statistical knowledge about Jews as a national community. As Mitchell Hart argues, Zionists believed that statistical and scientific knowledge about Jews was an integral part of the process of national regeneration. The knowledge itself was a vehicle for nation building.[7] This chapter examines how this double process of political assertion and nation building played itself out on a local level in interwar Czechoslovakia.

This study does not claim that the census results can be read as evidence of individuals' and groups' national belonging or their sense of national identification. At the time, there were competing interpretations of the census results among Jewish observers. The anti-Zionist Jewish

Conservative Party in Subcarpathian Rus', for example, claimed to have convinced a majority of the region's Jews to claim Jewish nationality in the 1921 census. To them this was a sign of loyalty to the state and hence *not* an expression of a commitment to Zionism or Jewish nationhood.[8] As the chapter shows, contemporary observers, activists, and respondents contested the 1921 and 1930 census results. This was due to the definitions employed, the categories included and excluded, and the census's highly politicized execution. Individuals' choices were likely shaped by a multiplicity of social, cultural, political, and legal considerations as well as by a general uncertainty as to the consequences of one's answer to the question about national affiliation. People's nationality, for example, determined not only in which schools their children belonged, but also what language they could use in correspondence with public offices.

Furthermore, it is unclear to what degree census commissioners influenced or overruled individuals' answers and even to what extent individuals and communities were actually visited by census commissioners, considering that the censuses took place in the winter months February (1921) and December (1930).[9] One observer, the scholar Emanuel Rádl (1873–1942), who was highly critical of the political weight and scientific authority awarded the census, pointed to the ways in which census commissioners adopted their own criteria for determining the accuracy of an individual's statement of national belonging. The regulations stated that mother tongue was the primary ethnic, and therefore national, marker and that commissioners should verify whether the respondent was answering truthfully. Yet, census takers routinely, according to Rádl's source, employed other methods:

> Among Jews we did not bother to persuade ourselves whether they really spoke Slovak at home. We knew that their language is Hungarian or German. This is still the case today and yet they would still declare themselves to be Czechoslovaks. The point is not whether they really speak Slovak at home, but what language the individual declares when asked, that is *what language he could speak* if he did not consider it a language of maids, something inferior, and thus unsuitable for the intimate sphere of the home.[10]

Although the census regulations were clad in a mantle of science and objectivity, as public servants census commissioners were well aware that their goal was to register as many "Czechoslovaks" as possible.

Indeed, the category "Czechoslovak" came about by merging respondents who declared Czech or Slovak languages as their mother tongue into one group. The census makers thereby attempted to maximize the number of "Czechoslovaks" vis-à-vis the country's other nationalities. This was a strategy they hoped would silence the voices critical of the fact that substantial German- and Hungarian-speaking minorities were included into the new state, populations that were thereby denied their right to national self-determination. Thus, when it came to Jewish respondents, in some instances, the census commissioners simply ignored the linguistic criterion, deeming it irrelevant. This practice reflected a broader understanding that when it came to national belonging, Jews were inherently opportunist *and* inherently other. The commissioners expected Jews to change their identifications in accordance with the shifting political winds. For the purposes of the census, Jews could be counted as "Czechoslovaks," thereby adding weight to the dominant nationality. This was a practice they adopted from the much despised Austro-Hungarian authorities, who counted many Jews among German-, Hungarian-, and Polish-speakers in the various provinces. They did so, at times, in accordance with Jews' language use; at others, in response to the authorities' own political need for a statistical majority. In short, the importance of the census for this study lies primarily in the meaning with which it was invested by activists, politicians, and social scientists rather than as a reflection of social reality.

A NOTE ON TERMINOLOGY

In studies such as the present one, which examines the discursive creation of a Jewish nation, it is difficult to avoid using terminology developed by scholars and other actors whose worldview was shaped by "groupism." Coined by the sociologist Rogers Brubaker in his critique of nationalism studies, "groupism" denotes the practice "to treat ethnic groups, nations, and races as substantial entities to which interests and agency can be attributed."[11] The experts and politicians discussed in this chapter assumed that races, ethnic groups, and nations existed as clearly bounded social actors whose members shared a number of characteristics, be they linguistic, biological, cultural, religious, or social – a sameness that defined distinct groups and the individuals belonging to them.

Although there were opposing voices, the aforementioned Emanuel Rádl being one, in interwar Czechoslovakia the social scientific establishment viewed ethnic origin and nationality as closely interconnected. This was a belief that found expression in legislation passed in those years. One representative of this view was Antonín Boháč. In 1919, he served as an expert witness at the postwar negotiations in Paris. Later that year, as the head of the State Statistical Bureau's demography section, Boháč was charged with the new country's population census. His views on the relationship between ethnic groups and nations can serve as an illustration of how social scientists, Zionists among them, thought about nationhood in the interwar years. Boháč defined ethnic groups as communities of kin.[12] Nations constituted communities of kin that were brought together by linguistic similarity and territorial proximity. A nation thus emerged out of a fusion of several ethnic groups. Over time, Boháč argued, a nation would manifest itself as a community of shared origin, language, homeland, economy, history, traditions, and culture and a common will to political sovereignty. Boháč distinguished between ethnic groups and nations as a way of explaining the linguistic and sociocultural differences within national communities. Yet, shared ethnic origin remained central to nationhood.

In interwar Czechoslovakia, the dominant social scientific community, empowered by the political elite to make recommendations regarding the census and other national identification practices, assumed that national belonging was inherited, not adopted. Such assumptions had far-reaching consequences. For example, the perceived link between ethnic origin and nationality shaped the census makers' designation of an individual's mother tongue as a primary national marker. This practice overruled an individual's own identifications and dismissed the significance of languages acquired later in life. In short, national belonging was ascribed to people in accordance with the ethnic evidence they were able to provide.[13] In 1925, officials were compelled to ascribe children a nationality at birth according to the mother's national belonging.[14] Nevertheless, even as they promoted discourses linking ancestry and nationality, Boháč and his colleagues also recognized a degree of fluidity due to intermarriage between individuals from different groups, to cultural adaptation, and to social and political pressures to assimilate with a group other than one's community of origin. These social scientists saw their task as one of uncovering everyone's real nationality as well as creating legislation and practices that subsequently hardened and fixed national boundaries. To them this was the key not only to a "Czechoslovak" majority in the country, but also to political and social stability in a country with a great deal of linguistic and cultural diversity.

STATISTICS IN THE SERVICE OF NATION BUILDERS

During their first meetings with Czech leaders in the last weeks of the war, the Jewish National Council had made it a priority to have the upcoming census include the category "Jewish nationality" as an option when respondents declared their national belonging. With minority rights on the international agenda, Zionists hoped that a census mapping Jews alongside the country's other nationalities would make the Jewish nation visible. The census, they believed, would demonstrate that Jews were a national community with valid demands for resources and representation.

In the immediate postwar months, as the borders of the new Czechoslovakia emerged on the drawing table in Paris, it was unclear whether the country's national minorities would be granted some form of political representation such as permanent parliamentary seats or officially recognized national governing bodies. Eventually, the provisions for minority rights that guaranteed equality before the law and equal civic and political rights regardless of race, language, and nationality were incorporated into the Czechoslovak Constitution prepared by the Czech and Slovak delegates of the so-called revolutionary National Assembly. This Czech-dominated leadership was determined not to name specific national minority groups or group rights in the constitutional documents, but only to commit themselves to the general minority rights. In addition to legal equality, the provisions included protection from "denationalization" and the right to public education in a minority language in areas where a "considerable faction" spoke this language.[15] The law specified that a minority language would be granted public status only in jurisdictions where minority language speakers constituted 20 percent or more of the population. The tradition for national cadasters in Moravia and in the Bohemian town of České Budějovice/Budweis, which fixed the numbers of Czechs and Germans in a jurisdiction and where Germans could vote only for German candidates, and Czechs for Czech ones, was abolished and replaced with a universal electorate. This was done to allow for the "uncovering" of as many "Czechoslovaks" as possible, people that Czech elites believed had been forcibly denationalized by the former dominant Germans.[16]

In June 1919, with the negotiations in Paris in full swing, local elections were held in the Bohemian Lands. With the ongoing tensions on the border between Slovakia and Hungary, this was the only part of the new state deemed stable enough to make elections feasible. Zionist candidates were elected to municipal councils in Bohemia and Moravia. The following year in the parliamentary elections held in the Bohemian Lands and Slovakia, the Zionist candidates collected 79,714 votes. Although Zionists considered this as an encouraging turnout, the number of votes was not enough to secure even one Zionist representative in the National Assembly.[17] Having lost this avenue for visibility and influence, Zionists refocused their attention on the upcoming population census.

The Prague-based State Statistical Bureau began preparations for the country's first census in the fall of 1918. This statistical event was defined in important ways by its Habsburg legacy. The Austrian census did not formally count nationalities; it asked only for language of daily use and therefore registered only linguistic communities. Yet, this was not how nationalists and other commentators interpreted the data. In the Bohemian Lands, German and Czech nationalists alike perceived one nation's gains as the other one's loss. Propaganda and intimidation were therefore part and parcel of the census days, when nationalists sought to capture as many souls for their nation as possible by ensuring that individuals declared this or the other language.[18] The battles were especially intense in mixed communities of Czech- and German-speakers, where nationalists used the census to measure the strength of the competing national groups and thereby each other's claim on public resources. In the previous decades, Czech nationalists had been fiercely critical of Austrian census practices, especially the registration of everyday language rather than mother tongue. According to Czech nationalists, the category of everyday language favored the dominant German population at the expense of the socially weaker Czechs. They claimed that Czechs were "forced" – for example, by employers or landlords – to use or declare German as their everyday language, thereby unjustly diminishing the Czech population's language rights and their access to Czech schools.[19] To Czech activists, who imagined their nation as a community of origin, mother tongue defined an individual's true national belonging. This historical experience, argued Antonín Boháč, had galvanized a consensus among Czech statisticians that in the new postwar census, mother tongue, "the most objective and stable marker of ethnic belonging," was to act as evidence of an individual's nationality. In contrast to the Austrian practice, which had shied away from defining national entities through language use, the Czechoslovak census would ask directly about national affiliation. Language (mother tongue) now enumerated national communities.[20]

The Czechoslovak census makers' search for objective ethnic markers was not as much a departure from Austrian practices as perhaps imagined. By the turn of the century, in Austrian legal practice, national belonging was increasingly understood in ethnic terms and believed to be verifiable through objective markers such as an individual's language, social and professional affiliations, and origin.[21] Furthermore, people's ability to choose national belonging was trumped by public and nationalist authorities' capacity to ascribe to individuals and their children a particular national affiliation. School boards, for example, were empowered to determine a child's nationality, overriding parents' claims, when determining whether a student belonged in a Czech- or a German-language school. Thus, even though Czech nationalists continued to imagine their nation to be under constant Austrian assimilating pressure, they and other nationalist activists had in fact succeeded in empowering public authorities to ascribe national belonging to people. By the turn of the twentieth century, the nation's rights trumped that of individual choice. Although it was contested by some legal experts, ethno-national ascription had increasingly become the legal practice in the Bohemian Lands during the last decades of Austrian reign.[22]

Despite the alleged consensus on the new census design among the Czech statisticians and politicians, once they were the ones in search of a statistical majority, considerable disagreement erupted among the members of the State Statistical Bureau. Some called for individuals' subjective choice of nationality. Others wanted objective criteria to govern national identification, either by listing nationality and language as separate categories or by making nationality dependent on corresponding ethnic evidence. In the end, a narrow majority decided on a procedure where "nationality is understood as ethnic belonging for which the main external marker is mother tongue."[23] While the Czech authorities claimed that the census "would provide correct, accurate, and honest information about the character of the population," there was significant uncertainty as to the census results' ability to document a substantial Czech and Slovak majority.[24]

To avoid embarrassment and ensure this majority, the Statistical Bureau created the category "Czechoslovak." As Jeremy King notes, by merging claims of Czech or Slovak nationality, the census "helped to paper over the inconvenient fact that ethnic Germans in the Slavic state numbered too many: only about 50 percent less than ethnic Czechs, and about 50 percent *more* than ethnic Slovaks."[25] There was therefore considerable uncertainty among Czech leaders as to Czechoslovaks' numerical strength, and by extension the census's utility in documenting the right of Czechs and Slovaks to national self-determination. This insecurity made them receptive to calls for the census to include special regulations for determining the nationality of the country's Jewish population. Czech statistical experts agreed that Jews, despite having "lost their national language," shared physical, socioeconomic, and religious characteristics constituting a distinct ethnic group yet a particular kind of national one. There was disagreement in the Statistical Bureau whether this particularity should find expression in the census.[26] In the end, Jews were awarded an exemption from the general rule ascribing nationality according to mother tongue, as the census regulations added that "Jews can declare Jewish nationality" regardless of their mother tongue.[27] Thus, Jews could choose either Jewish nationality or a nationality according to mother tongue. For the purposes of the census, religion was to act as the objective marker of an individual's ethnic Jewish origin.

In defining Jews' status as a nationality, the Statistical Bureau sought to balance multiple, contradictory political demands and legal restrictions. According to the Austrian Legal Code, the provisions of which remained in place in many instances, Jews were recognized collectively only as a religious community. In the years before the First World War, Jewish interest groups and the Austrian courts had sunk Jewish nationalists' attempts to have Jews recognized as one of the monarchy's nationalities by arguing that ascribing Jewish nationality to Jews deprived them of the right to belong to other nations. Jewish citizens (whom the state authorities perceived as a religious group) would thereby be denied rights enjoyed by other Austrian citizens merely on the basis of a difference in religion, a breach of the 1867 Constitution that awarded Jews' equal rights.[28] After 1918, the Statistical Bureau upheld this liberal tradition but added "that Jews could not be forced to declare other ethnic national belonging than Jewish during censuses, elections, and other public events," thereby effectively recognizing Jews as a nationality.[29] The bureau guaranteed individual Jews' right not to have their options limited by their religious affiliation yet allowed the census to reflect that Jews were considered, by many within the political and social scientific community, to be a separate ethnic group. Jews' ancestry thus precluded them ethnographically if not formally from belonging among other national groups.[30] Before the war, some Austrian judicial and political voices had been keen to "retain" Jews within the community of German-speakers in the Austrian monarchy. Now, a majority of the Statistical Bureau's experts, tasked with designing a census that documented a Czechoslovak majority, were eager to either "neutralize" Jews' presence by letting Jews opt for Jewish nationality or allow Jews to choose Czechoslovak national belonging.

The Jewish National Council actively sought to influence the census makers in order to secure the exemption for Jews. In late October 1920, just days before the Statistical Bureau was to publish the census guidelines, Artur Kauders (1867–?) and Max Brod, as representatives of the council, submitted a memorandum to the government warning that failure to consider Jews' particularity would produce "unwelcome results."[31] If members of the Statistical Bureau decided to register individuals' mother tongue and not ask about national belonging, then, the authors warned, the census "might falsely strengthen certain nationalities with members of the Jewish nationality whose mother tongue is one of these nationalities'."[32] Leaving no doubt as to what groups might benefit, they suggested that registering language would "strengthen the domination of the Hungarian and German nationalities." Drawing on the Czech nationalist trope of the Austrian state's manipulative and denationalizing census practices, they pointed out that polling language rather than nationality would make the census scientifically inaccurate. Since Jews spoke the language of other nationalities, a question about language would effectively erase the Jewish nation statistically. Equally as significant, it would be unconstitutional, as Jews, contrary to the guarantees made just months earlier, would be counted as members of other ethnic communities. Instead, Kauders and Brod proposed, in order to ensure "satisfactory results," the census ought to include questions about national belonging as well as mother tongue. Aware of the census makers' disagreement regarding objective markers or subjective choice of nationality, the Jewish leadership insisted that Jewish nationality could be defined objectively by ethnic origin (*kmenová příslušnost*) *and* subjectively by national consciousness (*uvědomění národní*).[33] Only by asking directly about national belonging in the census, the memorandum concluded, would it be possible for "the majority of people of Jewish origin who identify as Jewish nationals" to express their true national belonging. A few days later, the census regulations were passed defining nationality according to mother tongue, but explicitly exempting Jews from this general rule, thereby effectively meeting the Jewish National Council's demands.

Historians who have pondered the question of the Czech leaders' receptiveness to Zionists' arguments point to ideological as well as pragmatic answers. Hillel J. Kieval and Kateřina Čapková alike argue that Tomáš Masaryk's active support for the Zionists' demands and wider program played an important part in ensuring Jews' inclusion as a religious *and* national community in the census. Yet, as Kieval, Čapková, and other scholars have noted, there were also more immediate and pragmatic motives at play.[34] Considering the importance of the census results, ideological sympathies, such as Masaryk's, were only likely to gain a political life if the government perceived them as enhancing the Czechoslovak cause, in this case minimizing the numbers of Germans and Hungarians in relation to the "Czechoslovak" majority. Much like the census commissioner quoted earlier, many observers believed that Jews preferred German and Hungarian to Slovak (and presumably Czech) and therefore made up a significant part of the German- and Hungarian-speaking communities in the Bohemian Lands and Slovakia. Some German leaders feared that allowing Jews to opt for Jewish nationality would harm German minority language and nationality rights as German-speaking Jews "withdrew" from the German nationality.[35] As language rights were dependent on minority language speakers constituting 20 percent or more of a jurisdiction's total population, German nationalists worried about their ability to obtain rights in communities with a Czech majority. Likewise, Czech leaders believed that recognizing Jewish nationality and distinguishing between ethnic belonging and language in the case of Jews would significantly diminish the number of Germans.[36] The potential for "withdrawing Jews from the German numbers" was, according to the prominent German demographer and member of the Statistical Bureau Heinrich Rauchberg (1860–1938), decisive. The bureau's Czech members opted to register nationality rather than mother tongue, he claimed, so "that Jews could be separated from Germans."[37] In Slovakia, it was Hungarian activists who believed they had much to lose by Hungarian-speaking Jews' "withdrawal." Similar to the situation in the Bohemian Lands, in Slovakia, Rebekah Klein-Pejšová shows, Jews' weight was not statistically significant, but locally, Jews' choice of nationality could tip the scale below 20 percent for Hungarian-speakers in many municipalities.[38]

The German and Hungarian activists were right to be concerned. Between 1910 and 1921, the number of Jews who declared German as their language of everyday use or later mother tongue declined by 14,438 in Bohemia (from 48% to 35% of the region's Jews). In Moravia, 29,676 fewer Jews opted for German in 1921 than in 1910 (from 86% to 35%). To most observers, and certainly the interpretation promoted by Zionists, many German-speaking Jews had opted for Jewish national belonging when given the opportunity in 1921. In Bohemia, 15% of the Jewish population opted for Jewish national belonging (11,156), and in Moravia, 49% of the region's Jews declared Jewish national belonging

(18,955).[39] The "loss" of Jews in absolute numbers was not as significant as the potential impact of Jews' so-called "withdrawal" in communities where German-speakers were a minority and had to qualify for German-language public institutions and practices. In Slovakia, the drop in the number of Hungarian-speakers was also very significant. Here, there were 325,423 fewer "Hungarians" in 1921. Significantly, the number of Jews who declared Hungarian nationality (formerly mother tongue) went from 106,552 to 21,584.[40] A slight majority of Jews in Slovakia opted for Jewish nationality in 1921. As in the Bohemian Lands, in Slovakia Jews' choices of nationality appeared yet again to have an adverse impact on other nationalities. The counting of national souls was, from the perspective of Hungarian- and German-speaking activists, a zero sum game. From the perspective of the Czechoslovak authorities, however, a decline in the numbers of Germans and Hungarians was a win regardless of whether the "side switchers" chose Jewish or Czechoslovak nationality.

As time passed and the country's second census came around in 1930, some Czech politicians began to doubt that the exemption for Jews diminished German or Czech numbers in the Bohemian Lands. During this debate over the census design, some suggested that Hebrew and Yiddish be designated as Jewish national languages and hence as the ethnic evidence required to claim Jewish nationality. This was a proposal that would annul the 1921 census's exemption for Jews.[41] Zionist leaders were quick to mobilize *against* this proposal. Since few Jews in the Bohemian Lands and parts of Slovakia could claim Hebrew or Yiddish as their mother tongue, the Jewish nation would be erased statistically precisely in those regions where the competition to claim Jews for other nations was fiercest. Responding to the Jewish National Council's letter protesting this initiative, President Masaryk's office made no bones about Czech leaders' motivations for including "Jewish" on the list of nationalities: "The inclusion of the Jewish nationality in 1921 was the outcome of the fact that in that census nationality was to be defined according to language. Thus, for political reasons, namely in order to weaken the Hungarian and German communities, Jews were exempted from this general rule." But it has become clear, the letter continued, that the "creation of a new sixth nationality" had also decreased the numbers of "Czechoslovaks." Despite the sense among Czech nationalist members of the Statistical Bureau that "the anticipated political gains [of the exemption] had been overestimated," the 1921 census regulations regarding Jewish nationality remained in place.[42] Even though the presidential office might have felt secure about Jews' "Czechoslovak" identity, some Czech circles did not.[43] Czech nationalists were not convinced that Jews had let go of their alleged German and Hungarian loyalties. They worried that removing the exemption for Jews would weaken the Czechoslovak position.[44]

ZIONISTS AND THE CENSUS

The Zionist leadership was as adamant about the importance of the statistical representation of Jewish nationality in 1930 as it had been in the immediate postwar period. The category "Jewish nationality" allowed Zionists to articulate Jews' difference in national terms. They relied on the census's homogenizing effects to erase sociocultural, regional, and linguistic differences among Jews and represent Jews as one national entity. In this way, Jews' statistical representation was crucial in validating Zionists' posturing as representatives of one of the country's national minorities.

When addressing Jewish audiences, Zionists promoted "Jewish nationality" as the most immediate and effective way of pushing back against antisemitism. It was precisely the Austrian census's assimilation of Jews into "foreign" nations by way of Jews' language that had fueled the competition for their loyalties between different groups of nationalists, Zionists argued. By choosing Jewish nationality, they suggested, Jews could assert their neutrality, opt out of the battle between Czechs and Germans, Slovaks and Hungarians, and eliminate one of the root causes of antisemitism. Addressing the Jewish public preceding the 1921 and 1930 censuses, Zionist leaders assured their readers of the legality of claiming "Jewish" as national belonging as well as of the secrecy of their choice. Meanwhile they also warned of the consequences of "unwelcome results" whose publication, they claimed, would lead to an increase in antisemitism.[45] The intense politicization of the census only heightened the importance of Jews considering the consequences of their statement of national belonging. "Everybody is trying to recruit Jews for themselves today," and, one author cautioned, if Jews fail to opt for neutrality, "in the same way, they will *all* [my emphasis] turn against the Jews accusing them of siding with their enemies."[46] In the current climate, Jews could not afford to be nationally indifferent or loyal to any other nation but the Jewish one.

In 1921, despite the census makers' claims that the census was registering objective ethnic markers, nationalist groups acted to persuade individuals of their "true" nationality, much as in an election campaign. Zionists were no exception. In the Zionist press, the census was presented as an opportunity, much like the recent elections, to express Jews' "will to Jewish nationhood," "a commitment to neutrality in the nationality conflict," and loyalty to the new order.[47] The census could be another forceful public statement of Jews' unity, these writers suggested, making it impossible for the authorities to ignore the interests of this "sizable minority."[48] Almost a decade later, neutrality and public Jewish unity remained central themes in Zionists' campaign to mobilize Jews to "vote" for Jewish nationhood in the 1929 parliamentary elections and in the country's second census the following year.[49]

The statistical representation of a Jewish ethnic collective was also an important step in legitimizing Zionists' claim that Jews were a nation. As the public debate preceding the two censuses showed, the notion that Jews constituted a religious *and* a national minority was a contested one.[50] Weeks before the 1921 census, the Association of Czech-Jews (Svaz Čecho-židů) issued a statement in which they welcomed the opportunity to express their Czech national belonging directly rather than simply answering a question about everyday language. Dismissing Zionism as veil for some Jews' continued loyalty to German language and culture and as a derailment of a natural fusion of Jews with their environment, they noted:

> Jews who were born in Czech regions, and especially Jews whose families have lived here for generations, are in our opinion an inseparable part of the Czech nation. . . . Is it really necessary to point out again that two thousand years of history separates us from other Jews and ties us to our surroundings? We don't deny that there are certain differences between us and other Czechs or that we have ties (mostly emotional ones) to other

> Jewish communities, but these differences only make us a somewhat recognizable subset of the Czech nation, much like Czech aristocrats and Czech Protestants.[51]

Even though the tone of the official Czech-Jewish statement implied that they did not see Zionists' initial success in shaping the design of the census as a threat nor felt the need to rehash the arguments for or against Zionism, Czech-Jews were well aware of the importance of the census in establishing Jewish nationhood as a social fact. In the week following the 1921 census, Otto Bondy, writing in the Czech-Jewish weekly *Rozvoj*, lamented:

> In accordance with the results of the census, our schools will now be teaching with textbooks that declare that in our republic alongside so and so many Czechs, there are this many Germans, this many Hungarians, and this many Jews. It is only natural that in a child's mind Germans, Hungarians, as well as Jews are going to be considered foreigners . . . and the only ones who can take the credit for this are the Zionists. . . . Through their petitions they made the ministry include a fake [*fingované*] Jewish nationality in the census regulations, which have been distributed in the millions across the country.[52]

If Czech-Jews saw the recognition of Jewish nationality as detrimental to Jews, marking them as outsiders, as foreigners who did not belong, Zionists were convinced that creating firm boundaries between Jews and non-Jews was the first step in revolutionizing the relations between them.[53] By depicting the country's Jews as a community of ethnic origin, a notion supported by widespread belief that Jews were culturally and racially different from non-Jews, Zionists positioned Jews as equal to the country's other nationalities defined similarly as ethnic groups.

In a series of articles on the results of the first census, Gustav Fleischmann (1896–?), a Zionist activist and high-ranking bureaucrat in Prague's Jewish community, analyzed the success of Zionist efforts by comparing the numbers of ethnic Jews – that is, Jews by religion (Israelites) – to the number of Jews who had declared Jewish nationality in each locality across the Bohemian Lands.[54] Using religion to demarcate the *real* Jewish nation, Fleischmann focused on the reasons for the discrepancy between the numbers in the two columns. By suggesting that Jews' choice of national belonging other than Jewish was the result of intimidation, conformity, or indifference, Fleischmann depicted any inconsistency between ethnic and national identities as untruthful and opportunist.[55] "Either out of habit or fear," he argued, "many Jews who are both subjectively and objectively members of the Jewish nationality chose to declare their nationality according to their language."[56]

This blurring of boundaries between religious and national Jewish communities, a practice that ascribed Jewish national belonging to *all* Jews by way of their religion, was common among Zionists. Like many of their nationalist peers, they believed that their nation was a "community of blood."[57] Individuals fancying themselves as part of a nation different from their ethnic community simply suffered from a sort of "false consciousness."[58] To Zionists, the only authentic national option for Jews was the one that corresponded to their ethnic origin.[59] By ascribing all Jews Jewish nationality, Zionists could claim to represent a countrywide constituency. In a parliamentary speech criticizing the proposed changes to the 1930 census, Ludvík Singer, then a newly elected MP for the Jewish Party, claimed that he represented "the country's 350,000 Jews, of which 180,000 identify as Jews nationally."[60] Similarly, in a lecture presented to the Society for the Study of the Minority Question, Emil Margulies (1877–1943), a prominent German-speaking Zionist leader, discussed the issues facing "the 365,000 Jews who live here, the fellow citizens of Jewish nationality in this state," likewise referring to the approximate number of Jews as defined by religion in Czechoslovakia as constituting the country's Jewish nation.[61] Although the census allowed Jews a choice of nationality, Zionists did not.

For Zionists, the right to claim Jewish nationality was a benchmark for the state's commitment to Jews' individual as well as collective rights. Individual Jews' civil equality had to include their right to express their ethnic national belonging, a right the country's non-Jewish citizens enjoyed.[62] Furthermore, Zionists expected that as one of the country's national minorities, Jews were now entitled to state support for Jewish national minority schools in places where there was sufficient demand. Indeed, Zionists hoped to begin to roll back the so-called denationalization that Jewish society had been subjected to by Habsburg authorities with the help of the Czechoslovak state. Like German and Czech nationalists, Zionists believed that their nation's children needed to be "reclaimed" from "foreign" national environments, especially schools, and educated among their own. They looked to the census to document Jews' entitlement to Jewish national institutions.

Even though the parallels between Jews and Czechoslovakia's German, Hungarian, Polish, and Rusyn minorities were important, Zionists were determined that Jews stand out. Zionists rewarded the government's recognition of their national aspirations by downplaying criticism of the authorities' execution of the census. In the aftermath of both the 1921 and 1930 censuses, some national minority activists denounced the results as false, citing systematic abuse and misconstruction by census commissioners determined to increase the number of Czechoslovaks.[63] Similar criticisms were also raised in an article in *Židovské zprávy* shortly after the first census. "The census results regarding nationality will in no way reflect the truth – that much we can already say with confidence," the author stated. Recounting several instances where the Jewish National Council was called on to intervene when Jews were not allowed to declare Jewish nationality, the author accused the census officials of systematic manipulation of people's answers, even hinting that the abuse was sanctioned by the authorities.[64] However, aside from this initial criticism, the Zionist press embraced the event itself as well as the statistical material that it produced. Zionists thereby consciously set themselves apart from other minority activists. Uncertain of Jews' choices in the census, the Jewish National Council continued its strategy of cultivating an alliance between itself and the Czech authorities. After all, the government had been forthcoming in meeting Zionists' demands. In return, they were now expected to fulfill their role as a loyal partner of the state.

THE LACK OF A NATIONAL LANGUAGE AND JEWS' RIGHTS

The Statistical Bureau's adoption of the notion that Jews had "lost their national language" paved the way for the inclusion of an exemption for Jews in the census. If the Jewish National Council had succeeded in securing statistical visibility for the country's Jewish nation, then the path to equality as a national minority was fraught with challenges. In some cases, national collective visibility would come at the expense of individual rights. And in the long run, it was the lack of a national language that ended up being a major obstacle in achieving national minority rights for Jews in the ways Zionists imagined. Not only did the courts deny minority language rights to individuals of Jewish nationality, but as chapter 5 discusses in greater detail, bureaucrats in the Ministry of Education also used the absence of a Jewish national language to reject Zionist activists' demands for public Jewish national schools. Furthermore, by allowing Jews alone to choose a nationality other than their ethnic origin, the census nurtured the perception that Jews' nationality was a choice rather than an ethnographical fact. Zionists had hoped for quite the opposite result.

Even though census makers considered Jews a separate ethnic group, they permitted Jews alone to adopt a national identity different from their perceived ethnic origin. The census regulations defined Jews' national flexibility by their ethnic origin and allowed them "backward-looking" as well as "forward-looking" national identification (in other words, "original" or "adopted" identities).[65] In the case of Jews, national belonging corresponded either to an individual's ethnic origin (marked by adherence to Judaism) or to a choice of another nationality whose language the person had adopted. In other words, outside observers considered Jews' language use a choice rather than an integral part of Jewish identity, thereby making change or continuity a sign of political or cultural loyalties. Although many Jews considered German a Jewish language, Jews' use of German in Moravia and some parts of Bohemia was viewed by many observers as a sign of Jews' German national and Austrian loyalties rather than an integral part of their Jewishness.[66]

Since 1880, when language was first introduced as a category in the census in Austria-Hungary, respondents' claims had been surrounded by controversy. In this region, where multilingualism was widespread among Jews and non-Jews alike, the authorities insisted that individuals declare only one language as their language of daily use. This in turn fueled nationalists' fight for people's linguistic allegiance. In Czechoslovakia, Jews' formalized national flexibility ensured that the contest continued. As one Zionist author commented, "Czechs and Germans of every political orientation . . . are preoccupied with the question how they can increase their own numbers at the expense of the other nation.

They both agree that the Jews are the only ones that can enlarge the size of their nation [*Volkszahl*]."[67] Even though Zionist leaders were eager to demonstrate the existence of a Jewish nation through the census results, they also understood the precariousness of the exemption made for Jews in the census regulations. In anticipation of the censuses, the Jewish National Council called on Jews to opt for Jewish nationality if not for any other reason than "to withdraw" from the contest between Czechs and Germans, thereby refusing "to become the foot soldiers [*trabanty*] of other nationalities."[68] Ten years, later the battle for Jewish souls had not abated. A writer in the Brno/Brünn-based *Jüdische Volksstimme,* anticipating "an increase in the number of Jews choosing Jewish nationality," called on readers to opt for Jewish nationality and thereby make it "pointless for the other nationalities to attempt to restore their own ranks by decimating the Jewish nation in Czechoslovakia."[69]

The legacy of the national conflict in Habsburg Austria shaped the debate and legal practice regarding minority rights in Czechoslovakia in different ways. As mentioned earlier, the Statistical Bureau's choice of mother tongue as the defining ethnic marker was one. Another was the policies that governed education, in particular the rules determining in what school a child belonged. The 1869 Imperial School Law had recognized individuals' right to an education in their own language (as long as this was one defined as a language of common use in a region [*Landessprache*]). In addition, the Habsburg state expanded public education by demanding that municipalities fund elementary schools in places where there were at least forty children (over five years) within a radius of four kilometers.[70] In the course of the 1880s, Austrian courts determined that the 1869 law guaranteed linguistic minorities the right to public elementary schools in which the minority language was the language of instruction.[71] This change came about in part due to German and Czech nationalists' focus on children and schools as particularly important for their nation's fortunes. They insisted that children be educated in schools according to their nationality and staged fierce battles over funding for Czech- and German-language schools as well as over parents' school choices in the Bohemian Lands. As Tara E. Zahra has observed, the Habsburg state "recognized nationality in order to diffuse nationalism."[72] Rather than weakening national conflicts, these regulations intensified national strife as activists and politicians sought to win over people to their nation and to dominate individual town councils, the main local venues for these political battles.[73]

The nationalist campaigns of Czech and German activists came to a head in Moravia in 1905. The Moravian Compromise passed that year called for a division of the region's population into national public bodies. Now, people (or as it were, heads of households) had to choose national affiliation so they could be registered in either the Czech or the German national cadasters. Their choice determined what schools they could send their children to and what political parties they could vote for. While registration as one or the other nationality was easy, subsequently it was difficult for individuals to change their national belonging.[74] As a rule, the region's urban and German-speaking Jewish population was registered in the German national cadaster, thereby adding to the number of Germans in a specific jurisdiction, much to the anger of Czech nationalists.

The 1905 legislation also weighed in on educational matters in its paragraph 20, known as Lex Perek. It specified that children could attend only schools in whose language of instruction they were proficient.[75] By 1910, courts and school boards were interpreting this statute as meaning that a child should attend schools according to nationality and not merely language proficiency. As Tara E. Zahra argues, Lex Perek became the legal basis for the courts' assertion that a nation has a right to its children. Increasingly, parental rights and choice were limited by the courts in favor of school boards' claim that children attend school according to their objectively ascertained ethnic belonging.[76] Indeed, since an individual could only belong either to the German or the Czech nation and since Moravia's population was divided along national lines, parental choice other than the one assigned by their national affiliation was eliminated. It was this practice that was carried over into the postwar order.

After 1918, children in the Bohemian Lands had to attend a school that corresponded to their nationality; language proficiency was no longer a requirement.[77] The belief that the nation's right overruled parents' educational priorities and choice of school ensured that nationalists' annual late summer campaigns "to reclaim" children for one or another nationality continued unabated.[78] National belonging was now ascertained by the courts according to so-called objective ethnic evidence, such as a family's language use, political choices, readings habits, and social circles (but not necessarily people's own declaration of national affiliation). By contesting parents' school choices, nationalist activists sought to "uncover" children who had been enrolled in schools other than the ones demanded by their alleged ethnic belonging. In doing so, they sought to "reclaim" children for their "real" nation or school. As Zahra shows, in Czechoslovakia, a child's ethnic origin rather than language ability determined in which school he or she belonged. By 1925, the state authorities began registering the nationalities of all engaged couples as well as that of every newborn (derived from the mother's national belonging). These practices allowed authorities to fix individuals' nationality earlier. It made it possible for them to monitor more closely the demographic developments among the country's national groups than the census every ten years allowed for.[79]

As a result of the abolition of the national cadasters in Moravia in 1918 as well as the introduction of "Jewish nationality" as a category of ethnic belonging, the courts eventually had to consider in which schools children of Jewish nationality belonged. The fact that the Jewish national minority officially lacked a national language allowed parents who claimed Jewish national belonging a degree of autonomy over their children that parents of Czech and German nationality did not formally possess in the interwar years. In the late 1920s, a German school board in Moravia took the question of Jewish national children to the country's Supreme Administrative Court.[80] In the case of the child Zuzana Fríednerová, the German school board in Brno/Brünn argued that Zuzana was a German-speaker and therefore belonged not in her Czech school, but in a German one. Seeking to assess the merit of the school board's claim, the court obtained information from the parents in order to assess the child's Jewish nationality:

> According to the testimony of the child's mother, Berta Fríednerová, the child's father was born in Těšín and is of Jewish nationality. His parents were and are of Jewish nationality. The child's father attended German elementary school and uses Czech and German with his father and relatives. The child's mother is of Jewish nationality, as were and are her parents;

> she uses Czech and German with her relatives. At home, the child speaks both Czech and German and knows both languages well. The family reads Czech and German newspapers and books. In their day-to-day life they socialize with Czechs as well as Germans.[81]

Based on this evidence, the court concluded that parents and child were of Jewish nationality and thus Zuzana could not be reclaimed by the German school board through Lex Perek, as she did not belong to the German nation.[82] Since there were no public elementary schools with Jewish language of instruction and since Zuzana was proficient in both Czech and German, the court concluded, Zuzana's parents were not restricted in their choice of school for their child. In a similar case concerning the child František Fríed, the court dismissed the German school board's attempt to delegitimize Jewish nationality and have language use overrule national belonging. Citing the census regulations of 1920 and the notion that "the majority of Jews had not preserved their original national language," the court confirmed Jews' right to claim Jewish nationality regardless of language.[83] Thus, Jewish nationality status allowed these Moravian parents to make their own decisions regarding their children's education, something that Czech and German parents could no longer do if they sent their children to public schools.[84] In these two cases involving children of Jewish nationality, the parents stressed their families' bilingualism in general, and of the children in question in particular, thereby signaling that their children were equally at home in both languages. Whether a conscious strategy or a reflection of social reality, the parents pointed to their ethnic origin as well as a family tradition for multilingualism as evidence of their Jewish nationality. Indeed, while bilingualism was accepted among Jews – even used as a marker of Jewish national belonging – nationalist experts agreed that among non-Jews such linguistic behavior was immoral and detrimental to a child's development.[85]

Jewish national parents do not appear to have wasted this opportunity to provide their children with what was essentially a bilingual elementary and middle school education. In Bohemia, more than 60% of children of Jewish nationality attended Czech-language schools, including the region's only Jewish national school in Prague.[86] They did so already by the early 1920s, and the trend held steady in Bohemia.

In Moravia, children of Jewish national parents, the majority of whom would have been counted as Germans before 1918, enrolled in increasing numbers in Czech-language elementary schools. Between 1921 and 1925, there was an increase of 30% (from 18% to 48%). In both Bohemia and Moravia, once they were ready for middle school, some children of Jewish national parents continued their education at German-language institutions. For the country as a whole, there was a significant increase in the number of Jewish children who received a Czech- or Slovak-language education. This was a trend that Zionists routinely depicted as a result of parents of Jewish nationality choosing to enroll their children in Czech- and Slovak-language schools. As more Jews identified nationally as Jews, they argued, more Jewish children were educated in Czech and Slovak.[87]

Whether Jewish parents' choice to enroll their children in Czech- and Slovak-language schools was pragmatic or idealistic is hard to know, but the change was a significant one. In 1921, 32% of the country's Jewish children attended Czechoslovak-language schools. By 1930, this number had almost doubled to 59%. In the same decade, fewer Jewish children attended German-language schools (reduced from 14% to 9%) and Hungarian-language schools (reduced from 21% to 10%). Indeed, the enrollment data show that in terms of school choices, Jewish parents across national and regional divides were becoming more alike by sending their children to Czech- and Slovak-language elementary schools.

This freedom to choose was, however, a double-edged sword. It strengthened the notion that Jews' choice of language and school was a question of political loyalty and was guided by opportunism and cultural preferences. Thus, although the subjective character of Jewish nationality did allow Jews to "withdraw" and perhaps "transform their relations to the Czechs," as Zionists hoped, it also placed Jewish parents under scrutiny for their educational choices, now interpreted as a sign of political loyalty. In the context of intense national struggle, competing school boards, journalists, and politicians called on individuals of Jewish nationality to cast their lot with their particular linguistic group. Meanwhile Zionists sought to recruit Jewish children for the handful of Jewish national schools that were established in the 1920s. No matter their choice of school, Jews' formal flexibility made them more exposed to surveillance and denunciation, especially in towns and regions where linguistic communities mixed and where people's educational choices mattered in the competition for resources and representation.

Even if the belief that Jews lacked a national language allowed people of Jewish nationality to escape some constrictions, it also restricted German- and Hungarian-speaking Jewish nationals' right to use these minority languages publicly, a development that complicated the Zionist movement's agenda in several ways. In early December 1929, the German-language, government-sponsored newspaper *Prager Presse* announced that the country's Supreme Administrative Court had reached a verdict ending a yearlong strife over the question whether Jewish nationals were entitled to claim minority language rights.[88] The court's ruling determined that Czechoslovak law considered "language an expression of national belonging" and concluded that minority language speakers could claim minority language rights only if they were members of the corresponding national community. Members of the Jewish nationality could therefore not claim minority language rights even if their mother tongue was a minority language in the community in which they lived.[89]

In the case before the court, a German-speaking Jewish national from Moravská Ostrava/Mährisch Ostrau, Philip Rauchberger (1895–1942), and his lawyers argued that Czechoslovak law recognized the "fact" that Jews had lost their own national language and adopted the languages of the people among whom they lived. They thereby became members of linguistic communities that did not, however, correspond to their national belonging. Considering that large parts of the Jewish nationality were German- and Hungarian-speakers, now minority languages, the litigants argued, denying them language rights effectively amounted to discrimination. In their view, Jewish nationals were denied rights that they would otherwise have enjoyed had they declared German or Hungarian nationality.[90]

The decision was important to the Zionist movement. The Jewish National Council did not play a public part in the case, but Rauchberger's lawyers had consulted them.[91] The previous year, in a series of letters discussing Rauchberger's chances of winning the appeal, Emil Margulies and Paul März (1894–1981) speculated that Germans and Czechs alike would benefit from a negative outcome for Rauchberger. März, a Zionist leader from Moravská Ostrava/Mährisch Ostrau (where German-speakers constituted about half of the city's population), suggested that the minister of justice, Robert Mayr-Harting (1874–1948), whose decision was being challenged, was seeking to damage the prospects for the Zionist movement of gaining a stronger foothold among Jews, particularly in "mixed communities."[92] By limiting the rights for German-speakers of Jewish nationality, Mayr-Harting, a member of the German Christian Socialist party, sought to compel Jews to claim German nationality. The Czech authorities, Margulies believed, were also interested in a negative result for Rauchberger. Despite the same court's ruling on the autonomy of parents of Jewish nationality, Margulies feared that a negative outcome would enable the state authorities "to force us to send our children to Czech schools in German areas," thus claiming Jewish children for Czech schools.[93] In Margulies's view, both Germans and Czechs were attempting to boost their numbers in areas where they constituted a minority with Jewish souls. Margulies, himself a German-speaker from Litoměřice/Leitmeritz (where three-quarters of the population was German-speaking) in the Sudetenland, feared that in German-speaking areas, the threat of forced "Czechification" would be detrimental to the Zionist movement.[94] Critical of the Zionist leadership's decision to pursue the question of Jews' minority language rights through a legal rather than a political process, Margulies warned that the minister's decision

> threatens our political activity, indeed, our Zionist activity as a whole with complete extinction. If this was to become practice [denying Jewish nationals the right to use German publicly] then the result could be that we will be required to speak Czech in the town councils, this is how they will push us out of office and thereby push out our party all together. For you over there [in the Zionist headquarters in Moravská Ostrava/Mährisch Ostrau] this is a theoretical and abstract question – for us here, however, it is a vital matter [*Lebensfrage*].[95]

Margulies's lament reflects that the perception that Jews as a collective lacked a shared national language, the most significant marker of nationhood, could potentially entail fewer rights for people of Jewish nationality. In addition, this anomaly also opened up new avenues for competing nationalist activists to obstruct the work of Zionist politicians, some of whom, including Emil Margulies himself, did not master the state language, Czech. The case tested the state's tolerance for Jews' national particularity as defined by Zionists leaders. They in turn bemoaned the court's unwillingness to accept Jews' distinctive linguistic conditions as out of touch with the spirit of the Czechoslovak Constitution.[96] As *Jüdische Volksstimme* suggested, this decision threatened to revert the gains that Jewish nationalism had achieved in limiting the influence of the German and Hungarian minorities. Yet, a few months later, when the Statistical Bureau proposed to count linguistic rather than national communities in the upcoming census, a change that would in fact award Jewish nationals minority language rights, Zionists opposed the motion.[97]

For Zionists, the problem with Hebrew and Yiddish was twofold: practical and political. Yiddish and Hebrew were recognized as Jewish languages in public discourse, but Jews' uneven command or lack of use of either of these languages was a problem for the Zionist movement. Hebrew was, of course, the language of choice for Zionists and the symbol of the Jewish national revival. But in Czechoslovakia, the number of Hebrew-speakers was miniscule aside from the anti-Zionist, religious communities, who could not be counted on to declare their holy tongue a national one. Yiddish was spoken in Subcarpathian Rus' and eastern Slovakia, but not in the Bohemian Lands and large parts of Slovakia. Here, Jews spoke German, Hungarian, Slovak, and Czech. These were well-known ethnographical facts. To Zionists, the Statistical Bureau's proposal appeared as yet another conspiracy to claim Jews for other national communities by simply adding Jews to other national groups in accordance with Jews' mother tongue.

There were, however, also deeper cultural and acute political reasons for Zionists' opposition to Yiddish. Indeed, if Zionists in the Bohemian Lands did not waste any ink on this matter, it was perhaps because it was obvious to most that adopting Yiddish as Jews' national language was politically impossible, culturally undesirable, and simply impractical. In Habsburg Austria, Yiddish had been categorized as a German dialect and denied status as an independent language. In the interwar years, the link to German persisted as reflected in the common word, including in Czech and German, for Yiddish jargon (*žargon/jargon*), a rather unflattering label that also implied a debased, hybrid character, a derivative of German rather than an autonomous language. It was a language that for many middle-class Jews in Central Europe was strongly associated with the ghetto, with the shame of social denigration and religious traditionalism. Yiddish thus had undesirable political optics for Zionists working hard to contest the perception that Jews were a Germanizing force in the country and to create a new image of Jews as a modern, cultured people.[98] In contrast to Hebrew, Yiddish could probably have qualified as a mother tongue, according to the Statistical Bureau's criteria (the language a person learned first or the language that a person was most familiar with), among many Jews in eastern Slovakia and the majority in Subcarpathian Rus'. Yet, in Subcarpathian Rus', Zionist activists created schools with Hebrew as the language of instruction rather than Yiddish.[99] Only a handful of the region's Jewish students attended these privately funded schools. Although Czech and Slovak made very significant inroads in the interwar years among young Jews, German and Yiddish were probably the closest the country's Jews came to shared languages. Yet, this was a fact for which Zionists had little use.

Many of the obstacles faced by Zionists reflected that the state authorities' recognition of Jews' nationality status was a somewhat reluctant decision. It was not a result of the state's acceptance of Jewish nationhood and willingness to accommodate Jews' particularity. The decision to recognize Jews as a national minority was driven by the Czech leadership's desire to minimize the number of Germans and Hungarians, not by a commitment to national rights for Jews. Through the interwar years, the state authorities, faced with court challenges regarding Jews' language rights and political demands for public Jewish national schools, did not act to remove the obstacles that Zionists encountered in exercising their rights as members of a national minority. As long as the half-measure strengthened Czechoslovak hegemony in the state, it was, from the state authorities' point of view, fulfilling its purpose.

IMAGINING CZECHOSLOVAK JEWRY

While the Jewish nation's presence in the official census was a significant step in establishing the existence of a Jewish nation as a social fact, it was only the first step. The next was for Zionist experts to put the data to use

Table 3.1. The Jewish population of Czechoslovakia (religion) in absolute numbers and Jews' nationality according to the population censuses of 1921 and 1930 (percentages)

NATIONALITY	CZECHOSLOVAK	CZECHOSLOVAK	GERMAN	GERMAN	JEWISH	JEWISH	HUNGARIAN	HUNGARIAN	RUSYN	RUSYN	TOTAL # OF JEWS	
	1921	1930	1921	1930	1921	1930	1921	1930	1921	1930	1921	1930
BOHEMIA	50%	46%	35%	31%	15%	20%	-	1%	-	-	79,777	76,301
MORAVIA	16%	18%	35%	29%	49%	52%	-	1%	-	-	45,306	41,250
SLOVAKIA	22%	32%	7%	7%	48%	52%	17%	7%	-	-	135,918	136,737
SUBCARPATHIAN RUS'	1%	1%	-	-	87%	93%	8%	6%	4%	1%	93,341	102,542
TOTAL	22%	25%	15%	13%	54%	57%	9%	5%	1%	-	354,342	356,830
TOTAL # OF PEOPLE WITH JEWISH NATIONALITY											180,616	204,427

Sources:

1921: Table 1, pp. 3–4, in *Československá statistika,* svazek 37, řada VI, Sčítání lidu ze dne 15. 2.1921, sešit 6 III. díl (Praha, 1927);

1930: Table 4, pp. 104–107, in *Československá statistika,* svazek 98, řada VI, Sčítání lidu v republice československé ze dne 1. prosince 1930, díl I (Praha, 1934).

creating new, authoritative knowledge about the Jewish national collective. Zionist observers awaited the 1921 census with a mix of excitement and trepidation. And, the 1921 census results did not play right into the hands of Zionists. Even though over half of the country's Jews declared Jewish national belonging, the results also attested to Jews' diverse linguistic and national loyalties.

If the number of people who chose Jewish nationality in Bohemia (15%) was smaller than Zionists had hoped, then the census results were much more encouraging in the rest of the country.[100] In Moravia (47%) and Slovakia (54%), just around half of the regions' Jewish populations chose Jewish nationality. In Subcarpathian Rus', 87% did (see Table 3.1). At the same time, Jews did continue to appear among so-called foreign nationalities, especially in Bohemia. Just over 50% of the country's Jews opted for Jewish national belonging. Yet, so that the diversity of Jews' nationality, especially in Bohemia, not be constructed as a setback for Zionists, they spun the outcome in their favor. In fact, by using religion to trace the *real* Jewish nation, the difference in the number of ethnic and national Jews in the country's various regions became evidence for Jews' particular sociology. In lectures, journals, and newspaper articles, Jewish experts explained that Jews in Czechoslovakia – despite their apparent lack of not only a unifying national language but also a shared Jewish national consciousness – were indeed a nation. In their hands, statistics and social science served to make the country's Jews legible as a distinct nation whose religious, cultural, and linguistic differences only momentarily obscured their collective sameness. Some Jewish experts embarked on their work primarily as a defense against political opponents and antisemitism. Yet, it was through their preoccupation with statistics, historical documentation, and Jewish sociology that they came to imagine their Jewish nation. Over the course of the interwar years, Zionist experts invented Czechoslovak Jewry as a unique branch of the Jewish nation as well as a natural part of Czechoslovakia's ethnographical topography.

One of the central figures among the Jewish social scientists in Czechoslovakia was the Zionist activist and writer František Friedmann (1897–1945). Friedmann became involved in Prague Zionist circles at the end of the First World War. Having returned from service at the front,

Friedmann, then in his early twenties, began studying law at Charles University in the fall of 1918.[101] Soon he served as an editor and contributor to *Židovské zprávy* and *Selbstwehr* and as a member of the Jewish National Council. In the 1930s, Friedmann was a representative of the Jewish Party on Prague's Municipal Council and was involved in the Zionist sports movement as the chair of the local club Hagibor.[102] From the outset, Friedmann showed a keen interest in Jewish statistics and sociology, and he gradually established himself as the local Jewish statistician par excellence.[103] He wrote extensively on Jewish statistics in Czechoslovakia, and while he did not shy away from pointing his numerical guns at Jewish opponents and non-Jewish critics, he was particularly preoccupied with what he believed was the uniquely complex composition of Czechoslovak Jewry. Friedmann often directed his works at several different audiences simultaneously. At times when he addressed the Jewish reading public, among whom there were both critics and supporters, Friedmann clearly crafted his text with an eye to the piece's possible wider distribution among journalists and in political circles.[104] He also lectured and wrote for non-Jewish audiences specifically in the form of overtly polemical pamphlets and scholarly articles.[105] Friedmann was eager to establish himself as the authority on Czechoslovak Jewish statistics in the broader Jewish social scientific community, in addition to his readership at home. He sought to advertise his expertise as significant by questioning the work on this particular community of the foremost authority on Jewish statistics, Arthur Ruppin, as well as by emphasizing the wider importance of Czechoslovak Jewry for the advancement of Jewish statistics.[106] Because of its uniquely complex character, on the crossroads between east and west, the Jews of Czechoslovakia, argued Friedmann, formed a microcosm through which scientists could study Diaspora Jewry as a whole. His studies of Czechoslovak Jewry led him to believe, in contrast to other Zionist writers, that territorial relocation was not necessary for the future of the Jewish nation here. In fact, to Friedmann, Czechoslovakia, with its bridging and blending of eastern and western Jewries, was the Promised Land. In the early 1930s, his relationship with the Zionist leadership became increasingly strained.[107] Friedmann, who had been a rising star on the Zionist political stage, saw his ascent halted not so much by political issues as by the Zionist political leadership's discomfort with Friedmann's marriage to the non-Jewish Hana Silvanová (1901–?).[108] He did, however, remain a central figure in the capital's Jewish society as the editor of the Prague Jewish community's bulletin, *Věstník pražské židovské náboženské obce,* a member of the Prague City Council, and the chair of Hagibor.

In much of his work, František Friedmann used statistics and social science to further the cause of Jewish nationalism within Jewish society and to shape the way in which Jews and non-Jews alike perceived Czechoslovakia's Jewish Question. Friedmann's 1927 polemical pamphlet *Mravnost či Oportunita?* (Morality or Opportunity?) is a case in point. In this piece, Friedmann intended to fight off the Czech-Jewish movement's latest efforts to expand their activities in Moravia, Slovakia, and Subcarpathian Rus' by accusing Czech-Jews of denationalization. Since a majority of Jews in these regions had claimed Jewish nationality, Czech-Jews were, according to Friedmann, trying to strip them of their authentic national feelings in favor of an opportunist Czech national identity.

Drawing on the power of numbers to convey objectivity and truth, Friedmann used data derived from the 1921 census as well as recent elections to support his claim that the majority of the country's Jews identified nationally as Jews and had thus remained loyal to their ancestral community. In charting the boundaries of the Jewish nation, Friedmann adopted religion as the marker of nationhood, not individuals' declaration of Jewish national belonging. Thus, in Friedmann's hands, the census's counting of 79,777 Jews (according to religion) in Bohemia, 45,306 in Moravia-Silesia, 135,918 in Slovakia, and 93,341 in Subcarpathian Rus' recorded Jewish nationhood as an objective social fact.[109] To Friedmann, the census's question regarding nationality allowed him to measure the character of Jews' national consciousness, not the size of the nation – the latter was already determined in the column recording religion. In the eastern regions, Friedmann claimed, Jews had spontaneously chosen Jewish nationality, having been spared the pre-census denationalization efforts of Czech-Jewish activists, since they, in contrast to Zionist leaders, had not "dared" to travel to the remote region in the tumultuous postwar months.[110] In the Bohemian Lands, however, the situation was quite different. Here, Czech-Jewish and German-Jewish assimilationists alike had unleashed a "campaign of terror and propaganda," intimidating Jews by suggesting that expressing their "real" Jewish national feelings would label them as "foreigners."[111] This was why, Friedmann explained as he lumped together the results from Bohemia and Moravia, here as many as 50% of the region's Jews opted for Czechoslovak nationality, while 35% chose German national belonging.

The so-called terror campaign's effects on Jews in Bohemia, especially the statistical distortion of the real character of Jews' national feelings caused by it, were evident, according to Friedmann, when one compared census and election results. Only 15% of Bohemian Jews opted for Jewish nationality in the census meanwhile 52% of Jewish voters in Bohemia, he claimed, chose a Jewish nationalist candidate on their ballot. This was a typical rhetorical strategy employed by Friedmann in his work. By simultaneously insisting on and questioning the ability of statistics to capture social reality, he attempted to persuade his readers of his expertise and commitment to the truth. In the case of Bohemia, where a relatively small number of Jews (15%) opted for Jewish national belonging, he defined the census data as unreliable because of the politicization of the process and the lack of secrecy surrounding people's answers to the census questions (this in stark contrast to his evaluation of the census results in Subcarpathian Rus', where he accepted the census's count of 87% of the region's Jewish population opting for Jewish nationality as truthful).[112] The election results, assuming that each vote gained by a Jewish nationalist candidate was cast by a Jewish voter, provided Friedmann with a much more useful picture of Jews' ethnic loyalty in Bohemia. Similarly, he insisted, while "50.97% of all Jewish citizens in Czechoslovakia declared Jewish nationality, 72% voted for a Jewish party."[113] Despite Jews' overwhelming support for the Zionist program as well as the other objective signs of the existence of a Jewish nation in Czechoslovakia, Friedmann mocked the Czech-Jews, "You still insist that the Jewish nation was dissolved two thousand years ago?" Yet, Friedmann's statistical acrobatics aside, the fact remained that Jews in Czechoslovakia shared neither a national language nor national affiliation. He and other Zionist experts had to turn to other accepted markers of nationhood, such as shared origins, historical continuity, and territorial unity, in order to construct the country's Jewish nation.

THE ETHNIC NATION

Like most other minority nationalists in the region suspicious of the assimilating pressure of the state, Zionists defined their nation as a community of origin. By claiming national belonging as inherent rather than chosen or adopted, minority nationalists envisioned themselves as pushing back against assimilation by restoring an alleged natural order of distinct ethnic nations.[114] This backward-looking notion of national belonging not only projected ethnic identities onto historical communities, but also legitimized these nationalists' attempts to reclaim individuals and communities for their "real" nation. By ascribing national belonging according to "objective criteria," experts and other observers claimed to uncover artificial identifications.[115] To them, one's true national belonging was an inherited attribute, not an adopted political or cultural identification.

Zionists' image of their nation was shaped by these broader ethnonationalist discourses. As noted earlier, statistical experts and other observers agreed on Jews' ethnic distinctiveness but differed on the question whether Jews were a nation. In making their case for the authenticity of Jews' nationhood, Zionist experts depicted Jews' historical experience of denationalization as similar to that of Czechs and Slovaks. They argued that much like these former stateless nations, whose national distinctiveness was suppressed and their right to national self-expression denied by Austrian and Hungarian authorities, Jews had also been the victims of the former regime's denationalization efforts. Using this familiar narrative of denationalization, Friedmann explained the 1921 census's exposure of Jews' different national identifications as a result of their historical experience in Austria-Hungary.[116] Yet, Friedmann did not blame the Habsburg state alone for undermining Jews' nationhood. He also pointed to the damaging influence of "renegades," Jews acting as fervent and chauvinist Czech and German nationalists, who renounced their "own blood."[117] Inspired by the Czech politician and philosopher František Krejčí (1858–1934) and his work on ethnic loyalty as an ethical obligation, Friedmann suggested that "they [so-called assimilationist Jews] denied the existence of their own nation in order to ease their conscience and avoid being accused of immorality."[118]

If denationalization policies accounted for some of the diversity of national identifications among Jews, so did regional differences.[119] In Friedmann's view, Bohemian Jews constituted a typical western Jewry, characterized by secularization, assimilation, and a somewhat eroded sense of Jewish national consciousness.[120] He identified Moravia and Slovakia as "transitional" types.[121] Here, assimilation had undermined Jewish national culture and identity in some areas, but the majority of communities had withstood these pressures and retained a sense of Jewish national belonging.[122] In contrast to the communities in the Bohemian Lands and Slovakia, the Jews of Subcarpathian Rus' constituted an authentic Jewish national community, complete with a national language and distinct Jewish customs, beliefs, and worldview.[123] The socioeconomic backwardness and traditionalism of these Jews, and the region as such, Friedmann believed, had left their organic national life intact. This was documented by the more than 85 percent of the region's Jews who declared Jewish nationality "spontaneously and without any propaganda [campaigns]" in the country's first census.[124]

To Friedmann, the genuine Jewish national life found in Subcarpathian Rus' was not only a result of traditionalism and underdevelopment. The density of the community, composing about 15 percent of the region's population, created large and compact Jewish communities able to nurture vibrant and organic Jewish life. The correlation between the density of Jews' ethnic community and the level of Jewish national consciousness was noted as a feature of Jews' particular sociology by Jewish and non-Jewish experts alike. Indeed, Friedmann and others observed this phenomenon among western-type Jews as well.[125] In Bohemia, the movement of Jews from the countryside to the region's cities, first and foremost to Prague "has made it possible for Bohemian Jews to preserve their unique national character to a much greater degree than Jewish societies in other countries where Jews make up a similar percentage of the overall population."[126] Much the same could be said for Moravia, where compact Jewish settlements were believed by scholars to have acted as a bulwark against assimilation.[127] If urbanization had sustained Jews' nationhood historically, then the recent concentration of Jews in the country's capital and a few other major cities made a Jewish national awakening a sociological inevitability. As Friedmann predicted, "New Jewish centers have emerged, new urban communities that are more resistant to assimilation. The disappearing [village and small town] communities do not signal the dissolution of Jewry, but rather the possibility for new life."[128] Thus, although eastern and western Jews appeared different on the surface, these communities were, according to Friedmann's narrative, governed by the same particular sociology, one that sustained them as a national community despite differences in language and culture.[129]

Revealing shared sociological laws governing Jewish life was not the only way in which Friedmann sought to establish Jews' national distinctiveness and the truth of Zionist ideology. As his work developed, he coined a social scientific term, "fluctuation" (*fluktuace*), to describe the process whereby Jews opportunistically adopted and switched national identities different from their "real" one. He thereby sought to distinguish this phenomenon from assimilation.[130] In Czech nationalist discourse, people who "switched sides" were known as "hermaphrodites" or "renegades."[131] Friedmann used "renegades" about Jews who adopted a national identity different from their Jewish one. "Fluctuation," on the other hand, described Jews' exchanging one foreign nationality for another at moments of political change, such as after the collapse of Austria-Hungary, when Magyar Jews became Slovak and German ones Czech.[132] In *Mravnost či Oportunita?* Friedmann denounced Czech-Jews' efforts to expand their activities promoting Czech among Jews in Moravia as encouraging fluctuation. Claiming that Czech-Jews were making German-speaking Jews adopt Czech nationality in response to the new political order, Friedmann attacked the Czech-Jewish campaign for urging a superficial and insincere reorientation among Jews. He denounced these activities for harming Czech as well as Jewish interests by encouraging Jews to fake a Czech national commitment.[133]

The term "fluctuation" and its use embodied the way in which politics and social science were intertwined in Friedmann's work. On the one hand, its reference to national side switching, indifference, and opportunism cast Czech-Jews as promoting immorality aside from causing antisemitism. At the same time, Friedmann's admission that fluctuation took place among Jews and his denunciation of such opportunism gave the impression that Zionists were honest and ready to put an end to Jews' misguided behavior. On the other hand, as a social scientific term Friedmann used it to neutralize the incriminating effects of the widespread perceptions of Jews' opportunism and insincerity.[134] When addressing scholarly audiences, Friedmann depicted "fluctuation" as the result of historical, state policies that had encouraged Jews to abandon their ethnic nationality and adopt that of the state-nation.[135] He thereby presented Jews' changing national identifications as an outcome of their recent historical experience with denationalization rather than an enduring aspect of Jews' collective character.[136] The term's scientific appearance disguised its political origin. It strengthened the position of Zionists like Friedmann by presenting their ideological stance as objectively moral in contrast to the deviance of fluctuation.

The statistical exposure of a noticeable gap in the overlap between the country's ethnic and national Jewish communities was an irritant for Zionists. But the practice of collecting and reproducing the statistical data about Jews was much more important than the specific results of the census. The statistical knowledge collected facilitated the notion that Jews' collectively constituted a distinct social body governed by a particular sociology. The typology of eastern and western Jewry, which Friedmann borrowed from Jewish sociology, in turn provided him with an interpretative framework that ordered and explained the cultural variations among Jews, a temporary deviation from the natural state of ethnic, religious, cultural, linguistic sameness that he imagined Jewish nationhood to be.

Like his colleagues among Czech and German nationalist experts, Friedmann was seeking order in the seeming chaos of divergent cultures, languages, and loyalties in the newly unified territories. By elevating ethnic origin to the most important aspect of identity, Friedmann sought to unify the country's Jewish communities through a process of internal homogenization and external differentiation. In doing so, Friedmann divested Jews discursively from their local environments, loyalties, and identifications and marginalized the importance of other categories of identification among Jews. What mattered to Friedmann was not the intense rivalry between different Hasidic dynasties or the profound divisions between Neolog and Orthodox communities, between Jews in Prague and Brno/Brünn, Bratislava/Pressburg/Pozsony, and Mukačevo/Munkács/Munkatsch/Mukacheve, nor was he interested in Jews' other, overlapping, and at times conflicting identifications defined by place, language, class, political conviction, or gender.[137] Friedmann sought a homogenous and legible ethnic whole, not the chaos of individuals' identities and loyalties. In Czechoslovakia, the ethnification of individuals and communities was forcefully expressed in the census design. Census makers explicitly prescribed a set of legitimate ethnic identities. They prohibited people from giving answers that indicated, for example, an individual's multiple national or spatial identities and thereby formally marginalized and erased the significance of other forms of identification. In this way, statistics produced ethnic groups. Even though Jews could formally choose their nationality, the census categories and definitions prescribed Jews ethnic distinctiveness. Not only did numbers and officially sanctioned categories make Jews visible as an ethnic and national community, but they also lent this image objectivity and truth. Statistics "revealed" Jews' sociological distinctiveness, a characteristic of a real nation.

THE HISTORICAL NATION

The privileging of ethnic boundaries was not only a way in which experts and nationalist activists ordered and made sense of their present. It also shaped how they imagined their nation's past. Zionists justified their claims to nationhood by projecting ethnic boundaries and loyalties backward in time, presenting their current state as a loss of nationhood. They built anachronistically uniform notions of Jewishness, casting them onto diverse Jewish societies and cultures. Doing so allowed them to produce a narrative of the nation's historical continuity.

In the interwar years, urbanization and perceived assimilation intensified efforts to preserve the Jewish past. Local Jewish museums had already been established in Mikulov/Nikolsburg, Mladá Boleslav/Jungbunzlau, and Prague in the early 1900s. In the 1920s more museums and Judaica collections followed, in addition to several scholarly journals and numerous books devoted to the history of Jews in Czechoslovakia.[138] As the long list of authors, both Jewish and non-Jewish, engaged in Jewish historical research attests, František Friedmann was part of a much broader community of scholars uncovering Czechoslovakia's

Jewish past. The multiplicity of agendas driving this scholarship, such as local patriotism, Jewish nationalism, nostalgia, personal and professional ambitions, as well as resistance to antisemitism, reflects that these endeavors were not limited to Zionist circles. Rather, the search for a usable past was a way in which Jews imagined themselves at home in Czechoslovakia.[139] By documenting the longevity of multiethnic societies in the country's different regions, scholars made the case for minorities' belonging in Czechoslovakia. In this context, Friedmann's historical studies are particularly telling, precisely because his work recast Jews' past in ways that were personally meaningful as well as politically useful.

In 1929, as Philip Rauchberger's case for minority language rights for Jews was making its way through the courts and as the debate raged about whether to retain the exemption for Jews in the upcoming census, Friedmann published a historical study examining the relationship between nationality and language among Prague Jews. In it, he created a narrative of national survival and cultural adaptation that challenged the stereotype of the city's Jews as a bastion of Germanness in the so-called heart of the Czech nation. He constructed an image of a Jewish society that "since the earliest times considered itself part of a Jewish nation and was perceived as a national community by the [city's] non-Jewish population."[140]

Drawing on contemporary notions of the relationship between language and nationhood, Friedmann made the use of Hebrew as "a cultural and national language" the central marker of Jews' nationhood. Only with the introduction of the Austrian state's Germanization policies in the 1780s, he claimed, were Jews forced to adopt the German language *collectively*. However, because Jews continued to live socially and culturally separate from non-Jews, Friedmann argued, their "Germanness" was only a "veneer."[141] Contrary to popular belief, Prague's German schools were not vehicles for assimilation. Rather, because Jews were concentrated in a few areas of the city, the schools in these neighborhoods had an overwhelmingly Jewish student body. In such an environment, Friedmann insisted, "they could not lose their national consciousness, because in the schools, where they could have been denationalized, they found themselves among their own kind."[142] These

German-language schools strengthened social ties between Jews and nurtured rather than destroyed Jewish national consciousness.[143]

Friedmann's teleological notion about the transmission of nationhood through early socialization and shared language privileged the primacy of national identities over other collective categories of identification. He invented Prague's Jewish nation. Friedmann was unable to locate the accepted objective marker of nationality, namely a Jewish national mother tongue, among contemporary Prague Jews. Instead, he employed historical evidence and statistical material to show that although forced to adopt a foreign tongue, Prague Jewry had remained an organic Jewish national society. Its national cohesion was only obscured by the community's German language use, a result of state coercion, not an expression of German national belonging or cultural loyalty.

Friedmann's narrative thus painted an image of historical continuity, a pointed challenge to the voices that questioned Jews' nationhood precisely because they believed that Jews lacked a national tongue. Indeed, Friedmann's work showed not only how Jews' ethnic mother tongue was destroyed by Austrian oppression, but also that the subsequent collective adoption of a foreign language (German) had actually sustained Jews' ethno-national cohesion. Thus, in the case of Jews, mother tongue did not denote membership of a national community as it did, Friedmann agreed, for other nationalities such as Germans and Czechs.

Even though the 1930 census makers eventually, as discussed earlier, chose to count national rather than linguistic communities, the threat of statistical erasure moved Zionists to evoke Jews' and Czechs' shared memory of Austrian denationalization practices. In an essay on Jewish statistics in Bohemia, Friedmann observed that until the late 1800s, Jews both self-identified as a nation and were perceived as such by the scientific community. "It is interesting to note," he observed, that in 1851 "all Jews in the Bohemian Lands declared Jewish nationality. Indeed, in official works, published on the basis of this census, Jews are treated as a religious group as well as a national community." The foremost representative of nineteenth-century Austrian ethnography and statistics, Karl Freiherr von Czoernig (1804–1889), a native of Bohemia, "dealt with Jews both historically and statistically as a nation."[144] By 1880,

Friedmann argued, as the census became a political tool rather than a search for truth, the authorities deliberately erased the Jewish nation as a statistical fact. By counting language of use instead of nationality and by defining Yiddish as German (or simply counting Yiddish-speaking Jews as Polish, as was the case in Galicia), Jews across the Habsburg Lands were assigned a nationality foreign to them regardless of their origin and national feelings.[145]

As the historical studies discussed above show, Friedmann challenged incriminating discourses about Jews by employing well-known tropes from the Czech nationalist narrative. His uncovering of the Austrian state's assimilationist policies and statistical manipulations was a not so subtle hint that the Czech authorities were toying with the same oppressive tools they had denounced in the past. His use of sociology and statistics to explain Jews' particularity made Jews legible as a nation to audiences unfamiliar with Jewish culture. The way in which he imagined the Jewish past enabled him to take pride in the Jewish nation's cultural resilience, withstanding attempts to erode its national unity. Significantly, his work cast Jews as victims of denationalization rather than opportunist "Germans" and "Czechoslovaks." Indeed, this image of the historical continuity of the Jewish nation positioned the Zionist project as the Jewish nation's rebirth, *not* its invention as some critics claimed.

THE TERRITORIAL NATION

In the same way that the narratives of shared origin and historical continuity bound the image of Czechoslovak Jewry, writers also constructed the territorial boundaries of the country's Jewish nation. In their works, Friedmann and other authors chronicled well-established historical networks of scholarship and kinship between the Jewish communities in the Bohemian Lands, Slovakia, and Subcarpathian Rus'. They presented the community in the Bohemian Lands as a "historical reservoir" from which Jewish migrants ventured out, strengthening Jewish societies in the neighboring regions.[146]

Challenging the claim, allegedly spread by "Magyar Jews," that Jews in Slovakia and Subcarpathian Rus' were "the descendants of Judaized Khazars who colonized Hungary with the Magyars," Friedmann traced the origins of Jewish settlement in these regions to the migration of Bohemian and Moravian Jews following the enactment of the Familiant Laws in Austria. "There was not a substantial community here until the eighteenth century," Friedmann insisted, "[when] Northern Hungary became the destination for Jews from the Bohemian Lands. The community leaders, especially, originated in our region."[147] What he uncovered in his work were centuries-old kinship ties and a long-standing cultural affinity that bound Jews together across the boundaries of the newly amalgamated territories. Thus, in Friedmann's hands, the history of these Jewish societies documented that the regions that made up the new Czechoslovakia were in fact one historical entity, albeit one whose boundaries and integrative networks Hungarians had attempted to dismantle. Eager to distinguish Jews from "colonizers" like the Germans and Hungarians, he suggested that the historical ties between the Jews in the country's various regions attested to the Jewish nation's integrative qualities, to Jews' belonging in Czechoslovakia.[148] While the German and Hungarian national minorities "pulled" Czechoslovakia apart, the Jewish *and* the Czechoslovak nations' cultural and physical cohesion straddling the country from east to west attested to the authenticity and true character of Czechoslovakia's borders.

Friedmann created this Jewish version of the Czechoslovakist trope of the Great Moravian state as the first Czechoslovakia to make Jews tribal unity and historical continuity legible to his readers. According to Czechoslovakist ideology, the historian Elisabeth Bakke shows, Czechs and Slovaks traced their shared origin and linguistic sameness to Great Moravia, a national and political unity that was destroyed by more powerful Hungarian "invaders."[149] According to this discourse, the Czechoslovak nation's unity was disrupted territorially, historically, and linguistically by external forces. The two tribes' affinity was maintained by cultural exchanges in which the Czechs, as the allegedly more developed branch of the Czechoslovak nation, sustained the Slovaks.[150] Similarly, Friedmann constructed a narrative in which Moravia was the place of origin of Czechoslovakia's Jews. According to his view, the affinity between western and eastern Jewries was sustained by a continuous influx of western cultural and intellectual elites to the east. Friedmann thereby employed familiar and legitimate narratives from the Czech context to document Jews' territorial cohesion and belonging to a wider readership.[151]

Although scholars' construction of Jews' ethnic sameness created firm boundaries between Jews and non-Jews, they also made the case for Jews' deep-rooted presence, especially in the Bohemian Lands. Narratives about Jews' cultural coherence and achievements, the longevity of the communities, and their importance to the local environment formed a significant part of the scholarly endeavors and publishing projects of Jewish activists. This tendency was perhaps most prominently embodied in Hugo Gold's multivolume book project published between 1929 and 1934.[152] Hugo Gold (1895–1974), a Brno/Brünn-based Zionist in charge of the publishing house Jüdischer Buch- und Kunstverlag, edited and published these encyclopedic volumes, which he dedicated to its deceased founder Max Hickl (1874–1924), a prominent Zionist cultural entrepreneur and Gold's uncle.

Written by multiple Jewish and non-Jewish authors, these substantial books chronicled the histories of communities, listing their rabbis and dignitaries, depicting their synagogues, schools, and cemeteries, and continuously inscribing Jews as a nation living alongside, but separate from, Czechs and Germans.[153] Documenting the history of vanishing rural communities as well as some of the growing urban ones – Prague was conspicuously absent – Hugo Gold intended the volumes to "awaken in Jews a love for their past, one that is closely linked with the history of their native country, in an effort to preserve [the history] so that future generations will not forget the roots from which their strength grows."[154] In addition to the alphabetically organized entries on individual communities, each volume contained essays concerned with Bohemian and Moravian Jewries' particular history and characteristics as well as statistical essays. As Hugo Gold noted in the preface to the Moravian volume, this was a conscious attempt to preserve the memory of a vanishing culture uniquely its own in both its Moravian and Jewish contexts.

If Jews were to imagine themselves as deeply rooted in Bohemia and Moravia through these local narratives of ethnic, historical, and territorial unity, so were non-Jews. In the early 1930s, as antisemitism gained ground in Czechoslovakia and neighboring countries, this was a particularly important message. In the preface to the Bohemian volume published in 1934, Gold noted, "I present this third volume of my life's work to the public, at a time when a tempest batters the Jewish nation . . . hoping that *non-Jews* [*sic*] will become aware of the great contribution that the Jewish population has made and that the Jewish nation will draw new love and renewed strength and faith from a past so rich in honor and glory."[155] Characteristically, these works constructed a "Moravian Jewry" and a "Bohemian Jewry" by projecting backward modern notions of ethnic community. This was a narrative that glossed over centuries of intercommunal conflict, especially in Bohemia, where there were deep divisions between Prague and the region's other Jewish communities. The authors thereby created homogenous Jewish societies whose physical boundaries corresponded to those of Czechoslovakia's regions and reinforced the image of western and eastern Jews' distinct histories. Through these narratives of ethnic sameness, historical continuity, and territorial belonging, Zionists imagined their community as one whose physical boundaries coincided with those of Czechoslovakia.

At the same time, however, the boundaries of the Jewish nation also extended well beyond Czechoslovakia. Jews were, after all, widely perceived as dispersed across the globe and, as Zionists were at pains to demonstrate, constituted one people regardless of their difference in language, customs, and physical appearance.[156] Friedmann did adopt elements of the Zionist narrative that linked exile, the condition of Diaspora Jews, with social dysfunctions and demographic implosion, a perceived pathology embedded in much of Jewish social science. Yet, he did not embrace the "negation of the Exile" characteristic of much of Zionist ideology. Rather, he employed the tropes of western Jewry's pending dissolution and eastern Jewry's authentic nationhood to construct Czechoslovakia as a Promised Land. Czechoslovakia, Friedmann suggested, constituted a Jewish laboratory contributing in important ways to Jewish social scientific knowledge. Its significance was neither in its size nor its density, but in the unique circumstance that the community united an eastern (*Ostjudentum*) and western Jewry (*Westjudentum*). It thereby formed a microcosm "through which we can obtain an informative picture of the development trends within European Diaspora Jewry as such. On the basis of this [knowledge] we will be able to extract conclusions regarding the general nature of the Jewish problem and its possible solution."[157] If Jewish social scientists in Berlin and elsewhere had yet to take notice of Czechoslovak Jewry, Friedmann was there to correct this oversight.

* * *

František Friedmann's emphasis on his community's unique complexity contained a controversial subtext. He believed that the simultaneous trends of intense urbanization, creating large and vibrant Jewish communities, and westward migration, resulting in a physical and spiritual replenishing of the otherwise dwindling Jewish society in the Bohemian Lands, created the right conditions for a sustainable Jewish national future in Czechoslovakia. He thereby distanced himself from mainstream Zionist sociology that argued that territorial relocation was necessary for Jews' national regeneration and rejected the Diaspora as a viable Jewish national space. Rather, through his work, Friedmann discovered Jews' continuous national life hidden under a veneer of assimilation as well as social and political developments that would sustain a Jewish nation in Czechoslovakia. His work offered an alternative Zionist narrative, one that affirmed the Diaspora. At the same time, it was perhaps also a personal quest. By the mid-1930s, the Friedmanns had two children, Mirjam and Karel, and František Friedmann was perhaps in search of ways in which to resolve the dissonance between Zionism's negation of the Diaspora experience and his own sense of belonging, at home in Czechoslovakia.[158]

Jewish social science was central to Czechoslovak Zionists as a mode of nation building as well as a political and tactical device. Drawing simultaneously on Zionist and local social scientific discourses on statelessness, assimilation, and language behavior, Jewish experts constructed new, usable knowledge about Jews' past, present, and future. Although these narratives were novel, they were not unfamiliar to Jewish and non-Jewish audiences alike. For decades, political and ethnographical debates on nationhood had centered on assimilation policies, statistics, language use, and individuals' ability and willingness to make "true" choices of national belonging. These new histories explained Jews' ethnic, religious, and cultural differences as national ones and therefore not evidence of Jews' foreignness, disdain for non-Jews, or pathology.

Rather, Jews' difference reflected a distinct sociology and historical experience, one that could be compared and discussed alongside the histories of other nations. These narratives thus emphasized and legitimized Jews' difference, meanwhile constructing Jews' belonging as part of the ethnographical and political fabric of Czechoslovakia – a process of simultaneous differentiation and integration.

In interwar Czechoslovakia, statistics paradoxically served both to prescribe Jews' national belonging according to their perceived ethnic origin and to disseminate the notion that Jews had flexible national identities. On the one hand, the census and its interpreters represented Jews as a community of origin, a separate ethnic group fundamentally different from other ethnic communities such as the Czech and Slovaks, Germans and Hungarians. On the other, Jews' perceived lack of a national language and their right to choose a nationality different than the one their ethnic origin would otherwise prescribe formalized and disseminated the notion of Jews' national flexibility. In the context of intense national rivalry, such national flexibility made Jews targets of competing demands for their loyalty, an impossible position that perhaps furthered Jews' isolation rather than ensured their integration, as Zionists had hoped.

For nationalist entrepreneurs, stabilizing and fixing individuals' national belonging was of outmost importance. During census days, elections, and school enrollment weeks, nationalists depended on individuals acting loyally to their nation. As Jews continued to enroll their children in non-Jewish schools, to choose national belonging other than Jewish, and to vote for non-Jewish parties, Zionists turned increasingly to practices such as the census that ascribed Jews' ethnic sameness and hence Jewish national belonging. With few incentives at their disposal and as committed Jewish nationalists, Zionist experts promoted discourses that racialized national belonging in an effort to legitimize their nation-building project. To them, a choice of national identity different from one's community of origin was not legitimate. Yet, as Jews – and among them leading Zionist social scientists such as František Friedmann – continued to marry non-Jews or simply chose a nationality other than Jewish, the ethnic Jewish category was destabilized. It was destabilized even as more and more Jews identified as "Jewish" in the census.

Despite their efforts to fix Jews' nationality, in the end the future of the Jewish nation depended on Jews choosing to belong to it. This was not an issue that concerned Zionists alone. In Czechoslovakia, state authorities and minority entrepreneurs were eager to fix national belonging and monitor people's national behavior. Yet, individuals such as the ones who intermarried, educated their children in multiple languages, and shifted nationality as they saw fit challenged the very possibility of erecting hard boundaries between the country's national communities as long as it remained a liberal democracy.

Some contemporary observers and later historians pointed to the Czechoslovak government's decision to award Jews' national minority status in the census as a reflection of a Czech tradition for justice and tolerance. They implied that the new Czech elite's alleged commitment to democracy made them "naturally" sympathetic to Zionism.[159] Indeed, at times, this decision alone is held up as evidence of the favorable conditions for Jews in interwar Czechoslovakia. This chapter challenges this view by showing that the state authorities' recognition of Jewish nationhood was at best a half-measure. Contrary to what is often implied, yet never fully examined in the aforementioned narratives, the inclusion of Jewish nationality in the census did not reflect a granting of national minority rights to Jews in equal measure as to the country's other minority groups. By making an exemption for Jews for the purposes of the census alone and therefore not making room for Jews' national particularity – the lack of a shared national language – Jews did not enjoy the same rights and access to public resources as other national minorities. Furthermore, individuals of Jewish nationality who were also minority language speakers were denied minority language rights. They thus enjoyed fewer rights than those citizens whose mother tongue overlapped with their national identification. By not making further accommodations for Jews in the legislation on language rights and thus not taking into account the broader implications of their difference or "impairment," Jews who chose Jewish national affiliation were denied individual and collective access to public funds and rights that other citizens enjoyed. This included the right to state-funded Jewish national minority schools. The Hebrew-language Jewish national schools in Subcarpathian Rus' as well as the Czech- and German-language ones in the

Bohemian Lands remained private institutions through the interwar years.

In granting Jews' national minority status, the Prague authorities remained motivated by one priority alone: to diminish the number of German- and Hungarian-speakers in the country by "withdrawing" Jews from these communities into a separate category. This withdrawal was intended to neutralize Jews' presence as minority language speakers. In short, the authorities were willing to award Jews full national minority status only when this recognition strengthened Czechoslovak hegemony. As we shall see, when Zionists demanded funding for schools and minority language rights, intended to place Jewish national culture on a firmer footing on par with the country's other nationalities and thereby sustain, even strengthen, linguistic and national diversity in the country, the authorities then denied Jews equal status.

Well aware that they, as representatives of a relatively small minority without its own language, were at a disadvantage in their negotiations with the Prague authorities, Zionists used social science to construct an image of the Jewish nation as distinct from the country's other national minorities. Rather than a threat to Czechoslovakia, Jews were, Zionists proposed, an integrative force whose historical and territorial boundaries attested to the truth of Czech and Slovak "reunification." On their map of Czechoslovakia, the Jews constituted the one nation that straddled the country's westernmost regions to its easternmost ones; Jews were the human material that held together Czechoslovakia. Jews were perhaps "the only real Czechoslovaks," as a popular saying went.

This vision of Czechoslovak Jewry's historical and cultural cohesion was an integral part of Zionists' political project of belonging. As we shall see in the next chapters, during the interwar years, Zionists worked to create countrywide Jewish institutions. As it turned out, for Zionists, the negotiations with the Statistical Bureau as well as the production of new historical and cultural narratives about Jews proved to be much easier undertakings than creating Czechoslovak Jewish institutions. The next chapter examines Zionists and other Jewish activists' efforts to modernize the most historically significant Jewish institution, the Jewish community (*náboženská obec/Kultusgemeinde*). Zionists set out to transform the Jewish community from a religious to a national institution, and they would in large measure succeed. Paradoxically, however, in doing so they soon found themselves part of a reform process designed to strengthen the cultural sameness of Jews in the Bohemian Lands, meanwhile articulating these western communities' distinct character vis-à-vis the Jews in Slovakia and Subcarpathian Rus'. As we shall see, nation building was indeed a project fraught with challenges and contradictions.

FOUR

Conquering Communities

ZIONISTS, CULTURAL RENEWAL, AND THE STATE

IN EARLY JANUARY 1919, AS THEY PREPARED FOR CZECHOSLOVAKIA'S first Jewish Congress, the Jewish National Council published its program for a revolution in Jewish life. Paradoxically, the manifesto's authors began not by looking to create new Zionist institutions, but by turning to the one social and cultural space that more than any other embodied Jewish tradition, declaring, "The Jewish community is the organic center of Jewish life."[1] In their quest for a national revolution, Zionists looked for continuity in the one institution that had historically provided Jews with a social, legal, economic, political, and cultural framework – indeed they argued, a national structure – in the absence of state institutions: the Jewish community. They immediately set out to transform the existing *Kultusgemeinde,* an institution with religious ritual obligations alone, into a *Volksgemeinde,* a community that served Jews as a people, with an extensive social welfare, educational, and cultural agenda. At stake was the very survival of the Jewish nation.

In the Bohemian Lands in the interwar years, one of the Zionists' most successful projects was the recasting of the formal Jewish community as an institution that served not only Jews' religious needs, but their ethnic and cultural ones as well. From the outset, Zionists placed the community at the center of their program for cultural renewal. They believed that previous generations of leaders, bent on promoting assimilation, had let this, the most significant Jewish institution, decay. Now, communal lay and religious leaders were to be the driving force in a renaissance of Jewish culture. Since the Jewish community was the only representative, legal institution, the reform efforts involved close cooperation between Zionists and the state authorities, a partnership facilitated by the parties' shared desire to modernize the country's Jewish communities.

In their January 1919 manifesto, Zionists outlined several major goals: a reform of Jewish education meant to deepen Jews' attachment to their ancestral community; the creation of a rabbinical and teacher seminary in Czechoslovakia that would bring forth a cohort of rabbis and teachers ready to take charge of the transmission of Jewish culture to new generations of Jews; the preservation of Jewish heritage sites that embodied the unique history and culture of the region's Jews; and the creation of a federation uniting Jewish communities across the country, a union that would represent Jews' interests vis-à-vis the state in Czechoslovakia. Although their path was full of twists and turns, in the course of the 1920s and '30s, Zionists made significant strides toward realizing the Jewish National Council's early vision. Contrary to their initial expectations, Zionists found allies among their political opponents within the Jewish communities, among so-called assimilationists and religious traditionalists. Indeed, the project succeeded because a group of Jewish activists, who were in many ways political adversaries, agreed that Jewish continuity in the Bohemian Lands depended on modernization. For example, by reforming Jewish education and thereby ensuring that young Jews gained a solid foundation in history, literature, and Hebrew, Jewish leaders hoped to reconnect more Jews to Jewish culture and community. They believed that by awakening Jews' sense of ethnic belonging, the communities would become sites for positive cultural identification. To these activists, the future of Jewish life in the region required them to make Jewish culture and community resonate with contemporary Jews.

In 1898, Zionist leader Theodor Herzl commanded activists "to conquer the communities."[2] In Habsburg Austria, Zionists understood this decree to mean that Zionists should work to achieve political control of the Jewish communities by ousting anti-Zionist leaderships. In doing so, they would transform the communities into centers for Jewish national life in the Diaspora.[3] The conquest of the community was front and center in Austrian Zionists' program in the years before the war. The First World War heightened Zionists' revolutionary zeal and placed conquest at the top of their agenda in the Bohemian Lands.[4] Already in

October 1918, the Jewish National Council here called for a democratization of community governance. They demanded that universal suffrage be introduced in the communities and that leaderships be elected rather than appointed. They trusted that "the people" would elect Zionist candidates to positions of power. For Zionists, the democratization of the community went hand in hand with an expansion of its mandate. The new Volksgemeinde was to be built on three pillars: social welfare, education, and religion. Although they envisioned the expansion as a necessary step in modernizing the community and making it relevant to Jews, activists also framed the Volksgemeinde as a return to a more authentic form of Jewish community, where individuals' religion and national belonging were inseparable.

Indeed, Zionists depicted their Volksgemeinde as a traditional yet revolutionary institution. To reconcile the seeming paradox, they invoked the memory of the premodern, semi-autonomous Jewish community, the *kehilah.* In many parts of Europe, the kehilah formed the center of Jewish society, with extensive legal, political, social, cultural, and economic functions until the nineteenth century. Then, government reforms reduced the kehilah's authority and reach, in part to facilitate Jews' integration into the societies in which they lived. These reforms, along with social and cultural changes among European Jews, transformed the kehilah into a religious organization first and foremost, a Kultusgemeinde.[5] The community was reduced to serving Jews' religious needs, since, theoretically at least, this was the only aspect that set Jews apart from their fellow citizens. Even though charitable and educational institutions continued to be an important part of the Jewish community, by the late nineteenth and early twentieth century, Jewish activists across Central Europe looked to expand the communities' formal mandates by including social welfare, cultural, and educational tasks in addition to religious activities.[6] By then, at a time of great socioeconomic, cultural, and demographic changes among Jews, the kehilah became a symbol of earlier cultural authenticity, vibrancy, and social cohesion. Activists seeking to reinvigorate Jewish life did so by creating new institutions as well as modernizing existing ones such as schools and seminaries, hospitals, social welfare programs, and libraries. They thereby lay what they hoped would be the foundation for Jewish social and cultural renewal and continuity. Rather than a community based on religion, they imagined one centered on shared ethnicity, a Volksgemeinde.[7]

After the First World War, in the Bohemian Lands, it was Moravian activists who took the lead in transforming their communities into Volksgemeinden. Already in the fall of 1919, Moravská Ostrava/Mährisch Ostrau's community board adopted new statutes that outlined its commitment "to foster Jewish peoplehood [*Pflege des jüdischen Volkstums*]." The board proposed to support new Jewish educational and cultural institutions, providing Hebrew language education and arranging for public lectures on Hebrew literature and Jewish history.[8] The community was also responsible for defending "Jewish honor" and Jews' rights and interests. About a year later, the Jewish community in Brno/Brünn adopted similar statutes.[9] These large Moravian communities moved quickly to redefine their mandate, but similar efforts were met with more resistance in Bohemia. Nevertheless, by the late 1930s, the Volksgemeinde had become the norm in Bohemia as well. Yet, as this chapter shows, unlike Zionist narratives of conquest and strife, the transformation of the Jewish communities in the Bohemian Lands was achieved by extensive and persistent cooperation between Zionist and non-Zionist activists. These activists agreed that strengthening Jews' ethnic identity – a sense of shared history and culture, of being a community of fate – constituted the foundation for modern Jewish life, indeed was the key to Jewish continuity. Yet, the modernization of the Jewish community that began after the First World War was not a rejection of the integrationist paradigm that had shaped earlier reforms. Rather, the changes made reflected that Jewish activists and state authorities alike viewed Jewish cultural renewal as a way to further Jews' integration into Czechoslovak society.

This chapter situates the Bohemian and Moravian Zionists' effort to conquer their communities within its proper contexts. First, the Zionist vision with its focus on Jews' ethnicity and on Jewish continuity was part of a broader and shared discourse among Jewish activists concerned with what they saw as a crisis in Jewish life. Thus, this Zionist undertaking was shaped in profound ways by local conditions that facilitated the alliance between Zionists and other Jewish activists. Second, Zionists had initially set their eyes on a countrywide revolution. It soon became clear, however, that even if unification of Czechoslovakia's Jewish communities were achieved, it might make nationalization impossible and impede cooperation between Jewish leaderships. This was due to the profound cultural and religious differences between the Jewish societies across Czechoslovakia as well as strong opposition to any perceived secular Jewish agenda among Jewish authorities in Slovakia and Subcarpathian Rus'. Furthermore, the state authorities' decision to retain both the Austrian and Hungarian legal codes that governed relations between Jewish communities and the state also made it impractical to unite them. From the outset, Zionists' goals and strategies were thus shaped by pragmatism and, ironically, by a sense of the cultural distinctiveness of Bohemia and Moravia's Jewish culture vis-à-vis the rest of the Jewish nation in Slovakia and Subcarpathian Rus'. And last, the urgency with which Jewish activists and their state partners approached the modernization of the country's Jewish communities has to be understood in its broader political and cultural context, namely that of a postwar order that called into question Jews' loyalties and their linguistic and cultural practices in several ways.

Bohemian and Moravian Jewry's place within the German-language Jewish cultural sphere, a characteristic particularly manifest in Jewish religious and communal life in the early twentieth century, became both ideologically and practically awkward in the postwar years. Since the 1780s, Jewish society in the Bohemian Lands had undergone a process of cultural and linguistic Germanization, in part due to state legislation and in part due to socioeconomic and cultural changes. This meant that Jewish communities kept their records and conducted their affairs in German, provided their members with elementary religious education in Hebrew and German, and rabbis gave their sermons in German. Over time, German replaced Yiddish as the everyday language of most Jews in the Bohemian Lands. For decades, Jewish communities in the Bohemian Lands had hired rabbis, cantors, and other religious personnel who were educated at the prestigious theological seminaries in Vienna, Breslau, and Budapest.[10] Students from across Austria-Hungary (including the Bohemian Lands), Germany, and beyond attended these prestigious institutions. Their graduates were German-speakers and thus able to find work in communities in Bohemia and Moravia. The establishment of Czechoslovakia profoundly disrupted this tradition. Now, the state demanded that rabbis and others in positions of authority be citizens of Czechoslovakia and expected them to be Czech-speaking. Furthermore, even though the rabbis' German-language seminary and university training retained its prestige, their foreignness and especially the fact that many candidates did not know Czech became politically and culturally suspect. Reconfiguring Judaism as Czech, one element of which was the education of a Czech-speaking, homegrown rabbinate, was only one of a series of challenges that Jewish leaders faced in the Bohemian Lands in the 1920s and '30s. Indeed, the Czechoslovak state's new demands on its religious communities only exacerbated and brought starkly into public view what Jewish activists had long sensed was a profound crisis in Jewish life in the Bohemian Lands, a crisis that predated the Great War.

This chapter explores how a group of Jewish leaders, secular and religious, Zionist and non-Zionists, responded to this crisis by working to modernize Jewish communal life. It was an effort that involved not only a cultural renaissance, but also changes in the relationship among communities and between community leaders and the state. At the core of the reformers' vision was the creation of a Prague-based Jewish authority that would act as a partner to the state in matters concerning the country's Jews.

The modernization of the Jewish communities in the Bohemian Lands went hand in hand with efforts to accentuate and display Jews' belonging in the region. In the years after the war, the memory of rural Jewish life, the centuries-old village and small-town communities that had thrived until the mid-nineteenth century, assumed increasing importance as symbols of Jews' ties to Bohemia and Moravia. To urbanized Jewish observers, these Jewish spaces, void of Jews yet rich in evidence of Jewish life, embodied the unique Jewish culture that had evolved over the centuries in the Bohemian Lands. At a time when Czech nationalists claimed the region as the heartland of their nation – marginalizing and delegitimizing the presence of other communities – these traces of Jewish history bore witness to Jews' deep roots in the Bohemian Lands.

Yet, at the same time, as the memory of the old way of Jewish life was revered, the existing rural communities struggling with dwindling numbers of members and resources became an eyesore for Jewish activists from larger communities such as those from Prague. They resented what they perceived as the decline, neglect, and chaos among rural Jews. As young Jews left for the cities, no one remained who could pick up the mantle from the older generation. In the name of preserving Jewish heritage for future generations, these urban leaders set about eroding the tradition for communal independence and the local customs of rural Jews. The concern over the fate of the rural village and small-town communities, their elderly residents, the synagogues, cemeteries, and other communal institutions and assets tied to the specific locales, reflected a sense of decay in Jewish life widespread among Jewish observers. Beginning in the 1920s, urban Jewish leaders were at the forefront of efforts to conserve the remnants of the old Jewish way of life as well as to recast their own growing communities as centers for Jewish cultural renewal.[11]

In the Bohemian Lands, a new Jewish authority, known as the Supreme Council of the Jewish Religious Communities in Bohemia, Moravia, and Silesia (Nejvyšší Rada svazů židovských náboženských obcí v Čechách, na Moravě, a ve Slezku/Oberster Rat der Kultusgemeinde-Verbände Böhmens, Mährens und Schlesiens; hereafter, the Supreme Council), became the main representative of the regions' Jews. Although the institution itself was politically neutral, the Jewish activists involved in this governing body were anything but. They represented a range of ideological, regional, and national traditions and loyalties. Its chair, August Stein (1854–1937), was a well-known Czech-Jewish activist, while his closest daily collaborator, the Supreme Council's secretary, Gustav Fleischmann, was a Zionist activist and employee of Prague's Jewish community. Yet, they and the other members of the Supreme Council shared a desire for Jewish renewal that nurtured historical awareness and cultural familiarity among Jews. Their work focused on creating a meaningful secular Jewish culture centered in the most historically significant institution in Jewish life, namely the community. They did so through strategies intended to make the Jewish community relevant to Jews as well as worthy of the respect of non-Jews. At the heart of the efforts, which Jewish reformers undertook with the support of the state authorities, was the desire to create their vision of an ideal Jewish citizenry – people who were loyal to the state, equally at home in German, Czech, and Jewish culture, and whose traditions and history were firmly rooted in its Czechoslovak homeland.

THE POSTWAR CRISIS IN THE JEWISH COMMUNITIES IN THE BOHEMIAN LANDS

The postwar order posed multiple challenges to Jewish society in Czechoslovakia. The collapse of Austria-Hungary undermined traditional cultural and religious networks. The new political boundaries cut off the Jews of Bohemia and Moravia from the German, Austrian, and Hungarian Jewish religious and cultural institutions upon which they had relied. Like the Jews in the Bohemian Lands, the Jews in Slovakia belonged to multiple cultural and religious worlds. Although Vienna, Berlin, and Budapest were important centers, some Jews, including many wartime refugees, looked further east to Hasidic communities in Polish Galicia. These were cultural, religious, and kinship connections that were rendered suspicious in the postwar political climate when insecure state authorities looked with suspicion at communities that straddled the new political borders.

In the Bohemian Lands, the political changes exacerbated already existing problems within the Jewish communities. For decades, rural and small-town Jewish communities had struggled to maintain their religious institutions in the face of a rapidly diminishing and secularizing Jewish population. As Jews abandoned villages and small towns for the region's fast-growing cities, the old communities, as physical evidence of Jews' long-time presence in the Bohemian Lands, were invested with new meaning. The prospects of the disappearance of rural Jewish life in the Bohemian Lands, of the demise of this anchor of cultural identification, generated unease among some Jews. By the mid-1920s, rabbis and other communal leaders concerned with what they saw as a floundering Jewish religious life in the old rural communities as well as in the growing urban ones raised the alarm.

In Austria-Hungary, the Jewish societies in Bohemia, Moravia, and Silesia had been governed by distinct provincial laws as well as statewide legislation. Although the communities continued to have somewhat separate historical experiences, after the Habsburg state's collapse, Jewish activists from these regions increasingly came to see themselves as part of one Jewish community. This integrative process was facilitated by Bohemian and Moravian Jewish activists' efforts to distance themselves from what they perceived as the culturally backward Orthodox Jews in Czechoslovakia's east. Their sense of common fate was also strengthened by the view that the communities in the Bohemian Lands, despite their distinct traditions, faced similar challenges in the postwar years.[12]

In Moravia, Jewish communities had historically formed compact and urban settlements, a structure that shaped Moravian Jewry's distinct institutions and culture. In some Moravian towns, Jewish communities constituted both religious and political entities where Jews maintained a municipality separate from the general municipality in which they resided. These "Jewish townships" were known as Jewish political communities, a unique phenomenon among European Jews.[13] Furthermore, Moravian Jewry had a well-established tradition for intra-communal cooperation and problem solving. Since 1787, Jewish leaders oversaw the Moravian Jewish *Landesmassafond*. Although originally established for tax purposes, this fund, according to the historian Michael Miller, was used for "support for the religious, educational, and communal needs of Moravian Jewry well into the twentieth century."[14] Significantly, it allowed smaller communities with dwindling populations to continue to meet their obligations to their members.[15]

By the second half of the nineteenth century, almost two-thirds of the non-Jewish population in Moravia were Czech-speakers. Yet, Moravia's Jews, living mainly in towns and cities, favored German language over Czech, which was mainly spoken by the rural majority. This was a result not only of historical government reforms, such as the German-Jewish schools, but also the fact that German-speakers remained dominant in Moravia's urban centers. From 1861, the political Jewish communities, most of which were urban electoral districts, became a heated issue in the intensifying German and Czech political struggle in Moravia's cities. Jews, Miller argues, were thought to "tip the scales in favor of the German candidates."[16] Indeed, in Moravia, and unlike Bohemia,

German was unrivaled as a language of high culture, education, and social mobility until 1918. In time, Moravian Jews' "Germanness" became a distinct characteristic of the region's Jewish culture.[17]

The Jewish political communities remained in place until the Czechoslovak state authorities abolished them between 1919 and 1925 (all but two were dissolved in 1919).[18] By then, Moravian Jewry's traditional political and religious institutions had already been weakened as Jews moved from small towns to the region's growing industrial centers in the second half of the nineteenth century. By 1921, 47 percent of Moravia's Jews resided in Brno/Brünn (10,866) and Moravská Ostrava/Mährisch Ostrau (6,872). These were communities that had only been established in the 1850s.[19] In the decades before the First World War, thousands of Moravian Jews moved to nearby Vienna. Thus, between 1890 and 1921, the number of Jews in the region dropped from 45,324 to 37,989.[20] This flight from small towns to the industrial centers challenged the economic, social, and religious viability of many of Moravia's fifty-two communities.[21]

In contrast to the compact Jewish communities in Moravia, Jews in Bohemia had historically lived in hundreds of villages and small towns, forming a network of numerous small communities, with Prague as the major center. In 1921, the province's 79,777 Jews composed 203 communities (almost four times the number of communities in Moravia).[22] By the turn of the twentieth century, as in Moravia, most Jews lived in the urban centers. Prague alone claimed 40 percent of Bohemian Jewry (31,751 in 1921), while another 30 percent lived in the region's other large cities, such as Teplice/Teplitz, Plzeň/Pilsen, and Karlovy Vary/Carlsbad.[23] The Bohemian communities were more divided and estranged from each other than were their Moravian counterparts. This was due both to the tradition of small independent communities and to the significant social and cultural differences between urban and rural Jewries. By the late 1800s, the influx of Czech-speaking rural Jews to Bohemia's industrial and urban centers challenged the hegemony of the German-speaking Jewish establishments.[24] As in Moravia, Bohemia's Jews had also adopted German language and culture, but as a result of the dispersion of Jewish settlement here, more Jews had a greater familiarity with Czech language and culture, because many lived in villages and small-town communities populated predominantly by Czech-speakers. Furthermore, in Bohemia, many larger towns and cities had both Czech- and German-speaking middle classes. This facilitated the retention of bilingualism among many urbanizing and socially mobile former rural Jews. In short, in Bohemia, Czech increasingly rivaled German as a language with social and political advantages, and bilingualism was invested with cultural significance as a characteristic of Bohemian Jews' particular historical experience.

The last, and by far the smallest, of the three former Austrian crown lands that now constituted Czechoslovakia's western half was the province of Silesia. It had a relatively small Jewish population. In 1921, Silesia's 7,317 Jews lived in nine communities.[25] These were German-speaking communities, and the geographical proximity to Moravian Jewry facilitated close cooperation between Jewish leaders in the two provinces. In practice, state authorities and Jewish observers alike treated the Jews of Moravia and Silesia as one sociocultural entity.[26] Despite the communities' distinct historical experiences, after the First World War Jewish communal leaders and activists in Bohemia, Moravia, and Silesia faced similar sociocultural and institutional challenges.

The Jewish communities in the Bohemian Lands were governed by the Law of March 21, 1890 (Law for the External Legal Conditions of the Jewish Religious Community/*Gesetz der äusseren Rechtsverhältnisse der israelitischen Religionsgemeinschaft*), as was the rest of Habsburg Austria, except for Galicia. The law defined the communities' territorial boundaries, degree of independence, and responsibilities vis-à-vis both its members and the state authorities. After 1918, the Czechoslovak state, now in charge of territories governed by Austrian as well as Hungarian legal codes, left the existing laws regarding Jews' religious communities in place.[27] The Austrian Law of 1890 specified, as had previous legislation, that a certain town or geographic area could have only one Jewish community.[28] Thus, while there could be multiple synagogues and prayer rooms within a certain area, they all belonged to the same community, whose leaderships were, according to the law, required to respect "different ritual directions" in their midst.[29] Similarly, all Jews who had not formally given up their membership belonged to the Jewish community where they resided. Members were obligated to pay community taxes, an obligation that could be enforced by the local state authorities. The community in turn was responsible for meeting its members' religious needs. Each community was therefore required to employ a rabbi and expected to maintain institutions, such as a synagogue or prayer room, a cemetery, a ritual bath, and a ritual butcher, and to provide elementary religious education. With the establishment of Czechoslovakia, new citizenship requirements were placed on communal leaders. Although all Jews regardless of citizenship belonged to the community in which they resided, only Czechoslovak citizens were eligible to hold positions of authority within it. Now, religious functionaries, including rabbis, were also required to have Czechoslovak citizenship in addition "to a flawless moral and civic character [*mravní a státoobčanskou bezzávadnost*]."[30]

In Czechoslovakia's eastern half, in Slovakia and Subcarpathian Rus', the legislation stemming from the Kingdom of Hungary remained in place. In contrast to the Bohemian Lands, the Jews in the former Hungarian territories had been organized along denominational lines – Neolog and Orthodox – since 1868.[31] In addition, some communities chose to remain unaffiliated. They became known as Status Quo communities.[32] If in the western provinces each locality had one unified community that accommodated different types of observance, then in Slovakia there were parallel communities within one jurisdiction. In 1920, the Orthodox communities in Slovakia organized a regional association, which expanded a few years later to include communities from Subcarpathian Rus' (Organisace autonomních ortodoxních židovských obcí).[33] By the mid-1920s, the association Jeschurun (Svaz židovských náboženských obcí na Slovensku Jeschurun) emerged as the representative of the region's Neolog and Status Quo communities. These territorial and denominational federations continued a prewar tradition for extensive intra-communal cooperation within each denomination.

Yet, at the same time, the social and religious division within this former Hungarian Jewry was significant. As the historian Jacob Katz remembers, by the early twentieth century, Neolog and Orthodox Jews formed separate social units, and coming from an Orthodox family, he "was taught to think of the Neologs as members of a different religious community." To illustrate the divisions, he notes, "Entry into a Neolog synagogue was considered no less taboo in our circles than a visit to a Catholic Church."[34] In Slovakia and Subcarpathian Rus', Orthodoxy remained dominant in the interwar years. In 1930, Slovakia had an estimated 217 communities, of which 165 were Orthodox and 52 Neolog and Status Quo (the majority of which were Neolog ones). In Subcarpathian Rus', there were 21 Orthodox (these included Hasidic communities) and only 1 Neolog.[35]

The relationship between the Jewish communities and the state was also different in Slovakia and Subcarpathian Rus', another remnant of the area's Hungarian past. In contrast to the former Austrian regions, the Jewish communities in Slovakia and Subcarpathian Rus' had received state subsidies for their clergy and for Jewish schools since 1895. Even though funds were withheld for some time in the immediate postwar years, the Czechoslovak authorities decided to uphold the right of the regions' Jewish communities to receive these subsidies.[36] The old Hungarian legal code remained in place in Slovakia and Subcarpathian Rus' through the interwar period, much in the same way that the Austrian one with regard to the Jewish communities was left fairly intact in the western provinces.

Looking east, Jewish observers in the Bohemian Lands, including many rabbis, had a somewhat ambivalent relationship to the religious traditionalism there. They viewed the Orthodox Jewish societies in Slovakia and Subcarpathian Rus' as backward and did their utmost to distance themselves, and their communities, from the so-called eastern Jews and their alleged religious fanaticism. At the same time, they held up images of empty synagogues and dilapidated cemeteries in villages and small towns across Bohemia as the embodiment of the profound material and spiritual crisis of Jewish society in the Bohemian Lands. For decades, they argued, Bohemia's old communities had floundered, their leaders unable or unwilling to maintain the most basic religious institutions and services for their diminishing and increasingly secularized memberships.[37] In the cities, where the majority of Jews now lived, most Jews were ignorant of and indifferent to their religious tradition and cultural heritage.[38] To activists committed to Jewish religious and communal life, the postwar crisis in the Jewish communities was an outcome of decades of neglect by incompetent leaderships and indifferent members, who disregarded the most basic tenets of Jewish tradition. This was a state of affairs, they warned, that threatened the future of Jewish life in many parts of the Bohemian Lands.

By the mid-1920s, rabbis, social scientists, community administrators, and others committed to and with a vested interest in organized Jewish life regularly debated the causes of the crisis in the Jewish press and at public meetings. Most agreed that the "decimation" of the old communities was a result of emancipation, the lifting of restrictions on Jews' residence and professions, and the subsequent move by thousands of Jews to cities across the Bohemian Lands and further afield to other parts of Austria-Hungary and to North America. But to these observers, the communities were plagued not only by a demographic crisis, but also by a spiritual one.

In the Jewish press, writers called readers' attention to the chaos prevailing in rural and small-town communities. Responding to a survey initiated by the Zionist *Židovské zprávy,* one writer, claiming to represent a rural Jewish perspective – "a voice in the desert" – pointed to the incompetence of the oligarchic communal leaderships. Tradition and law dictated that the largest taxpayers had the most influence rather than people most dedicated or competent to govern the community.[39] Indifferent to Judaism and to their congregants' needs, according to the author, many boards refused to hire rabbis or even religious teachers, thereby eroding religious life in their communities.[40] In a series of articles in the Czech-Jewish newspaper *Rozvoj* around the same time, Rabbi Isaac Eisenberg also painted an image of disorder, ignorance, and stagnation in Bohemia's rural communities. He too described how community boards looking to save money chose not to employ rabbis and teachers in blatant disregard of the law, which indeed required communities to have a rabbi and to provide elementary religious instruction.[41] These lay leaders, thriving on the local authorities' indifference to or ignorance of Jewish affairs, claimed Eisenberg, instead hired rabbis from neighboring communities on an ad hoc basis to perform specific tasks. Preying on the desperate financial situation of the small-town and village rabbis, these lay leaders lacked both social responsibility and respect for Jewish and state laws.[42] Not surprisingly, to Eisenberg and other rabbis writing about rural life, the secular boards' indifference and corruption were yet another reflection of the moral decline that stemmed from secularization and the abandonment of Jewish traditions.[43]

Even though Eisenberg placed much of the responsibility for the decline in Jewish life on the secular leaders, he also noted the devastating effects of the postwar land reforms on rural Jewish life. Enacted in 1919, the reforms were intended to distribute land held by large landowners such as the Catholic Church and the German and Hungarian nobility to the country's land-hungry Czech, Slovak, and Rusyn populations. But, Eisenberg argued, these new government policies had, albeit unintentionally, eroded the material basis for Jewish life outside Bohemia's urban centers.[44] The land reforms divided large estates among local users, thereby forcing the previous owners or tenants off the land, depriving rural Jewish communities of their major taxpayers: the Jewish owners, renters, or managers of large agricultural estates.[45] Once the latter lost their livelihoods, they moved to the cities, leaving behind community boards unable to make ends meet.[46] "While the law is not directed against Jews, even though Jewish families have been the renters and managers of such estates for generations," Eisenberg claimed, "in the end the Jews are the victims of this law."[47] If Jews' indifference to Judaism were to blame for much of the decline in the communities, then the postwar land reform was the nail in the coffin for rural Jewish life in Bohemia.

Others believed that it was the proliferation of very small Jewish communities, often made up of only a few families, that constituted the problem. These miniscule communities – comprising one to two hundred members, and often much less – were not equipped to handle the demanding administrative and educational tasks of the present day.[48] Thus incompetence and indifference were only part of the explanation put forward. At the heart of the problems that the small communities were struggling with was simply the lack of people. Although these communities might have thrived in the past, they did not have the resources to cope with the cultural and social challenges of the times.

Eisenberg and others were well aware that it was the increasing urbanization among Jews that posed the greatest challenge to the old Jewish way of life in the Bohemian Lands. The statistician František Friedmann, always a keen observer of social change, depicted a community near his hometown Sedlčany/Seltschan as illustrative of the transformation of

Jewish life in the region. "[In 1871], the largest community [in the region] was Kosová Hora, with 400 members (185 men and 215 women), one rabbi, two teachers, its own synagogue, and a school with 100 students. In 1921, this community had only about 50 souls left, and out of all the institutions, the only one remaining is the cemetery."[49] Even as Jews' move to the cities eroded the existence of traditional communities, new Jewish centers were emerging in large towns and cities in the Bohemian Lands. But to some observers, these urban communities were ill-equipped to become centers for Jewish life, because they lacked cultural and educational institutions that would suit the needs of a new generation of Jews.

In the postwar years, new forms of Jewish education were held up by a variety of activists as the key to a regeneration of Jewish communal life across the Bohemian Lands. The centrality of education rested to some degree on these observers' shared belief that local Jews were extraordinarily indifferent to and ignorant of their religious and cultural heritage. One such critic was the Zionist rabbi Gustav Sicher (1880–1960). Sicher, a member of Mizraḥi (the most prominent religious Zionist organization), became the rabbi for Prague's large Vinohrady/Weinberge community in 1927 and the city's chief rabbi in the early 1930s. According to the historian Kateřina Čapková, Sicher was the public face of Judaism in Prague, and as a Czech-speaker and talented orator, he made occasional appearances on the radio.[50] Sicher believed strongly in the importance of developing Czech-language Jewish educational materials and was instrumental in the translation of the Torah into Czech, a project he began in the mid-1920s together with his colleague Isidor Hirsch (1864–1940) from Prague's Karlín/Karolinenthal community. As an editor and contributor to *Židovské Zprávy,* Sicher commented extensively, and mostly critically, on religious life. In 1921, for example, he noted about Bohemia's Jewish communities:

> When it comes to religion, Jews in Bohemia – even more so than anywhere else in Western Europe – are done for. There is no question about it. The synagogues are empty and religious institutions are rotting away. . . . What is happening in the countryside [i.e., in the rural communities] on a small scale is happening in Prague on a larger one. Today, in Prague, the city of ancient Jewish life, Jewish heritage sites serve only as a testament to the vibrant religious life of the past.[51]

For Sicher, Bohemian Jews held the dubious honor of being Europe's most de-Judaized Jewry.[52] The disregard for the Jewish tradition in his community was particularly apparent, in Sicher's mind, in the lack of religious and educational texts in Czech. In a favorable review of his colleague Richard Feder's Jewish stories in Czech, Sicher noted that "except for the first volume of Jewish stories [*Židovské besídky: pro zábavu a poučení dospělejší mládeže židovské,* published in 1912–1913], we do not have any other books from which a child who knows only Czech can learn something about Jews and Judaism and thus escape the complete ignorance that prevails among us to a much greater degree than among other European Jews."[53] Indeed, to Sicher the solution to Jews' indifference to Judaism was not religious reform, as was being suggested from some quarters, but bringing forth, through education, a new Jewish consciousness rooted in religious traditions as well as in a sense of historical and cultural belonging.

Richard Feder (1875–1970), a well-known Czech-Jewish activist and the rabbi of Kolín, about fifty kilometers east of Prague, also believed that the future of religious life in the Bohemian Lands depended on a collective recommitment to Jewish education.[54] Like Sicher, Feder did his rabbinical training in Vienna and then went on to complete his doctorate at the Czech-language Charles University in Prague. In debates on Jewish education among secular and religious Jewish leaders in the mid-1920s, Feder advocated for the establishment of a new kind of Talmud-Torah, the traditional Jewish religious school. A symbol of traditionalism and ignorance for many reformers and parents, many Talmud-Torahs had been closed due to dwindling student numbers. Feder envisioned the creation of a modern institution with well-qualified teachers that would provide both children and adults with a sound Jewish education.[55] The needs of Jews living in small communities could be served, Feder proposed, by mobile Jewish educators, traveling lecturers covering a wide range of topics in Jewish history and culture.

Despite their political differences, the Czech-Jew Richard Feder and the Zionist Gustav Sicher alike agreed that the new Jewish curriculum should not focus on religion alone, but also on students' acquiring broader knowledge of Jewish history and literature. Furthermore, they believed that the creation of a Czech Judaism, a Jewish liturgy and religious literature in the Czech language, constituted a crucial step in making Judaism meaningful to Jews. For both men, this Czechification went hand in hand with, in Feder's words, "a reacquisition of Hebrew, which would bring Jews closer to their Jewishness."[56] The Jewish renaissance, as imagined by these two rabbis, was thus defined by the coexistence of Czech and Hebrew as tools through which the Jewish tradition could be reacquired by Jews whose primary language was Czech as well as maintained for future generations.[57] As Richard Feder continued to expand and develop his Hebrew-language textbooks for use by both Czech- and German-speaking Jewish children, Sicher and his colleagues embarked on the translation of the Torah into Czech.

By the mid-1920s, the sense of crisis and decay strengthened the voices coming from different corners of the Jewish political spectrum that called for Jewish unity and, in particular, for the establishment of a centralized leadership institution that could act as a representative of Jews to the outside world. This call for unification was not just a postwar phenomenon. In the 1850s, Moravian Jewish leaders had attempted and failed to create a unified leadership for the region (even so, they continued to work together to keep small communities afloat through the *Landesmassafond,* an institution that no doubt served as an inspiration to the postwar reformers). In the late 1890s, Jewish communal leaders in the Austrian provinces had tried to establish a unified leadership in Vienna that would be the public representative of Austria's Jews, an initiative that ran aground due to internal Jewish differences.[58] In the Bohemian Lands in the decades that followed, some Jewish communities succeeded in establishing voluntary federations along political, national, and regional lines, such as the Federation of Czech Israelite Communities (Svaz českých israelských náboženských obcí) in 1909 and, during the First World War, an organization for the Jewish communities in Moravia (Der Landesverband der israelitischen Kultusgemeinden in Mähren).[59]

After the war, proponents of unity, who were aware of the profound sociocultural divisions among Czechoslovakia's Jews but were convinced of the importance of centralization, turned to the state for support in establishing a central leadership for the country's Jews.

The Jewish National Council's public demands for unity of the Jewish communities across Czechoslovakia in 1918 and 1919 were seconded by a Czechoslovak assembly of rabbis convening in the late summer of 1920.[60] Yet, nothing came of these proclamations in practice. Only in the mid-1920s did the efforts to establish some degree of cooperation between the Jewish communities in the Bohemian Lands succeed. Although federations for all the communities in Moravia and Silesia had existed since the end of the First World War, the Bohemian communities remained deeply divided.[61] Unable to overcome their social, cultural, and national differences, in Bohemia three federations emerged.[62] Jewish communities in and on the outskirts of Prague established an organization for Greater Prague that were joined by some of Bohemia's other large urban communities, namely Plzeň/Pilsen and České Budějovice/Budweis (Svaz Pražských židovských náboženských obcí/ Verband der jüdischen Kultusgemeinden in Prag).[63] This federation consisted of communities committed to bilingualism. It was flanked by German and Czech federations representing German-speaking (Verband der Kultusgemeinden mit deutscher Geschäftssprache) and Czech-speaking (Svaz českých náboženských obcí židovských v Čechách) communities in Bohemia, respectively.[64] Even though the Prague federation represented some of Bohemia's major Jewish centers, Prague being the most significant one, the German-language federation also included important communities such as Teplice-Šanov/Teplitz-Schönau, the largest Bohemian community outside Prague.[65] The Moravian and Silesian federations represented all the Jewish communities within their regions. Meanwhile, in Bohemia, some of the more than two hundred communities remained unaffiliated.[66]

As Jewish leaders and activists struggled to navigate the postwar challenges to Jewish religious institutions and their cultural traditions and networks, they fell back on well-known strategies for religious and cultural continuity. As in the 1780s, when German education and modernized religious instruction was introduced in Jewish schools, these reformers envisioned a simultaneous strengthening of Jewish education alongside a cultural-linguistic transformation of Judaism and its institutions.[67] This Jewish renaissance would both embody Jews' return to Judaism and signal Jews' moral respectability and their suitability as citizens. This was an effort that required education of ordinary Jews as well as a new generation of Czech-speaking and well-educated rabbis and other spiritual leaders. It was a task that Jewish reformers could solve only in unison and in close cooperation with the state authorities.

THE CREATION OF A CENTRAL JEWISH AUTHORITY

From the outset of their postwar work, Zionists in the Bohemian Lands had envisioned a centralized Jewish leadership, representing the country's communities, as playing a central role in the Jewish national revival movement.[68] They believed that the community as defined in strictly religious terms had lost its appeal to most Jews.[69] A new modern institution, serving Jews as a people, as a national community, should take on broader educational, cultural, and social welfare tasks. Furthermore, as had become clear during and immediately after the war, some situations, in this case the Galician refugee crisis, made cooperation between Jewish communities necessary.[70] In their calls for communal reform, Zionist activists rallied against what they viewed as entrenched oligarchs and assimilationist leaderships. But once they gained seats on community boards, they negotiated and cooperated with existing leaderships regardless of their ideological differences. The Supreme Council, for example, whose members represented Jewish communities in the Bohemian Lands, was the result of successful and sustained partnership between a politically diverse group of Jewish activists committed to creating a central Jewish leadership. And if Jewish community leaders believed there was a need for a new organizational structure for Bohemian and Moravian Jewry, so did the state authorities overseeing the country's religious groups.

Since the early 1920s, the Ministry of Education had pondered the possibility of creating a Czechoslovak Jewish institution that would unite the Jewish communities in the Bohemian Lands, Slovakia, and Subcarpathian Rus'. This was an organization that was supposed to connect the newly amalgamated territories with each other by breaking down the legal, administrative, and cultural differences that complicated the authority of the central government. In early 1921 in a substantial internal report, the Ministry of Education's civil servants investigated the French and German experiences for a model for a centralized Jewish leadership with statewide authority.[71] The issue, however, remained unresolved. Then, in the summer of 1926 as Jewish communities became eligible for state subsidies for clergy, the question of creating a Czechoslovak Jewish organization reemerged in the Ministry of Education.[72]

In an internal report, a civil servant recommended that a central Jewish administration be established, an institution similar to those representing other religious societies such as the Catholic and Orthodox Churches. This body would then receive state subsidies on behalf of the Jewish communities. A Jewish central administration was crucial, the author noted, in order "for Jews not to be left behind everybody else again."[73] Subsequently, the Ministry of Education in Prague solicited the opinions of the regional authorities regarding the question of a Czechoslovak Jewish organization. The state authorities in Bohemia, Moravia, and Silesia unanimously favored centralization and a countrywide organization. The ones in Slovakia and Subcarpathian Rus', however, deemed such plans wholly unfeasible.[74] The Ministry of Education's office in Mukačevo/Munkács/Munkatsch/Mukacheve dismissed the unification plans, noting that "considering the mentality of the Jews here," the leaders of the predominantly Orthodox and Hasidic Jewish societies of Slovakia and Subcarpathian Rus' were unlikely to voluntarily join an organization that included non-Orthodox members.[75] The office in Bratislava/Pressburg/Pozsony concurred that the religious differences between east and west were so profound that Jewish leaders in Slovakia were unlikely to even consider a proposal prepared by the Prague federation.[76] The idea was shelved, but the desire for statewide unification among civil servants remained, a pressure that the Supreme Council, looking only to unite the communities in the Bohemian Lands, was determined to resist.[77]

From the outset, the Supreme Council did not discourage the belief, circulating among the Ministry of Education's civil servants, that unification of the eastern and western Jewish communities in a Czechoslovak institution was impossible because of the vast religious and cultural differences among the country's Jews.[78] The Zionist activists on the council thus had to downplay their usual claim that the country's Jews constituted one nation, whose interests they rightfully represented.[79]

The Supreme Council was concerned about the Ministry of Education creating a dysfunctional, but Czechoslovak Jewish authority, powerful yet unable to address any of the challenges facing Jews in the Bohemian Lands.[80] They worried, first, because historically the Orthodox and non-Orthodox communities in the former Hungarian regions had been unable to overcome their differences and reach a consensus on substantive issues.[81] There was little indication that it would be any easier now. Second, just as the social, cultural, and religious differences between the Orthodox and Neolog communities in Slovakia and Subcarpathian Rus' were substantial, so were the ones between Jews in the country's eastern and western regions. Both council members and state bureaucrats appeared to have little hope that these differences could be overcome. Last, the Supreme Council's reservations probably also reflected unease about the political consequences of statewide Jewish unity. Not only were the eastern Jewish populations significantly larger than the western ones, but they also had a historical tradition of unity and cooperation across communal boundaries that added to their political strength vis-à-vis the Jews in the Bohemian Lands. Indeed, as mentioned earlier, the majority of Jewish communities in Slovakia and Subcarpathian Rus' had joined a forceful representative organization already in 1920. If unity was enforced by the state, the eastern, Orthodox communities would have the upper hand over the western ones.

Despite their reservations about state intervention, once the legislation making Jewish communities eligible for state subsidies was on the table, Jewish activists were being offered an opportunity to inject financial resources into Jewish religious life that they could not afford to pass up. As the new legislation passed through the legislative and administrative offices of the state in early 1926, representatives of the five community federations in the Bohemian Lands worked to appoint a leadership that would act as a public representative of the Jewish communities in the region.[82] Established in November 1926, this leadership institution was known as the Supreme Council of the Jewish Religious Communities in Bohemia, Moravia, and Silesia.[83] By the end of that year, the Ministry of Education had granted the Supreme Council status as a provisional representative of the Jewish communities in the Bohemian Lands.[84]

The Supreme Council's board members included both lay and religious leaders, some of whom remained part of the council until its dissolution at the end of 1939.[85] The composition of this first board illustrates the way in which this institution brought together a cross section of activists with complex political, cultural, and regional allegiances.[86] The council's chairmanship was assumed by August Stein, the prominent Czech-Jewish activist from Prague. By then already in his seventies, Stein, a lawyer by training, had had a long career in the Prague Municipality and had played a central role in the so-called ghetto clearing in Prague's old Jewish quarter Josefov/Josephstadt at the turn of the century.[87] In the 1920s, he acted as chair of Prague's Jewish community. Stein was deeply involved with the city's Jewish Museum and had been committed to the creation of a "Czech" Judaism for decades, a project that included the compilation of an influential Czech-Hebrew prayer book in 1884.[88] Stein remained at the head of the Supreme Council until 1931, when the physician Josef Popper (1871–1942) took over. Popper, like Stein, had been with the Supreme Council from the beginning and was one of the four members from Prague on the council's nine-member board. In contrast to Stein, Popper was sympathetic to Zionism and was considered a representative of German-speaking Jews in Prague. Popper, who also chaired the Czechoslovak chapter of the fraternal organization B'nai B'rith and represented his country in the Jewish Agency, remained at the helm of the Supreme Council until 1938.[89] The well-known Prague Zionist Norbert Adler acted as the council's executive director while pursuing a career in municipal politics.[90]

Bohemia's Czech and German communities were represented by Hugo Rindler (1887–?) (Benešov/Beneschau) and Emil Margulies (Litoměřice/Leitmeritz), respectively.[91] Margulies, a Zionist leader and chair of the Jewish Party from 1931 to 1935, was also, as we have seen, an outspoken defender of the rights of German-speaking Jews in Czechoslovakia.[92] While the Bohemian communities had six seats on the board, the Moravian and Silesian communities held two and one, respectively. Alois Hilf (1851–1934), the longtime chair of the community in Moravská Ostrava/Mährisch Ostrau, and Leopold Goldschmied (1867–?), a rabbi from Prostějov/Prossnitz, represented Moravia. Known for their Zionist activism, Hilf and Goldschmied had both been instrumental in transforming their communities from religious to national institutions.[93] Thus, out of the nine members on the Supreme Council's executive, five were well-known Zionists.

The list of important actors is, however, not yet complete. As a career Jewish bureaucrat, Gustav Fleischmann, the Supreme Council's secretary from 1926 to 1939, played a key role in the institution's work and activities. Fleischmann, then in his early thirties, was, like Margulies, Adler, and Stein, a lawyer and at the time working as the top bureaucrat in the Prague Jewish community, a position he held from 1922 until he left for Palestine in 1939.[94] He began his Zionist career on the Jewish National Council and continued as a contributor to *Židovské zprávy* in the 1920s and '30s. With the Supreme Council headquartered in the offices of Prague's Jewish community in the Jewish Town Hall on Maisel Street, Fleischmann was an indispensable part of the everyday affairs of the council, for which he authored statistical surveys, minutes of meetings, and correspondence.[95]

The Supreme Council's executive thus consisted of several generations of well-educated, politically and administratively experienced, and Jewishly committed activists.[96] Many of them shared Zionist sympathies or commitments, but they still had to overcome their regional, linguistic (at least four and perhaps more of the nine council members were bilingual), and ideological differences. The predominance of Zionists appointed to the Supreme Council indicated that by the mid-1920s they were considered respectable leaders in communities across the Bohemian Lands. Even if they did not dominate the community boards on the local level to the same extent as they did the Supreme Council, Zionists were nevertheless considered competent and trustworthy representatives of the regions' Jews, even by a grand-old man of the Czech-Jewish movement like August Stein.

Zionist activists' influence in Jewish communal politics is testimony not only to their commitment to Jewish renewal, but also to the pragmatism that they adhered to. During the election of the first chair of the Supreme Council, for example, Leopold Goldschmied and other Zionists chose the Czech-Jewish candidate over the Zionist one in a move that asserted their autonomy vis-à-vis broader Zionist priorities as well as helped consolidate the council's legitimacy as an all-Jewish rather than a Zionist institution.[97]

If representatives from the five Prague communities dominated the Supreme Council's executive, then the seats on the council's general assembly were more evenly distributed, with each federation, regardless of its size, sending five representatives. In addition to these lay delegates, six representatives of the associations for rabbis and religious functionaries attended the assembly.[98] A reflection of the secular activists' self-confidence vis-à-vis the regions' religious leaders, the Supreme Council awarded the latter an advisory role in an effort to restore to traditional Jewish leaders a degree of respectability as well as to soothe the Orthodox "pockets" that were still influential within the communities in the Bohemian Lands.[99]

A few days after its inaugural assembly in early November 1926, the Supreme Council, at this point a body approved only to receive and distribute state subsidies to the region's Jewish communities, appealed to the Ministry of Education to recognize formally its authority as a representative of the Jewish communities. "As the authorized spokesman for the Jewish religious societies in Bohemia, Moravia, and Silesia," the Supreme Council pledged in return "to place our efforts and our influence at the disposition of the honorable Ministry and other government offices in matters regarding the Jews of these regions."[100] The Ministry of Education complied, and as an officially recognized institution, the Supreme Council was now eligible to apply for state subsidies for its administrative expenses, the employment and education of Jewish clergy, and the maintenance of synagogues and other communal sites.[101] Thus, by the late 1920s, the Jewish cultural renewal movement stood to receive a substantive infusion of resources from the state.[102]

THE STATE AND ITS JEWS

As a voluntary association with no legal basis or any formal power, the Supreme Council's authority and eligibility for state support depended on the Ministry of Education recognizing it as a useful partner.[103] Uncertain of the support among Jewish community boards, the council looked to mobilize the authority and the resources of the state for its modernization program. Headed by experienced administrators and lawyers, the council presented itself as well-equipped to form a Jewish central administration committed to correcting the "terrible state of affairs" in the communities through rational and centralizing management practices.[104] Although the Ministry of Education was eager to pass on the supervision of the Jewish communities, including the oversight of the annual state subsidies, to a trusted Jewish partner, it needed assurances that this leadership prioritized "the state before all else! [*Stát nade vše!*]."[105]

From the perspective of the Ministry of Education, a central Jewish administration would not only ease the pressure on its own resources, but also play an important role in shaping Jews into loyal and Czech-speaking citizens.[106] Among the ministry's civil servants there was a perception that Jews in the Bohemian Lands (and the rest of Czechoslovakia) were not Czech enough, a belief nurtured by the so-called lack of a "native" Czech rabbinate as well as the absence of a Czech translation of the Torah. It was a perception perhaps encouraged by their colleague Edvard Lederer (1859–1944), a prominent Czech-Jewish writer, journalist, and political activist, who worked in the Ministry of Education's section on religious affairs from 1919 to 1926. Although the extent of his involvement in Jewish matters within the ministry is unclear, he did travel on official business to Slovakia's Jewish communities in the summer of 1920. Lederer strongly favored centralization, and his support for the establishment of a central Jewish authority was echoed in the appeals made over the years by various Jewish lobby groups.[107]

In postwar Czechoslovakia, one of the most contested political issues was the separation of church and state. Some Czech nationalists viewed the Catholic Church as a Habsburg institution used to assert Austrian dominance over the Czech nation. In contrast, their Slovak counterparts perceived Catholicism as integral to Slovak nationhood. In the revolutionary atmosphere of the state's first few years, the government passed legislation meant to undermine the church's legal and cultural dominance by, for example, introducing civil marriage and divorce, limiting religious instruction in public schools, and expropriating church property.[108] The educational policies in particular became the stage for bitter confrontation between Catholics and anti-clerical factions. By the mid-1920s the radicals had lost out. Since the Catholic Church continued to enjoy considerable popular support across the country, and as the issue threatened to damage relations between Czechs and Slovaks, the government backed off.[109]

It was not only the Catholic Church that felt the effects of the drive for the separation of church and state. Other religious communities, such as the Jewish one, also saw their religious infrastructure come under attack. The new legislation that limited religious instruction in public schools is a case in point. For decades, the majority of Jewish children in the Bohemian Lands received their formal Jewish education through the mandatory religious instruction in the public school system.[110] Rather than maintaining separate Jewish educational institutions, Jewish teachers worked predominantly within the general public system.[111] The reduction in the number of hours for religious instruction in the public schools was thus set to have a significant impact on Jewish education. Rabbis and religious instructors warned of a complete collapse of Jewish education. As their livelihoods and moral authority came under attack, they appealed to the state to consider Jewish educators as partners in making Jews into good citizens.

In late August of 1920, rabbis from the Bohemian Lands and some from Slovakia gathered in Prague to establish an organization for rabbis in Czechoslovakia. In their public memorandum to the Ministry of Education, the rabbis warned of the dire effects of making religious instruction in public middle schools voluntary.[112] The authors were particularly concerned with the erosion of the authority and stature of teachers. If religious instruction became voluntary, then teachers would depend financially on the whims of Jewish children and their parents. They pointed to the dangers of weakening traditional moral authority. "In this postwar era where wicked violence, moral decline, and chaos is the order of the day," they argued, it was in the state's interest to strengthen rather than weaken religious education and authority. The rabbis were not looking to uphold the status quo with regard to the state's involvement in Jewish education. Rather, they were seeking the authorities' assistance in strengthening Jewish religious leadership and authority by asking the Ministry of Education for support for a rabbinical seminary in Prague.

It was their hope that well-educated Czech-speaking teachers and rabbis would bestow new political and cultural prestige on Jewish education, a crucial step, in their minds, in creating upright Jewish citizens. Unsure whether their moral appeal would resonate with the ministry, the rabbis invoked the newly passed Czechoslovak Constitution's guarantees of equality for its minorities. If the state supported some religious educational institutions, such as the new Protestant theological seminary in Prague, then, the assembly demanded, it had to consider the needs of its Jews, because "the four hundred thousand citizens of the Jewish faith deserve the state's attention, participation, and support."[113]

The rabbis mobilized in response to an immediate threat to Jewish education. Their plea also reflected that the new political boundaries had disrupted cultural and educational networks upon which the Jewish communities in the Bohemian Lands and Slovakia depended. As mentioned earlier, communities in Bohemia and Moravia and the Neolog ones in Slovakia had traditionally recruited rabbis from the Jewish theological seminaries in Breslau, Berlin, Vienna, and Budapest, while Orthodox communities relied on yeshivas to train their rabbis. In the postwar period such institutional ties became problematic.[114] Few graduates from these institutions met the new requirements for religious clergy: Czechoslovak citizenship and proficiency in the Czech or Slovak languages. As a result it became increasingly difficult for community boards to find suitable rabbis, teachers, and other religious functionaries for their congregations. Consequently, communities continued the "import" of clergy from abroad. This practice worried some Jewish observers who feared that, to outsiders, it appeared as if Jews (stubbornly) continued to recruit their spiritual leaders from the German and Hungarian cultural sphere. This might not have been a concern in Bohemia's and Moravia's German-speaking areas, but in mixed and predominantly Czech-speaking communities the presence of so-called Germanizing rabbis was "impossible."[115] Similarly in Slovakia, critical observers saw the presence of Hungarian- and German-speaking rabbis as a reflection of Jews' continued disdain for their Slovak neighbors. A state-sponsored, Czech-language rabbinical seminary in Prague would enable communities to provide their congregants with suitable spiritual leaders by producing a Czechoslovak rabbinate, whose political loyalties and cultural familiarity would satisfy the authorities as well as members of Czech-speaking and bilingual Jewish communities.

The disruption in the practice of recruiting rabbis educated in Austria, Hungary, and Germany exacerbated the so-called deficit of rabbis that communities in the Bohemian Lands had faced for some time. In the mid-1920s, 40 percent of the Jewish communities in Bohemia did not have a rabbi, while another 40 percent employed rabbis who were between sixty-five and eighty years old.[116] Similarly, more than half of Moravia's communities did not have an ordained rabbi.[117] To some critics, the many vacant positions were more than just a result of recent government legislation.[118] Rather, the lack of religious leaders was a sign of the material and spiritual erosion of Jewish life. To them, the new political order had exposed rather than caused the profound structural crisis plaguing communal Jewish life in the Bohemian Lands.[119]

Responding to the assembly of rabbis' request for a state-sponsored rabbinical seminary in Prague, one civil servant recommended that the Ministry of Education extend funds for such an institution so that "[rabbinical] candidates would no longer be forced to attend seminaries abroad from where they would bring foreign beliefs into our society [*odkud by přinášeli do života názory cizí*]."[120] Ten years later, the "import" of foreign Jewish clergy, "the current unhealthy state of affairs," remained a concern among the bureaucrats overseeing the work of the Supreme Council. And they were strongly in favor of creating a rabbinical seminary.[121] The plans for a seminary did not materialize until 1938.

Another issue that concerned the authorities was the notion that Judaism in the Bohemian Lands was too German, an image particularly powerfully embodied by the lack of a Czech translation of the Five Books of Moses, the Torah. The Supreme Council's work to translate Jewish religious texts into Czech and create new textbooks for religion and Hebrew-language instruction in public schools was applauded and financially supported by the Ministry of Education. One civil servant believed that the lack of a Czech translation of the Torah "obstructs the efforts of the Supreme Council to educate the Jewish youth in the state language and in the spirit of the Czechoslovak nation." The translation project's religious and patriotic (*státotvorné*) significance went hand in hand from the authorities' point of view.[122] Through its commitment to shape Jews into respectable citizens, a process that involved making them more Czech, the Supreme Council succeeded in demonstrating its worthiness as a partner of the state.

The Supreme Council's vision for Jewish communal life and its own role in it, however, involved more than a linguistic and cultural transformation. Responding to the sense of a crisis and decay, the council appealed to the state for support for its plans to modernize the structure of the Jewish communities in the region. This process involved the redrawing of communal boundaries and thus constituted a challenge to individual communities' independence. The Supreme Council therefore looked to the Ministry of Education for the legal authority to assume power over all Jewish communities in the Bohemian Lands. By depicting scenes of mismanagement and corruption in the rural communities, this group of Jewish leaders, not the state, engineered the gradual erosion of the long-standing tradition for communal independence in the Bohemian Lands in the course of the 1930s.

The Supreme Council launched its first major attempt to implement a plan for modernization in January 1928.[123] Its proposed restructuring of the Jewish communities in Bohemia included the dismantling of the small and so-called unsustainable communities. These communities would be attached to nearby larger ones or merged with other similarly small communities into one new entity. According to this plan, the number of communities in Bohemia would drop from 198 to 79. With a sense of urgency the Supreme Council pleaded with the Ministry of Education to enforce the reform without any further consultation with individual communities:

> The only way to correct the terrible state affairs is through the merger of communities into units that can sustain themselves and fulfill their duties as stipulated by religious as well as state law. We [the Council Executive] are aware that the enforcement of this proposal will be difficult and that it will be necessary to overcome the resistance of various officials who will be unwilling to give up their misunderstood autonomy and positions of power. However, the conditions have deteriorated to such a degree that it will not be possible to correct them with less radical measures than the ones proposed here.[124]

The state authorities, perhaps concerned about the lawfulness of such an intervention, did not enforce the structural reform, nor did they award the Supreme Council authority over the communities.[125]

Despite the Supreme Council's thinly veiled disdain for what they considered the cultural backwardness of the Jewish societies in the eastern provinces, these leaders' plans for restructuring the Jewish communities in the Bohemian Lands resembled the Slovak model of large so-called mother communities in the center of a network of affiliated communities.[126] Theoretically, the mother community not only employed rabbis, teachers, and ritual butchers, but also maintained institutions such as ritual baths and elementary religious schools. This system allowed communities to pool resources and provide "subordinate" communities with access to a wide range of religious services and institutions.[127] In the 1928 reform proposal, the Supreme Council similarly envisioned the creation of district rabbinates that would act as religious and cultural centers for a series of smaller communities, thereby preserving the individual communities yet improving their access to education and public worship. By 1937, there were five such district rabbinates in Bohemia and more under way in Moravia.[128]

Even if the Ministry of Education hesitated to endorse the Supreme Council formally as a central authority, in practice it did recognize the council as a Jewish central administration for the Bohemian Lands. For its day-to-day administrative needs, the council relied primarily on funding from its federations, but the Ministry of Education did extend grants on an annual basis.[129] Beginning in 1931, the Supreme Council was entrusted with the distribution of state subsidies for rabbis on behalf of its member communities.[130] The Ministry of Education did not, however, act to curb the traditional independence of Jewish communities. This lack of authority remained a sore point for the Supreme Council, undercutting its prestige and ability to restore order, something its leaders drew the Ministry of Education's attention to over and over again. And the council's authority remained contested. Not only did individual communities insist on preserving their boundaries and independence, but some, like Hradec Králové/Königgrätz, a community of almost six hundred in central Bohemia, refused to join all together.[131]

In the early 1930s, Alois Hilf and Gustav Fleischmann began working on a formal proposal for an amendment of the Law of 1890 that would create an officially recognized central Jewish leadership institution in the Bohemian Lands.[132] The Supreme Council handed the proposal to the country's two Zionist parliamentarians, Chaim Kugel (1897–1953) and Angelo Goldstein (1889–1947), both representatives of the Jewish Party in the National Assembly. In the summer and fall of 1936, the two MPs ushered the proposal through Prague's bureaucratic and political offices and corridors. The bill arrived on the National Assembly's agenda in late January 1937.[133] In practice the proposed bill formalized and expanded the Supreme Council by creating a central office with authority over all Jewish communities in the Bohemian Lands. Although individual communities retained some independence, the central office was to be responsible for meeting Jews' collective religious needs and for distributing state subsidies for Jewish clergy. The institution was to act as an advisor to the state, and the law required public offices to consult it in matters concerning the Jewish communities.[134] The fact that the Supreme Council was able to step in immediately and assume the role as a central Jewish authority reflected, according to one of its members, that the office "had gained much recognition in political and administrative circles who will not intervene in Jewish matters without first asking for the wishes and point of view of the Supreme Council."[135] Thus, after a decade of lobbying, the Supreme Council had succeeded in eroding Jewish communal independence and creating a formal, unified Jewish representative body in the Bohemian Lands.[136]

Angelo Goldstein was quick to highlight what he saw as a timely restructuring of Jewish communal life when the bill came to a vote in late January 1937. By then, as German and Slovak nationalists called for increasing self-governance in their regions, in Prague local autonomy had had become synonymous with disloyalty. Goldstein saw an opportunity to equate a strong central Jewish authority with the defense of Czechoslovakia's political and territorial integrity. It was an opportunity not to be missed.[137] At a time of increasing tension over separatism in Slovakia and the German borderlands, Goldstein called on the state to grant the new Jewish authority far-reaching executive powers, enabling it "to carry out its tasks and break the resistance that has emerged out of a misunderstood will to autonomy and unhealthy local patriotism." He was nevertheless disappointed in what he saw as the reform's weakness: it did not create a Jewish authority for all of Czechoslovakia. Goldstein agreed with other MPs that such a bold move would have strengthened the country's territorial and political unity, a weapon against "the separatism and revisionism that is fed by the persistence of legal dualism."[138] What was in Goldstein's opinion an unnecessarily cautious reform reflected, however, that the Ministry of Education had accepted the Supreme Council's preference over its own desire for a countrywide institution.[139]

The Supreme Council's resistance to a Czechoslovak organization – its refusal to enter into an organization that would include the Orthodox and Hasidic communities in Slovakia and Subcarpathian Rus' – was guided in no small part by a concern about upholding a particular image of Jews and their communities in the Bohemian Lands. This was an image that, to them, had very little to gain politically and culturally from being associated with the Jews in the east. The Bohemian and Moravian communities had a tradition for moderate religious reforms and acculturation, meaning that even in the interwar years, communities followed the so-called Viennese rite, which adopted aesthetic changes to Jewish ritual, but largely preserved halakhic norms. This enabled the coexistence of progressive and traditionalist members within the same community.[140] According to this model as well as state law, the communities' rabbis had to have formal rabbinical ordination and university training. Jewish activists imagined the ideal rabbi, highly educated and cultured, in the Bohemian Lands, as in stark contrast to the figure of the yeshiva-trained and culturally isolated rabbi from Slovakia. To Jewish leaders in the Bohemian Lands, the eastern rabbis lacked the respectability expected of a communal leader, as well as the language, knowledge, and mind-set necessary to reach and guide their flocks. In Moravia, religious leaders were worried that community boards, desperate for rabbis and eager to save money, would jump at the opportunity to hire Slovak rabbis. They informed the state authorities that despite their Czechoslovak citizenship, rabbinical candidates trained in Bratislava "lack the kind of general education and knowledge required in Moravian communities."[141] While these rabbis might be able to perform their ritual duties, the letter writers argued, their Orthodox training with its lack of secular education did not prepare them to officiate in communities in the Bohemian Lands.

And the requirements were indeed demanding. A 1921 advertisement for a rabbinical position in the Jewish community in Hodonín/Göding is a case in point. This town with fewer than one thousand Jews in southern Moravia requested that prospective candidates hold Czechoslovak citizenship, have a doctorate, and be proficient in German as well as Czech. In particular, the text stressed, the candidate should be able to both speak and write Czech, as religious education in the state language was especially important to the local community.[142] More than a decade later, the character of rabbis' education was still more important to the Supreme Council's rabbinical committee than the candidates' citizenship.[143] Insisting that formal rabbinical ordination along with a completed high school degree constituted a minimum requirement for rabbis in the west, the council sought to guard their community's respectability against a potential influx of eastern Jews. Although they were equipped with Czechoslovak citizenship, eastern Jews did not have the social and cultural prestige bestowed by university education and middle-class stature so important to acculturated, urban Jewish societies in Central Europe.[144]

Through the 1930s, the Ministry of Education did indeed accept the Supreme Council's insistence that only candidates ordained at reputable theological seminaries, mainly the ones in Berlin and Breslau, were acceptable as rabbis in the Bohemian Lands.[145] The ministry supported the council's sponsorship of rabbinical students receiving the majority of their training abroad as well as its pleas for leniency in the enforcement of the citizenship requirements for the rabbis applying for positions in Czechoslovakia. In the 1930s, applicants from Germany especially looked for work in the Bohemia and Moravia's German-speaking communities. Indeed, the Supreme Council preferred to negotiate hard with the authorities for work permits for so-called foreign rabbis, who "due to internal and external political conditions . . . were unwanted," than have "Orthodox" Jews arrive from Slovakia as spiritual leaders in the Jewish communities in the Bohemian Lands.[146]

MAKING JEWS CZECH

The question of what kind of rabbis to "import" highlighted one of the central concerns of the Supreme Council, namely the way in which religious leaders reflected on Jewish society more broadly. Indeed, one of the key preoccupations of the council in the interwar years was to make Jews and their communities more Czech. Although this was partly an effort to improve Jews' image, it also revealed a desire on behalf of these Jewish leaders to become a fully integrated, yet culturally distinct community of worthy citizens. Furthermore, since an increasing number of Jewish children attended Czech-language schools and used Czech as their primary language, Jewish leaders knew that Czech-speaking teachers and Czech-language Jewish texts were crucial if young Jews were to get a solid Jewish education. Beginning in the late 1920s, the Supreme Council embarked on a program for cultural and religious renewal among Jews, a program that was undertaken with the financial and, more importantly, political support of the state.

The Supreme Council's work centered on creating a new rabbinate steeped in what they saw as the Czech spirit of the times. Inspired by President Masaryk's example, the council promoted respect for religion as an ethical tradition, a moral compass, meanwhile distancing itself from religious dogma and the institutions of power that maintained them.[147] Thus, the new rabbinate would play a central role in the Jewish renaissance as transmitters of Judaism as a religious as well as an ethical and cultural tradition. The creation of a Czech rabbinate was part of the Supreme Council's broader effort to recast Judaism and Jews as a Czech cultural community rather than a vestige of German culture unable to shake the ties to the Austro-Hungarian past. In addition, by casting the country's eastern communities as hotbeds of religious fanaticism, the council insisted on *their* Judaism as the model Jewish tradition. The Czech Torah translation and the documentation and conservation of Jewish heritage sites across the Bohemian Lands sponsored by the Supreme Council became forceful statements about Jews' belonging in Czechoslovakia.[148]

Among the foremost priorities for the Supreme Council was the creation of a homegrown rabbinate. The Ministry of Education's decision to create a state-sponsored Czechoslovak rabbinical seminary in Prague in the fall of 1938 followed a ten-year campaign by the council. In their letters to the ministry, the executive stressed the importance of a native rabbinate, fluent in the state language and familiarity with the culture of his community. Critical of the proposals to locate the new seminary in Bratislava, they argued that "in Prague, more so than anywhere else, the city's atmosphere will contribute to the education of rabbis in the spirit of patriotism [*státotvorném*; lit. "state building"]."[149] The proposal for a Prague seminary bore evidence of Jewish leaders' commitment to Czechoslovakia. At the same time, it also promised to be an institution that would ensure a favorable civic and cultural image for a new generation of rabbis, teachers, and other Jewish clergy.[150]

When it began its seminary campaign in 1928, the Supreme Council did not ask the authorities to make an exception for Jews. They insisted that Jews as citizens were entitled to a state-sponsored Jewish theological seminary. The Supreme Council demanded equality for Jews. "May we remind the ministry," the council noted, "that we are the only religious group that still has not received any state support for the training of its spiritual leaders despite the demands placed on them by the state. . . . If Jewish taxpayers' money is being spent on the seminaries of other religious communities, then it would only be just that the state commit itself to the establishment and upkeep of a [rabbinical] seminary."[151] It would be another ten years before the Ministry of Education committed itself to state sponsorship of a Prague seminary.[152]

The plans for the Prague seminary had to be placed on hold in 1928 due to the lack of funds. In response, the Supreme Council devised a plan that would be the first step in the creation of somewhat homegrown rabbis and teachers. Beginning in 1929 and continuing through the 1930s, the council sponsored between five and twelve rabbinical candidates who undertook studies at the seminaries in Breslau and Berlin. The study by Czechoslovak students at the rabbinical seminaries in Germany did meet with the Ministry of Education's approval and financial support.[153] Over time, the council's wards did part of their training at institutions in Czechoslovakia before they went to Germany to complete their studies and receive their ordinations. This was a measure that not only saved the council money, but also limited the problematic "foreign" influence on these young men.[154] In 1936, a provisional seminary (Pedagogia pro výchovu učitelů náboženství a prosemináře v Praze) was established in Prague, where the rabbinical students completed their first two years of studies and where the much-needed religious teachers for public schools were trained.[155] Furthermore, in advance of their studies abroad or during summer holidays, the council shepherded the students through Czech-language courses meant to ensure they had a suitable command of the state language. In return for their stipends, these young men committed themselves to serve communities in the Bohemian Lands for at least ten years following their ordination, placements that would be made at the discretion of the Supreme Council.[156] Yet, the continued reliance on foreign rabbinical seminaries remained a sore point for the council, one that was exacerbated by the increasingly difficult conditions for Jews in Germany. Through the 1930s, the executive allocated a portion of its state resources to a seminary fund.[157] Eventually, in 1937, the Ministry of Education got on board as well and committed itself to the creation of a Jewish theological seminary in Prague. The seminary never got off the ground. By the time it was ready to open its doors for the fall semester in 1938, Czechoslovakia was crumbling, and the state authorities' attitude toward the Jewish minority was about to change.[158]

Pursuing a program for Jewish cultural renewal, the Supreme Council also devised programs that were to have a more immediate impact on Jewish education in the Bohemian Lands. Since the public elementary and high schools were the main sites for Jewish education, the council focused on creating a pool of Jewish teachers with adequate Jewish knowledge, with modern pedagogical skills, and equipped with a command of Czech language as well as with Czechoslovak citizenship.[159] For this purpose, the council sponsored long- and short-term courses for teachers at the Jewish high school in Brno/Brünn and the Hebrew-language high school in Mukačevo, summer seminars in various locations in Bohemia, and from 1936 onward more extensive training at the provisional seminary in Prague.[160] As part of these efforts to strengthen Jewish education in the broadest sense, the council also funded Richard Feder's work preparing suitable textbooks for instruction in Hebrew and Judaism for use in elementary and middle schools.[161]

Similarly, in an effort to address the lack of religious leadership in the majority of the regions' communities, the Supreme Council arranged and funded a program to train religious functionaries, especially cantors. Like the teachers and rabbis, these functionaries had to be Czechoslovak citizens, and the council recruited graduates from the Mukačevo high school, as they possessed a modern Jewish education and were "already fluent in the state language and with the basic Hebrew training necessary for this profession."[162] The council's focus on educating minor Jewish clergy was partly a response to the lack of any religious leadership in many places and the need to train clergy who could serve smaller and less resourceful communities. The demands placed on individuals who went to work in these communities were staggering. One community in Moravia was, according to a critical article in *Židovské zprávy,* looking for a cantor who "was musically educated, able to conduct a service with organ and choir, read from the Torah, act as *shohet* [ritual butcher], teach lessons in religion in the elementary school, be authorized to keep the community's registry, as well as be under the age of forty and unmarried."[163] As communities in the Bohemian Lands struggled to find and afford suitable clergy, it was no wonder that community boards employed Jews from Slovakia with some degree of religious studies behind them to provide wide-ranging religious services for local Jews.[164] Seeking to stem the stream of Slovak Jews seeking employment as religious functionaries in the west, the Supreme Council invested in the training of a development professional communal clergy, who like the Czech-speaking ordained rabbis and well-qualified teachers, were expected to reinvigorate Jewish religious and cultural life.

Another major priority for the Supreme Council in the interwar years was the creation of a modern religious canon in Czech. While it funded new textbooks and August Stein's translation of the High Holiday prayer book into Czech, it was the creation of a Czech Torah that carried particular importance.[165] The council presented the translation of the Five Books of Moses into Czech as a step as momentous as Moses Mendelssohn's translation of the Torah into German. Mendelssohn's translation and commentary was considered by contemporary observers, and later by historians, as a major step in the modernization of Jewish culture and religion and hence Jews' integration into society more broadly.[166] According to the Supreme Council, Torah translations were part and parcel of Jews' historical experience. As in the past, the translation of the Torah would open the door for Jews into the culture of other peoples as well as reacquaint Jews with the text. The translation, the council predicted, would transform Czech from an everyday language to Jews' language of worship.[167] Even though the council highlighted the importance of Torah translations in Jewish history, it also evoked a more local and familiar trope. In the dominant Czech nationalist narrative, the translation of the Christian Bible into Czech and Jan Hus's use of the Czech vernacular in his sermons were considered significant achievements in Czech national history, a moral weight that the Supreme Council now sought to bestow on its own translation project.[168]

The translation of the Torah, like the creation of a Czech-speaking rabbinate, was central to the Supreme Council's efforts to modernize Jewish religious life in the Bohemian Lands. On the one hand, these priorities were a response to political changes that demanded that Jewish clergy and teachers adopt the language of the state. On the other, however, the council's focus on educating new spiritual leaders and on making Judaism Czech was also a response to the widespread perception among Jewish activists that Jewish religious culture in the Bohemian Lands had become stagnant, a decaying relic with little appeal to current and future generations of Jews. Only a new spiritual leadership would be able to reestablish the connection between modern Jews and the Jewish religious tradition, a desirable moral pursuit from a Jewish and civic standpoint. Concerned with the image of Judaism as inherently German, something they believed estranged the tradition from young Jews, Jewish activists pursued the Czechification of their spiritual leadership and religious canon. It was a transformation intended to make Jews and their communities into social and cultural entities that belonged in the Bohemian Lands.

The Supreme Council's commitment to Czech was, however, not one that severed the ties to German language and culture. Rather, it embraced a form of trilingualism. Czech was the official, but not the only, language of use, a position also adopted by the Prague Federation of Jewish Communities, which refused to choose sides in the "language struggle."[169] In practice, German continued to play an important role in Jewish religious, communal, and cultural life. At the same time, the council supported the teaching of Hebrew as a language through which Jews could connect to their distinct cultural and religious heritage. This commitment to trilingualism, the coexistence of German, Czech, and Hebrew within Jewish society, was important to the council. By facilitating Jews' acquisition of Hebrew and Czech, the council sent an important message about Jews' distinctiveness and adaptability. To the council, trilingualism signaled that Jews, like their Czech- and German-speaking Christian neighbors, had local roots, that they were an integral part of the Bohemian and Moravian cultural landscape.

If Jews' multiple languages were to act as "evidence" of their history in the region, so were the many remnants of Jewish life that dotted the countryside in the Bohemian Lands. Indeed, precisely at the time that Jewish society became decidedly urban, Jewish activists looked to the rural past as a site for cultural identification.[170] As centuries-old communities were abandoned for the city, they were reinvested with meaning as sites of organic and authentic Jewish life. Nevertheless, the image of the old Jewish way of life in the Bohemian Lands was fraught with contradictions. On the one hand, the small communities were associated, in the minds of Jewish critics, with neglect, decay, and dysfunction. On the other, however, village Jews and the old kehilah bore testimony to a particular Jewish cultural tradition and history and documented the longevity of Jewish life in the area.[171]

From the outset, the Supreme Council fashioned itself as the custodian of Jewish cultural heritage in the Bohemian Lands. While it supported initiatives already under way such as the Jewish Museum in Prague or the newly established Society for the History of Jews in Czechoslovakia (Společnost pro dějiny židů v Československé republice/Gesellschaft für Geschichte der Juden in der Čechoslovakische Republik), it established its own Heritage Committee (Památková komise/Denkmalkommission) in 1928.[172] The council's chair, August Stein, was a veteran supporter of the efforts to preserve the Jewish past and was joined on the committee by other museum experts and activists, such as the Jewish scholar Salomon H. Lieben (1881–1942), who had worked with Stein to create the Jewish Museum in Prague in the early 1900s. Beginning in 1928, the Heritage Committee began a project to document, preserve, collect, and display the material culture, from synagogues and tombstones to ritual objects and letters, of the regions' past and present Jewish societies.[173]

The Heritage Committee's conservation project reflected a growing scholarly and public interest in Jewish history and culture in the interwar years. Literary scholars, such as Oskar Donath (1882–1940), published works on the region's Jewish literature, Hugo Gold oversaw the compilation and publication of two encyclopedic volumes on the Jewish communities of Bohemia and Moravia, and Jewish museums were established in Mikulov/Nikolsburg (in Moravia) and in Prešov/Eperies/Eperjes and Košice/Kaschau/Kassa (both in Slovakia) in the 1920s and '30s. Among Jews living in cities, far removed physically and culturally from traditional Jewish life, Jewish community leaders detected a steady growing interest in Jewish heritage sites and in the lives and customs of past Jewish societies in the Bohemian Lands. Indeed, as Norbert Adler, the executive director of the Supreme Council noted, the Heritage Committee was responding to the needs of a new generation of Jews looking to connect with their past. Much like their Czech neighbors, Adler noted, Jews needed to know their roots in order to develop a vibrant and creative Jewish community for the present and the future. A new generation of Jews was returning to the community, according to Adler, less for their religious needs than for a desire for cultural identification and ethnic belonging, a need for rootedness in the present day. This was precisely the kind of awakening that Zionists had hoped to bring about.

The urgency of the Supreme Council's efforts to collect sources "that attest to the artistic, historical, and cultural contribution of the Jewish culture that emerged in this area and was preserved in communities here" was brought on by fear of actual physical dissolution or dispersion of the Jewish heritage due to mismanagement and financial difficulties among rural Jews.[174] Stories of synagogues being sold off and turned into cinemas and dance halls highlighted the need of the Heritage Committee's work.[175]

In 1933, the Heritage Committee published a short book that appeared in both Czech and German editions in which it showcased some of its conservation efforts to the public.[176] The narrative embedded in the book's text and images was one that told a story of creativity and authenticity as well as decline and neglect. The architect Leopold Ehrmann (1887–1951), who had remodeled synagogues in Prague's Smichov/Smichow and Karlín/Karolinenthal districts in the 1920s, discussed the types of synagogues found in rural Bohemia. He noted the evidence of shared aesthetic norms among Christians and Jews, reflected in the similarities between synagogues and churches and the influence of Christian craftsmen and builders on the Jewish sites.[177] At the same time, he explained, the Jewish community boards, who had commissioned the work, had found ways to embed Jewishness in the design through inscriptions or decorative motifs. The photographs accompanying the text showed the different types of synagogues, a testament to the intertwined lives of Christians and Jews in rural Bohemia.

At the same time, however, the images – much like the conservation project itself – appeared to communicate the dissolution of this Jewish world. The photographer centered on the individual synagogue, most often leaving out the building's surroundings. The spaces, the building itself and the street in front of it, appeared empty, of people and life. Only occasionally did a group of barefooted village urchins pose for the photographer. At times, the camera snapped an image just as a goose or chicken entered the frame. Seemingly void of Jewish life, revealing the absence of the community that would have filled the synagogue and the street in front of it, the images projected a sense of abandonment. In much the same way, Salomon Lieben's essay showed, the rural cemeteries, the most ancient and threatened Jewish spaces, fell into disrepair as the Jewish population dwindled. The age-old cemeteries, in which the dead were to rest undisturbed, their peace protected by their descendants, were being desecrated. The graveyards were robbed of their stones by thieves, appropriated as public spaces by the locals, and even used as communal pastures. It was high time, Lieben called out, that the Jewish public came to the rescue of abandoned synagogues, violated cemeteries, neglected community archives, and commodified ritual objects, "the endangered witnesses to the Jewish past."[178]

The unease about the dissolution of rural Jewish life and appropriation of Jewish spaces for other purposes coexisted with a sense of optimism and pride among the scholars involved in the conservation project.

They marveled at the reinvigorated Jewish life in the growing urban communities and saw their own efforts as making the past available to new Jewish audiences eager to familiarize themselves with their Jewishness. By the early 1930s, the Heritage Committee saw itself as merely directing a Jewish renaissance already under way. By facilitating Jews' access to their own past, its physical spaces, its literature, and knowledge of Jewish history, they were putting the chain connecting Jews' past, present, and future back together. Indeed, a usable past, one distinctively Jewish yet at home among non-Jews, one of belonging and cultural creativity rather than alienation and persecution, was to Norbert Adler and his Zionist and non-Zionist colleagues alike essential in fostering a new generation of publicly self-aware and respected Jews. Nevertheless, even as they celebrated the work already undertaken by the Heritage Committee and the growing public interest in Jewish culture and history, these activists' and experts' work was infused with an anxiety over the potential for the dissolution of the very sites that anchored the memory of Jews' presence in the region – and with that, the erosion of Jews' claim to belonging.

Jewish activists invoked the memory of the kehilah, of the old Jewish way of life, to recast Jewish community as a site for cultural identification. Although religious observance was part of the Jewish renaissance, it was only one aspect of a broader transformation of Jewish identity and community. The new rabbis and teachers were to act primarily as transmitters of Jewish culture, teaching Jews about their history, culture, and religion, not merely as religious authorities. Similarly, synagogues, cemeteries, and Torah scrolls were reinterpreted as sources to a rich and creative Jewish history rather than objects for religious observance. By recasting the Jewish collective as an ethnic fellowship, a community bound by its shared heritage and fate, the Supreme Council returned the kehilah to the center of Jewish life in the Bohemian Lands.[179]

COOPERATION OR CONQUEST? THE TWISTED ROAD FROM *KULTUS-* TO *VOLKSGEMEINDE*

Although Zionists imagined the creation of the Volksgemeinde as indicative of a democratic ethos, an expression of the will of the Jewish people, in the Bohemian Lands it was hardly a process undertaken using democratic means. As the Supreme Council succeeded in eroding the historical independence of individual Jewish communities, once the council was transformed into a state-sanctioned Jewish authority in 1937, it imposed an expansion of the communities' formal obligations in Bohemia and Moravia.

Through the 1920s and '30s, Zionists did face local opposition to their efforts to broaden the communities' social welfare, cultural, and educational activities from Czech-Jews and other community activists. The opponents were wary that Zionists were seeking to take control of communal institutions and resources in order to harness them to their political agenda. In Prague, for example, Czech-Jewish activists policed the use of communal resources, ensuring that the board funded only so-called religious activities.[180] Thus, the community board supported religious education but did not generally fund Prague's Jewish national school. Similarly, while Czech-Jewish activists supported the Jewish hospital's use of communal grounds near the new Jewish cemetery in Prague's Strašnice neighborhood, they fought long and hard to expel the Zionist sports club Hagibor from this property.[181] The Czech-Jewish activists might very well have had reasons to be suspicious of the Zionist board members' political intentions. In Brno/Brünn, where the community was committed to the broader social and cultural agenda, the board extended subsidies not only to the local Jewish national school, but also to Zionist political organizations such as Mizraḥi and Po'ale Tsiyon (a socialist-Zionist party).[182] Writing on the eve of the community elections in the Czech-Jewish bastion of Hradec Králové/Königgrätz, a community that had resisted the Supreme Council's centralization efforts, one observer claimed that "in those places where they [the Zionists] are in charge, they have introduced community regulations that pertain to the care for the 'Jewish nation' or 'the Jewish national whole,' which is against very clear laws."[183] Accusing Zionists of using "totalitarian methods," the writer pointed to Zionism as the cause of Jewish disunity, warning that Zionist board members directed funds intended for religious activities into political ones, such as projects in Palestine, Zionist youth groups, and Jewish national schools. Although these local struggles between Czech-Jews and Zionists were not unusual, the mandatory unification of the Jewish communities in the Bohemian Lands added to this familiar battle a new, stronger player, one that some Czech-Jews saw as having a Zionist agenda.

The union of Jewish communities enforced by the 1937 bill was, not surprisingly, welcomed in Zionist circles. Not only did writers take pride in the Jewish parliamentarians' role in creating "the first Jewish law in the republic," but they also saw it as the first step in overcoming "the chaotic fragmentation in favor of Jewish unity."[184] Zdeněk Landes, the editor of *Židovské zprávy,* noted that the constitution for the new Jewish authority, which had been prepared by none other than Gustav Fleischmann and Alois Hilf, allowed communities to expand into new areas such as social welfare and cultural activities, a proposal that no doubt caused alarm among Czech-Jewish activists.[185]

Furthermore, while the Supreme Council's power depended on the authority of the state, the council made use of its constitution to strengthen the authority of rabbis vis-à-vis the lay community boards. It did so by creating a new rabbinical court that would act as the supreme religious authority in the Bohemian Lands. Thus, in contrast to Zionist tactics in Slovakia and Subcarpathian Rus', where they were primarily battling rabbinical authorities and where their rhetoric had a distinct anti-clerical tone, in the west Zionists sang a different tune.[186] Here co-operation with rabbis and so-called orthodox circles not only was a sign of Zionists' commitment to the Jewish tradition, but also served to bring the observant circles, still influential in some communities in the late 1930s, in line with the unification efforts.[187]

The Supreme Council had mobilized support for a united leadership among religious activists and in Zionist circles. The response to the proposed reform bill in the Czech-Jewish weekly *Rozvoj* was at first surprise and apprehension.[188] Caught unaware that a proposal had been readied for the parliamentary senate committee in the summer of 1936, Czech-Jewish activists first sought to mobilize political opposition to the bill.[189] When that failed, they called for extensive community consultation once the details for the role of the council were to be negotiated.[190] However, Czech-Jews' opposition to the council would spark a confrontation that would become a turning point in Jewish communal politics in the Bohemian Lands.[191]

Since 1936, there had been a public rift among Czech-Jews and Zionists in Moravská Ostrava/Mährisch Ostrau over whether it was appropriate for the community to use its funds for Jewish social and cultural institutions. The latter were, according to the complaint, activities that did not qualify as care for Jews' religious needs.[192] In early 1937, after months of intense and public verbal clashes between Czech-Jewish and Zionist activists, the local state authorities in Moravská Ostrava/Mährisch Ostrau ruled in favor of the Czech-Jews. Zionists were outraged over the decision. The battle was not yet lost, however, because the Supreme Council decided to issue an expert opinion.[193]

The Supreme Council was annoyed that it had been bypassed as an advisor to the state on matters concerning a Jewish community, a role it had been formally awarded a few months earlier by the National Assembly. The council handed the case to its rabbinical court for an authoritative decision.[194] The rabbis concluded "that social welfare and cultural activities are and can be the responsibility of religious communities . . . indeed the rabbinical court considers social and cultural activities an important part of our religion and therefore a religious need, which the communities are obligated to care for." Furthermore, seeking to stake out a stronger position vis-à-vis secular authorities – a nod to the old kehilah – the council's rabbinical committee declared that "no disgruntled individual or state office" could decide what constituted religious obligations. This was the prerogative of the Supreme Council and its rabbinical court alone.[195]

Thus, by the late 1930s, the Volksgemeinde had become a reality. It had been a process full of contradictions. Zionists from across the Bohemian Lands alongside traditionalist and certain Czech-Jewish and German-speaking Jewish activists, groups usually at odds in Jewish politics, had worked together to erode the authority of existing Jewish communities. They had done so to empower a centralized leadership dominated by members from the region's large, urban communities, most prominently among them Prague, Brno/Brünn, and Moravská Ostrava/Mährisch Ostrau. These activists had pursued the abolition of individual community's historical independence in the name of a Jewish renaissance that centered on the revival of the community as a locus for Jewish life. Ironically, Jewish activists' efforts to elevate the memory of the kehilah as an organic, vibrant, and deep-rooted institution depended on the removal of the most significant historical tradition embodied by the community: its independence vis-à-vis other Jewish communities.

Having enlisted the help of the state to enforce the centralization of Jewish communities, this Jewish leadership used its newfound legitimacy as a representative of the region's Jews to push back against both the authorities *and* dissenting Jewish activists' interpretation of the parameters for the Jewish community's mandate. The Supreme Council legitimized its power grab in part as an effort to secure compliance with state law and the education of a loyal, Czechoslovak Jewish citizenry. But it used this new authority, propped up by its rabbinical court, to limit state encroachment into internal Jewish affairs. At the same time as the council promoted an image of Jews as belonging in and committed to Czechoslovakia, there was also consensus among some of the most influential secular and religious leaders in the Bohemian Lands that Jews were a *Volk,* a community of origin with particular religious, social welfare, and cultural needs.

* * *

A little more than a year later, by the late spring of 1939, the Supreme Council would be a thing of the past. With the occupation of the Bohemian Lands by Nazi Germany, some council members left their home, along with thousands of other Jews from Bohemia and Moravia, seeking safety elsewhere. Emil Margulies, Norbert Adler, and Gustav Fleischmann left for Palestine within a few months of the German occupation. Until the very end, Fleischmann carefully attended to his duties, fulfilling the council's obligation to its dependents and to the state, taking care of pension payments to rabbis and their families until shortly before he left the country.[196] The Supreme Council had dissolved. The challenges that lay ahead were of a character than no one could have imagined.

Despite its tragic end, the Supreme Council was in many ways a success story. The institution's goal was Jewish unity and renewal, and its achievement has, like so much else in Jewish history, been overshadowed by its demise. The Supreme Council succeeded in expanding and modernizing Jewish education, in translating Jewish texts into Czech, and in securing the creation of a public rabbinical and teachers' seminary. It had managed to create an institution that could speak with authority on Jewish matters and acted as a trusted advisor to the state. It was in fact a Jewish leadership that successfully influenced the policies of the state authorities vis-à-vis the country's Jews. It secured public funds for new and existing Jewish institutions and developed projects that made the state a partner in a program for Jewish cultural renewal.

The activists on the Supreme Council, a closely knit group with different political and national loyalties and religious commitments, people who often appeared as absolutely at odds, cooperated for years to revive Jewish communal life. They shared a desire to turn the communities into centers for a new vibrant Jewish culture. In the name of Jewish continuity and Jews' social and cultural respectability, these activists turned to education as the key to Jewish renewal. They invested much effort and money into the education of a Czech-speaking rabbinate, a new cultural elite that could act as spiritual leaders, as well as into the training of highly qualified teachers ready to fan out and reinvigorate Jewish education in the country's public schools. The council also looked to nurture Jews' and non-Jews' awareness of Jewish history and culture, especially the memory of long-established and flourishing Jewish communities in Bohemia and Moravia. Much like Jews in neighboring Germany, Jews in the Bohemian Lands turned to their past as a way of making a claim about belonging in the present.[197] Old synagogues and cemeteries dotting the countryside in every corner of the Bohemian Lands served to reassure Jews of their place in Czechoslovakia, their belonging embedded in the country's cultural landscape.

Jewish activists searched for respectability and identity by nurturing the memory of a harmonious and organic past. At the same time, they also shared a belief that Jews' future depended on the modernization of their communities as well as a deepening of the relationship between Jews and the state. Convinced that the fragmentation of Jewish communities, embodied by the historical tradition of communal independence, was outdated and a source of decay and stagnation, these Jewish leaders sought to establish a modern central administration for the Jewish communities, harnessing the authority of the state for a program of modernization. Presenting itself as an agent for the state, the Supreme Council worked to centralize the governance of Jewish life, rightfully, in their minds, now in the hands of experienced bureaucrats, to regulate and control the affairs of individual communities, and to impose among Jews in the Bohemian Lands a cultural and political orientation in sync with that of the state's ethos.

Zionists generally fashioned themselves as the leaders of a popular revolt against an assimilationist or traditionalist oligarchy in charge of the Jewish communities in Czechoslovakia. This study of a long-standing point of cooperation makes clear that in the Bohemian Lands, Zionists pursued the creation of the Volksgemeinde together with so-called assimilationist activists equally committed to Jewish continuity. Even though these activists might have disagreed on the question of Jews' national identification, they shared a desire for cultural renewal. These lawyers, physicians, and rabbis, united by their Jewishness and by their education and class, constituted a bureaucracy whose legitimacy as leaders rested in their expertise and social status. Their political differences mattered less than their shared commitment to Jewish continuity. By the late 1930s, this cohort of Jewish activists thus succeeded in establishing the Volksgemeinde – a communal organization whose raison d'être was its members' shared ethnicity and whose scope encompassed social, cultural, *and* religious institutions – as the ideal for Jewish communal life in the Bohemian Lands.

The success of the Supreme Council in creating a partnership with the state rested to a large extent on the fact that the council did not seek to redefine Jews' status. They acted as representatives of Jews as a religious minority, not a national one. The council did not seek to redefine the relationship between Jews and the state, but worked within the already existing legal parameters. Indeed, by de facto transforming the communities into institutions committed to "care for the Jewish people," the council did not challenge the status quo but nevertheless still managed to secure state support for what was for all intents and purposes activities meant to strengthen Jews' religious as well as secular ethnic identities. For their part, the state authorities most likely acted on what they saw as a social fact, namely that Jews constituted a community of shared religion *and* ethnicity. Yet, it was in the state authorities' interest to retain the status quo rather than supporting a formal transition to nationality status for Jews. A change in Jews' status, from a religious to a national minority, was, from the authorities' perspective, a policy that caused more fragmentation by adding another minority nationality to the country's already large minority populations. Furthermore, by recognizing Jews as a nationality, the state would be on the hook for much greater expenditures, for Jewish national schools and social welfare programs, than what they were committing to Jews' religious institutions. And last, while there was consensus among Jews and non-Jews alike that Jews constituted an ethnic community, there was disagreement within and outside Jewish society whether Jews were a national minority. According to the census, almost half of the country's Jews had a national identity other than Jewish. From the state authorities' and the Supreme Council's point of view, a change in Jews' status promised to be divisive and therefore counterproductive.

The Ministry of Education's forthcoming posture on matters regarding the Jewish communities stood in stark contrast to their unwelcoming of Zionist projects that aimed to create institutions on the premise that Jews constituted a *national* minority. As a result, the Jewish national schools met with resistance from state bureaucrats. The next chapter, which focuses on Zionists' struggle to create public Jewish national schools, explores the contradictions in Zionists' strategy of integration through national distinctiveness as well as the resistance of the central administration to efforts that appeared to weaken Czech cultural and linguistic hegemony in interwar Czechoslovakia.

FIVE

A Stateless Nation's Territory

ZIONISTS AND THE JEWISH SCHOOLS

IN MID-JUNE 1921, AS CZECH, GERMAN, AND JEWISH NATIONALISTS in the Bohemian Lands were getting ready for the annual campaigns to recruit children for their nation's schools, František Friedmann reported on his recent visit to Prague's new Jewish national school. Impressed with what he found, Friedmann noted that if only Jewish parents could see the happiness of these children, at ease with each other and their teachers, learning Hebrew through song and play, they "would no doubt care much more about Jewish schools." At the end of his tour, the teacher invited little Frischmann and little Winternitzová to the class podium. From up there, they recited "proudly and straight from the heart":

Born in Bohemia, I speak Czech
And I take pride in being of Bohemia
I am a Jew and I will remain a Jew
I shall not forget my nation
The one who is ashamed of his own nation
deserves to be scorned by all people
I will not be silent about my nation,
I am proud of belonging to the Jewish nation
Our nation is a glorious one
With an ancient life
I want to love it faithfully,
Never to disown it[1]

The performance had left him barely able to hold back tears, Friedmann confessed to his readers. His depiction of the Jewish school as a place where Jewish children frolicked among their peers and teachers, where there was harmony between their Hebrew song and Czech poetry, where they could be Jews *and* at home in Bohemia, embodied the utopian image of the Jewish school that Zionist activists in the Bohemian Lands harbored in the interwar years.

In the Bohemian Lands, schools and the children who attended them had been at the center of nationalist politics since the mid-nineteenth century. In a region where multilingualism was the norm, not the exception, and where little else but language distinguished Czech-speakers and German-speakers, Czech and German nationalists intent on mobilizing "their" nations rallied around schools as national "fortresses."[2] The historian Tara E. Zahra has shown that the intense national mobilization around children reflected nationalists' anxiety about the population's national ambiguity and indifference, attitudes and behaviors that threatened to undermine claims about inherent and important differences between German- and Czech-speakers. Zahra notes that "German and Czech nationalists in the Bohemian Lands feared that children 'born' to their nation could literally be 'exchanged,' 'lost,' or 'kidnapped' from the national community through education in the wrong national milieu or by nationally indifferent parents." Thus, even though nationalists believed that one was born into a nation, that "nationality was an inherent quality," they worried about the fragility of these ties.[3]

Among Jewish activists – and Zionists were not alone in this matter – fear of assimilation, of Jews becoming indistinguishable from non-Jews, went hand in hand with Jews' gradual legal emancipation and acculturation. Since the late eighteenth century, as social barriers between Jews and non-Jews became less pronounced and as traditional religious practice became less important, every generation of Jewish leaders predicted an imminent end to Jewish life. They mostly pointed to materialism and social opportunism as the reason why Jews abandoned religious observance, communal life, and other customs that tied them to Jewish society. Later, psychological terms like "self-hatred" became popular among activists critical of what they perceived to be Jews' indifference to their "ancestral" community. When Jewish activists turned to the Jewish national school after the First World War, they were motivated by fears that were similar to those of their German and Czech nationalist colleagues. They feared that without national schools, without a national education and early socialization, children would be lost to their nation. As we saw in the previous chapter, this anxiety about assimilation, articulated by Zionists in national terms, was widespread among Jewish activists.

Zionist activists shared with many politicians, educators, social workers, and professional child experts, among others, a concern about the physical, moral, and spiritual state of the postwar generation of youth. Furthermore, Zionist experts believed that due to Jews' historical experience of dispersion, their youth were particularly affected by feelings of alienation and moral disorientation. In their minds, the Jewish national school promised to restore Jewish children's emotional, psychological, physical, and moral health by creating a close-knit national community. They believed that this miniature national community, or *Volksgemeinschaft,* was the space in which a new generation of Jews would emerge, committed simultaneously to their Jewish nation and the broader community of loyal Czechoslovak citizens.

The success of Jewish national education depended on Jewish activists' ability to mobilize parents to entrust their children to the Jewish schools. In this, their work was shaped in important ways by prewar modes of minority nationalist activism in the Bohemian Lands. Despite their efforts to rally parents for the Jewish schools, most Jewish children in the interwar years attended public Czech- and Slovak-language elementary schools, a development both welcomed and encouraged by the state. Although Zionist believed that having been granted national minority rights Jews were entitled to public Jewish national schools, the state authorities did not support the establishment of such schools. The Jewish schools remained private, modest institutions attended by a relatively small number of Jewish children, despite Zionist activists' persistent lobbying of politicians and bureaucrats. Czech leaders paid lip service to the Zionist cause and acknowledged as sincere Zionists' pledges of loyalty and patriotism. Nevertheless, the authorities rejected their request for funding for – what was widely believed to be the most important institution for any nationalist movement – the national school.

A NATIONALIST BATTLEGROUND: SCHOOLS AND NATION BUILDING IN HABSBURG AUSTRIA

In September 1920, at the opening ceremony for the Jewish elementary and high schools in Brno/Brünn, teacher and the school's first principal Joseph Lamm (1882–1941) thanked the assembled parents and supporters for having stood by the project in face of opposition and ridicule from its "enemies."[4] Controversy surrounding Jewish schools was nothing new in the Bohemian Lands. For more than a century, state-mandated Jewish education had caused controversy within Jewish societies. Beginning in the 1780s, some parents, rabbis, and teachers feared that the education Jewish children received in the new German-language Jewish schools (*Normalschulen*) would erode the youngsters' Jewishness. Children now had to make time for a secular, state-supervised education alongside the familiar religious curriculum of the traditional Jewish elementary school, the *heder.* These misgivings intensified after 1868, when Jews began attending general schools in ever-greater numbers.[5] When after the First World War Zionists introduced the plans for Jewish national schools, some critics deplored the idea as a "return to the heder," an institution they associated with the "ghetto," with ignorance and isolation.[6] At the same time, Czech-Jewish activists and Czech nationalists also suspected that the new Jewish national schools were simply a resurrection of the earlier German-Jewish schools, symbols of Jews' Germanness and distancing from Czech culture.

The German-Jewish elementary schools in Bohemia and Moravia were established in accordance with an Austrian state directive in the 1780s.[7] The schools were supervised by the state but funded by the Jewish communities, a situation that bore some resemblance, one might add, to the Jewish schools in Bohemia and Moravia in the interwar years. Even as some Jewish children began attending public schools, these Jewish schools remained a feature of many communities. As the numbers of Jewish children dropped and as German nationalists looked to retain German-language schools in areas where German-speakers were in the minority, Jewish schools were in some places transformed into German elementary minority schools.[8] Reforms opening the door to public education for Jews, the increasing urbanization among Jews, and Czech and German nationalists' campaigns aimed to convince Jewish parents to sign their children up for either Czech- or German-language schools contributed to the decline of the Jewish schools in the late 1800s.[9] In Bohemia, it was the Czech-Jewish movement, argues Hillel J. Kieval, that delivered the deathblow.[10] In a decade-long campaign against the Jewish schools between 1894 and 1907, Czech-Jewish activists, in an effort to distance Jews from Germanness, facilitated the closure of almost all the remaining Jewish schools in the region.[11] In contrast, in Moravia, most German-Jewish schools retained a Jewish student body, and the school boards in charge of them resisted efforts to merge the Jewish schools with local German ones until the end of the Habsburg Monarchy.[12]

By the 1890s, the German-Jewish school had become a symbol to Czech nationalists of Jews' German loyalties. This belief was further strengthened by claims that Jewish parents preferred German schools over Czech ones, even in areas that were predominantly Czech, such as Prague.[13] In the minds of Czech nationalists, Jews were guilty of maintaining German institutions in otherwise Czech communities. Not only did Jewish parents choose German-language schools for their children, who then made up a disproportionate number of the students in these schools, but Jewish communities also funded these private Jewish schools.[14] Jews' preference for German-language schools was, on the one hand, a pragmatic choice, opting to educate their children in Austria-Hungary's dominant language, a language of high culture and social mobility. On the other, as Marsha L. Rozenblit has recently argued, many Jews also viewed German as a Jewish language. By the 1860s, Jews had been German-speakers for two generations. This linguistic transformation from western Yiddish to German was an inextricable part of the modernization of Jewish culture in Habsburg Austria.[15] According to Rozenblit, while the German-Jewish schools did signal "that Jews belonged to the German-speaking world," they were Jewish spaces first and foremost, not German nationalist ones, an observation that applies equally to Bohemia's Jewish schools as to the Moravian ones that Rozenblit studies. Significantly, she notes, the German-Jewish schools continued to teach Czech language when that was abandoned by other

German-language schools.[16] To Jewish community leaders and teachers, "German was the language they spoke, even a Jewish language."[17] German-language education, acquired at a Jewish school or a general one, did form an important part of Jewish culture in the Bohemian Lands. This helps explain why Jews continued to prefer German-language schools even as Czech became the dominant language in many parts of Bohemia and Moravia. As the nationalist struggle over schools intensified, Czech and German nationalists' tolerance for such non-national, multilingual practices dissipated. In the last decades of Austria-Hungary, Czech and German nationalists' competition for Jewish children fueled the perception that Jewish parents' educational choices were flexible, a notion that mirrored critical narratives of Jews' national loyalties as fluid and inherently opportunist.

To the postwar Jewish National Council, the creation of Jewish national schools was an important step in their efforts to "withdraw" Jews from the national conflict.[18] In their reading of the minority rights embedded in the Czechoslovak Constitution, Zionists expected to receive state funding for their educational, cultural, and social welfare institutions. The exemption made for Jews with regard to language in the census raised Zionists' hopes. They thought that Jews, despite their lack of a national language, would now be entitled to publicly funded minority schools on par with other national minorities in Czechoslovakia. Nevertheless, in Czechoslovakia as in Habsburg Austria, Jews' perceived lack of a shared national language turned out to pose a significant obstacle for their ability to obtain equal minority rights.

Since 1867, the Austrian state had recognized the right of a national community to "the means for an education in its language."[19] By the mid-1880s, this commitment guaranteed linguistic minorities the right to state-funded elementary schools in their language. Thus, if the parents of more than forty children (living within four kilometers) signed a request for a school in which children would receive an education in one of the province's commonly used languages (*Landessprache*), according to Austrian law the local municipality had to provide it.[20] From 1880 onward, as Pieter M. Judson and Tara E. Zahra have shown, in the Bohemian Lands, German and Czech nationalists mobilized tremendous financial and popular support for their respective minority schools that were established in communities where German- and Czech-speakers mixed. Beginning in the 1880s, the German and Czech school associations mobilized hundreds of thousands of activists and supporters and successfully established and helped maintain minority schools in mixed communities and in the border regions of the Bohemian Lands.[21]

Drawing on this historical experience, Jewish school activists established Jewish School Associations (Židovská matice školská/Jüdischer Schulverein) in Bohemia and Moravia, seeking to mobilize Jewish parents for Jewish national schools in the immediate postwar period.[22] Seeking to roll back what they saw as a century of "denationalization" of Jewish children, forced into the schools of nations other than their own, the school activists urged Jewish parents to sign on. They called on them "to make their voices heard" and demand that the government support Jewish national schools.[23] "It is the responsibility of every nationally conscious Jew," they argued, "to support this important institution by becoming a member and recruiting new members and students."[24] Only Jewish schools would ensure "that the Jewish child will never become an object in the national battle again."[25]

ZIONISTS AND THE JEWISH NATIONAL SCHOOLS IN INTERWAR CZECHOSLOVAKIA

In the turbulent months after the end of the First World War, Zionists optimistically embarked on the foundation for a Jewish national society in the new multinational state. They immediately set out to lay the groundwork for what was in their view the most vital institution: the school. By 1920, new Jewish national elementary schools emerged in the two largest cities in the Bohemian Lands, Prague and Brno/Brünn. The latter also boasted a Jewish national high school.[26] Beginning in 1924, the Czechoslovak Zionist Organization ran a Jewish trade school in Moravská Ostrava/Mährisch Ostrau.[27] These four institutions constituted the Jewish national school system in the Bohemian Lands until the end of the 1930s.[28] One of the most well-established Jewish schools was a private German-language institution run by the Jewish community in Moravská Ostrava/Mährisch Ostrau since 1863. It did not become a Zionist institution after the First World War, but remained a private

Jewish school that taught German and some Czech, thus continuing the tradition of the German-Jewish schools in Moravia.[29]

Unlike in neighboring Germany, where Jewish urban communities experienced a clear revival of Jewish schools in the 1920s, in the Bohemian Lands the numbers of students attending these schools remained more modest.[30] In Prague, where the Jewish population grew from 31,751 in 1921 (these numbers refer to Jews according to religion) to 35,425 in 1930, the Czech-language Jewish elementary school had 17 students in 1922, 121 by 1928 (in that year, only about 7% of the city's Jewish children in elementary school attended the Jewish one), and 200 by 1934.[31] As Jews fleeing persecution in Germany began arriving in Prague, after 1933 more children enrolled in the school.[32] In Brno/Brünn, where there were 10,866 Jews in 1921 and 11,003 in 1930, the German-language Jewish elementary school had 110 students in 1928 and 158 in 1933 (about 7% of the Jewish children in elementary schools in all of Moravia).[33] The German-language Jewish high school, which primarily attracted local students with diverse Jewish backgrounds (many, although not the majority, were born in other parts of the former Habsburg Empire), became the most significant Jewish educational institution in the Bohemian Lands. In 1922, the high school had 55 students. This number grew to 155 in 1928, 228 by 1934 (less than 20% of the region's Jewish middle school students), and 244 by 1937.[34] In the 1920s especially, male students outnumbered female ones three times. The Jewish schools in Brno/Brünn gradually transitioned from German to Czech language of instruction in the late 1920s, completing the switch in 1928/1929. In Moravská Ostrava/Mährisch Ostrau, where there were 6,872 Jews in 1921 and 7,482 in 1930, the non-Zionist German-language Jewish elementary school had 131 students in 1922, 172 in 1928, and 235 in 1934.[35] This school began the shift from German to Czech in the school year 1933–1934, partly in response to the ascent of Nazism in Germany and among German-speakers in the Bohemian Lands, and became a Czech-language school in 1935–1936.[36] Less than 20 percent of Moravia's Jewish children attended Jewish elementary schools.

The school in Prague was created through cooperation between Zionist and religious or "orthodox" activists, the latter hoping to strengthen elementary Jewish religious education. Nevertheless, in the 1920s, it received funding from the board of the Prague Jewish community only occasionally, because members of the board considered the school a national and not a primarily religious institution.[37] By the 1930s, when the school began absorbing children from Germany, the community board began supporting the school. In contrast, in Brno/Brünn, the Jewish community board helped fund the schools from the outset, as did the Moravian Federation of Jewish Religious Communities.[38] In Moravská Ostrava/Mährisch Ostrau, the school was supported entirely by the Jewish community.[39] This difference in communal support reflected the greater unity within the Moravian communities on the question of language use and Jewish identity. Here, German-language education and Jewishness was mutually reinforcing rather than at odds. That was not the case in Prague, where successive community boards fought fierce battles over Czech, German, and Jewish nationalist loyalties in the 1920s. Furthermore, the school in Brno/Brünn, unlike Prague, also received substantial support from the city's municipal council, which had several Jewish members. One author claimed that it was only thanks to these Jewish representatives that the schools received regular and undiminished subsidies from the local municipality.[40]

As private institutions, the Jewish schools also relied on tuition fees. In Brno/Brünn, however, more than 20% of the students attending the *Gymnasium* had their fees waived. In some years, this number increased to more than 30% (in 1923/1924 it was 34%; in 1932/1933, it was 32%, up from 23% the previous school year), but most students between 1920 and 1938 paid tuition.[41] While Jewish activists were keen to remove obstacles to Jewish children's enrollment in Jewish national schools, the funds generated through tuition fees appear to have made up a significant part of the institutions' budgets. At the Brno/Brünn high school, for example, in 1928, tuition fees brought in Kč 48,650 to the school's coffers. In 1928, the local Jewish community contributed Kč 60,000 to the elementary school and high school. The previous year, the city council had awarded them Kč 165,000. Even though waiving fees might have increased enrollment, it was hardly something the school boards could afford to do on a broad scale.

Although Zionists invested this handful of Jewish national schools with great hope for the future, the majority of Czechoslovakia's Jewish children did not live in the Bohemian Lands, but in Slovakia and Subcarpathian Rus'. Throughout the interwar years, Zionists in the west were intensely focused on establishing Hebrew-language schools in Subcarpathian Rus'.[42] Beginning its work just after the war, by 1922 the Hebrew-Language School Association had managed to establish eight elementary schools in the region. Three years later it opened a Hebrew-language high school in Mukačevo/Munkács/Munkatsch/Mukacheve, a city that had a Jewish population of 11,313 in 1930.[43] The number (between seven and nine) of Hebrew-language elementary schools remained relatively stable through the 1920s, yet the number of students enrolled appears to have fluctuated considerably. Thus, in 1924 about 1,000 students attended the Hebrew-language elementary schools, 286 did so by 1928, and about 775 by 1930.[44] The Mukačevo high school had 130 students in 1928 and 372 by 1934. By 1935, a second high school was being planned in Užhorod/Ungvár/Uzhhorod, the region's administrative center. As we shall see, through the 1920s and 1930s, the Zionist leadership pursued the transformation of these private Hebrew-language schools into a public – and thus state-funded – Jewish national minority school system. They did not succeed. The schools remained private institutions throughout the interwar years, as did the Jewish schools in the Bohemian Lands. Similarly to the situation there, only a minority of the region's Jewish children attended the Jewish schools.

Although the Zionist press regularly ran full articles and substantial editorial pieces dealing with the question of Jewish schools in Czechoslovakia, writers were unusually silent when it came to Jewish schools in Slovakia, the region with the largest Jewish population (136,737 in 1930).[45] As discussed in the previous chapter, in Slovakia, the Hungarian legislation, which provided annual state subsidies for religious communities including education, remained in place. In Czechoslovakia, the Slovak communities were therefore able to retain the public Jewish confessional schools, the equivalent to the historic German-Jewish schools in the Bohemian Lands. In 1931, there were sixty-one such schools in Slovakia; most used Slovak as the language of instruction, some used Hungarian and German. That year, 6,571 Jewish children attended these schools, almost half (45%) of the region's school-age Jewish youth.[46] Zionist activists did not pay much attention to the Slovak confessional schools, which they considered to be Hungarian, German, or Slovak assimilationist institutions, much like the German-Jewish schools. Ironically, the Slovak Jewish schools were the closest Jews came to state-funded minority schools in interwar Czechoslovakia.[47]

It is hard to know why children ended up in the schools they did. The fact that Jewish schools had to charge tuition would have been an obstacle for many Jewish parents not only in impoverished Subcarpathian Rus', but also among Jews in the Bohemian Lands. Some parents, eager to see their children take advantage of the possibilities for higher education in Czechoslovakia, might have had concerns about the Jewish schools' accreditation and respectability. Despite the Jewish schools careful compliance with state regulations, parents might have worried that their children would be at a disadvantage once they applied for admission to general middle and high schools, professional schools, apprenticeships, and universities. A Jewish education did after all advertise their child's Jewishness. To the extent that the large Orthodox and Hasidic communities in Slovakia and Subcarpathian Rus' sent their children to secular schools, they appear to have enrolled them either in the Slovak confessional schools or in Czech- and Slovak-language public schools. Influential rabbis and many observant Jews considered the Hebrew-language schools and their Zionist teachers heretical, but they viewed the state schools as less threatening and more socially advantageous. Lastly, for poor, working-class, and middle-class Jews alike, education was the most important way in which to secure a good livelihood and strengthen their family's social and cultural credentials. At a time of increasing uncertainty and growing antisemitism, Jewish parents took advantage of the free and respected public education available to them in a way that was increasingly off-limits to Jews in other parts of Central and Eastern Europe.

Regardless of the modest number of Jewish children enrolled in the Jewish schools in the Bohemian Lands and Subcarpathian Rus', Zionist activists considered the Jewish schools to be the lifeblood of the Jewish national renaissance. They were public manifestations of Jews' will to "reclaim" their children. Much as Czech nationalists had claimed that Austria's language policies and the dominant socioeconomic position of Germans in Bohemia and Moravia had led to forced Germanization of

Czech children, Jewish activists now set out to encourage Jewish parents to return their children to Jewish schools. Unlike Czech and German activists, who could launch wide-ranging investigations of the background of the children and force a school choice on parents (and thereby "reclaim" the child), Jewish activists could merely appeal to Jewish parents to correct the assimilationist patterns of the past. They could, however, draw on the moral and political legitimacy of reclaiming children for their "real" nation. The Jewish schools were tangible symbols of Jews' nationhood and a familiar first step in the process of national revival in the Bohemian Lands.[48] In preparation for the summer campaigns to mobilize parents for the Jewish schools, one activist reminded his audience of their responsibility to the nation: "The school is the most valuable [institution] that a people can be given and at the same time a most reliable weapon that no nation relinquishes voluntarily – without a school, no youth, without a youth, no nation and no future."[49]

THE JEWISH SCHOOL AS HOMELAND

Like other adherents of nationalist movements, Zionists invested the education of the nation's youth with particular importance for the broader nationalist project.[50] Imagining that a national community had been lost in the process of modernization, nationalist activists looked to the schools as spaces in which a past purity of language and culture could be restored. Jewish school activists envisioned the nation's school as an ideal, protected environment in which children could be raised in an authentic national community. They believed that Jewish children educated among their own would remain faithful to their nation. For Jewish nationalists, the school was a utopian space where Jewish youths were protected from the polluting effects of the mixing of peoples and cultures, the temptations of opportunism and assimilation, and the psychological damage caused by antisemitism – all dangers that lured on the outside.

Zionist teachers and child experts believed that they played an extraordinarily important and difficult role in the national renaissance. Josef Freund, a frequent contributor to *Židovské zprávy* on pedagogical questions, noted, "In the *Galut* [Exile], the Jewish teacher has a special mission. The teacher must fill the absence of a homeland with a spiritual world and a spiritual homeland."[51] Eduard Drachmann (1888–1944), teacher and later principal of the Brno/Brünn *Gymnasium* as well as a leading school activist, described the so-called absence of Jewish national life, of a living nation, as the greatest challenge for Jewish pedagogues. "Everything a Jewish teacher teaches seems unreal," Drachmann argued, "it comes from the past and passes into the future through an empty space of the present."[52] It was up to the teacher to create "a national present." Indeed, to activists like Drachmann the school was an opportunity for students to experience what it meant to be part of a *Volksgemeinschaft*, an organic national community. Non-Jewish schools, Joseph Lamm believed, "cannot offer them [Jewish children] the Jewish spirit and the feeling of unity and love that is created through a shared rhythm of the blood; this is what the Jewish teacher can provide."[53] In the Jewish school they will learn, he continued, "that it is good to be a Jew. . . . In our school, they will find their intellectual and spiritual homeland [*Heimat*]."[54]

Zionist pedagogues did not believe that the creation of a national community should be achieved through isolation or self-confinement, by restricting children physically and spiritually to a Jewish world. Rather, their pedagogy was one that taught children how to engage the world as Jews. In the Jewish schools' curriculum, there were no special Jewish subjects aside from instruction in Judaism and the voluntary study of Hebrew. Instead, the teachers were expected to infuse the general curriculum with a distinct Jewish worldview, with Jewish values, and with a Jewish spirit.[55] In Brno/Brünn, for example, the high school curriculum listed one book on a Jewish subject and only did so in the first three grades of the eight-year high school.[56] Nevertheless, in the lists of new acquisition to the *Gymnasium*'s library, there were plenty of materials on Jewish subjects alongside Czech and German classics of every sort. By learning in a Jewish environment, from Jewish teachers, among Jewish fellow students, pedagogues believed, the child would acquire an understanding and familiarity with Jewish culture and a strong Jewish self-awareness, "a deep, true, and responsible understanding of one's own position that will replace opportunism as the basis for our children's relationship to other nations and above all to the state."[57] Indeed, in the

Jewish schools, children would become not only better Jews, but also better citizens.[58]

Although Jewish national schools had the potential of producing good Jews and even better citizens, the project relied in every way on Jewish parents. Not only did the school activists' work depend on parents sending their children to the private Jewish school, but their pedagogical vision demanded that parents cooperate with teachers to reinforce the Jewish atmosphere of the school at home. Eduard Drachmann believed that only within a close-knit circle of home and school could teachers, children, and parents together create a national community. In the absence of a living Hebrew language and a real Jewish national life, "Jewish customs and manners, Jewish books and the Jewish language (Hebrew) [*sic*], Jewish religious ideas and Jewish ethics must come alive everywhere in the child's surroundings. . . . As in the past, the studious father and the wise and modest mother must be living examples and supporters of the efforts to preserve [our] cultural heritage."[59]

In the minds of Jewish school activists, the so-called crisis of Jewish youth was in no small way brought on by irresponsible Jewish fathers and mothers.[60] Even though Joseph Lamm acknowledged that the Austrian state's so-called assimilation efforts, such as mandatory German-Jewish schools, were in part responsible for the so-called dejudaization (*Entjudung*) of the Jewish communities in the Bohemian Lands, he also pointed his finger at the failures of Jewish parents:

> Whatever the [German-Jewish] schools could not destroy in our children, the Western Jewish home hungry for assimilation [*assimilationslüsterne*] has thoroughly taken care of. What is left for our children? We older ones are connected to the Jewish past by the memories of our parents and grandparents' Sabbath table, but in many cases we cannot even give these [memories] to our children. It is here that the work of the Jewish school begins.[61]

As Jewish children were learning to be Jews in the new Jewish school, their parents were also summoned to the school bench. At the *Gymnasium,* informal evening events allowed parents to consult with educational experts on "questions on upbringing" and offered them an opportunity to engage contemporary Jewish issues through popular lectures.[62] The task at hand required "harmony between school and home." Experts such as Josef Freund left little doubt though about who was going to be in charge in "bringing down the walls separating the school from the family and spreading the atmosphere of the school to the private sphere."[63] But disciplining Jewish parents proved to be harder than perhaps first imagined. In the mid-1930s, Eduard Drachmann complained that despite years of work he and his colleagues had failed to convince parents to create homes supportive of students' national education.[64]

The Jewish schools served an internal purpose by creating a tangible Jewish national community. But they were also a visible embodiment of Jewish nationhood, one that reflected the nation's cultural and political loyalties. Here, the Jewish activists had to tread carefully. They assumed that most parents would want to educate their children in German. German was after all an integral part of Jewish culture in the Bohemian Lands, especially among Moravia's Jews, and remained an unrivaled language of high culture in Central Europe during the 1920s and '30s. This preference for German was risky for Jews' public image as a loyal minority, because in the postwar environment state loyalty was most convincingly demonstrated though the use of the Czech language. In Prague, the Jewish school adopted Czech as the language of instruction from the outset. In Brno/Brünn, it took a decade. In Moravská Ostrava/Mährisch Ostrau, the non-Zionist Jewish school used German as the language of instruction but taught Czech, as it had for decades. After 1918, and even more so after 1928, the number of hours of Czech increased for students at all levels. The school began the transition to Czech as a language of instruction in the mid-1930s, completing the process in 1935–1936.[65] In the 1920s, Jewish school activists legitimized the use of German, which they assumed was the mother tongue of most of Moravia's Jewish children, by pointing to the accepted and now legal pedagogical norm that dictated that children should be educated exclusively in their mother tongue.[66]

In Brno/Brünn, where the language of instruction in the Jewish schools' was German until 1928, the school activists were careful to distinguish their German-language schools from German national schools by emphasizing the tripartite – Czech, German, and Hebrew – linguistic and cultural identification of the Zionist movement in the Bohemian Lands. The Brno/Brünn high school's yearbook, for example, highlighted that the teachers ensured that the students were immersed equally in Czech, German, and Jewish culture, noting that students visited Czech, Jewish, and German events and art exhibitions during the school year.[67] Similarly, the sign on the school's façade prominently displayed its name to the Brno/Brünn public in all three languages. In so doing, the school leaders "advertised" Jews' tradition for trilingualism in the Bohemian Lands, a tradition for familiarizing Jewish youths with German, Hebrew, and Czech language that had been established by the German-Jewish schools.[68]

Zionists recognized that Modern Hebrew could not be the language of instruction in the Jewish schools in Moravia and Bohemia. Few Jewish children here had any proficiency in the language, and few parents were interested in substituting their children's German- and Czech-language education with a Hebrew-language one. Instead, Modern Hebrew became part of the Jewish school curricula in the Bohemian Lands as a "voluntary subject," in accordance with government regulations.[69] Conscious of the weakness that the lack of a national language constituted in the early 1920s, Czechoslovak Zionists contemplated ways in which they could strengthen Hebrew in Czechoslovakia. They committed themselves to work to make Hebrew a mandatory subject for Jewish children in schools that had more than fifty Jewish students, to introduce mandatory Hebrew in the country's Jewish schools, and to create public schools with Hebrew as the language of instruction.[70] They were, however, unsuccessful in convincing the state authorities that Hebrew-language instruction had any educational merit.[71] Yet, if Hebrew played an important, albeit largely symbolic and decorative role in the west, Jewish activists in the Bohemian Lands believed that in the east, in Subcarpathian Rus', new Hebrew-speaking Jewish communities could emerge with the help of Hebrew-language schools.

Zionist activists in Bohemia and Moravia encountered the eastern Hebrew-language schools primarily in the pages of the Jewish press, where they were depicted as part civilizing, part nationalizing institutions. They, like most outside western observers, viewed the region and its population, Jews and non-Jews alike, as backward and primitive.[72] In 1935, Irma Pollaková (1892–1983), a journalist and one of the leading members of the Tarbut office in Prague (a Zionist organization promoting Hebrew among Jews in the Diaspora), described, in a retrospective on Hebrew-language education in Czechoslovakia, the schools' impact on Jewish life there:

> [In Subcarpathian Rus'] Jews were, and for the most part still are, incredibly culturally backward and ruled by miracle rabbis [Hasidic spiritual leaders believed to perform miracles]. . . . The Jewish street appeared as if still in the darkest Middle Ages and 40 percent of the Jews were illiterate (1920). . . . All efforts to improve their level of culture had to happen in a language that they considered separate from the modern world or any civilization, but that for them was a living one and through which their trust could be gained. . . . Thanks to the Hebrew-language schools entire towns and villages are today Hebraized in part or in whole and the number of Hebrew speakers is about four thousand.[73]

Activist Chaim Weisz, reporting on "life in the Hebrew schools," described the students as pioneers spreading the light of modern education to their families and communities: "In many families parents are learning Hebrew from the children. . . . In a number of places, the children have taken the initiative to establish Hebrew libraries; they want to be able to read Hebrew books outside of school."[74] The stories of a Hebrew revival in the east served as inspiration and documentation of a Jewish national renaissance to Zionists. They were evidence that Jews had a national mother tongue and hence were a real nation, a claim that was after all called into question repeatedly by the country's demographers and bureaucrats, including Jewish critics. By the early 1930s, the Hebrew-language high school in Mukačevo, the crown jewel of the Hebrew-Language School Association, assumed a central role in the modernization of Jewish religious communities in the Bohemian Lands.

In June 1928, Alfred Engel (1881–1944), a leading Zionist pedagogue and school activist, reminded the Brno/Brünn high school's first graduating class that they had a responsibility to become "*ḥalutsim* of the Galut" (pioneers in Exile). In gratitude to the ones who made their education possible, Engel argued, these graduates should become teachers themselves.[75] Other Jews could go to Palestine if they wished, but they – the elite of the nation's youth – had a task to fulfill at home in Czechoslovakia. Engel's speech echoed a 1920 article by none other than Hugo Bergmann, the most famous early Palestine-bound pioneer from

Prague, who appealed to Jewish youth in the Bohemian Lands to write their chapter in the Zionist story by becoming teachers in the Diaspora.[76] As we have seen, beginning in the mid-1920s, the leadership of the Jewish communities in the Bohemian Lands, the Supreme Council, looked first to the Brno/Brünn high school and later to Mukačevo for graduates who would make up a new generation of Jewish teachers and rabbis.[77] Thus, in the course of the interwar years, the Jewish national schools were transformed from Zionist projects to cornerstones in Jewish leaders' efforts to modernize the Jewish communities and thereby secure the continuity of Jewish life in the Bohemian Lands. The Jewish schools might have attracted a minority of Jewish children and youth, but Jewish leaders hoped that these youths would take the lead in the renewal of Jewish life and culture.

"IN WHICH SCHOOL DOES A JEWISH CHILD BELONG?"

Even though the Jewish School Association promoted its schools as Jewish national institutions, activists were careful to focus on questions of Jewish cultural continuity rather than potentially divisive political sympathies when seeking to mobilize parents for the schools. In Prague and Brno/Brünn, Zionists worked with other groups in the community to establish the first school.[78] In Brno/Brünn and Moravská Ostrava/Mährisch Ostrau, the Jewish community boards supported the local Jewish schools. Although Zionists emphasized that the new Jewish schools in Prague and Brno/Brünn were national institutions first and foremost and not religious ones, which the school in Moravská Ostrava/Mährisch Ostrau formally remained, there was an emphasis on students acquiring Jewish religious knowledge and celebrating Jewish holidays.[79] Furthermore, considering the political turmoil and ideological polarization in general and within the Zionist movement in particular in the interwar period, the Jewish School Association in Prague was compelled to remind parents and potential supporters that "our Jewish elementary school . . . is a cultural institution, not a political one; it is open to Jewish children from all circles regardless of the party affiliation of their parents, it does not predispose students to one political party, but seeks to raise self-aware Jews, honest people and loyal citizens, committed to the Jewish people's past and future, because they value and know its language, history, and teachings."[80]

Jewish parents' enthusiasm for the Jewish School Association left – judged by the laments of Jewish activists – much to be desired. Commenting on the development of the Jewish School Association in Bohemia, activist Oskar Lieben complained "that if only we Jews would show even a fraction of the interest that Germans and Czechs do, our desire for a quick development [of national schools] would be fulfilled much quicker."[81] Indeed, the number of Jewish School Association members in the Bohemian Lands was small. In Bohemia, the association had about 1,000 members in 1928, 560 in Prague alone.[82] Ten years later, in 1937, the number had grown to 1,125, with 547 in Prague.[83] In Moravia, the association had about 350 members.[84] In the late 1930s, Josef Pollak, then the association's chair, complained that the majority of the Jewish public was unaware of the work undertaken by the organization.[85] One part of Jewish activists' mission was to mobilize parents collectively for Jewish schools by joining the school association. Another was to convince them individually to enroll their children in the Jewish school.

Every summer, Jewish school activists campaigned to mobilize Jewish parents to register their children in the Jewish schools, an effort that ran parallel to similar campaigns conducted by Czech and German nationalists seeking to influence and police parents' school choices.[86] School activists assumed that Jewish parents would be reluctant to send their children to a Jewish institution. To persuade them, the activists offered up chilling stories of the alienation and humiliation that Jewish children suffered in non-Jewish schools, formative experiences that threatened to derail their psychological, emotional, and moral development from an early age. The Jewish School Association's campaign portrayed "resistant" parents as misguided, ignorant, and outright cruel. Joseph Lamm recounted his "conversations" with parents opposed to Jewish schools:

> "Isolation is not good, one must have contact with Christian students," says a father who wants his son to become a prosperous businessman. . . . One lady honestly believed that "it is never too early for a Jewish child to be beaten up by others, this way the child learns to live with antisemitism from an early age and can adapt accordingly." . . . "The Jewish school is a

> betrayal of the Germans," says a man who engages a Czech teacher for his children. . . . "I will not let my child be taught in Yiddish," says another, and "I don't believe in confessional schools," says a father who sends his son to a Protestant school.[87]

Lamm considered some of these parents hypocritical. Others, he noted, did simply not understand the consequences of their ignorance. School activists dismissed the belief that Jewish children benefited from going to school with non-Jews. They argued that in contrast to parents' wishful thinking, Jewish students remained profoundly isolated within these "foreign" environments. This isolation had far-reaching psychological, social, and moral consequences. Lamm called on parents to remember what it felt like "in high school when the class was reading *The Merchant of Venice* and the Aryan students' eyes glared with an outright malicious pleasure."[88] Tapping into what they believed to be shared experiences of embarrassment and isolation, school activists appealed to parents to protect their "unsuspecting and innocent" children from antisemitism by sending them to a Jewish school "where they would come to know the word 'Jew' as something other than a swear word."[89]

This early exposure to antisemitism left behind more than just unpleasant memories. School activists believed that Jewish children's experiences of shame and alienation had deep effects on their psychological and moral constitution as well as their familial and social relationships. By sending the Jewish child to a foreign nation's school, warned one author writing during the 1920 summer campaign, parents violated the child's trust and set in motion a process of estrangement and isolation:

> The child learns that belonging to the Jewish people is a stigma . . . and feels only a sense of ostracism and contempt for Judaism. Thus, emotionally torn, our child cannot find its place and wavers between indifference toward and contempt for its heritage, family, Judaism, without a clear firm direction. . . . This evil can be uprooted only if we let our child grow in soil that is suited for its own emotional world – and that is the Jewish school![90]

Parents were told that the internal turmoil felt by Jewish children affected their character and behavior. Eduard Drachmann observed that problems like nervousness and exaggerated zealousness "are often found among Jewish children who have been among other children and is caused first and foremost by a sense of degradation." In a Jewish school, "this presumed need to hide oneself and to pretend disappears, and they are no longer driven to be on constant guard. . . . Once they are free of these other pressures they are more susceptible to the moral guidance by our teachers."[91] Assuring parents of the advantages for their children's moral education and respect for authority, Jewish school activists insisted that only among their own kind would Jewish children learn "to love both their father's house and their fellow citizens."[92]

In making their case for the moral value of the Jewish schools, activists also tapped into material from broader debates about education. They modified the pedagogical dogma, promoted by Czech nationalists and often referred to as the Komenský principle, that dictated that elementary education in the mother tongue was a precondition for children's harmonious intellectual, spiritual, and emotional development. Leaving behind mother tongue as a precondition, they highlighted the moral significance of Jewish education – an education among one's own – for the nation and for its children.[93] If Czech children belonged in Czech schools, as a well-known slogan went, then Jewish children belonged in the Jewish ones.[94]

Jewish school activists employed an emotional strategy focused on parents' anxiety about antisemitism and its effects on their children's psychological and moral well-being, but they also catered to more pragmatic concerns for academic standards and qualifications. Activists detected that Jewish parents presumed that the Jewish school offered a substandard education and that Jewish teachers were academically unqualified and pedagogically inept. Working to dispel this image, they assured parents of the schools' "very good academic standards," confirmed year after year by favorable state inspections.[95] Similarly, Jewish teachers' external credentials were upheld as proof of their respectable qualifications. Thus, in the 1920s, the yearbooks for the Brno/Brünn high school listed alongside each teacher's name the public educational institution that served as his main employer. Eduard Drachmann, for example, also taught at a German-language high school in Brno/Brünn.[96]

Furthermore, activists battled what they believed was a widespread perception of Jewish teachers as incompetent pedagogues. According to Joseph Lamm, one woman recalling her own education in a Jewish school claimed, "The Jewish child has no respect for Jewish teachers."[97] Admiring the modern educational methods employed by the Hebrew-language teacher in Prague's Jewish school, where Hebrew was taught in accordance with modern pedagogical methods using the so-called natural Hebrew language system (*ivrit be-ivrit*), František Friedmann recalled his own experience with Jewish teachers: "The rabbi came in, we had to read some kind of prayer, he underlined certain words and wrote what they meant next to them, dull routine work, uninteresting; after all we did not understand the meaning of these philosophical sentences that we were reading. Here it is different."[98] Although Friedmann and others argued that the traditional Jewish elementary school, the heder, was a place of ignorance – a view shared widely by educational reformers in Eastern Europe, they idealized the modern Jewish school as a pure and nationally regenerating environment.[99]

The teaching of Hebrew was an important symbolic and practical element in the Jewish schools in the Bohemian Lands, but this was not the language question that preoccupied Jewish parents. They wanted their children to know Czech as well as German. In their recruitment ads, school activists assured parents that their children, regardless of the particular language of instruction used in the local Jewish school, would be well versed in both Czech and German. Indeed, even the Czech-Jewish campaigners, who insisted that Jewish children belonged in Czech-language schools, thought it necessary to assure parents that their children would still learn German.[100] In Prague, where the Jewish school's language of instruction was Czech, parents were promised that German would not be neglected.[101] Similarly, in Brno/Brünn, where the Jewish schools used German as the language of instruction in the 1920s, Joseph Lamm stated that "German, Czech, and Hebrew will get equal attention."[102] Although children were supposed to attend schools where their mother tongue was the language of instruction, there was, historian Blažena Przybylová argues, significant pressure from the state authorities on the Jewish school boards to introduce Czech as the language of instruction.[103] Thus, in the late 1920s, the Brno/Brünn schools gradually switched to Czech as a language of instruction, completing it by 1928. The Jewish high school started up its first class in Czech in the fall of 1929. By 1937, German had been phased out as a language of instruction in Brno/Brünn.

In Moravská Ostrava/Mährisch Ostrau, where the language of instruction was German and where classes in Czech had long been part of the curriculum, the Jewish school board initially pushed back against official pressure to switch to Czech as the language of instruction. They did so by insisting on the practical obstacles to such a change. These included the lack of state-approved Czech-language textbooks for Jewish schools and the difficulties in finding qualified Jewish teachers who could teach in Czech.[104] In 1928, parents at the school shot back at the local authorities when the latter demanded that the school teach in Czech only:

> For those who want to educate children for the small country of the Czechoslovak republic only, it would be enough to raise them in Czech [*v duchu českém,* lit. "in the Czech spirit"]. We, however, want to educate and bring up [children] for the world, and for that an education in Czech will not suffice. We consider it unwise to educate our children in Czech only, the same way that it would not be right if they were taught exclusively in German.[105]

Jewish parents, however, were not alone in demanding bilingual education for their children. In the mid-1920s, Czech school activists called for a strengthening of the German-language education in Czech schools in the borderlands. They warned that Czech parents, concerned that their children might be at a disadvantage in the German environment, were sending their children to German schools in order for them to become bilingual.[106] Indeed, as historian Tara E. Zahra shows, in the interwar years parents continued to resist the efforts of nationalists and state authorities to eradicate formal and informal bilingual educational practices.[107]

In the Bohemian Lands, some Jewish parents might have pursued a bilingual strategy by sending their children to Czech elementary schools only to enroll them subsequently in German middle schools. In Bohemia, 62% of Jewish children (as defined by religion) went to the ubiquitous Czech-language elementary schools, while 38% attended German ones in 1930.[108] In Moravia, the numbers were similar, with

61% attending Czech and 39% German schools. The distribution shifted slightly for Jewish children enrolled in middle school with 57% attending German schools in Bohemia and 56% in Moravia. In both regions, Jewish students made up about 10% of the student body in the German middle schools. While more Jewish children attended Czech schools in the interwar years, German education continued, as did the German language, to play an important role among Jews in the Bohemian Lands, something that did not go unnoticed by Czech nationalists.

A few years later, the ascent of the radical right-wing Sudeten German Party (Sudetendeutsche Partei) in the Bohemian Lands and the rise of Nazism in neighboring Germany placed the issue of Jews' language on the front pages. In the spring of 1933, the right-wing newspaper *Venkov* reported from Moravská Ostrava/Mährisch Ostrau on local Jews' response to the political developments in Germany. Recounting how the Jewish community, seeking to rid itself of German, was turning to Czech institutions for help in arranging Czech-language courses for children and adults as well as teacher training programs, the reporter gleefully remarked:

> No one is as flexible when it comes to their [national] orientation as the Jews and thus to everybody's surprise Jews [*židovstvo*] came out united in front of the Ostrava public and expressed clearly that they will exchange their German language and cultural orientation for the patriotic Czech language. . . . At this time groups are being formed seeking to discourage Jews from speaking German in the streets and in public places.[109]

A few months later, in Bohemia, Czech-Jews and Zionists alike encouraged Jews to stop using German in public, calling on them to affirm both their Czechness *and* Jewishness. Calling out from his pulpit, the Czech-Jewish rabbi Richard Feder implored, "Brothers and sisters! If you live in Czech towns and villages or in areas with a Czech majority – speak Czech! If you don't know it well, then learn it." "Our Czech neighbors are provoked by every German word," he warned, "and you depend on their friendship and goodwill, so don't speak German in public or at home and see to it that your children learn Czech well and are familiar with Czech culture."[110] It was time, the rabbi impassionedly pleaded, for all Jews to return to their ancestral community and defend Jewish honor by distancing themselves from all things German. As Feder's appeal shows, there was a meeting of minds between Czech-Jews and Zionists on the language question. They believed it was crucial for Jews to adopt Czech as their everyday language and appealed to the state authorities for support in their efforts.

"A SAD CHAPTER" – THE STATE AND THE JEWISH SCHOOLS

Following the Paris Peace Conference and the recognition of Jewish nationality in the Czechoslovak Constitution, Zionists expected that the state authorities would be forthcoming with support for Jewish national schools. They were bitterly disappointed. Through the 1920s and 1930s, Zionists were dismayed by the Czechoslovak state authorities' lack of support for Jewish national schools in the country's eastern and western regions. They saw it not only as a betrayal of the trust upon which the alliance between Jews and Czechs was based, but also as a breach of Jews' rights as a national minority.[111] The Jewish national schools received some public subsidies in the interwar years, but they were largely maintained by private Jewish funds. Yet, Zionists persisted in lobbying the government for recognition of the Jewish schools as public minority schools.

In 1919, when the Czechoslovak government adopted the Austrian model with regard to minority schools – a model that defined national minorities as linguistic communities – Zionists were concerned. The state authorities thereby maintained that the right to public schools under this legislation applied to linguistic minorities alone – and this time there was no exemption made for Jews as there had been in the census.[112] At first, Zionists interpreted the authorities' refusal to extend funding to Jewish schools as a reflection of widespread antisemitism in the state administration. Later, they conceded that the Jewish schools in the Bohemian Lands, where the language of instruction was either Czech or German, would not qualify for state support under the minority school legislation.[113] They insisted, however, that the Jewish schools in Subcarpathian Rus', which used Hebrew as their language of instruction, did meet the requirements for state support.[114] The authorities countered that minorities had the right to state support for their schools only if their language was one commonly used in the region, which Hebrew was not.

To Zionist ideologues Hebrew was the language of Antiquity, an era of Jewish sovereignty and imagined cultural purity. By the interwar years it had also become the official language of the *Yishuv* (the Jewish society in Palestine). Zionist activists in the Bohemian Lands and elsewhere could thus point to the living Hebrew language in Palestine as evidence for the legitimacy of Jews' assertion that Hebrew was the language of a national minority.[115] Although Hebrew was indeed recognized as a Jewish language by the state authorities, sympathetic Jewish and non-Jewish observers alike understood that the claim that Hebrew constituted a mother tongue among Jews in Subcarpathian Rus' was a stretch.[116] Regardless, they promoted Hebrew-language schools by pointing to what they perceived as the unusually backward cultural conditions among the region's population as well as political expediency. The Czech writer František Svojše noted that in the "chaos of languages and nationalities" that governed the region, it was justified to suspend the usual commitment to mother tongue.[117] In the case of the Jews, whose mother tongues were Yiddish (widely considered a form of broken German, hence the use of the term "jargon" for Yiddish) and Hungarian, he praised Zionists for understanding that "these languages were not desirable" to the new authorities. They had therefore chosen Hebrew as the language of instruction for their schools. Through Hebrew, Svojše concluded, Zionists had "detached Jews from Hungarian" and brought about no less "than a miracle."[118] Further evidence of the Hebrew-Language School Association's patriotism and moral significance was reflected by "the spirit of the Hebrew schools, which is completely loyal; there the children do not hear any attacks on the state or unfriendliness toward Czechs, something that is unfortunately the case elsewhere."[119]

Similarly, Jaromír Nečas (1888–1945), a Czechoslovak social democratic parliamentarian who represented Subcarpathian constituents and worked and traveled in the region in the early 1920s, supported the creation of the Hebrew-language high school in Mukačevo in 1924. As the Ministry of Education contemplated whether to allow the high school to be established, Nečas stated:

> There are almost 100,000 Jews in Subcarpathian Rus', a region the Jewish public abroad is increasingly taking an interest in. The Czechoslovak Social Democratic Party welcomes the efforts of Jews, working under the banner of a Jewish national renaissance, to liberate Subcarpathian Jewry from an atmosphere of superstition and alcohol through enlightenment and productive work. We therefore oppose any attempt to halt the creation of Hebrew-language schools in Subcarpathian Rus'.[120]

Jewish and non-Jewish activists highlighted the Hebrew-language schools' moral and social significance, especially their potential in directing the "Jewish masses" toward so-called productive occupations. Nevertheless, the state authorities insisted that the schools did not qualify as minority schools. They rejected Zionists' requests for help to consolidate the Hebrew-language schools using state funds in the interwar years.

The Hebrew-Language School Association tried to bolster its case with the authorities in other ways as well. According to state law, if the parents of forty students in a school district wanted a minority-language school (a language that not only had to be in common use in the region, but also in which their children had to be proficient), then the state had to provide one. The proponents of Hebrew-language education, however, had difficulties mobilizing sufficient numbers of parents for their schools. Jewish parents were requesting Czech-language schools rather than Hebrew-language ones. This was a choice Zionists blamed on local Jews' ignorance and subjugation by anti-Zionist rabbis.[121] The Zionist schools were indeed met with significant resistance by the local traditionalist religious authorities, who were fiercely opposed to Modern Hebrew–language education and to Zionism.[122] *Židovské zprávy* brimmed with stories of rabbis' "terror campaigns" and excommunications of Jewish parents whose children attended these new Jewish schools. Other parents were allegedly denied religious honors, such as being called upon at services to read a portion of the Torah, subject to economic boycotts, and refused the right to sell kosher products in their stores and stalls.[123] Thus, if parents were not coming out demanding Hebrew-language schools, Zionist writers implied, it was because they were being prevented from doing so by powerful religious authorities whose influence reached deep into the community's social and economic life. By the mid-1930s, the evidence of Jewish parents' requesting Czech-language schools had become so abundant that even Chaim Kugel (1897–1953), the principal of the Mukačevo high school and member of the National Assembly for the Jewish Party since 1935, could no longer dismiss it and demanded Hebrew-language schools in Subcarpathian Rus' only in "places where the parents want them."[124] A good number of the region's Jewish parents no doubt viewed the Hebrew-language schools as heretical institutions. But they probably also believed that the new, well-equipped and well-funded Czech-language schools were their children's ticket to further education and social mobility, a path that did not require a rejection of traditional Jewish authorities. Given the difficult socioeconomic conditions in Subcarpathian Rus' and the constant trickle of Jews leaving for the country's more prosperous western provinces, a Czech-language elementary and high school education would have been an attractive proposition for Jewish parents. In stark contrast to the images of Jewish parents terrorized by traditionalist rabbis and their supporters into sending their children to public Czech-language schools in the east, Zionists did not dwell on the reasons why, in the Bohemian Lands, the majority of Jewish parents, even ones claiming Jewish nationality, chose to do so as well.

By the late 1920s, after almost a decade of failed efforts to secure state support under the minority legislation, the financial difficulties facing the Hebrew-language schools were so significant that local Zionists were ready to employ measures other than the usual lobbying and fundraising to keep them afloat. In June 1928, the central political committee of the Czechoslovak Zionist organization met in Prague to discuss a proposal submitted by Chaim Kugel, at the time acting only as the principal of the high school and not yet as a member of the National Assembly, and Zeev Sternbach, a Zionist activist and editor of the Yiddish-language Zionist weekly *Yiddishe Stimme* in Subcarpathian Rus'. The plan, they proposed, would solve the financial difficulties of the Hebrew-language schools once and for all.[125] The proposal, which was the outcome of negotiations between Jewish activists and representatives of an unnamed political party in the region, suggested a deal whereby the Jewish Party withdrew from participating in the Subcarpathian regional elections in exchange for public funds for the Hebrew-language schools. The committee, consisting of Angelo Goldstein, Emil Margulies, Ludvík Singer, and František Friedmann, all Bohemia-based activists, dismissed the idea on moral and political grounds. They reiterated "our demands for funding for these schools is legally justified based on the character of the Jews as a minority population – by forfeiting this right now, its permanent fulfillment can never be ensured."[126] It was a plan doomed to fail.

The committee instead suggested that their colleagues in the east step up their political campaigns and thereby secure more influence in the local and national legislative assemblies. This was an answer that most likely confirmed Kugel and Sternbach's belief that their western colleagues had little understanding for the dire socioeconomic conditions in which they worked to keep the private Hebrew-language schools staffed and open. Even though the Hebrew-Language School Association had secured an annual state subsidy of Kč 30,000 by 1924, in 1926 its budget for the region's eight elementary schools and one high school amounted to Kč 500,000. Every year, the difference had to be made up by private Jewish funds.[127]

A year later, in 1929, when the Jewish Party won two seats in the National Assembly, Zionists believed that the establishment of public Jewish national schools was within reach. When in 1935, Chaim Kugel took up his seat in the National Assembly, he made state funding for the Hebrew-language schools his top priority. Despite the Jewish parliamentarians' numerous meetings with ministers and even then president Edvard Beneš, their requests for state-funded Hebrew-language schools or, alternatively, a substantial increase in state subsidies for the schools were dismissed by the Ministry of Education.[128] In a 1936 report, one ministry official insisted "that these schools do not serve a nationality, but rather a specific religious group and hence if they were granted public status would amount to more privileges than those awarded to other religious communities."[129] Furthermore, the official noted, "teaching children Hebrew is not in the state's interest; it is a language that is not of general use and is known only to some members of a particular religious group." Despite Zionists' assurances that Hebrew was a commonly used language in Subcarpathian Rus', the authorities were not convinced that a few thousand students in the Hebrew-language schools sufficed to give Hebrew status as a *Landessprache*. Hebrew-language schools also presented a practical problem. There were no school inspectors familiar with Hebrew, and it would thus be impossible for the Ministry of Education to undertake the necessary oversight of the Hebrew schools. Insisting that it would not be fair to make an exception for Jews when it came to schools, the report concluded, "The state does not usually create schools according to students' religion . . . and does not support private middle schools; an exception cannot be made for the Hebrew-language ones."[130] Thus, after more than seventeen years of lobbying and campaigning for the schools, neither the Hebrew-Language School Association nor the Zionist activists and politicians in Prague had managed to convince the state authorities that the modern Jewish national school with Hebrew as its language of instruction – so often held up since as evidence of the Czechoslovak state's recognition of Jewish nationhood – constituted anything but a heder.

WHEN DO JEWISH CHILDREN BELONG IN CZECH SCHOOLS?

In the Bohemian Lands, the battle over Jewish children that had been part of the late Habsburg era continued in the interwar years, in particular between Zionist and Czech-Jewish activists.[131] Armed with statistical evidence, Zionists and Czech-Jews alike cast themselves as promoting Czech among Jews and their opponents as clinging to Germanness.[132] While Jewish activists were preoccupied with fundraising campaigns, petitions, and battles in the Jewish press over the question in which schools Jewish children belonged, in the course of the 1920s, most Jewish children found their way into the public Czech- and Slovak-language elementary schools. In 1921, 32% of the country's Jewish children attended Czechoslovak schools, 26% Rusyn schools, 14% German, 21% Hungarian, and 7% "other" (a category that included Polish- and Romanian-language schools as well as schools with multiple languages).[133] By 1930, 60% were enrolled in Czechoslovak schools, 11% in Rusyn ones, 9% in German, 10% in Hungarian, 2.5% in Hebrew schools, and 8% went to Polish and multi-language schools.

In the Bohemian Lands, the shift from German-language education to Czech was particularly dramatic in Moravia. In 1921, 54% of Bohemia's Jewish children went to Czech-language elementary schools, 46%

to German-language ones. Ten years later, there had been only a small increase in the percentage of Jewish children who attended Czech-language schools, up from 54% to 59% (1930). In Moravia, however, a much starker change occurred in the 1920s. In 1921, 29% of Moravia's Jewish children attended Czech-language schools, while 71% went to German-language ones. In 1930, the percentage of Jewish children receiving an elementary German-language education had dropped by almost half, to 38%. By then, 62% went to Czech-language schools. Thus, in the course of the 1920s, Moravian Jews, who had been predominantly German-speaking in 1918, began to look a lot more like the bilingual Jewish society that Zionist school activists had hoped for, with a linguistic competency that had historically been more widespread among Jews in Bohemia. This emerging cultural and linguistic similarity was also reflected in the fact that by the early 1930s, the same proportion of Jewish students in Bohemia and Moravia went to Czech-language middle school (43%–44%), while a slim majority attended German-language ones.[134]

As Jewish children were funneled into the Czechoslovak schools, Zionists were quick to articulate a response. In the Zionist German-language press in the postwar era, activists called for Czech-language Jewish national schools in communities that were majority Czech-speaking as well as ones with a mix of German- and Czech-speakers. The goal of language instruction in all Jewish national schools was, according to these proponents, that Jews become bilingual, completely fluent in Czech and German.[135] In the Bohemian Lands, Zionists thus cast themselves as promoters of Czech among Jews. Interpreting Czech antisemitism primarily as a reaction to Jews' perceived Germanness, Zionists believed that Jews could best show their loyalty to the state by adopting Czech language and culture.[136] This was, however, a position on the Czech political stage already "inhabited" by the Czech-Jewish movement. Through the 1920s and early 1930s, Zionists and Czech-Jews competed to take the credit for Jews' so-called reorientation from German to Czech in the Bohemian Lands, a precondition, although not necessarily a guarantee, for their inclusion in the fold of equal citizens.[137]

Since German functioned as a lingua franca for Zionists in Czechoslovakia and Central Europe, Czech-Jews insisted that Zionism and the new Jewish national schools were a disguise for some Jews' continued adherence to German language and culture.[138] In response, Zionists highlighted the new Jewish schools' commitment to educating Jewish children in German as well as Czech. Despite these assurances, the critical voices did not subside, and "Germanization" was an accusation that Zionists had to take seriously in the climate of the 1920s and even more so in the '30s. They responded by bringing out the well-known statistical guns. In his 1927 pamphlet *Mravnost či Oportunita?* (Morality or Opportunity?), František Friedmann retaliated. He revealed that, in contrast to the Czech-Jews' claims, Jews who identified nationally as Czechs continued to send their children to German-language schools.[139] Indeed, contrary to Czech-Jews' misconstruction, it was the Zionist movement that was successfully reorienting Jews from German- to Czech-language schools. Drawing on statistics generated in the country's elementary schools at the start of every school year, Friedmann demonstrated that in Moravia, 48.1% of children of Jewish nationality went to Czech-language schools. In contrast, only 20% of Jewish children of "assimilationist parents" attended Moravia's Czech schools, while 80% went to German schools.[140] Even in Bohemia, where Czech-Jews had long been active, there was little evidence that Czech-Jewish assimilationism ensured that Jews enrolled in Czech schools. In the early 1920s, a third of Jewish parents of Czech nationality continued to send their children to German schools, a public embarrassment even the Czech-Jewish leaders had not been able to deny.[141] Similarly, in Slovakia and Subcarpathian Rus', where, Friedmann claimed, "Zionists had been in charge" – needless to say a wildly exaggerated assertion – 74% and 80%, respectively, of children of Jewish nationality attended Czech-, Slovak-, or Rusyn-language schools.[142] Thus, rather than allowing Jews to cling to their old ways, Friedmann concluded, the Zionist movement was at the forefront of the efforts to transform Jews into loyal Czech- and Slovak-speaking citizens of Czechoslovakia.

By the early 1930s, Zionists no longer so readily celebrated the advent of Czech-language education among Jews in Subcarpathian Rus'. By then, about 60 percent of the school-age Jewish children in the region attended Czech-language schools. At a time when the controversial private Hebrew-language schools were struggling to stay afloat in the impoverished region, the government was establishing new Czech schools.

Jewish children were then enrolled, according to Zionists, since there were not enough children of Czechoslovak nationality around to fill the classrooms.[143] Already in the mid-1920s, one author claimed, in order to "Czechify" the region, the state authorities established Czech schools in areas with no Czech children and lured Jewish children into the otherwise almost empty schools, a process that allegedly was turning the region's Rusyn majority against both Czechs and Jews. This "cultural assault on Rusyns and Jews," the author warned, "will bear bitter fruit."[144]

By the mid-1930s, Zionists believed that the Czech authorities were engaging in a full-scale denationalization process in their efforts to modernize and Czechify the east.[145] In an article on the Jewish national minority in Subcarpathian Rus' published in the prestigious state-sponsored *Národnostní obzor,* František Friedmann invoked the trope of Czechs' and Jews' shared experience of denationalization in Habsburg Austria to highlight the harmful effects of the Czechoslovak state's policies. Friedmann presented data that showed that children of Jewish nationality constituted 80% to 90% of the students in Subcarpathian Rus's Czech-language schools.[146] Although he welcomed the increased number of Jewish children receiving a modern education, Friedmann accused the government of using Jews to enhance the "Czech" character of the region much as Austria had used the Jewish minority to Germanize otherwise Slav areas. The denationalization and "Czechification" of children of Jewish nationality, Friedmann warned,

> will deepen the abyss between the Jewish minority and the Rusyn majority population. The outcome of this development could be that the Czech minority in Subcarpathian Rus' will consist predominantly of Jews, which, considering the economic and cultural conditions in the region, will not endear "Czechs" to the local population. It is likely that as time goes by, thousands of "Czech" Jews will migrate to the capital, Prague, where the Jewish minority will grow rapidly, as it did in Budapest, multiplying its current size many times. The appearance of these representatives of "Czechness," in journalism and generally in society, could lead to a significant increase in antisemitism of a kind that we have so far been spared.[147]

Thus, Friedmann argued, not only was denationalization immoral, but it was also undermining Czech authority in the province. It threatened to increase inter-ethnic tension, with destabilizing effects across Czechoslovakia. Zionists were not alone in this critique. Another vocal opponent of Czech "colonization" policies and the authorities' use of Jewish children to fill the region's Czech-language schools was the Communist writer Ivan Olbracht, who reported extensively from the region in the 1930s.[148]

If Jewish nationalists believed that Czechness among Jews in the Bohemian Lands made them better citizens, in the east it was considered a sign of moral corruption and government hypocrisy. "These [Czech] schools are in deep conflict with the Komenský tradition," argued the Prague-based Zionist editor Zdeněk Landes. "The [Jewish] child is raised to become a cultural Levantine [*levantínec*] who has a thin varnish of Czechness but lacks a sense of his own traditional values."[149] Pointing to the shortsightedness of the authorities' position denying Jews public Hebrew-language schools in favor a policy of Czech cultural colonization, Landes concluded, "It is impossible that such human material can become a solid component of Czech or any other culture." Thus, in the interwar years Zionists promoted and applauded the adoption of Czech language and culture among Jews in the west, the only acceptable response if they were to uphold the image of an alliance between Czechs and Jews. Meanwhile in the east, where Czech cultural and political domination was contested, Zionist writers, employing well-known tropes from Czech nationalist discourse, deplored Czech education for Jewish children as denationalization, a process of moral and cultural degeneration for Jews and Czechs alike.

* * *

For Zionists, the state authorities' refusal to concede that Jews had either a legal or moral entitlement to public Jewish national schools was a bitter disappointment. Already in the mid-1920s, Ludvík Singer accused the government of betraying the trust upon which the alliance between Jews and Czechs was founded.[150] Jewish activists had been optimistic that the "liberated" Czech nation would honor its leaders' promises to the country's Jewish nation. They soon learned that Czechs did not act on noble principles alone. As Zionists discovered, the state leaders were willing to give concessions to Jews only when it did not involve circumscribing Czech dominance. Furthermore, Zionists were frustrated by the indifference and laxness of Jewish parents and faced stiff and sustained opposition from the religious authorities and their communities in the east – a resistance they never managed to overcome.

As in other parts of Eastern Europe, Jewish parents in Czechoslovakia preferred to send their children to non-Jewish public schools.[151] Regardless of Zionists' efforts to paint "foreign" schools as harmful to Jewish children, without government support there was little Jewish activists could do to compete with the state-funded public schools. In some ways, the failure of the Jewish national school project reflected that in Czechoslovakia the public educational system remained open and attractive to Jewish parents. Unlike Jews in neighboring states, Jews here were not subject to formal quotas, restrictions, or unbearable harassment. In this country, the dominant elite did not see Jews as a threat. Rather Czech leaders, acting on the notion of Jews' malleable loyalties and potential for respectability, appear to have encouraged Jews' Czechification in the public schools as a means to consolidate Czech linguistic and cultural hegemony in all of Czechoslovakia.

Regardless of the challenges facing Zionists in securing this most important institution, the Jewish schools played an important role in the modernization and renewal of the Jewish communities in the Bohemian Lands. The Jewish national school was a symbol of and a vehicle for the nationalization of Jewish life and thus an important part of Zionists' politics of belonging. Zionists' deep integration into the institutional, cultural, and political framework of the Jewish communities in the Bohemian Lands, as well as their active participation in the broader political process, deepened their investment in and commitment to the continuity of Jewish life in the Diaspora. Although disappointed in Czechoslovakia's failure to correct the "wrongs" committed by Habsburg Austria, by the late 1930s Zionists were well aware that they had few other options than to trust that their loyalty would eventually be rewarded.

Yet, in Eastern Europe, minority nationalists did not view national schools as the only institutions that could facilitate collective awakening. Indeed, through the nineteenth century gymnastic organizations had served as significant vehicles for mass mobilization. By the early twentieth century, as nationalists invested children and youths with increasing importance in securing the nation's future, youth groups and sports clubs alongside gymnastics societies assumed growing prestige as valuable national institutions. Thus, in spite of the importance Zionists placed on schools, they did develop other organizations through which they sought to mobilize the nation's youth. The next chapter examines the Zionist alternative to the Jewish national schools, the Jewish gymnastics and sports movement.

SIX

Making New Jews

MACCABI IN CZECHOSLOVAKIA

IN THE MONTHS PRECEDING THE 1936 OLYMPICS IN BERLIN, debates raged in several European and North American countries about whether or not their athletes should be allowed to boycott the Games. No country pulled out of the event, but individual athletes did. Some Jewish athletes decided not to participate; others traveled to Berlin with their non-Jewish team members.[1] In Czechoslovakia that summer, audiences followed the boycott debate with great interest. Months earlier the Czechoslovak Jewish sports organization Makabi ČSR (Maccabi Czechoslovakia) had announced that its members would not participate in the Berlin Games.[2] This decision was met with support in Jewish and non-Jewish circles.[3] It might have gone unnoticed had it not been the case that some of the country's top swimmers and water polo players belonged to the Jewish clubs Hagibor Praha/Prag, Bar Kochba Bratislava, and Maccabi Brno/Brünn. In addition, several other Jewish athletes, who belonged to non-Jewish clubs, were also members of the Olympic swim and water polo teams.[4] Sports commentators believed that the Czechoslovak teams had a good chance of bringing home medals from Berlin. They predicted that the Jewish athletes' withdrawal would weaken the national teams considerably.

The Czechoslovak Amateur Swimming Association fought long and hard to prevent the Jewish athletes from withdrawing from its Olympic team.[5] Branding the boycott movement a political conspiracy and claiming that the athletes had been coerced into withdrawing, the organization's leaders sowed suspicion as to Maccabi's patriotism. To the Swimming Association's board members, Jewish athletes, like all members of the Swimming Association, had a duty to defend their country's colors. But the board could not force the Jewish athletes to Berlin, because the Czechoslovak Olympic Committee had decreed that Jewish athletes were allowed to withdraw. Yet, the association's leadership decided to make an example out of what they viewed as Maccabi's collective breach of associational discipline. They threatened to fine and disqualify the clubs from competitions for two years. In the end nothing came of the sanctions. At the Czechoslovak Swimming Championships that July, Bar Kochba Bratislava replaced Hagibor Praha/Prag as the national champions. Two weeks later the Czechoslovak Olympic team headed to Berlin without the majority of its Jewish athletes.

Journalists were quick to make more of the broader issues at play in the dispute between Maccabi and the Czechoslovak Amateur Swimming Association. Before long, they turned their readers' attention to the question of Jews' divided loyalties by asking if the Jewish organization's decision to withdraw its athletes from the national team exposed a deeper, more troubling flaw in Jews' loyalty to Czechoslovakia. Were Jews (and by extension Czechoslovakia's other national minorities) capable of being good and trustworthy Czechoslovak citizens? Writers in the right-wing *Venkov* and *České Slovo* scolded the Jewish clubs for their open defiance of the national swimming body's authority. They decried the potential harm the clubs' decision had done to the Olympic team as well as the athletes' alleged lack of loyalty to the state.[6] The author of the article "An Athlete like a Soldier Must Not Retreat: Why the Jewish Swimmers Should Participate in the Olympics" argued that since the idea of Czechoslovakia was to unite all its different nationalities, national minorities had a responsibility to this higher, civic duty, one that trumped partisan interests. In fateful moments for Czechoslovakia, the author demanded, "a soldier must remain a soldier – and the same is true for an athlete."[7] War imagery pervaded the debate. One writer likened the Jewish clubs' decision to mutiny, noting, "The interest of the nation, the state, the collective must always trump that of individuals." Playing on the military analogy, the author continued, "For these amateur athletes there is an unwritten law that demands that Czechoslovak athletes regardless of their nationality or conviction defend the Czechoslovak flag on the international playing field."[8] Like the Swimming Association executive, some writers declared that Jews were mixing sports with politics and thereby failing to fulfill their civic duty. The articles questioned Jews' loyalties as well as contemplated the extent to which national minorities generally could be trusted as committed citizens in times of war and peace.

The public debate and the tense negotiations behind closed doors between Maccabi, the Swimming Association, and representatives from the Ministry of Health and Physical Education touched a raw nerve among Zionist sports activists. Not only did Jewish solidarity appear at odds with Czechoslovak patriotism, but Jewish nationality was depicted as a political choice, an opportunist move, a sense of loyalty and unity that Jews could exchange for something else should they wish to do so. This was precisely the perception of Jews' nationhood that Zionists had worked hard to undo for years. Although some commentators supported Jewish athletes' display of national unity and solidarity, critics played up the stereotype of Jews' opportunist, untrustworthy, and even treasonous character.

Zdeněk Landes, a well-known Zionist editor and member of Maccabi's executive, wasted no time responding to the damaging criticism. He rejected the claim that the boycott was a sign of Jews' disloyalty to their country, evidence that Jews' ethnic particularity was incompatible with their duties as citizens.[9] At a time when there was open war between Jews and the Third Reich, Landes argued, it would be a disgrace for any self-respecting Jew to attend the Games. The clubs' refusal to participate in the Olympics in Germany, a place where Jews were being wronged and humiliated, was not a question of politics; it was a question of honor. By refusing to participate in the Games, Maccabi and its athletes were not prioritizing minority interests over the common good. Rather, they were making a moral choice to defend their nation's honor. Thus, even as critics portrayed Jews as wanting in loyalty, discipline, and fighting spirit and as ministerial officials privately noted that Maccabi had damaged Czechoslovakia's image abroad, Jewish activists insisted that their defense of Jews' honor reflected their respectability. To them, Jews' determination to protest Nazi Germany's antisemitism, to take a stand against the regime's assault on Jews' dignity, proved that Jews were upright citizens.

For more than a decade, Maccabi had promoted the Jewish sports and gymnastics organization as an institution that transformed Jews from opportunist and unreliable subjects into disciplined, nationally committed, and patriotic citizens of Czechoslovakia. As representatives of one of the country's national minorities, Maccabi leaders had been keen to establish a political alliance with the Czechoslovak authorities by casting gymnastics and sports as key to the creation of useful and loyal Jewish citizens. The "new Jew," a masculinized individual and collective ideal, embodied the symbiosis between Jewish nationalism and Czechoslovak patriotism promoted by Maccabi. The decision to go through with the boycott was a high-stakes game for Maccabi leaders, putting their hard-fought public image as model citizens on the line. Their decision reflected how significant the defense of Jews' honor, the insistence of Jews' equality and dignity, was to their own sense of what it meant to a respectable Czechoslovak citizen.

In interwar Czechoslovakia, gymnastics and sports were a social and symbolic space where the discourses on citizenship, nationhood, and gender intersected. In contrast to older interpretations of nationalism that viewed nationalist sports and gymnastics organizations as evidence of mass national awakening and of the nation's existence, I argue that the nation existed only as performance. Whether during afternoon training, evening get-togethers, or weekend-long spectacular events, these performances were rites that established the nation's boundaries and rehearsed over and over the nation's ideals and values. Maccabi's institutional structures, its neighborhood clubs, the sports journals, the shared symbols and commands, the uniforms, and the summer camps, were all part of the performance. Jews' collective loyalties, their readiness for civic equality and nationhood, only came to life as performance, what some scholars have also referred to as rites of citizenship.[10]

Sports and gymnastics clubs were particularly important to Zionists because of their potential for mass mobilization and their legibility as national institutions. Furthermore, through the establishment of Maccabi, a countrywide umbrella organization, Zionists demonstrated Jewish nationalism's potential as an integrative force in Czechoslovakia. They thus affirmed one of the pillars of the alliance between Jews and the state. Zionists viewed the sports movement, much as they did the Jewish schools, as the "nation's territory." It was within the clubs and on the teams that a tangible national community could be created. For Zionists, Jewish gymnastics and sports were the social and symbolic space where personal bonds between Jews were formed, where they shared each other's struggles and hopes, and where the individual experienced what it meant to be part of a greater whole, part of a national community. Indeed, over time, Zionists came to see Maccabi as especially significant because of the absence of a Jewish national school system in Czechoslovakia.[11] Viewing the dispersal of Jewish children and youths in Czech, German, Slovak, and Hungarian schools as detrimental to a national rebirth, Maccabi activists imagined themselves on the front line in the battle for Jewish children's souls. As Maccabi leader and chief ideologue Ernst Fuchs declared, "In Exile, Maccabi must act as a school, [an institution] that is available to people of other nationality from childhood on. At evening gatherings, through courses, on the exercise grounds, playing fields, and in the tests to acquire the gymnastics- and sports badge, we must carry out our program [of regeneration]."[12] In contrast to the Jewish schools, Maccabi found greater support among the country's Jews as well as among state bureaucrats and politicians. Thus, the story of Jewish sports reveals the complex ways in which Zionists sought to construct Jews' belonging in Czechoslovakia and allows us to gauge to what extent they succeeded in doing so.

This chapter focuses on the work of the organization's leaders, who were based in the Bohemian Lands and headquartered in Prague, to transform a handful of Jewish gymnastics and sports clubs into a mass movement. As we have seen earlier, the quest to become the model loyal minority was an ideological as well as a strategic choice. As representatives of a new grassroots organization with the ambition to become the country's dominant Jewish sports institution with units in communities across Czechoslovakia, Jewish sports activists needed money. For that they turned to the state. Gymnastics and sports were intrinsically connected to military traditions. The health and discipline of soldiers were a constant subtext for the state's investment in physical education. In the 1930s, in step with the government and the wider culture, Maccabi turned to military matters as yet another expression of Jews' loyalty to the state and their desire for inclusion – a demand for equality that had to be continuously stated and restated.

JEWS, MASCULINITY, AND MARGINALIZATION

Until recently, historians of modern Jewry and the Zionist movement in Europe have paid little attention to the role of sports and gymnastics in Jewish societies. When they did, they would often include references to gymnastic clubs and sports teams as piquant illustrations or curious anecdotes. Few scholars studied these often large and certainly widespread Jewish institutions.[13] Along with an increased interest in social and cultural history and issues of race, class, and gender, however, recent scholarship has brought Jews and sports under serious investigation, adding to the understanding of issues such as integration, acculturation, self-assertion, and responses to antisemitism.[14]

Middle-class male Jews joined in the general involvement in gymnastics and physical education in the nineteenth century. Not until the fin de siècle did exclusively Jewish clubs emerge in Europe. Most famously, the Berlin Bar Kochba was established in 1898 and was soon followed by numerous other clubs in Germany and Habsburg Austria, including the Bohemian Lands.[15] Within a few years, Jewish women joined in.[16] The Jewish clubs, scholars suggest, emerged as a response to antisemitism as well as Zionism.[17] These institutions were founded by men eager to participate in gymnastics (physical and mental discipline was, after all, key to the masculine ideal) but who found themselves excluded from the general increasingly nationalist and antisemitic associations.[18] Some scholars emphasize the push factor, while others have argued for more of a pull effect. With the emergence of Zionist ideas, they argue, Jews created their own clubs as an expression of their sense of Jewish national belonging and commitment to Jews' national regeneration. Even if Zionist ideology motivated many pioneers of Jewish gymnastics and sports, in some parts of Central Europe, the clubs they helped establish kept a cautious distance from the Zionist movement. Wary of the divisive nature of Zionism at the time and unsure of its appeal among Jews, these sports and gymnastic clubs focused on Jewish renewal and health. Their leaders emphasized physical and moral reform and ethnic Jewish unity rather than nationalist goals.[19]

The emergence of Jewish gymnastics and sports clubs was, however, more than a process of push and pull. And Jewish gymnastics was more than a Zionist and Jewish nationalist endeavor. Jewish clubs with German nationalist, socialist, and so-called neutral profiles also dotted the Central European landscape.[20] In Galicia, as Joshua Shanes has shown, the Jewish nationalist gymnasts were driven by opposition to religious authorities as well as a desire to invigorate and discipline the body of their nation. In this they were inspired by similar efforts among their Polish and Rusyn peers.[21] In the German context, Jacob Borut has examined German nationalist, Zionist, and neutral Jewish clubs and showed that some Jews joined up for ideological reasons, while others participated for pragmatic ones – perhaps a friend was already a member or the club facilities were in a convenient location.[22] These studies suggest that one of the central impulses behind the emergence of Jewish sports and gymnastic clubs was a search for Jewish community and a way to establish Jews' social respectability.[23] Whether Jews insisted on performing rites of manhood such as fencing and gymnastics, seeking out an environment free of antisemitic slurs and intimidation, or pursuing the Jewish nation's rebirth, their involvement was in many cases acts of resistance against perceived attacks on their honor.[24]

In his work on modern masculinity, the historian George L. Mosse shows that at the turn of the twentieth century, the masculine ideal was at the core of societies' self-definition. Drawing primarily on examples from Central and Western Europe, Mosse suggests that men's bodies became sites for utopian longings; the male ideal symbolized social and moral order.[25] The manly stereotype fused virtues such as discipline, honor, and will power with ideals of bodily health and beauty, making the male body a sign of moral respectability.[26] However, the emergence of the normative masculine stereotype, Mosse contends, went hand in hand with the construction of its countertype, the symbol of physical and moral disorder.[27] Social outsiders, Jewish and homosexual men in particular, were marginalized through narratives that cast them as unmanly, even incapable of becoming men.[28] Mosse shows how negative Jewish stereotypes were infused with gendered meanings that cast Jewish men as weak-willed, cowardly, and passive and their bodies as effeminate and unpleasing contrasts to the normative ideals of manly beauty.[29] Practices and discourses enforcing and popularizing the image of unmanly Jews denied Jewish men honor, a virtue at the heart of manhood.[30]

Having internalized the manly ideal and its countertype and seeking to restore their respectability, Jews responded, as did gay men, Mosse argues, by co-opting the dominant ideals of manliness. The impetus behind the efforts to create a "new Jew," an embodiment of the masculine ideals and a vision shared by Jewish reformers of different ideological colors, was an attempt to resist these marginalizing narratives. The "new Jew" would restore Jews' honor and facilitate their social equality. The emergence and spread of Jewish gymnastics and sports clubs was one instance of Jews' co-optation of the masculine ideal. Gymnastics, at the heart of the manly project, cultivated physical rigor, beauty, and skill and instilled virtues such as willpower, restraint, and courage. Gymnastics was central to the desire of Zionists, nationalists, socialists, and others to create new Jews in the decades before and after the First World War.[31]

Among the Jewish political movements, masculinity was particularly important to Zionists.[32] Zionist activists worked to transform Jews into a nation – an assertive and fit *Volk* – by doing away with the unhealthy and powerless people of the ghetto. This contrast between old and new Jews, the ghetto and the nation, Exile and the Land of Israel, was at the heart of Zionist ideology and iconography. At the second Zionist Congress in 1898, the Zionist leader and cultural critic Max Nordau (1894–1923) laid out his vision for a muscular Jewry.[33] To Nordau, new Jews, physically fit individuals who were morally committed to Jewish nationhood, embodied as well as facilitated the process of national regeneration, a process of empowerment and normalization of Jews and Jewish culture. Nordau and other leaders' visions of the Jewish body as a utopian site were popularized in Zionist iconography on postcards, posters, and artwork and through gymnastics performances at the annual Zionist Congresses. Zionist heroes were idealized, virile men of Jewish antiquity such as Bar Kochba, the leader of a Jewish revolt against the

Romans in 133 CE, and the Maccabees, the Jewish fighters celebrated for having reconquered and re-Judaized the Land of Israel in the second century BCE.[34] By doing away with the heroes of Exile – the rabbis, scholars, and communal intermediaries – Zionists offered up masculine heroes deeply connected to physical assertiveness and to the Land of Israel. The imagined aggressive Jewishness and masculinity of these ancient heroes embodied the Zionist quest to restore Jews' dignity, defend their honor, and become a nation ready to assume statehood.[35]

Zionists, Bundists, and other Jewish reformers believed that gymnastics and sports were indispensable for the physical and mental regeneration of Jews, but they also recognized the utility of these popular pastimes in mobilizing the broader Jewish public politically. They believed that men and women, indifferent to and unaware of their own social, national, or political interests, could be won over for the cause through their gymnastics and sports activities, their admiration for certain teams, and their exposure to the movements' ideology through public spectacles.[36]

Much like these nongovernmental groups, military and political authorities had long recognized the importance of physical education in disciplining and mobilizing their populations.[37] After the First World War, in a climate of widespread anxiety over the physical and psychological condition of the postwar generation in Europe and the related popularity and influence of the eugenics movement, state involvement in the funding and organization of physical education increased.[38] Funds for athletic facilities, for institutes of physical education, and for sports and gymnastics organizations increased across Europe in an effort to promote physical and moral health in the aftermath of the war. Mass spectacles and spectator sports, soccer in particular, became enormously popular, and national and international sports institutions, governing bodies, and competitions were consolidated in the interwar years. The popularity of sports in the decades after the First World War, scholars argue, reflected a profound militarization of societies.[39] Sports arenas became settings for national and ideological rivalries, and audiences and authorities alike invested considerable prestige in their sports teams, viewing their performances as a reflection of the strength of their nation or political party.[40]

In Central Europe, gymnastics was a social space and a cultural practice intimately connected to the nation-building experience of stateless peoples. The Czech gymnastics movement, Sokol, for example, was widely admired by nationalists for its perceived role in "awakening" and "empowering" the slumbering Czech nation beginning in the 1860s. According to Zionist writers, in the Bohemian Lands, the pioneers of Jewish gymnastics and sports were keen observers of Sokol.[41] In 1899, local activists established the region's first Jewish club in Moravská Ostrava/Mährisch Ostrau.[42] In the decade before the First World War, clubs with names such as Bar Kochba, Maccabi, and Maccabea sprung up in towns across Moravia, including in the regional center Brno/Brünn in 1908.[43] That same year, Maccabi was established in Prague.[44] By 1914, there were thirty-two Jewish nationalist clubs in Habsburg Austria; more than half of them (seventeen) were in the Bohemian Lands.[45] Further east, in what would become Slovakia, Jewish soccer clubs were particularly widespread.[46] Along with other Jewish clubs in Central Europe, the ones in the Bohemian Lands joined in the Berlin-based international Jewish Gymnastics Movement (Jüdische Turnerschaft).[47]

After the First World War, at the twelfth Zionist Congress in Karlovy Vary/Karlsbad in 1921, the Jewish Gymnastics Movement reconstituted itself as the Maccabi World Union (Makkabi-Weltverband). The World Union and its member associations remained formally independent from the World Zionist Organization and its local branches.[48] Yet, every Zionist Congress featured gymnastics performances by Maccabi units, activists crisscrossed between Maccabi and Zionist federations, and Maccabi cultivated a strong connection to the Zionist project in Palestine through fundraising and Zionist education. Its most spectacular event, the Maccabiah (the so-called Jewish Olympics), was held in Palestine in 1932 and 1935 and attracted thousands of Jews from abroad as participants and spectators.[49]

The creation of international federations such as the Maccabi World Union was not a unique phenomenon in interwar Europe. The international Socialist Sports Movement and the Slav Sokol were similar transnational federations established to represent and strengthen particular nationalist or political movements.[50] Mass spectacles such as the Slav Olympics, the Workers' Olympics, and other mass rallies were put on to display the unity, assertiveness, and strength of a class or nation. Thus, Jews, much like other Europeans, were looking to the nation's body for redemption.

MACCABI ČSR – CREATING A CZECHOSLOVAK MOVEMENT

In the aftermath of the First World War, Jewish nationalist sports and gymnastics enthusiasts were, much like their colleagues in other branches of the Zionist movement, quick to respond to the new political reality. Anticipating the recognition of Jews as a national minority, activists set out to position Jewish clubs as national institutions with a legitimate claim to public resources in Czechoslovakia. For Zionists, who had watched Czech and German nationalists thrive as recipients of public funds for their nation-building work in Austria-Hungary, state support was the key to success. In light of the uncertainty that persisted with regard to Jews' minority status as well as the surge in antisemitism after the war, Jewish sports activists focused on convincing the new authorities that the Jewish gymnastics and sports movement would be an integrative force, uniting Jews across the country under a Czechoslovak and Jewish banner. Jewish reformers, such as the founders of the Council for the Health of Jewish Youth (Židovský výbor mládeže pro tělesnou péči), believed that with the help of the state they could transform Jews into "healthy and disciplined citizens."[51] This connection between healthy Jews and good citizens remained at the heart of the Jewish gymnastics and sports movement in Czechoslovakia in the interwar years.

State-makers and citizens alike were well aware that the real work to establish the legitimacy of Czechoslovakia was to take place in communities across the newly amalgamated territories. Alongside the renaming of streets, squares, and cities, the new flags and state symbols hoisted on public and private buildings, and the redrawn maps adorning classrooms, activists of various political and national persuasions created institutions that matched the new reality. As the monarchies crumbled, people also transformed their voluntary organizations in ways that would serve them best in the new political order.[52]

At the end of World War I, as Jewish men returned to their communities and some to their prewar gymnastics and sports clubs, activists worked to establish a statewide organization that could act as a unified voice for Jewish gymnastics and sports in Czechoslovakia. Beginning in November 1920, Jewish activists Robert Heller from Maccabi Chomutov/Komotau and Egon Štern, the soon-to-be chair of the Jewish Soccer League, participated in several meetings of the newly established Czechoslovak Sports Society (Československá sportovní obec). This organization's leaders were considering ways in which sports clubs and leagues in Bohemia, Moravia, and Slovakia could be enticed to organize themselves within one statewide federation.[53] The proposal on the table was to create federations and sports leagues along national lines that would be united through a Czechoslovak supra-governing body. Thus, German clubs in the Sudeten region and Subcarpathian Rus' would belong to one German federation. Zionists were eager to sign on to this model. After all, the bulk of the country's Jews, and hence their potential members, lived in the country's eastern region, and they were already, based on Slovakia's numerous Jewish soccer clubs, excited about sports. Considering the contested nature of Jews' national belonging in the immediate postwar period, Oskar Kaminsky, a leading member of the Council for the Health of Jewish Youth, Robert Heller, and Egon Štern wanted to make clear that Jews, just like other national minorities, belonged rightfully in their own national sports federation.

When the Czechoslovak Sports Society's aspirations to assume leadership of the country's sports clubs and leagues met resistance from Hungarian and German clubs, Heller and Štern made sure to draw clear distinctions between Jews and the other national minorities. In one meeting in early January 1921, Egon Štern, who had just returned from a trip to Košice/Kaschau/Kassa in eastern Slovakia, reported on the state of affairs in the east.[54] He recounted vividly to the assembly how Jewish nationalist sports activists who wanted to join the Czechoslovak Sports Society were intimidated by Hungarian nationalists. The latter had threatened to exclude the Jewish clubs from the Hungarian league, and thus, Štern argued, from every sports competition in a region dominated by the Hungarian sports federation. Jews were not, according to Štern, free to express their Jewish nationality nor their loyalty to Czechoslovakia in the face of the Hungarian clubs' dominance and power.[55] Seeking to cure the assembly of any mistrust of Jews, Štern made it clear that the Jewish nationalist clubs in Slovakia were not separatist, anti-Slovak, or pro-Hungarian, but important allies for the Czechoslovak Sports Society.

At stake for the Jewish sports activists were not only political respectability but also funding. Faced with the momentous task of building up a statewide Jewish organization, they were looking for tangible, material support. Subsidies for Jewish clubs to rent public sports facilities, for example, would reduce these clubs' dependence on playing fields owned by Hungarian clubs. They also suggested that the Czechoslovak Sports Society sponsor games between visiting Czech and local Jewish teams. The Jewish activists' motions were well received by the society's leaders. One board member, Josef Fikl, who was also on the Czechoslovak Olympic Committee, welcomed "these guarantees of Jewish and Czechoslovak cooperation" and noted that "the Jews in Slovakia are valuable material for us . . . hence the Jewish federation should not encounter any obstacles [in its efforts to organize Jewish clubs in Slovakia]."[56]

A few months later, the Jewish Sports and Gymnastics Society in Czechoslovakia was established in Prague.[57] The society was Jewish nationalist in its outlook. Its purpose was "to promote systematic physical education among the Jewish people and to awaken their national consciousness."[58] The founders imagined that the society would work as a unifying, umbrella organization that protected and represented Jewish sports and gymnastics clubs' shared interests. Like their peers among Zionist politicians, these activists consciously moved to create an institution that emphasized Jews' status as a national minority on par with the recently established German and Hungarian counterparts.

The loose organization and ideological neutrality that characterized the Jewish Sports and Gymnastics Society was a bone of contention among some members. In October 1927, a more ideologically committed, Zionist faction already organized as Maccabi Czechoslovakia under the umbrella of the society replaced its mother organization as the country's only Jewish sports and gymnastics federation. Arthur Herzog (1896–?), a longtime member of the local Prague Maccabi club, assumed the position at the helm of Jewish gymnastics and sports, where he remained until he emigrated to Palestine in 1939.[59]

To Maccabi activists, their organization's new role was a momentous step.[60] By assuming the position as a representative of the country's organized Jewish clubs, Maccabi was eligible for state support and came one step closer to cement the image of Zionism as the natural expression of Jewish nationalism, a depoliticized, neutral form of ethno-national identification.[61] From the outset, Maccabi formulated a controlled and centralized program with a focus on uniformity, community, and visibility. In contrast to its predecessor, the Maccabi executive aimed to create a uniform organizational structure within each regional district and enforce uniformity among member clubs by demanding the adoption of a standard set of statutes as well as the name Maccabi.[62] The Prague executive also reserved the right to exclude member clubs for breach of discipline.[63] Like other nation-makers, Maccabi's leaders were well aware that their nation had to be built on more than symbols of nationhood. In the program published after the takeover in Brno/Brünn in the bilingual monthly *Židovský sport – Hamakkabi,* they committed themselves to the creation of a community of gymnasts, a *Turngemeinschaft.*[64] Summer camps, local, regional, and national sports and gymnastic events, as well as frequent, informal outings, were designed to strengthen the personal bonds among young Jews and create a direct relationship and unity of purpose among members, clubs, and the Maccabi executive.[65]

As in other parts of Central Europe, the Czechoslovak Maccabi experienced a steady increase in member clubs.[66] From the late 1920s through the 1930s, the organization expanded its network of gymnastics and sports clubs in all parts of the country, becoming one of the largest Jewish non-communal institutions in Czechoslovakia. In 1919, there were fourteen Maccabi clubs. By 1921, this number had more than doubled to thirty-one. In 1928, Maccabi oversaw forty-four clubs, and by 1933, eighty-three.[67] The number of clubs settled around eighty, and some clubs expanded their membership base substantially as the number of actual members continued to grow through the 1930s.[68] In 1921, the organization had about 2,000 members; in 1928, 4,000; and by 1933, 8,000. This number had grown to 10,000 in 1936 and by 1937 to 11,000. As Jews made up the smallest of the country's national minorities, Maccabi was not surprisingly smaller than most of the other national organizations.

The Czechoslovak groups organized a total of 841,635 members; the German ones, 424,083; and the Hungarian federation, 7,800.[69]

Like its predecessor, the Prague-based Maccabi's leadership viewed the Jewish societies in Slovakia and Subcarpathian Rus' as an important "arena" on which to establish the organization's Czechoslovakness as well as enhance its deserving nature in the eyes of the state authorities. In their annual applications for financial support from the Ministry of Health and Physical Education, which made up the bulk of the correspondence between Maccabi and the state authorities, Maccabi leaders consistently presented the organization's work as "aimed at securing the well-being of the Czechoslovak state."[70] In report after report, they cast themselves as overseeing a conscientious program to improve the Jewish population in the east. They noted Maccabi's self-funded success establishing new clubs in areas where Jews had no other opportunity for physical education and highlighted the annual inspections undertaken by educators and representatives from Prague on visits to these units.[71] Maccabi's spokesmen argued that the impetus for their perseverance rested in the belief that in the country's poorest and most densely populated Jewish areas, physical education facilitated desirable social changes among Jews. In areas where socioeconomic tensions between Jews and Christians were rife, and where many Jews were poor, Maccabi was, according to its executive's self-representation, part of a program preparing young Jews for physical and agricultural labor. By facilitating "the transfer [*převrstvení*] [of Jews] from commerce and intellectual occupations to productive ones," Maccabi was doing its part "to ease the immense destitution among Jews in the eastern parts of the republic."[72] The success of this project of physical and social transformation, the authors of the report did not fail to point out, depended on its access to public resources.

Although the archival sources to Maccabi's history are far from complete, it is possible to gauge the extent to which the Ministry of Health and Physical Education was forthcoming with financial support for Maccabi.[73] In the years 1928–1938, Maccabi received what is best described as symbolic but consistent support from the ministry. The organization's annual income hovered between Kč 70,000 and Kč 100,000, with the vast majority of funds being generated from membership fees and private donations.[74] State contributions made up between Kč 2,000 (1933) and Kč 7,000 (1937). In its early days, Maccabi's leaders imagined sums five or six times those numbers, yet they continued to apply for funds every year. The authorities dutifully dispensed small amounts of money to the organization. If the actual support received from the state appeared to have made little difference in Maccabi's budget, the potential for more state support was important. As long as the authorities were forthcoming, there was the possibility that the trickle could grow into a stream. As we shall see, aside from direct financial support, there were other ways in which Maccabi could tap into state resources for physical education, especially in the country's eastern regions.

As Maccabi gained a more secure foothold in Slovakia, boasting several large clubs with access to sports facilities, the organization's leadership put on display their role as an integrative force by staging high-profile events in cities and towns across the region. These events served to cast Jews as a Czechoslovak element in Slovakia, as well as the region itself as a Czechoslovak space. In 1934, the Slovakian division of Maccabi held a regional gathering in Bratislava/Pressburg/Pozsony featuring local military units and the commander of the Czechoslovak army in Slovakia, along with the Maccabi gymnasts and athletes from across the country.[75] Two years later, in February 1936, the international Maccabi World Winter Games took place in Banská Bystrica/Neusohl/Besztercebánya, a resort town in central Slovakia. The following year, Maccabi athletes gathered for gymnastic performances, sports competitions, and parades at Maccabi's third national meeting in Žilina/Sillein/Zsolna in northwestern Slovakia. Hundreds of participants from other parts of Czechoslovakia and from abroad flocked to the 1936 and 1937 gatherings in Slovakia. The programs featured parades and sports competitions as well as multiple daily excursions up into the mountains on skis or in hiking boots, introducing the visitors to the region's splendors.[76] Thus, not only did the events themselves support the local economies, but the organizers made sure to advertise the region as a tourist destination and to spread out the economic opportunities for local vendors.[77] At the same time, all these events in Slovakia served as public displays of the Czechoslovak identity and civic loyalty of the Maccabi community precisely at a time when Slovak separatist nationalism was on the rise. Slovakia remained an important territory both practically and symbolically for Maccabi and strengthened the image of the organization's Czechoslovakness.

This search for political respectability in the eyes of state authorities and the public was also at the heart of Jewish gymnastics leaders' admiration for and cooperation with Sokol, the Czech(oslovak) nationalist gymnastics movement.[78] From the outset, Maccabi activists presented the organization as an apprentice of Sokol. Although this was a strategy that added familiarity and prestige to their own cause, it also reflected a genuine admiration among these activists of Sokol's projection of virility. Uniformed, disciplined, and manly, Sokol was known as the "Czech national army" prior to the First World War.[79] After the war, Sokol was celebrated for its alleged role in the fight for Czech "liberation," securing the German and Slovak borderlands for Czechoslovakia.[80] Like the pre-state Sokol, its most prominent ideologue and editor of the Jewish sports paper *Hagibor – Hamakkabi* Ernst Fuchs imagined, Maccabi was on the front line in the struggle for the nation's rebirth.[81]

This parallelism between Maccabi and Sokol was also expressed in the former's adoption of forms and traditions associated with Sokol, such as the gymnastics festivals known as *slets*.[82] These had been major events in Sokol's pre-state period. As performances of Czechoslovak nationhood, in the interwar years, the slets became spectacular public performances, complete with participation of the army and the president. The nation was represented by tens of thousands of gymnasts from across Czechoslovakia and the Czech diaspora. They were joined by participants from other Slavic countries.[83] Maccabi held three slets in the interwar years, the first in Brno/Brünn in 1921, then in Moravská Ostrava/Mährisch Ostrau in 1929, and the last in Žilina in 1937.

The adoption of this Sokol tradition made Maccabi's slets legible as performances of nationhood. At the same time, the slets' tradition for emphasizing Czechness as well as pan-Slavism served to legitimize the international character of the Maccabi movement. This precedent facilitated Maccabi's ability to perform its distinct Czechoslovak identity as well as its belonging within a broader Jewish nation. It was a connection that was particularly important at the 1929 slet, which combined a Maccabi event with the congress of the Maccabi World Union.

Thus, the hoisting of the Czechoslovak and the Zionist flag, the performance of the state anthem and "Hatikvah" (the Zionist anthem), and the presence of Maccabi athletes from Czechoslovakia and from across Central Europe were a play on familiar pan-nationalist traditions in Czechoslovakia.

The relationship between Maccabi and Sokol did not remain merely symbolic and rhetorical. The Maccabi leadership and the gymnastics director Paul Hirsch from Brno/Brünn cooperated closely with prominent gymnastics experts from Sokol, like František Trnka (1900–1943). Trnka was a well-known high school teacher and gymnastics expert, who ran seminars and courses for gymnastics instructors from his hometown in Prešov/Eperies/Eperjes in eastern Slovakia. From the early 1930s on, aspiring instructors from Maccabi attended Trnka's courses and seminars, and Trnka himself occasionally contributed articles on Jews and physical education to *Židovské zprávy* and the newsletter of the Maccabi instructors, *Doar Meamlenu* (News from Our Toil). Although Maccabi's cooperation with Trnka in professionalizing Jewish gymnastics reflected an ideological affinity, the relationship was also informed by more pragmatic concerns. Sokol received significant state funds for its educational program and facilities, resources that Maccabi activists could draw on, if only indirectly.[84] Furthermore, as national tensions increased in Czechoslovakia and gymnastics and sports clubs were suspected of irredentist activities, Maccabi's leaders flagged their collaboration with František Trnka as evidence that their gymnastics instructors were competent and loyal.[85] Trnka's involvement added weight to Maccabi's stated commitment to professionalize their activities through tight control of the education of instructors, a development that went hand in hand with the Prague executive's attempts at still closer surveillance of its local units in the 1930s.[86] By playing up the similarities between the two movements and working closely with Sokol experts, Maccabi leaders made their organization legible as a nation-building institution and assured the authorities of its political respectability. Despite Maccabi's leaders' efforts to project an image of national unity and discipline, the rank and file proved to be more difficult to command than perhaps first imagined.

In the late 1920s, some of the member clubs in Slovakia displayed what appeared to the Maccabi leadership in Prague to be a disturbing indifference to national discipline and self-sacrifice. Adolf Jellinek, a prominent Zionist activist and youth leader from Bratislava working in Slovakia, reported that local activists were unlikely to remain within the Maccabi movement as long as the Prague headquarters was not forthcoming with material assistance to their clubs.[87] They saw little reason to dispatch their membership fees – a not insignificant financial burden in this poor region, Jellinek pointed out – to Prague when the federation offered nothing in return. Jewish clubs were abundant in Slovakia, yet their members were unconvinced that membership in Maccabi was worth the sacrifice.

It was precisely such evidence of national indifference that convinced Maccabi leaders that their movement's success depended on state support. Public resources would enable Maccabi to provide incentives for Jewish clubs to join in. Only then could the process of instilling national discipline necessary to transform individuals into members of a nation begin. Much like Jewish parents who hesitated sending their children to Jewish schools, Jewish athletes did not flock to Maccabi. Instead, they weighed the pros and cons of that particular national commitment, looking for incentives to sign up.[88] Although the chair Arthur Herzog threw up his hands at Jellinek's critique, he was not unfamiliar with the calculations done by the local activists in Slovakia. Only a few months earlier, he had asked the Maccabi World Union leadership a similar question. In the wake of its congress in Brno/Brünn in late August 1927, Arthur Herzog publicly criticized Zionist leaders for placing undue financial demands on Maccabi in Czechoslovakia and its fellow federations in other countries. Even though many Maccabi clubs were struggling, Herzog noted, "the Zionist executive still expects them to do fundraising for all kinds of Zionist causes."[89] Herzog praised the fundraising done by the German and Czechoslovak Maccabi but was critical of the lack of reciprocity, noting that "the support of Zionists for the Maccabi organizations has so far been only platonic."[90] Faced with financial uncertainties, the rank and file as well as their leaders were asking what they were getting in return for their national commitment.

The "existential" need for state support shaped Maccabi's relationship to the Zionist movement. There were close personal and institutional ties between Czechoslovak Zionist institutions and individuals and Maccabi. Many Maccabi activists belonged to Zionist organizations, and Maccabi had its main office in Beth Ha'am (House of the People), a Zionist community center in Prague where many Zionist organizations as well as the editorial offices for the Zionist papers *Selbstwehr* and *Židovské zprávy* were housed in the 1930s.[91] But the sports and gymnastics movement guarded its status as a "non-political" organization committed first and foremost to Jewish unity.[92] According to its statutes, the organization's purpose was "to strengthen the physical vigor [*zdatnost*] of Jews and elevate their moral standards [*mravní úroveň*] whereby it aspires to build and maintain the Jewish nation and its homeland."[93] Maccabi was explicitly prohibited from "conducting political activities and from participating in political events."[94] This kind of political neutrality could have been problematic for Zionists in Poland, where they competed with Bundist and other Jewish political sports organization for the souls of young Jews. In Czechoslovakia though, there were no formal Jewish political rivals. Hence, here it was possible for Maccabi activists to focus on Jewish unity rather than partisan political commitments.[95]

The state's restriction of political activities was the result of a series of legislation in the early 1920s and '30s, intended to outlaw groups considered a threat to Czechoslovakia. In the years after the First World War, the Prague government sought to curb what they considered extremist groups, mostly Communists and separatist German nationalists. The 1923 "Law for the Protection of the Republic" also prohibited "incitement of hatred or violence against groups because of their nationality, language, race, and religion." It also outlawed the formation of armed groups and training in the use of arms, a role closely associated with gymnastics, as Sokol's activities reflected, in those turbulent postwar years. Ten years later, in October 1933, in light of the rise of Adolf Hitler and the political mobilization of German nationalists in the Sudetenland, the Czechoslovak authorities passed legislation that prohibited organizations considered to be endangering the territorial integrity of the state.[96] Cognizant of the close link between the German Gymnastics Movement (Deutscher Turnverein) and the emergence of the Sudeten German Party, in 1933, the government also restricted the access of nongovernmental organizations to the country's children and youth.

The state authorities were concerned that young people were vulnerable to influence by irredentist Communists, German, Hungarian, and Slovak nationalists and other perceived destabilizing elements.[97] They therefore restricted school-age children and youths' rights to membership in associations other than ones promoting physical education. In addition, youths were barred from participating in political demonstrations and parades.[98] Thus, in the interest of gaining access to the nation's youth and to continue to build up the organization with public support and thus pose as a neutral Jewish national organization, Maccabi was not formally affiliated with the Zionist movement in the interwar years. When the state authorities, suspecting the politicization of youth and gymnastics groups, stepped up their surveillance of sports and gymnastics federations in 1933–1934, political neutrality became yet another virtue Maccabi's executive could flag in their quest for state resources.[99] They wasted no time connecting their organization's reliance on membership fees and private donations as its main source of income – evidence of its political independence – to its pressing financial needs.[100]

Maccabi's public image, its ideological priorities and political alliances, was shaped by the organization's relationship to the state. Drawing on the experience of Czech and German minority nationalists, Maccabi activists saw access to public resources as key to the success of their national movement. The organization's patriotism, its institutional Czechoslovakness and reverence for the state, was not an outcome of some natural affinity between Czechs and Jews, but a strategy to position the institution as deserving of funding, respect, and trust. A new organization with ambitious goals yet few resources, Maccabi activists worked to become a practical and ideological partner of the Czechoslovak state. Like their colleagues in the Jewish schools, these activists worked to hold the state's political elite to its promises of equality for the country's national minorities.

ZIONIST OR JEWISH?

It was not the need to remain politically neutral and eligible for state resources alone that defined Maccabi's relationship to the broader Zionist movement. Activists' concern about widespread national indifference among young Jews also informed the decision to remain unaffiliated. In March 1927, as Maccabi activists were positioning themselves to replace the Jewish Sports and Gymnastics Society, Ernst Fuchs outlined his position that the statewide organization should remain separate from the World Zionist Organization. He believed that a Zionist institutional identity would be detrimental to Maccabi's work among Jewish youths in Czechoslovakia. "Physical education is in and of itself non-political," Fuchs argued, and the Maccabi organization reflected Jews' ethnic belonging (*Volkszugehörigkeit*) alone.[101] Although he believed that Zionism was the natural expression of Jews' national feelings, he cautioned that "the crisis within postwar Jewish youth" had made the union between Maccabi and Zionism untenable. Due to "the spiritual disorientation" and disunity among the country's Jews, a Zionist commitment would "be little more than an empty gesture and as a result there would be a far-reaching reduction in the number of members." Fuchs recommended that for now Maccabi focus on Jewish unity first and foremost, a goal that he believed would eventually pave the way for Jewish athletes to Zionism.

Other prominent Maccabi activists seconded this call for non-partisanship in the interest of national unity. Adolf Jellinek, already concerned with the lack of national commitment among Jewish athletes in Slovakia, followed suit, noting that Maccabi should remain open to all Jews by "caring for all things Jewish" and not push anyone away with demands for ideological commitments.[102] In the early 1930s, as divisions within the international Zionist movement deepened, Arthur Herzog reiterated his organization's commitment to non-partisanship.[103] "In Maccabi as well as in Maccabi ha-Tsa'ir no socialist, no revisionist, or any other ideas should be promoted," Herzog declared. "Each individual should decide their own political conviction. Maccabi is only Maccabi and will only remain so if we keep far away from party politics. ... In Maccabi there is room for everybody, regardless of his [*sic*] convictions."[104] Despite the fact that the Czechoslovak Zionist Organization promoted itself as a non-partisan, Jewish national organization, Maccabi leaders clearly believed that Jews did not consider Zionism politically neutral. Thus, in the name of national unity Maccabi's leaders saw it as prudent to remain independent from the Zionist Organization, yet fully committed to the Zionist project in Czechoslovakia and Palestine.

Although Maccabi activists cultivated this image of neutrality and non-partisanship, the organization retained strong ties to Zionist institutions in Czechoslovakia throughout the interwar years. The Zionist press, *Židovské zprávy, Selbstwehr,* and *Jüdische Volksstimme,* devoted either sections or entire supplements to news about Jewish gymnastics and sports and the Maccabi movement. The annual *Židovský Kalendář* published by the Jewish National Fund also included articles on Jews and sports in general and Maccabi in particular. Furthermore, in the mid-1930s, the longtime editor of *Židovské zprávy,* Zdeněk Landes, joined the Maccabi executive.[105] Paul März, a member of the Zionist executive and part of the Zionist political elite from its early days, chaired Maccabi's winter sports section from 1933 onward.[106] The Zionist veteran and Jewish Party parliamentarian Angelo Goldstein acted as a representative of Maccabi in the 1920s. Goldstein routinely appeared at Maccabi's gymnastics and sports events and traveled with the Czechoslovak team to the Maccabiah in Tel Aviv in 1932 and 1935.[107] Despite the continuous complaints of lack of funds for local clubs, Maccabi encouraged its members to buy the *Shekel,* the certificate of membership in the World Zionist Organization, and, as mentioned earlier, participated in fund-raising campaigns for the Jewish National Fund.[108]

Even though Maccabi activists warned against emphasizing Zionism in the interest of inclusiveness, efforts were made to provide members with a Jewish national education with significant Zionist content. Claiming non-partisanship, Maccabi's leaders nevertheless served up the Zionist movement as the agent of the Jewish national rebirth. Knowing to tread lightly on matters of politics and ideological convictions, Maccabi activists designed a two-tier membership system that allowed for the inclusion of athletes with different degrees of national commitment. The system was institutionalized by allowing studious and nationally conscious members to obtain the Gymnastics and Sports Badge, a rite of passage making them full-fledged members of Maccabi.[109] To obtain the badge, individuals had to demonstrate their physical skills and mastery of Zionist and Jewish knowledge, the culmination "of a period of systematic exercises and studies, a physical and spiritual development." Indeed,

Maccabi leaders intended the badge to serve as evidence of members' commitment to national regeneration, noting that "only those who express the will to develop their entire personality can become full-fledged *maccabim.*" Thus, as a way of compromise between the Maccabi World Union's calls for intensification of national education in the federations and the local leaders' warning about the dangers of emphasizing Zionism, Maccabi struck a balance between the ideologues and pragmatists and retained the organization's formal neutrality.

Yet, Maccabi did step up its efforts to institutionalize Zionist education as well as to homogenize and centralize the Maccabi community. The 1931 publication of the *Makkabi Handbuch* (Maccabi Handbook) was intended to provide new and existing members with a manual that outlined basic guidelines for physical education, uniforms, parading, and management. Soon after its release, headquarter representatives were dispatched to oversee the work being done in local clubs across the country. The manual was also meant to serve as a study guide for members preparing to test for the badge. Its content was threefold: knowledge of the Maccabi movement and Zionist institutions, Jewish knowledge, and general gymnastics guidelines. The authors situated Maccabi on the front line of Jews' national regeneration. If individual Maccabi units and members played a key role in facilitating this process, their efforts were focused by the Zionist project in Palestine, the destination for Maccabi's most committed members. Essays dealt with the history of the Zionist movement, the Jewish National Fund, and the Palestine Foundation Fund (the former an organization funding land purchase and immigration and the latter an institution meant to unite Zionist and non-Zionist Jews for a Jewish homeland in Palestine), as well as the history and geography of Palestine. The editors, assuming to be writing for an audience with widely varying forms of Jewish knowledge, included topics such as Judaism, the Jewish people's holidays, Jewish statistics and history, and hygiene. Maccabi's history and ideology were also discussed at length and were, along with a list of Hebrew gymnastics commands, a central part of the curriculum. The manual's only map depicted Palestine. The handbook was entirely in German, the assumed lingua franca of Jews in Czechoslovakia, except for the lyrics for "Hatikvah," printed in Hebrew transliteration with a German translation. Maccabi units formally used

Hebrew commands, but German was the language shared by most Jews in Czechoslovakia. Yet, the language of use in clubs in Bohemia and increasingly in Moravia would also have been Czech, and in Slovakia, Hungarian and Slovak. Nevertheless, German was the language that facilitated communication among Jews not only across regions but also across generations. In the interwar years, Zionists strove to produce parallel Czech and German or at least bilingual editions. It was probably financial and practical constraints that dictated the publication of the handbook in German only. With it, Maccabi's leaders hoped that they could enhance the quality of national and physical education and provide standards for appearance, cleanliness, and behavior, thereby strengthening the movement's respectability and internal homogeneity and cohesion.

As the Maccabi Handbook reflected, the leadership might have allowed for some flexibility in the commitment to national education, but their goal was to create a disciplined and centralized institution. Obedience and discipline were idealized as signs of national commitment on the individual and collective level. The attention that the overseers dispatched by the executive paid to the dress of gymnasts and athletes is a case in point. In advance of the Brno/Brünn summer slet in 1928, Ervin Goldschmid emphasized the importance of strict adherence to the dress code, noting that "every Maccabi embodies a disciplined member of our great community and this is expressed through uniform clothing; unduly independence with regard to dress reflects lack of order and discipline."[110] Uniformity in dress was not only a way of creating sameness in appearance, a visual manifestation of unity, but also a way of teaching collective discipline and obedience. Similarly, gymnastics director Richard Pacovsky on an inspection tour of Slovakian units in late 1931 reported a "surprising unfamiliarity with the content of the Maccabi Handbook." He was particularly appalled that members showed up in the gymnasium in their street clothes and shoes. Aside from the affront to hygiene, he noted, "the lack of uniform dress signals disorder, disunity, and heterogeneity."[111] Maccabi athletes had to be taught how to be a nation. The carefully planned lesson in national homogeneity was obstructed by the very same social and cultural differences that it was meant to erase.[112]

Maccabi's work was inhibited not only by their own members' indifference to ideological priorities and symbols of nationhood. It was also undermined by Jewish gymnastics and sports clubs and individual Jews who, in the eyes of Maccabi activists, refused to sign up among their "own." In Northern Bohemia, for example, there were several Jewish clubs that, according to Egon Štern, were not Jewish nationalist and therefore remained outside Maccabi. In Prague, the unaffiliated Hakoah sports club maintained a brief, antagonistic relationship to the city's other Jewish clubs.[113] In Slovakia, as Adolf Jellinek implied, some clubs were unwilling or unable to meet the financial demands of Maccabi and simply remained unaffiliated.[114] Perhaps more significantly, young Jews joined the gymnastics and sports clubs of "other nationalities." In laments similar to those of their colleagues involved with the Jewish schools, Zionist activists complained about Jews' resistance to joining Jewish clubs.[115] Indeed, Jewish nationalist activists believed that their cause was particularly difficult precisely because non-Jewish clubs remained open to Jews.[116] In an article on Jews and sports, activist Kurt Bloch lamented, "Maccabi is not a united front of Jewish athletes, because many continue to fight for the colors of other nations even though they are often only tolerated."[117] Jewish men and women participated in non-Jewish sports and gymnastics clubs until the late 1930s. The well-known DFC Prag (Deutscher Fussball Club), for example, was a magnate for Jewish players and audiences before and after the First World War. And it was only in October 1938, as a sign of the changing times, that the Prague Sokol began excluding Jews from its gymnastics and sports units. Jews in the Bohemian Lands and Slovakia, gripped by Central Europe's "sports craze," participated in gymnastics and sports in Maccabi, but many chose to enjoy sports with and alongside non-Jews through the 1920s and '30s.[118]

Maccabi's pragmatic attitude toward ideological diversity and different levels of national commitment reflects that it was perhaps more difficult than first imagined to mobilize Jewish youths around an ethnonationalist agenda. Although Maccabi managed to establish itself as a state-supported, countrywide national minority organization, it did not become a dominant institution in young Jews' lives the way its leaders had hoped. Throughout the 1920s and 1930s, a multiplicity of social circles and institutions remained open to Jews and allowed individuals to make choices based on other priorities than ethnicity – a state of affairs that Jewish nationalists could only lament.

MAKING NEW JEWS

In his welcome address to Maccabi athletes assembling in Banská Bystrica for the 1936 Maccabi World Winter Games, Angelo Goldstein described the importance of Maccabi for the Jewish nationalist movement. He described how from within the ranks of Maccabi, a new Jewish youth was emerging, a generation with healthy bodies and minds, respectable citizens and proud Jews. "The Games," Goldstein noted, "the struggle on the slopes, is an opportunity for us to demonstrate the progress we have made."[119] Like other nationalists, Zionists believed that national regeneration necessitated a physical as well as a moral transformation, a process that would reshape slumbering individuals into national collectives.[120] Rejecting the stereotype of the weak-willed and scrawny Jewish male, Maccabi activists imagined the new Jew as the embodiment of the bourgeois male ideal. To Maccabi activists, Jewish honor, empowerment, and social equality came in the form of disciplined, physically capable, and morally upright men. Fit Jews, and especially fit Jewish men, embodied the fundamental search for respectability and inclusion at the heart of Zionism in Czechoslovakia in the interwar years.[121]

Within Maccabi, Ernst Fuchs undertook most of the programmatic writing on the making of new Jews. He believed firmly in Maccabi as an educational and socializing institution creating the foundation for a new Jewish national community, much as Jewish school activists and pedagogues saw the schools as just such nationalizing spaces. In an essay in the Maccabi Handbook, Fuchs defined a normative male self, the new Jew, whose commitment to self-education and nation embodied as well as spearheaded the quest for the Jewish people's regeneration. According to Fuchs, self-education was to be achieved through continuous self-criticism and self-restraint. This constant perfection of the self involved physical exercises and discipline as well as the cultivation of virtues such as honesty, helpfulness, trustworthiness, courage, and willingness to sacrifice.[122] Individuals' commitment to self-improvement "upon which rested the nation's survival" had to permeate every aspect of life. As Fuchs noted, "We are not only *maccabim* on the exercise ground or the playing field, but everywhere and all the time in our lives. If Maccabi means the "hammer," the "fighter," then that means that we must be determined to hammer out our own fate and to fight for a better self."[123]

This personal autonomy, however, had to be balanced with the individual's commitment to community. The individual, Fuchs noted, must fit into and be subordinate to the national community.[124] The Turngemeinschaft in the making within Maccabi was thus a trailblazer for the broader Jewish awakening.[125] In order to foster community, Fuchs argued, Maccabi leaders needed to nurture national awareness as well as personal bonds and friendships between Maccabi members, thereby forming "a community – a group of people who seek the same in life." In his mind, the national community had to become tangible for young people to sign on. Activities that fostered these personal ties such as summer camps, excursions, social evenings, and larger local and regional gatherings were crucial and had been a priority for Maccabi since the mid-1920s.

Another precondition for the creation of community was the dismantling of social hierarchies. Fuchs advocated making the tone within Maccabi units familiar, substituting the formal with informal address, in an attempt to bridge age and social divisions within the organization.[126] Only then could Maccabi become a close-knit "friendship circle, a real *Volksgemeinschaft*."[127] The importance of social ties, of "reconstituting" community, was shared widely among Zionist activists. After decades of urbanization that brought thousands of people, and Jews especially, to the cities in the Bohemian Lands, they imagined the sports clubs as spaces where young Jews could experience a sense of belonging and shared fate, an institution as significant to Jewish life and identity as the synagogue and the community had been in the past. As Evžen Justic, a longtime Jewish sports activist, noted, sports did not require "a decision, conviction, or consciousness," but invited young Jews to participate in sports "here, among equals, among friends."[128] In short, through Jewish sports "a boy becomes a Jew." For Justic, Fuchs, and others, the Maccabi Turngemeinschaft was a site for utopian longings. Here they could foster and guide the nucleus of a Jewish nation, populated by beautiful young men, working in disciplined unison for their nation, the health of their bodies and minds the symbol of Jews' regeneration. The Jewish nationalist project depended in every way, they imagined, on the daily work undertaken in gymnasiums and on playing fields.

Maccabi ideologues wrote and spoke about new Jews and Jewish nationhood in decidedly masculine terms. They idealized the new Jew as assertive, self-confident, and proudly Jewish. Although female members and instructors were active in Jewish sports and gymnastics in large numbers, the organization was infused with a masculine ethos.[129] It was the male body that symbolized Jews' reclaimed agency and power. Activists imagined Jewish men first and foremost as inadequate nation builders without dignity and strength.[130] This discursive marginalization of women within Maccabi also reflected that citizenship was primarily imagined as a male domain.[131] Although women had been active in Jewish sports and gymnastics since its early days and had stepped into leadership roles during the First World War, they were sidelined as male power was re-imposed amid the social turmoil brought on by the war.

At the first postwar meeting of Maccabi Prag/Praha's executive in December 1918, a writer reporting from the event noted, "It was clear that the sisters of our unit have taken on great responsibilities in the absence of many of our brothers.... Our sisters have managed not only to preserve the club, but also made Maccabi bloom."[132] During the First World War, women across the Bohemian Lands, much like the women in Maccabi Prag/Praha, had taken charge of the organizations in which they were already active as members.[133] Once men returned from the front, they resumed their leadership positions and relegated women in whole or in part to their prewar roles. In December 1918, only weeks after the armistice, Maccabi members in Prague elected six men and three women to the new board, placing the most important positions in the hands of men.[134] Thus, as part of the normalization of life in the wake of the war, the reins held by Maccabi's women were promptly handed over to men and remained there throughout the interwar years.[135]

Girls and women most likely constituted half or more of the Maccabi members, yet the leaders of Maccabi hardly ever made direct reference to female members.[136] On the rare occasion that an article on women and women's issues was published in the Jewish sports press, the writers concerned themselves with general women's issues rather than addressing matters that might have been of particular interest to Jewish women. For the ideologues, women's participation in sports and gymnastics was first and foremost the means to a reproductive end. The purpose of physical education for women was to "create strong and robust mothers" in order to secure the nation a healthy future.[137] Women participated in Maccabi as gymnasts, competitive athletes, and instructors; nevertheless writers and other activists depicted them as mothers first and foremost. The central character in the performance of the new Jew was the new Jewish man.[138] The Zionist project was meant to establish Jews' manliness and thereby the Jewish nation as one among equals. On a discursive and a practical level, women were assigned supporting roles as Jewish men handled the masculinizing task of making new Jews. The increased focus on military fitness within Maccabi in the 1930s would only exacerbate this dynamic.

Although Maccabi leaders agreed on the manly ideal, they disagreed on how to achieve their goal. This tension was most starkly exposed by conflicts fueled by Maccabi's dual identity as a gymnastics *and* sports movement.[139] The debates over whether sports trivialized and debased the movement or whether gymnastics repelled Jewish youths appear at first glance to reflect a generational clash between ideological traditionalists and youthful sports enthusiasts. But they were in fact the site of a minor Kulturkampf within Maccabi. Both factions agreed that physical education was central to Jewish nationhood. They disagreed on the importance of image, publicity, and elitism for the process of national awakening. The gymnastics faction insisted on prioritizing internal regeneration and Jewish national unity. The sports proponents viewed the transformation of the image of Jews through athletic achievement and performance as indispensable for mass mobilization as well as equality.[140]

In the spring of 1937, a series of articles discussing the balance between gymnastics and sports within Maccabi appeared in *Doar Meamlenu,* the magazine for Jewish gymnastics teachers.[141] František Trnka was dismayed that international Maccabi executive had decided to rebrand the Maccabiah, the gathering of Maccabi athletes from across the world in Palestine every three years, as an Olympics rather than a gymnastics festival.[142] Pointing specifically to plans for the 1938 Maccabiah, Trnka argued that emphasizing sports rather than gymnastics was a significant and unfortunate step away from the organization's basic goals and values. The Maccabiah, in the tradition of the slet, should, according to Trnka, be a demonstration of the internal work – the systematic physical and mental discipline exercised every day – to improve Jews' physical condition. In contrast, sports focused only on records and trophies. By making the Maccabiah a competitive event like the Olympics, the Maccabi World Union chose to celebrate the work of sports organizations where physical fitness was driven not by a collective national commitment, but by individual ambition.[143] Although he recognized the utility of sports for its physical benefits, Trnka lamented the increasing influence of sports' non-ideological ethos.

Trnka's lament reflected the views of some gymnastic leaders within Maccabi. To them, gymnastics as a discipline and as a social institution was the only form of physical education that fostered nation building. Focusing on the need of the collective and on physical and mental discipline, writers noted how gymnastics erased social differences between members and created a sense of national unity.[144] Writing from Slovakia, Ervin Kovač argued that in the gymnasium there were no differences between rich and poor, between the educated and the uneducated. In here, the focus on ethnic sameness obliterated social divisions. Similarly, the individual's submission to the group during exercises taught gymnasts voluntary obedience, which in turn was translated into a sense of responsibility for the whole outside of the gymnasium. Thus, as did Ernst Fuchs, these gymnastic teachers believed that there was a direct connection between the practices and values taught and exercised in the gymnasium and gymnasts' competence as Jews and citizens. Within the Maccabi *Turnhalle* (gymnasium) Jews learned to identify nationally above all else by relinquishing the importance of all other differences, most prominently those of social hierarchy.[145] Faced with competition from socialist clubs and tasked with creating community among young people from different regions in addition to an increasing number of German-Jewish refugees, Maccabi leaders believed that neglecting gymnastics in favor of sports – and doing so precisely at the time when overcoming class and cultural divides was particularly urgent – was detrimental to the Jewish nationalist project.

Trnka and his colleagues were responding to what they believed was a widespread tendency within Maccabi to favor sport over gymnastics. In their view, this was a sign that Maccabi leaders and members alike were not taking seriously the national goals of Maccabi. One critic wrote about his colleagues' lack of commitment that "only among us [Jews] is national education in the gymnastics clubs considered unimportant, [at times] even completely neglected."[146] Pointing to Germany's string of medals at the Berlin Olympics, the author held up Germany as an example of the broader athletic benefits reaped from a serious effort to infuse physical education with nationalism. The increasing popularity of sports challenged precisely the most central values of the gymnastics movement. If gymnastics programs sought to unify individuals into one harmonious whole, then sports emphasized and celebrated the achievements of individuals or a select few. Similarly, gymnastics focused on the needs of the whole over those of individuals, while sports emphasized individualism and personal ambitions. These critics observed with little disguised distaste the entertainment and celebrity culture that was part and parcel of the sports world.

Sports and gymnastics enthusiasts had clashed over the respective merits of their clubs' work since Maccabi's early days, when critics admonished the sports clubs for not prioritizing national education in their programs and for an overall lack of commitment to Zionism. Zdeněk Landes, for example, noted that in contrast to the work of prewar Zionist gymnasts "who wanted to defend the colors of their own nation," many clubs had lost touch with their Zionist origins.[147] Indeed, so much had been forgotten, he lamented, "the blue and white flag has just become a symbol of the club, not of the nation!" Although Maccabi promoted neutrality and ethnic unity above all else, Landes bemoaned how many sports clubs' previously strong Zionist commitment had deteriorated into a foggy, nationally uncommitted, "all-Jewish" identity. He warned:

> In most cases this is the path that our sports clubs have taken, and my voice warning of the dangers is neither the first nor the only one. Jewish sports has a great responsibility, as it has in fact managed to attract a significant part of Jewish youth. Thus, the leaders of true Jewish sports cannot ignore

> the questions whether our youth grow up to become nationally indifferent [*indifferenty*] or people with a firm national consciousness. This is not the time to neglect serious cultural work. Much time has already been wasted. More than ever before, the club leaderships need to realize that it is necessary to make cultural work part of their program.[148]

Despite the discomfort of Zdeněk Landes and other critics with the ideologically undisciplined sports clubs, by the early 1930s, it was clear that sports in and of itself had become indispensable to the Zionist movement.

In the eyes of sports activists, competition was necessary for the restoration of Jews' dignity and the assertion of their equality. Jews' battles against other teams and athletes on the playing field and in the pool were vital to Maccabi's mission to restore Jews' honor. What mattered most to these activists were not the victories, although they were always welcome, but the fact that by competing against other athletes, against other nationalities, Jews asserted their right to compete as social equals. These performances, they argued, were what attracted young Jews to Maccabi's clubs. More than anything it was the feelings of pride and excitement evoked by Jewish athletes such as the champion diver Julius Balasz (1901–1970), Hagibor Praha/Prag's championship water polo team and top swimmers, Bar Kochba Bratislava's legendary Dr. Steiner (Paul/Pavol Steiner, 1908–1969), and other celebrities that paved the way for many young Jews to the Jewish nationalist movement. These spectacular performances, demonstrations of the merits of Jewish nationalism, were only possible through the intense and focused work undertaken by the sports clubs. Even Beda Brüll, a leading member of the executive and a firm believer in national education, admitted, "Sports games and victories have a significant effect on the national self-confidence of our youth. At a time when sports is not only a means to health and strength, it has turned out to be rather useful in the promotion of the Jewish regeneration movement."[149] Some Maccabi leaders scoffed at sports activists' focus on changing Jews' image. Brüll viewed precisely this dynamic as having a profound effect on Jewish youth's sense of a national self and pride. "From a Zionist point of view," he noted, "the publicity produced by sports has gained us many new friends and members."[150] A story in the Czech-language Brno/Brünn-based journal *Makabi Sport* celebrating the achievements of Jewish swimmers reflected some of this new self-confidence and sense of community among young Jews. The writer noted:

> They [the Jewish athletes] have dutifully pursued their goal on behalf of us all. . . . It is a long time since we stopped being these weaklings portrayed in Humor News [*Humoristické listy*]. It is the obligation of all individuals – at a time when athletic vigor seems to be the most persuasive form of publicity in the eyes of the world – to perfect ourselves, to invest all our strength in the education of even better, even stronger, even healthier, and more self-conscious Jewish youths.[151]

Sports had captured the imagination of young Jews. As Jewish athletes transformed Jews' image and thereby asserted Jews' respectability as social equals, youths joined in, attending events, cheering their teams, and participating in sports in their free time. In the eyes of some activists, sports had the potential of transforming Maccabi – and by extension Zionism – into a mass movement.

Even though the sports enthusiasts challenged the voices questioning the merits of competition, they shared the distaste for individualism and celebrity culture expressed by their critics. Athletes who did not submit to the discipline of the collective and who seemed to favor personal ambitions and success over that of the team and club were mockingly ridiculed as "prima donnas," an emasculated contrast to the disciplined and respectable Jewish athlete. It was a character that "appeared" most often among soccer celebrities, the most popular sport in Europe in the interwar years. Pointing to these athletes' damaging lack of team spirit, one writer noted, "The soccer prima donna always arrives late on the playing field (if at all), with new soccer shoes, in shorts pulled up high, and in snow-white kneepads. . . . He loves exposing his prima donna figure to camera lenses."[152] This type of athlete disregards, the author continued, the value of the voluntary work to regenerate body and soul, the democratic nature of sport, and basic values of modesty and courage inherent in true sportsmanship. On the one hand, the sports writers' denigrating depictions of the overly individualistic and hence unmanly athletes were intended to uphold the respectability of sports by distancing it from its low elements, the money-grubbing celebrity culture, and the rowdy crowds in the stands. On the other, they sought to restrain individual ambition and interests, upon which excellence in sport also depended, by ridiculing individualism and reminding the broader community of athletes of the priority of the team, the clubs, and the nation over that of personal ambition.[153]

Despite the distaste for sports among some Maccabi leaders, Jews' individual and collective athletic achievements took on increased importance in Maccabi's public self-representation in the course of the interwar years. Considering the prominence of Jews in swimming, diving, and water polo in particular, Maccabi's executive did not squander the opportunity to present these athletes' contributions to Czechoslovakia's national teams as evidence of a model citizenry. In the early 1930s, the reports that accompanied Maccabi's funding applications to the Ministry of Health and Physical Education gradually shifted their focus from the merits of gymnastics to the achievements of Maccabi's swimmers, tennis players, and track-and-field athletes.[154] The reports presented the prominence of Maccabi's athletes in Czechoslovak sports as a sign of the thorough transformation Jews underwent within the clubs. Careful not to overplay the superiority of the Jewish athletes, the reports' authors emphasized the significance of Maccabi's participation in international events and competitions as a representative of Czechoslovakia.[155] The achievements of Jewish athletes, the authors noted, heightened Czechoslovakia's prestige on the international stage. In the swimming world, "our athletes are first-class and their names well-known abroad," the author boasted. "They have always defended the Czechoslovak republic with dignity and honor."[156] These Jews, emerging from the ranks of Maccabi, were physically fit, reliable, ready and able to defend their country. In short, these Jews were model citizens.

The bureaucrats reviewing the applications were responsive to the depiction of Maccabi as serving Czechoslovak interests. During the 1930s, the Ministry of Health and Physical Education did increase state funds for Maccabi when its athletes were slated to compete abroad or in international Maccabi events in Czechoslovakia.[157] Writing a memo in support of funding for Maccabi's participation in the 1935 Maccabiah in Palestine, one official noted that the preparation of Jewish athletes for this event should, because of the prominent place of Jewish swimmers in Czechoslovakia, be considered part of these athletes' training for the Czechoslovak national team set to attend the Berlin Olympics in 1936.[158] As we know, the road to Berlin was to be more twisted than first imagined.

TESTING THE WATERS: THE MILITARIZATION OF MACCABI

In the interwar years, Zionists tirelessly declared their loyalty to Czechoslovakia. Jewish nationalists upheld the alleged shared reverence of Czechs and Jews for democracy and justice as evidence of their "natural" partnership in a struggle against common enemies. As tension mounted within Czechoslovakia in the 1930s, the state authorities became more and more suspicious of the loyalties and agendas of national minority groups. In response, Zionists worked even harder to present a public image of Jews' undivided and dependable loyalty to the state. In the name of democracy and patriotism, Maccabi adopted an increasingly militarist stance in the course of the 1930s.

In Central Europe, gymnastics and sports were closely linked with the military tradition. With the convergence of discourses on masculinity and nationalism in the early nineteenth century, the gymnastics movement and the army emerged as the manly institutions par excellence.[159] Existing in a symbiotic relationship, gymnastics was imagined as alleviating the wanting fitness and fighting abilities of men destined for army service. This role of physical education increased in importance in the minds of civil and military authorities in countries that were denied armies, as was Weimar Germany, or were building new ones, as were the successor states.[160] At the same time, sports, especially team sports, became sites where men watched and performed their masculinity by celebrating strength, sacrifice, courage, and other manly virtues.[161] Preparing Jewish men for military service was a constant subtext for Maccabi's activities. The physical and mental discipline and assertiveness performed by its athletes in sports competitions or exhibitions were symbolic statements about Jews' aptness for citizenship and the military duties this responsibility entailed. The connection between physical education and military service was further underlined by the blending of slets and military parades. Indeed, in 1934, Sokol was reinstated as a militia, its members charged with protection of the country's sovereignty.[162] As we have seen, the previous fall, legislation was passed that outlawed organizations suspected of endangering the country's territorial integrity, and Sokol's "promotion" to militia cast a shadow of suspicion on national minority organizations. In response to the uncertainty, that summer the Jewish Party MP Angelo Goldstein, in an appearance at the regional Maccabi gathering in Bratislava alongside local military dignitaries, announced publicly that "Czechoslovak Jewry is opposed to a revision of the borders."[163] By then, sports and gymnastics had taken on new, more acute significance as performances of Jewish citizens' loyalty.

The militarization of Maccabi was not a diversion from the organization's ideological stance or its political alliances. It was driven by the masculine ideal so central to Maccabi activists' self-perception. If called upon, they declared, Jews would respond as men to defend their country, one that had not let them down as so many others did their Jewish citizens. Czechoslovakia was after all one of the few states in the region whose government had not sponsored antisemitic legislation and actions and where Jewish refugees from Germany had found a safe haven, even if an uneasy and cool one. In response, Maccabi stepped up its public display of Jews' Czechoslovakness and patriotism.

Maccabi's 1937 slet in Žilina was an opportunity to do just that. For a few days in early July, local military and municipal dignitaries, representatives of the local Sokol units, Zionist leaders from across Czechoslovakia and abroad, and more than fifteen hundred active participants gathered in this tourist town located on the crossroads between the country's eastern and western provinces.[164] This was only the third statewide Maccabi slet and the first one to be held in Slovakia, where the year before Maccabi organizers had pulled off a successful Winter Olympics. The 1937 convention was infused with militarist themes. The slet opened with marching members of the youth movement Maccabi ha-Tsa'ir raising the Czechoslovak flag while singing the state anthem. This was followed by gymnastics exercises by Maccabi Bratislava and a unit from the local garrison. The opening ceremony culminated with gymnastics performances by female and male athletes, Hebrew song, and the entrance of women and children dressed in blue and white into the stadium.

If the Jewish gymnasts' performance in the stadium attested to the military readiness of the country's living Jews, the contribution of fallen

Jewish soldiers to the Czechoslovak cause was not forgotten. An entourage consisting of the local Neolog rabbi Hugo Stransky (1905–1983), various Jewish and non-Jewish dignitaries, representatives of the military, the Czech legionaries, the National Guard, and Slovak volunteers paid tribute to the war dead in the town's Jewish cemetery. This ceremony was followed by the placing of a wreath by Arthur Herzog at the memorial for the fallen soldiers of the First World War in the adjacent military cemetery. In this way, one reporter noted, "the Maccabi movement gave thanks to those who prepared the way for Czechoslovak independence."[165] That summer, the Maccabi gathering in Žilina was envisioned and performed as a demonstration of Jews' military preparedness and loyalty to Czechoslovakia. Post–World War I accusations of Jews' disloyalty and Czech and Slovak violence against Jews in the months following the collapse of Austria-Hungary were conveniently forgotten as Jews, Czechs, and Slovaks alike looked to assert their readiness to defend the republic.[166]

The performance in Žilina was the culmination of a concerted effort by Maccabi leaders to infuse their organization with an ethos of military readiness. In the late 1920s, Jewish gymnastics and sports activists had pointed implicitly to the importance of their work in preparing young men for military service by emphasizing athletics' promotion of discipline and moral and physical health.[167] By the mid-1930s, Maccabi's executive was looking to play a much more direct role in inducting young Jews into military service. In December 1935, they attempted to amend the organization's stated purpose to include "paramilitary training of Jewish youths according to the directives of the Ministry of National Defense."[168] This was in many ways a daring move, since it asked the authorities to exempt Maccabi, alongside Sokol, from the laws that prohibited weapons training. But the Ministry of Interior rejected Maccabi's bid to assume this new responsibility, arguing that the defense of the country, including "paramilitary training of youths," was the responsibility of the state alone.[169] Their first attempt rebuffed, Maccabi nevertheless persisted in devising ways in which they could bolster their organization's contribution to the defense of Czechoslovakia.

Beginning in January 1936, with the Berlin Olympic controversy already under way, Maccabi decided to incorporate civil defense training into the regular activities of its gymnastics clubs.[170] In a series of articles in *Židovské zprávy,* František Trnka discussed the plans in detail, carefully and publicly, making distinctions between civil defense training (*branná výchova*) and civil defense exercises (*branný výcvik*). The latter were formal military exercises under the auspices of the army, while civil defense *training* was aimed more generally at "strengthening an individual's ability to defend himself."[171] The program that Trnka outlined focused on building character, improving physical abilities and endurance, and teaching technical skills necessary for civilians to participate in the defense of the country in case of an attack or invasion. Civil defense training included the use and maintenance of weapons, maps, and compasses, as well as first aid, food emergency preparedness, and an understanding of the structure of the army and its various units. In addition to teaching technical skills and strengthening individuals' physical and mental abilities, Trnka's program also aimed to shore up individuals' "national and civic feelings" by emphasizing reverence for state symbols, the rights and duties of citizens, and the meaning of the state and democracy. These were goals meant to dispel any misgivings the watchful authorities might have had.

Since gymnastics exercises were already designed to heighten individuals' mental and physical discipline, Trnka and his colleagues believed that the incorporation of the defense training into club activities would be seamless. All that the instructor needed to do was "to push the gymnasts harder in every activity, thereby improving their endurance and hardening their self-discipline."[172] Through significant but smooth adjustments, instructors could make civil defense training part of their daily activities throughout the year. An excursion or camping trip, for example, could easily include long strenuous hikes through different terrain, teaching youths day- and night-orienteering skills, and familiarizing them with a range of weather conditions. By always pushing the groups through challenging and surprising exercises, Trnka claimed, "we will be strengthening both endurance and toughness." It is important, he noted, to create an atmosphere of struggle and danger in order to cultivate readiness and determination. He even conceded that brief sports games were useful in cultivating individuals' aggression, courage, and endurance, molding the desired tough character. "This tone," he argued, "would bring an element of danger to the exercises and teach the individuals to defend themselves by being able to make decisions in such [challenging] situations."[173] Maccabi's civil defense training was designed to instill a militarist ethos into every aspect of the clubs' activities, readying young Jews for what seemed an inevitable future struggle. Unsure of the state's intentions vis-à-vis its minorities, Zionists promoted Jews' worthiness as insiders, as allies of the Czechs, by infusing Maccabi with militarism and adopting an even more pronounced masculine ethos.[174]

Not surprisingly, Maccabi activists did not fail to align their organization's need for funds with the shifting priorities of the state authorities. In an application filed with the Ministry of Health and Physical Education in October 1936, just a few months after the Olympic boycott debate, Maccabi's representatives asked for funds to assist with the slet in Žilina, the education of instructors, and the expansion of civil defense training to all units within Maccabi.[175] The next summer, in their welcome to the participants and guests in Žilina, Maccabi leaders emphasized their organization's commitment to broader civic goals:

> We have always been mindful that Jewish youths devoting themselves to physical training and spiritual education should become familiar with Czechoslovak culture and the idea from which our state was born. . . . our members must at all times in both word and deed demonstrate their loyalty to the Czechoslovak republic. Therefore, as a natural outcome of the Maccabi spirit, civil defense training is a commandment for us to follow [*příkaz*]. We are raising disciplined citizens and recruits for the Czechoslovak state who are prepared to defend the independence of Czechoslovakia and its democratic and just foundation at all times. . . . Our parade [*přehlídka*] is a test before the Czechoslovak public and before ourselves. Parades and gymnastics competitions are nothing but a preparation of disciplined, ready, and loyal individuals.[176]

In his address, Angelo Goldstein noted that Maccabi's work "prepares Jews to contribute to the improvement of the military capability of the republic" – a task Maccabi units had undertaken so successfully, he beamed, that they had "received special recognition by the Czechoslovak army."[177]

As tension between Czechoslovakia, the Sudeten German leadership, and Nazi Germany intensified in the spring of 1938, the government issued a partial mobilization order. That summer the tenth Sokol slet served as a show of determination to resist the international and domestic pressures to secede the borderlands to Germany. Hundreds of thousands of people listened to and watched spectacular patriotic performances by men and women gymnasts, military parades including cavalry and air force units, and processions of allies from abroad, including a Maccabi delegation from Palestine.[178] By then, the Ministry of Defense had already given the Sokol movement and other "loyal" organizations such as Maccabi an even more prominent role in mobilizing civil society, an effort that brought Maccabi leaders into direct and regular contact with the military authorities. During these months, the Zionist press ran its own war bonds campaign, advertising Jews' financial and material contribution to the defense of Czechoslovakia.[179] In these same pages, activists evoked the "Žilina oath" (*žilinský slib*) as a way of reiterating publicly Jews' commitment to the defense of Czechoslovakia. Readers' morale was shored up by reports from a Jewish conscript who relayed how Maccabi athletes' skills and fitness had impressed military commanders hitherto suspicious of Jews and their ability and willingness to do their military service.[180] To some Jewish observers it was thanks to Maccabi's work that Jews were ready to defend their country. Indeed, because of Maccabi, the Czechoslovak authorities counted the Jewish sports and gymnastics movement as an ally – and the country's Jews among its loyal citizens.[181] If Jewish athletes' boycott of the 1936 Olympic had sowed doubt about Jews' loyalty among some political elites and the public more broadly, then once an actual war loomed, the state authorities trusted that Maccabi and perhaps Jews more broadly would stand with them as they faced the German threat.

* * *

The story of Maccabi embodies several of the elements that characterized Zionism in interwar Czechoslovakia. Drawing on a local tradition for national minority organizations and on familiar symbols of nationhood, Maccabi was an institution that made Jewish nationalism legible to Jewish and non-Jewish audiences alike. It was a language that allowed Jews to participate in the negotiation of collective rights and access to resources and representation. This tradition alongside Czechoslovakia's commitment to national minority rights provided the legitimacy that Maccabi needed to undertake its nation-building project with public support. To Maccabi, the state's willingness to do so served as a litmus test of the authorities' recognition of Jews' national minority rights. Yet, state support was not of symbolic importance alone. Maccabi's ambition to create Jewish clubs across the country – a Jewish national realm in which a new generation of healthy and empowered Jews would emerge – depended, in the minds of Maccabi activists, on state resources. They looked to the successes of German and Czech minority nationalists in establishing national institutions with public funds and took seriously the Czech elite's commitment to equal right for national minorities in Czechoslovakia.

It would be a mistake, however, to interpret Maccabi's patriotism as primarily opportunist. Maccabi activists' quest to create model citizens – their faith in the promise of new Jews – was shaped by their own gender and class identities and by the masculinized ideals embedded in the Zionist ideology. The ideal of new Jews served as the impetus for these Jewish nationalists' efforts. It was a symbol of Jews' transformation from marginalized and despised outsiders to respectable citizens and social insiders. Indeed, the ideal of the new Jew brought Jews' collective image in line with these activists' own sense of self. Performance was central to this process. By adopting familiar, dominant physical ideals, creating legible national institutions, and choreographing public display of Jews' prowess on the playing field, in the pool, and on the ski slopes, Maccabi activists and athletes performed Jewish nationhood. Like a ritual, it was an act that had to be repeated over and over to make the nation come to life and to remind participants and spectators alike of Jews' readiness for insider status.

Maccabi's quest for hegemony among Jewish clubs and athletes is one example of the attempts by political activists to nationalize the social realm in the interwar years. In Czechoslovakia, nationalist activists of all colors sought to erect distinct national spheres by creating separate schools, gymnastics and sports clubs, scouting groups, kindergartens, social welfare institutions, and political parties – each nation to its own, so to speak. The coexisting discourses of national self-determination and minority rights facilitated the establishment of political and social institutions claiming to represent national communities and seeking to assert their authority as semi-public bodies over their nations. The sports and gymnastics movement was one among many disciplining techniques employed simultaneously by grassroots activists and state authorities. In the case of the Zionist project, this nationalizing process was fraught with challenges, not least from Jews themselves who resisted Jewish nationalists' demands for the primacy of ethnicity in determining individuals' community. Like their Czech and German nationalist peers, Jewish activists were frustrated by obstructions to their efforts caused, in their minds, by the opportunism, indifference, and narrow individualism rampant among their nation's young and old. Their laments reflect that in the interwar years Jews searched for community in a variety of social spaces, guided by personal interests and relationships, class, locale, political convictions, and national and ethnic identity. The often repeated claim that young Jews were streaming into "foreign" clubs in great numbers suggest that young Jews – eager to participate in the thrill of sports and in pursuit of health, physical and mental strength, and the camaraderie that was part and parcel of sports and gymnastics clubs – did not necessarily feel the need to do so among other Jews or in exclusively Jewish clubs. In fact, even Maccabi members needed incentives to stay on board. Nevertheless, thousands of Jewish men and women, youngsters as well as more mature athletes, participated in the formation of a new kind of Jewish community, one that taught and advertised the symbiosis between Czechoslovak patriotism and Jewish nationalism; one that asserted Jews' belonging in Czechoslovakia.

Yet, the alliance between Czechs and Jews, between Sokol and Maccabi, was not always easy to uphold. The debate about the Jewish athletes' boycott of the Berlin Games reflects that even observers who had some sympathy for the injustices experienced by German Jews believed that "their" Jews had let down their country, that their minority identity prevented them from being good citizens. Although these critics paid lip service to individual athletes' democratic right to abstain, they scolded them for their lack of commitment to the collective, to the Czechoslovak flag. Indeed, as one author put it "as long as we have fifty nationalities in this country, we will never all be Czechoslovaks."

SEVEN

Promised Lands

ZIONISM AND COMMUNISM IN INTERWAR CZECHOSLOVAKIA

IN 1937, THE WELL-KNOWN COMMUNIST WRITER AND TRANSLATOR Jiří Weil (1900–1959) published his first novel *Moskva-hranice* (Moscow to the Border). A longtime left-wing activist, Weil had returned to his native Prague the previous year from the Soviet Union. He had spent the last three years there, first in Moscow, followed by a six-month "re-education" exile in Soviet Central Asia. Critical of Stalinism, the novel was in part inspired by Weil's experience in the Soviet Union. Not surprisingly, it was received with scathing criticism from his Communist colleagues in Prague. Yet, in *Moskva-hranice,* the Soviet Union was not the only collectivist experiment the author scrutinized. Weil, who had grown up in a poor, observant Jewish family in the village of Praskolesy/Praskoles near Prague, was perhaps eager to preempt accusations of being a bourgeois-Zionist agent, so he began his account in Palestine.

In the novel's opening chapters, the reader follows one of the main protagonists, Ri, a young Jewish woman from a small town in Moravia, and her ill-fated experience as a *ḥaluts* (a Zionist pioneer) in Palestine. Ri had been introduced to Zionism by a friend who jokingly invited her to a meeting with "some local lunatics, Zionists, who call themselves ḥalutsim." Much to her surprise, Ri is swept off her feet by that evening's speaker, the "Zionist agitator" Karel Geisinger, "this young man, strong, with broad shoulders, an energetic figure, with fair hair, he cannot possibly be a Jew."[1] Driven less by ideological conviction than emotional attraction, Ri joins the "self-confident and proud" Zionist youngsters in her town and soon finds herself at a training farm, a *hakhsharah,* in Slovakia. Before long Ri has left behind her middle-class life, her tennis lessons, pretty dresses, and coffee, for the unfamiliar, dirty, and exhausting physical labor on the farm. Once in Palestine, Ri and Karel, now a married couple, and their Zionist group join a kibbutz, an agricultural collectivist settlement.

In Weil's account, Palestine is a dystopia. Ri dreams of "the promised land . . . after all the filth and humiliation, a sweet home . . . a home where the land will be kind."[2] But as Weil shows, Palestine is nothing like the home Ri longs for. It is, in Weil's account and faithful to Soviet doctrine, an imperialist project. Ri witnesses the dispossession of the Arab peasants, whom she watches starve to death, destroyed physically and spiritually, by the loss of their land. The Arab tragedy is high-handedly dismissed by her fellow Zionists, who treat their Arab neighbors with the same disdain and distance as the British authorities. Soon, violence sweeps the community first during the Arab Revolt and then as the kibbutz attacks the idealistic, Jewish Communist Eissenfuss and hands him over to the British authorities. As Ri expresses her disgust with the injustice and immorality of the Zionists' violence against Arabs and fellow Jews, her husband Karel, the kibbutz's leader, explains patronizingly, "Communists are worse than the Arabs, malaria, and all of the rest of it."[3] For Ri, Palestine had become "a glistening salt lake, whose waters one cannot drink, her faith had been washed away by the blood on the roads edged by the eucalyptus trees."[4] Disgusted and disillusioned, Ri leaves Palestine. Returning to familiar Vienna, the pregnant Ri aborts her unborn child. As Ri emerges from her hospital bed, learning how to walk again, she meets and falls in love with Robert, a Jewish engineer from Poland. Soon she follows him to the Soviet Union. Having symbolically killed the illusion of a "sweet home" in Palestine, a society unworthy of new life, Ri is reborn, cleansed, before her journey to the land of socialism.

Weil's juxtaposition of the Zionist project in Palestine and the Soviet Union was no coincidence. Neither was his depiction of young Jews traveling between the Zionist and the Soviet utopias. The political landscape in interwar Europe was dominated by political extremes, by revolution and reaction, by the quest for national and social utopias. It was a political culture that celebrated the image of youth, and especially the image of the New Man, as an embodiment of the renewal, strength, and future promise embedded in political ideologies. Among Jews, it was Zionism and Communism that "competed for the hearts and minds of the young." For the first half of the twentieth century, the historian Anita Shapira observes, "in the sphere of ideals and ideas . . . these two movements were the opposing focal attractions of Jewish youth."[5] In some parts of Europe, most significantly Poland, anti-Zionist Jewish parties, such as the Orthodox Agudas Yisroel (Union of Israel) and the socialist Jewish workers' movement, the Bund, posed a significant political challenge to the Zionist movement. In interwar Czechoslovakia, Zionist leaders viewed Communism, a movement that made substantial political gains here, as the greatest threat to Zionism.

In the 1920s and '30s, Communism and the Soviet Union threatened to drain Zionism of its "human material" and financial resources.[6] In the 1920s, young Jews, from poor and middle-class backgrounds, joined the Communist movement. It is a phenomenon that scholars have contributed to the widespread radicalism among youths in the postwar years. Indeed, before the rise of Nazism sent thousands of German Jews fleeing to Palestine, Zionist activists worried that Palestine would be surpassed by the Soviet Union as the Jewish Promised Land. The 1920s was a decade of crisis in Palestine. The fourth wave of Jewish immigration, which lasted from 1924 to 1929, happened at a time of severe economic difficulties. It was a time when the number of Jews immigrating to Palestine declined, thousands of Jews left the British Mandate, and tension between Jews and Arabs intensified. During these troublesome years for the Zionist movement, in the Soviet Union the authorities sponsored what appeared to be Jewish nation-building projects, first in the Crimea, then in Birobidzhan. These Soviet colonization projects were not the only concern to Zionists, who also feared that large numbers of young Jews were attracted to Communism's promise of universal emancipation of humanity. By the 1930s, at a time of intensifying antisemitism in Europe and deepening socioeconomic marginalization of Jews, the Soviet Union and Europe's Communist organizations appeared to many as the most assertive anti-fascist force, a development that caused new unease among Zionists.

In Czechoslovakia, Zionist activists carefully cultivated an image of Zionism as a politically neutral or non-partisan movement, one that by virtue of being a national organization *naturally* represented the interests of all Jews regardless of their ideological beliefs. Because they were unsure of Zionism's appeal among Jews and eager to create a unified Jewish political voice, Zionist leaders articulated a so-called "all-Jewish" platform that focused on Jews' equality and dignity and their withdrawal from the battle between the country's nationalities. In short, Zionism was presented as a way for Jews to neutralize their presence by untangling themselves from the nationality conflict as well as participate on their own terms in political life in Czechoslovakia. Zionists believed that the pragmatic non-partisan position was effective in gaining them wider support among Jews, a consensus that, as shown in the previous chapter, existed within the Zionist sports and gymnastics movement. Yet, at the same time, they worried that Jewish youth, radicalized by years of war and revolution and imbued with utopian longings, would instead turn to Communism. Therefore, despite the Zionist Organization's continued formal political neutrality, its leaders supported a variety of Zionist youth groups that had strong left- and right-wing identities. It was not until 1935, when the Zionist movement's political arm, the Jewish Party, entered into an election agreement with the influential Czechoslovak Social Democratic Party, that Zionists abandoned what they considered a neutral stance. That year, amid fears of a possible victory at the polls for the country's right-wing parties and sensing the need for a Jewish alternative to Communism's forceful anti-fascism, the Zionist elite abandoned its non-partisan position for a socialist one, even as the alliance with the Social Democrats split its own ranks.

Elsewhere, away from the national political stage, a new, more forceful Zionist response to Communism had already emerged by the late 1920s in Czechoslovakia. Beginning in 1929, the Zionist economist Solomon Goldelman (1885–1974), an émigré from the Ukraine, a seasoned anti-Communist, but a newcomer to Jewish politics in Czechoslovakia, led a counteroffensive against Communists' anti-Zionist propaganda and activism. In 1934, Goldelman established the Zionist Propaganda Bureau, imagined as the command center for Zionists' battle with Communists. Located in Beth Ha'am, Prague's Zionist community center, the bureau encompassed an adult education program, a correspondence school, a publishing house, and a youth organization division. Goldelman created the bureau with the intention of equipping the largest number of Zionists with the knowledge, education, and ideological discipline needed to withstand the barrage of Communist propaganda.

If a defense against so-called red assimilation (Communists' promotion of Jews' assimilation into the proletariat) in Czechoslovakia had been Goldelman's initial focus, he quickly broadened the Zionist Propaganda Bureau's scope. With support from Prague's Zionist leaders and the Jewish National Fund in Jerusalem, Goldelman created an institution that offered Jews across Central and Eastern Europe the opportunity for "spiritual hakhsharah," an education intended to strengthen their Jewish and Zionist identities, prepare them for emigration to Palestine, and create an ideological bulwark against Communism. It was an institution meant to shore up Jews' defenses against the threat of Communism to Jewish national life in the Diaspora as well as in Palestine. It was an institution intended to harness what Goldelman viewed as the radicalism of Jewish youth to the Zionist cause. By strengthening Zionism from within, by creating a unified, ideologically disciplined, and battle-ready Zionist movement, he would be able to halt the defection of Jewish youths to the red banner.

ZIONISM AND POLITICAL NEUTRALITY

Writing a few days after the first parliamentary elections in Czechoslovakia on April 18, 1920, in which the United Jewish Parties received almost eighty thousand votes, Hugo Bergmann cautioned the Zionist Executive in London about undue optimism. The Palestine-bound Zionist and writer, "who had been unwillingly detained in my home country," noted that the Zionist movement, despite the astonishing success of the Jewish candidates, was facing serious challenges in the country. The large number of votes cast for Jewish nationalist candidates, Bergmann argued, was not a sign of Jews' commitment to Zionism, but rather reflected a "crude form of opportunism." It was, he claimed, merely a signal of Jews' desire for national and political neutrality.[7] It was a form of opportunism that had been encouraged by insecure Jewish candidates who had not asked voters to commit to a Zionist agenda but merely to vote for neutrality. At the same time, Bergmann noted that this so-called neutrality had divided the Zionist groups by allowing the socialist Zionist party, Po'ale Tsiyon (Workers of Zion), to call on Jews to support the Czech and German Social Democratic Parties and distance itself from the other Jewish candidates. It was a split that had robbed the Jewish parties of four parliamentary seats. Even more worrisome, Bergmann observed, "the youth is not as open to us now as they were during the war. Since the Zionists do not have a clear social program, youths are attracted to socialism." What Bergman outlined in this letter was what would become one of the Zionist movement's most important dilemmas in the interwar years: how to appeal to the Jewish masses and their disparate interests while mobilizing Jewish youths, the nation's future, who were more enamored with the promise of socialist than national revolution.

In the revolutionary atmosphere of the postwar years, a time marked by left- and right-wing extremism and nationalist and socialist revolutions, Jewish and non-Jewish voters alike, many of them newly enfranchised, faced a political landscape that was divided along ideological, religious, national, and social lines. As in Austria-Hungary, in Czechoslovakia political parties were organized along axis of nationality, class, and religion. For example, German and Czech Catholics, Social Democrats, and Agrarians were divided into parallel movements. These large political parties maintained a wide-ranging sociopolitical network that reached deep into ordinary people's everyday lives. Kindergartens, credit unions, gymnastics clubs, newspapers, and consumer cooperatives among other institutions were maintained by the strongest parties, creating parallel societal structures.[8] It was a system that was both dependent on and the source of fragmentation, such as the divide between German- and Czechs-speakers. In addition, in interwar Czechoslovakia, politics at the parliamentary level was run by a working group of the leaders of the five largest Czech political parties. Within this group, known as the *pětka* (for the five [*pět*] leaders), these politicians reached binding compromises among themselves, determined the legislative agenda, and dominated government posts as well as the state administration.[9] This system, historians believe, helps explain why Czechoslovakia experienced relative political stability in the interwar years despite its fragmented sociopolitical character and the marginalization of national minorities and the Communists.[10] As among the other nationalities, there also were several Jewish parties. Despite a series of internal splits, in the 1920s and '30s, the most significant Jewish party with countrywide ambitions was the Jewish Party (Židovská strana/Jüdisde Partei), the domestic political arm of the Zionist Organization of Czechoslovakia. In interwar Czechoslovakia, the only explicitly multinational movement was the Communist Party of Czechoslovakia.

From the outset, Zionist leaders prioritized Jewish national unity over other political goals. For them, the unification of the Jewish electorate behind one party – the creation of a Jewish political voice – was crucial for their nation-building project. In light of the diversity of the new country's Jewish societies and their divergent social, economic, cultural, and national interests, Zionist chose to develop the aforementioned non-partisan or "neutral" all-Jewish platform. This program focused on the state authorities' formal recognition of Jews as a national minority, access to public funds for Jewish schools and other national institutions, protection against antisemitism, and a democratization of the governance of the country's Jewish communities.[11] As a minority nationalist movement, they were keen to appear as a loyal and constructive political force to the state authorities. Zionist leaders believed that a partisan stance would undermine their claim to be the natural representatives of the country's Jews – and hence deserving of public resources for their national institutions – and not merely a marginal, partisan Jewish voice.

In the summer of 1919, Zionist candidates ran in municipal and regional elections in the Bohemian Lands.[12] According to their own estimates, the "Jewish Candidates' List" received as much as 60 percent of the Jewish vote in Bohemia and Moravia.[13] The Zionist press, eager to spread the news of the emergence of a Jewish political voice, described how in the Zionist headquarters in Prague, "the crowd welcomed the election results with jubilation because the Jewish *people* [*sic*] is behind us."[14] The following year, in the country's first parliamentary elections, the United Jewish Parties (Sdružené židovské strany/Vereinigten jüdischen Parteien) collected 79,714 votes in the Bohemian Lands and

Slovakia. Although not enough to secure a parliamentary seat, Zionists were encouraged by what they considered to be a forceful show of support for their program of neutrality and national unity. They considered the result "an honorable defeat."[15] In 1925, the Jewish Party, now running in all parts of the country, received 98,845 votes. Finally in 1929, in an alliance with representatives of the country's small Polish minority, two Jewish Party candidates secured seats in the National Assembly, Ludvík Singer from Bohemia and Julius Reiz (1880–1976) from Slovakia (the parties received a total of 104,539 votes). The Jewish Party retained its two MPs, then Angelo Goldstein and Chaim Kugel, in the 1935 election, now in a working alliance with the Czechoslovak Social Democrats, part of the governing coalition.

During the election campaigns, the historian Marie Crhová has shown, the Jewish Party focused on articulating an all-inclusive Jewish platform. Activists called on Jews to vote for the Jewish Party to express Jews' unity in the fight against antisemitism, Jews' neutrality in the competition between the country's other nationalities, and Jews' loyalty to Czechoslovakia. These remained important priorities through the 1920s. By the 1930s, antisemitism, the difficult economic conditions in the country's eastern Jewish communities, and Jews' commitment to Czechoslovakia were at the center of the Jewish Party's election campaigns. More than anything, Crhová suggests, it was the desire to express simultaneous loyalty and neutrality in the national struggle that motivated many to cast a vote for the Jewish Party.[16] Although we cannot know who the people were who voted for the Jewish Party, much less their motivations, the Jewish Party leadership believed it prudent to focus on addressing Jews' concerns about antisemitism and threats to Jews' equality in the election campaigns. Both issues were potential obstacles to Jews' integration and prosperity in Czechoslovakia.

PRESSURE FROM BELOW

By the late 1920s, the Zionist leadership was increasingly confronted with demands from within the Zionist ranks for the organization to assume a more partisan political position. Activists such Hans Lichtwitz (1906–1989), a socialist Zionist youth activist and member of the

Zionist Executive, pointed to "neutrality" as the reason for the Zionist movement's inability to attract Jewish youths. He argued that "the youth will join the Zionist ranks only once Zionism has a clear stance on social issues. Only then will Zionism also be able to keep young people in its ranks." These calls from the younger Zionist to embrace socialist Zionism were met with patronizing disdain by older Zionists. The chairman of the Zionist Executive, Josef Rufeisen (1887–1949), rejected the push for "factional politics" and declared it "unreasonable that the Zionist Organization should feint a swing [*Scheinmanöver*] to the left in order to win over the youth. . . . They will accomplish something only if they join, as much as possible, the work of adults."[17] Despite the leadership's insistence on unity, on maintaining the "non-ideological" general Zionist stance, rank-and-file activists were already pursuing more partisan Zionist options.

In the mid-1920s, a new radical right-wing faction appeared within the World Zionist Organization, known as Revisionists. In 1925, a Czechoslovak branch was established in Brno/Brünn.[18] Among other issues, the Revisionists opposed the dominance of labor Zionism in Palestine and developed a militant nationalist and anti-socialist stance most prominently embodied in its youth organization Betar.[19] In 1935, the Revisionists split off from the World Zionist Organization and created a separate organization. That year, the New Zionist Organization in Czechoslovakia was established and attracted some senior Zionist leaders, including Emil Margulies, the most prominent German-speaking Zionist and until 1935 the chairman of the Jewish Party.

At the other end of the political spectrum, socialist Zionists formed an alternative to the neutrality of the Jewish Party and the Zionist Organization as well as an opposition to Revisionism. In 1928, activists reestablished the social democratic Po'ale Tsiyon. By the early 1930s, within the Zionist Organization in Czechoslovakia, the non-partisan General Zionists held about a third of the membership votes cast, and many of the most prominent leaders, including Josef Rufeisen, belonged to this faction. The left received 25–30 percent, and the remainder was split between the Revisionists and Mizraḥi, the former being the more prominent of the two. Thus, despite the appearance of neutrality, the Zionist movement had very strong and fiercely opposed factions, and these divisions were felt in the country's Zionist youth movements.[20] It was a factionalism that reflected the broader political polarization in interwar Europe.

Throughout the interwar years, the Zionist Jewish Party in its various incarnations attracted at least three or four times as many voters countrywide than there were members of the Zionist Organization.[21] Activists deduced that Jewish voters supported an assertive Jewish political voice but were not committed to Zionism and its vision for a Jewish homeland in Palestine. Yet, Zionist leaders – and many Jews – did not lose sight of the Palestine project.

PALESTINE

In interwar Czechoslovakia, relative economic prosperity and social and political stability made the need for a Jewish homeland elsewhere less urgent. Activists thought of Palestine as a refuge for Jews in Czechoslovakia's impoverished east and for the less fortunate Jews in neighboring countries. Nevertheless, the Jewish homeland in Palestine was important to Zionist activism in a variety of ways. Zionists here were committed to the expansion and strengthening of the fundraising institutions for land acquisition, emigration, and settlement, the Jewish National Fund (Keren Kayemeth LeIsrael) and the Palestine Foundation Fund (Keren Hayesod). They also stated and restated their commitment to recruiting and training young Jews for emigration to Palestine.[22]

The number of Jews leaving Czechoslovakia for Palestine was small in the 1920s. A few groups of youngsters left in the early 1920s. Some participated in the establishment of agricultural settlement and otherwise managed to make a life for themselves in Palestine. Others returned to Czechoslovakia. By the early 1930s, the number of emigrants did pick up as the broader socioeconomic and political instability was felt in Czechoslovakia, a trend that intensified later in the 1930s.[23] The majority of the emigrants were from Slovakia and Subcarpathian Rus'. In 1934, for example, out of 159 people (90 men and 69 women) who received immigration certificates, 11 were from Bohemia, 15 from Moravia, 44 from Slovakia, and 89 from Subcarpathian Rus'.[24] Scholars and contemporaries estimate that about 4,000 to 6,000 Jews from Czechoslovakia immigrated to Palestine before 1938.[25] It is unclear how many returned, but the "returnee" was a topic of internal debate among Zionist activists.[26]

In general, Zionist leaders scorned opportunist emigrants, people they viewed as motivated not by Zionism but by dreams of escaping poverty. Nevertheless, by the late 1930s, the Jewish National Fund did not shy away from promoting Palestine as a destination for Czechoslovakia's poor Jews. Jews from Slovakia and Subcarpathian Rus' flocked to the towns and cities of the Bohemian Lands, and some observers worried that this influx of "eastern" Jews threatened the position of Bohemia's and Moravia's Jews. In preparation for their spring 1937 fundraising campaign, representatives of the Jewish National Fund instructed their volunteer fundraisers to stoke this anxiety. In an imaginary conversation between Herr NEIN (Mr. No), the reluctant Jewish donor, and Herr JA (Mr. Yes), the Zionist volunteer, the Fund provided its volunteers with talking points and responses to possible excuses not to donate to the Fund.[27] In response to someone's objection "There are enough poor [Jews] in this country. Why send the money abroad?" the volunteer was instructed to dismiss Jewish charity and welfare programs in Czechoslovakia as simply creating professional welfare recipients. Unless these migrants were directed to Palestine – something a donation to buy land would facilitate – they would flood the western communities. Rather than warning of antisemitism, the author presented a rational economic argument for a diversion of these migrants to Palestine:

> All these elements from the east, who are tough, energetic, and flocking to Bohemia, Moravia, and Silesia in massive numbers, endanger the economic and social position of Jews in these regions. They eke out a living as junk dealers and peddlers. They aggravate the mutual competition among Jews. The result is a battle between east and west that threatens to completely undermine the already fragile Jewry in this country.[28]

Tranquility and prosperity at home thus depended on the expansion of Jewish settlements in Palestine.

As in other countries in Europe and the Americas, even though local Jews' desire for emigration to Palestine was negligible, they were very willing to contribute money for other Jews' emigration to and settlement in the British Mandate. Between 1918 and 1938, the Jewish National Fund, which raised money for land purchase and settlement, collected almost 31 million crowns (Kč) in Czechoslovakia. The Palestine Foundation Fund, which was established to fund raise among the non-Zionist Jewish public, collected Kč 3.3 million in 1929/30 alone.[29] The annual sums collected grew consistently throughout the interwar years (the collected sums increased from Kč 1 million in 1920/21, Kč 2.1 million in 1929/30, to Kč 3.7 in 1937/38). Donations to the Zionist foundations were particularly generous in times of crisis in Palestine or Europe.[30] Thus, as in other Jewish communities, in Czechoslovakia donations increased in the aftermath of the August 1929 riots in Palestine as well as in the period from 1933 to 1938, when the persecution of German Jews was felt keenly in Czechoslovakia as refugees streamed across the country's western borders. If Jewish solidarity motivated donors, so did patriotism. In addition to general fundraisers, the Jewish National Fund also ran local patriotic campaigns for "Czechoslovak" projects in Palestine. These included the collection of funds in 1930 for the Masaryk Forest and in 1935 for the kibbutz Kfar Masaryk, with tree planting and agricultural pioneering being important legitimizing symbols of Jews' settlement of Palestine. Zionist leaders hoped that such "Czechoslovak" Palestine projects would increase donations – and they did.[31]

Zionists also engaged with the Jewish homeland in Palestine through lectures, films, art exhibitions, and the Zionist press, which brought news and stories from the *Yishuv* (the pre-state Jewish society in Palestine) to Jewish and non-Jewish audiences in Czechoslovakia.[32] In the 1930s, Jews went to Palestine as tourists, and some published travelogues or articles about their experiences.[33] So did the Maccabi sports teams that represented Czechoslovakia at the Maccabiah, the Jewish Olympics, in 1932 and 1935. As we shall see, some Zionist youth groups were intensely preoccupied with images and narratives from Palestine that formed the basis for war games and other activities that were intended to provide children and youngsters with psychological and practical skills.[34] In other words, while Palestine was not a physical destination for many Jews from Czechoslovakia, it was nevertheless a project, an imaginary space, that many Jews, Zionists and non-Zionists alike, encountered and engaged with in different ways.

ZIONISM AND ITS DISCONTENTS: YOUTH BETWEEN ZION AND EXILE

In the interwar years Zionist ideology and iconography centered on a cult of youth. Films and photography "documenting" Jewish life in Palestine was abundant with young, tanned, strong bodies working the land and building its towns, founding a new society. Indeed, youth and labor were the central Zionist ideals. For Europeans, youth embodied power and dynamism, health and a promise of renewal. After the First World War, political activists of all stripes looked to the mobilization of youth as a vehicle for social change. In the age of mass politics, activists looked to youth movements as agents for social and national revolution.[35]

Youth movements mushroomed across Czechoslovakia in the interwar years. Some were affiliated with political parties, such as the Social Democrats; others sought to distance themselves from party politics under a national or religious umbrella, such as the German Catholic group Staffelstein and the Czech Catholic group Orel.[36] In the Bohemian Lands, many of these youth groups had emerged before the First World War at a time of rapid urbanization and industrialization. Their number and membership grew rapidly in the 1920s and '30s, and some branched out and established affiliates in Slovakia and Subcarpathian Rus'. Thus, much like the country's political landscape, they formed a tapestry of groups that were organized along national, religious, and social lines. While some early twentieth-century youth movements in Central Europe had emphasized a certain degree of distance to and autonomy from adult society, in the interwar years adult activists and their junior helpers sought to mobilize children and adolescents in the name of national renewal, moral and social reform, or revolution. In search of community, hiking and scouting adventures, and spiritual and ideological self-fulfillment, or prodded by parents and peers, tens of thousands of children and adolescents flocked to youth groups in those years.[37]

In Czechoslovakia, there were a handful of Jewish youth movements. Most of them were affiliated with Zionism.[38] As in much of Central and Eastern Europe, these groups were inspired by the German Wandervogel and the scouting movements. Wandervogel, which became immensely popular in Central Europe in the years before the First World War, invited youths to return to a more authentic, natural, ascetic way of life in an autonomous youth community. It was a community imagined as in revolt against the urban, bourgeoisie, and materialist culture of adults.[39] Wandervogel and its many offshoots idealized nature hiking, known as "expeditions," communal experiences, and a commitment to youth leadership. In the Bohemian Lands, the Jewish youth group Blau Weiss, whose members were predominantly German-speaking Jewish youth, drew inspiration from the Wandervogel movement.[40] After the First World War, the Blau Weiss organization in the Bohemian Lands changed its name to the Hebrew Tekhelet Lavan (Blue White).

The internationalist scouting movement was another important influence on Zionist youth groups.[41] In contrast to the Wandervogel's focus on youth autonomy, the scouting movement emphasized hierarchy, obedience, and individual and collective discipline. In Czechoslovakia, the socialist Ha-Shomer ha-Tsa'ir (the Young Guard) and the right-wing Betar (acronym for Berit [alliance] Yosef Trumpeldor) modeled their ideals, symbols, and rituals on the scouting movement. These two organizations were especially active in Slovakia and Subcarpathian Rus' and were part of broader international organizational networks.[42] In addition to these secular groups, the Orthodox Zionist Tse'irei Mizraḥi (Mizraḥi Youth) also gained a following in Slovakia and Subcarpathian Rus' in the 1930s.[43]

In 1926, in response to the increasingly partisan left- and right-wing politics of the existing Zionist youth groups, activists from the gymnastics and sports organization Maccabi Czechoslovakia created a new explicitly neutral and "all-Jewish" organization known as Maccabi ha-Tsa'ir (Maccabi Youth). Much like its mother organization, Maccabi ha-Tsa'ir emphasized Jewish national rather than Zionist loyalties. Its founders hoped that Maccabi ha-Tsa'ir would appeal broadly to young Jews eager to join Jewish clubs but not ready to become Zionists. Furthermore, Maccabi activists hoped to assuage Jewish parents uncomfortable with the perceived radicalism of the existing Zionist youth groups. Yet, the creation of Maccabi ha-Tsa'ir also had a practical purpose. By providing a Jewish national community for children and young adolescents, an alternative to the non-Jewish groups in their hometowns, Maccabi activists hoped that Maccabi ha-Tsa'ir would funnel a new generation of Jews into the Jewish sports and gymnastics movements.[44] Maccabi ha-Tsa'ir soon had chapters across Czechoslovakia.

Unlike the sports organization Maccabi, which appealed broadly to Jewish youth, Zionist youth activists created a self-image as a Zionist elite, as the vanguard of the Jewish nation. They shared with older Zionist leaders a view of Jewish youth as confused, individualist, undisciplined, politically ignorant, and indifferent to national boundaries. In contrast, Zionist youth was imagined as disciplined, imbued with a will to decisive action, and committed to the national collective. While they differed on a range of ideological and cultural issues, all the Zionist youth groups idealized the ḥaluts, the Zionist pioneer.

The image of the pioneers – physically strong, working the land, building Palestine's roads and cities, living a life of simplicity and hard work, cultivating direct and honest relationships, and devoting their lives to the creation of the Jewish homeland – was constructed as the antithesis to the Diaspora Jew. Downtrodden, weak, and victimized, peddling in money and wares, this old Jewish type, according to Zionist ideology, embodied the degeneration caused by the severing of a people from its land. Indeed, in Zionist ideology Jews' reclaiming of the ancestral land was imagined as transformative on a collective and an individual level. By directing Jews into productive occupations – farming, crafts, and industrial work – Zionists envisioned a normalization of the Jewish nation's socioeconomic structure as well as the spiritual and physical regeneration of the Jewish people. Although there were a myriad of varieties of Zionist economic, social, and political theories spanning the political spectrum from left to right, they shared the heroic image of the pioneer as a trailblazer for the Zionist project.

The pioneering life was, however, easier to imagine in theory, in songs, stories, and speeches, than it was to carry out in reality. By the mid-1920s, the Zionist project in Palestine ran into serious obstacles that affected the Zionist youth movements in the Diaspora in profound ways. Rumors began making their way from Palestine to Czechoslovakia indicating that the ḥalutsim, who had left years earlier expecting to work in agricultural settlements, were stuck in training facilities unable to find a place in a kibbutz or ended up working in the city.[45] Hugo Bergmann, who had emigrated in 1920 when he was in his late thirties, placed the blame in part on the youth groups themselves, for focusing on the romance of pioneering life rather than the reality of the difficult economic conditions in Palestine. In an open letter to the members of Tekhelet Lavan, he warned:

> The living standard of a laborer in Eretz Israel is only a little higher than that of an Arab fellah. This is the reality that awaits the ḥaluts, and your preparations must measure up to this reality. In your case, a new social status does not mean merely a change in profession, it also means a drop from a bourgeois way of life to a proletarian one. Is this clear to you? . . . I suppose that many of your members will leave Eretz Israel disappointed and embittered. Their departure will be your fault, for not educating them to cope with the harsh reality.[46]

Back home, Zionist leaders worried that if these young people, disappointed and having lost hope, returned to Czechoslovakia, it would have a devastating effect on the pioneering groups.

By 1927, the difficult economic conditions and British restrictions on Jewish immigration to Palestine had made it increasingly difficult to procure immigration certificates for young emigrants from Czechoslovakia. As a result, aspiring pioneers lingered in and eventually abandoned the hakhsharot, the farms and urban communes where young Jews received agricultural, industrial, and ideological training, in the Bohemian Lands.[47] By the end of 1928, He-Ḥaluts (the Pioneer), the organization tasked with youth emigration, gave up on running permanent training farms after at least three had failed. The training communes were plagued not only by a lack of money and immigration certificates. Activists also complained of a significant gender imbalance, with three times more boys than girls joining in, a problem He-Ḥaluts sought to rectify at one point by creating a training farm for girls near Bratislava.[48]

In the mid-1930s, when emigration picked up and training farms were reestablished, activists remembered the significant cultural and social differences between young Jews from different parts of the country. Yehuda Rezniczenko, a representative of He-Ḥaluts who spent time in Czechoslovakia in the 1930s, recalled that activists from the Bohemian

Lands experienced these differences as a civilizational gulf.[49] He noted that Jews from the "eastern areas," who traveled west to join hakhsharot in the Bohemian Lands, were ignorant about Zionism and what was expected of pioneers, and "many of them lacked even the most elementary knowledge of the progress of civilization. Very often it was necessary to urge them to wash after work. It was difficult for them to get used to reading a newspaper. No wonder then that the members of Tekhelet Lavan had little affection for those ḥalutsim."[50] As a result, He-Ḥaluts gave up on running hakhsharot that brought together aspiring pioneers from all parts of the country and instead created regional centers.

Although the situation in Palestine contributed to the difficulties recruiting pioneers, so did the relative prosperity and opportunity available to Jews in Czechoslovakia. Some parents resisted letting their sons and daughters participate in what was mostly socialist communes of youths, let alone immigrate to Palestine. Instead, some young Jews worked as hired laborers on farms and in industrial workshops, and often they did so only during vacation time before returning to school or looking for other work. In response to the dwindling interest in emigration among youth and the Jewish public's lackluster support, upon whom the financial viability of the farms depended, the He-Ḥaluts leadership began promoting time spent at a hakhsharah as a vehicle for the productivization of Jewish youth in Czechoslovakia.[51]

Despite the practical difficulties of emigration, some youth activists were preoccupied with the merits of Zionist activism in the Diaspora versus Palestine. Some rejected the notion of ascribing equal value to all Zionist work, which was the official position of the Zionist Organization in Czechoslovakia. A member of Tekhelet Lavan, Fritz Flussmann, writing in the organization's newsletter *Bundesblätter* in April 1930, declared "a member of the youth movement will not equate Diaspora Zionism with pioneering. The pioneer in Palestine does, day in and day out, what the Zionist in the Diaspora does only in his spare time."[52] Anyone not committed to emigration, who chose to live in the Diaspora, he noted, fell short of the movement's expectations.[53] This view strengthened among some activists in the 1930s. In 1932, the leaders of Maccabi ha-Tsa'ir could not resist the draw of socialist Zionism and the ḥaluts ideal. They abandoned the organization's hitherto neutral all-Jewish stance.[54]

As the youth activists explained, "The youth wants not only to dream and to watch yearningly, but to join the front lines of their people's struggle for freedom and a future."[55] Sports and games were wonderful for children, but as they were coming of age, members of Maccabi ha-Tsa'ir needed a greater cause. In the following years, Maccabi ha-Tsa'ir defied the protests of the adult leaders of Maccabi Czechoslovakia, who insisted that the organization remain "non-political and non-partisan." As the leaders of Maccabi Czechoslovakia learned the hard way, to these youth activists, "the autonomy of the youth community" was not merely an empty phrase.[56]

Even though some circles cultivated an increasing "Palestinocentrism" in the 1930s, Zionist youth groups retained their tradition for Zionist "work in the present," providing a new form of community for young Jews. Activists promoted young Jews' self-productivization through hiking, scouting, adopting an ascetic and healthy lifestyle, and engaging in occasional physical labor. By making the break with the past more attainable, they hoped to create a community wherein young activists could let words be followed more immediately by deeds.[57] And for some, the tension between the present and the future, between the Diaspora and the Jewish homeland, was not an obstacle but rather an inspiration. Heinrich Hoffmann (1905–1974), a youth leader in Tekhelet Lavan, recalled that as a teenager his Zionist activism was inspired by this dichotomy:

> In my mind, Zionism was not bound up with the immediate negation of the Diaspora. Of course, I wanted to do away with the Diaspora, for I saw it as a way of life forced on the Jewish people and therefore not in keeping with its dignity [but] I saw Zionism as a process of national awakening, a protracted process which would need the project of realization in Eretz Israel, on the one hand, and the undertaking of an extensive educational program in the Diaspora, on the other.[58]

But Zionist leaders were troubled by the idealization of the pioneer and the radical Palestinocentrism among some youth activists. They believed that the radicalism of a small minority threatened to push other young Jews away from Zionism altogether.[59] Jakob Edelstein (1903–1944), a socialist Zionist activist and from 1933 onward the head of the Palestine Office in Prague, which distributed immigration certificates to the British Mandate, assessed that most young Jews who joined Zionist youth groups did not wish to emigrate. Rather, they were looking for an opportunity to participate in the creation of a new society, to find self-fulfillment and community. At a meeting in October 1932, Edelstein noted:

> Everyone who does not become a ḥaluts sees themselves as inferior. We must work to ensure that the non-ḥalutsim realize that their work is important for Zionism. Without a hinterland there will be no victory for the ḥalutsim. This is what we should be teaching. It is also up to the youth groups to value these young people more and not simply reduce them to errand boys [for the Zionist movement].[60]

Indeed, for some young Jews who did not desire to leave Czechoslovakia, the obsession with emigration became just another factor that pushed them away from Zionism in the political landscape. Eduard Goldstücker (1913–2000), who became a leading Communist student activist in Prague in the 1930s, felt out of place among his Hungarian-speaking comrades in Ha-Shomer ha-Tsa'ir. As a Slovak-speaker, from a poor family, and with no intention of emigrating, Goldstücker lasted only a few months as a Zionist. Much later in life, he remembered his time in Ha-Shomer as having laid the foundation for his Communist consciousness and activism. This was precisely the sequence of events that Zionist leaders worried about.[61]

RED ASSIMILATION

In early January 1927, a letter from London reached the headquarters of Czechoslovakia's Zionist Organization in Moravská Ostrava/Mährisch Ostrau. Its author demanded a response to allegations that the Zionist Organization in Czechoslovakia "had lost the Jewish youth." Quoting a "third-hand report," the letter relayed the claim that due to its focus on political neutrality and Jewish unity, Zionists leaders had failed to stem the spread of Communism within the Zionist youth movement in Czechoslovakia. In a country with "the strongest Communist party outside the Soviet Union," the majority of Zionist youths in the Bohemian Lands had transitioned to the "Communist camp." The report continued, "The Jewish student organization is in Communist hands, the leading members of Communist youth and cultural circles are former members of Po'ale Tsiyon and leaders in Tekhelet Lavan. In Pilsen, an entire Tekhelet Lavan group has gone over to the Communist Party." Furthermore, students from Slovakia and Subcarpathian Rus', "the children of Hasidic parents," who were attending schools and universities in the Bohemian Lands, were also joining the ranks of Communism.[62] Indeed, rather than being tapped for the Zionist movement, this great reservoir of Jewish youth, hitherto untouched by assimilation in the country's east, were succumbing to red assimilation.

The divisions among youth activists over emigration and the merits of Zionists' work in the present, in the Diaspora, were important. But in the interwar years, it was the so-called threat of "red assimilation" that dominated the debates about Jewish youth and the future of Zionism. From the top strata of the Zionist hierarchy to the grassroots in the youth groups, there was a widespread fear that young Jews generally and the young Zionist elite especially were joining the internationalist, anti-Zionist Communist movement. To Zionists, Communist Jews constituted a fifth column, one that created "cadres within the socialist Zionist youth movement" and then led them in defection.[63] It was a threat that destabilized the Jewish nation-building project by exposing its fragility, the porousness of its boundaries, and by challenging the nationalist paradigm. This was not a concern unique to Czechoslovakia. In the 1920s and '30s, Zionists worried that the Soviet Union would replace Palestine as the Promised Land. They feared that the dynamic and assertive Communist movement would eclipse Zionism in mobilizing the revolutionary potential of a new generation of Jews.

JEWS AND SOCIALISM

In the first half of the twentieth century, socialist Zionists' relationship to the broader socialist revolutionary movement was, in the words of Anita Shapira, "a drama of unrequited love."[64] After the Bolshevik Revolution, socialist Zionists admired the great revolutionary project under way in the Soviet Union. They yearned for Communists to acknowledge the Zionist project as one worthy of recognition as a revolutionary partner by the Soviet elite. But they received only undisguised hostility from Communists and the Soviet institutions toward the Palestine project.

Jewish activists had been part of the socialist movement in Europe since its earliest days. In most places, Jews were part of the general workers' organizations. In Russia and Austria-Hungary, where the majority of the world's Jews lived, activists created Jewish socialist parties. In Austria-Hungary, especially, national and social revolutions were closely intertwined among the monarchy's minorities, and socialists saw national rights as part and parcel of social justice. In Russia, the Jewish workers' union, the Bund, was the largest faction within the empire's socialist movement. By the early twentieth century, socialist Jews eager to mobilize the Jewish masses chose to join either the Diaspora-nationalist Bund or the socialist Zionist movement. At that time, socialist Jewish nationalists ran afoul of the broader socialist movement because of Lenin's rejection of Jews' status as a nationality.

The most significant socialist Zionist party, an international organization that spanned Europe, Palestine, and the Americas, was Po'ale Tsiyon.[65] Established in 1906 in Russia, Po'ale Tsiyon's founder Ber Borochov (1881–1917) combined Marxism and Zionism into a powerful revolutionary scheme. Borochov described Jews' socioeconomic abnormality as an inverted pyramid. Unlike other nations, only a small minority of Jews were farmers and workers. The majority of Jews worked in unproductive and increasingly marginalized sectors of the economy as peddlers, traders, and artisans. In some countries, Jews formed an abnormally large bourgeoisie. In order for a normal class differentiation and class struggle to occur among Jews – in order for Jews to become agents of history – Borochov argued, the Jewish people required land. Only in Palestine could a normal socioeconomic development take place and a Jewish proletariat emerge.[66] To Borochov, however, the revolutionary work took place both in the Diaspora and in Palestine. The struggle for national rights for Jews in the Diaspora would pave the way for the national renaissance in Palestine. As one slogan went, "Through freedom in the Diaspora to national renaissance in Palestine. Through renaissance . . . to socialism."[67]

The year 1917 was momentous for Jewish socialists and Zionist socialists alike. On the one hand, the October Revolution brought Lenin's Bolsheviks to power, a faction long opposed to the Bund's insistence on a Jewish national workers' movement and hostile to Zionism. But the Bolsheviks now stood as the undisputed leader of the revolution, a revolution that was immediately faced with violent resistance. It was time to choose. Some Bundists (Jewish socialists), Diaspora-nationalists, and Zionists left Russia, others joined the revolution. Jewish activists were soon recruited to establish the Jewish section of the Communist Party, the Yevsektia, to solidify support for the revolution among Jews.

Meanwhile, in November 1917, the British authorities issued the Balfour Declaration, which was interpreted as a promise to build a Jewish homeland in Palestine and was received with enormous jubilation by Jews around the world. To some socialist Zionists it appeared as if the conditions for a national renaissance were at hand. But the internationalist Communist movement, the Cominterm, renounced Zionist activism as "British imperialism," and by 1920 Po'ale Tsiyon had split. One faction, Po'ale Tsiyon Right, joined the social democratic Labor and Socialist International in 1923, while pro-Communist groups either organized a Po'ale Tsiyon Left or simply joined the broader Communist movement.[68] In accordance with Soviet doctrine, Communists were hostile to Bundists and socialist Zionists; both movements were suppressed in the Soviet Union itself. This was not a division unique to Jewish socialists, but one that affected socialist parties and movements everywhere. Despite the animosity between social democrats and Communists in the interwar years, the socialist experiment under way in the Soviet Union was admired widely and acted as a magnet for socialists of many different stripes. Yet, most admired the revolution from afar.

In Czechoslovakia, socialist Zionists were also divided over the question of national unity versus class struggle. In the aftermath of the First World War, Po'ale Tsiyon activists made up almost half of the Jewish National Council. In June 1919, the socialist Zionist candidates won 17 percent of the votes cast for Jewish parties in Prague.[69] By the time the campaign for the 1920 national election began, however, Po'ale Tsiyon activists encouraged their supporters to vote for the social democratic parties and not for the Jewish national ones. Czechoslovakia's socialist parties collected almost 48 percent of the votes in that first election. The following year, in 1921, the leader of Po'ale Tsiyon in Czechoslovakia, Rudolf Kohn, and some of his colleagues joined the newly established Communist Party of Czechoslovakia (Kommunistická strana Československa/Kommunistische Partei der Tschechoslowakei).[70] Thus, in Czechoslovakia, it was Po'ale Tsiyon Right that continued as an independent party, while the Left joined the Czechoslovak Communists and thereby dissolved as an independent Jewish party.

In interwar Czechoslovakia, the Communist Party was a legal political party. Like the country's other parties, its municipal and parliamentary work was supported by a network of cultural and economic associations and extensive publishing activity. More so than other political parties, in the 1920s, and to some extent in the 1930s, it attracted many of Czechoslovakia's most prominent writers, intellectuals, and artists. In the 1920s, the Communist Party's popularity was reflected in the numbers of voters as well as members. In its first election in 1925, Czechoslovakia's second national elections, it became the country's second largest party, winning 13.2 percent of the vote (934,223 votes and forty-one mandates in the assembly). The Communists attracted almost as many votes as the Czechoslovak and German Social Democratic Parties combined (15%). In 1929 and 1935, the Communist Party got 10 percent of the vote and thirty mandates in the National Assembly.[71] The party always remained outside of government. With its 150,000 members in 1928, the Communist Party of Czechoslovakia was the second largest party in the Comintern (after the Soviet one) and the strongest Communist party in Europe.[72] In 1929, the party took a Stalinist turn and imposed a new ideological discipline, expelling many of the founders. This old social democratic guard was replaced with young and more Moscow-oriented leaders. That year about three-quarters of the members left the party. In the 1930s, the party had substantially fewer members, reaching 55,000 in 1934.[73]

The Communist Party of Czechoslovakia was, until 1935, the only multinational party in Czechoslovakia. Yet, it did not recognize Jews as a nationality.[74] Unlike in the Soviet Communist Party, which had a Jewish section dedicated to mobilizing support for the Bolshevik regime among Jews until the late 1920s, in Czechoslovakia Jews were not on the Communist Party's agenda as a group with particular needs or rights of representation.[75] Even in the 1930s, when the Communist Party posed as a champion of Czechoslovakia's national minorities, it remained faithful to the position laid down by the Comintern and did not include Jews on the list of nationalities. As the historian Vít Strobach has shown, to the extent that the Communist Party concerned itself with Jewish matters, it was in taking a staunch anti-Zionist position.[76]

In the 1920s and '30s, there was a perception among a variety of Jewish observers that Jews were attracted to Communism in great numbers.[77] Yet, the link between Jews and Communism was not as strong in public discourse in interwar Czechoslovakia as in other parts of Central and Eastern Europe.[78] Nevertheless, since the Second World War, these perceptions have evolved into more sustained narratives. Some historians writing about the interwar years argue that Jews did support Communism in great numbers in Subcarpathian Rus'.[79] Historian Yeshayahu Jelinek describes the Subcarpathian branch of the Communist Party "as the preeminent representative of non-institutional Judaism. . . . It was an important force among the Jewish masses in Subcarpathian Rus'."[80] Similarly, Vít Strobach argues that in the 1930s, the Communist Party's anti-fascism attracted an increasing number of Jews.[81] One can also point to Jews in prominent positions in the Communist movement, such as political leaders Josef Guttmann (1902–1958) and Pavel Reiman (1902–1976) as well as journalists and editors Ivan Olbracht and Kurt Konrad (1908–1941). Some memoirs of Communist activists also appear "populated" with Jews.[82] Furthermore, it is perhaps a logical assumption that Jews would turn to the political left in light of an increasingly radical antisemitism. These observations might describe some Communist circles accurately, but they are hardly evidence of large numbers of Jews signing up for party membership or being fellow travelers in the interwar years. Indeed, one of the few studies that have examined left-wing leaderships in interwar Czechoslovakia suggests otherwise. While Jews were overrepresented in leadership positions on the political left, they had a much stronger presence in the country's German Social Democratic Party than in the Communist Party, at least until the 1930s, when they were about the same. Yet, it still remains unclear to what extent the leadership reflected the identities of voters and rank-and-file members.[83]

Thus, in light of the limited evidence available, it seems reasonable to assume, as historians have for other parts of Central and Eastern Europe, that while many Communists were Jews, most Jews were not Communists.[84] In Weimar Germany, the historian Karen Hartewig has argued, Zionism and Communism were Jews' options for radical political involvement. "Nonetheless," she concludes, "Communism remained the cause of no more than a very small minority among Jews."[85] The *perception* that young Jews were flocking to Communism was widely shared among Zionists in the 1920s and '30s. Zionists leaders felt under siege by Communists and worried continuously about Communist infiltration in the Zionist youth movement. It was a fear that shaped Zionist activism in important ways.[86]

In Czechoslovakia, Po'ale Tsiyon did not recover from the split between its pro- and anti-Communist wings in 1920 until almost a decade later. Yet, in the 1920s, the party's socialist Zionist tradition and ideology were carried forward by the Zionist youth movements, Tekhelet Lavan, Ha-Shomer ha-Tsa'ir, and He-Ḥaluts. According to the recollections of members from Tekhelet Lavan, the Zionist youth movement became the front line in the battle between Zionism and Communism in Czechoslovakia. They remember this fight as bitter and persistent and "as the most difficult of all."[87] This was in part because of these Zionists' and Communists' shared Marxist ideology. One activist recalls that "our most bitter struggles we waged against the Jewish Communists who used any anti-Zionist material they could lay their hands on quoting first and foremost from the writings of Lenin and Stalin. . . . All the generations of our youth movement were engaged in this a most bitter war of Communists against Zionism."[88] But the struggle was also bitter, because this was a familiar enemy. In the 1920s, the socialist Zionist groups experienced waves of "defections" to the Communist movement. At times, Heinrich Hoffmann remembered, one member would leave and an entire group would follow suit. Thus, the battle waged was against people who had been friends and fellow aspiring pioneers. It was a struggle that caused tension and anxiety among youth activists and resulted in a "bloodletting" that Zionist youth leaders were never really able to stop.[89]

SOVIET JEWISH NATION BUILDING

In the 1920s, the anxiety about young Jews' attraction to Communism, the sense of inferiority and vulnerability expressed by Zionist activists, was connected to simultaneous developments in the Soviet Union and Palestine. Indeed, the initial euphoria and optimism among Zionists sparked by the Balfour Declaration in 1917 was soon replaced by despair, infighting, and a growing panic that the Soviet Union would replace Palestine as the Promised Land. Even though the Soviet leadership, at home and abroad, generally rejected the notion that Jews constituted a nation, at times the Soviet state pursued policies that appeared to recognize a Jewish nation – that indeed appeared to be Jewish nation-building projects.

The first of these undertakings was launched in 1924 with a plan to create a network of Jewish agricultural settlements in the Ukraine and in the Crimea. The goal was to settle half a million Jews in modern farm cooperatives.[90] By the summer of 1925, 130,000 Jews were settled on the land.[91] Funded by the American Joint Distribution Committee's Agro-Joint, the Soviet settlements threatened to usurp Palestine as the solution to the Jewish Question. For socialist Zionists, some of whom left Palestine for the Ukraine, it appeared as if a Jewish proletariat could be created faster and in greater numbers there than elsewhere. Furthermore, at a time when Jewish society in Palestine was facing a severe economic crisis, unemployment, and a lack of "human material" or new immigrants, American Jewry chose to underwrite the Soviet Jewish project in addition to the Zionist one. The enthusiasm for the Soviet cooperatives among Jews in the Diaspora shocked the socialist Zionist movement and created a panic among Zionist leaders in Palestine.[92]

Although the Crimean project faltered by 1927, the Soviet authorities soon revealed plans for a Jewish colonization area in the far east of the Soviet Union, known as Birobidzhan. In Soviet propaganda, Birobidzhan was promoted as an alternative Jewish homeland and a direct competitor to Palestine. At the same time, the regime embarked on a more intense anti-Zionist course. The last remaining Zionist organizations in the Soviet Union, Po'ale Tsiyon Left and He-Ḥaluts, which had been part of the Crimean colonies, were disbanded in 1928 as part of a broader antinationalist campaign in the late 1920s.[93] In 1930, the Yevsektia, the Jewish section of the Communist Party that had spearheaded the internal anti-Zionist campaign, was liquidated. Birobidzhan did not generate the same kind of enthusiasm at home and abroad as the earlier Jewish colonization project, but it was a significant Soviet and Communist propaganda tool.[94]

In Czechoslovakia, this new, more intense Soviet anti-Zionism was felt in the Communist press, especially in the wake of the August 1929 violence in Palestine. As tensions between Arabs and Jews boiled over in the Mandate, the Communist daily *Rudé Právo* declared that "our sympathies are on the side of the oppressed Arab and Jewish workers and agricultural laborers in Palestine, but we must say to all Jewish workers that the current situation was caused by the Jewish population's role as 'British garrison.'"[95] With the crisis in Palestine and a new Jewish colonization project under way in the Soviet Union, Zionist youth was shaken. Amos Sinai recalls, "We were troubled by Communist propaganda which presented Birobidzhan in opposition to Palestine. . . . As we saw it, the Communists first tried to instill doubts in the minds of youngsters concerning Zionist fulfillment and to proceed from doubt to despair. Then they replaced democratic socialism with dogmatic Communism. This was the way of working among Jewish youth in an effort to bring about Red Assimilation."[96] For some Zionists, the Communist onslaught demanded a response, and in Czechoslovakia, it was members of Po'ale Tsiyon who took the lead.[97] Among them was a Ukrainian-Jewish immigrant, Solomon Goldelman.

ZIONISTS FIGHT BACK: SOLOMON GOLDELMAN AND THE ZIONIST COUNTEROFFENSIVE

In the early 1930s, Solomon Goldelman, an economist and seasoned Po'ale Tsiyonist, began mobilizing a counteroffensive against Communists' anti-Zionist campaign. In the course of the next few years, Goldelman developed a series of strategies intended to stem Communism's inroads among Jewish youth. From his post at the Zionist Propaganda Bureau in Prague's Beth Ha'am, Goldelman launched an education and organization offensive across Czechoslovakia and Central Europe.

Like many other émigrés, Solomon Goldelman's life was shaped by his old and new homes, the Russian Empire, Czechoslovakia, and Palestine. He was born in 1885 in Soroka in western Ukraine. From a well-to-do Jewish family, at seventeen Goldelman moved to Kishinev to complete his secondary education. In Kishinev, he helped establish the local chapter of Po'ale Tsiyon, where he operated under the code name Shalom Kishinever in the then illegal organization.[98] After graduating in 1907, Goldelman went to study economics at the Commercial Institute in Kiev.[99] By the time the First World War broke out in August 1914, the recently graduated Goldelman was working as an assistant at the institute. In 1915, he was appointed to head up the "Bureau of Employment for the Southwestern Front," an office set up to find work for war refugees. In wake of the revolution in March 1917, Goldelman became the director of the Central Labor Office in Kiev. That year Goldelman, as a representative of Po'ale Tsiyon, joined in the Central Rada, the provisional Ukrainian territorial assembly. Opposed to the Bolshevik takeover in November 1917, the Rada declared Ukrainian independence, signing a separate peace treaty with the Central Powers in January 1918.[100] In the dramatic and unstable months that followed, Goldelman served as secretary of labor and later as secretary of the Ministry of National Minorities in the briefly independent Ukrainian government.[101] In December 1918, he married the statistician Miriam Waksman (b. 1891), whom Goldelman had met at university and who had worked with him in Kiev. After a harrowing and tumultuous escape from the Ukraine, Goldelman and his wife found themselves in exile in Vienna in the summer of 1920.[102]

At that time, in Czechoslovakia, the Masaryk government, eager to assume a role in shaping the New Europe, was preparing a major effort to assist refugees from the Russian Empire. Launched in 1921, the "Russian Action" (*Ruská akce*) was intended to create a new elite ready to assume power in a post-revolutionary Russia. Run by the Ministry of Foreign Affairs, the Russian Action funded education and agricultural training programs for Ukrainian, Russian, and Belorussian émigrés in Czechoslovakia, a community of about twenty-five thousand people by 1925.[103] Many of these "Russians" were writers and intellectuals. In those years, Prague became known as the "Russian Oxford."[104] They were joined by thousands of workers, tradespeople, and peasants in the early 1920s.[105]

Among the émigrés were Ukrainian nationalists, socialists and conservatives, who jumped at the opportunity to establish state-sponsored education institutions in Prague and elsewhere in Czechoslovakia. They hoped to train a new Ukrainian intellectual, technical, and professional elite ready to assume power once the Bolshevik regime collapsed. In late 1921, Ukrainian activists in Prague began working on plans to create a Ukrainian institution of higher learning in Czechoslovakia, and they invited Solomon Goldelman to be part of the project.[106]

Goldelman, who had seen the Bolshevik regime destroy not only Ukrainian national aspirations, which he supported, but also bitterly divide Po'ale Tsiyon, jumped at the opportunity to resume his political and academic career. In January 1922, the Goldelmans moved to Prague.[107] That fall, they settled in the provincial town Poděbrady/Podiebrad, just fifty kilometers east of Prague, where the Ukrainian Commerce Academy had been established. Poděbrady/Podiebrad became the Goldelmans' home for the next seven years.[108]

As a Jewish member of the Ukrainian social democratic movement, Goldelman walked a fine line. During the Civil War in Russia and in the years that followed, relations between Jewish and Ukrainian activists in Europe deteriorated dramatically. Jewish activists accused Ukrainian nationalist forces of planning and perpetrating large-scale pogroms, while anti-Communist Ukrainians blamed Jews for supporting the Bolsheviks during the Civil War. Goldelman blamed the Bolsheviks for what he saw as the intertwined Ukrainian and Jewish tragedies. For him, Bolshevik opposition to Ukrainian independence had destroyed the prospects for a pluralistic, independent Ukraine and created a chaotic situation in which Jews fell victim to unprecedented violence. Goldelman disputed what many Jews believed at the time, that the Ukrainian nationalist leader Symon Petliura (1879–1926) was behind the devastating pogroms in the Ukraine, when at least fifty thousand Jews were killed. This was an unpopular position among many Jews, for which Goldelman was once verbally assaulted by Jewish students. During a lecture in Prague in 1924, they accused him of associating with *pogromchiki*.[109]

This episode aside, Goldelman appeared to have little to do with Jewish politics during his years in Poděbrady/Podiebrad. According to his own recollections, he devoted himself to teaching and research on general economic issues and on Jewish economy and sociology in the Ukraine.[110] Like his colleagues, he followed developments in the Soviet Union closely. By 1926, the Czechoslovak government began scaling back the funding for the Russian Action, which far exceeded the support offered by any other government, yet some support did continue.[111] By then, members of the émigré intelligentsia, including Goldelman, who depended on Czechoslovak government sponsorship for their livelihoods, had to rethink their futures. In late 1929, the Goldelmans moved to Prague in search of new opportunities.[112]

Although he continued to teach at the Ukrainian Commerce Academy in Poděbrady/Podiebrad and at Prague's Ukrainian Sociological Institute, Goldelman would spend the majority of the next decade deeply involved in the Zionist movement.[113] In fact, within a few years, he would become the main champion and organizer of Zionist education in Czechoslovakia. In 1929, at the time of his move to Prague, Goldelman joined the newly resurrected Po'ale Tsiyon and entered into the city's Zionist circles.[114] Writing in German, he contributed to *Selbstwehr* beginning in October 1931.[115] By then, he was also acting as the official spokesman for Po'ale Tsiyon. He began lecturing widely on topics of Jewish sociology and economics and the Jewish workers' movement in Palestine.[116] Goldelman remained committed to Marxist theory in his political and scholarly work. Unlike some socialist Zionists, he was a sharp, outspoken critic of Soviet Communism, and he reserved a particular hatred for Jewish Communists.

THE PROPAGANDA WAR BETWEEN COMMUNIST AND ZIONISTS

It was Communist circles in Germany that produced some of the most damaging anti-Zionist propaganda. In 1928, German communists established Geserd (Gesellschaft für die Landansiedlung werkstätigen Juden), a German branch of the Society for the Rural Placement of Jewish Toilers (OZET), the Soviet organization promoting Jewish colonization projects in Crimea. Although Geserd's purpose was to promote the new Soviet Jewish project in Birobidzhan, according to the historian George

L. Mosse, it soon became the leading Communist forum for the discussion of the Jewish Question, sponsoring lectures on and discussion of Communism and Zionism. At its helm stood Otto Heller (1897–1945). Born in Brno/Brünn into a wealthy Jewish family, Heller was a founding member of the Communist Party in Czechoslovakia. In the early 1920s, he was the editor for *Vorwärts,* the party's German-language newspaper published in Liberec/Reichenberg in northern Bohemia. Heller moved to Berlin in the mid-1920s, where he continued to write for the leading Communist papers. Having been dismissed from his post due to "some disagreement with the party," Heller's appointment to lead Geserd in 1928 was his return to the leading circles in the Communist fold, and he towed the party line faithfully.[117]

In 1931, Heller published *Der Untergang des Judentums* (The Decline of Jewry), known as "the breviary of the Geserd," since it was the only German-language Communist book on the Jewish Question.[118] In it, Heller argued, according to orthodox Marxist doctrine, capitalist society had created the conditions for Jews' assimilation. "Modern capitalism has destroyed the monopolistic economic position of Jews, disbanded the ghetto, uprooted religion," and, he declared, "unmasked the [Jewish] nation as a fiction."[119] With the end of capitalism and the advent of socialism, Jews would vanish as a separate group and become fully part of a new humanity. Heller, like Lenin and Stalin, insisted that Jewish nationality must be denied.[120] Indeed, he argued, while Jewish nationalism, and Zionism especially, was touted as the beginning of a new era in Jewish history, "Zionism is nothing more than the phenomenon that one can observe in someone on their deathbed who is filled for a moment with a new will to life just before they die."[121] Dismissing the Jewish society in Palestine as an imperialist and anachronistic project, Heller pointed to the August 1929 riots, "a large-scale pogrom against Jews," as the "the first fruit" of the collaboration between Zionists and British imperialists.[122]

The second half of the book was devoted to the Jewish colonization projects in the Soviet Union, and as George L. Mosse points out, Heller had to engage in "mental gymnastics" in order for readers not to confuse this with Soviet recognition of a Jewish nationality.[123] Heller presented Birobidzhan, a region to be settled with Jewish farmers and workers, as a step that would facilitate the assimilation of Jews into the Russian proletariat. Heller concluded his critique of Zionism and Jewish nationalism:

> Next year in Jerusalem? History has already answered that question. The Jewish proletarians and starving artisans of Eastern Europe ask a very different question: Next year in Socialism? What is Jerusalem to the Jewish proletarian? Are the harvesters in the Crimea and the tractors in Birobidzhan not of greater importance to the working Jews and non-Jews than Baron Rothschild's wine cellars [and] travel agencies' acclaim for Tel Aviv? Next year in Jerusalem? Next year in the Crimea! Next year in Birobidzhan![124]

A mixture of theoretical discussions and travelogue exulting Jewish life in the Soviet Union and Birobidzhan, Heller's book became an instant classic. Its message was disseminated through print as well as on Heller's lecture circuit throughout German-speaking communities, including Czechoslovakia.[125] On January 26, 1931, Heller spoke before an "enthralled crowd of Prague Jewish Communist men and women" at the city's public library, an event that included formal Zionist responses from none other than Max Brod and the youth activist Heinrich Hoffmann.[126]

Solomon Goldelman attended at least one of Otto Heller's presentations in Liberec/Reichenberg in November 1931.[127] Over the next few years, he devoted much of his work and writing to combating Heller and what Goldelman saw as the Communist movement's frontal attack on Zionism. Goldelman was not the only local Zionist remembered for his anti-Communist activism. Jakob Edelstein, a Po'ale Tsiyonist and a longtime member of the German Social Democratic Party in Teplice-Šanov/Teplitz-Schönau, was known, even though he was not a scholar, for challenging Communist propaganda in Marxist terms.[128] Goldelman was, however, an academic and economist, and he placed all his intellectual resources behind a series of detailed and carefully documented rebuttals of Soviet and Communist propaganda. From the outset, he positioned himself "within the Marxist fold" and worked to convince his audiences that Communists like Otto Heller did not have a monopoly on socialism – indeed, that Marxism and Zionism were not at odds. Goldelman focused on delegitimizing "red assimilation" by countering Communists' denial of Jews' nationhood and by exposing what he saw as the myth of Communism and the Soviet Union as paths to Jews' emancipation.[129]

In his writings, Goldelman drew on a Borochovian blend of Marxist and Zionist theory to show that Jews' nationhood rested in the economic position they inhabited in the Diaspora.[130] In every society, he argued, Jews' place in the economy was defined by the needs of the majority society. This was the fundamental condition that defined the Jewish people's abnormal economic constitution. Even as feudalism was replaced by capitalism, Goldelman contended, Jews' socioeconomic difference from non-Jews *and* the structural similarities among Diaspora Jewries remained constant. Thus, despite their dispersion and apparent differences, Jews shared a particular economic constitution (*Wirtschaftsverfassung*). This defined Jews as a "community of fate" (*Schicksalsgemeinschaft*), a nation.[131]

To make his point in objective terms, and drawing on a wide range of economic and statistical data, Goldelman compared recent developments among Jews in the largely agrarian economies of Romania and Poland to the industrialized societies in Germany and Czechoslovakia. Among these "eastern" and "western" Jewries, he observed the same socioeconomic abnormality. While most Jews were concentrated in commerce and crafts, the majority populations worked in agriculture and, in some cases, industry. While the latter had a proletariat, Jews did not. Across the board, Jews were experiencing an increasing economic marginalization, a process accompanied by intensifying antisemitism.[132] The decline of Diaspora Jewry, Goldelman argued, was indeed on the horizon. The end of the Jewish people, however, was not. With increasing economic competition followed by marginalization and antisemitism, Goldelman argued, Zionists alone held the solution to the Jewish Question. Only the Zionist project in Palestine that sought a social and economic restructuring of Jewish society, Goldelman predicted, "could re-create the conditions for general laws to govern the social and economic life of the Jewish people." Thus, Zionists held the key to Jewish emancipation, since only the creation of a Jewish workers' society in Palestine "will make the Jewish Question vanish [all together]."[133]

Goldelman devoted much of his work to counter a widespread perception among "gullible" Jewish and Zionist audiences that the Soviet

Jewish colonization projects in Crimea and Birobidzhan, what he disparagingly called "Soviet Zionism," constituted an alternative to Palestine.[134] Otto Heller's book and lectures did much to spread the word about the agricultural settlements in Crimea and Birobidzhan. Goldelman responded with articles that aimed to expose these Soviet Jewish nation-building projects as "Greek gifts," as harmful to Jews and merely masking the growing antisemitism and marginalization of Jews in Soviet society.[135]

Writing at a time when the magnitude (and potential) of the German Jewish crisis was beginning to dawn on Zionists, Goldelman warned that Soviet and Communist propaganda was deceiving Jewish donors and refugees alike with tales of Birobidzhan as a refuge.[136] Soviet propaganda presented Birobidzhan, the Soviet Jewish Autonomous Region, a place destined for mass Jewish colonization, as a homeland that would replace Palestine. This was, Goldelman argued, nothing but a tale. It was a bubble that burst once one looked beyond the glossy publicity and compared the numbers of Jews who immigrated to the two competing homelands. Goldelman showed that in the previous five years, between May 1928 and July 1933, 27,000 Jews had emigrated to Birobizdhan. Only 7,000 had settled, while more than 75 percent had returned to their old homes. In that same period, 35,000 Jews had entered Palestine, and 28,000 had remained.[137] Thus, while the Soviet authorities were promising to settle "one hundred thousand Jewish families," and "one million Jews in ten years," the reality was that fewer Jews went, and many decided not to stay in the "forests and swamps" of Birobidzhan.[138] It was clear, Goldelman noted, that Birobidzhan would not replace Palestine. After all, even Jewish Communists had to be forced to settle there.[139]

It was, however, a dangerous distraction. The Birobidzhan project was a tool, a potentially very effective one, Goldelman argued, to syphon off money from Jewish philanthropies eager to assist German and Russian Jews in need. Much like American Jewish funds had been wasted on the failed Crimean settlements, Soviet authorities were now mobilizing donors for Birobidzhan, money that would otherwise have gone to Palestine. Furthermore, he warned, these "Soviet Zionist" projects were luring "many young Jews, in search of answers to Jewish national and general social questions, toward the Moscow saviors for answers."[140]

Thus, Soviet propaganda posed a direct threat to the Zionist project in Palestine by draining its financial resources and human material.[141] And Goldelman was not alone in his concern. Beginning in the fall of 1932, *Selbstwehr* brought a series of articles by Ezriel Carlebach (1909–1956) to its readers. Carlebach, a well-known German-Jewish journalist, traveled in the Soviet Union in the summer of 1932. Upon his return to Germany, he wrote a widely read and highly critical series of articles about Jewish life in the Soviet Union. It appeared in *Selbstwehr* in the winter of 1932–1933.[142]

The Soviet Jewish nation-building projects were dangerous diversions for Jews and Zionists, and so was the Communist promise of universal emancipation, what Goldelman referred to as "red assimilation." Images of Soviet Jews working in factories or on the land, participating in the building of a new society as engineers, doctors, and journalists, the prominence of Jews among the top brass of the Soviet Communist Party, were presented in Soviet publicity and in the writings of Communists and admiring fellow travelers as evidence of the equality and opportunity enjoyed by Jews in Communist society. It was a myth, Goldelman believed, that not only lured young Jews to the red banner but also accounted for the pro-Soviet attitude he detected among broader Jewish audiences, a sympathy that only strengthened as the Soviet Union came to embody anti-fascism.

In a 1937 article entitled "A Russian-German Analogy (Jews and Communism)," Goldelman sought to challenge what he saw as the myth of the Soviet Union as a haven for Jews, as a place of Jewish emancipation and equal opportunity.[143] The Soviet promise rested on the assumption that Jews should assimilate (and thus vanish) into the Russian proletariat. And while Communists advertised the transformation of Soviet Jews into workers and farmers, the realty was that large numbers of Soviet Jews had funneled into white-collar positions as managers, professionals, educators, and journalists. To the naïve observer, this might appear as emancipation, but in reality, Goldelman argued, it was merely a mirage. Rather than making Jews "vanish," Soviet Jews were as conspicuous as ever, distinct in social and economic terms from the majority population. This ascent of Jews in Soviet society was not, Goldelman claimed, unlike that of German Jewry, and signs of its consequences – a marginalization of Jews in the economy and violent antisemitism – were already evident in the Soviet Union. A few years earlier, Jews had been pushed off the factory floor; now, Goldelman observed, they were being purged from the Soviet elite. Indeed, he warned, "the Jewish Question did not emerge out of capitalism and it will not be solved by socialism."[144]

In his memoirs, Goldelman claimed that he reentered Jewish politics in response to Communists' anti-Zionist campaign and in light of the disturbing inroads the movement was making among Jewish youths. Beginning in the early 1930s, he began traveling across the country lecturing on socialist Zionist topics. He founded the Czechoslovak chapter of the League for the Workers of Palestine (Liga für das arbeitende Erez-Israel/Palästina), a forum for lecture, debates, and political activism intended to act as a counterweight and alternative to Communist propaganda (Otto Heller had dismissed the German equivalent founded in 1928 as "fools" [*Dummköpfe*]).[145] Goldelman was convinced that in order to fight back against Communism, Zionism needed intellectual, organizational, and social fortifications. As he returned to Zionist activism, and in pursuit of a livelihood, Goldelman searched for ways in which to gain a firmer financial and institutional footing for his mission.

THE ZIONIST PROPAGANDA BUREAU

Goldelman arrived on the Zionist stage in Prague at a crucial time. Years of crisis in Palestine culminated in the August 1929 riots that caused new obstacles for Jewish emigration. At the same time, there was increasing disagreement within Zionist ranks regarding the future and character of the Jewish homeland in Palestine. In Czechoslovakia, divisions emerged between more assertive left- and right-wing factions that threatened the Zionist movement's carefully cultivated image of ideological neutrality. At the same time, Zionists were facing a dynamic, visible, and well-funded Communist movement that "took advantage of the ideological crisis among the Zionist youth and began attracting young Jews to Communism as a way of resolving the Jewish problem." It was a challenge to Zionism that had left the movement somewhat paralyzed, Goldelman believed, because "even the Zionist leaders in Eastern and

Central Europe were in some degree attracted to Communism by this Bolshevik propaganda of a happy life for Jews in the Soviet Union."[146] To Goldelman it was high time for an assertive Zionist response to young Jews' indifference to and ignorance of Zionism *and* their attraction to Communism, the two intertwined threats that led to "red assimilation."

Goldelman first pitched his idea to the Zionist Executive in Moravská Ostrava/Mährisch Ostrau.[147] To Goldelman, the answer to the crisis in Zionism was to be found in education and organization. Drawing on his experience as a socialist activist, Goldelman envisioned the creation of an ideological center, a youth commission, with strong ties to individual youth groups.[148] The commission would be tasked with propaganda, the production and dissemination of systematic knowledge about Zionism, and the training of individual members entrusted with education in their individual cells. Thus, organization, knowledge, and ideological discipline were the basis for the creation of a Zionist consciousness among youths. As young people searched for answers, the youth group, Goldelman envisioned, would serve to instill a Jewish (national) worldview (*Weltanschaung*).[149] Organizational and ideological discipline, Goldelman suggested, was the most effective defense of Zionist youth against Communism.

Yet, even though the threat of Communism had been a staple on the Zionist Executive's agenda for more than ten years, they were not interested in Goldelman's proposal. He was, after all, a foreigner, who had just recently entered Zionist circles. But Josef Rufeisen, the chair of the Executive and the Zionist Organization, was perhaps also uneasy about Goldelman's affiliation with Po'ale Tsiyon. In a report filed to the Zionist Executive in London in 1932, Rufeisen related his concern that the socialist Zionists were creating dissent and conflict by refusing to commit to a political platform along with other Zionist factions.[150] Much like they had a decade earlier, his report suggested, the socialist Zionists were unwilling to let the class struggle take the backseat to national unity.

Among Zionist leaders in Prague, there was more interest in Goldelman's experience and ideas. By 1932, around the time Goldelman was snubbed by the Zionist central leadership, the local Zionist chapter in Prague was already supporting his publication and lecture activities and had given him office space in Beth Ha'am.[151] One early supporter was Oskar Aschermann (1883–1966), a prominent Prague Zionist, member of the Zionist Executive, and head of the Jewish National Fund in Prague. Aschermann was adamant that "Communist propaganda is a great danger to our Zionist youth" and promoted Goldelman's vision and methods to his Zionist colleagues.[152]

In the spring of 1934, with support from Prague Zionist groups, Goldelman established the Zionist Propaganda Bureau (Sionistická informační služba a poradna/Zionistische Propagandastelle) in Prague.[153] From the outset the bureau was shaped by the needs of its sponsors and the anticipated needs of future ones. This was reflected in the bureau's mission statement "to promote Zionist ideological propaganda, to strengthen Zionist consciousness among youths through a deeper anchoring of their Jewish worldview [Weltanschaung] and to step up their practical work for Zionism and the Zionist foundations."[154] Goldelman emphasized that the bureau was focused on "internal propaganda" that "would strengthen and deepen the commitment to the Zionist idea and our movement within our own ranks."[155] And Goldelman did not lose sight of his own financial dependency on the bureau. From the outset, he made a plan that would ensure the bureau's financial independence within a few years, a plan that was reflected in the bureau's structure of multiple divisions: a Zionist School for Continuing Education (Sionistická lidová vysoká škola/Zionistische Volkshochschule), a correspondence school (Kursy písemného vyučování/Fernunterricht), a youth propaganda division (Služba mládeži/Jugendwerbedienst), a publishing house (Sionistická knihovnička/Kleine zionistische Bücherei), a lending library (Zprostředkování sionistické literatury/Vermittelung zionistischer Literatur), a speakers' bureau (Pořádání přednášek a seminářů na venkově/Veranstaltung von Vorträgen und Seminaren in der Provinz), and an information service (Informační služba/Informationsdienst). Indeed, the Zionist Propaganda Bureau, staffed by Goldelman and Leo Meller (c. 1915–?), a member of Tekhelet Lavan, was a multifaceted institution, and it quickly developed into much more than the youth office and information center that Goldelman had initially proposed.[156]

At the heart of the Zionist Propaganda Bureau was the Zionist evening school (*Volkshochscule*), with lectures on Mondays and Thursdays. The lectures were organized into three cycles, and students who completed them graduated with a diploma. The first cycle was entitled "The Problem of Nationality and the Jews" (ten units); the second, "Zionism" (six units); and the third cycle, "Palestine and the Construction of a Jewish homeland" (twelve units) – all in all a total of fifty lectures in the course of two semesters.[157] The units (consisting of one or two lectures) were taught by "the best Zionist minds" as well as by two of Goldelman's Ukrainian colleagues. Olgerd Bockovsky (1884/85–1939) and Panas Fedenko (1893–1981), well-known Ukrainian social democrats, intellectuals, and fellow émigrés, lectured on "The Foundation of the Nationality Question" and "The Nationality Question in the Soviet Union."[158] Max Brod tackled "Race Theory and the Jewish Question," František Friedmann lectured on Jews in Czechoslovakia and the Palestine Mandate, while Goldelman himself focused on Jewish social and economic conditions. Goldelman ensured that Zionist women were given space both on the course program and as lecturers. Mirjam Scheuer (1899–1983), a dentist and longtime Zionist activist, and Hanna Steiner (1894–1944), a social worker and the leader of WIZO (Women's International Zionist Organization), discussed Zionist women's work in Palestine and the Diaspora. The longtime youth activists and members of Tekhelet Lavan Hans Lichtwitz and Heinrich Hoffmann, now with completed doctorates, lectured on the Zionist youth and pioneer movement as well as Zionist attitudes to social questions. Adolf Pollak (1879–1951) and Arthur Bergmann (1881–?), representatives of the Jewish National Fund, covered the work of the Zionist foundations. In short, the Volkshochschule engaged a who's who of Zionism in Czechoslovakia. By 1936, Goldelman was planning a fourth cycle on Jewish history, economy, literature, politics, and religion. The Zionist Volkshochschule was in some ways becoming a forum for Jewish studies, the only such institution in Czechoslovakia and one that resembled, Goldelman boasted, a university environment.[159]

Goldelman's evening school was a real innovation in Prague's Zionist world.[160] It opened in October 1934, with 220 students signed up for the academic year. In his reports, Goldelman estimated that lectures were attended by 90 to 160 students, a retention rate he considered very satisfactory.[161] By the fall term 1936, 330 students were registered.[162] The lectures took place in Beth Ha'am, the Zionist building in the center of Prague. Located in Dlouhá street 41, the six-story, custom-built structure opened to the public in February 1930 and soon became an important Jewish social space in the city.[163] The administrative offices for the Zionist sports and gymnastic clubs, the youth groups, and student societies were housed here along with the Volkshochschule and the Zionist Propaganda Bureau. With the Zionist hangout Cafe Aschermann next door, the editorial offices of *Selbstwehr* and *Židovské zprávy*, a sizable gymnasium used by Maccabi Praha, and a host of Zionist offices, Beth Ha'am was at the heart of the kind of vibrant and dynamic national community that Zionists longed for. Much like the city's Czech National Theater or the German Casino, Beth Ha'am was a public, symbolic statement about Jews' presence as a nationality in Czechoslovakia.[164] With an appropriate distance to the old Jewish quarter's synagogues and cemeteries, but situated in an area where many Jews lived and worked, Beth Ha'am was meant to embody the aspirations of an ancient nation reborn.

While the Volkshochshule formed the basis for the Zionist Propaganda Bureau's other divisions, it was the correspondence school that, in Goldelman's view, would have the greatest impact. The curriculum consisted of the Volkshochschule's three cycles on the Jewish Question, Zionism, and Palestine. The lectures were mailed to subscribers, along with suggestions for further reading and examination questions. Goldelman hoped that in this way Zionist education would reach individuals and groups in even the remotest parts of Czechoslovakia and well beyond its borders. The correspondence school came under way a few months after the Volkshochschule, in December 1934. It had 340 subscribers in its first semester, 190 individuals and 150 "collectives," a variety of Zionist adult and youth groups. While two-thirds of the subscribers lived in Czechoslovakia, there were students in twelve other countries, including Germany, Austria, Hungary, Romania, Palestine and the United States.[165] By October 1935, there were 400 subscribers. By 1936, there were 449 in twenty countries. About three-quarters of the distance-learning students lived in Central Europe, the remainder in other parts of Europe.[166]

Funded in large part by the World Zionist Executive in London and the Jerusalem office of the Jewish National Fund, Goldelman's correspondence school had been tasked with extending Zionist education to all German-speaking Jewish communities, an area that included Germany, Austria, Hungary, and large parts of Czechoslovakia.[167] At a time of deteriorating conditions for Jews in Germany and Poland, increasing interest in immigration, but with a limited numbers of certificates, Zionist leaders were eager to recruit the most suitable people and weed out "opportunists."[168] Goldelman presented his correspondence school as "a real spiritual hakhsharah [*eine richtige geistiges haksharah*]," as an accessible and affordable way of preparing Jews for emigration to Palestine.[169] In his correspondence with his sponsors, Goldelman suggested that graduates of the correspondence school be given priority in certificate allocations and that "the subscribers that have completed all the cycles can take a test. Over time [we] should be able to establish a formal hakhsharah for pioneers and [other] certificate carriers. This will ensure that emigrants to Palestine consist of educated Zionist elements."[170] By 1936, the distance-learning division, now renamed Hachsharah-Korrespondenzschule, ensured, according to Goldelman, the deepening and systematization of Zionist knowledge, for thousands of young and adult Zionists."[171] By 1937, Goldelman began planning for an expansion of the correspondence school into the large Yiddish-speaking communities in neighboring states. At considerable expense to the bureau, Goldelman prepared Yiddish-language editions of the lectures "in an especially simplified form so that they are accessible to as broad a spectrum of youths in the eastern regions."[172] Goldelman even toyed with the idea of opening up a bureau in Warsaw.[173]

Alongside Zionist educational programs, the bureau also ran a publishing house, which distributed inexpensive pamphlets, booklets, and books. Through this division, Goldelman distributed the Volkshochschule lectures as well as many titles on socialist Zionism, Zionist political parties, and Palestine.[174] Some materials were intended as educational ones, while others, on Birobidzhan and "red assimilation," were more directly aimed at countering Communist propaganda.

Goldelman thought of his Zionist activism as a sort of rescue mission.[175] He did not merely blame Jewish youth's disillusionment on the severe economic crisis, unemployment, and rising popular and state-sponsored antisemitism. Youth flocked to Communism, in part, because of Zionist leaders' neglect. While the Zionist Organization supported all the youth movements financially and in equal measure, Zionist youth had been left ideologically adrift. It was thus not a surprise that young Zionists were satisfying their hunger for political activism elsewhere, Goldelman argued. The dangers of "red assimilation" were real, and if the neglect continued, it spelled the end of Zionism and of the Jewish people. As Goldelman declared in a call to action, "The youth belongs to the nation, the future of the nation is their future, [they] are the makers, the pioneers, and the agents of their nation's future."[176]

Through the bureau's youth propaganda division, Goldelman hoped to centralize and strengthen Zionist youth activism. Although the Zionist Propaganda Bureau had no formal authority, the Zionist youth movements were autonomous organizations; Goldelman and his collaborator Leo Meller hoped to rouse youths in a struggle against Zionism's enemies. In a letter "to all youth groups" circulated in May 1935, Goldelman and Meller called on Zionist youth to fight against the "inner enemy of ignorance and apathy."[177] In the tradition of self-criticism, Goldelman and Meller, who "were not afraid to speak the truth," accused youths of being content with "singing and hora dancing" rather than committing themselves to the hard and holy duty of Zionism. Considering the "dangers facing Zionism," they argued, "the inner superficiality of Zionist youth and their indifference to the need for a Jewish homeland is one of our most acute and painful challenges." It was time, they argued, for youths to become activist, responsible, and committed Zionists. They called on youth leaders to "become pioneers of the organization." As disciplined, responsible, and committed Zionists, they were to become a new "parallel type to the pioneers in Palestine."

Goldelman and Meller envisioned these new pioneers, appointed and monitored by their own groups, as responsible for Zionist education on the local level. They encouraged them and their units to sign up for the distance-learning program, advertised the bureau's discounted books and pamphlets, and offered tips on how to decorate meetings rooms with informative posters and other visual materials that the bureau could provide. Goldelman and Meller's initiative was an attempt to solve the tension between Palestine-bound and Diaspora-oriented Zionist youths. While they did not lose sight of the Palestine project, they sought to infuse everyday Zionist activism with meaning, community, and a sense for each individual member that they were participating in the creation of a new society.

In contrast to the interwar tradition for youth autonomy, Goldelman and Meller's vision focused on centralization, obedience, and surveillance. The hearts and minds of young Jews had to be captured early on and guarded diligently, using methods that resembled those of mass youth movements. Indeed, Goldelman and Meller encouraged Zionist youth to assume a more public, assertive, and unified stance. They called for joint campaigns in which Zionist youth across Czechoslovakia participated in "recruitment or battle weeks [against anti-Zionist agitation among Jewish youth], the redemption of a piece of land [in Palestine] through collective fundraising campaigns, and organized Jewish or Zionist holiday celebrations and so on."[178] Youth groups were no longer about independence and rebellion. Rather, Goldelman was pushing a new model in which a centralized leadership demanded unconditional obedience to its ideological vision as well as the individual's submission to the needs of the collective and sacrifice for the greater good. As one Jewish National Fund pamphlet put it, "Youths should be trained in a way so that they willingly give up part of their allowance to the Jewish National Fund, in a way that they understand that even with their limited means, they can also participate in the redemption of land in Palestine."[179]

In the summer of 1937, a satisfied Goldelman reported to his colleagues in Palestine:

> We began the Zionist Propaganda Bureau three years ago convinced that we were filling an important gap in Zionist life. We believed that through our work and activities we could create the financial basis for a further expansion of our activities. Our expectations have been fulfilled. Today our institution enjoys the recognition of the entire Zionist public as well as the material and moral support of the most important Zionist institutions and foundations. We hope that in the future we will be fortunate enough to expand so that the bureau can become the propaganda center for the entire Zionist movement.[180]

In interwar Czechoslovakia, Zionist activists' relationship to Zionist youth and to Palestine was rife with contradictions and tensions.

Zionist youth's idealization of the pioneer – young, strong, and powerful – and the rhetorical and practical dichotomy between old and new Jews, between Jewish power and powerlessness, between activism and passivity, between the past and present, cultivated a self-image of youth as a revolutionary force. For Zionist leaders, it was a double-edged sword. While they were eager to harness the energy of Zionist utopia to mobilize Jewish youth for Zionism, they were uncomfortable with its revolutionary implications. "The negation of the Diaspora" alienated from Zionism those young Jews who felt at home in Czechoslovakia at precisely the moment when their national and political consciousness was being shaped. And since the young Zionist elite was bent on emigration, the Zionist movement would be left without a new generation of leaders *and* with few prospects of becoming a mass movement. In short, "Palestinocentrism" threatened to undermine the Zionist project in Czechoslovakia.

Furthermore, even as Zionist leaders supported the work of a radical minority within the youth movements that focused on emigration, they remained committed to Jewish national life in the Diaspora. Their fear of "red assimilation" reflected anxiety about the instability of national boundaries and uncertainty with regard to the future of Jewish national life. Creating national spaces was a difficult undertaking. As they faced off with what they saw as the stronger enemy, the dynamic Communist movement, Zionist activists increasingly adopted their opponents' successful methods of propaganda and agitation. Goldelman's Zionist Propaganda Bureau sought to create a new form of political Jewish community, educating a Jewish national elite, and creating a tight network of groups disseminating this knowledge further and working in the day to day to build a Zionist consciousness among the Jewish "masses." Rather than autonomy, personal self-transformation, and an intimate youth community, this Zionist political culture emphasized discipline, ideological education, and surveillance. By the mid-1930s, Zionist activists formally abandoned non-partisanship and neutrality in favor of an alliance with the Czechoslovak Social Democratic Party, considered to be the moderate and patriotic left. For Zionists, as much as this alliance was a united front against the radical right, it was also a defense against the radical left.

* * *

By the summer of 1938, as war with Germany loomed on the horizon, Zionist education and emigration gained new urgency. The struggle against Communism faded in the months that followed as Goldelman and other activists threw themselves into frantic efforts to secure and distribute certificates for Palestine for as many Jews as possible, meanwhile contemplating their own and their families' future.

In mid-August 1939, Miriam and Solomon Goldelman went to Poděbrady/Podiebrad to visit with old friends and to say their goodbyes. On August 24, 1939, the couple left the Protectorate of Bohemia and Moravia for the Port of Trieste. Two weeks later they arrived in Haifa. When they disembarked, they discovered that most of what they owned, everything they had shipped, including Goldelman's extensive library, his published and unpublished work, diplomas, and manuscripts, had been confiscated or lost. They were penniless.[181] Goldelman assumed that his reputation as an educator and organizer would precede him and that he would be offered opportunities for work. But as he soon discovered, "in Palestine, no one had heard of a Ukrainian institution of higher learning in Czechoslovakia."[182] His contacts in the World Zionist Organization were of little help, and the Goldelmans found themselves spending all their energy on setting up a "primitive" household and learning Hebrew.

Within a year, however, Goldelman was active in Zionist education again. Always the fierce anti-Communist, when the German attack on the Soviet Union in June 1941 created a groundswell of pro-Soviet enthusiasm in Palestine, he struck out yet again on a campaign against "red assimilation." In his recollections, Goldelman's disillusionment was palpable. In recounting how during his early days in Jerusalem, one Prague colleague, told him, "Here people are turned into non-entities," Goldelman commented, "It is even worse. Here non-entities transform people into non-entities."[183] Although he had always been able to overcome "personal difficulties and misunderstandings (alongside moral and ideological successes)," Goldelman soon learned that here the opposite was true, "the independence of my character, and my feeling of self-respect – these qualities for which I was held in high esteem by non-Jews with whom I had worked for such a long time – became an obstacle for me in the country of my forefathers."[184]

Goldelman's disillusionment was not as much an ideological as a personal one. Despite his socialist Zionist commitment, Goldelman appears to have felt deeply alienated in Palestine. He did not speak the language; he was isolated, marginalized, and repulsed by the primitive conditions in the country. In short, "life was very difficult in Israel for the Goldelmans."[185] In the 1950s, when the political and economic conditions allowed for it, the Goldelmans renewed their contacts with Ukrainian émigré circles in Munich and traveled as much as they could in Europe on their small pension. In the mid-1960s, Goldelman withdrew from public life, with a sense that his generation had been "thrown out of the old junk pile, no longer useful or needed."[186] Much like the returning pioneers, Ri's real-life comrades, for Goldelman the Promised Land was not home after all.

Epilogue

"THE STORM OF BARBARISM"

ON MARCH 30, 1938, EMIL KAFKA (1880–1948), THE CHAIRMAN OF Prague's oldest Jewish community, and the community board gathered for their regular monthly meetings in the Jewish town hall. In his opening address, the prominent lawyer and Czech-Jewish activist turned his attention to the darkening political skies. At the time, Austrian-Jewish refugees were crossing the border seeking safe haven in Czechoslovakia and bringing with them harrowing tales of persecution and public humiliation at the hands of their neighbors and the German invaders. The unease among Jews in the Bohemian Lands was palpable, but Kafka reassured his colleagues that *here* things would be different. Invoking the memory of the Swedish army threatening Prague in 1648, Kafka reminded his fellow board members that back then Jews and Christians rebuffed their enemy by standing together. He noted:

> For more than one thousand years, Prague Jews have lived in this ancient place. Czech and Jews shared a common fate in good times and in bad ones. In this city, we have survived many dangers. The ancient symbol of the Prague Jewish community, the Swedish hat, remains a visible symbol of our unity in past defensive struggles. . . . We pledge that in this moment, we stand as one with the entire Czechoslovak nation, that we will devote all our strength to the grand task of ensuring peace, internal and external peace. . . . Without hesitation we will bring any sacrifice that is required of us.[1]

Standing at attention, the board applauded Kafka's words urging Jews to be ready to act yet remain calm. In the months that followed – as the crisis in the German-dominated borderlands loomed, as the army mobilized, and as people were called upon to prepare for war by donating money for defense, practicing evacuation drills, and preparing air-raid shelters – Kafka's vision for Czechoslovak unity was put to a test. When Germany annexed the Sudetenland in early October and as Hungary subsequently assumed control of southern Slovakia and later Subcarpathian Rus', thousands of refugees fled to Czechoslovakia's interior. Fifteen to twenty thousand Jews left the German-occupied areas for safety mainly in Bohemia and Moravia.[2] This new wave of refugees added to the pressure on Jewish social welfare, refugee, and other communal organizations in the Bohemian Lands already stretched by years of humanitarian efforts on behalf of German and Austrian Jews.[3]

Furthermore, that summer and fall, Jews in the Bohemian Lands and Slovakia faced a powerful wave of antisemitism that intensified after Czechoslovakia suffered territorial losses.[4] Jews were attacked in the press, fired from their jobs, and harassed in public. Jewish leaders implored German-speaking refugees from the Sudeten areas not to gather or speak to each other in public places, in order to avoid "irritating the Czechs."[5] This popular hostility was compounded by the new Czech authorities' initial refusal to grant Jewish organizations access to British funds intended to alleviate the refugee crisis and other hardships caused by the loss of the borderlands. By early November 1938, Emil Kafka's trust in the unity of Czechs and Jews had been severely shaken. His optimism was replaced by shock and dismay at the vehement anti-Jewish sentiments expressed by Czechs. Speaking to his board for the first time since mid-September, when war had seemed imminent, Kafka lamented:

> The Munich Agreement harmed the Czechoslovak nation. And to a large degree, it has hurt us Jews. We mourn alongside the Czech nation, and we mourn the sudden change in attitude among Czechs toward Jews living here in our dear homeland. You have all experienced the kind of anti-Jewish sentiment that is spreading here. Perhaps it is a reflection of what is going on elsewhere, perhaps it is a reaction to recent events, but we, Jews, we don't deserve it![6]

Kafka, who considered himself a Czech, ascribed the growing antisemitism to confusion, to the state of shock in which Czechs found themselves. He trusted that once the Czech nation "finds itself again," conditions for Jews would improve.

Within months of Kafka's mournful speech, Czechoslovakia had ceased to exist. Its territory divided among its neighbors and its people living under German or Hungarian rule or in a new, independent and antisemitic Slovakia. Soon the Jews of Czechoslovakia found themselves separated by new borders. Yet, they all faced intensifying public and popular antisemitism and an onslaught of anti-Jewish policies intended to dispossess and isolate them from society at large. While many left – an estimated twenty-seven thousand Jews fled the Bohemian Lands by the end of 1940 – most remained behind.[7]

In the Bohemian Lands, Jewish activists – many of whom had worked for years, as we have seen, to secure Jewish continuity and integrate Jews into the fabric of Czechoslovak society – now faced the choice whether to stay or to seek refuge elsewhere in Europe, Palestine, Shanghai, or the Americas. For Zionists, this choice was particularly acute. For some, the deteriorating conditions for Jews were a historical inevitability. For others, it spelled a more temporary crisis, one that demanded exceptional leadership. Unlike most Jews considering their options for emigration, Zionist activists had access to immigration certificates to Palestine through the World Zionist Organization and thus had a way out. But, like others, they were weighing the pros and cons of emigration, the uncertainties at home and elsewhere, and the responsibility to family and community.

Some Zionists left for Palestine, others for England. Many remained. Even for longtime Zionists, the decision to emigrate to Palestine was not one made easily. Max Brod, known not only as a critic and author but also as a Zionist ideologue in the 1920s and '30s, wanted to go to the United States. As the historian Gaëlle Vassogne shows, in the fall of 1938, Max Brod contacted the director of the New York Public Library.[8] In return for employment and hence a U.S. visa, Brod offered the library Franz Kafka's papers. As he anxiously awaited the American's response, which was negative, Brod made the decision to leave for Palestine by way of Poland. He did so, with Kafka's papers tucked into his suitcase, on a train that passed through Moravská Ostrava/Mährisch Ostrau just before the German army closed the border. It was March 14, 1939.

In what now became the Protectorate of Bohemia and Moravia, Jewish leaders scrambled to respond simultaneously to the needs of Jews and the demands of the German authorities. Within a few weeks of the occupation, chairs of Jewish communities across Bohemia and Moravia, asked the Prague leadership to act on their behalf as the representative of all Jews.[9] If the previous years had been characterized by bitter power struggles between Prague and other communities and by resistance to giving up local independence in favor of a centralized Jewish authority, now Jewish leaders were quick to unite. In this moment of crisis, they agreed, Jewish unity and solidarity was the best response. From then on, the Prague community oversaw a massive social assistance and refugee effort as well as the daunting task of negotiating with hostile German and Czech authorities. Among its first tasks was to provide the authorities with a detailed report about the Jewish population in Bohemia, Moravia, and Slovakia. No one knew what policies were forthcoming, but the threatening pose of the authorities was unmistakable. Proud of the trust invested in the Prague leadership, Emil Kafka promised, "Prague has always been ready."

Unlike in Germany, where anti-Jewish legislation and practices gradually made life intolerable for the country's Jews, in Bohemia and Moravia, Jews were hit with the full force of Nazi persecution almost overnight, an experience similar to that of Austrian Jews. While the Munich Crisis had unleashed popular antisemitism and government-sponsored efforts to take charge of Jewish-owned corporations, the German occupation brought with it physical attacks on Jews as well as a barrage of anti-Jewish policies. By late June 1939, the Nuremberg Laws were in effect and the "Aryanization" of Jewish property under way. Jews were denied access to public spaces such as parks, cinemas, and theaters; were restricted in their use of public transit and city streets; and had to abide by a curfew that restricted them to their homes at eight o'clock in the evening. From then on, a myriad of initiatives meant to isolate Jews from the rest of the population followed in a steady stream.[10]

In Prague, a new partnership emerged between Zionist and Czech-Jewish activists working within the community. Many Zionist leaders, such as Angelo Goldstein, Emil Margulies, and Josef Rufeisen, left in the months after the Munich Crisis, and more followed after the German occupation. Others such, as Franz Kahn (1895–1944), the longtime secretary of the Czechoslovak Zionist Organization, and Paul März from Moravská Ostrava/Mährisch Ostrau, relocated to Prague. Here, März, Kahn, Jakob Edelstein, František Friedmann, and Otto Zucker (1892–1944), an activist from Brno/Brünn – the most prominent Zionists remaining – joined forces with Czech-Jews Emil Kafka and František Weidmann (1910–1944).[11] These men oversaw the efforts to meet German demands for Jewish emigration – a process that carefully and meticulously stripped emigrating Jews of everything they owned – and to care for the Jews that remained. During the summer of 1939, Prague Jewish leaders negotiated with international Jewish organizations to fund the emigration of Jews from the Protectorate. Thus, in July 1939, František Friedmann and Emil Kafka traveled to Paris for meetings with the Joint Distribution Committee, an undertaking sanctioned by the German authorities. While Friedmann returned to Prague, Kafka went on to London for more aid negotiations in late July.[12] Unlike Friedmann, Kafka remained abroad.

At first, the Germans' efforts to force Jews into emigration, paradoxically, reinvigorated the Jewish community in the Protectorate. Emigration and the confiscation of Jews' property were priorities for the German authorities and thus demanded most of the Jewish leadership's attention. Vocational programs, language courses, agricultural training, and efforts to secure visas for Jews to Denmark, Britain, Shanghai, and the Americas consumed the community's resources. At the same time, Jewish teachers, gymnastic instructors, doctors, and administrators also sought to bolster a positive sense of Jewishness amid the intensifying persecution. In the winter of 1938–1939, Zionist activists and educators such as Jakob Edelstein, Solomon Goldelman, and Hanna Steiner organized language and vocational programs as well as theater, reading groups, and lectures aimed at strengthening prospective emigrants' Zionist commitment. Although Zionist leaders were somewhat uncomfortable with many people's sudden interest in emigrating to Palestine, they embraced the opportunity to strengthen Zionism especially among Jewish youths. Much as the threat from the German authorities paved the way for Jewish communal centralization and unity, in these early months, as more Jews joined Zionist programs and activities, the socioeconomic and cultural regeneration that Zionists had pursued in the decades earlier appeared within reach.[13]

The Jewish community mobilized enormous resources to assist the majority of Jews that either could not or would not leave the Bohemian Lands. Communal offices provided financial assistance and employment opportunities for Jews displaced from the borderlands, fired from their jobs, unable to practice their professions, or whose business had been "Aryanized." Now Jewish schools were overflowing with students eager to attend an environment less hostile than their public schools. Before long, the remaining Jewish children were expelled from their non-Jewish schools. Since many non-Jewish sports and gymnastics clubs, among them the widely popular Sokol, had expelled their Jewish members already before the German occupation, the Jewish sports clubs such as Maccabi and Hagibor assumed a central role in many young Jews' lives. Similarly, as more public spaces were off-limits to Jews, Jewish sports facilities, gymnasiums, schools, and community centers, such as Beth Ha'am in Prague, and other Jewish institutions became sites for employment, education, culture, and community. Even Jewish cemeteries came to life as Jewish children, young people, and families, excluded from the city's green spaces, sought respite from a society in which they were simultaneously isolated and exposed.

In the fall of 1941, the German authorities halted all emigration efforts. By mid-October 1941, thousands of Jews from Prague, Moravská Ostrava/Mährisch Ostrau, and Brno/Brünn were deported to ghettos and labor camps in Łódź, Riga, Minsk, and other cities in the German-occupied east. In Prague, Jewish leaders were tasked with the creation of the Protectorate's first and only ghetto in the fortress town of Terezín/Theresienstadt, about forty miles northwest of Prague. By December 1941, Jakob Edelstein took charge of the ghetto as the head of the German-appointed Jewish Council. Two years earlier, Edelstein had witnessed the brutal and chaotic deportation of Jews to Nisko, a failed German attempt at "resettling" Jews in Poland. He and his colleagues in Prague hoped that the ghettoization of the Jewish population in Terezín/Theresienstadt would prevent further deportations to the east and keep their community in the Protectorate. They were unaware that the Germans merely intended Terezín/Theresienstadt to become a transit point for transports to the killing centers in Poland. Thus, as Edelstein and Otto Zucker relocated to Terezín/Theresienstadt, they set out to make the ghetto a useful and valuable source of labor for the Germans. Edelstein's strategy, "Jewish work to save Jewish lives," was similar to the ones pursued by other ghetto leaderships in German-occupied Eastern Europe.[14] It was, however, as Livia Rothkirchen notes, the only ghetto leadership dominated by Zionists. Within the confines of the ghetto, they pursued Zionist priorities such as youth education and vocational training.[15] As in other ghettos in German-controlled territory, the Jewish Council's efforts to save their communities were to no avail even though they might have contributed to the survival of individuals. By early 1943, Edelstein and his colleagues were increasingly sidelined. On December 18, 1943, Edelstein, his wife Miriam (1908–1944), and twelve-year-old son Ari (1931–1944) were deported to Auschwitz. They were murdered there the following summer.

As ghetto elder, Edelstein had received the majority of the Protectorate's Jews in the Terezín/Theresienstadt in the course of 1942 and watched as thousands of them were sent on "to the east." By early 1943, almost all of the few thousands Jews who remained in Prague and elsewhere in Bohemia and Moravia were ones married to non-Jews and these couples' young children, protected from deportation by their "Aryan" ties.

As in the Bohemian Lands, the destruction of Slovakia's Jewish communities happened in stages. Here, between March and October 1942, the local Slovak authorities rounded up and handed over 57,000 (more than half of the country's Jews) to the Germans, who sent them to Auschwitz, Majdanek, and Sobibor for immediate extermination. After this first wave of deportations, the Slovak authorities stalled the deportation of the remaining 24,000 Jews for almost two years.[16] They, as well as most Jews living under Hungarian control, remained out of reach of the Germans until late spring and summer 1944, when the German army occupied first Hungary and then Slovakia. Before the end of that year, Germans deported about half of the remaining Jews in Slovakia as well as 140,000 from former Czechoslovak areas occupied by Hungary.[17]

In the Protectorate of Bohemia and Moravia, as the German authorities deported the Jewish population, spaces that had once been part of the fabric of the communities were converted into holding pens for the material remains of Jewish life. The old and new synagogues, once centers of religious life, were transformed into warehouses crammed full of objects stolen from the deported Jews and their communities. The Jewish schools, community centers, and sports facilities, which had embodied the emergence of a new form of Jewish society in the interwar years and offered respite for Jews during the first years of German occupation, were turned into storage facilities and forced labor camps. Thus, the pride of Prague Zionists, Beth Ha'am, became a depository for rugs, and the Hagibor stadium was turned into an internment camp and labor site for Jews married to non-Jews and people of mixed ancestry from across the Protectorate.[18] In the course of 1944, as many non-Jewish spouses were interned, people who had hitherto been protected from deportation by way of their "mixed marriage" were deported to Terezín/Theresienstadt.

One of the few Jews who remained in Prague until the end of the war was František Friedmann. His marriage to Catholic Hana Silvanová in 1929 had for all intents and purposes cost him a leadership position in the Zionist movement in Czechoslovakia and strained his relationship with some Zionists in the 1930s.[19] Yet, in the aftermath of the Munich Crisis, Friedmann took the lead in negotiating the so-called Czech Transfer, a program using British funds to enable the emigration of twenty-five hundred to three thousand Jews to Palestine in the spring and summer of 1939. By doing so, Friedmann earned the admiration of his Zionist colleagues. In an interview published in February 1939, Jakob Edelstein emphasized that Friedmann acted "as a genuine and courageous Zionist" during these difficult times.[20] In the wake of the German occupation, Friedmann took on the chairmanships of various Jewish organizations (among them Maccabi ČSR), traveled abroad to negotiate assistance from the American Jewish Joint Distribution Committee and other relief organizations, oversaw the community's finances, and met with German officials on behalf of the Protectorate's Jews.[21] In January and June 1943, the German authorities deported the chairmen of Prague's Jewish Council, first František Weidmann and then Salo Krämer (1899–1944), neither of whom were protected by a non-Jewish spouse. Friedmann now assumed this position and remained at the helm of Prague's Jews until the end of the German occupation in early May 1945.[22] By then, he was gravely ill, yet involved in plans to reestablish the city's Jewish community in the wake of the German defeat.[23] Friedmann died at the end of May 1945, leaving behind his wife and two children.

Edelstein and Friedmann responded to the onslaught of German persecution by drawing on their experiences as activists, elected officials, and administrators. While they sought to keep the ship afloat at home in the Bohemian Lands, their colleagues in Britain and Palestine worked to maintain the partnership between Zionists and the Czech elite, now in exile in London.

Although less than 10 percent of the Jews who left Czechoslovakia in the wake of the Munich Crisis went to Palestine, most of the country's Zionist leaders and activists emigrated to the British Mandate. These emigrants included the chair of Czechoslovakia's Zionist Organization, Josef Rufeisen; the leader of German-speaking Zionists and former chair of the Jewish Party, Emil Margulies, and his successor at the helm of the party, Arnošt Frischer (1897–1954); the parliamentarian Angelo Goldstein; Maccabi leaders Arthur Herzog and Beda Brüll; as well as the Prague Zionists Norbert Adler, Gustav Fleischmann, and Solomon Goldelman. For them, Palestine was an immediate opportunity for escape and, for some, offered the possibility of continuing their work within familiar Zionist circles. By the end of 1939, there were between six thousand and seven thousand Czechoslovak citizens in Palestine.[24]

Before long, it became clear that the delicate balance of patriotism and Jewish nationalism upheld by Zionists in Czechoslovakia could no longer be maintained. Tension between exiled Czech and Jewish leaders erupted almost immediately. In October 1939, a row broke out over whether Czechoslovak male citizens in Palestine should volunteer for the newly formed Czechoslovak army units in France and Britain or await the establishment of a Jewish army in Palestine.[25] The most prominent Czechoslovak Zionist, Angelo Goldstein, supported the latter. The disagreement continued for months and poisoned the atmosphere between Jewish and Czech exiles based in Britain. Here, Zionist and other Jewish exiles clashed with the Czechs over increasing antisemitism in the Czechoslovak army. The conflict was exacerbated by Edvard Beneš's refusal to negotiate with or appoint minority representatives to the state council, the precursor to the Czechoslovak government-in-exile.

The Czechs' hostility to their fellow German and Jewish exiles reflected, argues the historian Jan Láníček, that early on in the war, Edvard Beneš and his circle had already decided that a reconstituted, postwar Czechoslovakia would be a nationally homogenous state.[26] Adapting to a more radical, exclusionist, and xenophobic Czech nationalism that flourished at home in the Protectorate and in the exile community, Beneš blamed Czechoslovakia's minorities for having destabilized and eventually destroyed the country – an assessment Zionists' vehemently opposed. Beneš toyed early on with plans for population transfer and border realignments as vehicles for national homogenization. As Láníček shows, the vision for postwar Czechoslovakia that the exiled leadership pursued demanded that minorities assimilate or leave. Yet, in the fall of 1941, Beneš adopted a more conciliatory position vis-à-vis Zionist activists and appointed Arnošt Frischer to a seat on the state council. This did not, however, reflect a change in Beneš's position regarding Czechoslovakia's minorities. Frischer's appointment was preceded by interventions with Beneš by prominent British and American Jewish leaders. Furthermore, Beneš's cooperation with Zionist and other Jewish circles was motivated by his desire to facilitate emigration of the majority of the country's Jews after an Allied victory in the war. Although Beneš's state council and later government-in-exile posed as heirs of the interwar Czechoslovak state, the Czechs no longer viewed their Zionist colleagues as partners in a multinational society. Beneš had decided to rid Czechoslovakia of its minority question, a vision that at the time involved plans for transfer of the state's Germans, Hungarians, and Jews.[27] For the ones who remained, assimilation would be the only option.

In the wake of the war, upwards of three million Czechoslovak Germans and at least 80,000 Hungarians were driven out of the country and their property appropriated by the state and ordinary Czechs and Slovaks. As the scope of the wartime destruction of Jewish life in Czechoslovakia became clear to the authorities, they became less concerned with the size of the country's Jewish minority and more intensely preoccupied with claiming ownership of Jewish property stolen during and after the war.[28] In Czechoslovakia, the Jewish minority was a mere shadow of its former self. In the Bohemian Lands, about 85 percent of the

Jewish population had been murdered (about 14,000 survived the Holocaust). In Slovakia, more than two-thirds of the community was dead, leaving about 32,000 survivors.[29] In Subcarpathian Rus', 15,000 Jews survived the Holocaust (the rate of death was similar to the one in Bohemia and Moravia almost 85%). In all, 263,000 Jews from Czechoslovakia were murdered by the Germans and their helpers. In 1946, an estimated 55,000 Jews remained in Czechoslovakia.[30]

As elsewhere in Europe, Jews were "unwelcomed" as they returned home to rebuild their lives. In a context of radicalized nationalism, the brutal ethnic cleansing of Germans and Hungarians, and a terrifying increase in antisemitism, thirty thousand Jews left Czechoslovakia before 1948. Although survivors and exiled leaders such as Arnošt Frischer returned to begin the rebuilding of Jewish life in Czechoslovakia, the political climate of the postwar years – a context in which all minorities were treated with suspicion – made attempts to reestablish Jewish communal institutions difficult. With the advent of Communism and before long the regime's adoption of antisemitism and anti-Zionism, Jewish political activism had come to an end in Czechoslovakia. While Communism would provide the final nail in the coffin for Jewish national minority activism, the coffin itself had been prepared by the Czechoslovak leadership's embrace of a radical, xenophobic Czech nationalism. Postwar Czechoslovakia posed as the successor to the interwar republic, a state that had created a political, cultural, and social space in which national minorities could negotiate a place of belonging. It was anything but.

After the Second World War, it became painfully clear that the Wilsonian vision for a multinational Eastern Europe made up by states in which minority protection laws helped secure stability and democracy had failed. And, as is often the case with failures, historians have treated this history with a sense of inevitability. Yet, the exclusionary, nationally homogenous states that emerged after the Second World War were the result of the deliberate destruction of a legal and political framework that had envisioned state building as balancing the needs and interest of the state and its dominant elite with those of its linguistically, religiously, and ethnically diverse populations. In Czechoslovakia, the state authorities expected its citizens to recognize and accept Czech cultural, linguistic, and political primacy, but they did not demand uniformity.

While there were critics who clamored for national purity – and this discourse was the one that ultimately won out – the interwar years was a period of experimentation in state and nation building. Before the crisis of the late 1930s, there was a multiplicity of visions for the state. And among them were ones that viewed minority nationalism not only as compatible with the creation of a nation-state, but also as a vehicle for the consolidation and strengthening of Czechoslovak hegemony.

Influenced by events in the late 1930s and during the Second World War, historians and other observers have often depicted minorities either as powerless victims or as groups wielding extraordinary power. Parliamentary representation, international allies, and economic resources were ways in which observers measured minority populations' influence or lack thereof. This book has shown that Jewish minority representatives, rather than being powerless, managed to assert influence in a myriad of ways. While they were not always successful, activists helped shape Czechoslovak state authorities' policies toward its Jewish minority.

In the 1920s and '30s, Jewish demographers, historians, literary critics, and writers produced new knowledge about Jews' past and present. Part healers of imagined social ills, part defenders against slander and antisemitism, these scholars familiarized Jewish and non-Jewish audiences alike with Czechoslovakia's diverse Jewish societies and their cultural traditions. By shining the light of science and scientific methods on the Jewish minority, scholars entered into broader debates about the minority question in Czechoslovakia as members of scientific committees, as journalists, and as lecturers.

Jewish social science played out alongside protracted efforts to modernize the country's Jewish communities. The reform work was spearheaded by Jewish activists, some of whom were semi-professional administrators, eager to create a transparent, rational, efficient, and centralized framework to oversee the country's Jewish communities. Following a pattern that characterized the relationship between the Czechoslovak state and its Jews, public officials in close cooperation with Jewish representatives sought to update and adapt existing Habsburg legislation rather than abolish it altogether. While the state bureaucrats might have preferred one countrywide institution, they were sensitive to the rule of law that spelled out individual communities' independence, to Jews' distinct historical and legal traditions, as well as to the deep cultural and historical divisions among Czechoslovakia's Jews. After years of lobbying work and reform proposals, Jewish activists in the Bohemian Lands managed to create a new Jewish representative institution. On the one hand, this reform diminished Jewish independence. On the other, it invested Jewish representatives with a new, advisory authority and allocated state resources to a broad array of Jewish religious, cultural, and *national* activities, including plans for a state-sponsored rabbinical seminary. By working with the state bureaucrats to modernize Jewish communities, Zionists and other Jewish leaders reasserted their authority vis-à-vis the state in matters concerning the country's Jewish minority.

Indeed, it was the state-building process itself that created avenues for activists to influence policies that affected minorities. The relationship between Jewish activists and state authorities was dynamic, envisioned as mutually beneficial, and went beyond mere compliance with the law. Activists and bureaucrats alike imagined a Jewish citizenry served by modern, Czechoslovak institutions with a collective leadership acting as an accountable and respected partner to the state in matters regarding the country's Jews. By turning away from the parliamentary arena and looking at the multiple ways in which people and institutions produce and exercise power, this book shows that bureaucracies relied on and empowered minority representatives.

Czechoslovakia is often depicted as a uniquely welcoming and tolerant place for Jews in interwar Eastern Europe. Although this image is part of the myth of Czechoslovakia, it is fair to say that conditions for Jews were better here than in countries such as Poland, Hungary, and Romania. The country was plagued less by the social, political, and economic uncertainty and crisis that fed popular and state-sponsored antisemitism elsewhere. In Czechoslovakia, there were no targeted anti-Jewish economic policies or restrictive quotas for Jewish students in higher education. Although popular antisemitism existed, the state's leaders and officials did not nurture it in significant ways. In contrast to other successor states, Czech political elites had little to gain from antisemitism. They were certain that anti-Jewish rhetoric and policies would put at risk Czechoslovakia's international reputation. Furthermore, state-sponsored antisemitism would also have botched an opportunity to make Jews abandon their perceived German and Hungarian loyalties. As we have seen, Czech and Slovak nationalists viewed Jews' allegiances as inherently opportunist. In light of the new political order and the rising antisemitism among Germans and Hungarians, this was a chance to weaken the old elites that was too important to miss. Unlike the German- and Hungarian-speakers who dominated entire towns and regions and among whom there were vocal irredentists, the Jewish minority of Czechoslovakia was too small and too dispersed to constitute a political challenge. For Czech and Slovak elites and nationalists, the main conflict remained, as it had been in Austria-Hungary, with the country's Germans and Hungarians.

Although they did not promote antisemitism, Czech and Slovak politicians and bureaucrats often treated Jews with distrust. Officials considered so-called eastern Jews, migrants from parts of Slovakia and Subcarpathian Rus' as well as students, immigrants, and war refugees from other parts of Eastern Europe, especially undesirable, since they believed them to be morally and culturally suspect. But these suspicions had deeper roots than a mere sense of cultural superiority. Throughout the 1920s and '30s, Czechoslovak Jews' multilingualism and their ties to Jewish scholarly and religious networks in neighboring countries were seen by some critics as evidence of Jews' arrogant refusal to accept the new political and cultural order. This discourse, cast as a Czech and Slovak defense against Jewish agents of Germanization and Magyarization, was rife with antisemitic tropes – fantasies of Jews' hatred for Christians, treason, domination and exploitation, even acts of ritual murder. Although these voices were not dominant, they nurtured and recast old hatreds and stereotypes. This hostility was kept in check until the Munich Crisis, when it exploded in full force. By then, due to the redrawing of the borders, Jews had become not only the most significant minority in Slovakia and the Bohemian Lands, but also the most vulnerable one. It is tempting to suggest that by then hatred against Jews had also become an appealing, convenient, and safe way for Czechs and Slovaks to assert anti-German and anti-Hungarian sentiments while playing to their more powerful neighbor's antisemitism.

Histories of Zionism focus predominantly on Zionists' disillusionment with Diaspora Jewish life and their efforts to create a Jewish homeland in Palestine. For historians preoccupied with ideology and high politics, Zionism has come to be defined as a movement dedicated almost exclusively to the creation of a Jewish national society in Palestine and eventually a Jewish state. In interwar Eastern Europe, Zionists did support the project in Palestine, but Zionism also served a range of local functions – ones that, at first glance, might appear at odds with post-Holocaust conceptions of what Zionist activism entailed. In interwar Czechoslovakia, Zionism served multiple, parallel purposes. The most significant of these was as a vehicle for integration and cultural revival. Zionist activists were social and cultural entrepreneurs who wanted to create a new kind of Jewish society and a new type of Jew. They rejected the assimilationist paradigm as a path to equality. Instead, they believed that a strengthening of cultural boundaries – in the form of better Jewish education, the creation of new Jewish social spaces, and the promotion of Jewish history and material culture as sites for positive self-identification – was essential in securing real equality for Jews and collective Jewish continuity. At stake was the survival of the Jewish nation.

For Zionists, this nationalization of Jewish society depended on their ability to mobilize public resources for their projects. Nation building was costly. Throughout the interwar years, Zionists struggled to fund newspapers and other publication activities, youth and vocational programs, and the fledgling Hebrew-language schools. In the 1920s and '30s, while funds flowed in ever greater amounts from Czechoslovakia to Palestine, Zionist institutions at home struggled to stay afloat. Activists' promotion of Zionism as Czechoslovak patriotism was sincere, but it was also a way to appeal to the benevolence of the Czechoslovak authorities. Like other Jewish reformers that preceded them, Zionists sought to enlist the state's financial and legal support for their programs for cultural renewal by promising to make Jews loyal citizens. Ironically, it was as representatives of Jews as a religious minority, and not as a national one, that Zionists managed to mobilize the most public resources for their reform agenda. The Jewish schools, sports clubs, and other institutions received but a trickle of the state resources anticipated by activists. Yet, Zionists did not let up; the political, financial, and symbolic significance of public support was too great to be passed up – indeed, they had no alternative.

To be sure, one of the striking aspects of Zionism in Czechoslovakia was the movement's local character. Zionist goals, tactics, and narratives were shaped by activists' experience with local minority nationalist traditions. The legal and discursive continuities between the Habsburg state and Czechoslovakia meant that the census, schools, and voluntary associations remained central to activists' efforts to nationalize people's identities and behaviors. Zionists drew explicitly on Czech nationalist narratives of state oppression, awakening, and regeneration to make their national project legitimate and legible to Jews and non-Jews alike. They looked to statistical visibility as a way to document Jews' right to recognition and support. And they made Jews' local experience – the centuries-old communities, Jews' regional cultural and historical particularities and material culture – a site for Jewish national identification. Palestine was an important symbol of national regeneration, a source of inspiration for many. But, Zionists were most successful – and attracted the most Jews – when they created institutions that centered on Jews' shared ethnicity – history, religion, language, and family traditions – programs they often pursued in cooperation with non-Zionist Jewish activists. As we have seen, Zionism in Czechoslovakia was shaped as much by directives from London and Jerusalem as they were by local Zionist activists' sense of the needs and interests of their communities. Thus, within the sports and youth movement, dogmatic Zionism took a backseat to the creation of a broader, more inclusive Jewish ethnic community.

In interwar Czechoslovakia, Zionists were part of a broader process of nationalization by which activists increasingly demanded that people identify and behave in accordance with their perceived national belonging. The Jewish nation did not exist as a social fact. It had to be constructed, maintained, and naturalized. It was a contested process. Yet, with the help of social science and public performances of Jewish nationhood, Zionist activists shaped the image of Jews as a nation in powerful and tenacious ways. They made Jews legible as a nation – a community of ethnic sameness – whose perceived racial difference established their distinctiveness from other communities. By historicizing the nation and the process of nation building, this book reveals how state authorities and nationalist activists employed generalizing and homogenizing practices to assert their authority over individuals and groups. It was a development that empowered minority representatives while making members of minorities more vulnerable to intervention. It was a form of governance that in the name of individual and group rights imposed racial, national, and other collective identities – and in many ways continues to do so – with varying degrees of force and with more or less success, on individuals and communities.

Notes

Introduction

1. For Jews as insiders and outsiders, see Steven E. Aschheim, "Reflections on Insiders and Outsiders."

2. I am drawing on Nira Yuval-Davis's work on belonging, an emotional attachment, a sense of being at home, recognized by self and others, and the politics of belonging, the political projects undertaken to construct belonging to certain collectives. Nira Yuval-Davis, "Belonging and the Politics of Belonging."

3. For minorities in interwar East Central Europe, see the overview in Joseph Rothschild, *East Central Europe.* For empires and nation-states, see Karen Barkey and Mark von Hagen, eds., *After Empire;* and Aviel Roshwald, *Ethnic Nationalism and the Fall of Empires.*

4. For other minorities in Czechoslovakia, see Paul R. Magocsi, *The Shaping of a National Identity;* Jaroslav Kučera, *Minderheit im Nationalstaat;* Elisabeth Bakke, *Doomed to Failure;* Jörg K. Hoensch and Dušan Kováč, eds., *Das Scheitern der Verständigung;* Martin Schulze Wessel, ed., *Loyalitäten in der Tschechoslowakischen Republik, 1918–38.* For an example of another multinational state and its integration project, see the discussion on Romanian nation building in the interwar years, Irina Livezeanu, *Cultural Politics in Greater Romania.*

5. For a study on the identities and loyalties of Jews in Habsburg Austria, see Marsha L. Rozenblit, *Reconstructing a National Identity.*

6. For examples of these "partnerships" cultivated by Jewish enlighteners (*maskilim*) and other reformers in the modern era, see Michael Stanislawski, *Tsar Nicholas I and the Jews;* Derek J. Penslar, *Shylock's Children;* Ezra Mendelsohn, ed., *Jews and the State.*

7. For the expanding network of social welfare and educational institutions in Central Europe's modernizing Jewish communities beginning in the late nineteenth century, see Penslar, *Shylock's Children,* chapter 5. For the interwar years, see Michael Brenner and Derek J. Penslar, eds., *In Search of Jewish Community.* For the importance of the population census and national schools for activists in Imperial Austria, see Pieter M. Judson, *Guardians of the*

Nation; and Tara E. Zahra, *Kidnapped Souls.* For the significance of the census and ethnography in creating and managing multinational states, see Francine Hirsch, *Empire of Nations.*

8. This regional yet countrywide perspective is not unusual in the scholarship on Czechoslovakia's Jews. Kateřina Čapková did so in her exploration of Jewish identities in interwar Bohemia, in *Czechs, Germans, Jews?* In her recent work on interwar Slovakia, *Mapping Jewish Loyalties in Interwar Slovakia,* Rebekah Klein-Pejšová shows how the legacy of the Kingdom of Hungary continued to shape Jews' identities and cultures in the 1920s and '30s even as Jews there formed new attachments to Slovakia and by extension Czechoslovakia. For Subcarpathian Rus', see Yeshayahu A. Jelinek, *Carpathian Diaspora.* Hillel J. Kieval has recently made the case for the significance of the Czechoslovak context; see "Negotiating Czechoslovakia."

9. Kieval, *The Making of Czech Jewry;* and Kieval, *Languages of Community.*

10. For how Zionist intellectuals' experiences of national conflict in the Bohemian Lands shaped their attitudes to state building in Palestine, see Dimitry Shumsky, *Zweisprachigkeit und binationale Idee.*

11. For ethnic differences as innate, see, for example, the contributions in Peter F. Sugar and Ivo J. Lederer, eds., *Nationalism in Eastern Europe;* among the many works on nationalist mobilization in East Central Europe are Pieter M. Judson and Marsha L. Rozenblit, eds., *Constructing Nationalities in East Central Europe;* and Nancy M. Wingfield and Maria Bucur, eds., *Staging the Past.*

12. For works pointing to the importance of political and social alliances rather than preexisting ethnic loyalties or affinities for nation formation in the Bohemian Lands, see Gary B. Cohen, *The Politics of Ethnic Survival;* Jeremy King, *Budweisers into Czechs and Germans;* Eagle Glassheim, *Noble Nationalists.* For nationalist activism, the malleability of national identifications, and indifference to nation and nationalism in the Bohemian Lands, see Judson, *Guardians of the Nation;* Zahra, *Kidnapped Souls;* and Chad Bryant, *Prague in Black.*

13. Jeremy King, "The Nationalization of East Central Europe," 127.

14. For Germans and Jews in Prague, see G. Cohen, *The Politics of Ethnic Survival.* For Jews in German nationalist organizations, see Judson, *Guardians of the Nation,* 49–52; and for Czech nationalists and Jews, see Zahra, *Kidnapped Souls,* 21–23.

15. Michal Frankl, *"Emancipace od židů."*

16. This phrasing from Zahra, *Kidnapped Souls.*

17. This reading draws on George L. Mosse's work on masculinity and nationalism in which he argues that Zionism was a way for acculturated Jews to counter marginalizing stereotypes about Jews as weak, parasitical, and unmanly, by constructing a new form of Jewishness that conformed to the dominant social and cultural ideal; see Mosse, *The Image of Man.* In her work on interwar Bohemia, Kateřina Čapková has shown that Jews political loyalties,

whether they identified nationally as Czechs, Germans, or Jews, was shaped not by any meaningful objective differences such as class or profession, but by purely subjective factors, such as family or social circles; see Čapková, "Czechs, Germans, Jews – Where Is the Difference?"

18. Mark Cornwall has shown how Sudeten German nationalists sought to create such nationally separate spheres in the interwar years; see Cornwall, *The Devil's Wall.*

19. Andrea Orzoff's works explore the creation, dissemination, and use of the myth; see Orzoff, *Battle for the Castle.*

20. The origin of this saying is unclear. The earliest reference that I found is a somewhat curious one. In December 1944, a Jewish newspaper published in British Columbia, Canada, included a "little story" from the magazine *Pageant,* which concerned "the Czechoslovakia statesman Eduard Benes. . . . When his country was free some Nazi representatives called on him with the demands that he place restrictions on Jews . . . to which Benes replied: 'Why the Jews are the only Czechoslovaks we have. . . . All the others are either Czechs or Slovaks.'" *Jewish Western Bulletin,* December 8, 1944.

21. This notion of Zionism as neutrality has made its way into scholars' interpretations as well. Hillel J. Kieval argues that Zionism was a way in which Jewish activists could assume a neutral position in the political battle between German and Czech nationalists in the Bohemian Lands, while Dimitry Shumsky believes that Zionism allowed Jews to continue to identify with Czech as well as German language and culture. For neutrality, see Kieval, *The Making of Czech Jewry,* chapter 4. For Zionism as a product of the exceptional bilingualism of "Czecho-German Jews," see Dimitry Shumsky, "On Ethno-Centrism and Its Limits." Martin Wein has problematized Shumsky's claim that Jews' bilingualism set them apart from non-Jews; Martin Wein, "Only Czecho-German Jews?," 386–387.

22. For wartime developments, see Jan Láníček, *Czechs, Slovaks, and the Jews.*

23. For an overview of the development of Zionist thought in these early years, see Shlomo Avineri, *The Making of Modern Zionism.*

24. David Engel, *Zionism,*11.

25. For two important readings of nationalism, see Eric Hobsbawm, *Nations and Nationalism Since 1780;* and Benedict Anderson, *Imagined Communities.* For a critique of the continued dominance of the ethnic perspective, see King, "The Nationalization of East Central Europe."

26. For pre-state Zionist ideology, see Yael Zerubavel, *Recovered Roots,* 3–36.

27. The character Yudka in "The Sermon," by Ukrainian-born Israeli novelist Haim Hazaz (1898–1973), as quoted in Simon Rawidowicz, *Israel: The Ever-Dying People and Other Essays,* 75.

28. Ibid., 76.

29. For Galicia and the importance of contextualizing Zionism in its European environment, see Joshua Shanes, *Diaspora Nationalism and Jewish Identity in Habsburg Galicia.*

30. Matityahu Mintz, "Work for the Land of Israel and 'Work in the Present,'" 163–164.

31. For an assessment of Bund and Zionism in Eastern Europe, see the articles in Zvi Gitelman, ed., *The Emergence of Modern Jewish Politics.*

32. For prewar Prague Zionist intellectual circles, see Kieval, *The Making of Czech Jewry,* 93–153. Scott Spector's work looks at Zionism among Prague's fin-de-siècle Jewish writers; see Spector, *Prague Territories.*

33. For Zionists and other Jewish leaders at the Paris Peace Conference, see Carole Fink, *Defending the Rights of Others.*

34. For an in-depth discussion of this relationship, see chapter 7.

35. For an overview, see Bernhard Wasserstein, *The British in Palestine.*

36. The numbers are 126,349 and 228,170; see Jacob Metzer, "Jewish Immigration to Palestine in the Long 1920s."

37. Anita Shapira, *Israel: A History,* 115.

38. For Zionism's function in the Diaspora, see Stephen Poppel, *Zionism in Germany,* 76; and Michael Berkowitz, *Western Jewry and the Zionist Project,* 2.

39. For a comparative study of Jewish politics in interwar Eastern Europe and the United States, see Ezra Mendelsohn, *On Modern Jewish Politics.*

40. Marie Crhová, "Modern Jewish Politics in Central Europe."

41. For these intellectuals in Palestine, see Shumsky, *Zweisprachigkeit und binationale Idee.*

42. For studies on interwar German and Polish Zionism that adopt a traditional framework, see Celia Heller, *On the Edge of Destruction;* and Hagit Lavsky, *Before Catastrophe.* For a comparative perspective, see Mendelsohn, *On Modern Jewish Politics.*

43. Joshua Shanes made the case for contextualizing Zionist activism in *Diaspora Nationalism and Jewish Identity in Habsburg Galicia.* For earlier studies that looked at the meaning and function of Zionism for Diaspora Jews in the interwar years, see Poppel, *Zionism in Germany;* and Berkowitz, *Western Jewry and the Zionist Project.* Noam Pianko has recently introduced readers to marginalized voices from the interwar years, Zionist thinkers who sought an alternative to political sovereignty for Jews' national life; see Pianko, *Zionism and the Roads Not Taken.*

44. For the transformation of Jews' cultural allegiances and ethnic identity in Bohemia before the First World War, see Kieval, *The Making of Czech Jewry* and his *Languages of Community;* for the negotiation of identities among Jews in Bohemia in the interwar years, see Kateřina Čapková, *Czechs, Germans, Jews?;* for Habsburg Jews' tripartite identity and the reconfiguration of these identities in the wake of the war, see Marsha L. Rozenblit, *Reconstructing a National Identity;* and for the transfers and transformations of loyalties among Jews in Slovakia, see Rebekah Klein-Pejšová, *Mapping Jewish Loyalties in Interwar Slovakia.*

45. Brenner and Penslar, eds., *In Search of Jewish Community.*

46. For Habsburg Austria, see Judson, *Guardians of the Nation;* for the Bohemian Lands in the first half of the twentieth century, see Zahra, *Kidnapped Souls.*

47. František Friedmann, *Strana Židovská* (Praha: Kulturní odbor ústředního svazu českoslov. studentsva: Cyklus přednášek o ideologii českoslov. politických stran VII, 1931), 9.

48. For assimilation, Jews, and Czech nationalists, see Kieval, *Languages of Community,* 203–206.

49. See Avigdor Dagan, "The Press," 525–526.

50. For a list of place names in the languages of the communities that lived in these towns and cities in Slovakia and Subcarpathian Rus', see Paul Robert Magocsi, *Historical Atlas of East Central Europe*. For an example of a contested process of naming and renaming, see Peter Bugge, "The Making of a Slovak City."

1. The Jews of Czechoslovakia

1. Ivan Olbracht, *Golet v údolí* (Praha: Melantrich, 1937). I have used Iris Urwin Lewitová's English translation for the quotes, and page numbers refer to this edition: Ivan Olbracht, *The Sorrowful Eyes of Hana Karajich.* The collection was first translated into English in 1967 under the title *The Bitter and the Sweet.* The short story "The Sorrowful Eyes of Hana Karajich" was reissued as a novella by Central European University Press.

2. Olbracht, *The Sorrowful Eyes,* 99.

3. Ibid., 103–104.

4. Ibid., 112.

5. Ibid., 135.

6. Ibid., 142.

7. Ibid., 185.

8. Ibid., 188.

9. Ibid., 124–125.

10. Ibid., 185–186.

11. Jonathan Bolton, "Olbracht, Ivan," 1282. According to Jiří Opelík, Olbracht identified strongly with his mother's Jewishness; see Opelík, "Ivan Olbracht," 554–571.

12. Ruth Bondy (b. 1923), who grew up in Prague in the 1920s and '30s, notes that Olbracht's collection of stories was for many Jews in the Bohemian Lands their first 'encounter' with the Jews in the country's east; see Ruth Bondy, *Jakob Edelstein* (Praha: Sefer, 2001), 47; for other readers inspired by Olbracht's work, see Miroslav Holub's introductory essay in *The Sorrowful Eyes of Hana Karajich,* viii–x.

13. The American Jewish Joint Distribution Committee's representatives, who spent time in Subcarpathian Rus' and Eastern Slovakia after the war, commented on what they saw as the extraordinary backwardness of the region. They described its residents, Jews and Christians alike, as "uncivilized and void of any concept of morality and hygiene," and "in all of central and eastern Europe, there is no place in which the level of culture is as depressed as in Carpathian Rus," as quoted in Yeshayahu A. Jelinek, *The Carpathian Diaspora,* 115–116; for conflicts between the existing Jewish leadership and the newcomers, see 146–147.

14. In 1921, Catholics made up 76% of the population. Catholicism was the dominant religion among Czechs, Slovaks, Germans, and Hungarians in the country. Among these nationalities, Protestants were a minority (7% of the overall population). Rusyns were mainly Greek Catholic (4%), but with an Eastern Orthodox minority as well

(0.5%). The Czechoslovak National Church, whose members were mainly Czechs, made up 4% while Jews, who could be found among all of the nationalities, made up 3.6% of the population. Not insignificant was the number of people who declared themselves without religion (5%). See the list of the populations' religious affiliation in Joseph Rothschild, *East Central Europe,* 90.

15. Hillel J. Kieval, *Languages of Community,* 11–12.

16. Historians believe that Jews settled in Prague no later than the eleventh century, and Brünn/Brno had about one thousand Jews by the mid-fourteenth century. For Prague, see Kieval, *Languages of Community,* 10–13; for Brünn/Brno, see Michael L. Miller, "Brno," 238.

17. Kieval, *Languages of Community,* 13–14. For an overview of Moravia's medieval and early modern Jewish history, see M. Miller, *Rabbis and Revolution,* 11–59.

18. M. Miller, *Rabbis and Revolution,* 19, 22.

19. Kieval, *The Making of Czech Jewry,* 10.

20. One of the most spectacular of these expulsions, remembered for the suffering caused and the international response it stirred, was Maria Theresa's decision to expel the Jews from Prague and Bohemia in the winter of 1744–1745. For eyewitness testimonies and other sources, see the collection by Wilma Iggers, ed., *The Jews of Bohemia and Moravia.*

21. The state authorities fixed the number of Jewish families allowed to live in the Bohemian Lands (8,541 for Bohemia; 5,106 for Moravia; and 119 for Silesia); see Kieval, *Languages of Community,* 21.

22. In 1724, the census indicated that Jews lived in about 800 localities. By 1849, Jews were counted in 1,921 places in Bohemia; see Kieval, *The Making of Czech Jewry,* 11–12. Over time, the state authorities attempted to use the marriage restrictions to modify Jews' economic behavior – for example, by allowing a second son to marry if he engaged in agriculture as a tenant farmer or estate manager; see Iggers, *The Jews of Bohemia and Moravia,* 94. These exemptions could thus also have contributed to the dispersion of Jews to villages and small towns in Bohemia.

23. Although the Familiant Laws became a symbol of oppression and the regime's hostility toward Jews, the authorities did not succeed in reducing the Jewish population in the Crown Lands. Over the next 150 years, the number of Jews in the Bohemian Lands doubled. By 1849, when the Familiant Laws were abolished, there were 75,000–76,000 Jews in Bohemia (up from 42,000) and 38,000–39,000 (up from 25,000) in Moravia and Austrian Silesia; see Kieval, *Languages of Community,* 22.

24. At the time, the Kingdom of Hungary was a magnet for large numbers of immigrants looking for opportunity in areas that had recently come under complete Habsburg control. Historians believe that it was the Familiant Laws first and foremost that pushed more than thirty thousand Jews across the border from Moravia to Oberland between the 1730s and the 1780s; see

Kieval, *Languages of Community,* 22–23. For the number of migrants from Bohemia and Moravia, see Michael K. Silber, "Hungary before 1918," 771.

25. As in the Bohemian Lands, in the Kingdom of Hungary, Jews acted as mediators in the region's agricultural and natural resource economy, some administering estates, others making a living as innkeepers, moneylenders, tradespeople, and peddlers; see Ješajahu A. Jelínek, *Dávidova hviezda pod Tatrami,* 40.

26. Jelínek, *Dávidova hviezda pod Tatrami,* 40–41.

27. Kieval, *Languages of Community,* 27–28.

28. Hillel J. Kieval, "The Unforeseen Consequences," 110.

29. At the time, Jewish communities employed teachers or supported schools that provided Jewish children, mostly boys, with an elementary religious education. Gifted or well-off boys could continue their religious studies at a yeshiva; Kieval, "The Unforeseen Consequences," 115. For a recent study of these schools from 1848 to 1938, see Marsha L. Rozenblit, "Creating Jewish Space."

30. Louise Hecht, "Teaching Haskalah – Haskalah and Teaching," 95. Hillel J. Kieval notes that given that the majority of Jews lived in villages and small towns, many children did not attend German-Jewish schools, but were tutored privately or with other Jewish children. Some simply enrolled in the local general elementary school; Kieval, "The Unforeseen Consequences," 114.

31. Hillel J. Kieval, "Imperial Embraces and Ethnic Challenges," 4, 9–10.

32. Eva Kowalská argues that the Jewish population was so dispersed that most settlements and communities could not afford to run a *Normalschule.* By 1790, the Josephinian reforms were rescinded in Hungary, and the traditional Jewish religious education system consisting of elementary schooling and tutoring remained in place; see Eva Kowalská, "The Results of School Reforms in Upper Hungary," 126–128, 130–131.

33. Michael Silber, "The Historical Experience of German Jewry," 135.

34. Victor Karady shows that as a result Jews began using Hungarian language faster and to a greater extent than other ethnic minorities in Hungary in the late nineteenth and early twentieth century; see Victor Karady, "Religious Divisions, Socio-Economic Stratification," 169–171.

35. Indeed, by 1880, Michael K. Silber notes, "Hungarian Jewry was the largest German-speaking Jewish community in Europe"; see Silber, "The Historical Experience of German Jewry," 127.

36. Rozenblit, "Creating Jewish Space," 109.

37. Rebekah Klein-Pejšová, "Building Slovak Jewry," 26–27.

38. M. Miller, *Rabbis and Revolution,* 322.

39. By then, Jews' mediating position in the Hungarian economy had already begun to change. In villages, some Jews worked small plots of land, others leased or owned large estates. In the regions' growing towns, such as Žilina/Sillein/Zsolna and Košice/Kaschau/Kassa, Jews were active in the

processing and sale of agricultural and lumber products, and many worked as shopkeepers and professionals, especially doctors and lawyers; see Jelínek, *Dávidova hviezda pod Tatrami*, 57–60.

40. Jacob Katz, *A House Divided*, 37.

41. Theodor Haas, *Die Juden in Mähren: Darstellung der Rechtsgeschichte und Statistik unter besonderer Berücksichtigung des 19. Jahrhunderts* (Brünn: Jüdischer Buch- und Kunstverlag, 1908), 24–25; for more on this topic, see chapter 4.

42. Prague's Jewish population grew from 15,214 in 1869 (17% of Bohemia's Jews) to 29,107 in 1910 (34%); see Kieval, *The Making of Czech Jewry*, 14.

43. Ibid., 13–14.

44. Kieval, "Imperial Embraces," 12. In his family history, the Zionist activist and journalist Hugo Hermann (1887–1940), who was himself from Mährisch-Trübau/Moravská Třebová in Moravia, a town with a largely German-speaking population, noted about rural Jewish life in Bohemia that "all Bohemian country Jews spoke German and their not very extensive reading matter consisted of German books. But this was not really different from the socially and culturally higher-class Czechs, especially during the 'time of national revival' that lasted far into the nineteenth century, for they too, used German as much as Czech for their spoken language, and read German books, since there was too little high quality Czech literature. On the other hand, many Jews frequently spoke fluent Czech and took part as much as possible in the life of their fellow citizens." Hugo Hermann, *In Jenen Tagen* (Jerusalem: self-published, 1938), 215–216, as translated in Wilma Iggers, *The Jews of Bohemia and Moravia*, 221.

45. For the history of the Czech-Jewish movement before World War I, see Kieval, *The Making of Czech Jewry*. For the interwar years, see Kateřina Čapková, *Czechs, Germans, Jews?*, 93–102.

46. Kieval, *The Making of Czech Jewry*, 36. As Gary B. Cohen reminds us, this bilingualism was not unique to Jews, as "until 1945, most Czech-speakers in Prague and other Bohemian and Moravian cities studied German in school and spoke the language with varying degrees of competence"; see Gary B. Cohen, "Cultural Crossing in Prague, 1900," 11.

47. Miller observes that by 1869, 20% of Vienna's Jews were from Moravia, 44% from northern Hungary; M. Miller, *Rabbis and Revolution*, 321–322, 339.

48. In contrast to Bohemia, Moravia's German-speaking minority held on to economic and political power until the early twentieth century, which also helped sustain German culture and political affiliations among Jews; see M. Miller, *Rabbis and Revolution*, 333–334.

49. Rozenblit, "Creating Jewish Space," 117, 125.

50. The numbers are for Prague (31,751), Brno/Brünn (10,866), and Moravská Ostrava/Mährisch Ostrau (4,969). The cities were home to 38% of the regions' Jews. For data on Moravia, see Hugo Gold, ed., *Die Juden und Judengemeinden Mährens in Vergangenheit und Gegenwart* (Brünn: Jüdischer Buch- und Kunstverlag, 1929), 599.

51. In Slovakia, Bratislava (10,973) and Košice (8,792) were the largest

Jewish centers (about 15% of the province's Jews). The majority of Slovakia's Jews lived in midsized towns such as Bardějov/Bartfeld/Bártfa, Michalovce/Großmichel/Nagymihály, Nitra, and Prešov/Eperies/Eperjes (with populations of about 3,000 Jews or more); see Petr Brod, Kateřina Čapková, and Michal Frankl, "Czechoslovakia," 375–381. Rebekah Klein-Pejšová argues that the number of Jews in Košice after the First World War was substantially higher than the official data suggest; see "Building Slovak Jewry," 20.

52. Mukačevo's Jewish population was 26,100 in 1930 (43% of the city's population); see Paul R. Magocsi, "Muchaceve," 1209–1210.

53. František Langer wrote about Judaism and Jiří in his memoirs, *Byli a bylo.* The Zionist writer and journalist Max Brod (1884–1968) noted, like Langer, a similar distance yet fascination with Judaism that centered on family rituals; see Max Brod, *Streitbares Leben.*

54. For the construction of new synagogues and other Jewish communal institutions undertaken by all the Jewish denominations in Slovakia, see Klein-Pejšová, "Building Slovak Jewry," 22.

55. Jelinek, *The Carpathian Diaspora,* 213.

56. For the transformation of the Habsburg State, see Gerald Stourzh, *Die Gleichberechtigung der Nationalitäten;* for the Bohemian Lands, see Jeremy King, *Budweisers into Czechs and Germans.*

57. For Habsburg Austria, see Hannelore Burger, *Sprachenrecht und Sprachgerechtigkeit;* on Habsburg nationality politics and the Jews, see Joshua Shanes, *Diaspora Nationalism and Jewish Identity in Habsburg Galicia,* 35–36.

58. For a study of the role of language and education in the development of nationalism in the Bohemian Lands, see Tara E. Zahra, *Kidnapped Souls,* 15.

59. David I. Kertzer and Dominique Arel, "Censuses, Identity Formation, and the Struggle for Political Power." For a fascinating account of how this played out in the late nineteenth century, see Hugo Hermann's observation that Jews in Bohemia developed a "Marrano way of life" (Marrano refers to Jews who converted to Catholicism but continued to practice Judaism in secret at the time of the Spanish Inquisition) in order to navigate the conflict between Czech and Germans: "a large majority [of Jews] who hoped to accomplish the trick of being Czech in ordinary life and in business, but of remaining religious Jews and speaking German (the world language) at home where no other ears could hear them. Besides the Czech paper *Čas* [Time] they also subscribed to the *Prager Tagblatt,* the paper read by most Jews." Hermann, *In Jenen Tagen,* 216–217, as translated in Iggers, *The Jews of Bohemia and Moravia,* 222.

60. Zahra, *Kidnapped Souls,* 19–27.

61. Klein-Pejšová, "Building Slovak Jewry," 28.

62. Kieval, "Imperial Embraces," 15.

63. For the perception of Jewish schools as German institutions, and Czech nationalist Jews' efforts to close them down, see Kieval, *The Making of Czech Jewry,* 40–58. Marsha L.

Rozenblit argues that while Jews were attached to German language, they did not generally identify as members of the German nation; see Rozenblit, "Creating Jewish Space," 145.

64. Rebekah Klein-Pejšová, *Mapping Jewish Loyalties in Interwar Slovakia*, 25.

65. For Jews' primary and secondary school attendance in Bohemia, see Kieval, *The Making of Czech Jewry*, 194; for Moravia, see Rozenblit, "Creating Jewish Space," 146.

66. Kieval, *The Making of Czech Jewry*, 36.

67. Rozenblit, "Creating Jewish Space," 109.

68. For the Bohemian Lands, see Michal Frankl, *'Emancipace od židů'*; for Slovakia, see Jelínek, *Dávidova hviezda pod Tatrami*, 87–96.

69. For the meaning of ritual murder stories in the context of national struggle, see Kieval, *Languages of Community*, 181–197.

70. For an overview of antisemitism in the Habsburg Monarchy, see Bruce F. Pauley, *From Prejudice to Persecution*, 11–69. For the Bohemian Lands, see also Frankl, *'Emancipace od židů.'*

71. Catherine Albrecht, "The Rhetoric of Economic Nationalism."

72. For national indifference and overlapping populations in the Bohemian Lands, see Zahra, *Kidnapped Souls*, 13–48.

73. Kieval, *Languages of Community*, 182. Kieval has written extensively on Czech nationalist Jews in *The Making of Czech Jewry*. For Germans and Jews in Prague, see G. Cohen, *The Politics of Ethnic Survival;* for Jews in German nationalist organizations, see Judson, *Guardians of the Nation*, 49–52; and for Czech nationalists and Jews, see Zahra, *Kidnapped Souls*, 21–23.

74. For a comprehensive study of Czech, German, and Zionist Jews, see Kateřina Čapková, *Czechs, Germans, Jews?*

75. Marsha L. Rozenblit, *Reconstructing a National Identity: The Jews of Habsburg Austria during World War I.*

76. Ibid., 23–24, 29.

77. These data are based on the 1921 census's results on the population's nationality (mother tongue);, see Joseph Rothschild, *East Central Europe*, 89 (tables 12–13). For more on the census, see chapter 3.

78. *Československá statistika*, svazek 37, řada VI, Sčítání lidu ze dne 15.2.1921, sešit 6 III. díl (Praha: Státní úřad statistický, 1927), 3–4 (table 1).

79. Rogers Brubaker, "Nationalizing States in the old 'New Europe' – and the New," 412.

80. Ibid., 416–417. In Czechoslovakia, the 1919 land reform broke up large estates and distributed land formerly owned by people considered Germans and Hungarians, among them a not insignificant number of Jews, to Czech and Slovak farmers. Similarly, newly employed Czech civil servants fanned out across the country to assume political authority and assert Czechoslovak sovereignty in the country's borderlands inhabited by large minority populations; see Daniel E. Miller, "Colonizing the Hungarian and German Border Areas."

2. Jewish Power and Powerlessness

1. Viktor Fischl, *Jews of Czechoslovakia,* ill. Walter Herz (London: National Council of Jews from Czechoslovakia, 1940).

2. Ibid., 1.

3. Ibid.

4. For an insightful discussion of the relationship between Czech leaders and Zionists from Czechoslovakia in the years 1939–1941, see Jan Láníček, *Czechs, Slovaks, and the Jews: Beyond Idealisation and Condemnation, 1938–48,* here 50 note 49.

5. This narrative was vividly embodied in the anthology *Masaryk und das Judentum* that celebrated the president's many-sided relationship to Jews and Jewish culture. It was published simultaneously in German and Czech in 1931. It was published in English in New York in 1941. Ernst Rychnovsky, ed., *Masaryk und das Judentum/Masaryk a židovství* (Prag: Mars, 1931); *Thomas G. Masaryk and the Jews: A Collection of Essays* (New York: B. Pollak, 1941).

6. See the prefaces to the first two volumes of *The Jews of Czechoslovakia: Historical Studies and Surveys,* vols. 1–2; for a more recent example, Ezra Mendelsohn, *The Jews of East Central Europe,* 131–132, 148–151.

7. On the traditional interpretation of Czech leaders granting rights, see Václav Beneš, "Czechoslovak Democracy and Its Problems, 1918–1920," 41; Ladislav Lipscher, "Die soziale und politische Stellung der Juden in der ersten Republik," 272; Koloman Gajan, "T. G. Masaryk, idea sionismu a Nahum Sokolow," 78. For a critical look at Masaryk's and Beneš's mythmaking and cultural diplomacy during and after WWI, see Andrea Orzoff, *Battle for the Castle.*

8. Jonathan Frankel, "The Paradoxical Politics of Marginality," 3–6.

9. For the total numbers, see David Engel, "World War I," 2032–2037.

10. Beatrix Hoffmann-Halter, *"Abreisendmachung,"* 29.

11. Martin Welling, *"Von Hass so eng umkreist,"* 126.

12. For a detailed analysis on the impact of the war on Austrian Jews, focusing especially on how the wartime experience mobilized Jewish societies on the home front, see Marsha L. Rozenblit, *Reconstructing a National Identity.* For a comparison of Austrian and Czechoslovak refugee policies, see Rebekah Klein-Pejšová, "Beyond the 'Infamous Concentration Camps of the Old Monarchy.'"

13. Eric Lohr, "The Russian Army and the Jews."

14. Rozenblit, *Reconstructing a National Identity,* 65–66; for repatriation attempts, see Klein-Pejšová, "Beyond the 'Infamous Concentration Camps,'" 158–159.

15. Frankel, "Paradoxical Politics," 16; Carole Fink, *Defending the Rights of Others,* 89–90.

16. For estimates of the Jewish death toll in the Russian Civil War ranging from 50,000 to more than 200,000, see Henry Abramson, "Russian Civil War," 1620–1622; Orlando Figes, *A People's Tragedy,* 679; and Frankel, "Paradoxical Politics," 7.

17. For an account of the destruction of Jewish life in Galicia and Russia's western borderlands in 1914–1916, see the report by the Russian Jewish writer Ansky (Shloyme Zaynvl Rapoport), who traveled to the region as a representative of Russian-Jewish aid organizations; see S. Ansky, *The Enemy at His Pleasure: A Journey through the Jewish Pale of Settlement during World War I.* In 1916, the American Jewish Committee attempted to raise awareness of the conditions for Jews in Eastern Europe with the widely distributed booklet *The Jews in the Eastern War Zone.* The authors emphasized that their report was based "exclusively upon evidence furnished by the Russian government itself" or published with the approval of the Russian censors in order to dispel accusations of false atrocity stories; see American Jewish Committee, *The Jews in the Eastern War Zone* (New York, 1916).

18. Frankel, "Paradoxical Politics," 9.

19. For wartime mobilization of the home front in Vienna and the Bohemian Lands, including assistance to Jewish soldiers, see Rozenblit, *Reconstructing a National Identity,* 59–74; for amount spent, 68.

20. For the JDC's activities before and after the war, see Klein-Pejšová, "Beyond the 'Infamous Concentration Camps,'" 155.

21. Frankel, "Paradoxical Politics," 9.

22. For German Zionist activities during and after the war, see Egmont Zechlin, *Die deutsche Politik und die Juden im Ersten Weltkrieg;* Jay Ticker, "Max I. Bodenheimer"; and Francis R. Nicosia, "Jewish Affairs and German Foreign Policy."

23. American Jewish Committee, *The Jews in the Eastern War Zone,* 10.

24. Rozenblit, *Reconstructing a National Identity,* 43–58.

25. For the various efforts to unify Austrian Jews and especially the attempt to create an Austrian Jewish Congress, see David Rechter, *The Jews of Vienna,* 129–160.

26. Rozenblit, *Reconstructing a National Identity,* 127.

27. For Bodenheimer's proposal, see Ticker, "Max I. Bodenheimer," 16.

28. Ibid., 15; and Nicosia, "Jewish Affairs and German Foreign Policy," 262–263.

29. For Zionists and the British government and the attention paid by French and British authorities to American Jewish public opinion before the United States entered the war, see Mark Levene, *War, Jews, and the New Europe,* 78–107.

30. Fink, *Defending the Rights of Others,* 86–88.

31. For Zionism as a way of diminishing Bolshevism's appeal among Russia's Jews, see Levene, *War, Jews, and the New Europe,* 128–144; and Frankel, "Paradoxical Politics," 12, 16.

32. Orzoff, *Battle for the Castle,* 23–56.

33. Rechter, *The Jews of Vienna,* 169.

34. Fink, *Defending the Rights of Others,* 126. For the activities of the Jewish National Councils in the Bohemian Lands, see Rozenblit, *Reconstructing a National Identity,* 139–148.

35. In contrast to Bohemia, in Moravia and Silesia, the regional organization of Jewish congregations (Landesverbandes der israelitischen Kultusgemeinden) supported the

Jewish national program. See "Die Mährischen Juden für das nationaljüdische Programm," *Selbstwehr*, November 8, 1918; and "Die Forderungen der Landesverbände der jüdischen Gemeinden Mährens und Österreichisch-Schlesiens," in *Die Judenfrage der Gegenwart: Dokumentsammlung*, ed. Leon Chasanowitsch and Leo Motzkin (Stockholm: Bokförlaget Judäa A.B., 1919), 56. See also Ladislav Lipscher, "Die Lage der Juden in der Tschechoslowakei," 8.

36. "Der jüdische Nationalrat beim Národní výbor," *Selbstwehr*, November 1, 1918.

37. For the text of the Copenhagen Manifesto, see "Die Forderungen der zionistischen Organisation an die Friedenskonferenz: Erklärung des Kopenhagener Büros," in Motzkin, *Die Judenfrage der Gegenwart*, 68–69. For the Prague Jewish National Council's demands, see "Das Memorandum des Jüdischen Nationalrats an den Národní výbor," *Selbstwehr*, November 8, 1918; for an English translation, see Aharon M. Rabinowicz, "The Jewish Minority," 218–221.

38. Rozenblit, *Reconstructing a National Identity*, 125–126; Rechter, *The Jews of Vienna*, 166–173.

39. Kieval, *The Making of Czech Jewry*, 189–190.

40. See the documents in Motzkin, *Die Judenfrage der Gegenwart*.

41. Rozenblit, *Reconstructing a National Identity*, 68–71.

42. Klein-Pejšová, "Beyond the 'Infamous Concentration Camps,'" 156.

43. Rozenblit, *Reconstructing a National Identity*, 66–68.

44. Ibid., 69; Welling, *"Von Hass so eng umkreist,"* 126, 131, 137.

45. Kieval, *The Making of Czech Jewry*, 160–163.

46. Welling, *"Von Hass so eng umkreist,"* 84, 158; Lipscher, "Die Lage der Juden," 14–16.

47. Welling, *"Von Hass so eng umkreist,"* 99–101.

48. Kieval, *The Making of Czech Jewry*, 187.

49. For unification efforts during the war including those of Kaznelson, see Rechter, *The Jews of Vienna*, 137–160; see also Kieval, *The Making of Czech Jewry*, 187.

50. Rechter, *The Jews of Vienna*, 140–141, 144, 157–158.

51. Joseph Rothschild, *East Central Europe*, 76.

52. Mary Heimann, *Czechoslovakia*, 23–27.

53. Josef Kalvoda, "Masaryk in America in 1918," 98.

54. Heimann, *Czechoslovakia*, 33.

55. Rothschild, *East Central Europe*, 80.

56. Margaret MacMillan, *Paris 1919*, 237.

57. Ibid., 234; see also Rothschild, *East Central Europe*, 80.

58. MacMillan, *Paris 1919*, 237–238, 240.

59. "Masaryk für den Zionismus," *Selbstwehr*, November 8, 1918; "Der Wortlaut von Masaryks Botschaft," *Selbstwehr*, December 15, 1918; "Tschechische Staatsmänner über die jüdische Frage: Für Zionismus und Nationaljudentum–Für die Demokratisierung der Kultusgemeinden," *Selbstwehr*, January 31, 1919; "Die Pariser Delegation

des Prager Jüd. Nationalrates beim Minister Beneš," *Selbstwehr,* April 18, 1919.

60. "Der Wortlaut von Masaryks Botschaft," *Selbstwehr,* November 15, 1918.

61. On Singer's meeting, see Rozenblit, *Reconstructing a National Identity,* 125; and Rechter, *The Jews of Vienna,* 145.

62. "Der erste jüdische Nationalkongress," *Selbstwehr,* January 10, 1919. Among the Czech guests were Czech Social Democrats, members of the National Socialist and National Democratic Parties, along with journalists and writers.

63. "Der erste jüdische Nationalkongress," *Selbstwehr,* January 10, 1919.

64. Rozenblit, *Reconstructing a National Identity,* 145.

65. Fink, *Defending the Rights of Others,* 127–128, 158–160.

66. Ibid., 142.

67. Ibid., 196.

68. "Die Forderungen der jüdischen Delegationen an die Friedenskonferenz," in Motzkin, *Die Judenfrage der Gegenwart,* 74–78; Fink, *Defending the Rights of Others,* 200.

69. Ladislav Lipscher, "Die Pariser Friedensverhandlungen," 170; Fink, *Defending the Rights of Others,* 233, 269.

70. For the German Foreign Office's attention to Jewish interests in Eastern Europe and the United States after the war, see Nicosia, "Jewish Affairs and German Foreign Policy," 265. For German support for Jewish activists, the connection between Germany's fortunes in Paris and anti-Jewish violence in Poland, and that a connection between Zionists and Berlin was detected by diplomats in Paris, see Fink, *Defending the Rights of Others,* 107–113, 142–148, 160, 184.

71. On June 28, 1919, Poland signed a treaty known as the "The Little Versailles." It included a commitment to equality for those of its inhabitants who belonged to "racial, religious, or linguistic minorities." Despite the committee's efforts, Jews were not recognized as a national minority, did not get guaranteed political representation, but did get guarantees along with the country's other minorities that they had the right to state funding for minority schools (articles 10 and 11 of the treaty deal with Jews' rights). The treaty did afford freedom of religion and some protection of Sabbath observance. Fink, *Defending the Rights of Others,* 257–260.

72. Given Slovakia's Orthodox Jewish leaders' determined resistance to Zionism and the leadership of the Jewish National Council, this was a questionable assertion. "Bericht über die Plenarsitzung des Jüdischen Nationalrates am September 14," *Selbstwehr,* October 3, 1919. For Jewish politics in Slovakia in the immediate postwar period and Orthodox opposition to Zionists, see Rebekah Klein-Pejšová, *Mapping Jewish Loyalties in Interwar Slovakia,* 55–62.

73. Czechoslovakia gave assurances to minorities prior to the signing of the peace treaties. See Fink, *Defending the Rights of Others,* 126; and Frank Hadler, "'Erträglicher Antisemitismus'?," 189.

74. Letter from Edvard Beneš to Ludvík Singer, d. August 25, 1919, in A. Rabinowicz, "The Jewish Minority," 172–173; see also Kateřina Čapková, *Czechs, Germans, Jews?,* 29–30.

75. "Der Wortlaut von Masaryks Botschaft," *Selbstwehr,* November 15, 1918; "Die Pariser Delegation des Prager Jüd. Nationalrates beim Minister Beneš," *Selbstwehr,* April 18, 1919; interview with Hugo Bergmann, "Die Lage der Juden im tschechoslowakischen Staat," *Selbstwehr,* March 28, 1919. On the Czech propaganda campaign to sustain this image, see Fink, *Defending the Rights of Others,* 269. For a detailed analysis of Czech propaganda campaigns and cultural diplomacy during and after WWII, see Orzoff, *Battle for the Castle,* 23–56.

76. Schmuel Hugo Bergmann, *Tagebücher und Briefe,* vol. 1 (1901–1948), 125; Lipscher, "Die Pariser Friedensverhandlungen," 172.

77. The report from the meeting on August 28, 1919, quoted in A. Rabinowicz, "The Jewish Minority," 174–177. For Great Power leniency with regard to Czechoslovakia, see Fink, *Defending the Rights of Others,* 269.

78. Fink, *Defending the Rights of Others,* 127–128.

79. Rozenblit, *Reconstructing a National Identity,* 144.

80. Bergmann, *Tagebücher und Briefe,* 125; Lipscher, "Die Pariser Friedensverhandlungen," 173.

81. Bergmann, *Tagebücher und Briefe,* 125.

82. Letter from Hugo Bergmann to Leo Hermann August 26, 1919, quoted in A. Rabinowicz, "The Jewish Minority," 250–251.

83. Considering the Czech authorities' efforts to sustain an image abroad of a stable Czechoslovakia through propaganda and censorship, along with Bergmann's complaints about not receiving mail from Prague, one wonders to what extent those delegates who spent months abroad were aware of the situation at home. For examples of censorship of articles describing antisemitic events in Slovakia and the Bohemian Lands, see "V zoufalství nejvyšším," *Židovské zprávy,* July 11, 1919; "Doklady o Slovensku," *Židovské zprávy,* July 11, 1919; an untitled segment on page 3 in *Selbstwehr,* July 11, 1919; "Protižidovské bouře v Karlíně," *Židovské zprávy,* August 27, 1919; on letters, see Hugo Bergman to Else Bergmann, Bern March 12, 1919, and Paris April 7, 1919, in Bergmann, *Tagebücher und Briefe,* 118, 120.

84. Fink, *Defending the Rights of Others,* 160–161.

85. "Bericht über die Plenarsetzung des Jüdischen Nationalrates am 14. September 1919," *Selbstwehr,* October 3, 1919; Rozenblit, *Reconstructing a National Identity,* 144.

86. For the press campaign and its aftermath in relations to the Lemberg (Lwów) pogrom (November 22–24, 1918) and the Polish army's execution of thirty-five Jewish civilians in Pinsk (April 5, 1919), see Carole Fink, *Defending the Rights of Others,* 111, 125–128, 185–200.

87. "Die Ausschreitungen in Faltenau," *Selbstwehr,* November 29, 1918; "Jüdischer Nationalrat in Prag – Interventionen," *Selbstwehr,* November 22, 1918; "Mitteillungen des Jüd. Nationalrates in Brünn," *Jüdische Volksstimme,* November 22, 1918.

88. The communiqué was dated December 4, 1918, described two days of violence, and was published in *Selbstwehr,*

"Communique des jüdischen Nationalrats über die Ausschreitungen in Prag," *Selbstwehr,* December 6, 1918. The authors claimed to have sent their communiqué to Jewish National Councils, Zionist organizations, and Jewish press bureaus in various countries.

89. "Antisemitisches von der Prager deutschen Universität," *Selbstwehr,* November 22, 1918.

90. Letter from Max Brod to Leo Hermann d. October 18, 1918, as quoted in Brod's memoir *Streitbares Leben,* 237–238.

91. Rozenblit, *Reconstructing a National Identity,* 142.

92. "Denkschrift des jüdischen Nationalrats wegen des Holleschauer Pogroms," *Selbstwehr,* December 13, 1918.

93. The JNC reported numerous interventions to the WZO; see Rozenblit, *Reconstructing a National Identity,* 145.

94. For discussion of the earlier boycott, see Jeremy King, *Budweisers into Czechs and Germans, 1848–1948,* 127–128; for the early boycott and Jews, see Kieval, *Languages of Community,* 168, 189–190; and Catherine Albrecht, "The Rhetoric of Economic Nationalism."

95. "Wirtschaftlicher Boykott gegen die Juden," *Selbstwehr,* December 13, 1918.

96. "Antisemitische Ausschreitungen in Klattau und Strakonitz," *Selbstwehr,* January 17, 1919.

97. "Mitteilungen des Jüdischen Nationalrats in Prag," *Selbstwehr,* March 28, 1919; see also "Der Jüdische Nationalrat beim President Masaryk in Prag," *Jüdische Volksstimme,* April 4, 1919.

98. For Jewish activists' work to defend Jews against violence in Slovakia, see Klein-Pejšová, *Mapping Jewish Loyalties in Interwar Slovakia,* 41–48.

99. "Denkschrift des Jüdischen Nationalrats wegen des Holleschauer Pogroms," *Selbstwehr,* December 13, 1918.

100. Extract from the Report of Activities of the Jewish National Council in Prague, January 1919, in A. Rabinowicz, "The Jewish Minority," 222.

101. "Pravda o protižidovských výtržnostech v Karlíně," *Židovské zprávy,* May 23, 1919.

102. "Judenrecht," *Selbstwehr,* May 23, 1919; on the meeting, see Rozenblit, *Reconstructing a National Identity,* 143.

103. For a comparison of the postwar months in Poland and Czechoslovakia, see Anthony Polonsky and Michael Riff, "Poles, Czechoslovaks and the 'Jewish Question'"; for Zionists and the pogroms, see Rozenblit, *Reconstructing a National Identity,* 142.

104. "Der Lemberger Massenmord," *Selbstwehr,* November 29, 1918. This was a coordinated campaign, according to Carole Fink, and was fueled by a sense of urgency among Jewish leaders to demonstrate the need for both minority rights and a Jewish homeland in Palestine; see Fink, *Defending the Rights of Others,* 148–151.

105. "Der Vernichtungskrieg gegen die galizischen Juden," *Selbstwehr,* November 29, 1918; "Wie lange noch wollen unsere tonangebenden und massbegenden Führer die Agonie der böhm. Judenheit tatenlos mitansehen," *Jüdische Volksstimme,* January 24, 1919.

106. "Communiqué des Jüdischen Nationalrats über die Ausschreitungen in Prag," *Selbstwehr,* December 6, 1918.

107. Frankel, "Paradoxical Politics," 9–12.

108. For a good example of the perception of American Jews' influence, see "Zpráva o plenárním zasedání Národní Rady Židovské dne 3. května 1919," *Židovské zprávy,* May 16, 1919.

109. This was a well-established tradition among Zionist leaders. Theodor Herzl had employed the trope of international Jewish power when negotiating with state leaders since the Zionist movement's inception in the late 1890s. For a discussion of Herzl's methods, see Jacques Kornberg, "Theodore Herzl: A Revaluation," 239–240. David Rechter observes the same pattern among Viennese Zionist leaders in the postwar months as Austria's fate was being pondered by the Allies; see Rechter, *The Jews of Vienna,* 168.

110. Hadler, "'Erträglicher Antisemitismus'?," 177–178, 183, 190, 196.

111. Kieval, *Languages of Community,* 206–208. As Kieval shows, Masaryk was aware of this and admitted that he was not able to "overcome . . . the anti-Semitism of the common people." For a similar analysis, see Michael A. Riff, "The Ambiguity of Masaryk's Attitudes on the 'Jewish Question.'"

112. Kieval, *Languages of Community,* 206, 214.

113. Hadler, "'Erträglicher Antisemitismus'?," 178.

114. From Tomáš G. Masaryk's 1925 *Světová Revoluce,* as quoted in Felix Weltsch, "Masaryk und der Zionismus," in *Masaryk und das Judentum,* 67–116, here 77. See also the translation in Kieval, *Languages of Community,* 279. Masaryk might have been attempting to rationalize his 'pro-Jewishness' in the face of voices on the right critical of Jewish and German influence in Masaryk's circle in the interwar period. Christoph Stölzl, "Die 'Burg' und die Juden," 106–107.

115. Hadler, "'Erträglicher Antisemitismus'?," 186–187.

116. Letter from Masaryk to Beneš, as quoted in Hadler, "'Erträglicher Antisemitismus'?," 186. For full text of letter, see Zdeněk Solle, ed., *Masaryk a Beneš ve svých dopisech,* vol. 2, 146.

117. Letter quoted in Hadler, "'Erträglicher Antisemitismus'?," 187.

118. American Zionists implied that Masaryk's public commitment to equality for Jews and to "the rights of all minorities" demonstrated that the Czech leader was indeed "one of the noblest statesmen of the Allied Powers"; see the telegram as quoted in A. Rabinowicz, "The Jewish Minority," 244.

119. Letter from Chaim Weizmann to Minister Vavro Šrobár, d. July 8, 1919, as quoted in A. Rabinowicz, "The Jewish Minority," 223–224.

120. Report from meeting on August 28, 1919, between Nahum Sokolow and Edvard Beneš; see A. Rabinowicz, "The Jewish Minority," 174–177, here 174–176.

121. Beneš had stated earlier that he believed that the level of culture of a nation was reflected in its treatment of its Jews, implying that the "absence" of antisemitism in Czechoslovakia reflected the exceptionally cultured character of the state. "Die Pariser Delegation des Prager Jüd. Nationalrates beim Minister Beneš," *Selbstwehr,* April 18, 1919.

122. Both Beneš and Masaryk tended to plead ignorance of antisemitism or anti-Jewish violence when faced with complaints by Jewish activists, which served to dismiss these complaints as rumors and to exonerate the statesmen from any association with such accusations; see Hadler, "'Erträglicher Antisemitismus'?," 190, 193; Stölzl, "Die 'Burg' und die Juden," 99.

123. "Eine jüdische Massenversammlung in Prag," *Selbstwehr,* November 15, 1918; "Erste Jüdische Nationalkongress," *Selbstwehr,* January 10, 1919; "Brandeis Begleiter Wilsons," *Selbstwehr,* November 22, 1918.

124. "In Washington und in Prag: Brandeis, Bergson und Lord Reading für das tschechishe Volk," *Selbstwehr,* November 8, 1918.

125. Ibid.

126. "Masaryk für den Zionismus, Eine Botschaft an die amerikanischen Zionisten über die Juden im tschechoslowakischen Staat," *Selbstwehr,* November 8, 1918; see also the multiple articles on page 3 of that issue; "Der Wortlaut von Masaryks Botschaft," *Selbstwehr,* November 15, 1918; "Th. G. Masaryk," *Selbstwehr,* December 20, 1918. This admiration of the perceived accomplishments of American Jewry, many of whom were from Austria-Hungary and Russia, was common among Jews in Eastern Europe. See, for example, Rebecca Kobrin, "Rewriting the Diaspora," 15.

127. For instances of government censors' intervention when Jewish writers' self-censorship failed, see "V zoufalství nejvyšším," *Židovské zprávy,* July 11, 1919; "Doklady o Slovensku," *Židovské zprávy,* July 11, 1919; untitled, *Selbstwehr,* July 11, 1919; "Protižidovské bouře v Karlíně," *Židovské zprávy,* August 27, 1919.

128. Rozenblit also notes the depictions of "bad Poland and good Czechoslovakia"; see *Reconstructing a National Identity,* 142.

129. "Plünderungen," *Selbstwehr,* January 17, 1919.

130. "Ein tschechischer Eideshelfer der Polenlügen," *Selbstwehr,* February 21, 1919; for more examples, see also "Flüchtningslos – Judenschicksal," *Selbstwehr,* March 21, 1919; "Tschechoslowakischer Republik – Jüdischer Boykott," *Selbstwehr,* January 31, 1919.

131. "Die Tschechen und die Juden," *Selbstwehr,* October 25, 1918.

132. Minutes from the meetings of the provisional Czechoslovak National Assembly (Národní shromáždění československé) [NSČ], http://www.psp.cz/eknih/1918ns/index.htm, Karel Kramář, December 20, 1918, NSČ, 1918–1920.

133. Josef Stivín, December 20, 1918, NSČ, http://www.psp.cz/eknih/1918ns/index.htm.

134. Karel Kramář, December 20, 1918, NSČ, 1918–1920; for more examples, see Lipscher, "Die Lage der Juden," 23–24.

135. For more on the events in Slovakia, see Lipscher, "Die Lage der Juden," 26–35.

136. Josef Pekař, "Židé a bolševictví," *Národní listy,* August 31, 1919.

137. See, for example, "Jed z Judey," *Mír,* September 4, 1919; "Zhoubný kvas," *Mír,* November 13, 1919. For a list of antisemitic publications in Czech from

this period, see Lipscher, "Die Lage der Juden," 12–13, 16–19.

138. Klein-Pejšová, "Beyond the 'Infamous Concentration Camps,'" 153, 166.

139. Rozenblit, *Reconstructing a National Identity,* 139, 143.

140. Orzoff, *Battle for the Castle.*

141. "Židovská národnost v ústavě," *Židovské zprávy,* March 1, 1920.

3. Mapping Jews

1. Antonin Boháč, *Národní stát a světový mír: O zásady nového míru* (Praha: Melantrich, 1946), 42.

2. Benedict Anderson explored the census's role in constructing racial collectives and subsequent ethnic nationalisms in "Census, Map, Museum," in *Imagined Communities,* 163–170.

3. On the uses of statistics to map territories and populations, see James C. Scott, *Seeing Like a State,* 9–84.

4. Jacqueline Urla, "Cultural Politics in an Age of Statistics," 818.

5. Pieter M. Judson, *Guardians of the Nation,* 29.

6. John M. Efron, *Defenders of the Race;* Mitchell B. Hart, *Social Science and the Politics of Modern Jewish Identity;* Derek J. Penslar, *Shylock's Children;* Oren Soffer, "Antisemitism, Statistics, and the Scientization of Hebrew Political Discourse." When employing the term "Jewish statistics" or "Jewish social science," I am referring to the body of research on Jews as a social collective undertaken by Jewish experts from a broad range of disciplines beginning in the 1880s. As Mitchell Hart points out, the term "Jewish statistics" served as shorthand for a wide range of research categories relying methodologically on descriptive statistics, history, and ethnography. From 1902 to 1925, Berlin was the institutional focal point for Jewish social science. The organizing body, the Bureau for Jewish Statistics (Verein für jüdische Statistik), set up its main office here, and it was where its journal, *Zeitschrift für Demographie und Statistik der Juden,* was published. Furthermore, it was an institution closely connected to the Zionist project. Nevertheless, scholars from a wide variety of places and with very different interests and agendas used the methods and concepts of Jewish statistics; see Hart, *Social Science and the Politics of Modern Jewish Identity,* 3–4.

7. Both Hart and Efron locate this impetus in Max Nordau's 1901 speech calling for the collection, production, and publication of knowledge about Jews. Hart, *Social Science and the Politics of Modern Jewish Identity,* 29–31; Efron, *Defenders of the Race,* 168–169.

8. For the Jewish Conservative Party and the first census, see letter d. September 29, 1927, from Koloman Weisz to the Ministry of Interior, Národní Archiv–Ministerstvo školství a národní osvěty [MŠ] inv.č. 2086 sign. 47/VIII karton 3924.

9. For complaints about census commissioners, see Jaroslav Bubeník and Jiří Křesťan, "Zjišťování národnosti jako problém statistický a politický."

10. Emanuel Rádl, *Národnost jako vědecký problém* (Praha: Orbis, 1929), 48. Rádl insisted on citizens' right to choose nationality rather than be ascribed national belonging. He touched on the subject in his 1928 book-length analysis

of Czech-German relations, *Válka Čechů s Němci* (Praha, 1928), which was highly critical of Czech policies toward the country's German minority. His polemic with Czech statisticians, Antonín Boháč in particular, regarding the validity of nationality statistics was published in *Národnost jako vědecký problém.*

11. Rogers Brubaker, *Ethnicity without Groups,* 8.

12. Boháč, *Národní stát a světový mír,* 40–42.

13. Jeremy King, *Budweisers into Czechs and Germans,* 165.

14. Antonín Boháč, *Studie o populaci v Československé republice I: Rok 1927* (Praha: Melantrich, 1928), 14, 29.

15. King, *Budweisers into Czechs and Germans,* 162–163. Although the minority rights and language laws did not commit the state to fund national minority social, cultural, and educational institutions, that did become the practice in the 1920s as the country's most significant German political parties entered into coalition governments; see Tara E. Zahra, *Kidnapped Souls,* 145–146.

16. The authorities were alerted to the possibility for side switching by the results of the 1919 preliminary census; see King, *Budweisers into Czechs and Germans,* 141, 159, 172–173.

17. On the importance of the census in light of recent elections, see "Sčítání lidu," *Židovské zprávy,* January 21, 1921.

18. Judson, *Guardians of the Nation,* 29–33; for more on Austrian census practices and their effect on national competition in the Bohemian Lands, see Z. A. B. Zeman, "The Four Austrian Censuses," 37.

19. Mark Cornwall, "The Struggle on the Czech-German Language Border," 919.

20. Everyday language was dismissed by these experts as a flexible and adopted tool of communication, not an expression of national belonging; Antonín Boháč, "Národnost či jazyk?," *Československý statistický věstník* 2 (1921): 40–58, here 52. There was not consensus among social scientists as to what exactly constituted mother tongue. Some defined it as the language a person learned first, linking the person to his or her ancestral community; others, as the language that a person was most familiar with and in which he or she thought or spoke. For a discussion of the term and critique of mother tongue's status as an objective marker, see Dobroslav Krejčí, "Má se při našem příštím sčítání lidu zjišťovati národnost nebo řeč mateřská?," *Československý statistický věstník* 1 (1920): 275–285. As the Austrian census had, the authorities allowed respondents to claim only one language as an ethnic marker. The Czechoslovak census makers continued the Austrian practice of erasing multilingualism from the results, as they allowed respondents to record only one mother tongue; see "Instrukce pro sčítácího komisaře a revisora," *Československý statistický věstník* 2 (1921): 143–148, here 145. Statisticians also rejected national identities defined by space, citing examples such as Carpathian-Rus, Moravian, South Slav, or some other spatial rather than ethnic nationality as an unacceptable answer; see Krejčí, "Má se při našem příštím sčítání lidu zjišťovati

národnost nebo řeč mateřská?," 279–280.

21. For the ethnification of national belonging, see Gerald Stourzh, "Ethnic Attribution in Late Imperial Austria," 67–83; and T. Mills Kelly, "Last Best Chance or Last Gasp?"

22. Jeremy King, "Who Is Who?," 3.

23. Antonín Boháč, "První všeobecné sčítání lidu v Československé republice," *Československý statistický věstník* 2 (1921): 104–120, here 116.

24. Ibid., 104.

25. King, *Budweisers into Czechs and Germans*, 165.

26. In the scientific community, there was considerable discussion about whether Jews were a nation, precisely because of their perceived lack of a national language. The census makers attempted to accommodate multiple views by allowing Jews to choose Jewish nationality or any other nationality according to their mother tongue; see Boháč, "Národnost či jazyk?," 42. For the position that nationality should be a subjective choice, see Krejčí, "Má se při našem příštím sčítání lidu zjišťovati národnost nebo řeč mateřská?," 285. For the position that objective verifiable markers were necessary, see Antonín Boháč, "Příští sčítání lidu," *Československý statistický věstník* 1 (1920): 268–275, here 272–274. Both authors agreed that Jews constituted a distinct ethnic group. The discussion in Czechoslovakia reflected a more widespread uncertainty regarding the classification of Jews as a nationality; see, for example, the debate among Soviet ethnographers in Francine Hirsch, *Empire of Nations*, 132.

27. For regulations regarding the census's question of nationality, see Boháč, "První všeobecné sčítání lidu v Československé republice," 116. For the perception of the sociological importance of religion in preserving Jewish distinctiveness, thereby legitimizing it as an objective marker, see Boháč, "Národnost či jazyk?," 54.

28. For the Austrian court's decision on Jewish nationality status in connection with the Bukovina Compromise in 1909, see Gerald Stourzh, "Galten die Juden als Nationalität Altösterreichs?," 92.

29. This was included in the constitutional articles supplementing the Constitution's §128; see Ústavní listina, Národní shromáždění československé 1918–1920, tisk 2421 část č. 3, available electronically at www.psp.cz.

30. For examples of Austrian judges upholding the Legal Code's definition of Jews as a religious community yet recognizing that Jews are a separate ethnic and in some cases national group, and even that future legislation might change to reflect that, see King, "Who Is Who?," 45–48.

31. "Memorandum Národní rady židovské Prezidiu ministerské rady ČSR o zjišťování národnosti při prvním sčítání lidu v Československu 24. října 1920" (Memorandum from the Jewish National Council to the Ministerial Council of the Czechoslovak Republic regarding the identification of nationality in the first Czechoslovak census d. 24 October 1920) [Memorandum, October 24, 1920], reprinted (29–31) in Jaroslav Bubeník and Jiří Křesťan, "Zjišťování národnosti a židovská otázka," 29.

32. Memorandum, October 24, 1920, 29–30.

33. The Jewish National Council did not consider religion the only marker of Jewish descent, asking specifically for individuals with another or no religion to be allowed to claim Jewish nationality. In practice, however, this seems to be the only way in which Jewish descent could be determined aside from an individual's own statement or the census commissioners' observation of other "ethnic Jewish markers"; see Memorandum, October 24, 1920, 30.

34. As Hillel Kieval suggests, Masaryk was uncomfortable with Jews becoming Czech, and the endorsement of Jewish national rights was a way to avoid encouraging assimilation; Kieval, *Languages of Community,* 212. See also Kateřina Čapková, "Uznání židovské národnosti v Československu," 91, 101; Zahra, *Kidnapped Souls,* 119; Ezra Mendelsohn, *The Jews of East Central Europe,* 146; Václav L. Beneš, "Czechoslovak Democracy and Its Problems," 41.

35. *Židovské zprávy* denounced Heinrich Rauchberg for calling on Jews "not to endanger their own rights and those of their German fellow citizens" by opting for Jewish nationality in the upcoming census, a warning echoed by the German press; see "Židé a sčítání lidu," *Židovské zprávy,* February 3, 1921. Zionists were particularly incensed by Rauchberg's "Jewish origins." To them he served as an example of the chauvinistic character of assimilating Jews eager to prove their "Germanness"; see "K sčítání lidu (Návrh, který musí padnouti)," *Židovské zprávy,* February 14, 1930.

36. While *Židovské zprávy* generally cited Czech support for the Zionist cause, Brno/Brünn's *Jüdische Volksstimme* reported that both Czech and German nationalists were competing for Jewish "numbers"; see "Volkszählung," *Jüdische Volksstimme,* February 10, 1921.

37. Rauchberg wrote about his experience of the Statistical Bureau's decision-making process in an article published in mid-January 1921 in *Znaimer Tagblatt,* as quoted by Emanuel Rádl in *Národnost jako vědecký problém,* 43–44.

38. Rebekah Klein-Pejšová, *Mapping Jewish Loyalties in Interwar Slovakia,* 123.

39. For 1910: table 24, p. 34, in *Österreichische Statistik: Die Ergebnise der Volkszählung vom 31. Dezember 1910,* 1. Band, 2. Heft (Wien: K.K. Hof- und Staatsdruckerei, 1914); for 1921: table 1, pp. 3–4, in *Československá statistika: Sčítání lidu ze dne 15. 2.1921,* svazek 37, řada VI, sešit 6 III. díl (Praha, 1927); for 1930: table 4, pp. 104–107, in *Československá statistika: Sčítání lidu v republice československé ze dne 1. prosince 1930,* svazek 98, řada VI, díl I (Praha, 1934).

40. Klein-Pejšová, *Mapping Jewish Loyalties in Interwar Slovakia,* 134–137.

41. For the debate that preceded the 1930 census, see Bubeník and Křesťan, "Zjišťování národnosti a židovská otázka," 24–25; Bubeník and Křesťan, "Zjišťování národnosti jako problém statistický a politický," 119–139; Jaroslav Kučera, "Politický či přirozený národ?," 548–568. For a detailed critique of the Statistical Bureau's insistence on objective markers of nationality, see Rádl, *Národnost jako vědecký problém.*

42. This letter is quoted in Kateřina Čapková, *Czechs, Germans, Jews?*, 44. Letter d. 15.2.1930 from the President's Office to Ludvík Singer (Singer's letter to the President's Office was dated 10.2.1930), Archiv Kancelář prezidenta republiky [AKPR] D 1274/30.

43. Ludvík Singer noted publicly that there were "political" benefits in retaining the 1921 definition of Jewish nationality, i.e., fewer Germans and Hungarians, in his parliamentary speech on February 22, 1930; see NSČ, 1929–1935. See also his address to the parliament on Czech fears of "defeat" in mixed urban areas if the definition of Jewish nationality changed, as the Statistical Bureau had proposed earlier that year; Singer, November 26, 1930, NSČ, 1929–1935.

44. For Czech nationalist circles who believed Czechoslovaks were on the defensive against Germans and Hungarians, see comments in *Národní politika* as quoted in "Nationalität und Sprache," *Prager Tagblatt*, February 11, 1930. See also Cornwall, "Struggle on the Czech-German Language Border," 939; Tara Zahra, "Reclaiming Children for the Nation," 516. Čapková argues that both right-wing German and Czech nationalist parties supported the continued exemption for Jews; see Čapková, *Czechs, Germans, Jews?*, 45–46.

45. "Sčítání lidu," *Židovské zprávy*, January 21, 1921.

46. "Židé a sčítání lidu," *Židovské zprávy*, February 3, 1921; for similar sentiments in Moravia, see "Jüdisches Volk!," *Jüdische Volksstimme*, February 10, 1921; "Volkszählung," *Jüdische Volksstimme*, February 10, 1921.

47. See, for example, "Jüdische Wähler und Wählerinnen!," *Jüdische Volksstimme*, October 24, 1929.

48. "Sčítání lidu," *Židovské zprávy*, January 21, 1921.

49. "Jüdische Wähler und Wählerinnen!," *Jüdische Volksstimme*, October 24, 1929; "Volkszählung 1930," *Jüdische Volksstimme*, January 23, 1930.

50. See the sources on the debates preceding both the 1921 and 1930 census.

51. "Čeští židé a sčítání lidu," *Tribuna*, February 5, 1921.

52. Otto Bondy, "Antisemitský úspěch," *Rozvoj*, February 25, 1921.

53. The demand for statistical representation was included in the first memorandum the Jewish National Council delivered to the Czech government in October 1918; see English translation in Aharon M. Rabinowicz, "The Jewish Minority," 218–221.

54. Gustav Fleischmann's series appeared over the course of several months in 1922: "Výsledky sčítání lidu," *Židovské zprávy*, May 5, 1922; "Výsledky sčítání lidu II," *Židovské zprávy*, May 22, 1922; "Výsledky sčítání lidu III," *Židovské zprávy*, June 30, 1922; "Výsledky sčítání lidu," *Židovské zprávy*, August 25, 1922; "Výsledky sčítání lidu V," *Židovské zprávy*, October 6, 1922.

55. Fleischmann, "Výsledky sčítání lidu II," *Židovské zprávy*, May 22. 1922; see also "Výsledky sčítání lidu," *Židovské zprávy*, March 2, 1921.

56. Fleischmann, "Výsledky sčítání lidu II," *Židovské zprávy*, May 22, 1922.

57. "Jüdisches Volk!," *Jüdische Volksstimme*, February 10, 1921; "Die Volkszählung," *Jüdische Volksstimme*, February 10, 1921. For a later (1927),

but potent, example of this notion, see František Friedmann, *Mravnost či Oportunita? Několik poznámek k anketě akad. Spolku Kapper vBrně* (Praha: Sionistický výbor pro Čechy a Moravu v Praze, 1927), 54–55.

58. For this use of the term, see Zahra, "Reclaiming Children for the Nation," 521.

59. See Ludvík Singer's speech in the National Assembly on February 22, 1930, NSČ, 1929–1935.

60. Ibid. For Zionist MPs' constituency as including all Jews, see also "Was antwortet die Regierung," *Jüdische Volksstimme,* February 13, 1930.

61. Emil Margulies's lecture in the Society for the Study of the Minority Question, a state-sponsored institution founded in 1929, on March 21,1933, "Stenografisches Protokoll des Vortrages Dr. Emil Margulies 'Über die gegenwärtigen politischen Strömungen und Programme unserer Mitbürger jüdischer Nationalität,'" 4, Central Zionist Archives [CZA] A299/9.

62. "Die čechoslovakische Sprachenfrage und die Juden," *Jüdische Volksstimme,* July 11, 1929; "K sčítání lidu (Návrh, který musí padnouti)," *Židovské zprávy,* February 14, 1930. In anticipation of both censuses, Zionists stressed the importance of the census results for Jews' political and legal position; see "Sčítání lidu," *Židovské zprávy,* January 21, 1921; "Židé a sčítání lidu," *Židovské zprávy,* February 3, 1921; "Volkszählung 1930," *Jüdische Volksstimme,* January 23, 1930.

63. For critical voices within the Polish community, see Ellen L. Paul, "Czech Teschen Silesia and the Controversial Czechoslovak Census of 1921," 162–163, 165–167; see also Rádl, *Národnost jako vědecký problém.*

64. "Výsledky sčítání lidu," *Židovské zprávy,* March 2, 1921.

65. For the notion of backward- or forward-looking categories, see David I. Kertzer and Dominique Arel, "Censuses, Identity Formation, and the Struggle for Political Power," 25–27.

66. The view that German language was central to Jewish identity in the region was articulated by Jewish experts, such as František Friedmann, "Pražští Židé," in *Židovský kalendář 1929/1930:* 148–207, as well as more recently by Marsha L. Rozenblit, "Creating Jewish Space."

67. "Die Volkszählung," *Jüdische Volksstimme,* February 10, 1921.

68. See the Czech version of the Jewish National Council's address published as "Sčítání lidu," *Židovské zprávy,* January 21, 1921; and the German version, "Volkszählung," *Jüdische Volksstimme,* January 27, 1921. For a similar sentiment in 1930, see "Volkszählung 1930," *Jüdische Volksstimme,* February 13, 1930.

69. "Volkszählung 1930," *Jüdische Volksstimme,* January 23, 1930.

70. Zahra, *Kidnapped Souls,* 14.

71. Ibid. As Pieter Judson notes, while the 1867 Austrian Constitution envisioned the equality of languages as a basic individual civil right, over time language rights were increasingly interpreted as collective, national rights; see Judson, *Guardians of the Nation,* 12–13.

72. Zahra, *Kidnapped Souls,* 14.

73. Jeremy King, "The Municipal and the National in the Bohemian Lands."

74. King, *Budweisers into Czechs and Germans,* 152.

75. Zahra, *Kidnapped Souls,* 33–39.

76. Zahra, "Reclaiming Children for the Nation," 511.

77. Zahra, *Kidnapped Souls,* 126–127.

78. Over three hundred cases on contested children in Moravia reached the Supreme Administrative Court in the interwar years, two of which involved children of Jewish nationality, although others might have involved Jews with a different national belonging; see Zahra, "Reclaiming Children for the Nation," 504, for information on the collection as a whole. For the case of Wilhelm Trattner (of Czech nationality, but of Jewish origin) and of František Fríed, see also Zahra, *Kidnapped Souls,* 133. According to Zahra, every year, thousands of children were reclaimed for Czech schools in interwar Czechoslovakia; Zahra, *Kidnapped Souls,* chapter 4.

79. Antonín Boháč, *Studie o populaci v Československé republice I: Rok 1927* (Praha: Melantrich, 1928), 14, 29.

80. Case of Františk Fríed, NA–Nejvyšší správní soud [Nss] karton 858 doc. 58 case no. 16046/29 d. 7.9.1929 [Fríed]; case of Zuzana Fríednerová, NA–Nss karton 858 case no. 16836/30 d. 4.11.1930 [Fríednerová].

81. Fríednerová, 1–2.

82. Ibid., 4.

83. Fríed, 6.

84. Zahra, *Kidnapped Souls,* 129–131.

85. Ibid., 23–27.

86. František Friedmann, "Jaké školy navštěvují židovské dětí," *Židovské zprávy,* October 21, 1927.

87. Franz Friedmann, "Jüdische Kinder an Volks- und Bürgerschulen," *Selbstwehr,* October 7, 1932.

88. The Czechoslovak language law stipulated that if a national minority made up 20% or more of a jurisdiction's total population, minority language speakers had the right to the use of their own language in correspondence with public offices, courts, etc.; see articles related to section 129 of the Constitutional Charter, as quoted in A. Rabinowicz, "The Jewish Minority," 239.

89. "Jüdische Nationalität und Sprachenrecht," *Prager Presse,* December 5, 1929.

90. "Philipp Rauchberger erhebt Beschwerde gegen die Entscheidung des Justizministeriums vom 30.1.1928 Zahl: 47.899/27," submitted March 31, 1928, NA–Fond Emil Margulies inv.č. 25 karton 9, 1919–1928 doc. 10–16.

91. Letter from Paul März to Emil Margulies, d. April 12, 1928 NA–Fond Emil Margulies inv.č. 25 karton 9, 1919–1928 doc. 20.

92. Ibid.

93. Letter from Emil Margulies to Paul März, d. March 4, 1928 NA–Fond Emil Margulies inv.č. 25 karton 9, 1919–1928 doc. 17.

94. Letter from Emil Margulies to Paul März, d. April 21, 1928 NA–Fond Emil Margulies inv.č. 25 karton 9, 1919–1928 doc. 23.

95. Ibid.

96. "Die čechoslovakische Sprachenfrage und die Juden," *Jüdische Volksstimme,* July 11, 1929.

97. See the interview with the head of the Statistical Bureau, Jan Auerhan, in "President státního statistického

úřadu dr. Jan Auerhan o sčítání lidu," *České Slovo,* February 9, 1930; see also "Nationalität = Sprache: Nationaljuden nur Angehörige der hebräischen und jiddischen Sprache," *Prager Tagblatt,* February 5, 1930; "Nationalität und Sprache: Erklärungen des Präsidenten des Statistischen Staatsamtes," *Prager Tagblatt,* February 11, 1930.

98. This perception of Yiddish was common among many educated and middle-class Central European Jews; see Sander L. Gilman, *Jewish Self-Hatred: The Hidden Language of Jews.*

99. In 1921, the population census recorded 180,855 individuals who claimed Yiddish or Hebrew as their mother tongue. In 1930, 186,642 individuals were counted in that language category. The vast majority were Yiddish-speakers. For statistics, see Joseph Rothschild, *East Central Europe,* 89.

100. František Friedmann, *Mravnost či Oportunita? Několik poznámek k anketě akad. Spolku Kapper v Brně* (Praha: Sionistický výbor pracovní pro Čechy a Moravu v Praze, 1927), 24, 46.

101. Friedmann used the German equivalent of František, Franz, when writing for German-speaking audiences. For biographical details, see Magda Veselská, "František Friedmann."

102. Friedmann became a member of Prague's Municipal Council in 1931. He was the chair of Hagibor from 1933 to 1939, and he became the last chair of the Jewish nationalist sports organization Maccabi in Czechoslovakia in 1938. For a short biography, see "Skvělý úspěch židovské kandidátky v pražských volbách," *Židovské zprávy,* October 2, 1931; for involvement in Jewish sport, see Archiv hlavního města Prahy [AHMP]–Židovský sportovní klub Hagibor XIV/0367 and AHMP–Svaz Makabi v ČSR XIV/0685.

103. For an example of his command of local statistical data as well as Jewish statistics, see František Friedmann, "Pražští Židé," *Židovský kalendář 1929/1930:* 148–207; for his reputation as a statistician, see "Skvělý úspěch židovské kandidátky v pražských volbách," *Židovské zprávy,* October 2, 1931; and his essay on Bohemian Jewish statistics, František Friedmann, "Židé v Čechách," in *Židé a židovské obce v Čechách v minulosti a v přítomnosti,* vol. 1, ed. Hugo Gold (Brno-Praha: Židovské nakladatelství, 1934), 729–735.

104. This is especially true for his attacks on Czech-Jews and articles such as the ones challenging the efforts to institute a *numerus clausus* in Czechoslovak universities as well as his articles on Jewish children and schools. For Czech-Jews, see František Friedmann, *Mravnost či Oportunita?;* for the *numerus clausus* and schools, see, for example, "Jak to ve skutečnosti vyhlíží s cizinci na vysokých školách českých," *Židovské zprávy,* December 6, 1929; "Vysoké školy české ve světle číslic," *Židovské zprávy,* December 13, 1929; "Židovské děti na národních školách," *Židovské zprávy,* April 20, 1932.

105. Friedmann published a defense against the antisemitic attacks by the Czech social democrat Josef Hudec (1873–1957); František Friedmann, *Na obranu židovství, Kritické poznámky k brožuře poslance Josefa Hudce* (Praha: Židovské zprávy, 1920). For a lecture on the Jewish Party held as part of

a lecture series on the political parties in Czechoslovakia organized by the Union of Czechoslovak Student Societies, see František Friedmann, *Strana Židovská* (Praha: Kulturní odbor ústředního svazu českoslov. studentsva: Cyklus přednášek o ideologii českoslov. politických stran VII, 1931); for more scholarly endeavors, see the summary of his lecture held in November 1933 in the Society for the Study of the Minority Question, "Asimilace a sionismus u Židů v ČSR (Z přednášky dra F. Friedmanna dne 10. XI. 1933), *Národnostní Obzor* 4, no. 2 (1934): 159–160. For his two-part article published in the society's journal, the only study on the Jewish national minority in the journal's ten years, see František Friedmann, "Židovská národní menšina na Podkarpatské Rusi I," *Národnostní Obzor* 4, no. 3 (1934): 185–192, and "Židovská národní menšina na Podkarpatské Rusi II," *Národnostní Obzor* 4, no. 4 (1934): 269–277.

106. For critique of Ruppin's assessment of local nationality statistics, see Franz Friedmann, *Einige Zahlen über die tschechoslowakischen Juden: Ein Beitrag zur Soziologie der Judenheit* (Schriften zur Diskussion des Zionismus no. 9) (Prag: Jüd. Akad. Tech. Verb. Barissia, Prag, 1933), 28. For wider importance of Czechoslovak Jewry, see Franz Friedmann, *Die Juden in der Tschechoslowakei*, Zyklus: Nationalproblem und Judentum (Prag, 1936), 1. This is the German translation of a series of lectures given by Friedmann (in Czech) at the Zionist School for Continuing Education (Sionistická lidová vysoká škola/Zionistische Volkshochschule) in Prague in 1934/1935 (CZA BK 6970); *Einige Zahlen*, 9. These lectures were published in Prague in German and Yiddish editions but were intended for Jewish audiences across the German- and Yiddish-speaking Jewish world. For more on the Zionist distance learning program, see chapter 7.

107. Friedmann filed six legal complaints against the Zionist executive between 1935 and 1938 for misconstruction of his views or attempts to rid him of his position on Prague's Municipal Council; see "Nelze už mlčet," *Židovské zprávy*, February 25, 1938.

108. Kateřina Čapková's interview with Viktor Fischl entitled "Pak to ale dopadlo ještě jinak" was originally published in the monthly *Roš Chodeš* in March 2001. It is available online at http://www.holocaust.cz/cz2/resources/ros_chodes/2001/03/fischl (5–6).

109. Friedmann, *Mravnost či Oportunita?*, 45.

110. Ibid., 47–48.

111. Ibid., 29.

112. Ibid., 29.

113. Ibid., 71–72.

114. For the ethnification of national belonging, see Stourzh, "Ethnic Attribution in Late Imperial Austria"; Kelly, "Last Best Chance or Last Gasp?"

115. On the centrality of language in this process, see Dominique Arel, "Language Categories in Censuses: Backward- or Forward-Looking?," 96–102; Zeman, "The Four Austrian Censuses."

116. Friedmann, *Mravnost či Oportunita?*, 3.

117. Friedmann, *Strana Židovská*, 6–9.

118. Ibid., 6.

119. These distinctions accompanied almost all of Friedmann's longer studies of Czechoslovak Jewry; see, for example, Friedmann, *Mravnost či Oportunita?*, 45–46; *Einige Zahlen*, 9.

120. As explained earlier, Friedmann believed that the actual number of Jewish nationals in Bohemia was much higher than the census suggested, as more Jews voted for Jewish parties here than opted for Jewish nationality; see Friedmann, *Mravnost či Oportunita?*, 29; *Einige Zahlen*, 24.

121. Friedmann, *Tschechoslowakei*, 1.

122. Friedmann, *Mravnost či Oportunita?*, 40.

123. Friedmann, "Židovská národní menšina I," 188–192.

124. Friedmann, *Mravnost či Oportunita?*, 46–50.

125. Gustav Fleischmann "documented"' this trend in his study of the 1921 census results for the Bohemian Lands; see, for example, Fleischmann, "Výsledky sčítání lidu," *Židovské zprávy*, May 5, 1922; "Výsledky sčítání lidu III," *Židovské zprávy*, June 30, 1922. For non-Jewish experts' observations of this trend, see Antonín Boháč, "Hlavní město Praha: Studie statistická I. Část," *Československý statistický věstník* 3 (1922): 353–480, here 415; Friedmann drew explicitly on Boháč's study in his own work, see *Mravnost či Oportunita?*, 50–51.

126. František Friedmann, "Jak se změnilo rozsídlení Židů v Čechách za posledních 50 let," *Židovské zprávy*, December 2, 1927.

127. See the discussion in Michael L. Miller, *Rabbis and Revolution*, 339.

128. František Friedmann, "Jak se změnilo rozsídlení Židů v Čechách za posledních 50 let," *Židovské zprávy*, December 2, 1927. Friedmann also argued that the concentration of Jews in certain Prague neighborhoods such as the Old Town created the kind of densely populated community that allowed Jews to resist assimilation and denationalization; see Friedmann, "Pražští Židé."

129. For an article making a similar argument for all of Czechoslovak Jewry, see Friedmann, *Einige Zahlen*, 6–7.

130. "Asimilace a sionismus u Židů v ČSR (Z přednášky dra F. Friedmanna dne 10. XI. 1933)," 159.

131. Tara Zahra's work deals extensively with the creation of hard national boundaries and the methods used to marginalize people who were perceived to evade or to be indifferent to "their" nation. See Zahra, *Kidnapped Souls*.

132. Friedmann, *Na obranu židovství*, 49; *Strana Židovská*, 8–9.

133. Friedmann, *Mravnost či Oportunita?*, 43.

134. "Asimilace a sionismus u Židů v ČSR (Z přednášky dra F. Friedmanna dne 10. XI. 1933)," 159–160.

135. Friedmann, "Židovská národní menšina II," 271–272.

136. According to John Efron, the emphasis on historical experience over race in shaping Jews' character was typical for Jewish race scientists in the early 1900s; see Efron, *Defenders of the Race*, 174.

137. See, for example, Jeremy King's work for this process: King, *Budweisers into Czechs and Germans*.

138. For museums in interwar Czechoslovakia, see Magda Veselská, "Jewish and Related Museums in Czechoslovakia in the First Republic"; for the Prague museum, see Magda

Veselská, *Archa paměti;* examples of periodicals include *Ročenka Společnosti pro dějiny židů v ČSR/Jahrbuch der Gesellschaft für Geschichte der Juden in der Čechoslovakischen Republik* (published 1929–1938) and *Zeitschift für die Geschichte der Juden in der Tschechoslowakei* (published 1930–1938); for an overview of publications on Prague Jews for this period, see Otto Muneles's bibliographical index: Otto Muneles, ed., *Bibliografický přehled židovské Prahy.*

139. One example of this broader Jewish interest is the work of the Prague-born Josef Polák (1886–1945), who ran the Eastern Slovakia Regional Museum in Košice/Kaschau/Kassa in the interwar years. Polák, who had a lifelong interest in Jewish history and material culture, created ethnographical exhibits that highlighted that region's multiethnic character and religious diversity. See Magda Veselská, *Muž, který si nedal pokoj.*

140. Friedmann, "Pražští Židé," 192.

141. Ibid., 193–194.

142. Ibid., 195.

143. Ibid., 200–202. For a similar interpretation of the role of Moravia's Jewish schools, see Rozenblit, "Creating Jewish Space."

144. Friedmann, "Židé v Čechách," 733. Karl Freiherr von Czoernig (1804–1889) was president of the Austrian statistical service 1841–1865 and author of *Ethnographie der österreichischen Monarchie* (Wien, 1855–1857), to which Friedmann was referring. Prokop Závodský, "The National Museum and the Development of Statistical Science," 1–4; see also Kieval, *Languages of Community,* 138.

145. Friedmann, "Židé v Čechách," 733; "Sčítání lidu v duchu ústavy," *Židovské zprávy,* July 4, 1930. As Jews were not recognized as a *Volksstamm* (this category was defined by linguistic criteria, and Yiddish did not qualify as a legitimate language), they were often counted as belonging to other groups such as Germans and Poles. For Jewish activists' response in Galicia, see Joshua Shanes, "Neither Germans nor Poles," 196–197.

146. Friedmann, "Židé v Čechách," 729.

147. Friedmann, "Židovská národní menšina I," 190; this point was also made by the Moravian Jewish statistician Theodor Haas (1878–1942), also a Zionist activist, "Die Juden im Mähren nach den Ergebnissen der letzten Volkszählung," *Jüdische Volksstimme,* November 1, 1921. For a recent discussion of the links between Moravian Jews and the communities in what was then the northern part of the Kingdom of Hungary, see M. Miller, *Rabbis and Revolution,* 39–40.

148. The notion that Germans gradually Germanized the Slav heartlands is discussed in Cornwall, "Struggle on the Czech-German Language Border."

149. Elisabeth Bakke, "The Making of Czechoslovakism," 32.

150. Ibid., 28.

151. Similarly, the Jewish National Council had called on Jews to choose Jewish national identity and vote for Jewish parties by employing the Czechoslovakist trope "strength through numbers"; see "Sčítání lidu," *Židovské zprávy,* January 21, 1921.

152. Hugo Gold, ed., *Die Juden und Judengemeinden Mährens in Vergangenheit*

und Gegenwart (Brünn: Jüdischer Buch- und Kunstverlag, 1929); Hugo Gold, ed., *Die Juden und die Judengemeinde Bratislava in Vergangenheit und Gegenwart* (Brünn: Jüdischer Buchverlag, 1932); Hugo Gold, ed., *Židé a židovské obce v Čechách v minulosti a v přítomnosti/ Die Juden und Judengemeinden Böhmens in Vergangenheit und Gegenwart*, vol. 1 (Brno-Praha: Židovské nakladatelství, 1934). Hugo Gold saw this work as a step toward establishing a Jewish museum in Brno/Brünn encompassing both collections of artifacts and an archive, a process that needed to come under way "before it is too late"; see Gold, *Juden Mährens*, 3. While the Moravian volume was in German, the Bohemian one was in both Czech and German.

153. See, for example, the entry for Boskowitz/Boskovice, in Gold, *Juden Mährens*, 123.

154. Hugo Gold, "Slovo úvodem," in *Židé a židovské obce v Čechách v minulosti a v přítomnosti*, vol. 1, ed. Hugo Gold (Brno-Praha: Židovské nakladatelství, 1934).

155. Ibid.

156. Efron, *Defenders of the Race*, 126.

157. Friedmann, *Tschechoslowakei*, 1.

158. The Friedmanns' daughter was born in 1933, the son in 1936. See Friedmann's residence card held at NA.

159. For a recent example, see Livia Rothkirchen, *The Jews of Bohemia and Moravia*, 4–5.

4. Conquering Communities

1. "Das Gemeindeprogramm des Jüdischen Nationalrats: Thesen der Kultusgemeindekommission des J.N.R.," *Selbstwehr*, January 3, 1919.

2. For Herzl's intention and its subsequent interpretations in Germany and Austria, see Jehuda Reinharz, *Fatherland or Promised Land*, 112–113.

3. For the 1901 and later programs for the Zionist Organization for Habsburg Austria, see Adolf Gaisbauer, *Davidstern und Doppeladler*, 99–100, 312; for Zionism and the conquest more broadly, see Matityahu Mintz, "Work for the Land of Israel and 'Work in the Present,'" 161–170.

4. "Das Gemeindeprogramm des Jüdischen Nationalrats: Thesen der Kultusgemeindekommission des J.N.R.," *Selbstwehr*, January 3, 1919; and "Die Wahlen in die Kultusgemeinde," *Selbstwehr*, October 21, 1921. This was true more generally in Central Europe. For Weimar Germany, see Michael Brenner, "The Jüdische Volkspartei," 220.

5. In this chapter, when using "communal" or "community" I will be referring to this formal institution and its social, cultural, and religious infrastructure. For similar social and cultural modernization projects in Germany and Austria, see Michael Brenner and Derek J. Penslar, eds., *In Search of Jewish Community*.

6. For Zionists in Prague invoking the memory of the kehilah and the Volksgemeinde as the embodiment of more authentic Jewish community, see "Die Wahlen in die Kultusgemeinde," *Selbstwehr*, October 21, 1921.

7. Michael Brenner, *Renaissance of Jewish Culture*, 7, 49–65.

8. The statutes were adopted on September 16, 1919, *Statut der israelitischen Kultusgemeinde Mährisch Ostrau* (Mährisch Ostrau: Verlag des

Jüdischen Volksblattes, 1920), 3–4. Significantly, the statutes also required the community's rabbi to be qualified to lecture on Jewish literature and history and willing to do so in the winter months.

9. The Moravská Ostrava/Mährisch Ostrau community's statutes, authored by Alois Hilf, became the model for other Moravian Jewish communities such as Brno/Brünn; for Hilf's model statutes, see Theodor Haas, "Die Reform der Brünner Kultusgemeinde Statuten," *Jüdische Volksstimme,* January 23, 1921.

10. Jews in the former Hungarian territories that became Slovakia and Subcarpathian Rus' in 1918 had undergone a more limited form of Germanization centering on language use. Later, German was to some extent replaced by Hungarian among the region's Jews; see Michael Silber, "The Historical Experience of German Jewry." For the failed efforts in the mid-nineteenth century to create a rabbinical seminary in Mikulov/Nikolsburg in Moravia, the first in the historic Habsburg Lands, see Michael L. Miller, *Rabbis and Revolution,* 302–303.

11. This chapter studies modernization from the center and thus focuses on the Prague leadership. The communal archives for individual communities are kept at the Jewish Museum in Prague. For an overview of this collection, see Jan Heřman, "Jewish Community Archives from Bohemia and Moravia."

12. For the most detailed overview, see Hugo Gold's encyclopedic volumes on Moravia and Bohemia, *Die Juden und Judengemeinden Mährens in Vergangenheit und Gegenwart* (Brünn: Jüdischer Buch- und Kunstverlag, 1929); and *Die Juden und Judengemeinden Böhmens in Vergangenheit und Gegenwart* (Brünn: Jüdischer Buch- und Kunstverlag, 1934).

13. Twenty-seven of Moravia's fifty-two communities had Jewish political communities. Some of the larger ones had their own constable, fire brigade, and German-language Jewish school. The religious community and the Jewish municipality were not overlapping, as the latter was made up of homeowners and taxpayers within a certain district, while the former encompassed all Jews living within the territorial boundaries of the community; see Ruth Kestenberg-Gladstein, "The Jews between Czechs and Germans," 46–49.

14. Michael L. Miller, "Voice and Vulnerability," 161.

15. Ibid., 162.

16. M. Miller, *Rabbis and Revolution,* 311, 331–334.

17. Michael L. Miller and Marsha L. Rozenblit, authors of the most recent studies on Moravian Jews, agree on the significance of German for Moravian Jewish culture as well as the importance of specific institutions, such as the German-Jewish schools and the *Landesmassafond,* in maintaining Jews' sense of ethnic distinctiveness. Miller's argument is best summarized in M. Miller, "Voice and Vulnerability," and Rozenblit makes her case in, "Creating Jewish Space," 109.

18. Theodor Haas, "Statistische Bertrachtungen über die jüdische Bevölkerung Mährens," in *Die Juden und Judengemeinden Mährens in Vergangenheit und Gegenwart,* ed. Hugo Gold (Brünn:

Jüdischer Buch- und Kunstverlag, 1929), 594–596, here 594–595.

19. Ibid. For a discussion of the status of the "new" communities, i.e., ones that were not part of Moravia's original fifty-two communities, such as Brno/Brünn and Moravská Ostrava/Mährisch Ostrau, see Theodor Haas, *Die Juden in Mähren: Darstellung der Rechtsgeschichte und Statistik unter besonderer Berücksichtigung des 19. Jahrhunderts* (Brünn: Jüdischer Buch- und Kunstverlag, 1908), 45–46.

20. Haas, "Statistische Bertrachtungen," 594–595.

21. Ibid., 595.

22. Václav Paleček, "Izraelská náboženská společnost," in *Slovník veřejného práva československého,* ed. Emil Hácha et al., vol. 2 (Brno: Polygrafia 1932), 28–52, here 30. According to František Friedmann, the number of Jewish communities in Bohemia dropped from 274 to 199 between 1871 and 1921 (26% of the communities disappeared [75]); František Friedmann, "Jak se změnilo rozsídlení Židů v Čechách za posledních 50 let," *Židovské zprávy,* December 2, 1927.

23. If, in 1880, 50% (47,510) of Bohemian Jews lived in rural communities with a total population of less than 5000, by 1921 only 23% (18,108) did so; Friedmann, "Jak se změnilo rozsídlení Židů v Čechách za posledních 50 let."

24. The most significant work on Czech-speaking Jews and the social and cultural transformation of Bohemian Jewish life in the nineteenth and early twentieth centuries is Hillel J. Kieval's book *The Making of Czech Jewry,* 10–35.

25. Paleček, "Izraelská náboženská společnost," 30.

26. For example, the statistical data for the two provinces on language, religions, nationality, and so on were often merged and presented as one category, Moravia-Silesia, in scholarly as well as official state publications, a practice already in place during the late Habsburg period; see Haas, *Die Juden in Mähren,* 17; for more on this, see Fleischmann, "The Religious Congregation," 277.

27. Paleček, "Izraelská náboženská společnost," 29, the Law of March 21, 1890 no. 57.

28. The territorial definition was in line with previous legislation. For the changing legislation governing the Jewish communities in the Bohemian Lands until 1890, see Kieval, *Languages of Community,* 10–27.

29. Paleček, "Izraelská náboženská společnost," 35. There was a similar preference for such unified congregations (*Einheitsgemeinden*) in most communities in Weimar Germany; see Brenner and Penslar, *In Search of Jewish Community,* x.

30. The citizenship and character requirements for rabbis were adopted from the Austrian legislation, only Austrian citizenship was replaced with Czechoslovak; see Haas, *Die Juden in Mähren,* 40; and for new requirements, see Paleček, "Izraelská náboženská společnost," 30–33.

31. Neolog was particular to Jews in the Hungarian territories. It was a progressive form of Judaism that favored more secular education and moderate synagogue reforms but did not challenge halakhic norms. Most Neolog communi-

ties were larger urban ones, most prominently in Pest. For the Neolog movement and the schism in Hungary's Jewry, see Jacob Katz, *A House Divided: Orthodoxy and Schism in Nineteenth-Century Central European Jewry*, 41–45.

32. Status Quo was not a formal denomination, but a position of nonaffiliation, thus neither Orthodox nor Neolog. For a study of Status Quo communities, see Howard Lupovitch, "Between Orthodox Judaism and Neology: The Origins of the Status Quo Movement," 123–124, 127.

33. Zionists interpreted the expediency with which the Orthodox organization was established in the summer of 1930 as a deliberate act by Orthodox leaders in Slovakia to undermine early Zionist efforts to create a Czechoslovak federation; see "In der Slowakisch-Orthodoxen Zentralkanzlei," *Selbstwehr*, July 5, 1920; Klein-Pejšová, *Mapping Jewish Loyalties in Interwar Slovakia*, 142.

34. Katz, *A House Divided*, 230–31.

35. For Slovakia, see Klein-Pejšová, *Mapping Jewish Loyalties in Interwar Slovakia*, 142; and Paleček, "Izraelská náboženská společnost," 40.

36. Václav Müller, "Náboženské společnosti," in *Slovník veřejného práva československého*, vol. 2, 697–711, here 707.

37. See the report from the discussion at a meeting of Jewish leaders from Bohemia, "Svaz českých židovských náboženských obcí v Čechách," *Rozvoj*, April 18, 1924.

38. Otokar Kraus, "O úkolech židovských náboženských obcí," *Židovské zprávy*, January 23, 1925.

39. "Jak zastavit další úpadek židovství v Čechách?," *Židovské zprávy*, January 25, 1924. Interestingly, this debate did not get much attention in the German-language *Selbstwehr*.

40. "Jak zastavit další úpadek židovství v Čechách?," *Židovské zprávy* February 2, 1924.

41. J. Eisenberg, "Krise rabínského stavu I," *Rozvoj*, February 15, 1924.

42. Ibid.; Otokar Kraus, "Naše vedlejší příjmy," *Židovské zprávy*, May 29, 1925.

43. "K naší anketě o úpadku židovství v Čechách," *Židovské zprávy*, April 4, 1924.

44. J. Eisenberg, "Krise rabínského stavu II," *Rozvoj*, March 28, 1924.

45. In 1921, about 3.5% of the Jewish heads of households in Bohemia were owners, renters, or managers of large estates. By 1930, this number had dropped to 2.6%; see "Zanikají Židé v Čechách?," *Židovské zprávy*, August 27, 1934.

46. J. Eisenberg, "Krise rabínského stavu II," *Rozvoj*, March 28, 1924.

47. Ibid.

48. "K naší anketě o úpadku židovství v Čechách," *Židovské zprávy*, April 4, 1924.

49. František Friedmann, "Jak se změnilo rozsídlení Židů v Čechách za posledních 50 let," *Židovské zprávy*, December 2, 1927.

50. Kateřina Čapková, *Czechs, Germans, Jews?*, 196.

51. Gustav Sicher, "Náboženské reformy," *Židovské zprávy*, March 2, 1921. After his wartime Palestine exile, Sicher returned to Prague as chief rabbi in 1947 and remained there until his death in 1960. Kateřina Čapková, *Czechs, Germans, Jews?*, 196–197. See also the short biography in Blanka Rozkošná

and Pavel Jakubec, *Židovské památky Čech: historie a památky židovského osídlení Čech,* 474; and Efraim Sicher, "The Concept of Work in the Writings of Chief Rabbi Dr. Gustav Sicher," 136–143.

52. Gustav Sicher, "Náboženské reformy," *Židovské zprávy,* March 2, 1921. It is difficult to say whether Jews in the Bohemian Lands were more or less observant or ignorant of Judaism than similar communities in Germany and Austria, as few social or cultural historians have studied Jewish religious practice in this area in late Habsburg Austria and interwar Czechoslovakia.

53. Gustav Sicher, "Z naší pedagogické literatury," *Židovské zprávy,* March 22, 1920. The book under review was Richard Feder's *Židovské besídky:pro zábavu a poučení mládeže židovské,* vol. 2(Kolín n. Lab: Richard Feder, 1920). The first volume had been published just before the First World War; Richard Feder, *Židovské besídky:pro zábavu a poučení dospělejší mládeže židovské,* vol. 1 (Roudnice n. Lab.: Richard Feder, 1912–1913).

54. The two men's lives remained connected. After the Second World War, they chose to live in Communist Czechoslovakia, where Gustav Sicher served as Prague's chief rabbi and Feder took up a position as rabbi in Brno/Brünn. After Sicher's death in 1960, Feder moved to Prague, assuming Sicher's old post until he passed away in 1970. Kateřina Čapková, "Feder, Richard," 503–504.

55. "Sjezd českých izraelských náboženských obcí," *Židovské zprávy,* April 11, 1924. Feder's ideas bore a great deal of similarity to the reformed *heder* (a traditional Jewish elementary school) in Russia in the early twentieth century that, according to Steven Zipperstein, were to strengthen Jews' national awareness; see Zipperstein, *Imagining Russian Jewry,* 48.

56. "Sjezd českých izraelských náboženských obcí," *Židovské zprávy,* April 11, 1924. Feder published several Hebrew language textbooks for use in both Czech- and German-language schools in the interwar years; see, for example, Richard Feder, *Hebräisches Lehrbuch* (Prag: Staats. Verlagsamt., 1923); *Hebrejská učebnice: obrázky kreslil Ludvík Hermann* (Praha: Státní nakladatelství, 1923); *Haleluja: hebrejská řeč. Pro školy občanské, měšt'anské, a střední,* vol. 1 & 2 (Praha: Státní nakladatelství, 1936).

57. For a similar "return" to Hebrew among liberal Jews in Weimar Germany, see Brenner, *Renaissance of Jewish Culture,* 49–50.

58. Edvard Lederer, "Kongruový zákon a naši rabíni," *Rozvoj,* September 24, 1926.

59. For the Czech federation, see Richard Feder, "Svaz českých israelských náboženských obcí," *Rozvoj,* March 28, 1924. For the Moravian federation, see Alois Hilf, "Der Landesverband der israelitischen Kultusgemeinden in Mähren," in Gold, *Die Juden und Judengemeinden Mährens,* 72–74, here 72–73. For perceptions of Moravian unity as a model for the Bohemian communities, see Feder as listed above.

60. This call for territory-wide unity had also been part of the prewar Zionist agenda (1910); see Gaisbauer, *David-*

stern und Doppeladler, 313. For postwar calls for unity, see "Das Gemeindeprogramm des Jüdischen Nationalrats: Thesen der Kultusgemeindekommission des J.N.R," *Selbstwehr,* January 3, 1919. For the need for the Prague community to play a leading role in such a unification effort, see "Die Wahlen in die Kultusgemeinde," *Selbstwehr,* October 21, 1921.

61. Zemský svaz israelských náboženských obcí na Moravě/Der Landesverband der israelitischen Kultusgemeinden in Mähren was formally established July 24, 1924, although it had existed in practice since 1917; see Hilf, "Der Landesverband," 72. Svaz židovských náboženských obcí ve Slezku/Der Landesverband der jüdischen Kultusgemeinden in Schlesien was formally recognized March 11, 1925, even though the federation had existed longer; see Paleček, "Izraelská náboženská společnost," 37.

62. For Prague's withdrawal from the Czech federation in 1924 due to the Prague board's commitment to bilingualism, see Richard Feder's report, "Svaz českých israelských náboženských obcí," *Rozvoj,* March 28, 1924; see also Fleischmann, "The Religious Congregation," 297.

63. Svaz Pražských židovských náboženských obcí/Verband der jüdischen Kultusgemeinden in Prag was established November 26, 1925; see Paleček, "Izraelská náboženská společnost," 37. The Prague federation's official language was Czech, but anyone was allowed to participate and contribute in German; see letter d. October 29, 1925, from the Prague Federation to the Ministry of Education, NA–Mš sign. 47/VIII karton 3921.

64. These were committed to the use of either language in their affairs. Svaz českých náboženských obcí židovských v Čechách was recognized by the authorities on February 18, 1927, and Verband der Kultusgemeinden mit deutscher Geschäftssprache (known in Czech as Svaz israelských náboženských obcí s německým jednacím jazykem) was similarly recognized on February 18, 1927; see Paleček, "Izraelská náboženská společnost," 37.

65. Fleischmann, "The Religious Congregation," 297. Significantly, Emil Margulies, the prominent Zionist leader and the chair of the Litoměřice/Leitmeritz community, was initially opposed to the creation of federations. While this could have opened another rift among Zionists in the Bohemian Lands, Margulies soon joined the Prague Zionists on the Supreme Council.

66. The communities' membership in the federations was voluntary, and their boards could choose to withdraw any time. It is not clear how many communities remained outside the federations. Fleischmann notes that the Moravian federation established in 1918, but not ratified until 1924, had "most of the communities" within its fold; in Bohemia, he claims, "only a few congregations . . . mostly small ones, declined to enter any of the federations"; Fleischman, "The Religious Congregation," 296–298. Václav Müller stated in a 1934 article that all communities had joined; see "Náboženství a národnost v naší republice," *Národnostní obzor* 5, no. 4 (1934): 241–247, here 246.

67. For religious instruction in German-Jewish schools, see Rozenblit, "Creating Jewish Space," 116.

68. The plans for a statewide central organization for the Jewish communities were embodied in a resolution approved at the first Czechoslovak Zionist meeting in July 1919; see *VIII. Zionistentag Brünn 30.–31.7.1928: Rechenschaft über die Vergangenheit – Programm für die Zukunft* (Mährish Ostrau: Zionistischer Zentralverband für die čsl. Republik, 1928), 7.

69. Josef Pollak, "Reforma náboženských obcí," *Židovské zprávy,* July 30, 1921. See also the October 28, 1918 memorandum issued by the Jewish National Council.

70. In 1921, various Jewish factions came together to establish a social welfare organization, Jüdische Fürsorgezentrale für die Tschechoslowakei, in order to deal with the refugee crisis in the Bohemian Lands and the more general desperate conditions among Jews in the country's east; see "Programm der Jüdischen Fürsorgezentrale für die Tschechoslowakei" (Prag, 1921). In the 1920s and '30s, the American Jewish Joint Distribution Committee was active in Subcarpathian Rus' along with the Zionist Women's Organization, WIZO, in Czechoslovakia; for the Joint, see Yehuda Bauer, *My Brother's Keeper,* 218–219; and for WIZO, see Čapková, *Czechs, Germans, Jews?,* 235–237.

71. For similar efforts to centralize Jewish communities in Germany in the 1920s, see Max P. Birnbaum, *Staat und Synagoge.*

72. The subsidies for Jewish clergy was the offshoot of a deal negotiated between the Agrarian Party (Republikánská strana zemědělského a malorolnického lidu) and the Catholic Czechoslovak People's Party (Československá strana lidová) when state subsidies were committed in support of Catholic clergy; see Peter Heumos, "Konfliktregelung und Soziale Integration," 56.

73. Ministerial notes d. August 1926 in "Židovská náboženská společnost v RČS: vyšší organisace," NA–Mš inv.č. 2086 sign. 47/VIII karton 3921.

74. For response from the authorities in the Bohemian Lands, see letter d. September 30, 1926, from Zemská správa politická v Brně; letter d. September 11, 1926, from Zemská správa politická v Opavě; and letter d. September 16, 1926, from Zemská správa politická v Praze, in NA–Mš inv.č. 2086 sign. 47/VIII karton 3921.

75. From the authorities in Subcarpathian Rus', see letter d. August 15, 1926, from Presidium politické správy Podkarpatské Rusi, NA–Mš inv.č. 2086 sign. 47/VIII karton 3921.

76. From Slovakia, see letter d. August 26, 1926, NA–Mš inv.č. 2086 sign. 47/VIII karton 3921.

77. See recommendations made in Ministry of Education's internal report d. February 17, 1921; internal notes d. January 8, 1934, NA–Mš 47/VIII karton 3917.

78. Ministerial notes d. August 1926, NA–Mš inv.č. 2086 sign. 47/VIII karton 3921. For the Supreme Council encouraging this belief, see report of meeting between members of council and the Ministry of Education in January 1934 during which the Jewish rep-

resentatives explained their desire to remain a regional federation, allegedly claiming that the Jews in Slovakia and Subcarpathian Rus' were "too different," making unity impossible. Internal notes d. January 8, 1934, NA–Mš sign. 47/VIII karton 3917.

79. In the early postwar period, the Zionists called for a countrywide organization as well as several other priorities later adopted by the Supreme Council, such as the rabbinical seminary. The countrywide organization was not favored by the council members; for earlier Zionist priorities, see "Für einen Jüdischen Kultusgemeindebund," *Selbstwehr,* August 8, 1919.

80. See the carefully worded programmatic article by Gustav Fleischmann, "Der Oberste Rat der jüdischen Kultusgemeindeverbände und seine nächsten Aufgaben," *Selbstwehr,* January 6, 1928.

81. Katz, *A House Divided,* 217–224.

82. The legislation extending the subsidy was passed on June 25, 1926. August Stein was already corresponding with the Ministry of Education regarding the establishment of a central Jewish administration in early May 1926; see letter d. May 3, 1926, from August Stein to Ministry of Education, NA–Mš inv.č. 2086 sign. 47/VIII karton 3921.

83. Fleischmann, "The Religious Congregation," 308.

84. Internal ministerial notes d. December 16, 1926; the Supreme Council submitted its statutes on December 3, 1926, NA–Mš inv.č. 2086 sign. 47/VIII karton 3921.

85. Referáty z porad zástupců židovských náboženských obcí Protektorátu Čechy a Morava 1939, ŽMP Inv.č. 9 karton 1.

86. The positions on the first board were distributed as follows: chair, Dr. August Stein; vice-chairs, Dr. Leopold Goldschmied, Dr. Alois Hilf, Dr. Emil Margulies, and Dr. Josef Popper; secretary, Dr. Norbert Adler; assistant secretary, Hugo Rindler; accountant, Karel Schablin; and suppliant, Ignaz Wolf; "Ústavení Nejvyšší Rady," *Židovské zprávy,* November 12, 1926.

87. Magda Veselská, *Bestii navzdory,* 6; and for a broader study of Stein's role in the ghetto clearing, see Cathleen M. Giustino, *Tearing Down Prague's Jewish Town,* 191–192, 201–204.

88. Kieval, *Languages of Community,* 164–165.

89. The B'nai B'rith was a Jewish fraternal organization first established in the mid-nineteenth century in the United States. Popper had been the chair of the Czechoslovak Lodge since 1921. In Czechoslovakia, the B'nai B'rith was, according to Kateřina Čapková, decidedly pro-Zionist in the interwar years; see Čapková, *Czechs, Germans, Jews?,* 74. Fleischmann, in contrast, insists, albeit not very convincingly, that Popper was a "non-Zionist"; Fleischmann, "The Religious Congregation," 312. Popper was also the chair of the Jewish Committee for Aid to Refugees from Germany established in 1934; see Livia Rothkirchen, *The Jews of Bohemia and Moravia,* 53.

90. For Adler and his role, see Fleischmann, "The Religious Congregation," 309.

91. Hugo Rindler was the chair of the Czech federation through much of

the 1930s; Hugo Rindler, "Neudržitelné poměry v našich českých náboženských obcí," *Rozvoj*, May 18, 1933.

92. Kateřina Čapková, "Specific Features of Zionism in the Czech Lands in the Interwar Period," 131.

93. As president of the community in Moravská Ostrava/Mährisch Ostrau, Alois Hilf succeeded in securing early support for youth groups, sports clubs, and projects in Palestine, a decision that, as we shall see, was contested; see Hugo Gold, *Gedenkbuch der untergegangenen Judengemeinden Mährens* (Tel Aviv: Olamenu, 1974), 83. Leopold Goldschmied collaborated with Hugo Gold on the histories of the Jewish communities in Bohemia and Moravia and introduced Hebrew classes and courses in Jewish history in the community in Prostějov/Prossnitz; Gold, *Gedenkbuch*, 83.

94. Popper was a physician; Hilf, Stein, Adler, Rindler, Schablin, and Margulies were attorneys.

95. At times, Fleischmann delivered funding applications and reports in person to the Ministry of Education; see, for example, the two-volume report on the proposed reform of communal boundaries, Gustav Fleischmann, "Sídla Židů v Čechách." Fleischmann's mapping of Jewish communities was well-received among the civil servants in the Ministry of Education; see notes d. December 22, 1927, in "Úprava obvodů židovských náboženských obcí v Čechách, na Moravě a ve Slezsku, seznamy obsahující sídla židů podle sčítání lidu z15. II. 1921," NA–Mš inv.č. 2987 sign. 47/VIII karton 3922. After the war, Gustav Fleischmann wrote the only analysis of the work of the Supreme Council in "The Religious Congregation."

96. Fleischmann and Adler were among the Supreme Council's younger members, born in the 1890s. Popper and Margulies were about twenty years older. Stein was born in 1854 and thus seventy-two at the time of the Supreme Council's establishment. Rudolf M. Wlaschek, *Biographia Judaica Bohemiae*, vols. 1–2.

97. This was, according to one writer, an embarrassing display of disunity that prompted the Zionist leadership to issue a decree making its future decision binding and thus overriding its members' other institutional interests; *Zionistentag 1928*, 33–34.

98. The organization representing rabbis in Bohemia got two seats, the Moravian and Silesian associations had one each, and the organization for religious functionaries had two representatives on the assembly; "Ústavení Nejvyšší Rady," *Židovské zprávy*, November 12, 1926.

99. The Supreme Council established a rabbinical committee (Rabínská zkušební komise) already in 1926. Its members were primarily engaged in testing the qualifications of teachers and rabbis; see Hugo Rindler, "Organisace náboženské společnosti židovské a její další vybudování," *Bnai Brith* 2 (1934): 58–62, here 59. For Orthodox pockets in the Bohemian Lands, see Stransky, "Religious Life," 331–332.

100. Letter d. November 8, 1926, August Stein to Ministry of Education, NA–Mš inv.č. 2086 sign. 47/VIII karton 3921. The Supreme Council's statutes submitted on December 3, 1926,

and the recognition of its legitimacy by the regional authorities arrived in the ministry's office within a few weeks; see, for example, letter d. December 16, 1926, the Provincial Political Administration in Brno/Brünn to the Ministry of Education.

101. Müller, "Náboženství a národnost," 246.

102. Gustav Fleischmann, "Was bietet des Kongruenzgesetz den Rabbinern?" *Selbstwehr*, September 21, 1928.

103. The Supreme Council did not appear to have submitted an overview that listed the communities affiliated with the council. The Ministry of Education, in turn, never appears to have asked. However, somewhere in the ministry's offices there must have been a list, as the council received the state subsidies for Jewish clergy on behalf of its member communities only between 1931 and 1937. In any case, in the funding applications, the Supreme Council always described itself as "the representative of Jewish communities in Bohemia, Moravia, and Silesia"; see, for example, letter d. June 25, 1931, the Supreme Council to the Ministry of Education, NA–Mš inv.č. 2086 sign. 47/VIII karton 3921.

104. Quoted in letter d. January 24, 1928, the Supreme Council to the Ministry of Education, in NA–Mš inv.č. 2086 sign. 47/VIII karton 3922.

105. Vaclav Müller argued that the state authorities respected the independence of religious communities in their internal affairs as long as they respected the principle that the state comes before all else; Müller, "Náboženství a národnost," 247.

106. See the lengthy internal report d. February 17, 1921, NA–Mš sign. 47/VIII karton 3917.

107. For Lederer's travels to Slovakia as reported in *Židovské zprávy* (the report from his trip was originally printed in the newsletter *Služba*, issues 6–7), see "Židovstvo na Slovensku," *Židovské zprávy*, July 11, 1920 and August 11, 1920; see also Mš internal report d. February 17, 1921. For support of the Supreme Council and centralization, see Edvard Lederer, "Kongruový zákon a naši rabíni," *Rozvoj*, September 24, 1926. For more on Edvard Lederer, see Kieval, *Languages of Community*, 168–169, 175–176; Alexej Mikulášek et al., *Literatura s hvězdou Davidovou*, vol. 1, 225.

108. Jaroslav Šebek, "Der tschechische Katholizismus," 145–146. For the expropriation of church property as part of the 1919 land reforms, see Daniel E. Miller, "Colonizing the Hungarian and German Border Areas," 305.

109. Jaroslav Šebek notes that following the electoral success of conservative and Catholic parties in the 1925 elections, by 1926 the attempts at separating church and state were halted; Šebek, "Der tschechische Katholizismus," 148.

110. For Jewish children in public schools in the late nineteenth-century Bohemia, see Kieval, *Languages of Community*, chapter 6. Hugo Stransky argues that in 1918, the majority of Jewish children received no formal Jewish education beyond the weekly two hours in public schools; Hugo Stransky, "The Religious Life in the Historic Lands," 343.

111. According to Gustav Fleischmann, Jewish communities appointed the teachers, who were then supervised

and paid by the school board. He comments that religious education in and beyond the public schools was one of the most important functions of the Jewish community in the interwar period; Fleischmann, "The Religious Congregation," 290.

112. Letter d. September 10, 1920, signed by Dr. Isidor Hirsch (Karlín/Karolinenthal), Dr. Ignaz Ziegler (Karlovy Vary/Karlsbad), and Dr. Leopold Goldschmied (Prostějov/Prossnitz) on behalf of the Federation of Rabbis in Czechoslovakia (Svaz rabínů v Československé Republice) to Ministry of Education NA–Mš karton 3917 sign. 47/VIII [Svaz rabínů, September 10, 1920]; the public memorandum was published in the Jewish press, "Organisace rabínů v Československé republice," *Židovské zprávy,* September 10, 1920.

113. Ibid. For the government supporting the establishment of a state-sponsored Protestant theological seminary in 1919, see Šebek, "Die tschechische Katholizismus," 146.

114. Stransky, "The Religious Life," 345. He also notes that the German-speaking communities had access to plenty of well-qualified rabbis.

115. For comment on German-speaking communities not facing the same problems as the Czech-speaking ones, see Richard Feder, "Otázka svazu českých israelských náboženských obcí," *Rozvoj,* September 15, 1924.

116. Richard Feder, "Svaz českých israelských náboženských obcí," *Rozvoj,* March 28, 1924.

117. Letter d. June 11, 1924, Rabbi Jindřich Schwenger to the Provincial Political Administration in Brno/Brünn (Zemská správa politická v Brně), NA–Mš sign. 47/VIII karton 3917. These numbers are confirmed in an overview authored by the Supreme Council a few years later. According to this report, concerned both with the absence and qualifications of rabbis, in 1928, 104 communities in Bohemia had no rabbi at all. Of the 95 rabbis active in the region, 33 had a university education, 7 had not studied beyond high school, and 34 had only an elementary school education behind them. In Moravia, there were only 20 so-called fully qualified, meaning formally ordained, rabbis. In Silesia, four out of eight communities had an ordained rabbi; see reform proposal d. March 26, 1928, from the Supreme Council to the Ministry of Education, NA–Mš inv.č. 2086 sign. 47 karton 3921.

118. See, for example, Gustav Sicher, "Náboženské reformy," *Židovské zprávy,* March 2, 1921.

119. See, for example, Feder, "Svaz českých israelských náboženských obcí."

120. Mš internal report d. February 17, 1921. NA–Mš sign. 47/VIII karton 3917.

121. Ministerial notes d. December 31, 1930, NA–Mš inv.č. 2086 sign. 47 karton 3921.

122. Ministerial notes d. December 31, 1930, NA–Mš inv.č. 2086 sign. 47 karton 3921.

123. Reform proposal d. January 24, 1928, in "Úprava obvodů židovských náboženských obcí v Čechách, na Moravě a ve Slezsku, seznamy obsahující sídla židů podle sčítání lidu z15. II. 1921," NA–Mš inv.č. 2987 sign. 47/VIII karton 3922. The reform proposed to

create larger communities, citing 400 congregants as a minimum number for a viable community, establishing 14 communities with more than 1,000 Jews (up from 11), 34 with populations between 400 and 1,000 (up from 23), 31 between 100 and 400 (down from 164 [69 of which had less than 100 people]).

124. Ibid.

125. The Ministry of Education held off approving such an intervention until the Supreme Council had legal standing; see "Židovský organisační zákon v kulturním výboru poslanecké sněmovny," *Židovské zprávy,* November 13, 1936.

126. Reform proposal d. January 24, 1928, in "Úprava obvodů židovských náboženských obcí v Čechách, na Moravě a ve Slezsku, seznamy obsahující sídla židů podle sčítání lidu z15. II. 1921," NA–Mš inv.č. 2987 sign. 47/VIII karton 3922.

127. Paleček, "Izraelská náboženská společnost," 40–44.

128. "Deset let Nejvyšší Rady," *Židovské zprávy,* March 5, 1937.

129. The Supreme Council's budget as reflected in the reports submitted to the Ministry of Education listed total annual expenses ranging from Kč 71,375 (1929) to Kč 324,000 (1937). Not surprisingly, the council's expenses grew steadily between 1927 and 1938. The state subsidy covered only a fraction of the council's expenses, ranging from Kč 20,000 (1929), Kč 100,000 (1930 – a sum that greatly increased its expectations for future grants), Kč 85,000 (1931), Kč 20,000 (1932), and Kč 50,000 (1934–1937); see funding applications in NA-Mš inv.č. 2086 sign. 47/VIII karton 3921. Thus, for much of the 1930s, the state subsidy covered less than 20% of the Supreme Council's official expenses. The Ministry of Education did, however, treat the council quite leniently. For example, when the ministry's accountants recommended that promised subsidies for a rabbinical seminary be withheld in 1931, noting that the council had in fact not established the planned seminary, the ministry rejected their recommendation, claiming that stipends for rabbinical students served the same purpose as would a seminary. See the internal notes on decision d. December 31, 1930, in this file. Furthermore, the ministry's civil servants did not question the substantial deficit that the Supreme Council carried over from year to year.

130. Letter from the Supreme Council to the Ministry of Education d. June 25, 1931; see notes on ministerial decision d. September 8, 1931, NA–Mš inv.č. 2086 sign. 47 karton 3921.

131. On Hradec Králové/Königgrätz, see letter d. June 25, 1931, the Supreme Council to the Ministry of Education, NA–Mš inv.č. 2086 sign. 47 karton 3921. For size of community, see František Friedmann, "Jak mizejí Židé z českého venkova," *Židovské zprávy,* January 20, 1933.

132. Internal notes d. January 8, 1934, Ministry of Education, NA–Mš sign. 47/VIII karton 3917. In the internal notes, the civil servant who received Fleischmann stated that the latter had informed him that Alois Hilf was working on a similar overview of the communities in Moravia and Silesia; see notes d. December 22, 1927, in NA–Mš inv.č. 2987 sign. 47/VIII karton 3922.

133. See Goldstein's presentation of the bill and subsequent discussion d. January 21, 1937, "Zpráva výborů ústavně-právního a kulturního o usnesení senátu (tisk 628) k vládnímu návrhu zákona (tisky sen. 220 a 240), jímž se doplňuje organisace náboženské společnosti židovské v zemích České a Moravoslezské (tisk 676)" in NSČ 1935–1938, PS, 76. Schůze, www.psp.cz/eknih.

134. Goldstein, NSČ, January 21, 1937.

135. Rindler, "Organisace náboženského společenství," 61.

136. Fleischmann, "The Religious Congregation," 323.

137. Goldstein referred to "separatism and local patriotism" no less than four times in his initial presentation; Goldstein, NSČ, January 21, 1937.

138. Goldstein in exchange with MPs Dormin and Iváк; Goldstein, NSČ, January 21, 1937.

139. For persistent pressure from the Supreme Council not to create a Czechoslovak organization, see internal ministerial notes d. January 8, 1934, and ditto d. May 3, 1934, in NA–Mš 47/VIII karton 3917.

140. For the Viennese rite in the Bohemian Lands and in Hungary, see Silber, "The Historical Experience of German Jewry," 121.

141. Letter d. June 11, 1924, Rabbi Jindřich Schwenger to Zemská správa politická v Brně, NA–Mš sign. 47/VIII karton 3917.

142. "Konkurs," *Jüdische Volksstimme*, October 21, 1921.

143. One member of the rabbinical committee, Samuel Arje (1875–1950), asked the state authorities to show leniency in enforcing the citizenship requirements for rabbis because of these internal cultural differences between the Bohemian Lands and Slovakia; see letter d. May 23, 1937, from the rabbinical committee (Rabínská zkušební komise) to the Ministry of Education. The latter concurred and recommended that the Ministry of Social Welfare, responsible for the work permits, issue permits for German and Austrian rabbis applying to work in Bohemia and Moravia; see letter d. December 6, 1937, NA–Mš sign. 47/VIII karton 3917; for Arje, see Stransky, "Religious Life," 339.

144. Stransky, "Religious Life," 345; Fleischmann, "The Religious Congregation," 286. For an account of Prague's middle-class Jews' cool reception of the scholar Jiří Langer "passing" as a Hasid in Prague shortly before the First World War, see František Langer, "My Brother Jiří," in Jiří Langer, *Nine Gates to the Chasidic Mysteries*, ix–xxxiv. For Jewish middle-class ideals of respectability in Central Europe more broadly, see Marion A. Kaplan, *The Making of the Jewish Middle Class*.

145. Letter d. May 5, 1931, from the Supreme Council to the Ministry of Education on recruiting rabbinical candidates among graduates from Czech- and Slovak-language high schools, NA–Mš inv.č. 2086 sign. 47 karton 3921.

146. "Zpráva o činností Nejvyšší rady za rok 1934," *Rozvoj*, January 11, 1935; see also "Nedostatek českých rabínů," *Rozvoj*, March 15, 1935.

147. On Masaryk and his emphasis on religion and moral regeneration for the character of individuals and societies, see Kieval, *Languages of Community*, 174, 203.

148. In some ways, the attempt to make Judaism Czech was similar to Catholic activists' efforts to distance themselves from "Austrian" Catholicism and infuse Catholicism with Czech national themes in the postwar years. Some of these activists founded the Czechoslovak Church (Československá církev), which became the second largest religious community in Czechoslovakia within a few years (it had just under one million members). The Czech Protestant churches had an easier time incorporating Czech nationalism, as the Czech nationalist narrative celebrated Protestant and anti-Catholic heroes of the nation's past; see Martin Schulze Wessel, "Vyznání a národ v českých zemích," 130. See also Martin Schulze Wessel, "Tschechische Nation und Katholische Konfession."

149. Application for the establishment of a rabbinical seminary in Prague, d. March 26, 1928, from the Supreme Council to the Ministry of Education, NA–Mš sign. 47/VIII karton 3917.

150. Application for the establishment of a rabbinical seminary in Prague, d. March 26, 1928. For the memory of Rabbi Löw and the Golem, see Kieval, *Languages of Community*, 95–113; for the Landesrabbiner, see Michael L. Miller, "Crisis of Rabbinical Authority."

151. Application for the establishment of a rabbinical seminary in Prague, d. March 26, 1928, NA–Mš sign. 47/VIII karton 3917.

152. Ministerial notes d. May 21, 1928; in their seminary application, the Supreme Council pointed out that while Jews made up 3% of the country's population, they received (Bohemian Lands, Slovakia, and Subcarpathian Rus' combined) only 1.3% of the Ministry of Education's budget for religious communities (Slovakia and Subcarpathian Rus' accounted for Kč 840,000 and the Bohemian Lands for Kč 665,000). By 1934, the funding had not improved significantly. According to Václav Müller, in 1934, Jewish communities received almost Kč 1.8 million (in comparison, the Czechoslovak Church, whose congregation was double the size [about 800,000] of the Jewish one, received Kč 5.4 million); Müller, "Náboženství a národnost," 247. In the statement attached to the application, the Supreme Council's assembly stated, "Except for the seminary in Budapest, most Jewish seminaries were established using private funds and subsequently the state would begin subsidizing them or, as is the case in Paris, take over the administration completely. We do not want this institution in our state to be established with private funds, as citizens we ask that it be established using state funds . . . since our state acts in its own interest when it acts in ours"; declaration from meeting d. January 22, 1928. Letter d. November 30, 1928 letter from Ministry of Education to the Supreme Council, NA–Mš inv.č. 2086 sign. 47/VIII karton 3921.

153. The number of students at the seminaries abroad ranged from five (1931) to twelve (1937). In the early 1930s, the stipends were reported to be about Kč 8,000 per student; by the late 1930s, the stipends were just about half of that; see funding applications from the Supreme Council to the Ministry

of Education 1927–1938, NA-Mš inv.č. 2086 sign. 47/VIII karton 3921. Even though the ministry insisted that the basic funds for the seminary be raised privately among the Jewish communities, it allowed the council to funnel part of their annual state allowance into a "seminary fund." The ministry's subsidy was never enough to cover all of the Supreme Council's expenses. The Supreme Council was funded mainly by the federations. The "Seminary Fund" appeared on the list of expenses beginning in 1931. Amounts ranged from Kč 15,000 to 25,000; see funding applications NA–Mš inv.č. 2086 sign. 47 karton 3921.

154. For financial concerns, see Fleischmann, "The Religious Congregation," 314.

155. "Deset let Nejvyšší Rady," *Židovské zprávy,* March 3, 1937; Fleischmann, "The Religious Congregation," 314–315.

156. Letter (funding application 1930/1931) d. December 18, 1930, from the Supreme Council to the Ministry of Education, NA–Mš inv.č. 2086 sign. 47/VIII karton 3921.

157. On the lack of a seminary as a "painful gap" for the Supreme Council, see letter d. May 20, 1931, NA–Mš inv.č. 2086 sign. 47/VIII karton 3921.

158. The Supreme Council as well as the Slovak federation Jeschurun donated funds for this project in addition to the state funds committed by the government; "Rabínský seminář v Československu," *Židovské zprávy,* November 12, 1937.

159. In 1937, the expenses for teachers' training and rabbinical students' education was Kč 47,000 and Kč 60,000 respectively, letter d. November 10, 1937, from the Supreme Council to the Ministry of Education, NA–Mš inv.č. 2086 sign. 47 karton 3921.

160. The Mukačevo programs for religious functionaries began in 1931, then expanded to include teachers. The latter programs were generally two years long; see Fleischmann, "The Religious Congregation," 314; "Deset let Nejvyšší Rady," *Židovské zprávy,* March 3, 1937. For religious functionaries, see "Die Tätigkeit der Obersten jüdischen Rates," *Selbstwehr,* December 16, 1932.

161. For reference to Feder in budget, see letter d. May 31, 1935, from the Supreme Council to the Ministry of Education, NA–Mš inv.č. 2086 sign. 47/VIII karton 3921.

162. The cooperation between the Supreme Council and the explicitly Zionist Hebrew High School in Mukačevo is yet another example of the pragmatism that characterized the work of these so-called assimilationist and Zionist activists. The council had originally envisioned establishing a permanent educational institution (at the cost of Kč 80,000/year) for religious functionaries in Moravská Ostrava/Mährisch Ostrau but had to scrap the idea due to lack of funds; see letter d. December 18, 1930, from the Supreme Council to the Ministry of Education, NA–Mš inv.č. 2086 sign. 47/VIII karton 3921. Letter d. May 20, 1931, from the Supreme Council to the Ministry of Education, NA–Mš inv.č. 2086 sign. 47/VIII karton 3921. On the recruitment of graduates from Mukačevo, see Jelinek, *Carpathian Diaspora,* 220.

163. "Smutný zjev," *Židovské zprávy*, October 3, 1924.

164. This according to Rabbi Hugo Stransky (1905–1983). Stransky was educated at the seminary in Berlin and served as a rabbi in the interwar years in both the Bohemian Lands and Slovakia (Žilina/Sillein/Zsolna); see Stransky, "The Religious Life," 345.

165. For earlier attempts at making Judaism Czech through translations and change of liturgical language, see Kieval, *Languages of Community*, 159–180.

166. Moses Mendelssohn's status as an icon for non-traditional Jews in the nineteenth and twentieth century can hardly be overestimated; see Michael A. Meyer, *The Origins of the Modern Jew*, especially 11–56. For Moses Mendelssohn's and other Jewish translations of the Torah into the vernacular in the modern period, see Richard I. Cohen, "Urban Visibility and Biblical Visions," 40–61.

167. Letter d. December 27, 1927, from the Supreme Council to the Ministry of Education, NA–Mš inv.č. 2086 sign. 47/VIII karton 3921.

168. Martin Schulze Wessel, "Die Konfessionaliserung der tschechischen Nation," 135. The Supreme Council's subsidy for Richard Feder's textbook on Judaism, *Sinai: Učebnice izraelského náboženství*, vol. 1 (Praha: Státní nakladatelství, 1934), was Kč 3,000; "Zpráva o činnosti Nejvyšší Rady za rok 1934," *Rozvoj*, January 11, 1935. Isidor Hirsch and Gustav Sicher, *Pět knih Mojžišových*, vols. 1–4 (Praha: Svaz pražských náboženských obcí židovských, 1932–1939).

169. Letter d. October 10, 1925, from the board of the Federation of Jewish Communities in Prague to Ministry of Education submitting its statutes, NA–Mš sign. 47/VIII karton 3921.

170. This nostalgia was widespread in Jewish culture in late nineteenth- and early twentieth-century Europe and beyond; see, for example, Richard I. Cohen, *Jewish Icons*, 155–219, on Prague specifically, see 199–203; and Nils Roemer, "The City of Worms," 78–81.

171. Jewish activists remained invested in the particularity of regional Jewish history as reflected in the establishment of separate Jewish museums in Moravia (1936) and Slovakia (1928) in addition to the existing Prague one (1906); For the Moravian museum in Mikulov/Nikolsburg, see Magda Veselská, "Židovské ústřední museum pro Moravsko-Slezko v Mikulově." For the Prague Jewish Museum, see Magda Veselská, *Archa paměti*.

172. The Supreme Council's budget included "conservation" as a category listing expenses for the upkeep of heritage sites, support for the Jewish museum, and for the historical societies. According to the budgets submitted to the Ministry of Education, the amount ranged from Kč 10,000 to 40,000 annually from 1929 to 1933, and from 1934 to 1937 between Kč 200 and 10,000. These budgets included only the council's expenses, not what individual federations and communities might have been spending on conservation and museum work. For the council's involvement with the Society for the History of Jews in Czechoslovakia, see Samuel Steinherz, "Vorwort," *Jahrbuch der Gesellschaft für Geschichte der Juden in der Čechoslovakischen Republik* 1 (1929): v–vii, here v, 452.

173. For the establishment of the Heritage Committee, see Michal Bušek, ed., *"Naděje je na další stránce,"* 10.

174. In the reform proposal submitted in January 1928, the Supreme Council asked the government to intervene to prevent any community boards affected by the reform from selling communal property off; see reform proposal d. January 24, 1928.

175. See discussion at meeting May 31, 1931, as reported in "Nejvyšší rada židovských obcí," *Židovské zprávy,* June 8, 1931.

176. The booklet was published in one thousand Czech copies and two thousand German ones: *O židovských památkách v Československé republice* (Praha: Památková komise Nejvýšší rady Svazu židovských obcí náboženských v Čechách, na Moravě a Slezku, 1933); and *Die jüdischen Denkmaler in der Tschechoslowakei* (Prag: Veröffentlichungen der Denkmalkommission des Obersten Rates der jüdischen Kultusgemeinden in Böhmen, Mähren, und Schlesien, 1933). For number of copies, see "Nejvyšší Rada náboženských obcí v posledním roce," *Židovské zprávy,* January 5, 1934.

177. *O Židovských památkách v Československé republice* (Praha: Památková komise Nejvyšší rady svazu židovských obcí náboženských v Čechách, na Moravě a Slezku, 1933), 7 and the accompanying photographs, especially nos. 1, 26, 8, 13, 15, 19.

178. Ibid., 4.

179. "O významu Nejvyšší rady svazu náboženských obcí," *Židovské zprávy,* November 5, 1926; see also Edvard Lederer, "Kongruový zákon a naši rabíni," *Rozvoj,* September 24, 1926.

180. In the Prague community, Zionists held about a quarter of the seats on the Community Council in the 1920s; the rest were held by various non-Zionist groups, such as the Czech-Jews, the Middle Class Jewish Party, Jewish Progressives, Democrats (German-speaking Jews), and so on; for 1921 results, see "Das Resultat der Kultusgemeindewahlen," *Selbstwehr,* November 4, 1921; and for 1929, see "Die Wahlen in die israelitische Kultusgemeinde Prag," *Selbstwehr,* November 15, 1929.

181. For struggle between Hagibor and Prague's Jewish community, see Tatjana Lichtenstein, "'Heja, Heja, Hagibor!'"

182. For the Brno/Brünn community budget, see *Zionistische Organisation Brünn Berichtet* (Brünn: Verlag der Zionistischen Organisation in Brünn 1932), 10.

183. V. M., "K volbám do náboženské obce židovské v Hradci Králové," *Rozvoj,* November 13, 1936.

184. "Nový řád uzákoněn," *Židovské zprávy,* January 22, 1937; Zdeněk Landes, "Nová židovská ústava," *Židovské zprávy,* July 2, 1937.

185. Landes, "Nová židovská ústava," *Židovské zprávy,* July 2, 1937.

186. See, for example, the complaints of corruption and oppression allegedly committed by rabbis in the east: "Poražení," *Židovské zprávy,* November 20, 1925. Jewish leaders in the east also courted the central state authorities for recognition of their leadership, thereby resisting Zionist attempts to represent all of Czechoslovakia's Jews through the Jewish National Council;

see letter d. September 29, 1921, from the board of the Jewish Conservative Party in Subcarpathian Rus' (Židovská Konservativní strana v Podkarpatské Rusi) to Ministry of Interior, NA–MŠ inv.č. 2086 sign. 47/VIII karton 3921. For attitudes toward Zionism among eastern traditional leaders, see Jelinek, *Carpathian Diaspora*, 146–147.

187. Fleischmann argues that some Moravian and a few Orthodox communities were at first hesitant about giving up their autonomy but came around, he states, "in the interest of Jewry as a whole." Fleischmann, "The Religious Congregation," 319; for more on cooperation between Zionists and Orthodox circles in the Bohemian Lands, see also Čapková, *Czechs, Germans, Jews?*, 194–198.

188. "K osnově nové právní úpravy náboženské společnosti židovské," *Rozvoj*, July 24, 1936.

189. The influential Czech-Jew Maximilian Reiner (1864–1937), who was chair of the Prague Jewish community at the time, was allegedly unaware of the Senate's deliberations; see "Zpráva o mimořádné schůzi," *Rozvoj*, June 6, 1936; Lev Kohn, "K osnově nové právní úpravy náboženské společnosti židovské," *Rozvoj*, July 24, 1936; Dr. S., "Osnova organisace náboženské společnosti židovské," *Rozvoj*, November 28, 1936.

190. Dr. S., "Osnova organisace náboženské společnosti židovské," *Rozvoj*, November 28, 1936.

191. Fleischmann claims that Czech-Jews "were anything but delighted at the prospects of a new code . . . for [they] knew that eventually such an organization would be bound to stand in the way of assimilation"; Fleischmann, "The Religious Congregation," 319.

192. "Asimilanti proti obci," *Židovské zprávy*, December 24, 1937.

193. Matters become so heated in the spring of 1938 that Josef Popper, the chair of the Supreme Council, felt compelled to issue a public statement calling for restraint. He urged the opposing parties to consider the damaging effects on Jewry as a whole of the display of these bitter internal divisions and urged them "to use dignified language and manners in public and . . . avoid topics that could fuel anti-Jewish attitudes"; Josef Popper, "Provolání Nejvyšší rady," *Židovské zprávy*, March 4, 1938.

194. "Svědectví Nejvyšší rady," *Židovské zprávy*, March 11, 1938.

195. Ibid. Fleischmann also discusses this case in some detail, "The Religious Congregation," 321.

196. Fleischmann's salary was still listed for March 1939, but no longer for April 1939; ŽMP–Fond Nejvyšší rada sign 67352 Pokladní knížka II.

197. Roemer, "The City of Worms," 78–84.

5. A Stateless Nation's Territory

1. Iš Šalom (František Friedmann), "Návštěvou v pražské židovské škole," *Židovské zprávy*, June 13, 1921.

2. Pieter M. Judson, *Guardians of the Nation*, 19.

3. Tara E. Zahra, *Kidnapped Souls*, 3, 15.

4. Joseph Lamm, "Rede anlässlich der Eröffnung des Jüdischen Reformrealgymnasiums in Brünn," in *I. Jahresbericht des Jüdischen Reformrealgymnasiums in Brünn 1920/1921* (Brünn: Verlag

des Jüdischen Reformrealgymnasiums in Brünn, 1921), 3–4. Lamm felt the need to make this distinction even though the high school was in and of itself a first, as there had historically not been Jewish middle or high schools in the Bohemian Lands.

5. By the mid-1880s, two-thirds of Bohemia's Jewish children attended schools other than the German-Jewish ones; Hillel J. Kieval, *Languages of Community*, 142–143.

6. "Günstige Erledigung der Angelegenheit der jüdischen Schule," *Selbstwehr*, September 3, 1920.

7. For the history of German-Jewish schools in Bohemia, see Kieval, *Languages of Community*, 135–158. For the schools in Moravia, see Marsha L. Rozenblit, "Creating Jewish Space."

8. Rozenblit, "Creating Jewish Space," 142–143.

9. Zahra, *Kidnapped Souls*, 21–22.

10. Kieval, *Languages of Community*, 151. Tara Zahra notes that by 1885 only a third of Bohemia's Jewish children attended the Jewish schools; Zahra, *Kidnapped Souls*, 22.

11. In Bohemia, according to Kieval, there were 113 German-Jewish schools in 1885, 90 in 1895, and 5 in 1910; Kieval, *Languages of Community*, 151, 153–154.

12. Rozenblit, "Creating Jewish Space," 112.

13. Zahra, *Kidnapped Souls*, 21–22; for Jews in Prague, see Gary Cohen, *The Politics of Ethnic Survival*.

14. In Prague, the center of Czech nationalism, 97% of Jewish children went to German schools in 1890; Kieval, *Languages of Community*, 144, 147.

15. Rozenblit, "Creating Jewish Space," 110.

16. In 1868, schools could no longer "force" students to learn a second language. Until then, students had been required to learn both of the commonly used in languages in their province; see Hannelore Burger, *Sprachenrecht und Sprachgerechtigkeit*, 28, 38.

17. Rozenblit, "Creating Jewish Space," 110.

18. Memorandum, Jewish National Council, October 28, 1918, in Aharon M. Rabinowicz, "The Jewish Minority," 218–221.

19. Article 19, paragraph 3 of Austria's 1867 Constitution, as quoted in Zahra, *Kidnapped Souls*, 14.

20. Burger, *Sprachenrecht und Sprachgerechtigkeit*, 37–38.

21. For school associations in Habsburg Austria, see Judson, *Guardians of the Nation*, especially chapter 2. According to Tara Zahra, the German and Czech school associations (Deutsche Schulverein and Česká matice školská) constituted some of the largest voluntary associations in Central and Eastern Europe; Zahra, *Kidnapped Souls*, 14–16.

22. While the Bohemian and Moravian branches cooperated closely, they maintained somewhat separate identities. In the east, the activists organized in the Hebrew-Language School Association (Hebrejská matice školská).

23. Joseph Lamm, "Vom Geiste der jüdischen Schulen," *Jüdische Volksstimme*, March 18, 1920.

24. "Do které školy patří židovské dítě?," *Židovské zprávy*, July 4, 1921.

25. "Zur jüdischen Schulfrage," *Jüdische Volksstimme,* May 9, 1919.

26. In the Bohemian Lands, elementary schools encompassed the students' first four to five years. Then they could go on to four-year middle schools or eight-year high schools.

27. There is evidence that the Jewish school association tried to hold on to the already German-Jewish schools, but the documentation on this handful of communal schools is very scarce; see *Židovský Kalendář 1921/1922,* 120. See also "Stav sionistické práce a přiští úkoly naší organisace v Českoslov. republice," *Židovské zprávy,* November 17, 1922.

28. There were also kindergartens attached to the elementary schools in Prague and Brno/Brünn, but it is unclear if they remained continuously open during the interwar years; VIII. *Zionistentag Brünn 30–31.7.1928 – Rechenschaft über die Vergangenheit – Programm für die Zukunft* [Zionistentag 1928] (Mährisch Ostrau: Zionistische Zentralverband für die čsl. Republik, 1928), 59. For enrollment in the elementary school and kindergarten in Brno/Brünn in the early 1930s, see *Zionistiche Organisation Brünn Berichtet* (Brünn: Verlag der Zionistiche Organisation in Brünn, 1932), 19.

29. For a detailed study of this school from its establishment to the Second World War, see Rozenblit, "Creating Jewish Space," 131–145.

30. Michael Brenner, *The Renaissance of Jewish Culture,* 59. Brenner shows that in some cities, like Hamburg, one in two Jewish children attended a Jewish school in the 1920s.

31. For Prague numbers, see František Friedmann, "Jak se změnilo rozsídlení Židů v Čechách za posledních 50 let," *Židovské zprávy,* December 2, 1927; *Zionistentag 1928,* 59; and "Židovská škola v Praze," *Židovské zprávy,* April 16, 1937. By 1938, there were three elementary schools in Prague; "Židovská matice školská pro Čechy v Praze," *Židovské zprávy,* June 10, 1938. For population statistics for 1930, see Gustav Fleischmann, "Rozsídlení židovského obyvatelstva v Československu," *Židovské zprávy,* June 3, 1938; for percentage of the city's children in Jewish schools, see František Friedmann, "Židovské děti na pražských školách," *Židovské zprávy,* June 15, 1933.

32. Kateřina Čapková and Michal Frankl, *Nejisté útočiště,* 202.

33. For the Brno/Brünn and Moravská Ostrava/Mährisch Ostrau population, see Theodor Haas, "Statistische Betrachtungen über die jüdische Bevölkerung Mährens," 595; and "Zápis do židovských škol brněnských," *Židovské zprávy,* September 8, 1933. For percentage of Moravian children in Jewish school in Brno/Brünn and Moravská Ostrava/Mährisch Ostrau, see František Friedmann, "Odborná příprava k povolání mladé židovské generace," *Věstník židovské náboženské obce,* October 10, 1935: 2–3, here 2.

34. For data on Brno/Brünn students, see *Jahresbericht Gymnasium 1933/1934;* and Gustav Flusser, "Jüdische Kinder im Čechoslovakischen Schulwesen," *Bnai Brith* (1934): 190–195, here 192.

35. Blažena Przybylová, "Židovská škola v Moravské Ostravě," 342.

36. Rozenblit, "Creating Jewish Space," 144.

37. Early recruitment ads emphasized the good-quality religious instruction along with a solid general education; see also "Hovor o židovské škole," *Židovské zprávy*, June 18, 1937. The school received a small contribution from the Prague community (Kč 3,000) in 1927; see ŽMP–Protokoly ŽNO Budgets 1927; "Židovská matice školská," *Židovské zprávy*, December 16, 1927. In Brno/Brünn and Moravská Ostrava/Mährisch Ostrau, support for the Jewish schools appears to have been a regular item on the communities' budgets. For Prague in the 1930s, see *Věstník židovské náboženské obce* 1934, 3.

38. In the early 1930s, one source claimed, the Brno/Brünn Jewish community allocated Kč 50,000 annually to the Jewish schools; see *Zionistiche Organisation Brünn Berichtet*, 10. In 1928, the community provided Kč 60,000. The Moravian Federation of Jewish Religious Communities donated Kč 3,500; see *Zionistentag 1928*, 59.

39. Rozenblit, "Creating Jewish Space," 131.

40. The city of Brno/Brünn donated Kč 165,000 to the schools in 1927 (*Zionistentag 1928*, 59), by far the largest single subsidy that year.

41. For data about tuition and fees waived, see the statistical sections in the annual yearbooks from the school year 1920/1921 through 1937/1938, *Jahresbericht des Jüdisches Vereins-Reformrealgymnasium in Brünn/Výroční zpráva spolková – židovské reformní reálné gymnasium v Brně* [*Jahresbericht Gymnasium*].

42. In neighboring Poland, there were several parallel Jewish school systems. Aside from the different religious educational institutions, there were the Hebrew Tarbut system and the Yiddish TsYShO (Tsentrale Yidishe Shul Organizatsye) schools, as well as bilingual schools that taught in either Hebrew and Polish or Hebrew and Yiddish. For a short overview of schools in interwar Poland, see Miriam Eisenstein, *Jewish Schools in Poland;* for more on the TsYShO schools, see David E. Fishman, *The Rise of Modern Yiddish Culture.*

43. For the history of Hebrew-language schools in Subcarpathian Rus', see Aryeh Sole, "Modern Hebrew Education" Jelinek, *Carpathian Diaspora,* 214–224.

44. Sole, "Modern Hebrew Education," 409–410. For 1924, František Svojše, "Hebrejské školy na Podkarpatské Rusi," *Židovské zprávy*, August 29, 1924; for 1928, *Zionistentag 1928*, 61; for 1930, Zdeněk Landes, "Požadavky židovské menšiny," *Židovské zprávy*, March 5, 1937; for Mukačevo high school, in 1928, Václav Petera, "Několik poznámek o hebrejském gymnasiu v Mukačevě," *Židovský Kalendář 1928/1929*, 86.

45. For population figures, see Ezra Mendelsohn, *The Jews of East Central Europe*, 142.

46. František Friedmann, "Židovské konfesní školy na Slovensku," *Židovské zprávy*, February 10, 1933.

47. For Slovak Jews' gradual preference for Czechoslovak schools, see Rebekah Klein-Pejšová, *Mapping Jewish*

Loyalties in Interwar Czechoslovakia, 169–170.

48. For Czech and German nationalists reclaiming children in late Habsburg Austria and especially in Czechoslovakia, see Zahra, *Kidnapped Souls,* 106–141.

49. "Zur Schuleinschreibung," *Jüdische Volksstimme,* June 23, 1921. For the days of school registration as a battleground "in all areas where languages mix," see Ladislav Meyer, "Starý boj," *Rozvoj,* June 22, 1923; see also Zahra, *Kidnapped Souls.*

50. For nationalists and youth, see George L. Mosse, *The Image of Man.*

51. Josef Freund, "K židovské obecné škole II," *Židovské zprávy,* October 30, 1925.

52. Eduard Drachmann, *K otázkám židovského školství* (Brno: Spolek Židovská škola v Brně, 1936), 11.

53. *Jahresbericht Gymnasium 1920/1921,* 3–4.

54. Lamm, "Rede anlässlich der Eröffnung des Jüdischen Reformrealgymnasiums in Brünn," 4.

55. Ibid., 3.

56. *Jahresbericht Gymnasium 1930/1931,* 13.

57. Drachmann, *K otázkám židovského školství,* 5.

58. For statement about better Jews and better citizens, see "Menšinová práce svazu Čechů-židů," *Židovské zprávy,* September 7, 1926. While the school leaders presented their institution's dual loyalties, to the state and to the Jewish nation, as smooth and unproblematic, one wonders how the history teacher conducted the session on Romania – a country that Zionist writers routinely held up as the epitome of state antisemitism – on May 10, 1930, the official day celebrating "Czechoslovak-Romanian partnership"; *Jahresbericht Gymnasium 1929/1930,* 10.

59. Drachmann, *K otázkám židovského školství,* 11.

60. For perceptions of Jewish youth among educators and child experts, see Sharon Gillerman, "The Crisis of the Jewish Family in Weimar Germany," and Claudia Prestel, "'Youth in Need.'"

61. Joseph Lamm, "Rede anlässlich der Eröffnung des Jüdischen Reformrealgymnasiums in Brünn," 5.

62. Ibid., 5.

63. Josef Freund, "K židovské obecné škole II," *Židovské zprávy,* October 30, 1925.

64. Drachmann, *K otázkám židovského školství* 12.

65. Rozenblit, "Creating Jewish Space," 137.

66. For the legal norm, see Emil Svoboda, "Čtvrt století Perkova zákona," *Národnostní obzor* 2, no. 2 (1931): 88–98, here 91. In 1937, an article in *Národnostní obzor* boasted that "98.5% of schoolchildren are now attending schools of their own language," reflecting that the Komenský principle was believed to be guiding educational practices; "Národnostní školy v ČSR a národnostní poměry," *Národnostní obzor* 7, no. 3 (1937): 119–120, here 119. For more on the Komenský principle, see Zahra, *Kidnapped Souls,* 23, 127.

67. *Jahresbericht Gymnasium 1921/1922,* 8.

68. For the tradition for multilingual teaching, see Rozenblit, "Creating Jewish Space," 131.

69. The Jewish schools complied with the state curriculum and had state accreditation, something activists considered important for recruitment, as this allowed students to continue on in public middle schools and higher education.

70. For an overview of the different resolutions made by the Czechoslovak Zionist Organization in the 1920s, see *Zionistentag 1928,* 6–30, here 6–10, 19.

71. *Zionistiche Organisation Brünn Berichtet,* 18. For the request to make Hebrew mandatory in Jewish schools, "in order for students to take it seriously as a subject," see Drachmann, *K otázkám židovského školství,* 12.

72. For some of these sentiments, see Jelinek, *Carpathian Diaspora,* 144–145, 151.

73. Irma Pollaková, "Vývoj hebrejského hnutí v Československu," *Židovské zprávy,* February 1, 1935.

74. Chaim Weisz, "Ze života hebrejských škol na Podkarpatské Rusi," *Židovské zprávy,* February 26, 1926.

75. "První maturita na židovském gymnasiu v Brně," *Židovské zprávy,* June 22, 1928.

76. Hugo Bergmann, "Staňte se učiteli!" *Židovský Kalendář 1920/1921,* 48–51.

77. In their efforts to secure state-funding, Jewish parliamentarians also emphasized the role that the Jewish schools played in supplying candidates for a homegrown rabbinate, as we have seen, another key concern to Jewish and non-Jewish authorities alike. See, for example, Angelo Goldstein, "Požadavky židovské menšiny," *Židovské zprávy,* January 27, 1933.

78. For quote, see "Do které školy patří židovské dítě?" *Židovské zprávy,* July 4, 1921; for Prague, see "Židovská matice školská pro Čechy v Praze," *Židovské zprávy,* June 10, 1938.

79. The schools in Prague were not open on Saturdays and Sundays, respecting both Jewish and state law; see "Našim rodičům!," *Židovské zprávy,* June 17, 1931.

80. "Našim rodičům!," *Židovské zprávy,* June 17, 1931. For the factionalism within the Zionist movement in the interwar years, see Čapkova, *Czechs, Germans, Jews?,* 198–221. See also the overview in Oskar K. Rabinowicz and Yeshayahu Jelinek, "Zionism in Czechoslovakia," 304–310.

81. "Židovská škola v Praze," *Židovské zprávy,* October 26, 1928.

82. For Bohemian membership, see *Zionistentag 1928,* 58 (the Jewish population in Bohemia was 76,301 in 1930; Mendelsohn, *The Jews of East Central Europe,* 142).

83. "Židovská škola v Praze," *Židovské zprávy,* April 16, 1937.

84. For Moravian membership, see *Berichtet 1932,* 19 (the Jewish population in Moravia was 41,250 in 1930; Mendelsohn, *The Jews of East Central Europe,* 142).

85. "Židovská matice školská pro Čechy v Praze," *Židovské zprávy,* June 10, 1938.

86. Zahra, *Kidnapped Souls,* 106–141.

87. Joseph Lamm, "Unsere jüdische Schule," *Jüdische Volksstimme,* June 9, 1921.

88. Joseph Lamm, "Vom geiste der jüd. Schulen," *Jüdische Volksstimme,* March 18, 1920.

89. "Našim rodičům!," *Židovské zprávy,* June 17, 1931.

90. "Jüdische Eltern!," *Jüdische Volksstimme,* May 13, 1920 sign. Verein Jüdische Schule in Mähren.

91. Drachmann, *K otázkám židovského školství,* 10–11.

92. For languages, see "Židovským rodičům!," *Židovské zprávy,* June 18, 1926; for love, see "Židovským rodičům!," *Židovské zprávy,* August 29, 1924.

93. On Komenský and Czech nationalists, see Zahra, *Kidnapped Souls,* 23.

94. "Židovská škola," *Židovské zprávy,* June 11, 1925.

95. "Našim rodičům!," *Židovské zprávy,* June 17, 1931.

96. *Jahresbericht Gymnasium 1922/1923,* 5.

97. Joseph Lamm, "Unsere jüdische Schule," *Jüdische Volksstimme,* June 9, 1921.

98. Iš Šalom, "Návštěvou v pražské židovské škole," *Židovské zprávy,* June 13, 1920. For use of *ivrit be-ivrit* (a system that dictated that all communication in the classroom should be in Hebrew), see Zipperstein, *Imagining Russian Jewry,* 49.

99. Images of the heder run by a poor, ignorant, and often mean teacher (*melamed*), where children remained ignorant but were exposed to an unhealthy environment in "classrooms filled with death," was common in these reform circles; see Zipperstein, *Imagining Russian Jewry,* 42.

100. "Židovští souvěrci!," *Rozvoj,* August 27, 1924.

101. "Židovská škola," *Židovské zprávy,* June 11, 1925.

102. Joseph Lamm, "Unsere jüdische Schule," *Jüdische Volksstimme,* June 9, 1921.

103. Przybylová, "Židovská škola v Moravské Ostravě," 394. In Moravská Ostrava/Mährisch Ostrau, the first class with Czech as a language of instruction began in 1927.

104. Ibid. Czech-Jews did not consider such bilingual schools "really Czech." They claimed that German would inevitably become the dominant language; František Polák, "Zdatnost či národnost?," *Rozvoj,* July 17, 1920.

105. Letter d. February 9, 1928, Archiv města Ostravy–MŠV Ostrava–karton 148 sign. žid. 1935, as quoted in Przybylová, "Židovská škola v Moravské Ostravě," 394.

106. F. Borecký, "Zápas o menšinové děti," *ČSR,* June 25, 1925.

107. Zahra, *Kidnapped Souls,* 126–127.

108. In 1930, there were 6,116 Jewish children in elementary schools in the Bohemian Lands: 3,875 in Bohemia (2,390 in Czech schools; 1,485 in German ones) and 2,241 in Moravia (1,361 Czech; 880 German). There were 3,782 in middle schools: 2,266 in Bohemia (977 Czech; 1,289 German) and 1,516 (669 Czech; 874 German) in Moravia. Flusser, "Jüdische Kinder im Čechoslovakischen Schulwesen," 191–192.

109. "Židé v Moravské Ostravě," *Venkov,* April 19, 1933.

110. *Židovské zprávy* reprinted Feder's speech, noting that while they did not agree with his Czech-Jewish politics, they agreed with his remarks about using Czech; "Český rabín mluví k Židům," *Židovské zprávy,* June 9, 1933. For a similar appeal asking rabbis to

make their congregants speak Czech or at least not use German in public, see also "Slovo k rabínům," *Židovské zprávy,* September 21, 1933.

111. Quote from speech in National Assembly by Chaim Kugel, "Náše stárosti a požadávky," *Židovské zprávy,* December 4, 1936. While Tomáš G. Masaryk made a one-time pledge of Kč 10,000 to the Hebrew schools in 1921, this only reflected his personal goodwill toward the work of the Hebrew-Language School Association, and such occasional donations were not what the Jewish school activists were looking for. Indeed, it disguised the much more significant resistance to the creation of public Hebrew-language schools in the Ministry of Education. For resistance, see Sole, "Modern Hebrew Education," 409.

112. Law April 3, 1919, no. 189/19 Sb.; see Miloš Trapl, "Ke školské legislativě obecných a občanských škol a jejímu uplatňování v českých zemích v létech létech 1918–1922," 10.

113. Ludvík Singer, "Opávněnost hebrejského školství," *Židovské zprávy,* December 5, 1924. Czech-Jews maintained from the outset that Jews did not qualify for funding under the minority school legislation; see Dr. Kleiner, "Židovské školství," *Rozvoj,* July 17, 1920.

114. For claims of antisemitism, see Gustav Fleischmann, "Státní rozpočet a židovské školství národní," *Židovské zprávy,* January 13, 1922; for minority legislation, see Ludvík Singer, "Před deseti lety," *Židovské zprávy,* October 26, 1928.

115. For the construction of Hebrew as the nation's language, see Yael Zerubavel, *Recovered Roots,* 28–32.

116. For Czech-Jews' rejection of the claim that Hebrew is a Jewish mother tongue and hence that the schools are in violation of the Komenský principle, see "Židovské školy," *Rozvoj,* March 23, 1923.

117. František Svojše, "Hebrejské národní školy na Podkarpatské Rusi," *Židovské zprávy,* July 23, 1926.

118. František Svojše, "Hebrejské školy na Podkarpatské Rusi," *Židovské zprávy,* August 29, 1924.

119. František Svojše, "Hebrejské národní školy na Podkarpatské Rusi," *Židovské zprávy,* July 23, 1926.

120. Nečas's statement was quoted in *Židovské zprávy,* with the reservation that it was unfortunate that he had associated all Jews with alcohol; "Proti kulturnímu útlaku židovsko-národní menšiny," *Židovské zprávy,* December 5, 1924.

121. For ignorance, see Chaim Kugel, "Podkarpatsko žaluje," *Židovské zprávy,* December 13, 1935; and Zdeněk Landes, "Požadavky židovské menšiny," *Židovské zprávy,* March 5, 1937. For the opposition of rabbis, see, for example, Emil Waldstein, "Boj o hebrejské školství v čs. republice," *Židovské zprávy,* February 16, 1923; and "Židovská obec žádá uzavření hebrejských škol," *Židovské zprávy,* October 12, 1934 (the Jewish community in question was Mukačevo).

122. For more examples, see Jelinek, *Carpathian Diaspora,* 223.

123. For "terror campaigns" and excommunications, see Emil Waldstein, "Boj o hebrejské školství v Čs. republice," *Židovské zprávy,* February 16, 1923; and František Svojše, "Hebrejské školy na Podkarpatské Rusi," *Židovské zprávy,*

August 29, 1924. For denial of religious rights and boycotts, see Emil Waldstein, "Velká vymoženost," *Židovský Kalendář 1924/1925,* 36; Václav Patera, "Několik poznámek o hebrejském gymnasiu v Mukačevě," *Židovský Kalendář 1928/1929;* and "Židovská obec žádá uzavření hebrejských škol," *Židovské zprávy,* October 12, 1934.

124. Chaim Kugel, "Náše stárosti a požadávky," *Židovské zprávy,* December 4, 1936; and "Podkarpatoruští poslanci u presidenta republiky a ministerského předsedy," *Židovské zprávy,* March 6, 1936.

125. For Sternbach, see Avigdor Dagan, "The Press," 529; Jelinek, *Carpathian Diaspora,* 213.

126. Minutes from meeting of the Central Political Committee of the Czechoslovak Zionist organization d. June 11, 1928, in Prague, NA–Fond Emil Margulies–karton 9 inv.č. 94–100–104.

127. For funding in 1924, see František Svojše, "Hebrejské školství na Podkarpatské Rusi," *Židovské zprávy,* August 29, 1924; for 1926, see Chaim Weisz, "Ze života hebrejských škol na Podkarpatské Rusi," *Židovské zprávy,* February 26, 1926. By 1936, the annual subsidy had gone up to Kč 60,000; see the internal report dated March 30, 1936, and March 31, 1936. Letter to the government dated April 3, 1936, NA–Mš inv.č. 37.798 karton 3917 sign. 47/VIII. Jelinek argues that by 1927, the American Jewish Joint Distribution Committee, a major philanthropic organization active in most of Jewish Eastern Europe, offered to cover 12% of the Hebrew-language school system's expenses. The Joint's contribution along with donations from private Jewish individuals, according to Jelinek, made up the majority of the schools' income; Jelinek, *Carpathian Diaspora,* 218–219. For the work of the Joint, see also Yehuda Bauer, *My Brother's Keeper.*

128. Such meetings where not the only avenues for action. In spring 1933, for example, Emil Margulies gave a lecture in the Society for the Study of the Nationality Question, where he replayed the familiar complaints about the lack of funding for Jewish schools in the east; see "Emil Margulies Stenographisches Protokoll des Vortrages 'Über die gegenwärtigen politischen Strömungen und Programme unserer Mitbürger jüdischer Nationalität,'" d. March 21, 1933, CZA–A299/9.

129. Internal report d. March 30, 1936, and March 31, 1936. Letter to the government d. April 3, 1936, NA–Mš inv.č. 37.798 karton 3917 sign. 47/VIII.

130. For more evidence that social scientists and administrators did not consider Jews a national minority or at least not one that could be readily included in their studies alongside other national minorities, see Rudolf Stránský, "Účast naší státní péče na ochraně menšin v oboru školském," *Národnostní obzor* 2, no. 3 (1932): 161–167; and E. Čapek, "Střední školství národnostních menšin v českých zemích," *Národnostní obzor* 7, no. 3 (1937): 194–202.

131. For prewar surveillance and campaigning, see letter from the Association of Czech Progressive Jews in Bohemia and Moravia to Czech National Council requesting a list of Jewish parents and announcing that

they will publicize the names of Jewish parents who enroll their children in German schools, letter d. September 3, 1912, Svaz pokrokových židů v Čechách to Národní rada česká, NA–NRČ karton 509/2; see also Zahra, *Kidnapped Souls,* 21–22 for an earlier example. For non-Jews' claiming that Jews continue to attend German schools, see "Školská debata v sboru obecních starších," *Rozvoj,* December 30, 1920; for interwar surveillance, see "Zpráva o veřejné řádné schůzi," *Rozvoj,* October 25, 1935.

132. For statistics and denunciation, see Zahra, *Kidnapped Souls,* 30; for Zionists' commitment to Czech, "Sionisté a český jazyk," *Židovské zprávy,* April 14, 1933.

133. Numbers for elementary schools are based on František Friedmann's "Židovské děti na národních školách," *Židovské zprávy,* April 20, 1932.

134. Franz Friedmann, "Die jüdischen Mittelschüler in unserem Staate im letzten Schuljahr," *Selbstwehr,* June 18, 1933.

135. "Thesen für das Schulprogramm des Jüdischen Nationalrats," *Selbstwehr,* January 3, 1919; Max Brod, "Schulenquête," *Selbstwehr,* September 10, 1920; and "Günstige Erledigung der Angelegenheit der jüdischen Schule," *Selbstwehr,* September 3, 1920.

136. "K této školské akci," *Židovské zprávy,* September 7, 1926; Angelo Goldstein, "Projev posl. dra Goldsteina v parlamentě," *Židovské zprávy,* April 28, 1933. Zionists also held the view that Jews should speak the language of their surroundings and thus not strengthen linguistic (i.e., German- and Hungarian-speaking) minorities.

137. In the immediate postwar period, Czech-Jews feared that Jews would be forced into Jewish schools with Czech language of instruction due to their perceived Germanness; Dr. Kleiner, "Židovské národní školství," *Rozvoj,* July 10, 1920.

138. "Günstige Erledigung der Angelegenheit der jüdischen Schule," *Selbstwehr,* September 3, 1920.

139. František Friedmann, *Mravnost či Oportunita? Několik poznámek k anketě akad. Spolku Kapper v Brně* (Praha: Sionistický výbor pro Čechy a Moravu v Praze, 1927); see also František Friedmann, "Jaké školy navštěvují židovské děti," *Židovské zprávy,* October 21, 1927.

140. Friedmann, *Mravnost či Oportunita,* 39. Here Friedmann grouped Jewish parents of German and Czech nationality into one assimilationist category.

141. Ibid., 27–28.

142. Ibid., 47.

143. This was a development that Zionists were convinced was engineered by Czech-Jews and local rabbis who had worked together in the mid-1920s to establish Czech-language Jewish schools; "Ortodoxové v Podkarpatké Rusi pro židovské školství české, sionisté pro židovské školství hebrejské," *Rozvoj,* May 15, 1924; "Po zápisu do škol," *Rozvoj,* September 6, 1923.

144. "Doklady o čsl. kulturní politice na Podk. Rusi," *Židovské zprávy,* October 3, 1924.

145. One author argued that an alliance made up by the governing coalition parties and local rabbis conspired to fill Czech schools with Jewish children; Leo Strauss, "Školská politika," *Židovské zprávy,* January 24, 1936.

146. František Friedmann, "Židovská národní menšina na Podkarpatské Rusi II," *Národnostní obzor* 4, no. 4 (1934): 269–277, here 273; for part 1 of the study, see František Friedmann, "Židovská národní menšina na Podkarpatské Rusi I," *Národnostní obzor* 4, no. 3 (1934): 185–192.

147. Friedmann, "Židovská národní menšina II," 272.

148. See, for example, his 1932 essay "Židé" in Ivan Olbracht, *Hory a staletí* (Praha: Československý spisovatel, 1982, originally published in 1935), 44–61. For complaints that Czechs were colonizing German areas using Czech-language "school palaces" and underfunding or closing German ones, see Zahra, *Kidnapped Souls*, 115–116.

149. Zdeněk Landes, "Požadavky židovské menšiny," *Židovské zprávy*, March 5, 1937.

150. Ludvík Singer, "Oprávněnost hebrejského školství," *Židovské zprávy*, December 5, 1924. Jewish activists expressed this sense of betrayal on many occasions; see, for example, Angelo Goldstein, "Požadavky židovské menšiny," *Židovské zprávy*, January 27, 1933; and Zdeněk Landes, "Požadavky židovské menšiny," *Židovské zprávy*, March 5, 1937.

151. For an overview of the success of these schools in East Central Europe, especially in Czechoslovakia and Poland, see Mendelsohn, *The Jews of East Central Europe*, 160–161.

6. Making New Jews

1. Susan D. Bachrach, *The Nazi Olympics*, 67.

2. ČSR was a common Czech (Československá republika) and local German (Čechoslovakische) abbreviation for the Czechoslovak Republic. The organization's name appeared officially, according to Zionist practice, in Czech, German, and Hebrew simultaneously: Svaz Makabi v ČSR/Čechoslowakischer Makkabikreis/Histradut lehitamlut u-le-sport Makabi bčechoslovakia; see statutes 1924 in AHMP–PŘ–SK Svaz Makabi v ČSR XIV-685. By the mid-1930s, Maccabi leaders made little use of the German name publicly. Up until then all three names had adorned, for example, the organization's letterhead.

3. For broad support in the general press, see "Sportovec jako voják nesmí ustoupit: Proč by měli židovští plavci jeti na Olympiádu," *Lidový deník Večer*, July 17, 1936; and "Kolem olympiády v Berlíně," *Rozvoj*, May 15, 1936. For Czech-Jewish calls for Jewish athletes not to participate, see "Zájem světa," *Rozvoj*, March 20, 1936. For public protests supported by Czech-Jewish circles, see "Před berlínskou olympiádou," *Rozvoj*, July 24, 1936.

4. Kurt Epstein was a member of the Czech Swimming Club (Československý plavecký klub) and one of five Jews on the Czechoslovak national water polo team. Epstein was the only one of the five who decided to participate in the Berlin Olympics; see Helen Epstein, *A Jewish Athlete*.

5. The Ministry of Health and Physical Education acted as a mediator in the conflict between the Czechoslovak Amateur Swimming Association (Československý amaterský plavecký

svaz) and Maccabi ČSR. Maccabi leaders protested the swimming association's exclusion of Maccabi athletes from all competitions. The disqualification or exclusion of Maccabi athletes was presented as a disciplinary measure in response to breach of the Swimming Association's discipline. Similar sanctions were meted out against Jewish athletes in neighboring Austria. For the Ministry of Health and Physical Education's mediation, see documents pertaining to Svaz Makabi v ČSR and the Czechoslovak Amateur Swimming Association, d. December 1935 to November 1936, in NA–Ministerstvo veřejného zdravotnictví a tělesné výchovy [Mzd]–Svaz Makabi v ČSR inv.č. 3424/8/5 karton 913. For sanctions against Hakoah athletes in Austria, see William D. Bowman, "Hakoah Vienna."

6. "Naši židovští plavci a Olympiáda," *Venkov,* July 19, 1936; "Olympiáda pro a proti," *České slovo,* July 17, 1936.

7. "Sportovec jako voják nesmí ustoupit: Proč by měli židovští plavci jeti na Olympiádu," *Lidový deník Večer,* July 17, 1936.

8. "Naši židovští plavci a Olympiáda," *Venkov,* July 19, 1936.

9. "O neúčasti čs. židovských plavců na Olympiádě," *Lidové noviny,* July 18, 1936.

10. For sports as rite of citizenship, see Jack Kugelmass, "Why Sports?" For sports as "boundary work," see Noel Dyck, "Games, Bodies, Celebrations and Boundaries."

11. For examples of these statements, see Angelo Goldstein, "Cesta k uskutečnění," in *II. Svetové zimné hry Makabi Banská Bystrica 18–24. II 1936:* 31; and Ernst Fuchs, "Die Sokolbewegung; eine Parallele zum Makkabi," *Židovský sport,* June 1929: 17–19, here 18.

12. Ernst Fuchs, "Vom Wesen des Makabis," in *Makabi Handbuch* (Praha: Tschechoslowakischen Makabikreis im Makkabi Weltverband, 1931): 10–12, here 12.

13. In his classic history of Zionism, Walter Laqueur devotes half a page to the Zionist sports and gymnastics movement despite the fact that he acknowledges that "many boys and girls" became involved in Zionism through these institutions; see Laqueur, *A History of Zionism,* 485. Adolf Gaisbauer discusses the early establishment of sports and gymnastics clubs, focusing on the unification of these associations in Habsburg Austria; see Gaisbauer, *Davidstern und Doppeladler,* 424–440. In his work on Zionist bio-politics, Todd S. Presner devotes considerable attention to the Jewish sports and gymnastics movement; see Presner, *Muscular Judaism.*

14. In 1999, several articles examining Jews and sports in Europe and North America appeared in the *Journal of Sport History* 26, no. 2 (1999), and a few years later several edited volumes on Jews and sports appeared, including Dietrich Schulze-Marmeling, ed., *Davidstern und Lederball;* Jeffrey S. Gurrock, *Judaism's Encounter with American Sports;* Michael Brenner and Gideon Reuveni, ed., *Emancipation through Muscles;* Jack Kugelmass, ed., *Jews, Sports, and the Rites of Citizenship;* and Ezra Mendelsohn, ed., *Jews and the Sporting Life.*

15. For the early history, see Erik Friedler, *Makkabi Chai, Makkabi Lebt!*

16. Presner, *Muscular Judaism*, 120–121.

17. For examples of this narrative, see Haim Kaufman, "Jewish Sports in the Diaspora, Yishuv, and Israel: Between Politics and Nationalism," 148–150; and George Eisen, "The Maccabiah Games," 57–58, 264.

18. For examples of broader Jewish male desire to defend honor in response to antisemitism, see Gregory A. Caplan, "Germanizing the Jewish Male," 175; and Joachim Doron, "'Der Geist ist es, der sich den Körper schafft!,'" 240.

19. In Germany, Austria, and some of the successor states, this trend persisted among clubs inspired by various forms of Jewish nationalism in the interwar period. In Poland, however, where Jewish politics were very divisive, Jewish sports and gymnastic clubs were strongly affiliated with political organizations such as the Bund, Po'ale Tsiyon, and the Communist Party; see Jack Jacobs, "The Politics of Jewish Sports Movements," 93–105.

20. Studies of the Zionist clubs predominate, but scholars have also examined the Jewish socialist sports movement; see Roni Gechtman, "Socialist Mass Politics"; and Jack Jacobs, "Jewish Workers' Sports Movements."

21. Shanes shows that the Galician Jewish gymnastics movement was largely a Zionist endeavor. Its leaders' political goals were on gaining national rights for Jews in Galicia. It thus resembled parallel movements among the region's other national groups; Joshua Shanes, "National Regeneration," 78–84.

22. Jacob Borut, "'Verjudung des Judentums,'" 100–102.

23. For sports as a means of integration in Weimar Germany, see Jacob Borut, "Jews in German Sports during the Weimar Republic"; Shanes, "National Regeneration," 86–87; and Gechtman, "Socialist Mass Politics," 335.

24. For the discussion of gymnastics, Jews, and masculinity, I draw on George L. Mosse's *The Image of Man*. For more on Jews' adoption of these ideals, see Caplan, "Germanizing the Jewish Male."

25. Mosse, *Image of Man*, 3, 6.

26. For the link between a healthy body and soul where outward appearance reflects inward virtue and the establishment of "Greek" bodies as the manly ideal, see Mosse, *Image of Man*, 17–39. For an example of the dissemination of this "Greek" ideal in Czechoslovak government propaganda, see A. Očenáška, P. Bureš, and V. Rýpar, eds., *Tělesná výchova v Československu* (Praha: Ministerstvo veřejného zdravotnictví a tělesné výchovy, 1933).

27. Mosse, *Image of Man*, 57.

28. The use of gendered visual language went beyond the realm of social outsiders and was also used to ridicule or demonize nationalist or political opponents. For the use of the masculine heroes and their unmanly opponents in nationalist discourse, see for example, the analysis of the imagery produced by German and Czech nationalists in the Bohemian Lands in the collection of articles and images in Peter Becher and Jozo Džambo, eds., *Gleiche Bilder/Stejné obrazy*.

29. Mosse, *Image of Man*, 63; for a classic discussion of difference, antisemitism, and the Jewish body, see Sander L. Gilman, *The Jew's Body*. While the focus in Mosse's work is the male body, Jewish women's bodies were also depicted as opposite to the feminine ideal in antisemitic discourse. For examples from the Czech context, see Alexej Mikulášek, *Antisemitismus v české literatuře 19. a 20. století*, 168, 213.

30. Mosse uses the example of Jews' being denied the opportunity to defend their honor in dueling because Jews were perceived as having no honor; Mosse, *Image of Man*, 63.

31. Ibid., 151–152. In their efforts to create new men, nationalist and socialist activists shared the masculine ideal, although their utopias were different. Jewish efforts were thus part of these broader discourses on social reform, even though they addressed particular Jewish anxieties and desires. See, for example, Morgnshtern's ideals and iconography in interwar Poland in Gechtman, "Socialist Mass Politics," 327, 323–335. For Mosse's discussion of socialism and masculinity, see *Image of Man*, 123–132.

32. Mosse, *Image of Man*, 151–152; Daniel Boyarin, *Unheroic Conduct*, 274–276. For a critique of Boyarin's argument that this masculinity was heterosexual and for a further discussion of Zionism and Jewish masculinity, see Yaron Peleg, "Heroic Conduct."

33. Presner, *Muscular Judaism*, 1–3.

34. For the significance of "ancient" heroes like Bar Kochba in Zionist ideology, see Yael Zerubavel, *Recovered Roots*, 52–56.

35. Boyarin, *Unheroic Conduct*, 281.

36. For the discussion of gymnastics and sports as mobilization, see Gechtman, "Socialist Mass Politics." For similar ideas among other groups, see Claire E. Nolte, "'Every Czech a Sokol!'"; and Eisen, "The Maccabiah Games," 265.

37. See Mosse's discussion of the institutionalization of physical education in schools and armies, in *Image of Man*, 40–55, 133–146.

38. Mark Mazower, *Dark Continent*, 77, 92–96.

39. See the discussion in Gideon Reuveni, "Sports and the Militarization of Jewish Society," 45–46.

40. In Czechoslovakia, when dispensing funds in support of sports teams traveling to international competitions, the authorities and applicants alike placed great emphasis on the question of Czechoslovakia's prestige. See the funding applications from Maccabi ČSR to the Ministry of Health d. May 22, 1930, asking for funds in support of Jewish athletes' trip to the Maccabi World Union Congress in Antwerp in NA–Mzd–Svaz Makabi v ČSR inv.č. 3424/8/5 karton 913.

41. For inspiration from Sokol early on, see Ernst Fuchs, "Die Sokolbewegung; eine Parallele zum Makkabi," *Židovský sport*, June 1929: 17–19. See also Nolte, "'Every Czech a Sokol!'"

42. Beda Brüll, "Československý Makabi," *Židovský kalendář 1937/1938:* 97–107, here 98–99; Kurt Bloch, "Židé a sport," *Židovský kalendář 1933/1934:* 81–84, here 83.

43. Ernst Fuchs, "Jak jsme začínali . . . ," in *Slávnostný spis 3. slet čs. Svazu Makabi,*

ed. Beda Brüll (Praha: Svaz Makabi v ČSR, 1937), 40–45, here 42.

44. Ibid., 40–41.

45. Gaisbauer, *Davidstern und Doppeladler,* 432.

46. The historian Peter Bučka lists thirteen Jewish soccer clubs in Slovakia by 1921, some of which were established before the war; see Peter Bučka, "Futbal pod Dávidovou hviezdou," 45–46.

47. The Jewish Gymnastics Movement was established in Basel in 1903, with close links to Zionism, but remained independent from the Zionist movement as a national Jewish association working for the physical regeneration of Jews. It had its headquarters in Berlin and published the journal *Jüdischer Turnzeitung,* making Berlin, according to Daniel Wildmann, the center of the Jewish gymnastics movement in Europe. See Daniel Wildmann, "Jewish Gymnasts," 27. For claims of Bohemian and Moravian Jewry's heavy involvement in Jüdische Turnerschaft, see Beda Brüll, "Československý Makabi," 98; Ernst Fuchs, "Jak jsme začínali . . . ," 40.

48. Eisen, "The Maccabiah Games," 72. The members were Austria, Czechoslovakia, Palestine, and Germany. The Jewish Gymnastics Movement had adopted more explicit Zionist leanings shortly before the war (1913), with greater focus on the Zionist project in Palestine as a Jewish homeland and the adoption of Hebrew commands; Friedler, *Makkabi Chai, Makkabi lebt!,* 29–32.

49. For the history of the Maccabi World Union and the Maccabiah, see Eisen, "The Maccabiah Games."

50. For Sokol in the interwar years, see Mark Dimond, "The Sokol and Czech Nationalism."

51. Oskar Kaminsky, "Tělesná výchova naší mládeže," *Židovské zprávy,* March 2, 1919.

52. For the ways in in which Bohemian Germans worked to create new Sudeten German organizations, see Mark Cornwall, *The Devil's Wall,* 121, 134–135.

53. See the minutes from meetings taking place between November 9, 1920, and January 11, 1921, where Slovakia and Jewish clubs were on the agenda, NA–Fond Československá sportovní obec, 1918–1928 inv.č. 1 karton 1.

54. Minutes from meeting on January 11, 1921, 2, in NA–Fond ČsSO, 1918–1928 inv.č. 1 karton 1.

55. Ibid., 2.

56. Ibid., 3–4. Josef Fikl was also a member of the Czechoslovak Olympic Committee in 1919 and later wrote about his experience and change of heart regarding minority athletes as a result of Jews' example; Josef Fikl, "Poměr Židů k celostátnímu sportu," *Židovský sport,* January–February 1930: 7.

57. The society was formally established in 1921, and its name appeared in Hebrew (Aguda lehitamlut v lesport bčechoslovakia), Czech (Židovská tělocvičná a sportovní obec v ČSR), and German (Jüdische Turn- und Sportgemeinde in der ČSR), thus signaling its commitment to act as a nationally unifying force among the Jews of Czechoslovakia. Letter from Karel Friedmann and Oskar Kaminsky to Ministry of Interior d. June 29, 1921, announcing the establishment of the society, in NA–

Ministerstvo vnitra [Mv]–SR Židovská tělocvičná a sportovní obec v ČSR inv.č. 6/59/20 karton 1040.

58. The statutes were dated July 18, 1921, and were authorized by the Ministry of Interior on September 13, 1921; in NA–Mv–SR Židovská tělocvičná a sportovní obec v ČSR inv.č. 6/59/20 karton 1040.

59. For the takeover, see Fuchs, "Jak jsme začínali . . . ," 40–45. According to Egon Štern, Maccabi ČSR was established in Prague around 1919 by Richard Pacovsky, then moved to Brno/Brünn, where Karel Sonnenfeld (1883–1944) acted as chair in 1922. The subsequent chair was Robert Heller, and by 1924 Maccabi ČSR was back in Prague (which is when it is registered with the authorities there), with Arthur Herzog as chairman. Egon Štern, "Svaz Makabi v Československu," *Židovské zprávy,* September 2, 1927. For Arthur Herzog's time as chair, see affidavit given in Tel Aviv as part of Maccabi World Union's efforts to get restitution from Germany for property lost in the Sudeten area, Maccabi Archives box 146 4–37–12 affidavit by Arthur Herzog d. July 20, 1964.

60. On the formal dissolution, see letter d. December 29, 1927, from Arthur Herzog, vice chair of the Jewish Sports and Gymnastics Society and chair of Maccabi ČSR, to Ministry of Interior, in NA–Mv–SR Židovská tělocvičná a sportovní obec v ČSR, 1921–1928 inv.č. 6/59/20 karton 1040.

61. Erwin Goldschmid, "Zur Kreistagung des Makabi in der ČSR," *Židovský sport,* November 1927: 10–11

62. This was an attempt to enforce decisions made already in 1912 by the Jewish Gymnastics Movement; see Gaisbauer, *Davidstern und Doppeladler,* 431. Member clubs, however, preserved and continued to choose other names, such as Maccabea (established in Bratislava in 1912), Hagibor Praha/Prag (founded in 1914), Hagibor Plzeň/Pilsen (1923), and Bar Kochba Bratislava (1929).

63. Goldschmid, "Zur Kreistagung," 10.

64. In early 1927, Maccabi and the Prague sports club Hagibor reached an agreement to co-publish the existing monthly *Hagibor Židovský sport* as *Hagibor Židovský sport – Hamakkabi* [hereafter *Židovský sport*]. The first half of the magazine was in Czech, while the Maccabi section was in German; see announcements in *Hagibor Židovský sport,* February 1927. The first co-published issue followed in March 1927. The monthly was co-published until 1931, when it appeared as *Židovský sport – Hamakkabi.* It was discontinued altogether in 1933. *Hamakkabi* continued as a supplement to *Židovské zprávy.*

65. Goldschmid, "Zur Kreistagung," 10.

66. Bowman, "Hakoah Vienna," 643; for Germany, see Borut, "Jews in German Sports," 78–81.

67. Interestingly the number of clubs "jumped" from forty-five to eighty-three in two years between 1931 and 1933. This proliferation of clubs could be explained by an increase in antisemitism in German clubs in Czechoslovakia, by the newly arrived Jews from Germany establishing new clubs, as well as by the support extended to new clubs in Slovakia and Subcarpathian Rus' alleviating

them from membership fees in the first year. For documents suggesting the last, see funding application from Maccabi ČSR to Ministry of Health d. December 27, 1934. The numbers of clubs and members are the ones provided by Maccabi itself to the Ministry of Health in their funding applications in the period 1928–1938. The Ministry of Health apparently trusted the information provided by Maccabi, as it formed the basis for their internal memos and notes. See, for example, recommendations from the Municipality of Prague to the Ministry of Health d. March 9, 1929, and Ministry of Health internal memo recommending funding d. January 15, 1931, all in NA–Mzd Svaz Makabi v ČSR 1928–1952 inv.č. 3424/8/5 karton 913.

68. For number of clubs in 1936/1937 (eighty), see funding application Maccabi ČSR to Ministry of Health d. June 30, 1937, in NA–Mzd Svaz Makabi v ČSR 1928–1952 inv.č. 3424/8/5 karton 913.

69. The numbers bring together the memberships of organizations that identified as national ones; see *Tělesná výchova v Československu* (Praha: Ministerstvo veřejneho zdravotnictví a tělesné výchovy, 1930).

70. Mzd's file for Maccabi ČSR begins in 1928, when Maccabi ČSR established itself as the only Jewish organization working for Jews across the country. See application from Maccabi ČSR to Mzd d. December 24, 1928, in NA–Mzd Svaz Makabi v ČSR 1928–1952 inv.č. 3424/8/5 karton 913.

71. In some applications, the executive included letters of appreciation from clubs in Slovakia thanking the Prague executive for financial support. See, for example, letter from Maccabi ČSR to Ministry of Health and Physical Education d. May 31, 1937, and June 30, 1937, in NA–Mzd Svaz Makabi v ČSR 1928–1952 inv.č. 3424/8/5 karton 913; Maccabi to Ministry of Health and Physical Education d. December 27, 1934, in NA–Mzd Svaz Makabi v ČSR 1928–1952 inv.č. 3424/8/5 karton 913.

72. Letter Maccabi ČSR to Ludwig Czech d. April 22, 1936, in NA–Mzd Svaz Makabi v ČSR 1928–1952 inv.č. 3424/8/5 karton 913.

73. I have not been able to locate Maccabi ČSR's own archives, which were held in the main office in Prague until sometime in 1939. During his interrogation in February 1942, Leopold Hájek, who had been Maccabi ČSR's vice chair in 1937/1938, stated that the records had been seized by the Gestapo. Protokoll d. 21.2.1942 in AHMP–Svaz Makabi ČSR XIV 0685. The archival material available is from the state archives and documents correspondence between Maccabi ČSR and the police and ministerial authorities.

74. These numbers are according to Maccabi ČSR's own statements. In 1937–1938, Maccabi ČSR estimated that its total working budget would be Kč 102,229, with Kč 62,820 coming from memberships, Kč 27,159 from donations, leaving a deficit of Kč 12,159, which the organization hoped the ministry would help cover. That year Maccabi received Kč 2,000 in state support. Letter d. July 28, 1938, from Maccabi ČSR to Ministry of Health and Physical Education, in NA–Mzd Makabi ČSR karton 913 inv.č. 3424/8/5; and for Kč 2,000 support, notes d. June 29, 1938, in same file.

75. See an account from the event, "Armáda na naší půdě," *Židovské zprávy,* July 27, 1934.

76. See the programs for the 1936 Maccabiah, in NA–Mzd Svaz Makabi ČSR karton 913 sign. VIII/5/Praha/50 and 1937 slet NA–Mzd Svaz Makabi ČSR karton 913 inv.č 3424/8/5.

77. See reports highlighting this in letter from Maccabi ČSR to Ministry of Health and Physical Education d. April 22, 1936, and letter from Maccabi ČSR to Ministry of Commerce d. May 10, 1937, in NA–Mzd Svaz Makabi ČSR karton 913 inv.č. 3424/8/5.

78. According to Mark Dimond, the Czechoslovak Sokol Association "never really took off in Slovakia." It had no more than 32,000 members in a region with a population of 3.3 million; see Dimond, "The Sokol and Czech Nationalism," 192.

79. Nolte, "'Every Czech a Sokol!,'" 82.

80. See Andreas Luh, *Der Deutsche Turnverband,* 31; and Marek Waic, "Československá obec sokolská v politickém životě první republiky," 83.

81. Ernst Fuchs, "Die Sokolbewegung; eine Parallele zum Makkabi," 18.

82. For the origin of the word, see Claire E. Nolte, *The Sokol in the Czech Lands,* 180. Although the Sokol movement had its own founding father, Miroslav Tyrš (1832–1884), the ethos, structure, and ideals of Sokol (founded in 1862) mirror that of the earlier German *Turner* movement.

83. See the photographs of the 1932 slet in Prague in the booklet *IX. slet všesokolský 1932* (no publication data in Maccabi Archives Box 147 4–37–27).

84. For significant state investments in Sokol, see Luh, *Der Deutsche Turnverband,* 85.

85. See, for example, report submitted to Ministry of Health and Physical Education from Maccabi ČSR on its annual activities and future goals d. April 4, 1932, in NA–Mzd Svaz Makabi v ČSR 1928–1952 inv.č. 3424/8/5 karton 913. The authorities prosecuted the leaders of the German National Socialist youth organization Volksport in Czechoslovakia in the summer of 1932 and subsequently introduced more legislation seeking to crack down on "subversion"; see Cornwall, *The Devil's Wall,* 156.

86. For funding for courses to ensure adequate supply of instructors, see letter from Maccabi ČSR to Ministry of Health and Physical Education d. February 26, 1937. For central control of the units, see letter from Maccabi ČSR to Ministry of Health and Physical Education d. May 31, 1937, ditto d. July 28, 1938, in NA–Mzd Svaz Makabi v ČSR 1928–1952 inv.č. 3424/8/5 karton 913.

87. Adolf Jellinek, "Die Organisation des Makkabi in der Slowakei," *Židovský sport,* November 1927: 12–13.

88. Arthur Herzog responded that these demands were unrealistic, since Maccabi's budget was too small to fulfill the needs of its clubs, noting than many on the western parts of the country were struggling as well. His response was included immediately after Jellinek's account, *Židovský sport,* November 1927: 13.

89. Arthur Herzog, "Zur Makkabi Weltverbandtagung am 27. und 28.

August 1927 in Brünn," *Židovský sport,* September 1927: 11.

90. Herzog, "Zur Makkabi Weltverbandtagung," 11.

91. For a thorough description of Beth Ha'am, see "Beth-Haam-Beilage," *Selbstwehr,* February 7, 1930.

92. One instance when the debate flared up was around the suggestion that Maccabi Prag/Praha and Hagibor Praha/Prag merge in the name of Jewish unity. "Naše anketa II: Považujete sloučení Hagiboru a Makabi v Praze za možné a účelné?," *Židovský sport,* September 1926: 1. Arthur Herzog was among the opponents to the merger.

93. Svaz Makabi v ČSR statutes d. November 3, 1924 (as above).

94. For Maccabi ČSR statutes, see Isidor Brandt to Ministry of Interior d. November 3, 1924, submitting the final version of the statutes on behalf of the three founding gymnastic clubs, Židovská tělocvičná a sportovní jednota Makabi v Praze, Jüdischer Turn- und Sportverein Makkabi Teplitz-Schönau, and Jüdischer Turn- und Sportverein Makkabi, Komotau. The statutes were first submitted on June 11, 1924. For barring from political activities, see response to Maccabi ČSR from the Provincial Political Administration in Prague (Zemská správa politická v Praze) d. November 21, 1924, in AHMP–PŘ–SK XIV/685, Svaz Makabi v ČSR, 1924–1952.

95. In an article in the German Maccabi's monthly *Der Makkabi: Organ der deutscher Makkabi Kreises,* which also acted as the organ of the Maccabi World Union, Arthur Herzog explained that the Czechoslovak Maccabi was not affiliated with any Zionist institutions. Considering he made a special point of mentioning this, one wonders if this was perhaps an anomaly among the Maccabi federations; Arthur Herzog, "Der tschechoslowakische Makkabikreis," *Der Makkabi,* May 1929: 8–9, here 9. Haim Kaufman argues that the Maccabi World Union was openly Zionist in order to fight the Bund in the interwar years; Kaufman, "Jewish Sports in the Diaspora," 155. For evidence that Maccabi ČSR was indeed perceived as a non-Zionist organization by the leadership of the Czechoslovak Zionist Organization and denied funding because of it, see *VIII. Zionistentag in Brünn 30.–31.7.1928 Rechenschaft über die Vergangenheit – Programm für die Zukunft* (Mährisch Ostrau: Zionistischer Zentralverband für die čsl. Republik, 1928), 32.

96. Giovanni Capoccia, "Legislative Responses against Extremism," 707–710, 714.

97. Tara E. Zahra, "Your Child Belongs to the Nation," 381.

98. In early August 1935, Maccabi ČSR filed a complaint with the Ministry of Health and Physical Education, asking them to reiterate to a German school board that Maccabi ČSR was not a political organization and thus had the right to organize Jewish youths. According to Maccabi ČSR, the German school board was barring Jewish children's access on the grounds that Maccabi ČSR was a political organization. See letter from Maccabi ČSR to the Ministry d. August 1, 1935, and the positive response from the Ministry d. August 5, 1935, quoting the directive from the Ministry

of Education d. May 26, 1922, restricting activities of certain organizations in NA–Mzd Svaz Makabi v ČSR 1928–1952 inv.č. 3424/8/5 karton 913.

99. In 1934, authorities heightened their surveillance of gymnastics organizations; see Marek Waic, "Turnerské hnutí a československý stát," 248.

100. For the connection between independence and financial need, see letter from Maccabi ČSR to Mzd d. December 27, 1934, ditto d. June 30, 1937, ditto d. April 4, 1936, and ditto d. October 10, 1936, in NA–Mzd Svaz Makabi v ČSR 1928–1952 inv.č. 3424/8/5 karton 913.

101. Ernst Fuchs, "Unser Verhältnis zur zionistischen Organisation," *Židovský sport,* March 1927: 11–12, here 11.

102. Adolf Jellinek, "Protokoll der ordentlichen kreisvollversammlung des csl. Makkabikreises am 29. und 30. oktober 1927 in Brünn," *Židovský sport,* December 1927: 15–17, here 16.

103. Arthur Herzog, "Bericht auf der Makabi-Kreistagung," *Židovský sport,* September 1931: 4–5, here 4.

104. Ibid.

105. Landes was the editor of *Židovské zprávy* from 1925 to 1939 and a member of the Maccabi executive from September 1936, although he did write on behalf of the executive, as shown earlier, prior to that. For engagement with *Židovské zprávy,* see Avigdor Dagan, "The Press," 526. On the executive, see letter from Maccabi ČSR to police authorities in Prague d. September 16, 1936, announcing election of new board, AHMP–PŘ–SK Svaz Makabi v ČSR XIV/685.

106. The Maccabi Winter Sports Association was established in 1931 as a response, in the words of the founders, to the increasing antisemitism in other associations as well as the need for Jewish national unity; see "Židovským zimním sportovcům!" *Židovský sport,* September–October 1931: 7. For more on antisemitism in the German-Austrian Alpine Association (Deutsch-östereichischer Alpenverein) active in Germany, Austrian, and the Sudetenland, see Jacob Borut, "Jews in German Sports," 79.

107. Before gaining prominence within Zionist politics, Goldstein served on the board of both Maccabi Prag/Praha and Hagibor Praha/Prag. For examples of Goldstein's appearance at various sports events, see Bratislava event in 1934 in "Armáda na naší půdě," *Židovské zprávy,* July 27, 1934. Goldstein became honorary vice president of Maccabi ČSR in 1932, according to Arthur Herzog, "Erinnerungen und Eindrücke von der I. Makkabiah in Tel-Aviv im Jahre 1932," *Zeitschrift für jüdische Geschichte* (1964): 143–145, here 144. For Goldstein's visit to Palestine during the 1932 Maccabiah, see "Nachklänge zur Makabiah: Die Teilnehmer berichten," *Selbstwehr,* April 21, 1932.

108. Beda Brüll, "Československý Makabi," 105; Statutes, November 3, 1924; and for fundraising and monetary commitment to Zionist causes, see Prokop Bureš, *Sport a tělesná kultura v R.Č.S* (Praha: Alamanach sportu, 1931), 373; see also Arthur Herzog, "Der tschechoslowakische Makkabikreis," *Der Makkabi,* May 1929: 9.

109. This had been a requirement for full membership of Maccabi since 1925; see *Makabi Handbuch* (Praha:

Tschechoslowakischen Makabikreis im Makkabi Weltverband, 1931), 115.

110. Ervin Goldschmid, "Turn- und Sportfest 1928," *Židovský sport,* January 1928: 10–11, here 11.

111. Richard Pacovsky, "Reisebericht der Kreisturnvaters," *Židovský sport,* December 1931: 12–14, here 13.

112. Bedřich (Beda) Brüll, "Československý Makabi," 104–105. Brüll was the secretary of Maccabi ČSR from 1934 to 1939, editor of the *Hamakkabi* supplement in *Židovské zprávy;* see Yehuda Brüll to Arthur Hanak (director of the Maccabi Archives at the time) d. March 24, 1985, Maccabi Archives Box 147 4–37–19.

113. Egon Štern, "Makabi v Československu," *Židovské zprávy,* September 2, 1927. For Hakoah, see "Konec smutné historie," *Židovský sport,* July 1927: 5–6.

114. Jellinek, "Die Organisation des Makkabi in der Slowakei," *Židovský sport,* November 1927: 12.

115. For laments regarding Jews in other clubs, see, for example, Mc Loy, "Lehká atletika," *Židovský sport,* April 1926: 5; Kurt Bloch, "Židé a sport," *Židovský kalendář 1933/1934:* 81–84, here 84; and Evžen Justic, "Evropští Židé v sportu," *Židovský kalendář 1926/1927:* 80–84, here 81.

116. Mc Loy, "Lehká atletika," 5.

117. Bloch, "Židé a sport," 84.

118. The situation was the same in Weimar Germany; see Borut "Jews in German Sports," 78.

119. Angelo Goldstein, "Cesta k uskutečnění," in *II. Svetové zimné hry Makabi Banská Bystrica 18–24. II 1936:* 31.

120. See, for example, the comparison between the pre-state Czech Sokol and the interwar Zionist movement in Fuchs, "Die Sokolbewegung," 18.

121. Daniel Boyarin argues that honor and acceptance were the fundamental goals of Zionism, not cultural preservation; *Unheroic Conduct,* 281–282.

122. Ibid., 10. For George Mosse's examination of masculinity as embodying outward appearance and inward virtue, see *Image of Man,* 24–39.

123. Fuchs, "Vom Wesen," 10.

124. Ibid., 11.

125. Ernst Fuchs, "Schritte zur Turngemeinschaft," *Židovský sport,* September 1927: 1–2.

126. Fuchs, "Vom Wesen," 11; this was a symbol of egalitarianism adopted from Sokol, where the familiar "thou" was introduced early on in the 1860s; Nolte, "'Every Czech a Sokol!,'" 81.

127. Fuchs, "Vom Wesen," 11.

128. Justic, "Evropští Židé," 81.

129. Here, I am referring to the attention paid to women's issues or questions of women's participation in the club management. While women were involved in the executive, they did not hold prominent positions, and the main leaders were all male. For overview of executive 1924–1939, see AHMP–PŘ–SK Svaz Makabi v ČSR XIV/685.

130. Todd Presner also discusses the discursive absence on women in Zionist ideology and notes the physical presence of girls and women in the clubs from the turn of the century; see Presner, *Muscular Judaism,* 12, 120.

131. In Weimar Germany, Jewish women made up 38% of the membership (1924) in the German Maccabi.

For a discussion of Jewish women in the gymnastics and sports movement in Germany, see Gertrud Pfister and Toni Niewerth, "Jewish Women in Gymnastics and Sports in Germany," 298.

132. "Valná hromada těl. jednoty Makabi v Praze," *Židovské z právy*, December 18, 1918.

133. Despite "protests from younger members," women had been allowed to serve on the board of Maccabi Prag/Praha in 1914; Lise Tutsch, "Der Prager Makabi während des Krieges," *Židovský sport*, April 1931: 6. For similar developments within Sokol in the Bohemian Lands during the First World War, see Nolte, "'Every Czech a Sokol!,'" 100.

134. For members of the Prague club's board, see "Valná hromada těl. jednoty Makabi v Praze," *Židovské zprávy*, December 18, 1918.

135. For Maccabi Prag/Praha, see list of board members for the interwar period in AHMP–PŘ–SK Židovská tělocvičná jednota Makabi Praha XIII 54. The board of Maccabi was very similar in its gender distribution. Usually, on a ten-person board, two of the members would be women. For lists of board members 1925–1939, see AHMP–Svaz Makabi v ČSR.

136. The monthly reports on members' attendance, which unfortunately exist in only very limited numbers, is one way of getting at the gender distribution in the individual units. For example, in April 1937, 65 women and 30 men attended exercises in Maccabi Brno/Brünn. In Prague, an almost equal number of men (56) and women (52) partook in exercises that month. The total for Maccabi was 599 men and 672 women; see *Doar Meamlenu*, June 1937: 5.

137. Paul Holzer, "Der Wert der Leibesübungen für die Frau," *Židovský sport*, June 1929: 15–17. Similarly, the women's supplement to *Selbstwehr* did not cover sports and gymnastics in its pages.

138. For the marginalization of women within Zionist institutions more broadly, see the special issue of *Journal of Israeli History* on women and gender in Zionist and Israeli history and historiography, especially Rachel Rojanski, "At the Center or on the Fringes of the Public Arena."

139. The tension between gymnastic defenders and sports proponents was evident in many ideological organizations such as Sokol and the socialist movement. Gymnastic clubs had integrated some sports, such as swimming, ball games, and track-and-field into their programs, a move that was often presented as a utilization of the health benefits of sports. It was, however, as Gechtman shows, also a response to pressure from below. Thus, the line was not clear-cut between gymnastics and sports, and the balance between the two was contested among activists. For Sokol and the socialist DTJ (Dělnická Tělovýchovná Jednota) in interwar Czechoslovakia, see Marek Waic, "Dělnická tělovýchova," 141. For Bundist groups, see Gechtman, "Socialist Mass Politics," 343–344.

140. For the link between ideal and countertype, see Mosse, *Image of Man*, 56–76.

141. It was published by Maccabi ČSR and edited by the organization's gym-

nastics director Paul Hirsch in Brno/Brünn in the late 1930s.

142. František Trnka, "Ist der Makabi eine Turn oder Sportorganisation?" *Doar Meamlenu,* April 1937: 3–4.

143. Ibid., 4.

144. "Unsere aktuellen Aufgaben," *Doar Meamlenu,* July 1937: 9–10; reply to Trnka's "Ist der Makabi eine Turn-oder Sportorganisation?" (by Herbert Barber), *Doar Meamlenu,* July 1937: 11–12; and Ervin Kovač, "Niektore hodnoty tělocviku," *Doar Meamlenu,* July 1937: 12.

145. Kovač, "Niektore hodnoty," 12.

146. Reply to Trnka's "Ist der Makabi eine Turn-oder Sportsorganisation?," *Doar Meamlenu,* July 1937: 12.

147. Zdeněk Landes, "K poslání židovského sportu," *Židovský sport,* January 1927: 2–3.

148. Ibid.

149. Brüll, "Československý Makabi," 103.

150. Ibid., 106.

151. "Židovský plavecký klub Hagibor," *Makabi Sport: zprávy spolku pro tělocvik a sport,* April 5, 1936: 8.

152. Karvin, "Primadonství," *Židovský sport,* June 1927: 3; see also Arne Vínarský, "Sportsman a gentleman," *Židovský sport,* February 1927: 1.

153. For a discussion of the distaste for professionalism and business in sports among middle-class sports activists in interwar Central Europe, a distaste that was accompanied in some circles by an antisemitic bias, see Rudolf Oswald, "Nazi Ideology and the End of Central European Soccer Professionalism, 1938–1941." For the need to rid Hagibor of prima donnas, see Ginz, "Naše primadony," *Židovský sport,* December 1927: 4.

154. See letter Maccabi ČSR to the Ministry of Health and Physical Education d. April 4, 1932, ditto d. December 28, 1934, and ditto d. April 22, 1936, all in NA–Mzd Svaz Makabi v ČSR.

155. See, for example, Maccabi ČSR to the Ministry of Health and Physical Education d. December 30, 1931.

156. See Maccabi ČSR to the Ministry of Health and Physical Education d. May 22, 1933, and ditto d. December 27, 1934, for a similar statement.

157. Even though support was awarded repeatedly, the funding had a contingent character. Maccabi ČSR's executive submitted funding applications twice a year, and the ministry then decided on varying amounts, though never more than Kč 10,000 at any one time.

158. See Maccabi ČSR to the Ministry of Health and Physical Education d. December 27, 1934, and ditto d. October 24, 1934.

159. See Mosse, *Image of Man,* 51–53; Gideon Reuveni, "Sports and the Militarization of Jewish Society," 45–46; and Caplan, "Germanizing the Jewish Male," 167.

160. In Czechoslovakia, the Ministry of National Defense owned sports facilities such as pools and playing fields that could at times be used by civilian clubs, especially during larger tournaments. The ministry also produced physical education material on, for example, swimming, which were distributed among civilian clubs; see the reference to films on swimming on loan

from the Ministry of National Defense to Hagibor in Prague, "Propagační den plavecké sekce ŽSK Hagiboru v Praze," *Židovský sport,* February 1926: 4.

161. For more on this discourse, see Reuveni, "Sports and the Militarization Militarization of Jewish Society," 45.

162. Waic, "Československá obec sokolská v politickém životě první republiky," 85, 93.

163. "Armáda na naší půdě," *Židovské zprávy,* July 27, 1934.

164. "Velký slet čsl. Makabi," *Židovské zprávy,* July 16, 1937, and *Slávnostný spis– Žilina – III. Slet čsl. Makabi v Žilině 4.–6. VII 1937.*

165. Ibid.

166. Žilina had a distinct place in Czechoslovak mythology as the seat of the Slovak authority that remained loyal to Czechoslovakia during the fighting in the region just after the First World War; see Peter Bugge, "The Making of a Slovak City," 224.

167. See, for example, letter Maccabi ČSR to the Ministry of Health and Physical Education d. December 24, 1928, and ditto d. December 30, 1931. For more explicit references, see ditto d. December 27, 1934.

168. Maccabi ČSR to Ministry of Interior d. December 14, 1935; the proposed changes are included in the response from the Ministry of Interior to Maccabi ČSR d. January 10, 1936, in NA–Zemský Úřad–spolkové oddělení–Svaz Makabi v ČSR inv.č. 431–1936 karton 1098. Interestingly, according to Marek Waic, the German Gymnastics Federation came under increasing scrutiny in 1934, partly because they attempted to step up the military content of their activities; see Waic, "Turnerské hnutí," 249.

169. Letter from Ministry of Interior to Maccabi ČSR d. January 10, 1936. NA–Zemský Úřad–spolkové oddělení–Svaz Makabi v ČSR inv.č. 431–1936 karton 1098.

170. František Trnka, "Branná výchova v tělovýchovných organisacích (I)," *Židovské zprávy,* January 10, 1936; and František Trnka, "Branná výchova v tělovýchovných organisacích (II)," *Židovské zprávy,* January 17, 1936.

171. Trnka, "Branná výchova v tělovýchovných organisacích" I.

172. Ibid.

173. Ibid. These games and drills were already part and parcel of the culture of youth organizations in much of Central and Eastern Europe, where educators promoted war games as a way of readying youth for military service. For this youth culture in Imperial and Weimar Germany, see Jeffrey Bowersox, *Raising Germans in the Age of Empire,* 175–177; for Bohemia, see Cornwall, *The Devil's Wall,* 47.

174. See speeches from the Žilina slet on Czech and Jewish unity defending the republic, "Velký slet čsl. Makabi," *Židovské zprávy,* July 16, 1937. Maccabi was admitted into a group of organizations entrusted with the civil defense training of youths; see "Přípravy branné výchovy Makabi," *Židovské zprávy,* August 6, 1937. For courses for Maccabi instructors in civil defense training, see "Čs. Makabi připraven," *Židovské zprávy,* November 5, 1937. At this time, the Zionist press ran articles that described how well young Jews performed as soldiers in the Czecho-

slovak army. They touted these young men's time in Maccabi and the fitness and skills that they had acquired there as playing a central role in "shattering" Czechoslovak military leaders' preconceptions about Jews as inept soldiers. According to these reports, Maccabi had succeeded in preparing Jewish men to assume their primary civic responsibilities, namely soldiering. See, for example, M.J. "Makabi na vojně," *Židovské zprávy,* April 1, 1938.

175. Maccabi ČSR to the Ministry of Health and Physical Education d. October 10, 1936.

176. *Slávnostný spis 3. slet Čs. Makabi v Žilině 4.–6.VII 1937,* 8–9.

177. *Slávnostný spis 3. slet Čs. Makabi v Žilině 4.–6.VII 1937,* 21. In the following year, the authors topped off their account of Maccabi ČSR's accomplishments in the area of civil defense by citing letters from civil defense unit and army commanders thanking Maccabi for their participation. In one, the officer in charge of civil defense in Žilina, A. Andrášek, thanked Maccabi for their contribution to a successful drill "especially in serious times like these," while noting that he would be counting on Maccabi in the years to come. Likewise, Miloš Žák, head of the army's Ninth Division in Bratislava, thanked the local Maccabi club for its members' participation in a military parade overseen by the Minister of Defense in April 1938 (the letters were reproduced by Maccabi leaders in a subsequent letter to the Ministry of Health and Physical Education); Maccabi ČSR to the Ministry of Health and Physical Education d. June 28, 1938.

178. The authors of the reports from the slet in *Židovské zprávy* were excited about the display of the blue-and-white Zionist flag in the streets of Prague and took the opportunity to highlight their admiration for Sokol; see, for example, Beda Brüll, "Naše barvy mezi prapory," *Židovské zprávy,* July 8, 1938; and "Vaše radost je naše radost," *Židovské zprávy,* July 8, 1938.

179. Monetary contributions as well as collective resolutions were publicized in *Židovské zprávy;* see, for example, "Židé na obranu státu," *Židovské zprávy,* June 3, 1938; "První výkaz darů," *Židovské zprávy,* June 24, 1938; "Naše svědectví: Čísla místo slov – Židé na obranu státu," *Židovské zprávy,* July 1, 1938.

180. For conscripts, see M.J. "Makabi na vojně," *Židovské zprávy,* April 1, 1938.

181. Imrich Rosenberg (1913–1986) was involved in these consultations for Maccabi ČSR; see Imrich Rosenberg, *A Jew in Deed,* 14–15. The invitation from the Ministry of National Defense to Maccabi ČSR to take a more active role in preparations for civil defense by joining the Council for Civil Defense (*Výbor pro zvýšení brannosti lidu*) was mentioned in "Svaz Makabi ČSR: styk s veřejnými korporacemi," *Židovské zprávy,* July 10, 1936.

7. Promised Lands

1. Jiří Weil, *Moskva-hranice* (Praha: Mladá fronta, 1991, origl. 1937), 21.

2. Ibid., 22.

3. Ibid., 30.

4. Ibid., 29.

5. Anita Shapira, *Israel: A History,* 104.

6. Dan Diner and Jonathan Frankel, "Jews and Communism: The Utopian Temptation," 4.

7. Letter from Hugo Bergmann to the Zionist Organization in London d. April 23, 1920, Central Zionist Archives [CZA]-Z4/1886/I.

8. Peter Bugge, "Czech Democracy," 7–8; Tara E. Zahra, *Kidnapped Souls,* 73.

9. The five parties were the Republican Party of Agrarians and Peasants (Republikánská strana zemědělského a malorolnického lidu), the Czechoslovak National Democracy (Československá národní demokracie), the Czechoslovak People's Party (Československá strana lidová), the Czechoslovak Social Democratic Workers' Party (Československá sociálně-demokratická strana dělnická), and the Czechoslovak National Socialist Party (Československá národně socialistická strana); see Bugge, "Czech Democracy," 13.

10. Bugge, "Czech Democracy," 25. Thus, when the Jewish Party formed an alliance with the Social Democrats in 1935, it was one that promised a channel for influence, as the Czechoslovak Social Democratic Party was part of the *pětka.* It did, however, come at the expense of not running on a separate Jewish Party ticket but merely alongside other candidates on the Social Democratic roster.

11. For the history of the Jewish Party in Czechoslovakia, see Marie Crhová, "Modern Jewish Politics in Central Europe."

12. Although the national elections were significant, municipal politics were also important arenas for Zionist political activism. Considering that the majority of the country's Jews lived in towns and cities, it was here that Zionist activists could pursue specifically Jewish priorities. These included securing public funds for Jewish institutions, such as social welfare organizations, schools, and sports clubs, and equal access to municipal contracts and employment. At the same time, it was on the municipal level that Zionists faced competition from other Jewish political parties. This topic has only recently received some attention. For Prague's Municipal Council, see Inis Koeltzsch, *Geteilte Kulturen,* 89–177; and for municipal politics in Mukačevo, see Yeshayahu Jelinek, *The Carpathian Diaspora,* 140–176.

13. Crhová, "Modern Jewish Politics," 73.

14. "Der Erfolg bei den Gemeindewahlen," *Selbstwehr,* June 20, 1919.

15. Crhová, "Modern Jewish Politics," 88–89, 91.

16. Crhová, "Modern Jewish Politics," 218.

17. "Protokoll der Sitzung des Zionistichen Exekutivkomitees vom 23.V.1927," d. June 13, 1927, CZA–Z4/3564 I. A member of Tekhelet Lavan, Hans Lichtwitz (later Uri Naor) immigrated to Palestine in 1939 or 1940. Rufeisen was chairman of the Czechoslovak Zionist Organization from 1921 until 1938, when he left for Palestine.

18. For Revisionism in Czechoslovakia, see Oskar K. Rabinowicz, "Czechoslovak Zionism: Analecta to a History," 99–108.

19. For Revisionist ideology and organization in the interwar years, see Eran Kaplan, *The Jewish Radical Right,* 8–11.

20. For the relative strength of the different parties within the Zionist Organization in Czechoslovakia, see "Der IX. tschechoslowakische Zionistentag," *Selbstwehr,* January 1, 1930; and "Die Wahlen in der der ČSR," *Selbstwehr,* July 28, 1933. For factionalism among youth groups, see Kateřina Čapková, "Piłsudski or Masaryk?"

21. It is not clear how many people were formally members of Zionist organizations in the Bohemian Lands. In Czechoslovakia, the number of people paying membership fees (the *shekel*) was 18,693 in 1931 (in 1925, the Jewish Party got 98,845 votes). However, this number does not include everyone involved in the Zionist movement. For shekel payers, see *Židovský Kalendář 1932/1933,* 40.

22. The Jewish National Fund was established in 1901 and was primarily engaged in land acquisition, while the Palestine Foundation Fund, established in 1920, was an organization funding the activities of the World Zionist Organization and mobilized support from non-Zionist Jews. For a history of these organizations in Britain, the United States, and Germany, see Michael Berkowitz, *Western Jewry and the Zionist Project.* The Jewish National Fund was established in Czechoslovakia in 1919/1920 and the Palestine Foundation Fund in 1921; see O. Rabinowicz, "Czechoslovak Zionism: Analecta to a History," 36, 38.

23. The increase in emigration was part of a broader trend of increased emigration to Palestine from Eastern and Central Europe; see Alex Bein, *The Return to the Soil,* 443.

24. The author reporting on the emigration numbers complained that the Subcarpathian emigrants used Palestine as a "social asylum" and lamented that this group lacked Zionist education and motivation; see "Dvě statistiky," *Židovské zprávy,* July 19, 1935.

25. For estimation of 6,000 emigrants in 1937, see Simha-Manor-Mandelik, "Naši v Palestině," *Židovský kalendář 1937/1938,* 80–84, here 80; for 4,000, see Yeshayahu A. Jelinek, "Czechoslovak Jews in Israel," 311–312. Jelinek also reminds us that some of the emigrants were Jews who went to Palestine for religious reasons rather than Zionist ones; Jelinek, *Carpathian Diaspora,* 207. In comparison, 3,306 Jews left Weimar Germany for Palestine in the years 1920–1932. German Jewry was significantly larger (568,000 in 1925) than the Jewish population in Czechoslovakia (365,000 in 1930), but in the latter there were more poor Jews. It was these communities in the country's east that supplied the majority of emigrants to Palestine until the mid-1930s. For German Jewry, see Hagit Lavsky, *Before Catastrophe,* 34, 104.

26. For complaints about the demoralizing effects of returnees on pioneers preparing for emigration, see *Zionistische Organisation Brünn Berichtet* (Brünn: Verlag der Zionistischen Organisation in Brünn 1932), 67 [*Zionistische Organisation Brünn Berichtet 1932*]. For statement that re-emigration to Czechoslovakia was much lower than elsewhere in the west, see "Dvě statistiky," *Židovské zprávy,* July 19, 1935. Re-emigration from Palestine was quite significant in the late 1920s, even

exceeding immigration in some years. In 1926, for example, 13,081 Jews came to Palestine, while 7,365 left. In 1927, 2,313 entered Palestine, but 5,000 left the Yishuv; see Bein, *Return to the Soil,* 338.

27. Designed as a conversation between Herr NEIN and Herr JA, the list of seventeen imaginary excuses included ones such as "I am too busy," "What is the money really being used for?," "We have enough migrants to support here," "What is the point? It is all being destroyed in the riots," "The British are terrible; one doesn't feel like doing anything for Palestine," "There are better places for Jews to go," and "Palestine is too small." *Erez Israel: Orgán židovského národního fondu/Organ des Jüdischen Nationalfonds,* May 1, 1937, no. 47, CZA–KKL 5/7844.

28. *Erez Israel: Orgán židovského národního fondu/Organ des Jüdischen Nationalfonds,* May 1, 1937.

29. For the Palestine Foundation Fund 1929/30 collection, see *Židovský Kalendář 1932/1933,* 40.

30. For an overview of the Jewish National Fund numbers, see "Der Abschuss des Kontingentjahre 5698," d. November 27, 1938, CZA–KKL 5/9317. In comparison, in 1922, the Jewish National Council applied for Kč 300,000 from the state to support the country's Jewish schools; Gustav Fleischmann, "Státní rozpočet a židovské školství národní," *Židovské zprávy,* January 13, 1922. In 1931, the school association in Moravia's budget was Kč 520,000; *Zionistische Organisation Brünn Berichtet 1932,* 18. In 1934, the state's support for the country's Jewish religious communities amounted to Kč 1.8 million; see Václav Müller, "Náboženství a národnost v naší republice," *Národnostní obzor* 5, no. 4 (1934): 241–247, here 247. The increase in donations in times of crisis was not unique to Czechoslovakia. Alex Bein notes that Jews in the Diaspora expressed their solidarity with the Yishuv by giving more money, setting fundraising records in 1929; see Bein, *Return to the Soil,* 428.

31. For the launch of the Kfar Masaryk campaign, see *Eretz Israel: Zprávy židovského národního fondu/Mitteilungen des jüdischen Nationalfonds,* January 10, 1935 CZA–KKL 5/6509; and "Der Abschuss des Kontingentjahre 5698."

32. For an example of propaganda material for the Jewish National Fund distributed in the Zionist press, see "Obzory – příloha Židovských zpráv," *Židovské zprávy,* September 23, 1938. For images of "Czechoslovak" life in Palestine distributed as part of a fundraising campaign, see, for example, the pamphlet distributed as part of the campaign honoring Haim Arlosoroff, a Zionist leader killed in Palestine in 1933, *Arlosoroffová akce – půda a kolonisace* (Keren Kayemet LeIsrael, n.d.), CZA–DD 710. For a report discussing the showings of the film *The Promised Land* in Czechoslovakia, see the letter KKL Prague to KKL Jerusalem d. July 29, 1937, CZA–KKL 5/7835. The well-known Jewish painter Friedrich Feigl (1884–1965) traveled to Palestine in the late 1920s and exhibited his work depicting its life and landscape in Prague on several occasions; see *Friedrich Feigl: Paintings, Drawings, and Graphic Art.*

33. For travelogues and descriptions, see Felix Weltsch, *Palästina:*

Land der Gegensätze – Eindrücke einer Palästinareise (Prag: Selbstwehr Verlag, 1929); and Leopold Goldschmied, *Palästina: Ein Tagebuch von Rabbiner L. Goldschmied* (Prag: Verlag Erez Israel, 1933).

34. See, for example, *Makabi Handbuch* (Praha: Tschechoslowakischen Makabikreis im Makkabi Weltverband, 1931); for war games with Palestine themes, see "Makabi Hatzair Materialsammlung no. 2 5696/1936," 36, CZA–DD 709. See also Berkowitz, *Western Jewry and the Zionist Project*, 147–174.

35. For an example of such documentation, see the film *Land of Promise* (Palestine, 1935); for youth and mass politics, see George L. Mosse, *Masses and Man*.

36. Mark Cornwall, *The Devil's Wall*, 112–113. Although Cornwall looks specifically at German youth movements, it seems reasonable to assume that similar trends could be observed among other ethno-national and religious groups.

37. On nationalist and other youth groups, see Mosse, *Masses and Man*, 5.

38. Daniela Bartáková, "Comparative Study of Tchelet Lavan and Hashomer Hatzair in Czechoslovakia (1918–1938)," 33–34.

39. For a discussion of the Wandervogel movement in Bohemia, see Cornwall, *The Devil's Wall*, 40–50.

40. Richard Karpe, "The Beginnings of the Blau-Weiss in Bohemia and Its Development during the First World War," 16–17.

41. Elkana Margalit, "Social and Intellectual Origins of the Hashomer Hatzair Youth Movement, 1913–1920," 154–158.

42. For Ha-Shomer ha-Tsa'ir, see Pavol Meštan, ed., *Hašomer Hacair – Dějiny hnutia*. For Betar, see Čapková, "Pilsudski or Masaryk?"; Miryam Du-Nour, "Ideology, Education, and Realization," 138–139.

43. Du-Nour, "Ideology, Education, and Realization," 138.

44. For an indication of the goal of Maccabi ha-Tsa'ir, see the report by the Board of Maccabi ha-Tsa'ir (Hanhalat Makabi Hacair): *Makabi-Makabi Hazair* (Bratislava: October 1937), 1–2, CZA–DD710.

45. "Protokoll der Sitzung des Zionistichen Exekutivkomitees vom 23.V.1927," d. June 13, 1927, CZA–Z4/3564 I.

46. Hugo Bergmann in *Bundesblätter* 5 (5687/1926–1927), as quoted in *Rhapsody to Tchelet Lavan*, 55.

47. For complaints about Czechoslovakia's Zionist organization not being allocated sufficient immigration certificates, see the central committee resolution from meeting in Brno/Brünn July, 1926, as quoted in *Zionistische Organisation in Brünn Berichtet* (Brünn: Verlag der Zionistischen Organisation Brünn, 1932), 22. On young Jews abandoning the training camps, ibid., 67; "Resoluce přijaté v plenární schůzi ústředního výboru," *Židovské zprávy*, July 24, 1925; "Resoluce XII. Sjezd čsl. sionistů," *Židovské zprávy*, July 23, 1926; and Jelinek, *Carpathian Diaspora*, 207. For the decline of He-Ḥaluts and for demoralized groups of pioneers, see the letter from the Zionist Executive Committee for Czechoslovakia to the

Jewish National Fund d. May 30, 1927, CZA–KKL 5/1772.

48. The number of ḥalutsim was small to begin with, so any "disturbance" was devastating to the movement. According to reports from He-Ḥaluts, in 1923, 16 men left for Palestine; in 1924, 27 men; and in 1925, 70 men and 14 women. The number of members of He-Ḥaluts was greater, growing from 105 to 382 in that same period. The number of men was three times the number of women, and the leadership saw this as a major problem, even suggesting to "bring transports of girls [*Mädchentransporte*] from abroad to Czechoslovakia." The creation of the training farm for girls in Bratislava was part of an effort to recruit more young women, whose parents might be uncomfortable with the usual co-ed arrangements at the hakhsharot. "Bericht über die Weidah des čsl. Landesverbandes Hechalutz, 26–27 Dezember, 1925," CZA–Z4/2154. These numbers should to be treated with some skepticism, since the Zionist Organization's funding for He-Ḥaluts was tied to the number of emigrants.

49. Ruth Bondy, *Jakob Edelstein*, 81.

50. Yehuda Erez (Rezniczenko), "Hechalutz in Czechoslovakia," 69.

51. For failure of the training farms, see ibid., 65. The farms consisted of the one in Bratislava (for girls, 1924–1925), Nový Jičín/Neu-Titschein (1925–1926), and Chomutov/Komotau (1926–1928). The last had room for twenty h̩alutsim at a time; for productivization in Czechoslovakia, see Haim Yahil, "Tchelet Lavan in the Twenties," 51. For the lack of interest among youth, see the letter from Emil Margulies to A. Engländer d. September 9, 1924, NA–Fond Emil Margulies, Hechalutz: zemský svaz pro ČSR 1920–1931 karton 10 inv.č. 51. For the lack of interest among the Zionist and Jewish public for funding pioneers and the Palestine project, see Viktor Fischl, "Sionismus každodenní," *Židovské zprávy,* January 10, 1936. Balu Amir notes that socialist Zionist ideology prevented Tekhelet Lavan from enjoying broad public support; Amir, "Requiem to a Movement," 187.

52. Fritz Flussmann, writing in *Bundesblätter,* April 1930, as quoted in *Rhapsody to Tchelet Lavan*, 89.

53. Referring to Flussmann's dismissal of equality, Amos Sinai, "In the Face of a Changing World," 89.

54. Du-Nour, "Ideology, Education, and Realization," 138.

55. Hanhalat Makabi Hacair, *Makabi-Makabi Hazair* (Bratislava: October 1937), 1, CZA–DD710.

56. See the correspondence between Arthur Herzog, Maccabi ČSR, and leaders of Maccabi ha-Tsa'ir regarding the youth organization's participation in the upcoming Zionist Congress d. June 3 and June 8, 1937, in Hanhalat Makabi Hacair, *Makabi-Makabi Hazair* (Bratislava: October 1937), 4–5, CZA–DD710.

57. Many Zionist youth groups were deeply influenced by the Zionist thinker and activist Aaron David Gordon (1856–1922), who was a sort of Tolstoyan figure of wisdom, simplicity, and return to nature, who had emigrated to Palestine from Russia when in his early forties. Gordon argued that individual and national redemption could be

achieved only through manual labor. The socialist Zionist movements in particular celebrated Gordon's idealization of physical labor and agricultural life as a means to personal and collective transformation. It was a creed that could be put into practice immediately, and Gordon insisted that words and slogans be followed by deeds. For a brief overview, see Shlomo Avineri, *The Making of Modern Zionism*, 151–158. For a detailed description of an idealized program for "inner revolution among youths," see Makabi Hacair, "Klärung des Begriffes 'Jugendbewegung,'" d. April 7, 1938, CZA–DD710.

58. Yahil, "Tchelet Lavan in the Twenties," 50 (Heinrich Hoffmann, later Haim Yahil).

59. On the tension within youth groups between people who were planning to leave ("only the crazy ones went all the way") and the ones, "who for family or personal reasons stayed," see Philip Boehm, "Tchelet Lavan: A School for Practical Zionism (a Personal Story)," 28.

60. "Bericht die I. Konstituerende Sitzung des Landeskommittees vom 28. Oktober 1932 in Prag," CZA–Z4 3564/7.

61. Eduard Goldstücker, *Vzpomínky, 1913–1945*, vol. 1, 41–42.

62. Letter from the Central Zionist Office in London to the Zionistische Landeskommittee d. January 9, 1927, CZA–Z4 3564/I.

63. Sinai, "In the Face of a Changing World," 108.

64. Anita Shapira, "'Black Night – White Snow,'" 159.

65. Avineri, *The Making of Modern Zionism*, 141. For Po'ale Tsiyon in Habsburg Austria, see Adolf Gaisbauer, *Davidstern und Doppeladler*, 368–414.

66. Zvi Y. Gitelman, *Jewish Nationality and Soviet Politics*, 48–49; Shapira, "'Black Night – White Snow,'" 148.

67. From a 1905 Vitebsk Po'ale Tsiyon handbill, as quoted in Gitelman, *Jewish Nationality and Soviet Politics*, 49.

68. For more on the split in Po'ale Tsiyon and the afterlife of the Left in Poland, see Samuel D. Kassow, "The Left Poalei Tsiyon in Interwar Poland."

69. Kateřina Čapková, *Czechs, Germans, Jews?*, 205. Po'ale Tsiyon received 1,326 votes out of 8,012 cast for Jewish parties in Prague. "Grosse jüdische Wahlerfolge," *Selbstwehr*, June 20, 1919. *Selbstwehr* estimated the total number of Jewish voters to be 15,000, of which 8,046 voted for Jewish national candidates (according to the State Statistical Bureau 1922 publication, the Jewish parties collected 8,012 votes in Prague).

70. According to the historian Jacques Rupnik, Kohn and his colleagues first established a Jewish Communist Party and sought admission as a separate faction to the Communist Party. When this effort faltered, Kohn and the other former members of Po'ale Tsiyon simply joined the Communist Party; see Jacques Rupnik, *Dějiny Komunistické strany Československa*, 56.

71. For election statistics, see Věra Olivová, *Dějiny první republiky*, 332–333.

72. H. Gordon Skilling, "Gottwald and the Bolshevization," 645; Rupnik, *Dějiny Komunistické strany Československa*, 51.

73. Skilling, "Gottwald and the Bolshevization," 645; ordinary Commu-

nists' distaste with the 1929 purge and the subsequent Stalinization of the party was, according to Jacques Rupnik, reflected by a drop in membership from 100,000 to 25,000 in the course of 1929; see Rupnik, *Dějiny Komunistické strany Československa*, 79.

74. Rupnik, *Dějiny Komunistické strany Československa*, 57.

75. Many former social democratic members of the Communist Party came out of the Austro-Marxist tradition, which recognized social and national questions as intertwined in the multinational empire and therefore supported social parties created along national lines. Some leading Austro-Marxists, however, did not recognize Jews as a nationality, and the Communist Party continued this tradition. By the late 1920s and especially in the 1930s, the Communist Party cast itself as the champion of Czechoslovakia's national minorities, but its ideologues did not consider Jews a nationality; see Rupnik, *Dějiny Komunistické strany Československa*, 27–35.

76. Vít Strobach, "Zamyšlení nad 'rudou asimilací' českých Židů," 86.

77. Rabbi Richard Feder noted in his early postwar testimony, "Jewish youth was often – and why should we continue to hide it today – inclined toward Communism"; Richard Feder, *Židovská tragedie: Dějství poslední* (Kolin: 1947), 9.

78. Strobach, "Zamyšlení nad 'rudou asimilací' českých Židů," 86.

79. Crhová, "Modern Jewish Politics," 136.

80. Jelinek, *Carpathian Diaspora*, 184–185, 187.

81. Strobach, "Zamyšlení nad 'rudou asimilací,'" 121. Although this is perhaps a reasonable assumption, there were other (and earlier) anti-fascist groupings, including Jewish, social democratic, and humanitarian ones, which Jews might have joined.

82. Some examples include Pavel Reiman, *V dvacátých letech: vzpomínky*; Fritz Beer, "*. . . a tys na Němce střílel, dědo?*"; and Stanislav Budín, *Jak to vlastně bylo*.

83. The historian Thomas Weiser's work shows that Jews made up less than 2% of the Communist leadership until 1930, when it increased to 17%–23% (in absolute numbers these represent two and eight members). During that same period, Jews were far more strongly represented among the elite of the German Social Democratic Party, making up 24%–28% of the leadership; see Thomas Weiser, *Arbeiterführer in der Tschechoslowakei*, 245 (table 17).

84. In Eastern Europe, some historians agree, Jews participated in Communism in disproportionate numbers in the interwar years, as did other minorities. However, because the number of Communists was relatively small, they were a small group in Jewish society. Some have suggested that it was not until after the Second World War that Jews joined the Communist parties in greater numbers. Like many of their neighbors, and sometimes even more so, Jews were grateful for liberation and eager to take advantage of the possibilities afforded them by the new regime. See Diner and Frankel, "Jews and Communism," 4, 7; for an interesting analysis of the historiog-

raphy of "Judeobolshevism," see also André Gerrits, "Antisemitism and Anti-Communism."

85. Karen Hartewig, "A German Jewish Communist of the Second Generation," 267.

86. In light of Zionists' suspicions of Jewish Communists' subversion, it is somewhat ironic that during the 1952 Slánský Trial the eleven defendants "of Jewish origin" were accused of being Zionist infiltrators, plotting to destroy Communism. Among the defendants, the prosecutor singled out Rudolf Slánský (1901–1952), Otto Šling (1912–1952), and Bedřich Geminder (1901–1952) for their alleged time in Zionist youth groups, using this claim as evidence of their guilt. Needless to say, scores of less prominent Jews, some Communists, others not, and some former members of Zionist organizations, were affected by the antisemitic campaigns of the early 1950s.

87. The memoirs of members of Tekhelet Lavan now living in Israel was published in the volume *Rhapsody to Tchelet Lavan in Czechoslovakia*.

88. On Plzeň/Pilsen in the 1900s, see Uriel Nahari (Fritz Flussmann), "Everyone's Friend (in Memory of Kriebesch)," 77–78; and Pinda Shefa, "The Prague Gdud in the Twenties," 54.

89. Boehm, "Tchelet Lavan: A School for Practical Zionism (a Personal Story)," 27.

90. Shapira, "'Black Night – White Snow,'" 162.

91. Jonathan L. Dekel-Chen, *Farming the Red Land*, 55.

92. Shapira, "'Black Night – White Snow,'" 162–163. There were several articles on the topic of Soviet colonization in the late 1920s in the Zionist press; see, for example, "Die jüdische Kolonisation in Sowjetrussland," *Selbstwehr*, January 13, 1928.

93. These events were given careful coverage in the local Zionist press, as were acts of antisemitism in the Soviet Union; see "Die Sowjets lösen den Hechaluz auf," *Selbstwehr*, April 4, 1928; and "Die antisemitischen Bolschewisten," *Selbstwehr*, April 20, 1928.

94. Robert Weinberg, *Stalin's Forgotten Zion*; friendship societies were established across the world. In Czechoslovakia, the Society of Friends of Birobidzhan (Společnost přátel Birobidjanu) was established in 1934 (the archival folder for this organization at the Czech National Archives is empty).

95. *Rudé Právo*, September 6, 1929, as quoted in Strobach, "Zamyšlení nad 'rudou asimilací,'" 133.

96. Amos Sinai, a member of Tekhelet Lavan, remembers having encountered Soviet-sponsored anti-Zionist materials in the early 1930s; Sinai, "In the Face of a Changing World," 110.

97. Strobach, "Zamyšlení nad 'rudou asimilací,'" 141. For some time, a new socialist Zionist newspaper also emerged, *Der Jüdische Sozialist* (1929–1932, the dates of entire run are uncertain).

98. Lev Bykovsky (edited by Lubomyr R. Wynar), *Solomon Goldelman: A Portrait of a Politician and Educator, 1885–1974; A Chapter in Ukrainian-Jewish Relations*, 17. Lev Bykovsky had been Goldelman's student.

99. According to his own testimony, Goldelman's career was hampered by

quotas and anti-Jewish regulations at the Commercial Institute in Kiev, where he worked as an assistant from 1913 to 1915; see Bykovsky, *Solomon Goldeman*, 18–19.

100. Ibid., 20–24.

101. For positions held, see Solomon I. Goldelman, *Jewish National Autonomy in Ukraine*, 9.

102. Bykovsky, *Solomon Goldelman*, 25, 31.

103. Sam Johnson, "'Communism in Russia Only Exists on Paper,'" 377, 393.

104. For a study of one of the multinational academic environments that emerged in Prague at this time, see Jindřich Toman, *The Magic of a Common Language*.

105. Johnson, "'Communism in Russia Only Exists on Paper,'" 374, 379.

106. Bykovsky, *Solomon Goldelman*, 34.

107. Solomon Goldelman residency card, NA–Policejní ředistelství Praha II–evidence obyvatelstva.

108. Bykovsky, *Solomon Goldelman*, 35.

109. Goldelman volunteered to defend Symon Petliura's reputation at the Paris trial of the Ukrainian leader's assassin, Sholom Schwartzbard, in 1926–1927. He hoped to be a witness for both sides and explain the difficult conditions that precipitated the pogroms and the assassination. Ibid., 37–38.

110. In his memoirs, Goldelman notes, "A citizen of Ukraine of non-Ukrainian nationality – a nationally conscious son of the Jewish nation – had the opportunity to make a humble contribution to Ukrainian scholarship and education of a new generation of young Ukrainian economists that would work for a future independent Ukraine." "Memoirs from My Ukrainian Era" (1953), included in Bykovsky, *Solomon Goldelman*, 73–81, here 78.

111. Between 1921 and 1932, the Czechoslovak government allocated six times as much as the Yugoslav and French governments to the education of émigré youth from the Russian Empire. From 1924, it amounted to more than Kč100 million per year; Johnson, "'Communism in Russia Only Exists on Paper,'" 373. For comparison, see Jiří Vacek, *Ruská, ukrajinská a běloruská emigrace v Praze*, 3.

112. Bykovsky, *Solomon Goldelman*, 38; see also the Goldelmans' residency card.

113. Goldelman continued his involvement with his Ukrainian friends and colleagues. He taught at the Ukrainian Sociological Institute and helped re-launch the Ukrainian Commerce Academy as a correspondence school in 1936; Bykovsky, *Solomon Goldelman*, 35, 39. In many ways, he ran his Zionist and Ukrainian educational activities as parallel activities, drawing on methods within one movement to better the other. For example, he launched the Zionist correspondence school just a year before he engaged in similar efforts among Ukrainians in Czechoslovakia.

114. Ibid., 38. For Goldelman's renewed activity, see the brief mention in the report "Zionistischer Zentralverband für die Tschechoslowakische Republik: Exekutivkomitee Mährisch Ostrau," d. June 30, 1930 CZA–Z4 3564/V.

115. Several of Solomon Goldelman's articles in *Selbstwehr* were later reprinted in a collection of his lectures and essays entitled *Löst der Kommunismus der*

Judenfrage? Rote Assimilation und Sowiet-Zionismus (Gesammelte Aufsätze und Vorträge 1930–1936) (Wien: Heinrich Glanz, 1937); see, for example, "Der Weg der Jugend: Kommunismus und Zionismus," *Selbstwehr,* October 23, 1931; and "Im Kampfe gegen die Rote Assimilation," *Selbstwehr,* July 8, 1932.

116. It is not clear whether Goldelman spoke Czech, but he did know Russian, Ukrainian, German, and Yiddish. Goldelman founded the Czechoslovak branch of the League for the Workers of Palestine in Czechoslovakia (Liga für das arbeitende Erez-Israel in der Tschechoslowakei) and appears to have used this organization as a sort of springboard for speaking engagements in 1931. He founded a Zionist information and service and speakers' bureau sometime after he returned to Prague, which became the basis for the Zionist Propaganda Bureau; see the list of speaking engagements for 1933/1934 included in a letter asking for support from the Zionist Executive in London, letter Solomon Goldelman to Zionist Executive London d. April 8, 1934, CZA–Z4 3564/8.

117. Mosse, *Masses and Man,* 301–302.

118. Otto Heller, *Der Untergang des Judentums: Die Judenfrage/Ihre Kritik/Ihre Lösung durch den Sozialismus* (Berlin: Verlag für Literatur und Politik, 1931); for comment on significance, see Mosse, *Masses and Man,* 302.

119. Heller, *Der Untergang des Judentums,* 152.

120. Mosse, *Masses and Man,* 286–287.

121. Heller, *Der Untergang des Judentums,* 151.

122. Ibid., 163.

123. Mosse, *Masses and Man,* 303.

124. Heller, *Der Untergang des Judentums,* 173–174.

125. Mosse, *Masses and Man,* 302.

126. *Selbstwehr* reported from the event in great detail on its front page and printed Brod and Hoffmann's responses. See "'Untergang des Judentums': Kommunismus und Zionismus," *Selbstwehr,* January 29, 1932; Max Brod, "Erwiderung auf Otto Hellers Prager Vortrag," *Selbstwehr,* January 29, 1932; and Heinrich Hoffmann, "Die ökonomische Judenfrage," *Selbstwehr,* January 29, 1932.

127. Goldelman made a reference to this event in his book *Löst der Kommunismus der Judenfrage?,* 233.

128. Bondy, *Jakob Edelstein,* 41.

129. Goldelman claimed about his 1937 collected works *Löst der Kommunismus der Judenfrage?* that "this book was a great success and served as a guide in the struggle against Communist influence on the Jewish youth in the Jewish settlements." Bykovsky, *Solomon Goldelman,* 41.

130. He developed this analysis in several pieces, including "Jüdische Wirtschaftsverfassung als Schicksalsgemeinschaft: Die ökonomischen Grundlagen der exterritorialen jüdischen Nation," in *Löst der Kommunismus,* 45–65, here 48–49.

131. Ibid., 45–49.

132. Ibid., 55.

133. Ibid., 64–65.

134. In *Löst der Kommunismus der Judenfrage?* ten out of fifteen essays were devoted to Soviet Jewish policies and Soviet Jewish colonization projects,

which Goldelman referred to as "Soviet Zionism." About gullibility and widespread sympathies, see Goldelman, "Die Seifenblase platzt" (1933), in *Löst der Kommunismus der Judenfrage?*, 233–237, here 233.

135. Goldelman, "Ein Danaergeschenk" (1934), in *Löst der Kommunismus der Judenfrage?*, 237–241, here 241.

136. Goldelman, "Die Seifenblase platzt," 233.

137. Ibid., 236. Goldelman noted that even during the worst crisis in Jewish settlement in Palestine in 1922–1931, only 20% of the 95,000 immigrants left Palestine.

138. Ibid., 236.

139. Goldelman, "Ein Danaergeschenk," 240.

140. Goldelman, "Die Seifenblase platzt," 233–234.

141. Although emigration to Palestine had picked up by the mid-1930s, Zionist activists still saw Birobidzhan and the Soviet Union as a distraction to the Jewish public. At the time, Jews were being asked to donate funds to the Jewish National Fund for Czechoslovakia, to their own poor Jews as well as for persecuted Jews from Germany and Poland. In a set of guidelines for a Jewish National Fund fundraiser launched in May 1937, volunteers were instructed (it seemed to have Goldelman's fingerprints all over it, although the author remained anonymous) to challenge hesitant donors' claim that Birobidzhan is the best solution to "all Jewish questions." The self-confident reply went as follows: "We don't have anything against Birobidzhan as a reality, that is, if Birobidzhan really could absorb Jews from all over the world. In reality, despite the assistance of many million [dollars] from American Jews, the Soviets have succeeded in establishing only a very small settlement, with barely 15,000 Jewish souls. The borders of Russia are as closed to Jewish immigration as all other states. Let us remember that the promise was that by 1934, 100,000 Jewish families would be settled in Birobidzhan. Palestine, according to Communist-Jewish propaganda, was supposed to have been done with this year. By the end of this period [by 1934], there were 8,000 Jewish souls in Birobidzhan, while in Palestine during this year alone 42,000 Jews were taken in. In Birobidzhan, out of the 15,000 Jewish heads, 12,000 live in the city of Birobidzhan. In Palestine, over 100,000 Jews, 25% of the Jewish population, live on the land. We would gladly continue this comparison and also want to point you to the recently published book *Does Communism Solve the Jewish Question?* For us, Birobidzhan is not a problem, since there aren't really any immigration opportunities there." *Erez Israel: Orgán židovského národního fondu/Organ des jüdischen Nationalfonds,* May 1937, CZA–KKL5/7844.

142. Carlebach's series originally appeared in German in the Hamburg-based *Israelitisches Familienblatt,* for which he worked as a journalist, but the trip to the Soviet Union was funded by the Warsaw Yiddish paper *Haynt,* the organ for the Zionist Organization in Poland (and thus a Polish equivalent to *Selbstwehr*). His German-language articles appeared in *Selbstwehr* between November 4, 1932, and Febru-

ary 24, 1933, as "Reise zu den Juden Sowjetrusslands."

143. Solomon Goldelman, "Rusko-německé analogie (Židovství a komunismus)," in *Židovský kalendář 1937–1938*: 32–44, here 33. Goldelman's article was the lead piece in the annual that year.

144. Ibid., 35–38, 43, 44.

145. Heller, *Der Untergang des Judentums*, 170.

146. Bykovsky, *Solomon Goldelman*, 38; see Anita Shapira's observation on this among socialist Zionists in Palestine, "'Black Night – White Snow,'" 161.

147. Goldelman presented his ideas to the Zionist leadership sometime between 1930 and 1932. "Protokoll der Zionistiche Zentralverband in der ČSR," n.d. [1930–1932], CZA–Z4 3564/8.

148. Goldelman's ideas reflect his experience in Russian and consist of well-established socialist principles regarding organization, propaganda, and agitation. See, for example, Lenin's "The Tasks of Russian Social-Democrats" (1897), where he discusses socialist activism as being organized through a strong ideological center with a network of individual cells that would serve to create class consciousness among workers through propaganda (knowledge and education) and agitation (the framing of spontaneous events in ways that further workers' class consciousness and support for socialism).

149. Goldelman used "worldview" in the sense of an intellectual construction with one overriding hypothesis that solved all problems and left no questions unanswered. It was not merely an outlook on life, but a carefully constructed consciousness.

150. Rufeisen noted that Po'ale Tsiyon was not opposed to the Czechoslovak Zionist Organization's platform that afforded equal merit to the work for Jewish national rights in the Diaspora and work for the homeland in Palestine. They agreed with the basic tenets but refused to have their political program "dictated" by others on principle. "Referat von Dr. Josef Rufeisen (MO), 'Territorialverband oder territoriale Arbeitsgemeinschaft,'" d. 1932, CZA–Z4 3564/7.

151. Between September 1933 and April 1934, Goldelman, traveled across the Bohemian Lands and Slovakia, delivering more than forty-three lectures on topics such as "Zionism and Socialism," "Contemporary Socioeconomic and National Trends and the Jewish Problem," "The Jewish Economy in the Diaspora – The Jewish Economy in Palestine," and "Does Communism Solve the Jewish Question?" It was clearly an exhausting endeavor. In his correspondence with the Zionist Executive in London, Goldelman, who by then was in his mid-forties, mentioned that he had fallen ill at the end of his lecture circuit and noted, "I have devoted myself to the maximum of what can be expected of a single person to disseminate Zionist propaganda in this country." See letter from S. Goldelman to Zionist Executive in London d. April 8, 1934, CZA–Z4 3564/8. Bykovsky claims in his Goldelman biography that the latter's articles and lectures "soon became a very successful weapon against Communist propaganda among Jews in East Central Europe"; *Solomon Goldelman*, 40.

152. "Bericht der I. konstituerendes Sitzung des Landeskommittees vom 28. Oktober 1932 in Prag," CZA–Z4 3564/7.

153. Goldelman's vision struck a chord with Zionist leaders in Prague early on (sponsors included the Prague chapter of the Zionist Organization, WIZO, and the Czechoslovak Palestine Foundation office). By 1936, the Zionist Executive in London and the Jewish National Fund in Jerusalem were also supporting Goldelman's Zionist Propaganda Bureau. Yet, the Zionist leadership in Moravská Ostrava/Mährisch Ostrau held off on their support. They might have remained uncomfortable with the openly socialist orientation of the bureau as well as opposed to its Prague location, concerned as they always were with being upstaged by the capital. Over time, Goldelman established an especially close relationship with the Jewish National Fund, writing some of their publicity material and advertising the bureau's activities. For early funding, see Letter S. Goldelman to London Executive d. October 21, 1935 ("Bericht der Zionistische Propagandastelle Oktober 1935, Teil I–II"), CZA–Z4 3564/X; "Bericht der Zionistische Propagandastelle," CZA–Z4 3564/X.

154. "Bericht der Zionistischen Propagandastelle in Prag – Feber–Juni 1934," d. July 1, 1934, and signed S. Goldelman, CZA-Z5 3564/VIII.

155. "Bericht der Zionistischen Propgandastelle in Prag an den 19. Zionistenkongress in Luzern," d. early July 1935 and signed S. Goldelman, CZA–Z4 3564/X.

156. Leo Meller (later Yehuda Manor) grew up in Moravská Ostrava/Mährisch Ostrau. He was a member of Tekhelet Lavan or the Jewish socialist youth movement (associated with Po'ale Tsiyon and founded in Brünn c. 1928) – the two organizations merged in the early 1930s; see Yehuda Manor, "The Foundation of JSY and Its Amalgamation with Tchelet Lavan," 129–130. Meller was most likely tasked with the youth propaganda division, he and Goldelman co-signed letters addressed to the youth groups, and Meller also created the layout for Goldelman's book *Löst der Kommunismus der Judenfrage?* In his (brief) memoir included in *Rhapsody to Tchelet Lavan,* Manor does not mention Goldelman or the Zionist Propaganda Bureau even though he worked there for at least three or four years.

157. The following list is based on the bureau's advertisement in *Erez Israel: Zprávy židovského národního fondu,* August 12, 1935, 4–5, 8.

158. Olgerd Bockovsky (also Hyppolit Boczkowski) was a Ukrainian left-wing journalist and sociologist who lived in Bohemia from 1908 to his death in 1939; see Bohdan Ziljynskij, "Ukrajinská emigrace," in *Exil v Praze a Československu, 1918–1938/Exile in Prague and Czechoslovakia, 1918–1938,* 22–25. Panas Fedenko was a Ukrainian historian, publicist, and one of the leaders of the Ukrainian Social Democratic Party. After 1921, he taught at the Ukrainian Pedagogical Institute and the Ukrainian Free University in Prague and was a longtime associate of Goldelman's. After the Second World War, they reconnected in Munich, where Fedenko now lived. See biography at Special Collections of the Sla-

vonic Library, at the National Library in Prague, http://sbirkysk.nkp.cz/index.php?lang=en&page=sbirky&id=17.

159. The Jewish cycle would add an additional day of lecturing per week, from two to three days. For university environment and quality of lectures, "Bericht der Zionistischen Propgandastelle in Prag an den 19. Zionistenkongress in Luzern," signed S. Goldelman and dated beginning of July 1935, CZA–Z4 3564/X.

160. The Volkshochschule was entirely paid for by Prague Zionist organizations and provided the basis for other activities; "Bericht der Zionistischen Propagandastelle 1935/1936," CZA–Z4 3564/X.

161. "Bericht der Zionistischen Propagandastelle: Arbeitsplan für das Jahr 5696 (1935/1936)," d. October 1935, CZA–Z4 3564/X. Goldelman notes that lectures were orderly.

162. "Bericht der Zionistische Propagandastelle, 1936/1937," CZA–Z4 3564/X.

163. It took about five years to raise the money for the building, which had an additional two underground stories, office space, and dormitories for Jewish youths; see the description of the building in "Beth Haam v Praze odevzdán veřejnosti," *Židovské zprávy,* February 7, 1930.

164. For the German Casino and its meaning, see Gary Cohen, *The Politics of Ethnic Survival,* 53.

165. "Bericht der Zionistischen Propgandastelle in Prag an den 19. Zionistenkongress in Luzern," signed S. Goldelman and dated beginning of July 1935, CZA–Z4 3564/X.

166. "Bericht der Zionistischen Propagandastelle: Arbeitsplan für das Jahr 5696 (1935/1936)," d. October 1935, CZA–Z4 3564/X; for "the task given," see letter S. Goldelman to Zionist Organization in London dated May 20, 1935, CZA–Z4 3564/X; subscriber distribution: Central Europe, 73%; Eastern Europe, 11%; Western Europe, 9%; other, 7%; for 1936, "Bericht der Zionistische Propagandastelle, 1936/1937," CZA–Z4 3564/X.

167. Letter from S. Goldelman to Zionist Organization in London d. May 20, 1935, CZA–Z4 3564/X.

168. Letter SG to London Executive d. October 21, 1935, with "Bericht der Zionistische Propagandastelle Oktober 1935," CZA–Z4 3564/X.

169. "Bericht der Zionistischen Propgandastelle in Prag an den 19. Zionistenkongress in Luzern," signed S. Goldelman and dated beginning of July 1935, CZA–Z4 3564/X.

170. "Bericht der Zionistischen Propagandastelle in Prag: Feber-Juni 1934," d. July 1, 1934, and signed S. Goldelman, CZA–Z5 3564/8; and letter from S. Goldelman to London Executive d. October 21, 1935, with "Bericht der Zionistische Propagandastelle Oktober 1935," CZA–Z4 3564/X.

171. "Bericht der Zionistische Propagandastelle, 1936/1937," CZA–Z4 3564/X.

172. "Bericht der Zionistischen Propagandastelle: Arbeitsplan für das Jahr 5696/1935–1936," d. October 1935, CZA–Z43564/X.

173. "Bericht der Zionistische Propagandastelle, 1936/1937," CZA–Z4 3564/X.

174. Some of the titles in the Zionist Library included lectures from the

Volkshochschule, such as František Friedmann's *Einige Zahlen über die Juden der ČSR* and Goldelman's *Jüdische Galutwirtschaft*. Others were socialist Zionist "classics," such as David Ben-Gurion, *Chalutz Zionismus oder Revisionismus?*; Berl Locker, *Was ist Poale-Zionismus;* Mendel Singer, *Des Weg des jued. Arbeieter zum Sozialismus;* and Hugo Hermann, *Palästina-kunde*. In 1935, the number of titles was forty-seven, with 25% in Hebrew and Yiddish, the rest in German language; "Bücherlager Ausweis, Mai 1935," CZA–Z4 3564/X. The demand for literature in Czech was also being felt, and Goldelman anticipated an additional financial burden if he was going to meet it.

175. Bykovsky, *Solomon Goldelman,* 38–39.

176. Goldelman, "Der Weg der Jugend (1931)," in *Löst der Kommunismus die Judenfrage?*, 14–23, here 23.

177. Letter from S. Goldelman and L. Meller to all Zionist youth groups d. May 1935, CZA–Z4 3564/X.

178. Ibid.

179. Dow Biegun, "Jugendarbeit," *Erez Israel: Orgán židovského národního fondu/Organ des jüdischen Nationalfonds,* May 1937, 9; CZA–KKL5/7844.

180. "Bericht der Zionistische Propagandastelle, 1936/1937," CZA–Z4 3564/X.

181. Bykovsky, *Solomon Goldelman,* 42–43.

182. Ibid., 43–44.

183. Ibid., 45–46. The colleague was an unnamed former editor of *Selbstwehr.*

184. Ibid., 41, 44–45.

185. Ibid., 53–54.

186. Ibid., 54.

Epilogue

1. Židovská náboženská obec v Praze [ŽNOP], Protokoly [Minutes from the Board Meetings], March 30, 1938. Židovské museum v Praze [ŽMP]–Protokoly, 1918–1939.

2. Jewish observers estimated that more than 30,000 Jews would be at risk if the German-dominated areas were handed over to Germany, "Kolik Židů je v sudetském území?," *Židovské zprávy,* July 22, 1938. Most of the Jewish refugees left immediately, and 12,000 Jews had escaped by early November. Jews made up a small part of the more than 140,000 refugees from the Sudeten region; see Jörg Osterloh, *Nationalsozialistiche Judenverfolgung*, 203.

3. For a thorough study of various responses to Jewish refugees in Czechoslovakia, see Kateřina Čapková and Michal Frankl, *Nejisté útočiště.*

4. The rising antisemitism was felt already in the summer of 1938, as reflected in articles in *Židovské zprávy* seeking to defend Jews against attacks in the Czech press; see, for example, "Trojský kůň před branami," *Židovské zprávy,* August 5, 1938.

5. Livia Rothkirchen, *The Jews of Bohemia and Moravia,* 83.

6. ŽNOP–Protokoly, November 2, 1938.

7. Rothkirchen, *The Jews of Bohemia and Moravia,* 116.

8. Gaëlle Vassogne, *Max Brod in Prag,* 237–238.

9. The meeting took place on April 18, 1939, just a month after the German invasion. Information about the meeting of community leaders can be found in the minutes from the meeting of the

Prague community board on May 3, 1939; ŽNOP–Protokoly, May 3, 1939.

10. Rothkirchen, *The Jews of Bohemia and Moravia,* 102–103, 110.

11. Paul März (later Paul Meretz) testified about the German occupation of the Bohemian Lands at the Eichmann Trial in 1961. Eichmann had been active in Prague immediately after the establishment of the Protectorate as he arranged for creation of an emigration (and dispossession) center in Prague (Zentralstelle für jüdische Auswanderung in Prag) modeled on the one in Vienna. Paul März's testimony can be found in the trial's session 19, no. 1–3. März and his wife left Prague on November 15, 1939, and arrived in Palestine a week later; Eichmann Trial session 19, no. 2. The session can be found in "The Trial of Adolf Eichmann," vol. 1, April 11–May 8, 1961, sessions 1–30, and is available at http://www.nizkor.org/hweb/people/e/eichmann-adolf/transcripts/Sessions/index-01.html.

12. Paul März gave testimony about this at the Eichmann Trial, session 19, no. 2; ibid. Emil Kafka's arrival in London and information about the purpose of his trip was printed by the *Jewish Telegraph Agency* on July 24, 1939.

13. *Mitteilungen der Merkaz Lanoar,* late January 1939, 17–18, CZA–DD709.

14. Rothkirchen, *The Jews of Bohemia and Moravia,* 235.

15. Livia Rothkirchen, "The Zionist Character of the 'Self-Government' of Terezín," 59, 74.

16. Livia Rothkirchen, "The Situation of Jews in Slovakia between 1939–1945," 46–70, 56–57.

17. For deportations from Hungarian-occupied former Czechoslovak territory (southern Slovakia and Subcarpathian Ruthenia), see Randolp L. Braham, *The Politics of Genocide,* vol. 2, 604–608, 618–636.

18. On Beth Ha'am, see Eichmann Trial, session 44, no. 6; "The Trial of Adolf Eichmann," vol. 2, May 8–May 24, 1961, sessions 31–51. Ivana Dejmková notes that these were people of mixed ancestry whose status was being disputed or was still under consideration; Dejmková, "Hagibor aneb jak jedno místo v Praze získalo smutnou pověst," 258.

19. For the effects of Friedmann's marriage on his Zionist career, see Kateřina Čapková's interview with Viktor Fischl entitled "Pak to ale dopadlo ještě jinak," which was originally published in the monthly *Roš Chodeš* in March 2001. It is available online at http://www.holocaust.cz/cz2/resources/ros_chodes/2001/03/fischl (on intermarriage, pp. 5–6).

20. Interview with Jakob Edelstein, 6–8, in *Mitteilungen des Merkas Lanoar,* Prag, Mitte Feber, 1939, 8, CZA DD709.

21. Eichmann Trial, session 44, no. 6; "The Trial of Adolf Eichmann," vol. 2, May 8–May 24, 1961, sessions 31–51.

22. Rothkirchen, *The Jews of Bohemia and Moravia,* 130.

23. Kurt Wehle, "The Jews in Bohemia and Moravia, 1945–1948," 501.

24. Rothkirchen, *The Jews of Bohemia and Moravia,* 161.

25. Jews made up a significant number of exiled Czechoslovaks. According to Livia Rothkirchen, Jews made

up 25% of the first Czechoslovak army units formed in France in October 1939, some of whom had arrived there from Palestine; Rothkirchen, *The Jews of Bohemia and Moravia*, 163.

26. Jan Láníček, *Czechs, Slovaks and the Jews: Beyond Idealisation and Condemnation*, 47–48.

27. Ibid., 40–51, 75.

28. Anna Cichopek-Gajraj, "Limits to 'Jewish Power.'"

29. Yehoshua R. Büchler, "Reconstruction Efforts in Hostile Surroundings," 257.

30. For the estimated number of survivors and immigrants, see Petr Brod, Kateřina Čapková, and Michal Frankl, "Czechoslovakia," 380.

Bibliography

ARCHIVES

Czech Republic

PARLAMENT ČESKÉ REPUBLIKY/PARLIAMENT OF THE CZECH REPUBLIC

Minutes from the meetings of the provisional Czechoslovak National Assembly (*Národní shromáždění československé*) [NSČ], 1918–1938. http://www.psp.cz/eknih/1918ns/index.htm

Ústavní listina, Národní shromáždění československé 1918–1920, tisk 2421 část č. 3, available electronically at www.psp.cz

NÁRODNÍ ARCHÍV/NATIONAL ARCHIVES, PRAGUE

Ministerstvo školství a národní osvěty
- Inv.c. 2086 sign. 47/VIII karton 3917 (1920–1936)
- Inv.c. 2086 sign. 47/VIII karton 3921 (1921–1938)
- Inv.č. 2987 sign. 47/VIII karton 3922 (1921–1927)
- Inv.č. 2086 sign. 47/VIII karton 3922 (1928–1938)
- Inv.č. 2086 sign. 47/VIII karton 3924.

Ministerstvo veřejného zdravotnictví a tělesné výchovy
- Svaz Makabi v ČSR inv.č. 3424/8/5 karton 913 (1928–1952)

Ministerstvo vnitra
- Židovská tělocvičná a sportovní obec v ČSR inv.č. 6/59/20 karton 1040 (1921–1928)

Fond Československá sportovní obec, 1918–1928
- Inv.č. 1 karton 1.

Národní rada česká
- Karton 509/2

Zemský Úřad – Spolkové oddělení
- Svaz Makabi v ČSR inv.č. 431–1936 karton 1098.

Fond Československá sportovní obec, 1918–1928
- Inv.č. 1 karton 1.

Osobní Fondy
- Emil Margulies
- Inv.č. 25 karton 9, 1919–1928.
- Inv.č. 94–100–104 karton 9.
- Inv.c. 51 karton 10.

Nejvyšší správní soud
- Karton 858 case no. 16046/29 d. 7.9.1929 [Fríed]
- Karton 858 case no. 16836/30 d. 4.11.1930 [Fríednerová].

Policejní ředistelství Praha II – evidence obyvatelstva.
František Friedmann, 1897–1945
Solomon Goldelman, 1885–1974

ARCHIV KANCELÁŘ PREZIDENTA REPUBLIKY/ARCHIVES OF THE PRESIDENT OF THE REPUBLIC
D 1274/30]

ARCHÍV HLAVNÍHO MĚSTA PRAHY/ CITY OF PRAGUE ARCHIVES
Fond Policejni Ředitelstvi–Spolkový katastr
Židovský sportovní klub Hagibor XIV/0367
Svaz Makabi v ČSR XIV/0685. (1924–1952)
Židovská tělocvičná jednota Makabi Praha XIII 54.

ARCHÍV ŽIDOVSKÉHO MUZEA V PRAZE/ARCHIVES OF THE JEWISH MUSEUM
Židovská náboženská obec v Praze Protokoly, 1918–1939.
Referáty z porad zástupců židovských náboženských obcí Protektorátu Čechy a Morava 1939 inv.č. 9 karton 1.

ARCHÍV MĚSTA OSTRAVY/ CITY OF OSTRAVA ARCHIVES
MŠV karton 148 sign. žid. 1935 (1928)

Israel

THE CENTRAL ZIONIST ARCHIVES, JERUSALEM
Emil Margulies Collection A299/9
The Zionist Organization, Central Office, London, 1917–1955
Z4/1886/I (1920)
Z4/2154 (1925)
Z4/3564/I-X (1925–1937)
The Jewish Agency for Palestine, New York, 1939–1991
Z5 3564/8 (1934)
The Jewish National Fund, Head Office, Jerusalem, 1922–1980
KKL 5/1772 / 1927
KKL 5/6509 / 1935
KKL 5/7835 /1937
KKL 5/7844 /1937
KKL 5/9317 /1938
DD 710 (1937)
DD 709 (1936)
BK 6970

MACCABI ARCHIVES, RAMAT GAN
Box 147 4–37–27 (1932)
Box 147 4–37–19
Box 146 4–37–12 (1964)

ORAL TESTIMONIES
Kateřina Čapková's interview with Viktor Fischl, "Pak to ale dopadlo ještě jinak," available at *http://www.holocaust.cz/cz2/resources/ros_chodes/2001/03/fischl.*

FILMS
Land of Promise, Palestine, 1935.

TRIAL PROCEEDINGS
"The Trial of Adolf Eichmann," vol. 1, April 11–May 8, 1961, sessions 1–30, available at http://www.nizkor.org/hweb/people/e/eichmann-adolf/transcripts/Sessions/index-01.html.
"The Trial of Adolf Eichmann," vol. 2, May 8–May 24, 1961, sessions 31–51.

PRINTED PRIMARY SOURCES
II. Svetové zimné hry Makabi Banská Bystrica 18.–24. II 1936.

VIII. Zionistentag Brünn 30.–31.7.1928: Rechenschaft über die Vergangenheit – Programm für die Zukunft. Mährish Ostrau: Zionistischer Zentralverband für die čsl. Republik, 1928.

American Jewish Committee. *The Jews in the Eastern War Zone.* New York, 1916.

Ansky, S. *The Enemy at His Pleasure: A Journey through the Jewish Pale of Settlement during World War I.* New York: Henry Holt, 2002.

Beer, Fritz. *". . . a tys na Němce střílel, dědo?"* Praha: Paseka, 2008.

Bergman, Schmuel Hugo. "Staňte se učiteli!" *Židovský Kalendář 1920/1921:* 48–51.

———. *Tagebücher und Briefe.* Vol. 1 (1901–1948). Edited by Miriam Sambursky. Königstein: Jüdischer Verlag bei Althenäum, 1985.

Bloch, Kurt. "Židé a sport," *Židovský kalendář 1933/1934:* 81–84.

Boháč, Antonín. "Hlavní město Praha: Studie statistická I. Část." *Československý statistický věstník* 3 (1922): 353–480.

———."Příští sčítání lidu." *Československý statistický věstník* 1 (1920): 268–275.

———. "První všeobecné sčítání lidu v Československé republice." *Československý statistický věstník* 2 (1921):104–120.

———. *Národní stát a světový mír.* Praha: Melantrich, 1946.

———. "Národnost či jazyk?" *Československý statistický věstník* 2 (1921): 40–58.

———. *Studie o populaci v Českoslovanské republice I: Rok 1927.* Praha: Melantrich, 1928.

Brod, Max. *Streitbares Leben, 1884–1968.* Wien: F. A. Herbig, 1969.

Brüll, Beda. "Československý Makabi." *Židovský kalendář 1937/1938:* 97–107.

Budín, Stanislav. *Jak to vlastně bylo.* Praha: Torst, 2007.

Bureš, Prokop. *Sport a tělesná kultura v R.Č.S.* Praha: Alamanach sportu, 1931.

Čapek, E. "Střední školství národnostních menšin v českých zemích." *Národnostní obzor* 7, no. 3 (1937): 194–202.

Chasanowitsch, Leon, and Leo Motzkin, eds. *Die Judenfrage der Gegenwart: Dokumentsammlung.* Stockholm: Bokförlaget Judäa A.B., 1919.

Czoernig, Karl Freiherr von. *Ethnographie der österreichischen Monarchie.* Wien, 1855–1857.

Die jüdischen Denkmaler in der Tschechoslowakei. Prag: Veröffentlichungen der Denkmalkommission des Obersten Rates der jüdischen Kultusgemeinden in Böhmen, Mähren, und Schlesien, 1933.

Drachmann, Eduard. *K otázkám židovského školství.* Brno: Spolek Židovská škola v Brně, 1936.

Feder, Richard. *Haleluja: hebrejská řeč. Pro školy občanské, městanské, a střední.* Vols. 1–2. Praha: Státní nakladatelství, 1936.

———. *Hebräisches Lehrbuch.* Prag: Staats Verlagsamt., 1923.

———. *Hebrejská učebnice: obrázky kreslil Ludvík Hermann.* Praha: Státní nákladatelství, 1923.

———. *Sinai: Účebnice izraelského náboženství.* Vol. 1. Praha: Státní nakladatelství, 1934.

——. *Židovská tragedie: Dějství poslední.* Kolin, 1947.

——. *Židovské besídky:pro zábavu a poučení dospělejší mládeže židovské.* Vol. 1. Roudnice n. Lab.: Richard Feder, 1912–1913.

——. *Židovské besídky:pro zábavu a poučení mládeže židovské.* Vol. 2. Kolín n. Lab: Richard Feder, 1920.

Fischl, Viktor. *Jews of Czechoslovakia.* Illustrated by Walter Herz. London: National Council of Jews from Czechoslovakia, 1940.

Flusser, Gustav. "Jüdische Kinder im Čechoslovakischen Schulwesen." *Bnai Brith* (1934): 190–195.

Friedmann, František. "Asimilace a sionismus u Židů v ČSR (Z přednášky dra F. Friedmanna dne 10. XI. 1933)." *Národnostní Obzor* 4, no. 2 (1934): 159–160.

——. *Die Juden in der Tschechoslowakei.* Zyklus: Nationalproblem und Judentum. Prag: Jüd. Akad. Tech. Verb. Barissia, Prag, 1936.

——. *Einige Zahlen über die tschechoslowakischen Juden: Ein Beitrag zur Soziologie der Judenheit.* Schriften zur Diskussion des Zionismus 9. Prag: Jüd. Akad. Tech. Verb. Barissia, Prag, 1933.

——. *Mravnost či Oportunita? Několik poznámek k anketě akad. Spolku Kapper v Brně.* Praha: Sionistický výbor pro Čechy a Moravu vPraze, 1927.

——. *Na obranu židovství, Kritické poznámky k brožuře poslance Josefa Hudce.* Praha: Židovské zprávy, 1920.

——. "Pražští Židé." *Židovský kalendář 1929/1930:* 148–207.

——. *Strana Židovská.* Praha: Kulturní odbor ústředního svazu českoslov. studentsva: Cyklus přednášek o ideologii českoslov. politických stran VII, 1931.

——. "Židé v Čechách." In *Židé a židovské obce v Čechách v minulosti a v přítomnosti,* vol. 1, edited by Hugo Gold, 729–735. Brno-Praha: Židovské nakladatelství, 1934.

——. "Židovská národní menšina na Podkarpatské Rusi I." *Národnostní Obzor* 4, no. 3 (1934): 185–192.

——. "Židovská národní menšina na Podkarpatské Rusi II." *Národnostní Obzor* 4, no. 4 (1934): 269–277.

Gold, Hugo, ed. *Die Juden und die Judengemeinde Bratislava in Vergangenheit und Gegenwart.* Brünn: Jüdischer Buchverlag, 1932.

——, ed. *Die Juden und Judengemeinden Böhmens in Vergangenheit und Gegenwart.* Brünn: Jüdischer Buch- und Kunstverlag, 1934.

——, ed. *Die Juden und Judengemeinden Mährens in Vergangenheit und Gegenwart.* Brünn: Jüdischer Buch- und Kunstverlag, 1929.

——. "Slovo úvodem." In *Židé a židovské obce v Čechách v minulosti a v přítomnosti,* vol. 1, edited by Hugo Gold. Brno-Praha: Židovské nakladatelství, 1934.

——, ed. *Židé a židovské obce v Čechách v minulosti a v přítomnosti.* Vol. 1. Brno-Praha: Židovské nakladatelství, 1934.

Goldelman, Solomon. *Löst der Kommunismus der Judenfrage? Rote Assimilation und Sowiet-Zionismus (Gesammelte Aufsätze und Vorträge 1930–1936).* Wien: Heinrich Glanz, 1937.

——. "Rusko-německé analogie (Židovství a komunismus)." *Židovský kalendář 1937–1938:* 32–44.

Goldschmied, Leopold. *Palästina: Ein Tagebuch von Rabbiner L. Goldschmied.* Prag: Verlag Erez Israel, 1933.

Goldstücker, Eduard. *Vzpomínky, 1913–1945.* Vol. 1. Praha: GplusG, 2003.

Haas, Theodor. *Die Juden in Mähren: Darstellung der Rechtsgeschichte und Statistik unter besonderer Berücksichtigung des 19. Jahrhunderts.* Brünn: Jüdischer Buch- und Kunstverlag, 1908.

———. "Statistische Bertrachtungen über die jüdische Bevölkerung Mährens." In *Die Juden und Judengemeinden Mährens in Vergangenheit und Gegenwart,* edited by Hugo Gold, 594–596. Brünn: Jüdischer Buch- und Kunstverlag, 1929.

Heller, Otto. *Der Untergang des Judentums: Die Judenfrage/Ihre Kritik/Ihre Lösung durch den Sozialismus.* Berlin: Verlag für Literatur und Politik, 1931.

Hermann, Hugo. *In Jenen Tagen.* Jerusalem: self-published, 1938.

Herzog, Arthur. "Erinnerungen und Eindrücke von der I. Makkabiah in Tel-Aviv im Jahre 1932." *Zeitschrift für jüdische Geschichte* (1964): 143–145.

Hilf, Alois. "Der Landesverband der israelitischen Kultusgemeinden in Mähren." In *Die Juden und Judengemeinden Mährens, edited by Hugo Gold,* 72–74. Brünn: Jüdischer Buch- und Kunstverlag, 1929.

Hirsch, Isidor, and Gustav Sicher. *Pět knih Mojžišových.* Vols. 1–4. Praha: Svaz pražských náboženských obcí židovských, 1932–1939.

Krejčí, Dobroslav. "Má se při našem přístím sčítání lidu zjištovati národnost nebo řeč mateřská?" *Československý statistický věstník* 1 (1920): 275–285.

Makabi Handbuch. Praha: Tschechoslowakischen Makabikreis im Makkabi Weltverband, 1931.

Müller, Václav. "Náboženské společnosti." In *Slovník veřejného práva československého,* vol. 2, 697–711. Praha, 1938.

———."Náboženství a národnost v naší republice." *Národnostní obzor* 5, no. 4 (1934): 241–247.

Očenáška, A., P. Bureš, and V. Rýpar, eds. *Tělesná výchova v Československu.* Praha: Ministerstvo veřejného zdravotnictví a tělesné výchovy, 1933.

Olbracht, Ivan. *Golet v údolí.* Praha: Melantrich, 1937.

———. *Hory a staletí.* Praha: Melatrich, 1935.

———. *The Sorrowful Eyes of Hana Karajich.* Translated by Iris Urwin Lewitová. New York: Central European University Press, 1999.

O židovských památkách v Československé republice. Praha: Památková komise Nejvýšší rady Svazu židovských obcí náboženských v Čechách, na Moravě a Slezku, 1933.

Paleček, Václav. "Izraelská náboženská společnost." In *Slovník veřejného práva československého,* vol. 2, edited by Emil Hácha et al., 28–52. Brno: Polygrafia 1932.

Programm der Jüdischen Fürsorgezentrale für die Tschechoslowakei. Prag, 1921.

Rádl, Emanuel. *Národnost jako vědecký problém.* Praha: Orbis, 1929.

———. *Válka Čechů s Němci.* Praha, 1928.

Reiman, Pavel. *V dvacátých letech: vzpomínky.* Praha: Nakladatelství politické literatury, 1966.

Rindler, Hugo. "Organisace náboženské společnosti židovské a její další vybudování." *Bnai Brith* 2 (1934): 58–62.

Rychnovsky, Ernst, ed. *Masaryk und das Judentum/Masaryk a židovství.* Prag: Mars, 1931.

——, ed. *Thomas G. Masaryk and the Jews: A Collection of Essays.* New York: B. Pollak, 1941.

Slávnostný spis 3. slet Čs. Makabi v Žilině 4.-6.VII 1937.

Statut der israelitischen Kultusgemeinde Mährisch Ostrau. Mährisch Ostrau: Verlag des Jüdischen Volksblattes, 1920.

Stránský, Rudolf. "Účast naší státní péče na ochraně menšin v oboru školském." *Národnostní obzor* 2, no. 3 (1932): 161–167.

Svoboda, Emil. "Čtvrt století Perkova zákona," *Národnostní obzor* 2, no. 2 (1931): 88–98.

Tělesná výchova v Československu. Praha: Ministerstvo veřejneho zdravotnictví a tělesné výchovy, 1930.

Weil, Jiří. *Moskva-hranice.* Praha, 1937.

Weltsch, Felix. *Palästina: Land der Gegensätze – Eindrücke einer Palästinareise.* Prag: Selbstwehr Verlag, 1929.

Zionistische Organisation Brünn Berichtet. Brünn: Verlag der Zionistischen Organisation in Brünn 1932.

NEWSPAPERS, PERIODICALS, BULLETINS

Newspapers

Čas
České slovo
Českožidovské listy
Der Jüdische Sozialist
Jüdische Volksstimme
Jüdische Volkszeitung
Lidové noviny
Lidový deník Večer
Mír
Národní listy
Národní politika
Prager Presse
Prager Tagblatt
Rozvoj
Rudé právo
Selbstwehr
Tribuna
Venkov
Znaimer Tagblatt
Zsidó Néplap
Židovské zprávy

Periodicals and Yearbooks

Bnai Brith
Bundesblätter
Der Makkabi: Organ der deutscher Makkabi Kreises
Doar Meamlenu
Erez Israel: Orgán židovského národního fondu/Organ des Jüdischen Nationalfonds
Jahresbericht des Jüdisches Vereins-Reformrealgymnasium in Brünn/Výroční zpráva spolková židovské reformní reálné gymnasium v Brně.
Makkabi sport: zprávy spolku pro tělocvik a sport
Národnostní obzor
Ročenka Společnosti pro dějiny židů v ČSR/Jahrbuch der Gesellschaft für Geschichte der Juden in der Čechoslovakischen Republik
Věstník židovské náboženské obce v Praze
Zeitschrift für Demographie und Statistik der Juden
Zeitschift für die Geschichte der Juden in der Tschechoslowakei
Židovský kalendář

Židovský sport – Hamakkabi (also *Hagibor Židovský sport – Hamakkabi*)

SECONDARY SOURCES

Abramson, Henry. "Russian Civil War." In *The YIVO Encyclopaedia of Jews in Eastern Europe,* 1620–1622. New Haven: Yale University Press, 2008.

Albrecht, Catherine. "The Rhetoric of Economic Nationalism in the Bohemian Boycott Campaigns of the Late Habsburg Monarchy." *Austrian History Yearbook* 32 (2001): 47–67.

Amir, Balu. "Requiem to a Movement." In *Rhapsody to Tchelet Lavan in Czechoslovakia,* 185–202. Israel: Association for the History of Tchelet Lavan-El Al in Czechoslovakia, 1996.

Anderson, Benedict. *Imagined Communities: Reflections on the Origins and Spread of Nationalism.* 2nd ed. London: Verso, 2006.

Arel, Dominique. "Language Categories in Censuses: Backward- or Forward-Looking?" In *Census and Identity: The Politics of Race, Ethnicity, and Language in National Censuses,* edited by David I. Kertzer and Dominique Arel, 92–120. Cambridge: Cambridge University Press, 2002.

Aschheim, Steven E. "Reflections on Insiders and Outsiders: A General Introduction." In *Insiders and Outsiders: Dilemmas of East European Jewry,* edited by Richard I. Cohen, Jonathan Frankel, and Stefani Hoffman, 1–14. Portland, Ore.: Littman Library of Jewish Civilization, 2010.

Avineri, Shlomo. *The Making of Modern Zionism: The Intellectual Origins of the Jewish State.* New York: Basic Books, 1981.

Bachrach, Susan D. *The Nazi Olympics: Berlin 1936.* Boston: Little, Brown and United States Holocaust Memorial Museum, 2000.

Bahm, Karl F. "Beyond the Bourgeoisie: Rethinking Nation, Culture, and Modernity in Nineteenth-Century Central Europe." *Austrian History Yearbook* 29 (1998): 19–35.

Bakke, Elisabeth. *Doomed to Failure: The Czechoslovak Nation Project and Slovak Autonomist Reaction, 1918–38.* Oslo: Oslo University, 1999.

———. "The Making of Czechoslovakism in the First Czechoslovak Republic." In *Loyalitäten in der Tschechoslowakischen Republik, 1918–1938: Politische, nationale, und kulturelle Zugehörigkeiten,* edited by Martin Schulze Wessel, 23–44. München: Oldenbourg Verlag, 2004.

Barkey, Karen, and Mark Von Hagen, eds. *After Empire: Multiethnic Societies and Nation-Building: The Soviet Union and the Russian, Ottoman, and Habsburg Empires.* Boulder, Colo.: Westview Press, 1997.

Bartáková, Daniela. "Comparative Study of Tchelet Lavan and Hashomer Hatzair in Czechoslovakia (1918–1938)." MA thesis, Central European University, Budapest, 2011.

Bauer, Yehuda. *My Brother's Keeper: A History of the American Jewish Joint Distribution Committee, 1929–1939.* Philadelphia: Jewish Publication Society of America, 1974.

Becher, Peter, and Jozo Džambo, eds. *Gleiche Bilder, gleiche Worte: Deutsche, Österreicher und Tschechen in der Karikatur (1848–1948)/Stejné obrazy, stejná slova. Němci, Rakušané a Češi v karikatuře (1848–1948)*. München: Adalbert-Stifter-Verein, 1997.

Bein, Alex. *The Return to the Soil: A History of Jewish Settlement in Israel*. Jerusalem: Youth and Hechalutz Department of the Zionist Organization, 1952.

Beneš, Václav L. "Czechoslovak Democracy and Its Problems, 1918–1920." In *A History of the Czechoslovak Republic, 1918–1948*, edited by Victor S. Mamatey and Radomír Luža, 39–98. Princeton, N.J.: Princeton University Press, 1973.

Berend, Ivan T. *Decades of Crisis: Central and Eastern Europe before World War II*. Berkeley: University of California Press, 1998.

Berger, Natalie, ed. *Where Cultures Meet: The Story of the Jews of Czechoslovakia*. Tel Aviv: Beth Hatefutsoth, 1990.

Berkowitz, Michael. *Western Jewry and the Zionist Project, 1914–1933*. New York: Cambridge University Press, 1997.

Birnbaum, Max P. *Staat und Synagoge 1918–1938: eine Geschichte des Preussischen Landesverbandes jüdischen Gemeinden (1918–1938)*. Tübingen: J.C.B. Mohr, Paul Siebeck, 1981.

Boehm, Philip. "Tchelet Lavan: A School for Practical Zionism (a Personal Story)." In *Rhapsody to Tchelet Lavan in Czechoslovakia*, 22–31. Israel: Association for the History of Tchelet Lavan-El Al in Czechoslovakia, 1996.

Bolton, Jonathan. "Olbracht, Ivan." In *The YIVO Encyclopedia of Jews in Eastern Europe*, 1282. New Haven: Yale University Press, 2008.

Bondy, Ruth. *Jakob Edelstein*. Praha: Sefer, 2001.

Borut, Jacob. "Jews in German Sports during the Weimar Republic." In *Emancipation through Muscles: Jews and Sports in Europe*, edited by Michael Brenner and Gideon Reuveni, 77–92. Lincoln: University of Nebraska Press, 2006.

———. "'Verjudung des Judentums': Was There a Zionist Subculture in Weimar Germany?" In *In Search of Jewish Community: Jewish Identities in Germany and Austria, 1918–1933*, edited by Michael Brenner and Derek J. Penslar, 92–114. Bloomington: Indiana University Press, 1998.

Bowersox, Jeffrey. *Raising Germans in the Age of Empire: Youth and Colonial Culture, 1871–1914*. New York: Oxford University Press, 2013.

Bowman, William D. "Hakoah Vienna and the International Nature of Interwar Austrian Sports." *Central European History* 44, no. 4 (2011): 642–668.

Boyarin, Daniel. *Unheroic Conduct: The Rise of Heterosexuality and the Invention of the Jewish Man*. Berkeley: University of California Press, 1997.

Braham, Randolph L. *The Politics of Genocide: The Holocaust in Hungary*. Vol. 2. New York: Columbia University Press, 1981.

Brenner, Michael. "The Jüdische Volkspartei: National-Jewish Communal Politics in Weimar Germany." *Leo Baeck Institute Yearbook* 35 (1990): 219–243.

———. *The Renaissance of Jewish Culture in Weimar Germany*. New Haven, Conn.: Yale University Press, 1996.

Brenner, Michael, and Derek J. Penslar, eds. *In Search of Jewish Community: Jewish Identities in Germany and Austria, 1918–1933.* Bloomington: Indiana University Press, 1998.

Brenner, Michael, and Gideon Reuveni, eds. *Emancipation through Muscles: Jews and Sports in Europe.* Lincoln: University of Nebraska Press, 2006.

Brod, Petr, Kateřina Čapková, and Michal Frankl. "Czechoslovakia." In *The YIVO Encyclopedia of Jews in Eastern Europe,* 375–381. New Haven: Yale University Press, 2008.

Brubaker, Rogers. *Ethnicity without Groups.* Cambridge, Mass.: Harvard University Press, 2004.

——. "Nationalizing States in the Old 'New Europe' – and the New." *Ethnic and Racial Studies* 19, no. 2 (April 1996): 411–437.

Bryant, Chad. *Prague in Black: Nazi Rule and Czech Nationalism.* Cambridge, Mass.: Harvard University Press, 2007.

Bubeník, Jaroslav, and Jiří Křesťan. "Zjišťování národnosti a židovská otázka." In *Postavení a osudy židovského obyvatelstva v Čechách a na Moravě v letech 1939–1945 Sborník studií,* edited by Helena Krejčová and Jana Svobodová, 11–39. Praha: Ústav pro soudobé dějiny AV ČR & Maxdorf, 1998.

——. "Zjištování národnosti jako problém statistický a politický: zkušenosti ze sčítání lidu za první republiky." *Paginae Historiae* 3 (1995): 119–139.

Büchler, Yehoshua R. "Reconstruction Efforts in Hostile Surroundings – Slovaks and Jews after WWII." In *The Jews Are Coming Back: The Return of the Jews to Their Countries of Origin after WWII,* edited by David Bankier, 257–276. Jeruslaem: Yav Vashem, 2005.

Bučka, Peter. "Futbal pod Dávidovou hviezdou." *História* 1–2 (2011): 44–46.

Bugge, Peter. "Czech Democracy, 1918–1938: Paragon or Parody?" *Bohemia* 47 (2007): 3–28.

——. "The Making of a Slovak City: The Czechoslovak Renaming of Pressburg/Pozsony/Prešporok, 1918–19." *Austrian History Yearbook* 35 (2004): 205–227.

Burger, Hannelore. *Sprachenrecht und Sprachgerechtigkeit im Österreichischen Unterrichtswesen, 1867–1918.* Wien: Der österreichischen Akademie der Wissenschaften, 1995.

Bušek, Michal, ed. *"Naděje je na další stránce": 100 let knihovny Židovského muzea v Praze.* Praha: Židovské muzeum v Praze, 2007.

Bykovsky, Lev. *Solomon Goldelman: A Portrait of a Politician and Educator, 1885–1974; A Chapter in Ukrainian-Jewish Relations.* New York: Ukrainian Historical Association, 1980.

Čapková, Kateřina. *Češi, Němci, Židé? Národní identita Židů v Čechách, 1918–1938.* Praha: Paseka, 2005.

——. *Czechs, Germans, Jews? National Identity and the Jews of Bohemia.* New York: Berghahn Books, 2012.

——. "Czechs, Germans, Jews – Where Is the Difference? The Complexities of National Identities of Bohemian Jews, 1918–1938." *Bohemia* 46 (2005): 7–14.

——. "Feder, Richard." In *The YIVO Encyclopedia of Jews in Eastern Europe,* 503–504. New Haven, Conn.: Yale University Press, 2008.

——. "Piłsudski or Masaryk? Zionist Revisionism in Czechoslovakia 1925–1940." *Judaica Bohemiae* 35 (1999): 210–239.

——. "Specific Features of Zionism in the Czech Lands in the Interwar Period." *Judaica Bohemiae* 38 (2002): 106–159.

——. "Uznání židovské národnosti v Československu 1918–1938." *Český časopis historický* 102, no. 1 (2004): 77–103.

Čapková, Kateřina, and Michal Frankl. *Nejisté útočiště: Československo a uprchlíci před nacismem 1933–1938*. Praha: Paseka, 2008.

Caplan, Gregory A. "Germanizing the Jewish Male: Military Masculinity as the Last Stage of Acculturation." In *Towards Normality? Acculturation and Modern German Jewry*, ed. Rainer Liedtke and David Rechter, 159–184. Tübingen: Mohr Siebeck, 2003.

Capoccia, Giovanni. "Legislative Responses against Extremism: The "Protection of Democracy" in the First Czechoslovak Republic (1920–1938)." *East European Politics and Societies* 16, no. 3 (2002): 691–738.

Cerman, Ivo. "Familiant Laws." In The *YIVO Encyclopedia of Jews in Eastern Europe*, 493–494. New Haven, Conn.: Yale University Press, 2008.

Cichopek-Gajraj, Anna. "Limits to 'Jewish Power': How Slovak Jewish Leaders Negotiated Restitution of Property after the Second World War." *East European Jewish Affairs* 44, no. 1 (2014): 51–69.

Cohen, Gary B. "Cultural Crossing in Prague, 1900: Scenes from Late Imperial Austria." *Austrian History Yearbook* 45 (2014): 1–30.

——. *The Politics of Ethnic Survival: Germans in Prague, 1861–1914*. Princeton, N.J.: Princeton University Press, 1981.

Cohen, Richard I. *Jewish Icons: Art and Society in Modern Europe*. Berkeley: University of California Press, 1998.

——. "Urban Visibility and Biblical Visions: Jewish Culture in Western and Central Europe in the Modern Age." In *Cultures of the Jews*, vol. 3, ed. David Biale, 9–74. New York: Schocken Books, 2002.

Cohen, Richard I., Jonathan Frankel, and Stefani Hoffman, eds. *Insiders and Outsiders: Dilemmas of East European Jewry*. Portland, Ore.: Littmann Library of Jewish Civilization, 2010.

Cornwall, Mark. *The Devil's Wall: The Youth Mission of Heinz Rutha*. Cambridge, Mass.: Harvard University Press, 2012.

——. "The Struggle on the Czech-German Language Border, 1880–1940." *The English Historical Review* 109, no. 433 (1994): 914–951.

Cornwall, Mark, and R. J. W. Evans, eds. *Czechoslovakia in a Nationalist and Fascist Europe, 1918–1948*. New York: Oxford University Press, 2007.

Crhová, Marie. "Modern Jewish Politics in Central Europe: The Jewish Party of Interwar Czechoslovakia, 1918–1938." PhD diss., Central European University, 2007.

Dagan, Avigdor, ed. *The Jews of Czechoslovakia: Historical Studies and Surveys*. Vol. 3. Philadelphia: Jewish Publication Society of America, 1984.

———. "The Press." In *The Jews of Czechoslovakia: Historical Studies and Surveys*, vol. 1, 523–532. Philadelphia: Jewish Publication Society of America, 1968.

Diner, Dan, and Jonathan Frankel, eds. *Dark Times, Dire Decisions: Jews and Communism*. Studies in Contemporary Jewry 20. New York: Oxford University Press, 2005.

———. "Jews and Communism: The Utopian Temptation." In *Dark Times, Dire Decisions: Jews and Communism*, edited by Dan Diner and Jonathan Frankel, 3–12. Studies in Contemporary Jewry 20. New York: Oxford University Press, 2005.

Dejmková, Ivana. "Hagibor aneb jak jedno místo v Praze získalo smutnou pověst." In *Evropská velkoměsta za druhé světové války: každodennost okupovaného velkoměsta, Praha 1939–1945 v evropském srovnání*, vol. 26, 253–261. Praha: Archiv hlavního města Prahy, 2007.

Dekel-Chen, Jonathan L. *Farming the Red Land: Jewish Agricultural Colonization and Local Soviet Power, 1924–1941*. New Haven, Conn.: Yale University Press, 2005.

Dimond, Mark. "The Sokol and Czech Nationalism, 1918–1948." In *Czechoslovakia in Nationalist and Fascist Europe, 1918–1948*, edited by Mark Cornwall and R. J. W. Evans, 185–205. New York: Oxford University Press, 2007.

Doron, Joachim. "'Der Geist ist es, der sich den Körper schafft!' Soziale Probleme in der jüdischen Turnbewegung (1896–1914)." *Tel Aviver Jahrbuch für deutsche Geschichte* 20 (1991): 237–258.

Du-Nour, Miryam. "Ideology, Education, and Realization – Zionist Youth Movements in the CSR." In *Berlin-Vienna-Prague: Modernity, Minorities, Migration in the Inter-War Period*, edited by Susanne Martin-Finnis and Matthias Uecker, 127–141. New York: Peter Lang, 2001.

Dyck, Noel. "Games, Bodies, Celebrations and Boundaries: Anthropological Perspectives on Sport." In *Games, Sports and Cultures*, edited by Noel Dyck, 13–42. New York: Berg 2000.

Efron, John M. *Defenders of the Race: Jewish Doctors and Race Science in Fin-de-Siècle Europe*. New Haven, Conn.: Yale University Press, 1994.

Eisen, George. "The Maccabiah Games: A History of the Jewish Olympics." PhD diss., University of Maryland, 1979.

Eisenstein, Miriam. *Jewish Schools in Poland, 1919–1939: Their Philosophy and Development*. New York: King's Crown Press, 1950.

Engel, David. "World War I." In *The YIVO Encyclopedia of Jews in Eastern Europe*, 2032–2037. New Haven, Conn.: Yale University Press, 2008.

———. *Zionism*. New York: Pearson, 2009.

Epstein, Helen. *A Jewish Athlete: Swimming against Stereotype in 20th Century Europe*. New York: Plunkett Lake Press, 2011.

Erez (Rezniczenko), Yehuda. "Hechalutz in Czechoslovakia." In *Rhapsody to Tchelet Lavan in Czechoslovakia*, 64–71. Israel: Association for the History of Tchelet Lavan-El Al in Czechoslovakia, 1996.

Feigl, Friedrich: Paintings, Drawings, and Graphic Art. Prague: Jewish Museum in Prague, 2007.

Figes, Orlando. *A People's Tragedy: A History of the Russian Revolution 1891–1924.* New York: Penguin, 1998.

Fink, Carole. *Defending the Rights of Others: The Great Powers, the Jews, and International Minority Protection, 1877–1938.* New York: Cambridge University Press, 2006.

Fishman, David E. *The Rise of Modern Yiddish Culture.* Pittsburgh: University of Pittsburgh Press, 2005.

Fleischmann, Gustav. "The Religious Congregation, 1918–1938." In *Jews of Czechoslovakia: Historical Studies and Surveys,* vol. 1, edited by Avigdor Dagan, 267–329. Philadelphia: Jewish Publication Society of America, 1968.

Frankel, Jonathan. "The Paradoxical Politics of Marginality: Thoughts on the Jewish Situation during the Years 1914–1921." In *The Jews and the European Crises, 1914–1921,* edited by Jonathan Frankel, Peter Y. Medding, and Ezra Mendelsohn, 3–22. Studies in Contemporary Jewry 4. New York: Oxford University Press, 1988.

Frankl, Michal. *"Emancipace od židů": český antisemitismus na konci 19. století.* Praha: Paseka, 2007.

Friedler, Erik. *Makkabi Chai, Makkabi Lebt! Die Jüdische Sportbewegung in Deutschland, 1898–1988.* Wien: Brandstätter, 1998.

Gaisbauer, Adolf. *Davidstern und Doppeladler: Zionismus und jüdischer Nationalismus in Österreich, 1882–1918.* Wien: Böhlau Verlag, 1988.

Gajan, Koloman. "T.G. Masaryk, idea sionismu a Nahum Sokolow." *Židovská ročenka 5763/2002–2003:* 71–85.

Gartner, Lloyd P. *History of Jews in Modern Times.* New York: Oxford University Press, 2001.

Gechtman, Roni. "Socialist Mass Politics through Sport: The Bund's *Morgnshtern* in Poland, 1926–1939." *Journal of Sport History* 26, no. 2 (1999): 326–352.

Gerrits, André. "Antisemitism and Anti-Communism: The Myth of 'Judeo-Communism' in Eastern Europe." *East European Jewish Affairs* 25, no. 1 (1995): 49–72.

Gillerman, Sharon. "The Crisis of the Jewish Family in Weimar Germany: Social Conditions and Cultural Representations." In *In Search of Jewish Community: Jewish Identities in Germany and Austria, 1918–1933,* edited by Michael Brenner and Derek J. Penslar, 176–199. Bloomington: Indiana University Press, 1998.

Gilman, Sander. *Jewish Self-hatred: The Hidden Language of Jews.* Baltimore: Johns Hopkins University Press, 1986.

———. *The Jew's Body.* New York: Routledge, 1991.

Gitelman, Zvi, ed. *The Emergence of Modern Jewish Politics: Bundism and Zionism in Eastern Europe.* Pittsburgh: University of Pittsburgh Press, 2003.

———. *Jewish Nationality and Soviet Politics: The Jewish Sections of the CPSU, 1917–1930.* Princeton, N.J.: Princeton University Press, 1972.

Giustino, Cathleen M. *Tearing Down Prague's Jewish Town: Ghetto Clearance and the Legacy of Middle-Class Ethnic Politics around 1900.* New York: Eastern European Monographs, 2003.

Glassheim, Eagle. *Noble Nationalists: The Transformation of the Bohemian Aristocracy.* Cambridge, Mass.: Harvard University Press, 2005.

Gold, Hugo. *Gedenkbuch der untergegangenen Judengemeinden Mährens.* Tel Aviv: Olamenu, 1974.

Goldelman, Solomon I. *Jewish National Autonomy in Ukraine, 1917–1920.* Chicago: Ukrainian Research and Information Institute, 1968.

Gurrock, Jeffrey S. *Judaism's Encounter with American Sports.* Bloomington: Indiana University Press, 2005.

Hadler, Frank. "'Erträglicher Antisemitismus'? Jüdische Fragen und tschechoslowakische Antworten 1918/19." *Jahrbuch des Simon-Dubnows-Instituts* 1 (2002): 169–200.

Hart, Mitchell B. *Social Science and the Politics of Modern Jewish Identity.* Stanford, Calif.: Stanford University Press, 2000.

Hartewig, Karen. "A German Jewish Communist of the Second Generation: The Changing Personae of Klaus Gysi." In *Dark Times, Dire Decisions: Jews and Communism,* edited by Dan Diner and Jonathan Frankel, 255–271. Studies in Contemporary Jewry 20. New York: Oxford University Press, 2005.

Hecht, Louise. "Teaching Haskalah – Haskalah and Teaching: Jewish Education in the Czech Lands (a Power Play)." *Jewish Culture and History* 13, nos. 2–3 (August–November 2012): 93–107.

Heimann, Mary. *Czechoslovakia: The State That Failed.* New Haven, Conn.: Yale University Press, 2009.

Heller, Celia. *On the Edge of Destruction: Jews of Poland between the World Wars.* Detroit: Wayne State University Press, 1993.

Heřman, Jan. "Jewish Community Archives from Bohemia and Moravia: Analytical Registers to the Catalogues of Archive Materials from Jewish Communities with the Exception of That of Prague." *Judaica Bohemia* 7, no. 1 (1971).

Heumos, Peter. "Konfliktregelung und Soziale Integration: Zur Struktur der Ersten Tschechoslowakishen Republik." *Bohemia* 30 (1989): 52–70.

Hirsch, Francine. *Empire of Nations: Ethnographic Knowledge and the Making of the Soviet Union.* Ithaca, N.Y.: Cornell University Press, 2005.

Hobsbawm, Eric. *Nations and Nationalism since 1780.* New York: Cambridge University Press, 1990.

Hoensch, Jörg K., and Dušan Kováč, eds. *Das Scheitern der Verständigung: Tschechen, Deutsche, und Slovaken in der Ersten Republik.* Essen: Klartext, 1994.

Hoffmann-Halter, Beatrix. *"Abreisendmachung": Jüdische Kriegsflüchtlinge in Wien, 1914–1923.* Wien: Böhlau Verlag, 1995.

Holub, Miroslav. "Introduction." In *The Sorrowful Eyes of Hana Karajich,* by Ivan Olbracht, vii–xxii. New York: Central European University Press, 1999.

Iggers, Wilma, ed. *The Jews of Bohemia and Moravia: A Historical Reader.* Detroit: Wayne State University Press, 1986.

Jacobs, Jack. "Jewish Workers' Sports Movements in Interwar Poland: *Shtern* and *Morgnshtern* in Comparative Perspective." In *Jews, Sports, and the Rites of Citizenship*, edited by Jack Kugelmass, 114–128. Urbana: University of Illinois Press, 2007.

——. "The Politics of Jewish Sports Movements in Interwar Poland." In *Emancipation through Muscles: Jews and Sports in Europe*, edited by Michael Brenner and Gideon Reuveni, 93–105. Lincoln: University of Nebraska Press, 2006.

Jelínek, Ješajahu A. *Dávidova hviezda pod Tatrami: Židia na Slovensku v 20. storočí.* Praha: Vydavatelstvo Jána Mlynárika, 2009.

Jelinek, Yeshayahu A. *The Carpathian Diaspora: The Jews of Subcarpathian Rus and Mukachevo, 1848–1948.* New York: East European Monographs, 2007.

——. "Czechoslovak Jews in Israel." In *New Encyclopaedia of Zionism and Israel*, vol. 2, edited by Geoffrey Wigoder. Toronto: Associated University Presses, 1994.

Jewish Publication Society of America. *The Jews of Czechoslovakia: Historical Studies and Surveys.* Vol. 1. Philadelphia: Jewish Publication Society of America, 1968.

Jewish Publication Society of America. *The Jews of Czechoslovakia: Historical Studies and Surveys.* Vol. 2. Philadelphia: Jewish Publication Society of America, 1971.

Johnson, Sam. "'Communism in Russia Only Exists on Paper': Czechoslovakia and the Russian Refugee Crisis, 1919–1924." *Contemporary European History* 16, no. 3 (2007): 371–394.

Judson, Pieter M. *Guardians of the Nation: Activists on the Language Frontiers of Imperial Austria.* Cambridge, Mass.: Harvard University Press, 2006.

Judson, Pieter M., and Marsha L. Rozenblit, eds. *Constructing Nationalities in East Central Europe.* New York: Berghan Books, 2005.

Kalvoda, Josef. "Masaryk in America in 1918." *Jahrbücher für Geschichte Osteuropas* 27, no. 1 (1979): 85–99.

Kaplan, Eran. *The Jewish Radical Right: Revisionist Zionism and Its Ideological Legacy.* Madison: University of Wisconsin Press, 2005.

Kaplan, Marion. *The Making of the Jewish Middle Class: Women, Family, and Identity in Imperial Germany.* New York: Oxford University Press, 1991.

Karady, Victor. "Religious Divisions, Socio-Economic Stratification and the Modernization of Hungarian Jewry after the Emancipation." In *Jews in the Hungarian Economy, 1760–1945*, edited by Michael K. Silber, 161–184. Jerusalem: Magnes Press, 1992.

Karpe, Richard. "The Beginnings of the Blau-Weiss in Bohemia and Its Development during the First World War." In *Rhapsody to Tchelet Lavan in Czechoslovakia*, 16–20. Israel: Association for the History of Tchelet Lavan-El Al in Czechoslovakia, 1996.

Kassow, Samuel D. "The Left Poalei Tsiyon in Interwar Poland." In *The Emergence of Modern Jewish Politics: Bundism and Zionism in Eastern Europe*, edited by Zvi Gitelman, 71–84. Pittsburgh: University of Pittsburgh Press, 2003.

Katz, Jacob. *A House Divided: Orthodoxy and Schism in Nineteenth-Century Central European Jewry.*

Waltham, Mass.: Brandeis University Press, 1998.

——. *Out of the Ghetto: The Social Background of Jewish Emancipation, 1770–1870.* Cambridge, Mass.: Harvard University Press, 1973.

Kaufman, Haim. "Jewish Sports in the Diaspora, Yishuv, and Israel: Between Politics and Nationalism." *Israel Studies* 10, no. 2 (2005): 147–167.

Kelly, T. Mills. "Last Best Chance or Last Gasp? The Compromise of 1905 and Czech Politics in Moravia." *Austrian History Yearbook* 34 (2003): 279–301.

Kertzer, David I., and Dominique Arel, "Censuses, Identity Formation, and the Struggle for Political Power." In *Census and Identity: The Politics of Race, Ethnicity, and Language in National Censuses,* edited by David I. Kertzer and Dominique Arel, 1–42. Cambridge: Cambridge University Press, 2002.

Kestenberg-Gladstein, Ruth. "The Jews between Czechs and Germans in the Historic Lands, 1848–1918." In *Jews of Czechoslovakia: Historical Studies and Surveys,* vol. 1, edited by Avigdor Dagan. Philadelphia: Jewish Publication Society of America, 1968.

Kieval, Hillel J. "Bohemia and Moravia." In *The YIVO Encyclopedia of Jews in Eastern Europe,* 202–211. New Haven, Conn.: Yale University Press, 2008.

——. "Imperial Embraces and Ethnic Challenges: The Politics of Jewish Identity in the Bohemian Lands." *Shofar* 30, no. 4 (2012): 1–17.

——. "The Lands Between: The Jews of Bohemia, Moravia, and Slovakia." In *Where Cultures Meet: The Story of the Jews of Czechoslovakia,* edited by Natalia Berger, 23–52. Tel Aviv: Beth Hatefutsoth, 1990.

——. *Languages of Community: The Jewish Experience in the Czech Lands.* Berkeley: University of California Press, 2000.

——. *The Making of Czech Jewry: National Conflict and Jewish Society in Bohemia, 1870–1918.* New York: Oxford University Press, 1988.

——. "Negotiating Czechoslovakia: The Challenges of Jewish Citizenship in a Multiethnic Nation-State." In *Insiders and Outsiders: Dilemmas of East European Jewry,* edited by Richard I. Cohen, Jonathan Frankel, and Stefani Hoffman, 103–119. Portland, Ore.: Littman Library of Jewish Civilization, 2010.

——. "The Unforeseen Consequences of Cultural Resistance: Haskalah and State-Mandated Reform in the Bohemian Lands." *Jewish Culture and History* 13, nos. 2–3 (August–November 2012): 108–123.

King, Jeremy. *Budweisers into Czechs and Germans: A Local History of Bohemian Politics, 1848–1948.* Princeton, N.J.: Princeton University Press, 2002.

——. "The Municipal and the National in the Bohemian Lands, 1848–1914." *Austrian History Yearbook* 42 (Spring 2011): 89–109.

——. "The Nationalization of East Central Europe: Ethnicism, Ethnicity, and Beyond." In *Staging the Past: The Politics of Commemoration in Habsburg Central Europe, 1848 to the Present,* edited by Maria Bucur and Nancy M. Wingfield, 112–152. West

Lafayette, Ind.: Purdue University Press, 2001.

———. "Who Is Who? Group Rights in Liberal Austria and the Dilemma of Classificatory Procedure." Unpublished manuscript.

Klein-Pejšová, Rebekah. "'Abandon Your Role as Exponents of the Magyars': Contested Jewish Loyalty in Interwar (Czecho)Slovakia." *AJS Review* 33, no. 2 (November 2009): 341–362.

———. "Beyond the 'Infamous Concentration Camps of the Old Monarchy': Jewish Refugee Policy from Wartime Austria-Hungary to Interwar Czechoslovakia." *Austrian History Yearbook* 45 (2014): 150–166.

———. "Building Slovak Jewry: Communal Reorientation in Interwar Czechoslovakia." *Shofar* 30, no. 4 (2012): 18–40.

———. *Mapping Jewish Loyalties in Interwar Slovakia.* Bloomington: Indiana University Press, 2015.

Kobrin, Rebecca. "Rewriting the Diaspora: Images of Eastern Europe in the Bialystok Landsmanshaft Press, 1921–1945." *Jewish Social Studies* 12, no. 3 (2006): 1–38.

Koeltzsch, Inis. *Geteilte Kulturen: Eine Geschichte der tschechisch-jüdisch-deutschen Beziehungen in Prag, 1918–1938.* München: Oldenbourg Verlag, 2012.

Kornberg, Jacques. "Theodore Herzl: A Reevaluation," *Journal of Modern History* 52, no. 2 (June 1980): 226–252.

Kowalská, Eva. "The Results of School Reforms in Upper Hungary: Jewish Schools under State Control." *Jewish Culture and History* 13, nos. 2–3 (August–November, 2012): 124–133.

Kučera, Jaroslav. *Minderheit im Nationalstaat: Die Sprachenfrage in den tschechisch-deutschen Beziehungen, 1918–1938.* München: Oldenbourg Verlag, 1999.

———. "Politický či přirozený národ? K pojetí národa v Československém právním řádu meziválečného období." *Český časopis historický* 99, no. 3 (2001): 548–568.

Kugelmass, Jack, ed. *Jews, Sports, and the Rites of Citizenship.* Urbana: University of Illinois Press, 2007.

———. "Why Sports?" In *Jews, Sports, and the Rites of Citizenship,* edited by Jack Kugelmass, 3–30. Urbana: University of Illinois Press, 2007.

Lacquer, Walter. *A History of Zionism.* New York: Schocken Books, 1989.

Langer, František. *Byli a bylo.* Praha: Československý spisovatel, 1963.

———. "My Brother Jiří." In *Nine Gates to the Chasidic Mysteries,* by Jiří Langer, ix–xxxiv. Northvale, N.J.: Jason Aronson, 1961.

Láníček, Jan. *Czechs, Slovaks, and the Jews: Beyond Idealisation and Condemnation, 1938–1948.* London: Palgrave, 2013.

Lavsky, Hagit. *Before Catastrophe: The Distinctive Path of German Zionism.* Detroit: Wayne State University Press, 1996.

Levene, Mark. *War, Jews, and the New Europe: The Diplomacy of Lucien Wolf, 1914–1919.* Oxford: Littman Library of Jewish Civilization, 1992.

Lichtenstein, Tatjana. "'Heja, Heja, Hagibor!' Jewish Sports, Politics, and Nationalism in Czechoslovakia, 1923–1930." *Leipziger Beiträge zur jüdischen Geschichte und Kultur* 2 (2004): 191–208.

Lipscher, Ladislav. "Die Lage der Juden in der Tschechoslowakei nach deren Gründung 1918 bis zu den Parlamentswahlen 1920." *East Central Europe* 16, no. 1–2 (1989): 1–38.

———. "Die Pariser Friedensverhandlungen und der Minderheitenschutz für die Juden in der Tschechoslowakei." In *Das Jahr 1919 in der Tschechoslowakei und in Ostmitteleuropa*, edited by Hans Lemberg and Peter Heumos, 167–176. München: Oldenbourg Verlag, 1993.

———. "Die soziale und politische Stellung der Juden in der ersten Republik." In *Die Juden in den böhmischen Ländern*, edited by Ferdinand Seibt, 269–280. München: Oldenbourg Verlag, 1983.

Livezeanu, Irina. *Cultural Politics in Greater Romania: Regionalism, Nation Building, and Ethnic Struggle, 1918–1930*. Ithaca, N.Y.: Cornell University Press, 1995.

Lohr, Eric. "The Russian Army and the Jews: Mass Deportation, Hostages and Violence during World War I." *The Russian Review*, July 2001, 404–419.

Luh, Andreas. *Der Deutsche Turnverband in der Ersten Tschechoslowakischen Republik: Vom völkischen Vereinsbetrieb zur volkspolitischen Bewegung*. München: Oldenbourg Verlag, 1988.

Lupovitch, Howard. "Between Orthodox Judaism and Neology: The Origins of the Status Quo Movement." *Jewish Social Studies* 9, no. 2 (2003): 123–153.

MacMillan, Margaret. *Paris 1919: Six Months That Changed the World*. New York: Random House, 2003.

Magocsi, Paul R. *Historical Atlas of East Central Europe*. Seattle: University of Washington Press, 1993.

———. "Muchaceve." In *The YIVO Encyclopaedia of Jews in Eastern Europe*, 1209–1210. New Haven, N.J.: Yale University Press, 2008.

———. *The Shaping of a National Identity: Subcarpathian Rus', 1848–1948*. Cambridge, Mass.: Harvard University Press, 1978.

Manor, Yehuda. "The Foundation of JSY and Its Amalgamation with Tchelet Lavan." In *Rhapsody to Tchelet Lavan in Czechoslovakia*, 129–130. Israel: Association for the History of Tchelet Lavan-El Al in Czechoslovakia, 1996.

Margalit, Elkana. "Social and Intellectual Origins of the Hashomer Hatzair Youth Movement, 1913–1920." In *Essential Papers on Jews and the Left*, edited by Ezra Mendelsohn, 145–165. New York: New York University Press, 1997.

Mazower, Mark. *Dark Continent: Europe's Twentieth Century*. New York: Vintage, 2000.

Mendelsohn, Ezra, ed. *Jews and the Sporting Life*. Studies in Contemporary Jewry 23. New York: Oxford University Press, 2009.

———, ed. *Jews and the State: Dangerous Alliances and the Perils of Privilege*. Studies in Contemporary Jewry 19. New York: Oxford University Press, 2003.

———. *The Jews of East Central Europe between the World Wars*. Bloomington: Indiana University Press, 1983.

———. *On Modern Jewish Politics*. New York: Oxford University Press, 1993.

Mešt'an, Pavol, ed. *Hašomer Hacair – Dějiny hnutia.* Bratislava: Múzeum židovskej kultury, 2001.

Metzer, Jacob. "Jewish Immigration to Palestine in the Long 1920s: An Exploratory Examination." *Journal of Israeli History* 27, no. 2 (September 2008): 221–251.

Meyer, Michael A. *The Origins of the Modern Jew: Jewish Identity and European Culture in Germany, 1749–1824.* Detroit: Wayne State University Press, 1972.

Mikulášek, Alexej. *Antisemitismus v české literatuře 19. a 20. Století.* Praha: Votobia, 2000.

Mikulášek, Alexej, et al. *Literatura s hvězdou Davidovou: Slovníková příručka k dějinám česko-židovských a česko-židovsko-německých literárních vztahů 19. a 20. století,* vol. 1. Praha: Votobia, 1998.

Miller, Daniel E. "Colonizing the Hungarian and German Border Areas during the Czechoslovak Land Reform, 1918–1938." *Austrian History Yearbook* 34 (2003): 303–317.

Miller, Michael L. "Brno." In *The YIVO Encyclopedia of Jews in Eastern Europe,* 238. New Haven, Conn.: Yale University Press, 2008.

——. "Crisis of Rabbinical Authority: Nehemias Trebitsch as Moravian Chief Rabbi, 1832–1842." *Judaica Bohemiae* 43 (2007–2008): 65–92.

——. *Rabbis and Revolution: The Jews of Moravia in the Age of Emancipation.* Stanford, Calif.: Stanford University Press, 2011.

——. "Voice and Vulnerability: The Vagaries of Jewish National Identity in Habsburg Austria." *Simon Dubnow Institute Yearbook* 5 (2006): 159–171.

Mintz, Matityahu. "Work for the Land of Israel and 'Work in the Present': A Concept of Unity, a Reality of Contradiction." In *Essential Papers on Zionism,* edited by Jehuda Reinharz and Anita Shapira, 161–170. New York: New York University Press, 1996.

Mosse, George L. *The Image of Man: The Creation of Modern Masculinity.* New York: Oxford University Press, 1996.

——. *Masses and Man: Nationalist and Fascist Perceptions of Reality.* Detroit: Wayne State University Press, 1987.

Muneles, Otto, ed. *Bibliografický přehled židovské Prahy.* Praha: Státní židovské museum v Praze & ORBIS, 1952.

Nahari, Uriel (Fritz Flussmann). "Everyone's Friend (in Memory of Kriebesch)." In *Rhapsody to Tchelet Lavan in Czechoslovakia,* 77–78. Israel: Association for the History of Tchelet Lavan-El Al in Czechoslovakia, 1996.

Nicosia, Francis R. "Jewish Affairs and German Foreign Policy during the Weimar Republic: Moritz Sobernheim and the *Referat für jüdische Angelegenheiten.*" *Leo Baeck Institute Yearbook* 33 (1988): 261–283.

Nolte, Clair, E. "'Every Czech a Sokol!' Feminism and Nationalism in the Czech Sokol Movement." *Austrian History Yearbook* 24 (1993): 79–100.

——. *The Sokol in the Czech Lands: Training for the Nation.* New York: Palgrave, 2002.

Olivová, Věra. *Dějiny první republiky.* Praha: Karolinum, 2000.

Opelík, Jiří. "Ivan Olbracht." In *Dějiny české literatury: Literatura od konce 19. století do roku 1945,* vol. 4, edited by Přemysl Blažíček et al., 554–571. Praha: Victoria, 1995.

Orzoff, Andrea. *Battle for the Castle: The Myth of Czechoslovakia in Europe, 1914–1948*. New York: Oxford University Press, 2009.

Oswald, Rudolf. "Nazi Ideology and the End of Central European Soccer Professionalism, 1938–1941." In *Emancipation through Muscles: Jews and Sports in Europe*, edited by Michael Brenner and Gideon Reuveni, 156–168. Lincoln: University of Nebraska Press, 2006.

Paul, Ellen L. "Czech Teschen Silesia and the Controversial Czechoslovak Census of 1921." *Polish Review* 43, no. 2 (1998): 161–171.

Pauley, Bruce F. *From Prejudice to Persecution: A History of Austrian Antisemitism*. Chapel Hill: University of North Carolina Press, 1992.

Peleg, Yaron. "Heroic Conduct: Homoeroticism and the Creation of Modern Jewish Masculinities." *Jewish Social Studies* 13, no. 1 (2006): 31–58.

Penslar, Derek J. *Shylock's Children: Economics and Jewish Identity in Modern Europe*. Berkeley: University of California Press, 2001.

Pfister, Gertrud, and Toni Niewerth. "Jewish Women in Gymnastics and Sports in Germany, 1898–1938." *Journal of Sport History* 26, no. 2 (1999): 287–325.

Pianko, Noam. *Zionism and the Roads Not Taken: Rawidowicz, Kaplan, Kohn*. Bloomington: Indiana University Press, 2010.

Polonsky, Anthony, and Michael Riff. "Poles, Czechoslovaks and the 'Jewish Question,' 1914–1921: A Comparative Study," in *Germany in the Age of Total War*, edited by Volker R. Berghahn, 63–101. London: Croom Helm, 1981.

Poppel, Stephen. *Zionism in Germany: The Shaping of a Jewish Identity, 1897–1933*. Philadelphia: Jewish Publication Society of America, 1977.

Presner, Todd S. "'Clear Heads, Solid Stomachs, and Hard Muscles': Max Nordau and the Aesthetics of Jewish Regeneration." *Modernism/Modernity* 10, no. 2 (2003): 269–296.

———. *Muscular Judaism: The Jewish Body and the Politics of Regeneration*. New York: Routledge 2007.

Prestel, Claudia. "'Youth in Need': Correctional Education and Family Breakdown in German Jewish Families." In *In Search of Jewish Community: Jewish Identities in Germany and Austria, 1918–1933*, edited by Michael Brenner and Derek J. Penslar, 200–222. Bloomington: Indiana University Press, 1998.

Przybylová, Blažena. "Židovská škola v Moravské Ostravě." *Sborník Ostrava* 21 (2003): 378–398.

Rabinowicz, Aharon M. "The Jewish Minority." In *The Jews of Czechoslovakia: Historical Studies and Surveys*, vol. 1, 218–321. Philadelphia: Jewish Publication Society of America, 1968.

Rabinowicz, Oskar K. "Czechoslovak Zionism: Analecta to a History." In *The Jews of Czechoslovakia: Historical Studies and Surveys*, vol. 2, 19–136. Philadelphia: Jewish Publication Society of America, 1971.

Rabinowicz, Oskar K., and Yeshayahu Jelinek. "Zionism in Czechoslovakia." In *New Encyclopedia of Zionism and Israel*, edited by Geoffrey Wigoder, 304–310. Madison, N.J.: Fairleigh Dickinson University Press, 1994.

Rawidowicz, Simon. *Israel: The Ever-Dying People and Other Essays*, edited by Benjamin C. I. Ravid. Cranbury, N.J.: Associated University Presses, 1986.

Reuveni, Gideon. "Sports and the Militarization of Jewish Society." In *Emancipation through Muscles: Jews and Sports in Europe,* edited by Michael Brenner and Gideon Reuveni, 44–61. Lincoln: University of Nebraska Press, 2006.

Rhapsody to Tchelet Lavan in Czechoslovakia. Israel: Association for the History of Tchelet Lavan-El Al in Czechoslovakia, 1996.

Rechter, David. *The Jews of Vienna and the First World War*. Oxford: Littman Library of Jewish Civilization, 2000.

Reinharz, Jehuda. *Fatherland or Promised Land: The Dilemma of the German Jews, 1893–1914*. Ann Arbor: The University of Michigan Press, 1975.

Riff, Michael A. "The Ambiguity of Masaryk's Attitudes on the 'Jewish Question.'" In *T. G. Masaryk (1850–1937): Thinker and Critic*, vol. 2, edited by Robert B. Pynsent, 77–87. Houndsmills, UK: Macmillan, 1990.

Roemer, Nils. "The City of Worms in Modern Jewish Traveling Cultures of Remembrance." *Jewish Social Studies* 11, no. 3 (2005): 67–91.

Rojanski, Rachel. "At the Center or on the Fringes of the Public Arena: Ester Mintz-Aberson and the Status of Women in American Poalei Zion, 1905–1935." *Journal of Israeli History* 21, no. 1 (2002): 27–53.

Rosenberg, Imrich. *A Jew in Deed*. Ottawa: Penumbria Press, 2004.

Roshwald, Aviel. *Ethnic Nationalism and the Fall of Empires: Central Europe, Russia, and the Middle East, 1914–1923*. New York: Routledge, 2001.

Rothkirchen, Livia. *The Jews of Bohemia and Moravia: Facing the Holocaust*. Lincoln: University of Nebraska Press, 2005.

———. "The Situation of Jews in Slovakia between 1939–1945." *Jahrbuch für Antisemitismusforschung* 7 (1998): 46–70.

———. "The Zionist Character of the 'Self-Government' of Terezín (Theresienstadt): A Study in Historiography." *Yad Vashem Studies* 11 (1976): 56–87.

Rothschild, Joseph. *East Central Europe between the Two World Wars*. Seattle: University of Washington Press, 1998.

Rozenblit, Marsha L. "Creating Jewish Space: German-Jewish Schools in Moravia." *Austrian History Yearbook* (2013): 108–147.

———. *Reconstructing a National Identity: The Jews of Habsburg Austria during World War I*. New York: Oxford University Press, 2001.

Rozkošná, Blanka and Pavel Jakubec. *Židovské památky Čech: historie a památky židovského osídlení Čech*. Brno: ER group spol, 2004.

Rupnik, Jacques. *Dějiny Komunistické strany Československa: Od počátků do převzetí moci*. Praha: Academia 2002.

Schulze-Marmeling, Dietrich, ed. *Davidstern und Lederball: Die Geschichte der Juden im Deutschen und Interna-*

tionalen Fussball. Göttingen: Verlag die Werkstatt, 2003.

Scott, James C. *Seeing Like a State: How Certain Schemes to Improve the Human Condition Have Failed.* New Haven, N.J.: Yale University Press, 1998.

Šebek, Jaroslav. "Der tschechische Katholizismus im Spannungsfeld von Kirche, Staat, und Gesellschaft zwischen den Weltkriegen." In *Religion im Nationalstaat zwischen den Weltkriegen 1918–1939: Polen – Tschechoslowakei – Ungarn – Rumänien,* edited by Hans-Christian Maner and Martin Schultze-Wessel, 145–156. Stuttgart: Franz Steiner Verlag, 2002.

Shanes, Joshua. *Diaspora Nationalism and Jewish Identity in Habsburg Galicia.* New York: Cambridge University Press, 2012.

——. "National Regeneration in the Ghetto: The Jewish *Turnbewegung* in Galicia." In *Jews, Sports and the Rites of Citizenship,* edited by Jack Kugelmass, 75–94. Urbana: University of Illinois Press, 2007.

——. "Neither Germans nor Poles: Jewish Nationalism in Galicia before Herzl, 1883–1897." *Austrian History Yearbook* 34 (2003): 191–213.

——. "Yiddish and Jewish Diaspora Nationalism." *Monatshefte* 90, no. 2 (Summer 1998): 178–188.

Shapira, Anita. "'Black Night – White Snow': Attitudes of the Palestinian Labor Movement to the Russian Revolution." In *The Jews and the European Crisis, 1914–1921,* edited by Jonathan Frankel, Peter Y. Medding, and Ezra Mendelsohn, 144–171. Studies in Contemporary Jewry 4. New York: Oxford University Press, 1988.

——. *Israel: A History.* Waltham, Mass.: Brandeis University Press, 2012.

Shefa, Pinda. "The Prague Gdud in the Twenties." In *Rhapsody to Tchelet Lavan in Czechoslovakia,* 52–54. Israel: Association for the History of Tchelet Lavan-El Al in Czechoslovakia, 1996.

Shumsky, Dimitri. "Historiography, Nationalism, and Bi-Nationalism: Czech-German Jewry, the Prague Zionists, and the Origins of the Bi-National Approach of Hugo Bergmann." *Zion* 69, no. 1 (2004): 45–80.

——. "On Ethno-Centrism and Its Limits – Czecho-German Jewry in Fin-de-Siècle Prague and the Origins of Zionist Bi-Nationalism." *Simon Dubnow Institute Yearbook* 5 (2006): 173–188.

——. *Zweisprachigkeit und binationale Idee: Der Prager Zionismus 1900–1930.* Göttingen: Vandenhoeck & Ruprecht, 2013.

Sicher, Efraim. "The Concept of Work in the Writings of Chief Rabbi Dr. Gustav Sicher." *Shvut: Studies in Russian and East European Jewish History* 5, no. 21 (1997): 136–143.

Silber, Michael K. "The Historical Experience of German Jewry and Its Impact on Haskalah and Reform in Hungary." In *Toward Modernity: The European Jewish Model,* edited by Jacob Katz, 107–157. New Brunswick, N.J.: Transaction Books, 1987.

——. "Hungary before 1918." In *The YIVO Encyclopedia of Jews in Eastern Europe,* 770–782. New Haven, Conn.: Yale University Press, 2008.

——. "Josephinian Reforms." In *The YIVO Encyclopaedia of Jews in Eastern*

Europe, 831–834. New Haven, Conn.: Yale University Press, 2008.

Sinai, Amos. "In the Face of a Changing World." In *Rhapsody to Tchelet Lavan in Czechoslovakia,* 87–130. Israel: Association for the History of Tchelet Lavan-El Al in Czechoslovakia, 1996.

Skilling, Gordon. "Gottwald and the Bolshevization of the Communist Party of Czechoslovakia, 1929–1939." *Slavic Review* 20, no. 4 (December 1961): 641–655.

——. *T. G. Masaryk: Against the Current, 1882–1914.* Houndsville, UK: Macmillan, 1994.

Soffer, Oren. "Antisemitism, Statistics, and the Scientization of Hebrew Political Discourse: The Case Study of Ha-tsefirah."*Jewish Social Studies* 10, no. 2 (2004): 55–79.

Sole, Aryeh. "Modern Hebrew Education in Subcarpathian Ruthenia." In *The Jews of Czechoslovakia: Historical Studies and Surveys,* vol. 2, 401–439. Philadelphia: Jewish Publication Society of America, 1971.

Solle, Zdeněk, ed. *Masaryk a Beneš ve svých dopisech z pařížských mírových jednání v roce 1919,* vol. 2. Praha: Archiv Akademie Věd ČR, 1994.

Spector, Scott. *Prague Territories: National Conflict and Cultural Innovation in Franz Kafka's Fin de Siècle.* Berkeley: University of California Press, 2000.

Stanislawski, Michael. *Tsar Nicholas I and the Jews: The Transformation of Jewish Society in Russia, 1825–1855.* Philadelphia: Jewish Publication Society of America, 1983.

Stölzl, Christoph. "Die 'Burg' und die Juden. T. G. Masaryk und sein Kreis im Spannungsfeld der jüdischen Frage: Assimilation, Antisemitismus und Zionismus." In *Die "Burg": Einflussreiche politische Kräfte um Masaryk und Beneš,* vol. 2, edited by Karl Bosl, 79–110. München: Oldenbourg Verlag 1974.

Stourzh, Gerald. *Die Gleichberechtigung der Nationalitäten in der Verfassung und Verwaltung Österreichs 1848–1918.* Wien: Verlag der Österreichischen Akademie der Wissenschaften, 1985.

——. "Ethnic Attribution in Late Imperial Austria: Good Intentions, Evil Consequences." In *The Habsburg Legacy: National Identity in Historical Perspective,* edited by Ritchie Robertson and Edward Timms, 67–83. Edinburgh: Edinburgh University Press, 1994.

——. "Galten die Juden als Nationalität Altösterreichs?" *Studia Judaica Austriaca* 10 (1984): 73–117.

Stransky, Hugo. "The Religious Life in the Historic Lands." In *Jews of Czechoslovakia: Historical Studies and Surveys,* vol. 1, 330–357. Philadelphia: Jewish Publication Society of America, 1968.

Strobach, Vít. "Zamyšlení nad 'rudou asimilací' českých Židů." MA thesis, Univerzita Karlova, Praha 2007.

Sugar, Peter F., and Ivo J. Lederer, eds. *Nationalism in Eastern Europe.* Seattle: University of Washington Press, 1969; reissued 1994.

Ticker, Jay. "Max I. Bodenheimer: Advocate of Pro-German Zionism at the Beginning of World War I." *Jewish*

Social Studies 43, no. 1 (Winter 1981): 11–30.

Toman, Jindřich. *The Magic of a Common Language Jakobson, Mathesius, Trubetzkoy, and the Prague Linguistic Circle*. Boston: MIT Press, 2003.

Trapl, Miloš. "Ke školské legislativě obecných a občanských škol a jejímu uplatňování v českých zemích v létech 1918–1922." In *Z dějin českého školství 1918–1945*, edited by Ervín Koukal, 5–62. Praha: Státní pedagogické nakladatelství, 1970.

Urla, Jacqueline. "Cultural Politics in an Age of Statistics: Numbers, Nations, and the Making of Basque Identity." *American Ethnologist* 20, no. 4 (1993): 818–843.

Vacek, Jiří. *Ruská, ukrajinská a běloruská emigrace v Praze: Katalog výstavy*. Praha: Národní knihovna, 1995.

Vassogne, Gaëlle. *Max Brod in Prag: Identität und Vermittlung*. Tübingen: Max Niemeyer Verlag, 2009.

Veselská, Magda. *Archa paměti. Cesta pražského židovského muzea pohnutým 20. stoletím*. Praha: Academia – Židovské muzeum v Praze, 2012.

——. *Bestii navzdory: Židovské museum v Praze 1906–1940*. Praha: Židovské muzeum v Praze, 2006.

——. "František Friedmann." In *Biografický slovník českých zemí*, edited by M. Makarinsová a kol., vol. 18. Praha: Academia, 2015.

——. "Jewish and Related Museums in Czechoslovakia in the First Republic." *Judaica Bohemiae* 40 (2004): 78–92.

——. *Muž, který si nedal pokoj: příběh Josefa Poláka (1886–1945)*. Praha: Židovské museum v Praze, 2005.

——. "Židovské ústřední museum pro Moravsko-Slezko v Mikulově." *RegioM: Sborník Regionálního muzea v Mikulově*, 2005, 80–87.

Waic, Marek. "Československá obec sokolská v politickém životě první republiky." *Moderní dějiny* 3 (1995): 83–100.

——. "Dělnická tělovýchova v prvním desetiletí Československé republiky, 1918–1928." *Moderní dějiny* 4 (1996): 131–158.

——. "Turnerské hnutí a československý stát v letech 1934–1938." In *Češi a Němci ve světě tělovýchovy a sportu*, edited by Marek Waic, 247–263. Praha: Karolinum, 2004.

Wasserstein, Bernhard. *The British in Palestine: The Mandatory Government and the Arab-Jewish Conflict, 1917–1929*. London: Blackwell, 1991.

Wehle, Kurt. "The Jews in Bohemia and Moravia, 1945–1948." In *The Jews of Czechoslovakia: Historical Surveys and Studies* vol. 3, edited by Avigdor Dagan, 499–530. Philadelphia: Jewish Publication Society of America, 1984.

Wein, Martin. "Only Czecho-German Jews?" *Zion* 70 (2004): 386–387.

Weinberg, Robert. *Stalin's Forgotten Zion: Birobidzhan and the Making of a Soviet Jewish Homeland, An Illustrated History, 1928–1996*. Berkeley: University of California Press, 1998.

Weiser, Thomas. *Arbeiterführer in der Tschechoslowakei: Eine Kollektivbi-*

ographie sozialdemokratischer und kommunistischer Parteifunktionäre, 1918–1938. München: Oldenbourgh Verlag, 1998.

Welling, Martin. *"Von Hass so eng umkreist": Der Erste Weltkrieg aus der Sicht der Prager Juden.* Frankfurt am Main: Peter Lang, 2003.

Wessel, Martin Schulze, ed. "Die Konfessionaliserung der tschechischen Nation." In *Nation und Religion in Europa: Mehrkonfesionelle Gesellschaften in 19. und 20. Jahrhundert,* edited by Heinz-Gerhardt Haupt and Dieter Langwie, 135–149. New York: Campus Verlag, 2004.

——. *Loyalitäten in der Tschechoslowakischen Republik, 1918–38.* München: Oldenbourg Verlag, 2004.

——. "Tschechische Nation und Katholische Konfession vor und nach der Gründung des Tschechoslowakischen Nationalstaats." *Bohemia* 39 (1997): 311–237.

——. "Vyznání a národ v českých zemích." In *Češi a Němci: Dějiny – kultura – politika,* edited by Walter Koschmal et al., 126–131. Praha: Nakladatelství Paseka, 2002.

Wildmann, Daniel. "Jewish Gymnasts and Their Corporeal Utopias in Imperial Germany." In *Emancipation through Muscles: Jews and Sports in Europe,* edited by Michael Brenner and Gideon Reuveni, 27–43. Lincoln: University of Nebraska Press, 2006.

Wingfield, Nancy M., ed. *Creating the Other: Ethnic Conflict in East Central Europe.* New York: Berghahn Books, 2003.

Wingfield, Nancy M., and Maria Bucur, eds. *Staging the Past: The Politics of Commemoration in Habsburg Central Europe, 1848 to the Present.* West Lafayette, Ind.: Purdue University Press, 2001.

Wistrich, Robert S. *The Jews of Vienna in the Age of Franz Joseph.* Oxford: Oxford University Press, 1990.

Wlaschek, Rudolf M. *Biographia Judaica Bohemiae.* Vols. 1–2. Dortmund: Forschungsstelle Ostmitteleuropa, 1997.

Yahil, Haim. "Tchelet Lavan in the Twenties." In *Rhapsody to Tchelet Lavan in Czechoslovakia,* 47–52. Israel: Association for the History of Tchelet Lavan-El Al in Czechoslovakia, 1996.

Yuval-Davis, Nira. "Belonging and the Politics of Belonging." In *Patterns of Prejudice* 40, no. 3 (2006): 197–214.

Zahra, Tara E. *Kidnapped Souls: National Indifference and the Battle for Children in the Bohemian Lands, 1900–1948.* Ithaca, N.Y.: Cornell University Press, 2008.

——. "Reclaiming Children for the Nation: Germanization, National Ascription, and Democracy in the Bohemian Lands, 1900–1945." *Central European History* 37, no. 4 (2004): 501–543.

——. "Your Child Belongs to the Nation: Nationalization, Germanization, and Democracy in the Bohemian Lands, 1900–1945." PhD diss., University of Michigan-Ann Arbor, 2005.

Závodský, Prokop. "The National Museum and the Development of Statistical Science." *Bulletin of the Czech Statistical Society* 6 (English issue, 1995): 1–4. http://www.statspol.cz/bulletiny/ib-95-a.pdf.

Zechlin, Egmont. *Die deutsche Politik und die Juden im Ersten Weltkrieg.* Göttingen: Vandenhoeck & Ruprecht, 1969.

Zeman, Z. A. B. "The Four Austrian Censuses and Their Political Consequences." In *The Last Years of Austria-Hungary: Essays in Political and Military History, 1908–1918,* edited by Mark Cornwall, 31–39. Exeter: University of Exeter Press, 1990.

Zerubavel, Yael. *Recovered Roots: Collective Memory and the Making of Israeli National Tradition.* Chicago: University of Chicago Press, 1995.

Ziljynskij, Bohdan. "Ukrajinská emigrace." In *Exil v Praze a Československu, 1918–1938/Exile in Prague and Czechoslovakia, 1918–1938,* 22–25. Praha: Archiv hlavního města Prahy, 2006.

Zipperstein, Steven J. *Imagining Russian Jewry: Memory, History, Identity.* Seattle: University of Washington Press, 1999.

Index

Note: Pages numbers in *italics* indicate tables.

TATJANA LICHTENSTEIN is an assistant professor of Modern Eastern Europe in the Department of History at the University of Texas at Austin. She earned her PhD in history at the University of Toronto. Her research focuses on nationalism, minorities and state building, and relations between Jews and non-Jews in the Bohemian Lands in the twentieth century. At the University of Texas, she teaches courses on East European and Jewish history in the modern period.

www.ingramcontent.com/pod-product-compliance
Lightning Source LLC
Chambersburg PA
CBHW030920150426
42812CB00046B/418

* 9 7 8 0 2 5 3 0 1 8 6 7 0 *